Volume I – Fundamentals

Seventh Edition

CAY S. HORSTMANN • GARY CORNELL

Sun Microsystems Press
A Prentice Hall Title

Prentice Hall PTR offers excellent discounts on this book when ordered in quantity for bulk purchases or special sales. For more information, please contact U.S. Corporate and Government Sales, 1-800-382-3419, corpsales@pearsontechgroup.com. For sales outside of the U.S., please contact International Sales, 1-317-581-3793, international@pearsontechgroup.com.

Library of Congress Control Number: 2004109876

Editorial/production supervision: *Vanessa Moore*
Cover design director: *Jerry Votta*
Cover designer: *Nina Scuderi*
Cover illustration: *Karen Strelecki*
Manufacturing manager: *Alexis R. Heydt-Long*
Marketing manager: *Stephane Nakib*
Executive editor: *Gregory G. Doench*

Sun Microsystems Press Publisher: *Myrna Rivera*

Text printed on recycled and acid-free paper.

ISBN 0131482025

3 4 5 6 7 8 CRS 07 06 05

3 Printing February 2005

Sun Microsystems Press
A Prentice Hall Title

Contents

Chapter 2

Chapter 3

Chapter 5

Chapter 6

Chapter 7

Chapter 8

Chapter 9

Chapter 10

Chapter 11

Chapter 12

xi

List of Code Examples

Preface

To the Reader

In late 1995, the Java programming language burst onto the Internet scene and gained instant celebrity status. The promise of Java technology was that it would become the *universal glue* that connects users with information, whether that information comes from web servers, databases, information providers, or any other imaginable source. Indeed, Java is in a unique position to fulfill this promise. It is an extremely solidly engineered language that has gained acceptance by all major vendors, except for Microsoft. Its built-in security and safety features are reassuring both to programmers and to the users of Java programs. Java even has built-in support that makes advanced programming tasks, such as network programming, database connectivity, and multithreading, straightforward.

Since 1995, Sun Microsystems has released six major revisions of the Java Development Kit. Over the course of the last nine years, the Application Programming Interface (API) has grown from about 200 to over 3,000 classes. The API now spans such diverse areas as user interface construction, database management, internationalization, security, and XML processing. JDK 5.0, released in 2004, is the most impressive update of the Java language since the original Java release.

The book you have in your hand is the first volume of the seventh edition of the *Core Java 2* book. With the publishing of each edition, the book followed the release of the Java Development Kit as quickly as possible, and each time, we rewrote the book to take advantage of the newest Java features. In this edition, we are enthusiastic users of generic collections, the enhanced `for` loop, and other exciting features of JDK 5.0.

As with the previous editions of this book, we *still target serious programmers who want to put Java to work on real projects.* We still guarantee no nervous text or dancing tooth-shaped characters. We think of you, our reader, as a programmer with a solid background in a programming language. *But you do not need to know C++ or object-oriented programming.* Based on the responses we have received to the earlier editions of this book, we remain confident that experienced Visual Basic, C, or COBOL programmers will have no trouble with this book. (You don't even need any experience in building graphical user interfaces for Windows, UNIX, or the Macintosh.)

What we do is assume you want to:

- Write real code to solve real problems

and

- Don't like books filled with toy examples (such as toasters, fruits, or zoo animals)

In this book you will find lots of sample code that demonstrates almost every language and library feature that we discuss. We kept the sample programs purposefully simple to focus on the major points, but, for the most part, they aren't fake and they don't cut corners. They should make good starting points for your own code.

We assume you are willing, even eager, to learn about all the advanced features that Java puts at your disposal. For example, we give you a detailed treatment of:

- Object-oriented programming
- Reflection and proxies
- Interfaces and inner classes
- The event listener model
- Graphical user interface design with the Swing UI toolkit
- Exception handling
- Stream input/output and object serialization
- Generic programming

With the explosive growth of the Java class library, a one-volume treatment of all the features of Java that serious programmers need to know is no longer possible. Hence, we decided to break the book up into two volumes. The first volume, which you hold in your hands, concentrates on the fundamental concepts of the Java language, along with the basics of user-interface programming. The second volume goes further into the enterprise features and advanced user-interface programming. It includes detailed discussions of:

- Multithreading
- Distributed objects
- Databases
- Advanced GUI components
- Native methods
- XML processing
- Network programming
- Collection classes
- Advanced graphics
- Internationalization
- JavaBeans

When writing a book, errors and inaccuracies are inevitable. We'd very much like to know about them. But, of course, we'd prefer to learn about each of them only once. We have put up a list of frequently asked questions, bug fixes, and workarounds in a web page at `http://www.horstmann.com/corejava.html`. Strategically placed at the end of the errata page (to encourage you to read through it first) is a form you can use to report bugs and suggest improvements. Please don't be disappointed if we don't answer every query or if we don't get back to you immediately. We do read all e-mail and appreciate your input to make future editions of this book clearer and more informative.

We hope that you find this book enjoyable and helpful in your Java programming.

About This Book

Chapter 1 gives an overview of the capabilities of Java that set it apart from other programming languages. We explain what the designers of the language set out to do and to what extent they succeeded. Then, we give a short history of how Java came into being and how it has evolved.

In Chapter 2, we tell you how to download and install the JDK and the program examples for this book. Then we guide you through compiling and running three typical Java programs, a console application, a graphical application, and an applet, using the plain JDK, a Java-enabled text editor, and a Java IDE.

Chapter 3 starts the discussion of the Java language. In this chapter, we cover the basics: variables, loops, and simple functions. If you are a C or C++ programmer, this is smooth sailing because the syntax for these language features is essentially the same as in C. If you come from a non-C background such as Visual Basic, you will want to read this chapter carefully.

Object-oriented programming (OOP) is now in the mainstream of programming practice, and Java is completely object-oriented. Chapter 4 introduces encapsulation, the first of two fundamental building blocks of object orientation, and the Java language mechanism to implement it, that is, classes and methods. In addition to the rules of the Java language, we also give advice on sound OOP design. Finally, we cover the marvelous `javadoc` tool that formats your code comments as a set of hyperlinked web pages. If you are familiar with C++, then you can browse through this chapter quickly. Programmers coming from a non-object-oriented background should expect to spend some time mastering OOP concepts before going further with Java.

Classes and encapsulation are only one part of the OOP story, and Chapter 5 introduces the other, namely, *inheritance.* Inheritance lets you take an existing class and modify it according to your needs. This is a fundamental technique for programming in Java. The inheritance mechanism in Java is quite similar to that in C++. Once again, C++ programmers can focus on the differences between the languages.

Chapter 6 shows you how to use Java's notion of an *interface.* Interfaces let you go beyond the simple inheritance model of Chapter 5. Mastering interfaces allows you to have full access to the power of Java's completely object-oriented approach to programming. We also cover a useful technical feature of Java called *inner classes.* Inner classes help make your code cleaner and more concise.

In Chapter 7, we begin application programming in earnest. We show how you can make windows, how to paint on them, how to draw with geometric shapes, how to format text in multiple fonts, and how to display images.

Chapter 8 is a detailed discussion of the event model of the AWT, the *abstract window toolkit.* You'll see how to write the code that responds to events like mouse clicks or key presses. Along the way you'll see how to handle basic GUI elements like buttons and panels.

Chapter 9 discusses the Swing GUI toolkit in great detail. The Swing toolkit allows you to build a cross-platform graphical user interface. You'll learn all about the various kinds of buttons, text components, borders, sliders, list boxes, menus, and dialog boxes. However, some of the more advanced components are discussed in Volume 2.

After you finish Chapter 9, you finally have all mechanisms in place to write *applets,* those mini-programs that can live inside a web page, and so applets are the topic of Chapter 10. We show you a number of useful and fun applets, but more importantly, we look at applets as a method of *program deployment*. We then describe how to package applications in JAR files, and how to deliver applications over the Internet with the Java Web Start mechanism.

Finally, we explain how Java programs can store and retrieve configuration information once they have been deployed.

Chapter 11 discusses *exception handling,* Java's robust mechanism to deal with the fact that bad things can happen to good programs. For example, a network connection can become unavailable in the middle of a file download, a disk can fill up, and so on. Exceptions give you an efficient way of separating the normal processing code from the error handling. Of course, even after hardening your program by handling all exceptional conditions, it still might fail to work as expected. In the second half of this chapter, we give you a large number of useful debugging tips. Finally, we guide you through sample sessions with various tools: the JDB debugger, the debugger of an integrated development environment, a profiler, a code coverage testing tool, and the AWT robot.

The topic of Chapter 12 is input and output handling. In Java, all I/O is handled through so-called *streams.* Streams let you deal in a uniform manner with communicating with any source of data, such as files, network connections, or memory blocks. We include detailed coverage of the reader and writer classes, which make it easy to deal with Unicode. We show you what goes on under the hood when you use the object serialization mechanism, which makes saving and loading objects easy and convenient. Finally, we cover several libraries that have been added to JDK 1.4: the "new I/O" classes that contain support for advanced and more efficient file operations, and the regular expression library.

We finish the book with an overview of *generic programming,* a major advance of JDK 5.0. Generic programming will make your programs easier to read and safer. We show you how you can use strong typing with collections and remove unsightly and unsafe casts.

Appendix A lists the reserved words of the Java language.

Apppendix B tells you how to modify the code examples so that they compile on an older (JDK 1.4) compiler.

Conventions

As is common in many computer books, we use `monospace type` to represent computer code.

C++ NOTE: There are many C++ notes that explain the difference between Java and C++. You can skip over them if you don't have a background in C++ or if you consider your experience with that language a bad dream of which you'd rather not be reminded.

NOTE: Notes are tagged with "note" icons that look like this.

TIP: Tips are tagged with the "tip" icon that look like this.

CAUTION: When there is danger ahead, we warn you with a "caution" icon.

Application Programming Interface

Java comes with a large programming library or Application Programming Interface (API). When using an API call for the first time, we add a short summary description tagged with an API icon at the end of the section. These descriptions are a bit more informal, but we hope also a little more informative than those in the official on-line API documentation. We now tag each API note with the version number in which the feature was introduced, to help the readers who don't use the "bleeding edge" version of Java.

Programs whose source code is on the Web are listed as examples, for instance

Example 2–4: WelcomeApplet.java

Sample Code

The web site for this book at `http://www.phptr.com/corejava` contains all sample code from the book, in compressed form. You can expand the file either with one of the familiar unzipping programs or simply with the `jar` utility that is part of the Java Development Kit. See Chapter 2 for more information about installing the Java Development Kit and the sample code.

Acknowledgments

Writing a book is always a monumental effort, and rewriting doesn't seem to be much easier, especially with continuous change in Java technology. Making a book a reality takes many dedicated people, and it is my great pleasure to acknowledge the contributions of the entire Core Java team.

A large number of individuals at Prentice Hall PTR and Sun Microsystems Press provided valuable assistance, but they managed to stay behind the scenes. I'd like them all to know how much I appreciate their efforts. As always, my warm thanks go to my editor, Greg Doench of Prentice Hall PTR, for steering the book through the writing and production process, and for allowing me to be blissfully unaware of the existence of all those folks behind the scenes. I am grateful to Vanessa Moore for the excellent production support. My thanks also to my coauthor of earlier editions, Gary Cornell, who has since moved on to other ventures.

Thanks to the many readers of earlier editions who reported embarrassing errors and made lots of thoughtful suggestions for improvement. I am particularly grateful to the excellent reviewing team that went over the manuscript with an amazing eye for detail and saved me from many more embarrassing errors.

Reviewers of this and earlier editions include Chuck Allison (Contributing Editor, *C/C++ Users Journal*), Alec Beaton (PointBase, Inc.), Joshua Bloch (Sun Microsystems), David Brown, Dr. Nicholas J. De Lillo (Manhattan College), Rakesh Dhoopar (Oracle), David Geary (Sabreware), Angela Gordon (Sun Microsystems), Dan Gordon (Sun Microsystems), Rob Gordon, Cameron Gregory (olabs.com), Marty Hall (The Johns Hopkins University Applied Physics Lab), Vincent Hardy (Sun Microsystems), Vladimir Ivanovic (PointBase), Jerry Jackson (ChannelPoint Software), Tim Kimmet (Preview Systems), Chris Laffra, Charlie Lai (Sun Microsystems), Doug Langston, Doug Lea (SUNY Oswego), Gregory Longshore, Bob Lynch (Lynch Associates), Mark Morrissey (The Oregon Graduate Institute), Mahesh Neelakanta (Florida Atlantic University), Paul Philion, Blake Ragsdell, Stuart Reges (University of Arizona), Peter Sander (ESSI University, Nice, France), Paul Sevinc (Teamup AG), Devang Shah (Sun Microsystems), Bradley A. Smith, Christopher Taylor, Luke Taylor (Valtech), George Thiruvathukal, Kim Topley(author of *Core JFC*), Janet Traub, Peter van der Linden (Sun Microsystems), Burt Walsh, Corky Cartwright, Frank Cohen (PushToTest), Chris Crane (devXsolution), Bill Higgins (IBM), Hang Lau (McGill University), Angelika Langer, Mark Lawrence, Dr. Paul Sanghera (San Jose State University and Brooks College), and Steve Stelting (Sun Microsystems).

Cay Horstmann
San Francisco, 2004

Chapter 1

An Introduction to Java

- Java as a Programming Platform
- The Java "White Paper" Buzzwords
- Java and the Internet
- A Short History of Java
- Common Misconceptions About Java

The first release of Java in 1996 generated an incredible amount of excitement, not just in the computer press, but in mainstream media such as *The New York Times, The Washington Post,* and *Business Week.* Java has the distinction of being the first and only programming language that had a 10-minute story on National Public Radio. A $100,000,000 venture capital fund was set up solely for products produced by use of a *specific* computer language. It is rather amusing to revisit those heady times, and we give you a brief history of Java in this chapter.

Java as a Programming Platform

In the first edition of this book, we had this to write about Java:

"As a computer language, Java's hype is overdone: Java is certainly a *good* programming language. There is no doubt that it is one of the better languages available to serious programmers. We think it could *potentially* have been a great programming language, but it is probably too late for that. Once a language is out in the field, the ugly reality of compatibility with existing code sets in."

Our editor got a lot of flack for this paragraph from someone very high up at Sun who shall remain unnamed. But, in hindsight, our prognosis seems accurate. Java has a lot of nice language features—we examine them in detail later in this chapter. It has its share of warts, and newer additions to the language are not as elegant as the original ones because of the ugly reality of compatibility.

But, as we already said in the first edition, Java was never just a language. There are lots of programming languages out there, and few of them make much of a splash. Java is a whole *platform*, with a huge library, containing lots of reusable code, and an execution environment that provides services such as security, portability across operating systems, and automatic garbage collection.

As a programmer, you will want a language with a pleasant syntax and comprehensible semantics (i.e., not C++). Java fits the bill, as do dozens of other fine languages. Some languages give you portability, garbage collection, and the like, but they don't have much of a library, forcing you to roll your own if you want fancy graphics or networking or database access. Well, Java has everything—a good language, a high-quality execution environment, and a vast library. That combination is what makes Java an irresistible proposition to so many programmers.

The Java "White Paper" Buzzwords

The authors of Java have written an influential White Paper that explains their design goals and accomplishments. They also published a shorter summary that is organized along the following 11 buzzwords:

Simple	Portable
Object Oriented	Interpreted
Distributed	High Performance
Robust	Multithreaded
Secure	Dynamic
Architecture Neutral	

In this section, we will

- Summarize, with excerpts from the White Paper, what the Java designers say about each buzzword; and
- Tell you what we think of each buzzword, based on our experiences with the current version of Java.

NOTE: As we write this, the White Paper can be found at `http://java.sun.com/docs/white/langenv/`. The summary with the 11 buzzwords is at `ftp://ftp.javasoft.com/docs/papers/java-overview.ps`.

Simple

> *We wanted to build a system that could be programmed easily without a lot of esoteric training and which leveraged today's standard practice. So even though we found that C++ was unsuitable, we designed Java as closely to C++ as possible in order to make the system more comprehensible. Java omits many rarely used, poorly understood, confusing features of C++ that, in our experience, bring more grief than benefit.*

The syntax for Java is, indeed, a cleaned-up version of the syntax for C++. There is no need for header files, pointer arithmetic (or even a pointer syntax), structures, unions, operator overloading, virtual base classes, and so on. (See the C++ notes interspersed throughout the text for more on the differences between Java and C++.) The designers did not, however, attempt to fix all of the clumsy features of C++. For example, the syntax of the `switch` statement is unchanged in Java. If you know C++, you will find the transition to the Java syntax easy.

If you are used to a visual programming environment (such as Visual Basic), you will not find Java simple. There is much strange syntax (though it does not take long to get the hang of it). More important, you must do a lot more programming in Java. The beauty of Visual Basic is that its visual design environment almost automatically provides a lot of the infrastructure for an application. The equivalent functionality must be programmed manually, usually with a fair bit of code, in Java. There are, however, third-party development environments that provide "drag-and-drop"-style program development.

> *Another aspect of being simple is being small. One of the goals of Java is to enable the construction of software that can run stand-alone in small machines. The size of the basic interpreter and class support is about 40K bytes; adding the basic standard libraries and thread support (essentially a self-contained microkernel) adds an additional 175K.*

This is a great achievement. Note, however, that the graphical user interface (GUI) libraries are significantly larger.

Object Oriented

> *Simply stated, object-oriented design is a technique for programming that focuses on the data (= objects) and on the interfaces to that object. To make an analogy with carpentry, an "object-oriented" carpenter would be mostly concerned with the chair he was building, and secondarily with the tools used to make it; a "non-object-oriented" carpenter would think primarily of his tools. The object-oriented facilities of Java are essentially those of C++.*

Object orientation has proven its worth in the last 30 years, and it is inconceivable that a modern programming language would not use it. Indeed, the object-oriented features of Java are comparable to those of C++. The major difference between Java and C++ lies in multiple inheritance, which Java has replaced with the simpler concept of interfaces, and in the Java metaclass model. The reflection mechanism (see Chapter 5) and object serialization feature (see Chapter 12) make it much easier to implement persistent objects and GUI builders that can integrate off-the-shelf components.

NOTE: If you have no experience with object-oriented programming languages, you will want to carefully read Chapters 4 through 6. These chapters explain what object-oriented programming is and why it is more useful for programming sophisticated projects than are traditional, procedure-oriented languages like C or Basic.

Distributed

> *Java has an extensive library of routines for coping with TCP/IP protocols like HTTP and FTP. Java applications can open and access objects across the Net via URLs with the same ease as when accessing a local file system.*

We have found the networking capabilities of Java to be both strong and easy to use. Anyone who has tried to do Internet programming using another language will revel in how simple Java makes onerous tasks like opening a socket connection. (We cover networking in Volume 2 of this book.) The remote method invocation mechanism enables communication between distributed objects (also covered in Volume 2).

There is now a separate architecture, the Java 2 Enterprise Edition (J2EE), that supports very large scale distributed applications.

Robust

> *Java is intended for writing programs that must be reliable in a variety of ways. Java puts a lot of emphasis on early checking for possible problems, later dynamic (run-time) checking, and eliminating situations that are error-prone.... The single biggest difference between Java and C/C++ is that Java has a pointer model that eliminates the possibility of overwriting memory and corrupting data.*

This feature is also very useful. The Java compiler detects many problems that, in other languages, would show up only at run time. As for the second point, anyone who has spent hours chasing memory corruption caused by a pointer bug will be very happy with this feature of Java.

If you are coming from a language like Visual Basic that doesn't explicitly use pointers, you are probably wondering why this is so important. C programmers are not so lucky. They need pointers to access strings, arrays, objects, and even files. In Visual Basic, you do not use pointers for any of these entities, nor do you need to worry about memory allocation for them. On the other hand, many data structures are difficult to implement in a pointerless language. Java gives you the best of both worlds. You do not need pointers for everyday constructs like strings and arrays. You have the power of pointers if you need it, for example, for linked lists. And you always have complete safety, because you can never access a bad pointer, make memory allocation errors, or have to protect against memory leaking away.

Secure

> *Java is intended to be used in networked/distributed environments. Toward that end, a lot of emphasis has been placed on security. Java enables the construction of virus-free, tamper-free systems.*

In the first edition of *Core Java* we said: "Well, one should 'never say never again,'" and we turned out to be right. Not long after the first version of the Java Development Kit was shipped, a group of security experts at Princeton University found subtle bugs in the security features of Java 1.0. Sun Microsystems has encouraged research into Java security, making publicly available the specification and implementation of the virtual machine and the security libraries. They have fixed all known security bugs quickly. In any case, Java makes it extremely difficult to outwit its security mechanisms. The bugs found so far have been very technical and few in number.

From the beginning, Java was designed to make certain kinds of attacks impossible, among them:

- Overrunning the runtime stack—a common attack of worms and viruses
- Corrupting memory outside its own process space
- Reading or writing files without permission

A number of security features have been added to Java over time. Since version 1.1, Java has the notion of digitally signed classes (see Volume 2). With a signed class, you can be sure who wrote it. Any time you trust the author of the class, the class can be allowed more privileges on your machine.

NOTE: A competing code delivery mechanism from Microsoft based on its ActiveX technology relies on digital signatures alone for security. Clearly this is not sufficient—as any user of Microsoft's own products can confirm, programs from well-known vendors do crash and create damage. Java has a far stronger security model than that of ActiveX because it controls the application as it runs and stops it from wreaking havoc.

Architecture Neutral

The compiler generates an architecture-neutral object file format—the compiled code is executable on many processors, given the presence of the Java runtime system. The Java compiler does this by generating bytecode instructions which have nothing to do with a particular computer architecture. Rather, they are designed to be both easy to interpret on any machine and easily translated into native machine code on the fly.

This is not a new idea. More than 20 years ago, both Niklaus Wirth's original implementation of Pascal and the UCSD Pascal system used the same technique.

Of course, interpreting bytecodes is necessarily slower than running machine instructions at full speed, so it isn't clear that this is even a good idea. However, virtual machines have the option of translating the most frequently executed bytecode sequences into machine code, a process called just-in-time compilation. This strategy has proven so effective that even Microsoft's .NET platform relies on a virtual machine.

The virtual machine has other advantages. It increases security because the virtual machine can check the behavior of instruction sequences. Some programs even produce bytecodes on the fly, dynamically enhancing the capabilities of a running program.

Portable

Unlike C and C++, there are no "implementation-dependent" aspects of the specification. The sizes of the primitive data types are specified, as is the behavior of arithmetic on them.

For example, an `int` in Java is always a 32-bit integer. In C/C++, `int` can mean a 16-bit integer, a 32-bit integer, or any other size that the compiler vendor likes. The only restriction is that the `int` type must have at least as many bytes as a `short int` and cannot have more bytes than a `long int`. Having a fixed size for number types eliminates a major porting headache. Binary data is stored and transmitted in a fixed format, eliminating confusion about byte ordering. Strings are saved in a standard Unicode format.

The libraries that are a part of the system define portable interfaces. For example, there is an abstract Window class and implementations of it for UNIX, Windows, and the Macintosh.

As anyone who has ever tried knows, it is an effort of heroic proportions to write a program that looks good on Windows, the Macintosh, and 10 flavors of UNIX. Java 1.0 made the heroic effort, delivering a simple toolkit that mapped common user interface elements to a number of platforms. Unfortunately, the result was a library that, with a lot of work, could give barely acceptable results on different systems. (And there were often *different* bugs on the different platform graphics implementations.) But it was a start. There are many applications in which portability is more important than user interface slickness, and these applications did benefit from early versions of Java. By now, the user interface toolkit has been completely rewritten so that it no longer relies on the host user interface. The result is far more consistent and, we think, more attractive than in earlier versions of Java.

Interpreted

The Java interpreter can execute Java bytecodes directly on any machine to which the interpreter has been ported. Since linking is a more incremental and lightweight process, the development process can be much more rapid and exploratory.

Incremental linking has advantages, but its benefit for the development process is clearly overstated. In any case, we have found Java development tools to be quite slow. If you are used to the speed of the classic Microsoft Visual C++ environment, you will likely be

disappointed with the performance of Java development environments. (The current version of Visual Studio isn't as zippy as the classic environments, however. No matter what language you program in, you should definitely ask your boss for a faster computer to run the latest development environments.)

High Performance

> *While the performance of interpreted bytecodes is usually more than adequate, there are situations where higher performance is required. The bytecodes can be translated on the fly (at run time) into machine code for the particular CPU the application is running on.*

If you use an interpreter to execute the bytecodes, "high performance" is not the term that we would use. However, on many platforms, there is also another form of compilation, the *just-in-time* (JIT) compilers. These work by compiling the bytecodes into native code once, caching the results, and then calling them again if needed. This approach speeds up commonly used code tremendously because one has to do the interpretation only once. Although still slightly slower than a true native code compiler, a just-in-time compiler can give you a 10- or even 20-fold speedup for some programs and will almost always be significantly faster than an interpreter. This technology is being improved continuously and may eventually yield results that cannot be matched by traditional compilation systems. For example, a just-in-time compiler can monitor which code is executed frequently and optimize just that code for speed.

Multithreaded

> *[The] benefits of multithreading are better interactive responsiveness and real-time behavior.*

If you have ever tried to do multithreading in another language, you will be pleasantly surprised at how easy it is in Java. Threads in Java also can take advantage of multiprocessor systems if the base operating system does so. On the downside, thread implementations on the major platforms differ widely, and Java makes no effort to be platform independent in this regard. Only the code for calling multithreading remains the same across machines; Java offloads the implementation of multithreading to the underlying operating system or a thread library. (Threading is covered in Volume 2.) Nonetheless, the ease of multithreading is one of the main reasons why Java is such an appealing language for server-side development.

Dynamic

> *In a number of ways, Java is a more dynamic language than C or C++. It was designed to adapt to an evolving environment. Libraries can freely add new methods and instance variables without any effect on their clients. In Java, finding out run time type information is straightforward.*

This is an important feature in those situations in which code needs to be added to a running program. A prime example is code that is downloaded from the Internet to run in a browser. In Java 1.0, finding out runtime type information was anything but straightforward, but current versions of Java give the programmer full insight into both the structure and behavior of its objects. This is extremely useful for systems that need to analyze objects at run time, such as Java GUI builders, smart debuggers, pluggable components, and object databases.

NOTE: Microsoft has released a product called J++ that shares a family relationship with Java. Like Java, J++ is executed by a virtual machine that is compatible with the Java virtual machine for executing Java bytecodes, but there are substantial differences when interfacing with external code. The basic language syntax is almost identical to that of Java. However, Microsoft added language constructs that are of doubtful utility except for interfacing with the Windows API. In addition to Java and J++ sharing a common syntax, their foundational libraries (strings, utilities, networking, multithreading, math, etc.) are essentially identical. However, the libraries for graphics, user interfaces, and remote object access are completely different. At this point, Microsoft is no longer supporting J++ but has instead introduced another language, called C#, that also has many similarities with Java but uses a different virtual machine. There is even a J# for migrating J++ applications to the virtual machine used by C#. We do not cover J++, C#, or J# in this book.

Java and the Internet

The idea here is simple: users will download Java bytecodes from the Internet and run them on their own machines. Java programs that work on web pages are called *applets*. To use an applet, you need a Java-enabled web browser, which will execute the bytecodes for you. Because Sun is licensing the Java source code and insisting that there be no changes in the language and basic library structure, a Java applet should run on any browser that is advertised as Java-enabled. Unfortunately, reality has been different. Various versions of Netscape and Internet Explorer run different versions of Java, some of which are seriously outdated. This sorry situation made it increasingly difficult to develop applets that take advantage of the most current Java version. To remedy this problem, Sun has developed the *Java Plug-in*, a tool that makes the newest Java runtime environment available to both Netscape and Internet Explorer (see Chapter 10).

When the user downloads an applet, it works much like embedding an image in a web page. The applet becomes a part of the page, and the text flows around the space used for the applet. The point is, the image is *alive*. It reacts to user commands, changes its appearance, and sends data between the computer presenting the applet and the computer serving it.

Figure 1–1 shows a good example of a dynamic web page—an applet to view molecules—that carries out sophisticated calculations. By using the mouse, you can rotate and zoom each molecule to better understand its structure. This kind of direct manipulation is not achievable with static web pages, but applets make it possible. (You can find this applet at `http://jmol.sourceforge.net`.)

Applets can be used to add buttons and input fields to a web page. But downloading those applets over a dialup connection is slow, and you can do much of the same with Dynamic HTML, HTML forms, and a scripting language such as JavaScript. And, of course, early applets were used for animation: the familiar spinning globes, dancing cartoon characters, nervous text, and so on. But animated GIFs can do much of the same. Thus, applets are necessary only for rich interactions, not for general web design.

As a result of browser incompatibilities and the inconvenience of downloading applet code through slow connections, applets on Internet web pages have not become a huge success. The situation is entirely different on *intranets*. There are typically no bandwidth problems, so the download time for applets is no issue. And in an intranet, it is possible to control which browser is being used or to use the Java Plug-in consistently. Employees can't misplace or misconfigure programs that are delivered through the Web with each use, and the system administrator never needs to walk around and upgrade code on client machines.

Many corporations have rolled out programs such as inventory checking, vacation planning, travel reimbursement, and so on, as applets that use the browser as the delivery platform.

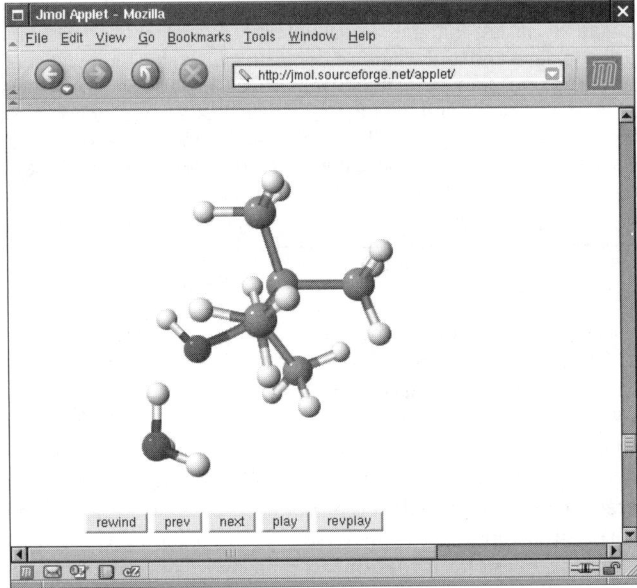

Figure 1–1: The Jmol applet

At the time of this writing, the pendulum has swung back from client-focused programs to *server-side programming*. In particular, *application servers* can use the monitoring capabilities of the Java virtual machine to perform automatic load balancing, database connection pooling, object synchronization, safe shutdown and restart, and other services that are needed for scalable server applications but are notoriously difficult to implement correctly. Thus, application programmers can buy rather than build these sophisticated mechanisms. This increases programmer productivity—programmers focus on their core competency, the business logic of their programs, and not on tweaking server performance.

A Short History of Java

This section gives a short history of Java's evolution. It is based on various published sources (most important, on an interview with Java's creators in the July 1995 issue of *SunWorld's* on-line magazine).

Java goes back to 1991, when a group of Sun engineers, led by Patrick Naughton and Sun Fellow (and all-around computer wizard) James Gosling, wanted to design a small computer language that could be used for consumer devices like cable TV switchboxes. Because these devices do not have a lot of power or memory, the language had to be small and generate very tight code. Also, because different manufacturers may choose different central processing units (CPUs), it was important that the language not be tied to any single architecture. The project was code-named "Green."

The requirements for small, tight, and platform-neutral code led the team to resurrect the model that some Pascal implementations tried in the early days of PCs. Niklaus Wirth, the inventor of Pascal, had pioneered the design of a portable language that generated intermediate code for a hypothetical machine. (These are often called *virtual machines*—hence,

the Java virtual machine or JVM.) This intermediate code could then be used on any machine that had the correct interpreter. The Green project engineers used a virtual machine as well, so this solved their main problem.

The Sun people, however, come from a UNIX background, so they based their language on C++ rather than Pascal. In particular, they made the language object oriented rather than procedure oriented. But, as Gosling says in the interview, "All along, the language was a tool, not the end." Gosling decided to call his language "Oak" (presumably because he liked the look of an oak tree that was right outside his window at Sun). The people at Sun later realized that Oak was the name of an existing computer language, so they changed the name to Java. This turned out to be an inspired choice.

In 1992, the Green project delivered its first product, called "*7." It was an extremely intelligent remote control. (It had the power of a SPARCstation in a box that was 6 inches by 4 inches by 4 inches.) Unfortunately, no one was interested in producing this at Sun, and the Green people had to find other ways to market their technology. However, none of the standard consumer electronics companies were interested. The group then bid on a project to design a cable TV box that could deal with new cable services such as video on demand. They did not get the contract. (Amusingly, the company that did was led by the same Jim Clark who started Netscape—a company that did much to make Java successful.)

The Green project (with a new name of "First Person, Inc.") spent all of 1993 and half of 1994 looking for people to buy its technology—no one was found. (Patrick Naughton, one of the founders of the group and the person who ended up doing most of the marketing, claims to have accumulated 300,000 air miles in trying to sell the technology.) First Person was dissolved in 1994.

While all of this was going on at Sun, the World Wide Web part of the Internet was growing bigger and bigger. The key to the Web is the browser that translates the hypertext page to the screen. In 1994, most people were using Mosaic, a noncommercial web browser that came out of the supercomputing center at the University of Illinois in 1993. (Mosaic was partially written by Marc Andreessen for $6.85 an hour as an undergraduate student on a work-study project. He moved on to fame and fortune as one of the cofounders and the chief of technology at Netscape.)

In the *SunWorld* interview, Gosling says that in mid-1994, the language developers realized that "We could build a real cool browser. It was one of the few things in the client/server mainstream that needed some of the weird things we'd done: architecture neutral, real-time, reliable, secure—issues that weren't terribly important in the workstation world. So we built a browser."

The actual browser was built by Patrick Naughton and Jonathan Payne and evolved into the HotJava browser. The HotJava browser was written in Java to show off the power of Java. But the builders also had in mind the power of what are now called applets, so they made the browser capable of executing code inside web pages. This "proof of technology" was shown at SunWorld '95 on May 23, 1995, and inspired the Java craze that continues today.

Sun released the first version of Java in early 1996. People quickly realized that Java 1.0 was not going to cut it for serious application development. Sure, you could use Java 1.0 to make a nervous text applet that moved text randomly around in a canvas. But you couldn't even *print* in Java 1.0. To be blunt, Java 1.0 was not ready for prime time. Its successor, version 1.1, filled in the most obvious gaps, greatly improved the reflection capability, and added a new event model for GUI programming. It was still rather limited, though.

The big news of the 1998 JavaOne conference was the upcoming release of Java 1.2, which replaced the early toylike GUI and graphics toolkits with sophisticated and scalable versions that come a lot closer to the promise of "Write Once, Run Anywhere"™ than their predecessors. Three days after (!) its release in December 1998, Sun's marketing department changed the name to the catchy *Java 2 Standard Edition Software Development Kit Version 1.2*.

Besides the "Standard Edition," two other editions were introduced: the "Micro Edition" for embedded devices such as cell phones, and the "Enterprise Edition" for server-side processing. This book focuses on the Standard Edition.

Versions 1.3 and 1.4 of the Standard Edition are incremental improvements over the initial Java 2 release, with an ever-growing standard library, increased performance, and, of course, quite a few bug fixes. During this time, much of the initial hype about Java applets and client-side applications abated, but Java became the platform of choice for server-side applications.

Version 5.0 is the first release since version 1.1 that updates the Java *language* in significant ways. (This version was originally numbered 1.5, but the version number jumped to 5.0 at the 2004 JavaOne conference.) After many years of research, generic types (which are roughly comparable to C++ templates) have been added—the challenge was to add this feature without requiring changes in the virtual machine. Several other useful language features were inspired by C#: a "for each" loop, autoboxing, and metadata. Language changes are always a source of compatibility pain, but several of these new language features are so seductive that we think that programmers will embrace them eagerly. Table 1–1 shows the evolution of the Java *language*.

Table 1–1: Evolution of the Java Language

Version	New Language Features
1.0	The language itself
1.1	Inner classes
1.2	None
1.3	None
1.4	Assertions
5.0	Generic classes, "for each" loop, varargs, autoboxing, metadata, enumerations, static import

Table 1–2 shows the growth of the Java *library* over the years. As you can see, the size of the application programming interface (API) has grown tremendously.

Table 1–2: Growth of the Java Standard Edition API

Version	Number of Classes and Interfaces
1.0	211
1.1	477
1.2	1524
1.3	1840
1.4	2723
5.0	3270

Common Misconceptions About Java

We close this chapter with a list of some common misconceptions about Java, along with commentary.

Java is an extension of HTML.

Java is a programming language; HTML is a way to describe the structure of a web page. They have nothing in common except that there are HTML extensions for placing Java applets on a web page.

I use XML, so I don't need Java.

Java is a programming language; XML is a way to describe data. You can process XML data with any programming language, but the Java API contains excellent support for XML processing. In addition, many important third-party XML tools are implemented in Java. See Volume 2 for more information.

Java is an easy programming language to learn.

No programming language as powerful as Java is easy. You always have to distinguish between how easy it is to write toy programs and how hard it is to do serious work. Also, consider that only four chapters in this book discuss the Java language. The remaining chapters of both volumes show how to put the language to work, using the Java *libraries.* The Java libraries contain thousands of classes and interfaces, and tens of thousands of functions. Luckily, you do not need to know every one of them, but you do need to know surprisingly many to use Java for anything realistic.

Java will become a universal programming language for all platforms.

This is possible, in theory, and it is certainly the case that every vendor but Microsoft seems to want this to happen. However, many applications, already working perfectly well on desktops, would not work well on other devices or inside a browser. Also, these applications have been written to take advantage of the speed of the processor and the native user interface library and have been ported to all the important platforms anyway. Among these kinds of applications are word processors, photo editors, and web browsers. They are typically written in C or C++, and we see no benefit to the end user in rewriting them in Java.

Java is just another programming language.

Java is a nice programming language; most programmers prefer it over C, C++, or C#. But there have been hundreds of nice programming languages that never gained widespread popularity, whereas languages with obvious flaws, such as C++ and Visual Basic, have been wildly successful.

Why? The success of a programming language is determined far more by the utility of the *support system* surrounding it than by the elegance of its syntax. Are there useful, convenient, and standard libraries for the features that you need to implement? Are there tool vendors that build great programming and debugging environments? Does the language and the tool set integrate with the rest of the computing infrastructure? Java is successful because its class libraries let you easily do things that were hard before, such as networking and multithreading. The fact that Java reduces pointer errors is a bonus and so programmers seem to be more productive with Java, but these factors are not the source of its success.

Now that C# is available, Java is obsolete.

C# took many good ideas from Java, such as a clean programming language, a virtual machine, and garbage collection. But for whatever reasons, C# also left some good stuff behind, most important security and platform independence. In our view, the biggest advantage of C# is its excellent development environment. If you are tied to Windows, C#

makes a lot of sense. But judging by the job ads, Java is still the language of choice for a majority of developers.

Java is proprietary, and it should therefore be avoided.

Everyone will need to make up their own mind on this issue. There are times when we are frustrated by some aspect of Java, and we wish that a competing open-source team could provide salvation. But the situation isn't that simple.

Although Sun has ultimate control over Java, they have, through the "Java Community Process" involved many other companies in the development of language revisions and the design of new libraries. Source code for the virtual machine and the libraries is freely available, but only for inspection, not for modification and redistribution.

Looking at the open-sourced languages out there, it is not clear that they are doing a better job. The most popular ones are the three "Ps" in "LAMP" (Linux, Apache, MySQL, and Perl/PHP/Python). These languages have their benefits, but they have also suffered from disruptive version changes, limited libraries, and a paucity of development tools.

On the other side of the spectrum we have C++ and C# that were standardized by vendor-independent standards committees. We agree that this process is more transparent than the Java Community Process. However, the results have not been as useful as you might think. It is not enough to standardize just the language and the most basic libraries. For real programming, you quickly go beyond string handling, collections, and files. In the case of C#, Microsoft has gone on record stating that they will keep most libraries outside the standardization process.

Perhaps the future of Java lies in an open-source process. But at this point, Sun has convinced a lot of people that it is a responsible steward of Java.

Java is interpreted, so it is too slow for serious applications.

In the early days of Java, the language was interpreted. Nowadays, except on "micro" platforms such as cell phones, the Java virtual machine uses a just-in-time compiler. The "hot spots" of your code will run just as fast in Java as they would in C++.

Java does have some additional overhead over C++ that has nothing to do with the virtual machine. Garbage collection is slightly slower than manual memory management, and Java programs are more memory-hungry than C++ programs with similar functionality. Program startup can be slow, particularly with very large programs. Java GUIs are slower than their native counterparts because they are painted in a platform-independent manner.

People have complained for years that Java is slower than C++. However, today's computers are much faster than they were when these complaints started. A slow Java program will still run quite a bit better than those blazingly fast C++ programs did a few years ago. At this point, these complaints sound like sour grapes, and some detractors have instead started to complain that Java user interfaces are ugly rather than slow.

All Java programs run inside a web page.

All Java *applets* run inside a web browser. That is the definition of an applet—a Java program running inside a browser. But it is entirely possible, and quite useful, to write standalone Java programs that run independently of a web browser. These programs (usually called *applications*) are completely portable. Just take the code and run it on another machine! And because Java is more convenient and less error-prone than raw C++, it is a good choice for writing programs. It is an even more compelling choice when it is combined with database access tools like Java Database Connectivity (see Volume 2). It is certainly the obvious choice for a first language in which to learn programming.

Most of the programs in this book are stand-alone programs. Sure, applets are fun. But stand-alone Java programs are more important and more useful in practice.

Java programs are a major security risk.

In the early days of Java, there were some well-publicized reports of failures in the Java security system. Most failures were in the implementation of Java in a specific browser. Researchers viewed it as a challenge to try to find chinks in the Java armor and to defy the strength and sophistication of the applet security model. The technical failures that they found have all been quickly corrected, and to our knowledge, no actual systems were ever compromised. To keep this in perspective, consider the literally millions of virus attacks in Windows executable files and Word macros that cause real grief but surprisingly little criticism of the weaknesses of the attacked platform. Also, the ActiveX mechanism in Internet Explorer would be a fertile ground for abuse, but it is so boringly obvious how to circumvent it that few have bothered to publicize their findings.

Some system administrators have even deactivated Java in company browsers, while continuing to permit their users to download executable files, ActiveX controls, and Word documents. That is pretty ridiculous—currently, the risk of being attacked by hostile Java applets is perhaps comparable to the risk of dying from a plane crash; the risk of being infected by opening Word documents is comparable to the risk of dying while crossing a busy freeway on foot.

JavaScript is a simpler version of Java.

JavaScript, a scripting language that can be used inside web pages, was invented by Netscape and originally called LiveScript. JavaScript has a syntax that is reminiscent of Java, but otherwise there are no relationships (except for the name, of course). A subset of JavaScript is standardized as ECMA-262, but the extensions that you need for real work have not been standardized, and as a result, writing JavaScript code that runs both in Netscape and Internet Explorer is an exercise in frustration.

With Java, I can replace my computer with a $500 "Internet appliance."

When Java was first released, some people bet big that this was going to happen. Ever since the first edition of this book, we have believed it is absurd to think that home users are going to give up a powerful and convenient desktop for a limited machine with no local storage. We found the Java-powered network computer a plausible option for a "zero administration initiative" to cut the costs of computer ownership in a business, but even that has not happened in a big way.

On the other hand, Java has become widely distributed on cell phones. We must confess that we haven't yet seen a must-have Java application running on cell phones, but the usual fare of games and screen savers seems to be selling well in many markets.

TIP: For answers to common Java questions, turn to one of the Java FAQ (frequently asked question) lists on the Web—see `http://www.apl.jhu.edu/~hall/java/FAQs-and-Tutorials.html`.

Chapter 2

The Java Programming Environment

In this chapter, you will learn how to install the Java Development Kit (JDK) and how to compile and run various types of programs: console programs, graphical applications, and applets. You run the JDK tools by typing commands in a shell window. However, many programmers prefer the comfort of an integrated development environment. We show you how to use a freely available development environment to compile and run Java programs. Although easier to learn, integrated development environments can be resource-hungry and tedious to use for small programs. As a middle ground, we show you how to use a text editor that can call the Java compiler and run Java programs. Once you have mastered the techniques in this chapter and picked your development tools, you are ready to move on to Chapter 3, where you will begin exploring the Java programming language.

Installing the Java Development Kit

The most complete and up-to-date versions of the Java 2 Standard Edition (J2SE) are available from Sun Microsystems for Solaris, Linux, and Windows. Versions in various states of development exist for the Macintosh and many other platforms, but those versions are licensed and distributed by the vendors of those platforms.

Downloading the JDK

To download the Java Development Kit, you will need to navigate the Sun web site and decipher an amazing amount of jargon before you can get the software that you need.

You already saw the abbreviation JDK for Java Development Kit. Somewhat confusingly, versions 1.2 through 1.4 of the kit were known as the Java SDK (Software Development Kit). You will still find occasional references to the old term.

Next, you'll see the term "J2SE" everywhere. That is the "Java 2 Standard Edition," in contrast to J2EE (Java 2 Enterprise Edition) and J2ME (Java 2 Micro Edition).

The term "Java 2" was coined in 1998 when the marketing folks at Sun felt that a fractional version number increment did not properly communicate the momentous advances of JDK 1.2. However, because they had that insight only after the release, they decided to keep the version number 1.2 for the *development kit*. Subsequent releases were numbered 1.3, 1.4, and 5.0. The *platform*, however, was renamed from "Java" to "Java 2." Thus, we have Java 2 Standard Edition Development Kit version 5.0, or J2SE 5.0.

For engineers, all of this might be a bit confusing, but that's why we never made it into marketing.

If you use Solaris, Linux, or Windows, point your browser to `http://java.sun.com/j2se` to download the JDK. Look for version 5.0 or later, and pick your platform.

Sometimes, Sun makes available bundles that contain both the Java Development Kit and an integrated development environment. That integrated environment has, at different times of its life, been named Forte, Sun ONE Studio, Sun Java Studio, and Netbeans. We do not know what the eager beavers in marketing will call it when you approach the Sun web site. We suggest that you install only the Java Development Kit at this time. If you later decide to use Sun's integrated development environment, simply download it from `http://netbeans.org`.

After downloading the JDK, follow the platform-dependent installation directions. At the time of this writing, they were available at `http://java.sun.com/j2se/5.0/install.html`.

Only the installation and compilation instructions for Java are system dependent. Once you get Java up and running, everything else in this book should apply to you. System independence is a major benefit of Java.

NOTE: The setup procedure offers a default for the installation directory that contains the JDK version number, such as `jdk5.0`. This sounds like a bother, but we have come to appreciate the version number—it makes it easier to install a new JDK release for testing.

Under WIndows, we strongly recommend that you do not accept a default location with spaces in the path name, such as `c:\Program Files\jdk5.0`. Just take out the `Program Files` part of the path name.

In this book, we refer to the installation directory as *jdk*. For example, when we refer to the *jdk*`/bin` directory, we mean the directory with a name such as `/usr/local/jdk5.0/bin` or `c:\jdk5.0\bin`.

Setting the Execution Path

After you are done installing the JDK, you need to carry out one additional step: add the *jdk*`/bin` directory to the execution path, the list of directories that the operating system traverses to locate executable files. Directions for this step also vary among operating systems.

- In UNIX (including Solaris and Linux), the procedure for editing the execution path depends on the shell that you are using. If you use the C shell (which is the Solaris default), then add a line such as the following to the end of your `~/.cshrc` file:

  ```
  set path=(/usr/local/jdk/bin $path)
  ```

If you use the Bourne Again shell (which is the Linux default), then add a line such as the following to the end of your `~/.bashrc` or `~/.bash_profile` file:

```
export PATH=/usr/local/jdk/bin:$PATH
```

For other UNIX shells, you'll need to find out how to carry out the analogous procedure.

- Under Windows 95/98/Me, place a line such as the following at the end of your `c:\autoexec.bat` file:

  ```
  SET PATH=c:\jdk\bin;%PATH%
  ```

  Note that there are *no spaces* around the `=`. You must reboot your computer for this setting to take effect.
- Under Windows NT/2000/XP, start the control panel, select System, then Environment. Scroll through the User Variables window until you find a variable named `PATH`. (If you want to make the Java tools available for all users on your machine, use the System Variables window instead.) Add the *jdk*`\bin` directory to the beginning of the path, using a semicolon to separate the new entry, like this:

  ```
  c:\jdk\bin;other stuff
  ```

  Save your settings. Any new console windows that you start have the correct path.

Here is how you test whether you did it right:

Start a shell window. How you do this depends on your operating system. Type the line

```
java -version
```

and press the ENTER key. You should get a display such as this one:

```
java version "5.0"
Java(TM) 2 Runtime Environment, Standard Edition
Java HotSpot(TM) Client VM
```

If instead you get a message such as "java: command not found", "Bad command or file name", or "The name specified is not recognized as an internal or external command, operable program or batch file", then you need to go back and double-check your installation.

Installing the Library Source and Documentation

The library source files are delivered in the JDK as a compressed file `src.zip`, and you must unpack that file to get access to the source code. We highly recommend that you do that. Simply do the following:

1. Make sure that the JDK is installed and that the *jdk*`/bin` directory is on the execution path.
2. Open a shell window.
3. Change to the *jdk* directory (e.g., `cd /usr/local/jdk5.0` or `cd c:\jdk5.0`).
4. Make a subdirectory `src`

   ```
   mkdir src
   cd src
   ```

5. Execute the command:

   ```
   jar xvf ../src.zip
   ```

   (or `jar xvf ..\src.zip` on Windows)

TIP: The `src.zip` file contains the source code for all public libraries. To obtain even more source (for the compiler, the virtual machine, the native methods, and the private helper classes), go to `http://www.sun.com/software/communitysource/j2se/java2/index.html`.

The documentation is contained in a compressed file that is separate from the JDK. You can download the documentation from `http://java.sun.com/docs`. Several formats (.zip, .gz, and .Z) are available. Choose the format that works best for you. If in doubt, use the zip file because you can uncompress it with the `jar` program that is a part of the JDK. Simply follow these steps:

1. Make sure that the JDK is installed and that the *jdk*/`bin` directory is on the execution path.
2. Download the documentation zip file and move it into the *jdk* directory. The file is called `j2sdk`*version*`-doc.zip`, where *version* is something like `5_0`.
3. Open a shell window.
4. Change to the *jdk* directory.
5. Execute the command

   `jar xvf j2sdk`*version*`-doc.zip`

   where *version* is the appropriate version number.

Installing the Core Java Program Examples

You should also install the Core Java program examples. You can download them from `http://www.phptr.com/corejava`. The programs are packaged into a zip file `corejava.zip`. You should unzip them into a separate directory—we recommend you call it `CoreJavaBook`. You can use any zip file utility such as WinZip (`http://www.winzip.com`), or you can simply use the `jar` utility that is part of the JDK. If you use `jar`, do the following:

1. Make sure the JDK is installed and the *jdk*/`bin` directory is on the execution path.
2. Make a directory `CoreJavaBook`.
3. Download the `corejava.zip` file to that directory.
4. Open a shell window.
5. Change to the `CoreJavaBook` directory.
6. Execute the command:

```
jar xvf corejava.zip
```

Navigating the Java Directories

In your explorations of Java, you will occasionally want to peek inside the Java source files. And, of course, you will need to work extensively with the library documentation. Table 2–1 shows the JDK directory tree.

Table 2–1: Java Directory Tree

Directory Structure	Description
jdk	(The name may be different, for example, `jdk5.0`)
├── `bin`	The compiler and tools
├── `demo`	Look here for demos
├── `docs`	Library documentation in HTML format (after expansion of `j2sdk`*version*`-doc.zip`)
├── `include`	Files for compiling native methods (see Volume 2)
├── `jre`	Java runtime environment files
├── `lib`	Library files
└── `src`	The library source (after expanding `src.zip`)

The two most useful subdirectories for learning Java are `docs` and `src`. The `docs` directory contains the Java library documentation in HTML format. You can view it with any web browser, such as Netscape.

TIP: Set a bookmark in your browser to the file `docs/api/index.html`. You will be referring to this page a lot as you explore the Java platform.

The `src` directory contains the source code for the public part of the Java libraries. As you become more comfortable with Java, you may find yourself in situations for which this book and the on-line information do not provide what you need to know. At this point, the source code for Java is a good place to begin digging. It is reassuring to know that you can always dig into the source to find out what a library function really does. For example, if you are curious about the inner workings of the `System` class, you can look inside `src/java/lang/System.java`.

Choosing a Development Environment

If your programming experience comes from using Microsoft Visual Studio, you are accustomed to a development environment with a built-in text editor and menus to compile and launch a program along with an integrated debugger. The basic JDK contains nothing even remotely similar. You do *everything* by typing in commands in a shell window. We tell you how to install and use the basic JDK because we have found that the full-fledged development environments don't necessarily make it easy to learn Java—they can be complex and they hide some of the interesting and important details from the programmer.

Integrated development environments tend to be more cumbersome to use for a simple program because they are slower, require more powerful computers, and often require a somewhat tedious project setup for each program you write. These environments have the edge if you write large Java programs consisting of many source files, and they integrate tools such as debuggers and version control systems. We show you how to get started with Eclipse, a freely available development environment that is itself written in Java. Of course, if you prefer a different development environment such as NetBeans or JBuilder that supports the current version of Java, then you can certainly use it with this book.

For simple programs, a good middle ground between command-line tools and an integrated development environment is an editor that integrates with the JDK. On Linux, our preferred choice is Emacs. On Windows, we also like TextPad, an excellent shareware programming editor for Windows with good Java integration. Finally, JEdit is an excellent cross-platform alternative. Using a text editor with JDK integration can make developing Java programs easy and fast. We used that approach for developing and testing most of the programs in this book. Because you can compile and execute source code from within the editor, it can become your de facto development environment as you work through this book.

In sum, you have three choices for a Java development environment:

- Use the JDK and your favorite text editor. Compile and launch programs in a shell window.
- Use an integrated development environment such as Eclipse, or one of many other freely or commercially available development environments.
- Use the JDK and a text editor that is integrated with the JDK. Emacs, TextPad, and JEdit are so integrated, as are many others. Compile and launch programs inside the editor.

Using the Command-Line Tools

Let us get started the hard way: compiling and launching a Java program from the command line.

Open a shell window. Go to the `CoreJavaBook/v1ch2/Welcome` directory. (The `CoreJavaBook` directory is the directory into which you installed the source code for the book examples, as explained on page 18.)

Then enter the following commands:

```
javac Welcome.java
java Welcome
```

You should see the output shown in Figure 2–1 in the shell window.

NOTE: In Windows, follow these instructions to open a shell window. Select the "Run" option from the start menu. If you use Windows NT/2000/XP, type `cmd`; otherwise, type `command`. Press ENTER, and a shell window appears. If you've never seen one of these, we suggest that you work through a tutorial that teaches the basics about the command line. Many computer science departments have tutorials on the Web, such as `http://www.cs.sjsu.edu/faculty/horstman/CS46A/windows/tutorial.html`.

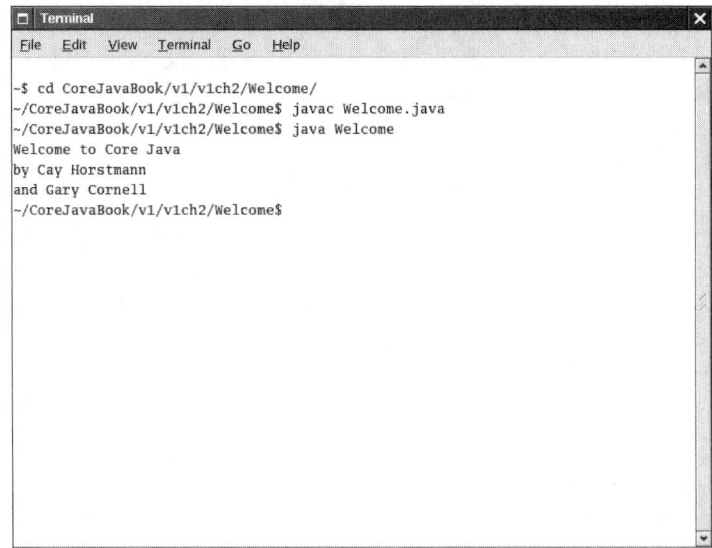

Figure 2–1: Compiling and running `Welcome.java`

Congratulations! You have just compiled and run your first Java program.

What happened? The `javac` program is the Java compiler. It compiles the file `Welcome.java` into the file `Welcome.class`. The `java` program launches the Java virtual machine. It executes the bytecodes that the compiler placed in the class file.

NOTE: If you got an error message complaining about the line

```
for (String g : greeting)
```

then you probably use an older version of the Java compiler. JDK 5.0 introduces a number of very desirable features to the Java programming language, and we take advantage of them in this book.

If you are using an older version of Java, you need to rewrite the loop as follows:

```
for (int i = 0; i < greeting.length; i++)
   System.out.println(greeting[i]);
```

In this book, we always use the language features of JDK 5.0. It is a straightforward matter to transform them into their old-fashioned counterparts—see Appendix B for details.

The `Welcome` program is extremely simple. It merely prints a message to the console. You may enjoy looking inside the program shown in Example 2–1—we explain how it works in the next chapter.

Example 2–1: Welcome.java

```
public class Welcome
{
   public static void main(String[] args)
   {
      String[] greeting = new String[3];
      greeting[0] = "Welcome to Core Java";
      greeting[1] = "by Cay Horstmann";
      greeting[2] = "and Gary Cornell";

      for (String g : greeting)
         System.out.println(g);
   }
}
```

Troubleshooting Hints

In the age of visual development environments, many programmers are unfamiliar with running programs in a shell window. Any number of things can go wrong, leading to frustrating results.

Pay attention to the following points:

- If you type in the program by hand, make sure you pay attention to uppercase and lowercase letters. In particular, the class name is `Welcome` and not `welcome` or `WELCOME`.
- The compiler requires a *file name* (`Welcome.java`). When you run the program, you specify a *class name* (`Welcome`) without a `.java` or `.class` extension.
- If you get a message such as "Bad command or file name" or "javac: command not found", then go back and double-check your installation, in particular the execution path setting.
- If `javac` reports an error "cannot read: Welcome.java", then you should check whether that file is present in the directory.

  Under UNIX, check that you used the correct capitalization for `Welcome.java`.

  Under Windows, use the `dir` shell command, *not* the graphical Explorer tool. Some text editors (in particular Notepad) insist on adding an extension `.txt` after every file. If you use Notepad to edit `Welcome.java`, then it actually saves it as `Welcome.java.txt`. Under the default Windows settings, Explorer conspires with Notepad and hides the `.txt`

extension because it belongs to a "known file type." In that case, you need to rename the file, using the `ren` shell command, or save it again, placing quotes around the file name: `"Welcome.java"`.

- If you launch your program and get an error message complaining about a `java.lang.NoClassDefFoundError`, then carefully check the name of the offending class.

  If you get a complaint about `welcome` (with a lowercase `w`), then you should reissue the `java Welcome` command with an uppercase `W`. As always, case matters in Java.

  If you get a complaint about `Welcome/java`, then you accidentally typed `java Welcome.java`. Reissue the command as `java Welcome`.
- If you typed `java Welcome` and the virtual machine can't find the `Welcome` class, then check if someone has set the *class path* on your system. For simple programs, it is best to unset it. You can unset the class path in the current shell window by typing

  ```
  set CLASSPATH=
  ```

  This command works on Windows and UNIX/Linux with the C shell. On UNIX/Linux with the Bourne/bash shell, use

  ```
  export CLASSPATH=
  ```

  Chapter 4 tells you how you can permanently set or unset your class path.
- If you get an error message about a new language construct, make sure that your compiler supports JDK 5.0. If you cannot use JDK 5.0 or later, you need to modify the source code, as shown in Appendix B.
- If you have too many errors in your program, then all the error messages fly by very quickly. The compiler sends the error messages to the standard error stream, so it's a bit tricky to capture them if they fill more than the window can display.

  On a UNIX system or a Windows NT/2000/XP system, capturing error messages is not a big problem. You can use the `2>` shell operator to redirect the errors to a file:

  ```
  javac MyProg.java 2> errors.txt
  ```

  Under Windows 95/98/Me, you cannot redirect the standard error stream from the shell window. You can download the `errout` program from `http://www.horstmann.com/corejava/faq.html` and run

  ```
  errout javac MyProg.java > errors.txt
  ```

TIP: The excellent tutorial at `http://java.sun.com/docs/books/tutorial/getStarted/cupojava/` goes into much greater detail about the "gotchas" that beginners can run into.

Using an Integrated Development Environment

In this section, we show you how to compile a program with Eclipse, an integrated development environment that is freely available from `http://eclipse.org`. Eclipse is written in Java, but because it uses a nonstandard windowing library, it is not quite as portable as Java itself. Nevertheless, versions exist for Linux, Mac OS X, Solaris, and Windows.

After starting Eclipse, select File -> New Project from the menu, then select "Java Project" from the wizard dialog (see Figure 2–2). These screen shots were taken with Eclipse 3.0M8. Don't worry if your version of Eclipse looks slightly different.

Click the "Next" button. Supply the project name "Welcome" and type in the full path name of the directory that contains `Welcome.java`; see Figure 2–3. Be sure to *uncheck* the option labeled "Create project in workspace". Click the "Finish" button.

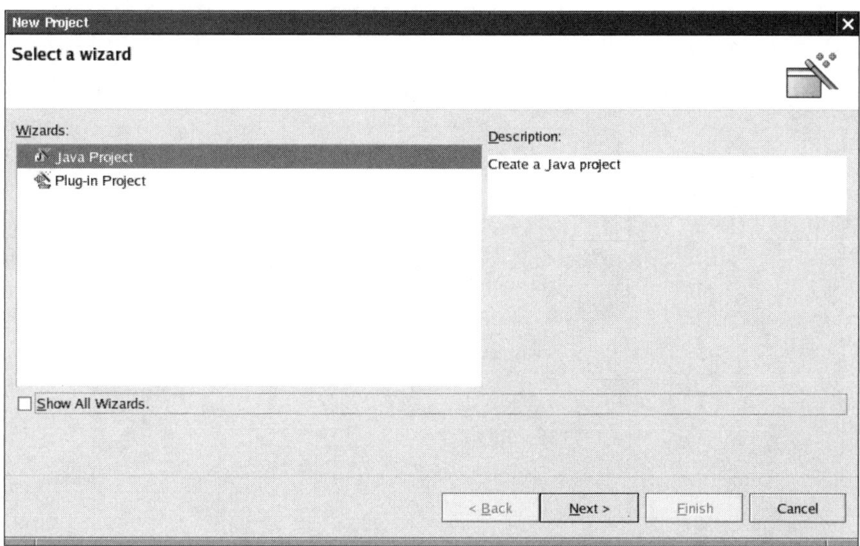

Figure 2–2: New Project dialog in Eclipse

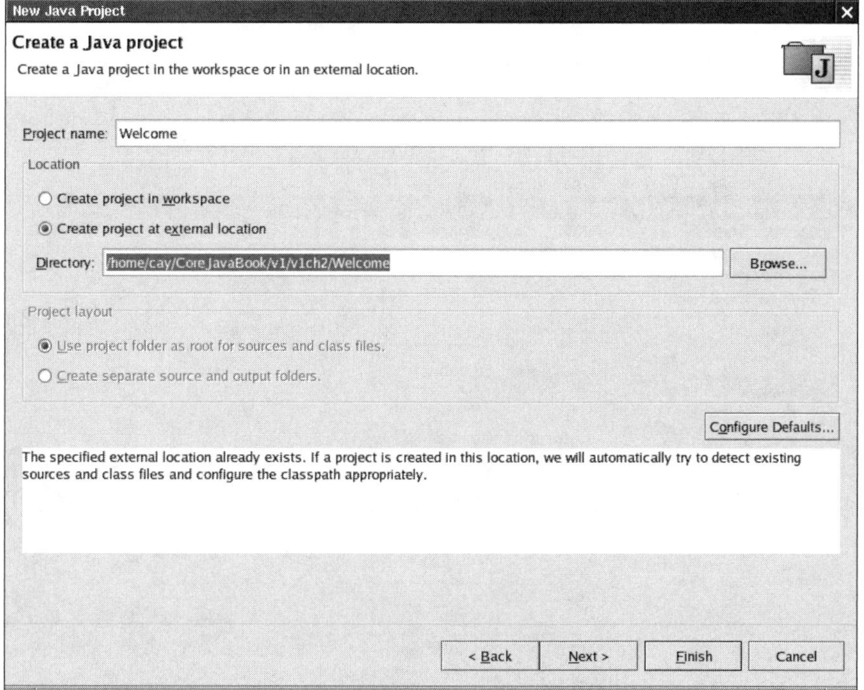

Figure 2–3: Configuring an Eclipse project

The project is now created. Click on the triangle in the left pane next to the project window to open it, and then click on the triangle next to "Default package". Double-click on `Welcome.java`. You should now see a window with the program code (see Figure 2–4).

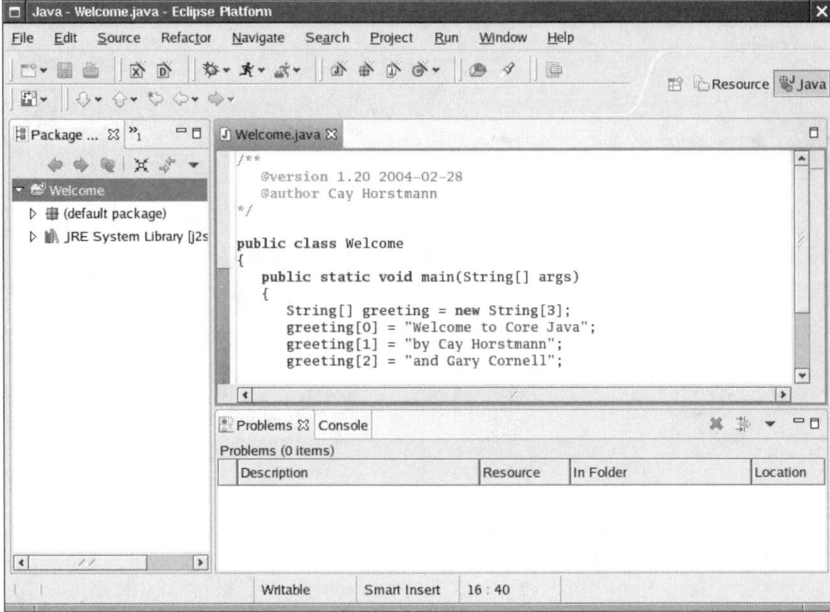

Figure 2–4: Editing a source file with Eclipse

With the right mouse button, click on the project name (Welcome) in the leftmost pane. Select Build Project from the menu that pops up. Your program is compiled. If it compiles successfully, select Run -> Run As -> Java Application. An output window appears at the bottom of the window. The program output is displayed in the output window (see Figure 2–5).

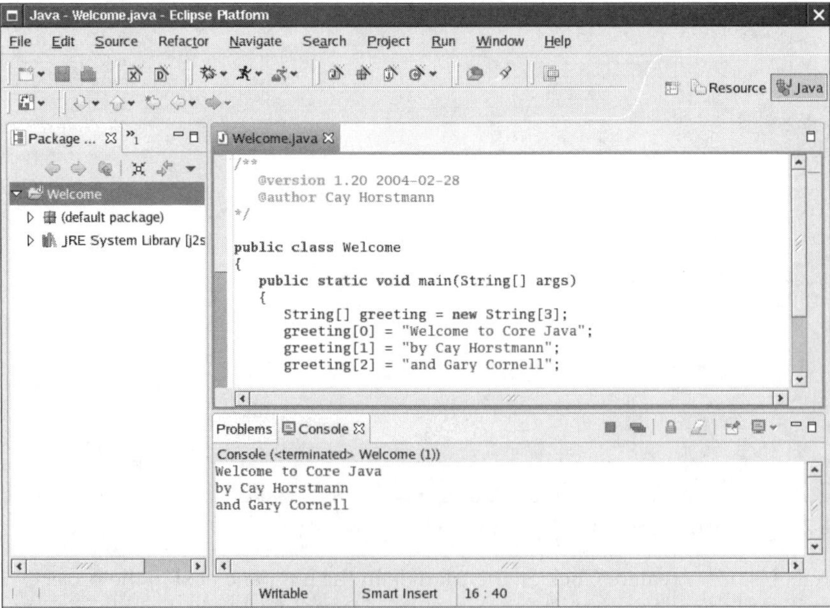

Figure 2–5: Running a program in Eclipse

Locating Compilation Errors

Presumably, this program did not have typos or bugs. (It was only a few lines of code, after all.) Let us suppose, for the sake of argument, that your code occasionally contains a typo (perhaps even a syntax error). Try it out—ruin our file, for example, by changing the capitalization of `String` as follows:

```
public static void main(string[] args)
```

Now, run the compiler again. You will get an error message that complains about an unknown `string` type (see Figure 2–6). Simply click on the error message. The cursor moves to the matching line in the edit window, where you can correct your error. This behavior allows you to fix your errors quickly.

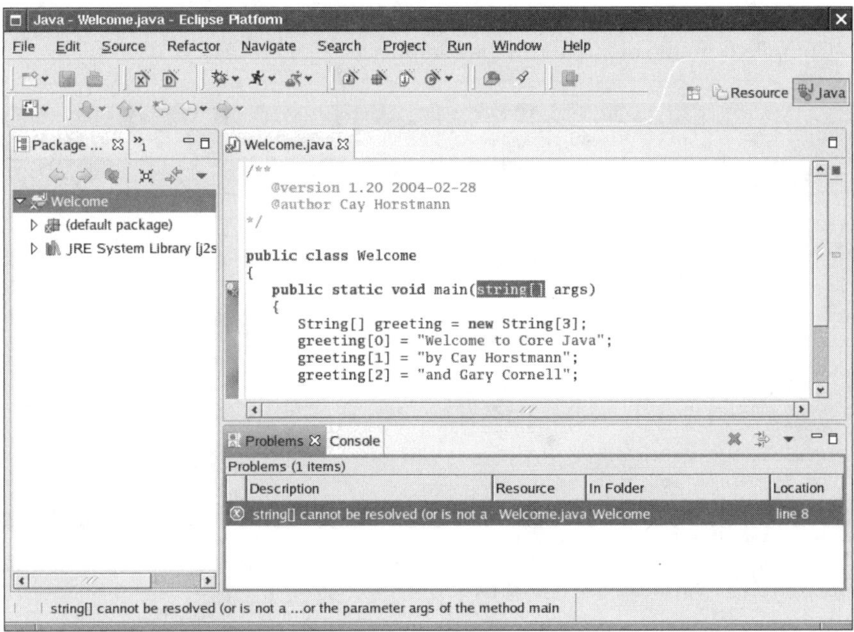

Figure 2–6: Error messages in Eclipse

These instructions should give you a taste of working in an integrated environment. We discuss the Eclipse debugger in Chapter 11.

Compiling and Running Programs from a Text Editor

An integrated development environment accords many comforts but also insinuates some drawbacks. In particular, for simple programs that are not distributed over multiple source files, an environment with its long startup time and many bells and whistles can seem like overkill. Fortunately, many text editors can launch the Java compiler, launch Java programs, and capture error messages and program output. In this section, we look at Emacs as a typical example.

NOTE: GNU Emacs is available from `http://www.gnu.org/software/emacs/`. For the Windows port of GNU Emacs, see `http://www.gnu.org/software/emacs/windows/ntemacs.html`. Be sure to install the JDEE (Java Development Environnment for Emacs) when using Emacs for Java programming. You can download it from `http://jdee.sunsite.dk`. You need JDEE 2.4.3beta1 or later with JDK 5.0.

Emacs is a splendid text editor that is freely available for UNIX, Linux, Windows, and Mac OS X. However, many Windows programmers find the learning curve rather steep. For those programmers, we can recommend TextPad. Unlike Emacs, TextPad conforms to standard Windows conventions. TextPad is available at `http://www.textpad.com`. Note that TextPad is shareware. You are expected to pay for it if you use it beyond a trial period. (We have no relationship with the vendor, except as satisfied users of the program.)

Another popular choice is JEdit, a very nice editor written in Java, freely available from `http://jedit.org`. Whether you use Emacs, TextPad, JEdit, or another editor, the concepts are the same. When you are done editing the source code, you invoke a command to compile the code. The editor launches the compiler and captures the error messages. You fix the errors, compile again, and invoke another command to run your program.

Figure 2–7 shows the Emacs editor compiling a Java program. (Choose JDE -> Compile from the menu to run the compiler.)

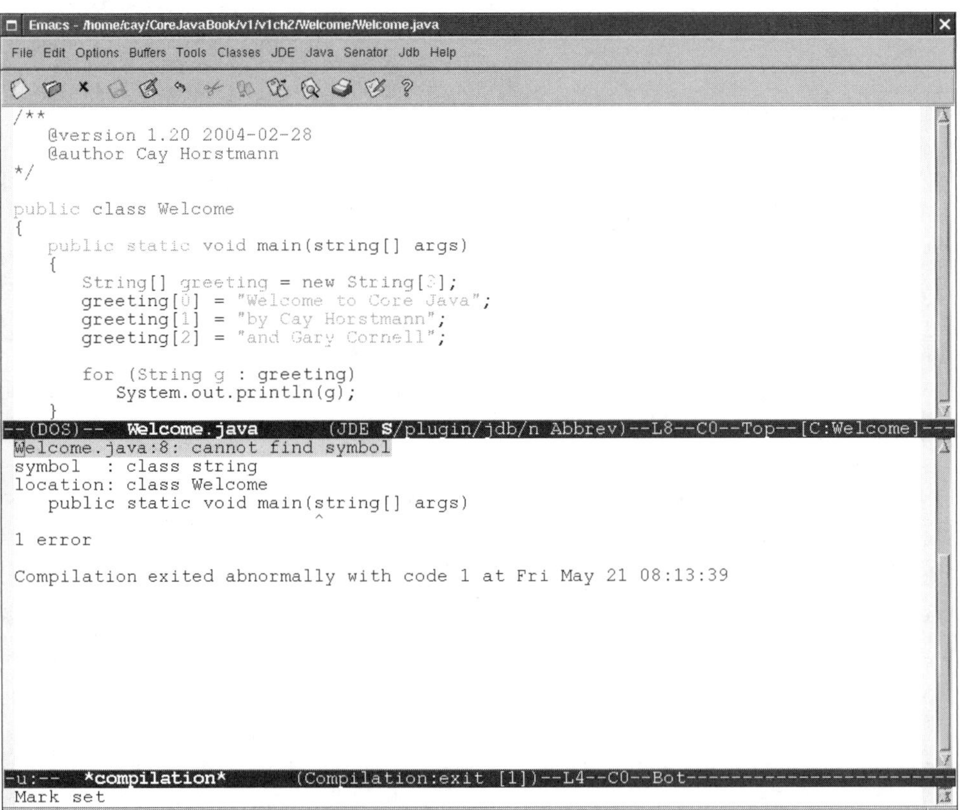

Figure 2–7: Compiling a program with Emacs

The error messages show up in the lower half of the window. When you move the cursor on an error message and press the ENTER key, the cursor moves to the corresponding source line.

Once all errors are fixed, you can run the program by choosing JDE -> Run App from the menu. The output shows up inside an editor window (see Figure 2–8).

```
Emacs - *Welcome*
File Edit Options Buffers Tools Complete In/Out Signals Help
/**
   @version 1.20 2004-02-28
   @author Cay Horstmann
*/

public class Welcome
{
   public static void main(String[] args)
   {
      String[] greeting = new String[3];
      greeting[0] = "Welcome to Core Java";
      greeting[1] = "by Cay Horstmann";
      greeting[2] = "and Gary Cornell";

      for (String g : greeting)
         System.out.println(g);
   }
--(DOS)--  Welcome.java      (JDE S/plugin/jdb/n Abbrev)--L6--C20--Top--[???]--------
cd /home/cay/CoreJavaBook/v1/v1ch2/Welcome/
/usr/local/j2sdk1.5.0/bin/java -ea Welcome

Welcome to Core Java
by Cay Horstmann
and Gary Cornell

Process Welcome finished
-u:**  *Welcome*        (JDE Run Mode:no process)--L9--C0--All--------------------
```

Figure 2–8: Running a program from within Emacs

Running a Graphical Application

The `Welcome` program was not terribly exciting. Next, we will demonstrate a graphical application. This program is a simple image file viewer that just loads and displays an image. Again, let us first compile and run it from the command line.

1. Open a shell window.
2. Change to the directory `CoreJavaBook/v1ch2/ImageViewer`.
3. Enter:

```
javac ImageViewer.java
java ImageViewer
```

A new program window pops up with our ImageViewer application (see Figure 2–9).

Now select File -> Open and look for a GIF file to open. (We supplied a couple of sample files in the same directory.)

To close the program, click on the Close box in the title bar or pull down the system menu and close the program. (To compile and run this program inside a text editor or an integrated development environment, do the same as before. For example, for Emacs, choose JDE -> Compile, then choose JDE -> Run App.)

Figure 2–9: Running the ImageViewer application

We hope that you find this program interesting and useful. Have a quick look at the source code. The program is substantially longer than the first program, but it is not terribly complex if you consider how much code it would take in C or C++ to write a similar application. In Visual Basic, of course, it is easy to write or, rather, drag and drop, such a program. The JDK does not have a visual interface builder, so you need to write code for everything, as shown in Example 2–2. You learn how to write graphical programs like this in Chapters 7 through 9.

Example 2–2: ImageViewer.java

```
import java.awt.*;
import java.awt.event.*;
import java.io.*;
import javax.swing.*;

/**
   A program for viewing images.
*/
public class ImageViewer
{
   public static void main(String[] args)
   {
      JFrame frame = new ImageViewerFrame();
      frame.setDefaultCloseOperation(JFrame.EXIT_ON_CLOSE);
      frame.setVisible(true);
   }
}

/**
   A frame with a label to show an image.
*/
class ImageViewerFrame extends JFrame
{
   public ImageViewerFrame()
   {
      setTitle("ImageViewer");
      setSize(DEFAULT_WIDTH, DEFAULT_HEIGHT);
```

```

      // use a label to display the images
      label = new JLabel();
      add(label);

      // set up the file chooser
      chooser = new JFileChooser();
      chooser.setCurrentDirectory(new File("."));

      // set up the menu bar
      JMenuBar menuBar = new JMenuBar();
      setJMenuBar(menuBar);

      JMenu menu = new JMenu("File");
      menuBar.add(menu);

      JMenuItem openItem = new JMenuItem("Open");
      menu.add(openItem);
      openItem.addActionListener(new
         ActionListener()
         {
            public void actionPerformed(ActionEvent event)
            {
               // show file chooser dialog
               int result = chooser.showOpenDialog(null);

               // if file selected, set it as icon of the label
               if (result == JFileChooser.APPROVE_OPTION)
               {
                  String name = chooser.getSelectedFile().getPath();
                  label.setIcon(new ImageIcon(name));
               }
            }
         });

      JMenuItem exitItem = new JMenuItem("Exit");
      menu.add(exitItem);
      exitItem.addActionListener(new
         ActionListener()
         {
            public void actionPerformed(ActionEvent event)
            {
               System.exit(0);
            }
         });
   }

   private JLabel label;
   private JFileChooser chooser;
   private static final int DEFAULT_WIDTH = 300;
   private static final int DEFAULT_HEIGHT = 400;
}
```

Building and Running Applets

The first two programs presented in this book are Java *applications*, stand-alone programs like any native programs. On the other hand, as we mentioned in the last chapter, most of the hype about Java comes from its ability to run *applets* inside a web browser. We want to show you how to build and run an applet from the command line. Then we will load the applet into the applet viewer that comes with the JDK. Finally, we will display it in a web browser.

First, open a shell window and go to the directory `CoreJavaBook/v1ch2/WelcomeApplet`, then enter the following commands:

```
javac WelcomeApplet.java
appletviewer WelcomeApplet.html
```

Figure 2–10 shows what you see in the applet viewer window.

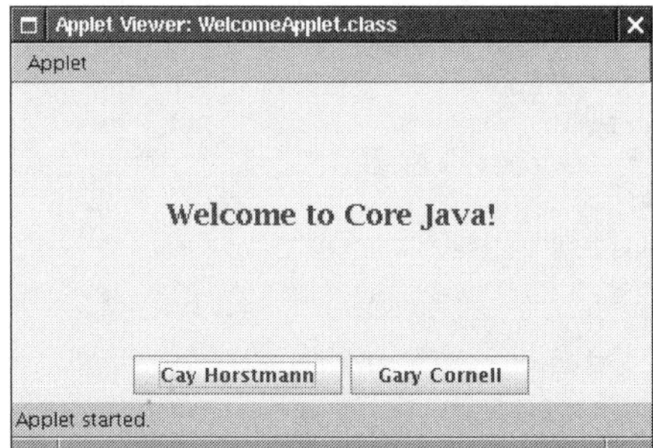

Figure 2–10: WelcomeApplet applet as viewed by the applet viewer

The first command is the now-familiar command to invoke the Java compiler. This compiles the `WelcomeApplet.java` source into the bytecode file `WelcomeApplet.class`.

This time, however, you do not run the `java` program. You invoke the `appletviewer` program instead. This program is a special tool included with the JDK that lets you quickly test an applet. You need to give this program an HTML file, rather than the name of a Java class file. The contents of the `WelcomeApplet.html` file are shown below in Example 2–3.

Example 2–3: WelcomeApplet.html

```
<html>
   <head>
      <title>WelcomeApplet</title>
   </head>
   <body>
      <hr/>
      <p>
         This applet is from the book
         <a href="http://www.horstmann.com/corejava.html">Core Java</a>
         by <em>Cay Horstmann</em> and <em>Gary Cornell</em>,
         published by Sun Microsystems Press.
      </p>
      <applet code="WelcomeApplet.class" width="400" height="200">
         <param name="greeting" value ="Welcome to Core Java!"/>
      </applet>
      <hr/>
      <p><a href="WelcomeApplet.java">The source.</a></p>
   </body>
</html>
```

If you are familiar with HTML, you will notice some standard HTML instructions and the `applet` tag, telling the applet viewer to load the applet whose code is stored in `WelcomeApplet.class`. The applet viewer ignores all HTML tags except for the `applet` tag.

The other HTML tags show up if you view the HTML file in a Java 2-enabled browser. Unfortunately, the browser situation is a bit messy.

- Mozilla (and Netscape 6 and above) support Java 2 on Windows, Linux, and Mac OS X. To experiment with applets, just download the latest version and make sure Java is enabled.
- Some versions of Internet Explorer have no support for Java at all. Others only support the very outdated Microsoft Java Virtual Machine. If you run Internet Explorer on Windows, go to `http://java.com` and install the Java Plug-in.
- If you have a Macintosh running OS X, then Safari and Internet Explorer are integrated with the Macintosh Java implementation, which supports JDK 1.4 at the time of this writing. OS 9 supports only the outdated version 1.1.

Provided you have a browser that supports the Java 2 platform, you can try loading the applet inside the browser.

1. Start your browser.
2. Select File -> Open File (or the equivalent).
3. Go to the `CoreJavaBook/v1ch2/WelcomeApplet` directory.

You should see the `WelcomeApplet.html` file in the file dialog. Load the file. Your browser now loads the applet, including the surrounding text. It will look something like Figure 2–11.

You can see that this application is actually alive and willing to interact with the Internet. Click on the Cay Horstmann button. The applet directs the browser to display Cay's web page. Click on the Gary Cornell button. The applet directs the browser to pop up a mail window, with Gary's e-mail address already filled in.

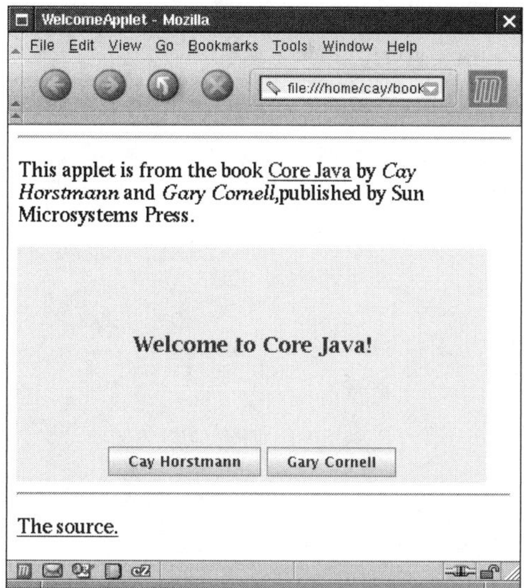

Figure 2–11: Running the WelcomeApplet applet in a browser

Notice that neither of these two buttons works in the applet viewer. The applet viewer has no capabilities to send mail or display a web page, so it ignores your requests. The applet viewer is good for testing applets in isolation, but you need to put applets inside a browser to see how they interact with the browser and the Internet.

TIP: You can also run applets from inside your editor or integrated development environment. In Emacs, select JDE -> Run Applet from the menu. In Eclipse, use the Run -> Run as -> Java Applet menu option.

Finally, the code for the applet is shown in Example 2–4. At this point, do not give it more than a glance. We come back to writing applets in Chapter 10.

In this chapter, you learned about the mechanics of compiling and running Java programs. You are now ready to move on to Chapter 3, where you will start learning the Java language.

Example 2–4: WelcomeApplet.java

```
import javax.swing.*;
import java.awt.*;
import java.awt.event.*;
import java.net.*;

public class WelcomeApplet extends JApplet
{
   public void init()
   {
      setLayout(new BorderLayout());

      JLabel label = new JLabel(getParameter("greeting"), SwingConstants.CENTER);
      label.setFont(new Font("Serif", Font.BOLD, 18));
      add(label, BorderLayout.CENTER);

      JPanel panel = new JPanel();

      JButton cayButton = new JButton("Cay Horstmann");
      cayButton.addActionListener(makeURLActionListener(
         "http://www.horstmann.com"));
      panel.add(cayButton);

      JButton garyButton = new JButton("Gary Cornell");
      garyButton.addActionListener(makeURLActionListener(
         "mailto:gary@thecornells.com"));
      panel.add(garyButton);

      add(panel, BorderLayout.SOUTH);
   }

   private ActionListener makeURLActionListener(final String u)
   {
      return new
         ActionListener()
         {
            public void actionPerformed(ActionEvent event)
            {
               try
               {
```

```
               getAppletContext().showDocument(new URL(u));
            }
            catch(MalformedURLException e)
            {
               e.printStackTrace();
            }
         }
      };
   }
}
```

Chapter 3

Fundamental Programming Structures in Java

At this point, we are assuming that you successfully installed the JDK and were able to run the sample programs that we showed you in Chapter 2. It's time to start programming. This chapter shows you how the basic programming concepts such as data types, branches, and loops are implemented in Java.

Unfortunately, in Java you can't easily write a program that uses a GUI—you need to learn a fair amount of machinery to put up windows, add text boxes and buttons that respond to them, and so on. Because introducing the techniques needed to write GUI-based Java programs would take us too far away from our goal of introducing the basic programming concepts, the sample programs in this chapter are "toy" programs, designed to illustrate a concept. All these examples simply use a shell window for input and output.

Finally, if you are an experienced C++ programmer, you can get away with just skimming this chapter: concentrate on the C/C++ notes that are interspersed throughout the text. Programmers coming from another background, such as Visual Basic, will find most of the concepts familiar and all of the syntax very different—you should read this chapter very carefully.

A Simple Java Program

Let's look more closely at about the simplest Java program you can have—one that simply prints a message to the console window:

```
public class FirstSample
{
   public static void main(String[] args)
   {
      System.out.println("We will not use 'Hello, World!'");
   }
}
```

It is worth spending all the time that you need to become comfortable with the framework of this sample; the pieces will recur in all applications. First and foremost, *Java is case sensitive.* If you made any mistakes in capitalization (such as typing `Main` instead of `main`), the program will not run.

Now let's look at this source code line by line. The keyword `public` is called an *access modifier;* these modifiers control the level of access other parts of a program have to this code. We have more to say about access modifiers in Chapter 5. The keyword `class` reminds you that everything in a Java program lives inside a class. Although we spend a lot more time on classes in the next chapter, for now think of a class as a container for the program logic that defines the behavior of an application. As mentioned in Chapter 1, classes are the building blocks with which all Java applications and applets are built. *Everything* in a Java program must be inside a class.

Following the keyword `class` is the name of the class. The rules for class names in Java are quite generous. Names must begin with a letter, and after that, they can have any combination of letters and digits. The length is essentially unlimited. You cannot use a Java reserved word (such as `public` or `class`) for a class name. (See Appendix A for a list of reserved words.)

The standard naming convention (which we follow in the name `FirstSample`) is that class names are nouns that start with an uppercase letter. If a name consists of multiple words, use an initial uppercase letter in each of the words. (This use of uppercase letters in the middle of a word is sometimes called "camel case" or, self-referentially, "CamelCase.")

You need to make the file name for the source code the same as the name of the public class, with the extension `.java` appended. Thus, you must store this code in a file called `FirstSample.java`. (Again, case is important—don't use `firstsample.java`.)

If you have named the file correctly and not made any typos in the source code, then when you compile this source code, you end up with a file containing the bytecodes for this class. The Java compiler automatically names the bytecode file `FirstSample.class` and stores it in the same directory as the source file. Finally, launch the program by issuing the command:

```
java FirstSample
```

(Remember to leave off the `.class` extension.) When the program executes, it simply displays the string `We will not use 'Hello, World'!` on the console.

When you use

```
java ClassName
```

to run a compiled program, the Java virtual machine always starts execution with the code in the `main` method in the class you indicate. Thus, you *must* have a `main` method in the source file for your class for your code to execute. You can, of course, add your own methods to a class and call them from the `main` method. (We cover writing your own methods in the next chapter.)

NOTE: According to the Java Language Specification, the `main` method must be declared `public`. (The Java Language Specification is the official document that describes the Java language. You can view or download it from `http://java.sun.com/docs/books/jls`.) However, several versions of the Java launcher were willing to execute Java programs even when the `main` method was not `public`. A programmer filed a bug report. To see it, visit the site `http://bugs.sun.com/bugdatabase/index.jsp` and enter the bug identification number 4252539. However, that bug was marked as "closed, will not be fixed." A Sun engineer added an explanation that the Java Virtual Machine Specification (at `http://java.sun.com/docs/books/vmspec`) does not mandate that `main` is `public` and that "fixing it will cause potential troubles." Fortunately, sanity finally prevailed. The Java launcher in JDK 1.4 and beyond enforces that the `main` method is `public`.

There are a couple of interesting aspects about this story. On the one hand, it is frustrating to have quality assurance engineers, who are often overworked and not always experts in the fine points of Java, make questionable decisions about bug reports. On the other hand, it is remarkable that Sun puts the bug reports and their resolutions onto the Web, for anyone to scrutinize. The "bug parade" is a very useful resource for programmers. You can even "vote" for your favorite bug. Bugs with lots of votes have a high chance of being fixed in the next JDK release.

Notice the braces { } in the source code. In Java, as in C/C++, braces delineate the parts (usually called *blocks*) in your program. In Java, the code for any method must be started by an opening brace { and ended by a closing brace }.

Brace styles have inspired an inordinate amount of useless controversy. We use a style that lines up matching braces. Because whitespace is irrelevant to the Java compiler, you can use whatever brace style you like. We will have more to say about the use of braces when we talk about the various kinds of loops.

For now, don't worry about the keywords `static void`—just think of them as part of what you need to get a Java program to compile. By the end of Chapter 4, you will understand this incantation completely. The point to remember for now is that every Java application must have a `main` method that is declared in the following way:

```
public class ClassName
{
   public static void main(String[] args)
   {
      program statements
   }
}
```

C++ NOTE: As a C++ programmer, you know what a class is. Java classes are similar to C++ classes, but there are a few differences that can trap you. For example, in Java *all* functions are methods of some class. (The standard terminology refers to them as methods, not member functions.) Thus, in Java you must have a shell class for the `main` method. You may also be familiar with the idea of *static member functions* in C++. These are member functions defined inside a class that do not operate on objects. The `main` method in Java is always static. Finally, as in C/C++, the `void` keyword indicates that this method does not return a value. Unlike C/C++, the `main` method does not return an "exit code" to the operating system. If the `main` method exits normally, the Java program has the exit code 0, indicating successful completion. To terminate the program with a different exit code, use the `System.exit` method.

Next, turn your attention to this fragment.

```
{
   System.out.println("We will not use 'Hello, World!'");
}
```

Braces mark the beginning and end of the *body* of the method. This method has only one statement in it. As with most programming languages, you can think of Java statements as being the sentences of the language. In Java, every statement must end with a semicolon. In particular, carriage returns do not mark the end of a statement, so statements can span multiple lines if need be.

The body of the `main` method contains a statement that outputs a single line of text to the console.

Here, we are using the `System.out` object and calling its `println` method. Notice the periods used to invoke a method. Java uses the general syntax

object.method(parameters)

for its equivalent of function calls.

In this case, we are calling the `println` method and passing it a string parameter. The method displays the string parameter on the console. It then terminates the output line so that each call to `println` displays its output on a new line. Notice that Java, like C/C++, uses double quotes to delimit strings. (You can find more information about strings later in this chapter.)

Methods in Java, like functions in any programming language, can use zero, one, or more *parameters* (some programmers call them *arguments*). Even if a method takes no parameters, you must still use empty parentheses. For example, a variant of the `println` method with no parameters just prints a blank line. You invoke it with the call

```
System.out.println();
```

NOTE: `System.out` also has a `print` method that doesn't add a new line character to the output. For example, `System.out.print("Hello")` prints "`Hello`" without a new line. The next output appears immediately after the "`o`".

Comments

Comments in Java, like comments in most programming languages, do not show up in the executable program. Thus, you can add as many comments as needed without fear of bloating the code. Java has three ways of marking comments. The most common method is a //. You use this for a comment that will run from the // to the end of the line.

```
System.out.println("We will not use 'Hello, World!'"); // is this too cute?
```

When longer comments are needed, you can mark each line with a //. Or you can use the /* and */ comment delimiters that let you block off a longer comment. This is shown in Example 3–1.

Example 3–1: FirstSample.java

```
/*
   This is the first sample program in Core Java Chapter 3
   Copyright (C) 1997 Cay Horstmann and Gary Cornell
*/

public class FirstSample
{
   public static void main(String[] args)
   {
```

```
        System.out.println("We will not use 'Hello, World!'");
    }
}
```

Finally, a third kind of comment can be used to generate documentation automatically. This comment uses a `/**` to start and a `*/` to end. For more on this type of comment and on automatic documentation generation, see Chapter 4.

CAUTION: `/* */` comments do not nest in Java. That is, you cannot deactivate code simply by surrounding it with `/*` and `*/` because the code that you want to deactivate might itself contain a `*/` delimiter.

Data Types

Java is a *strongly typed language*. This means that every variable must have a declared type. There are eight *primitive types* in Java. Four of them are integer types; two are floating-point number types; one is the character type `char`, used for code units in the Unicode encoding scheme (see the section on the `char` type); and one is a `boolean` type for truth values.

NOTE: Java has an arbitrary precision arithmetic package. However, "big numbers," as they are called, are Java *objects* and not a new Java type. You see how to use them later in this chapter.

Integers

The integer types are for numbers without fractional parts. Negative values are allowed. Java provides the four integer types shown in Table 3–1.

Table 3–1: Java Integer Types

Type	Storage Requirement	Range (Inclusive)
`int`	4 bytes	–2,147,483,648 to 2,147,483, 647 (just over 2 billion)
`short`	2 bytes	–32,768 to 32,767
`long`	8 bytes	–9,223,372,036,854,775,808 to 9,223,372,036,854,775,807
`byte`	1 byte	–128 to 127

In most situations, the `int` type is the most practical. If you want to represent the number of inhabitants of our planet, you'll need to resort to a `long`. The `byte` and `short` types are mainly intended for specialized applications, such as low-level file handling, or for large arrays when storage space is at a premium.

Under Java, the ranges of the integer types do not depend on the machine on which you will be running the Java code. This alleviates a major pain for the programmer who wants to move software from one platform to another, or even between operating systems on the same platform. In contrast, C and C++ programs use the most efficient integer type for each processor. As a result, a C program that runs well on a 32-bit processor may exhibit integer overflow on a 16-bit system. Because Java programs must run with the same results on all machines, the ranges for the various types are fixed.

Long integer numbers have a suffix `L` (for example, `4000000000L`). Hexadecimal numbers have a prefix `0x` (for example, `0xCAFE`). Octal numbers have a prefix `0`. For example, `010` is 8. Naturally, this can be confusing, and we recommend against the use of octal constants.

C++ NOTE: In C and C++, `int` denotes the integer type that depends on the target machine. On a 16-bit processor, like the 8086, integers are 2 bytes. On a 32-bit processor like the Sun SPARC, they are 4-byte quantities. On an Intel Pentium, the integer type of C and C++ depends on the operating system: for DOS and Windows 3.1, integers are 2 bytes. When 32-bit mode is used for Windows programs, integers are 4 bytes. In Java, the sizes of all numeric types are platform independent.

Note that Java does not have any `unsigned` types.

Floating-Point Types

The floating-point types denote numbers with fractional parts. The two floating-point types are shown in Table 3–2.

Table 3–2: Floating-Point Types

Type	Storage Requirement	Range
`float`	4 bytes	approximately ±3.40282347E+38F (6–7 significant decimal digits)
`double`	8 bytes	approximately ±1.79769313486231570E+308 (15 significant decimal digits)

The name `double` refers to the fact that these numbers have twice the precision of the `float` type. (Some people call these *double-precision* numbers.) Here, the type to choose in most applications is `double`. The limited precision of `float` is simply not sufficient for many situations. Seven significant (decimal) digits may be enough to precisely express your annual salary in dollars and cents, but it won't be enough for your company president's salary. The only reasons to use `float` are in the rare situations in which the slightly faster processing of single-precision numbers is important or when you need to store a large number of them.

Numbers of type `float` have a suffix `F` (for example, `3.402F`). Floating-point numbers without an `F` suffix (such as `3.402`) are always considered to be of type `double`. You can optionally supply the `D` suffix (for example, `3.402D`).

As of JDK 5.0, you can specify floating-point numbers in hexadecimal. For example, `0.125` is the same as `0x1.0p-3`. In hexadecimal notation, you use a `p`, not an `e`, to denote the exponent.

All floating-point computations follow the IEEE 754 specification. In particular, there are three special floating-point values:

- positive infinity
- negative infinity
- NaN (not a number)

to denote overflows and errors. For example, the result of dividing a positive number by 0 is positive infinity. Computing 0/0 or the square root of a negative number yields NaN.

NOTE: The constants `Double.POSITIVE_INFINITY`, `Double.NEGATIVE_ INFINITY`, and `Double.NaN` (as well as corresponding `Float` constants) represent these special values, but they are rarely used in practice. In particular, you cannot test

```
if (x == Double.NaN) // is never true
```

to check whether a particular result equals `Double.NaN`. All "not a number" values are considered distinct. However, you can use the `Double.isNaN` method:

```
if (Double.isNaN(x)) // check whether x is "not a number"
```

CAUTION: Floating-point numbers are *not* suitable for financial calculation in which roundoff errors cannot be tolerated. For example, the command `System.out.println(2.0 - 1.1)` prints `0.8999999999999999`, not `0.9` as you would expect. Such roundoff errors are caused by the fact that floating-point numbers are represented in the binary number system. There is no precise binary representation of the fraction 1/10, just as there is no accurate representation of the fraction 1/3 in the decimal system. If you need precise numerical computations without roundoff errors, use the `BigDecimal` class, which is introduced later in this chapter.

The char *Type*

To understand the `char` type, you have to know about the Unicode encoding scheme. Unicode was invented to overcome the limitations of traditional character encoding schemes. Before Unicode, there were many different standards: ASCII in the United States, ISO 8859-1 for Western European languages, KOI-8 for Russian, GB18030 and BIG-5 for Chinese, and so on. This causes two problems. A particular code value corresponds to different letters in the various encoding schemes. Moreover, the encodings for languages with large character sets have variable length: some common characters are encoded as single bytes, others require two or more bytes.

Unicode was designed to solve these problems. When the unification effort started in the 1980s, a fixed 2-byte width code was more than sufficient to encode all characters used in all languages in the world, with room to spare for future expansion—or so everyone thought at the time. In 1991, Unicode 1.0 was released, using slightly less than half of the available 65,536 code values. Java was designed from the ground up to use 16-bit Unicode characters, which was a major advance over other programming languages that used 8-bit characters.

Unfortunately, over time, the inevitable happened. Unicode grew beyond 65,536 characters, primarily due to the addition of a very large set of ideographs used for Chinese, Japanese, and Korean. Now, the 16-bit `char` type is insufficient to describe all Unicode characters.

We need a bit of terminology to explain how this problem is resolved in Java, beginning with JDK 5.0. A *code point* is a code value that is associated with a character in an encoding scheme. In the Unicode standard, code points are written in hexadecimal and prefixed with U+, such as U+0041 for the code point of the letter A. Unicode has code points that are grouped into 17 *code planes*. The first code plane, called the *basic multilingual plane*, consists of the "classic" Unicode characters with code points U+0000 to U+FFFF. Sixteen additional planes, with code points U+10000 to U+10FFFF, hold the *supplementary characters*.

The UTF-16 encoding is a method of representing all Unicode code points in a variable length code. The characters in the basic multilingual plane are represented as 16-bit values, called *code units*. The supplementary characters are encoded as consecutive pairs of code units. Each of the values in such an encoding pair falls into an unused 2048-byte range of the basic multilingual plane, called the *surrogates area* (U+D800 to U+DBFF for the first code unit, U+DC00 to U+DFFF for the second code unit).This is rather clever, because you can immediately tell whether a code unit encodes a single character or whether it is the first or second part of a supplementary character. For example, the mathematical symbol for the set of integers $\mathbb{Z}$ has code point U+1D56B and is encoded by the two code units U+D835 and U+DD6B. (See `http://en.wikipedia.org/wiki/UTF-16` for a description of the encoding algorithm.)

In Java, the `char` type describes a *code unit* in the UTF-16 encoding.

Our strong recommendation is not to use the `char` type in your programs unless you are actually manipulating UTF-16 code units. You are almost always better off treating strings (which we will discuss starting on page 51) as abstract data types.

Having said that, there will be some cases when you will encounter `char` values. Most commonly, these will be character constants. For example, `'A'` is a character constant with value 65. It is different from `"A"`, a string containing a single character. Unicode code units can be expressed as hexadecimal values that run from `\u0000` to `\uFFFF`. For example, `\u2122` is the trademark symbol (™) and `\u03C0` is the Greek letter pi (π).

Besides the `\u` escape sequences that indicate the encoding of Unicode code units, there are several escape sequences for special characters, as shown in Table 3–3. You can use these escape sequences inside quoted character constants and strings, such as `'\u2122'` or `"Hello\n"`. The `\u` escape sequence (but none of the other escape sequences) can even be used *outside* quoted character constants and strings. For example,

```
public static void main(String\u005B\u005D args)
```

is perfectly legal—`\u005B` and `\u005D` are the UTF-16 encodings of the Unicode code points for [and].

Table 3–3: Escape Sequences for Special Characters

Escape Sequence	Name	Unicode Value
`\b`	Backspace	`\u0008`
`\t`	Tab	`\u0009`
`\n`	Linefeed	`\u000a`
`\r`	Carriage return	`\u000d`
`\"`	Double quote	`\u0022`
`\'`	Single quote	`\u0027`
`\\`	Backslash	`\u005c`

NOTE: Although you can use any Unicode character in a Java application or applet, whether you can actually see it displayed depends on your browser (for applets) and (ultimately) on your operating system for both.

The `boolean` *Type*

The `boolean` type has two values, `false` and `true`. It is used for evaluating logical conditions. You cannot convert between integers and `boolean` values.

C++ NOTE: In C++, numbers and even pointers can be used in place of `boolean` values. The value 0 is equivalent to the `bool` value `false`, and a non-zero value is equivalent to `true`. This is *not* the case in Java. Thus, Java programmers are shielded from accidents such as

```
if (x = 0) // oops...meant x == 0
```

In C++, this test compiles and runs, always evaluating to `false`. In Java, the test does not compile because the integer expression `x = 0` cannot be converted to a `boolean` value.

Variables

In Java, every variable has a *type*. You declare a variable by placing the type first, followed by the name of the variable. Here are some examples:

```
double salary;
```

ı. The semicolon is necessary because a

e a sequence of letters or digits. Note that
va than in most languages. A letter is
er that denotes a letter in a language. For
n variable names; Greek speakers could
characters that denote a digit in
ide variable names, nor can spaces.
: and *case is also significant.* The length of

ıaracters are "letters" as far as Java is con-
isJavaIdentifierPart methods in the Character

able name. (See Appendix A for a list of

clare each variable separately, your pro-

‹ample, `hireday` and `hireDay` are two separate
that only differ in their letter case. However,
ne for a variable. Many programmers then
as

ariable name

ıe variable:

tialize it by means of an assignment
ılized variables. For example, the Java
ıs as an error:

```
int vacationDays;
System.out.println(vacationDays); // ERROR--variable not initialized
```

You assign to a previously declared variable by using the variable name on the left, an equal sign (=), and then some Java expression that has an appropriate value on the right.

```
int vacationDays;
vacationDays = 12;
```

You can both declare and initialize a variable on the same line. For example:

```
int vacationDays = 12;
```

Finally, in Java you can put declarations anywhere in your code. For example, the following is valid code in Java:

```
double salary = 65000.0;
System.out.println(salary);
int vacationDays = 12; // ok to declare a variable here
```

In Java, it is considered good style to declare variables as closely as possible to the point where they are first used.

C++ NOTE: C and C++ distinguish between the *declaration* and *definition* of variables. For example,

```
int i = 10;
```

is a definition, whereas

```
extern int i;
```

is a declaration. In Java, no declarations are separate from definitions.

Constants

In Java, you use the keyword `final` to denote a constant. For example,

```
public class Constants
{
   public static void main(String[] args)
   {
      final double CM_PER_INCH = 2.54;
      double paperWidth = 8.5;
      double paperHeight = 11;
      System.out.println("Paper size in centimeters: "
         + paperWidth * CM_PER_INCH + " by " + paperHeight * CM_PER_INCH);
   }
}
```

The keyword `final` indicates that you can assign to the variable once, and then its value is set once and for all. It is customary to name constants in all upper case.

It is probably more common in Java to want a constant that is available to multiple methods inside a single class. These are usually called *class constants.* You set up a class constant with the keywords `static final`. Here is an example of using a class constant:

```
public class Constants2
{
   public static void main(String[] args)
   {
      double paperWidth = 8.5;
      double paperHeight = 11;
      System.out.println("Paper size in centimeters: "
         + paperWidth * CM_PER_INCH + " by " + paperHeight * CM_PER_INCH);
   }

   public static final double CM_PER_INCH = 2.54;
}
```

Note that the definition of the class constant appears *outside* the `main` method. Thus, the constant can also be used in other methods of the same class. Furthermore, if (as in our example) the constant is declared `public`, methods of other classes can also use the constant—in our example, as `Constants2.CM_PER_INCH`.

C++ NOTE: `const` is a reserved Java keyword, but it is not currently used for anything. You must use `final` for a constant.

Operators

The usual arithmetic operators + – * / are used in Java for addition, subtraction, multiplication, and division. The / operator denotes integer division if both arguments are integers, and floating-point division otherwise. Integer remainder (sometimes called *modulus*) is denoted by %. For example, `15 / 2` is 7, `15 % 2` is 1, and `15.0 / 2` is 7.5.

Note that integer division by 0 raises an exception, whereas floating-point division by 0 yields an infinite or NaN result.

There is a convenient shortcut for using binary arithmetic operators in an assignment. For example,

```
x += 4;
```

is equivalent to

```
x = x + 4;
```

(In general, place the operator to the left of the = sign, such as *= or %=.)

NOTE: One of the stated goals of the Java programming language is portability. A computation should yield the same results no matter which virtual machine executes it. For arithmetic computations with floating-point numbers, it is surprisingly difficult to achieve this portability. The `double` type uses 64 bits to store a numeric value, but some processors use 80-bit floating-point registers. These registers yield added precision in intermediate steps of a computation. For example, consider the computation:

```
double w = x * y / z;
```

Many Intel processors compute `x * y` and leave the result in an 80-bit register, then divide by `z` and finally truncate the result back to 64 bits. That can yield a more accurate result, and it can avoid exponent overflow. But the result may be *different* from a computation that uses 64 bits throughout. For that reason, the initial specification of the Java virtual machine mandated that all intermediate computations must be truncated. The numeric community hated it. Not only can the truncated computations cause overflow, they are actually *slower* than the more precise computations because the truncation operations take time. For that reason, the Java programming language was updated to recognize the conflicting demands for optimum performance and perfect reproducibility. By default, virtual machine designers are now permitted to use extended precision for intermediate computations. However, methods tagged with the `strictfp` keyword must use strict floating-point operations that yield reproducible results. For example, you can tag `main` as

```
public static strictfp void main(String[] args)
```

Then all instructions inside the `main` method use strict floating-point computations. If you tag a class as `strictfp`, then all of its methods use strict floating-point computations.

The gory details are very much tied to the behavior of the Intel processors. In default mode, intermediate results are allowed to use an extended exponent, but not an extended mantissa. (The Intel chips support truncation of the mantissa without loss of performance.) Therefore, the only difference between default and strict mode is that strict computations may overflow when default computations don't.

If your eyes glazed over when reading this note, don't worry. Floating-point overflow isn't a problem that one encounters for most common programs. We don't use the `strictfp` keyword in this book.

Increment and Decrement Operators

Programmers, of course, know that one of the most common operations with a numeric variable is to add or subtract 1. Java, following in the footsteps of C and C++, has both increment and decrement operators: `n++` adds 1 to the current value of the variable `n`, and `n--` subtracts 1 from it. For example, the code

```
int n = 12;
n++;
```

changes `n` to 13. Because these operators change the value of a variable, they cannot be applied to numbers themselves. For example, `4++` is not a legal statement.

There are actually two forms of these operators; you have seen the "postfix" form of the operator that is placed after the operand. There is also a prefix form, `++n`. Both change the value of the variable by 1. The difference between the two only appears when they are used inside expressions. The prefix form does the addition first; the postfix form evaluates to the old value of the variable.

```
int m = 7;
int n = 7;
int a = 2 * ++m; // now a is 16, m is 8
int b = 2 * n++; // now b is 14, n is 8
```

We recommend against using `++` inside other expressions because this often leads to confusing code and annoying bugs.

(Of course, while it is true that the `++` operator gives the C++ language its name, it also led to the first joke about the language. C++ haters point out that even the name of the language contains a bug: "After all, it should really be called ++C, because we only want to use a language after it has been improved.")

Relational and `boolean` Operators

Java has the full complement of relational operators. To test for equality you use a double equal sign, `==`. For example, the value of

```
3 == 7
```

is `false`.

Use a `!=` for inequality. For example, the value of

```
3 != 7
```

is `true`.

Finally, you have the usual `<` (less than), `>` (greater than), `<=` (less than or equal), and `>=` (greater than or equal) operators.

Java, following C++, uses `&&` for the logical "and" operator and `||` for the logical "or" operator. As you can easily remember from the `!=` operator, the exclamation point `!` is the logical negation operator. The `&&` and `||` operators are evaluated in "short circuit" fashion. The second argument is not evaluated if the first argument already determines the value. If you combine two expressions with the `&&` operator,

expression$_1$ `&&` *expression*$_2$

and the truth value of the first expression has been determined to be `false`, then it is impossible for the result to be `true`. Thus, the value for the second expression is *not* calculated. This behavior can be exploited to avoid errors. For example, in the expression

```
x != 0 && 1 / x > x + y // no division by 0
```

the second part is never evaluated if x equals zero. Thus, 1 / x is not computed if x is zero, and no divide-by-zero error can occur.

Similarly, the value of *expression*$_1$ || *expression*$_2$ is automatically true if the first expression is true, without evaluation of the second expression.

Finally, Java supports the ternary ?: operator that is occasionally useful. The expression

```
condition ? expression1 : expression2
```

evaluates to the first expression if the condition is true, to the second expression otherwise. For example,

```
x < y ? x : y
```

gives the smaller of x and y.

Bitwise Operators

When working with any of the integer types, you have operators that can work directly with the bits that make up the integers. This means that you can use masking techniques to get at individual bits in a number. The bitwise operators are

& ("and") | ("or")   ^ ("xor")   ~ ("not")

These operators work on bit patterns. For example, if n is an integer variable, then

```
int fourthBitFromRight = (n & 8) / 8;
```

gives you a 1 if the fourth bit from the right in the binary representation of n is 1, and 0 if not. Using & with the appropriate power of 2 lets you mask out all but a single bit.

NOTE: When applied to boolean values, the & and | operators yield a boolean value. These operators are similar to the && and || operators, except that the & and | operators are not evaluated in "short circuit" fashion. That is, both arguments are first evaluated before the result is computed.

There are also >> and << operators, which shift a bit pattern to the right or left. These operators are often convenient when you need to build up bit patterns to do bit masking:

```
int fourthBitFromRight = (n & (1 << 3)) >> 3;
```

Finally, a >>> operator fills the top bits with zero, whereas >> extends the sign bit into the top bits. There is no <<< operator.

CAUTION: The right-hand side argument of the shift operators is reduced modulo 32 (unless the left-hand side is a long, in which case the right-hand side is reduced modulo 64). For example, the value of 1 << 35 is the same as 1 << 3 or 8.

C++ NOTE: In C/C++, there is no guarantee as to whether >> performs an arithmetic shift (extending the sign bit) or a logical shift (filling in with zeroes). Implementors are free to choose whatever is more efficient. That means the C/C++ >> operator is really only defined for non-negative numbers. Java removes that ambiguity.

Mathematical Functions and Constants

The Math class contains an assortment of mathematical functions that you may occasionally need, depending on the kind of programming that you do.

To take the square root of a number, you use the sqrt method:

```
double x = 4;
double y = Math.sqrt(x);
System.out.println(y); // prints 2.0
```

NOTE: There is a subtle difference between the println method and the sqrt method. The println method operates on an object, System.out, defined in the System class. But the sqrt method in the Math class does not operate on any object. Such a method is called a *static* method. You can learn more about static methods in Chapter 4.

The Java programming language has no operator for raising a quantity to a power: you must use the pow method in the Math class. The statement

```
double y = Math.pow(x, a);
```

sets y to be x raised to the power a (x^a). The pow method has parameters that are both of type double, and it returns a double as well.

The Math class supplies the usual trigonometric functions

```
Math.sin
Math.cos
Math.tan
Math.atan
Math.atan2
```

and the exponential function and its inverse, the natural log:

```
Math.exp
Math.log
```

Finally, two constants denote the closest possible approximations to the mathematical constants π and e:

```
Math.PI
Math.E
```

TIP: Starting with JDK 5.0, you can avoid the Math prefix for the mathematical methods and constants by adding the following line to the top of your source file:

```
import static java.lang.Math.*;
```

For example,

```
System.out.println("The square root of \u03C0 is " + sqrt(PI));
```

We discuss static imports in Chapter 4.

NOTE: The functions in the Math class use the routines in the computer's floating-point unit for fastest performance. If completely predictable results are more important than fast performance, use the StrictMath class instead. It implements the algorithms from the "Freely Distributable Math Library" fdlibm, guaranteeing identical results on all platforms. See http://www.netlib.org/fdlibm/index.html for the source of these algorithms. (Whenever fdlibm provides more than one definition for a function, the StrictMath class follows the IEEE 754 version whose name starts with an "e".)

Conversions Between Numeric Types

It is often necessary to convert from one numeric type to another. Figure 3–1 shows the legal conversions.

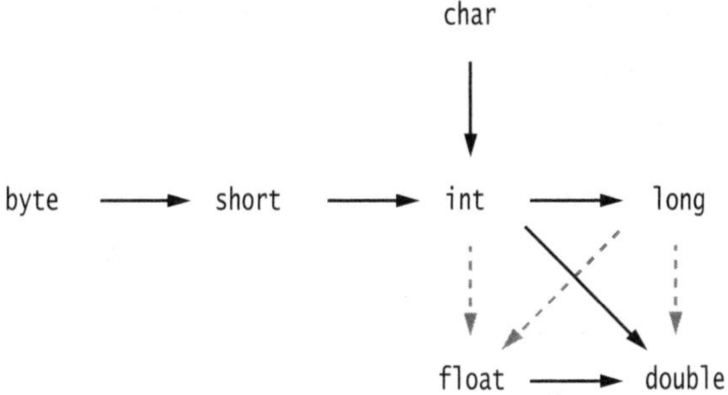

Figure 3–1: Legal conversions between numeric types

The six solid arrows in Figure 3–1 denote conversions without information loss. The three dotted arrows denote conversions that may lose precision. For example, a large integer such as 123456789 has more digits than the float type can represent. When the integer is converted to a float, the resulting value has the correct magnitude but it loses some precision.

```
int n = 123456789;
float f = n; // f is 1.23456792E8
```

When two values with a binary operator (such as n + f where n is an integer and f is a floating-point value) are combined, both operands are converted to a common type before the operation is carried out.

- If either of the operands is of type double, the other one will be converted to a double.
- Otherwise, if either of the operands is of type float, the other one will be converted to a float.
- Otherwise, if either of the operands is of type long, the other one will be converted to a long.
- Otherwise, both operands will be converted to an int.

Casts

In the preceding section, you saw that int values are automatically converted to double values when necessary. On the other hand, there are obviously times when you want to consider a double as an integer. Numeric conversions are possible in Java, but of course information may be lost. Conversions in which loss of information is possible are done by means of *casts.* The syntax for casting is to give the target type in parentheses, followed by the variable name. For example:

```
double x = 9.997;
int nx = (int) x;
```

Then, the variable nx has the value 9 because casting a floating-point value to an integer discards the fractional part.

If you want to *round* a floating-point number to the *nearest* integer (which is the more useful operation in most cases), use the Math.round method:

```
double x = 9.997;
int nx = (int) Math.round(x);
```

Now the variable nx has the value 10. You still need to use the cast (int) when you call round. The reason is that the return value of the round method is a long, and a long can only be assigned to an int with an explicit cast because there is the possibility of information loss.

CAUTION: If you try to cast a number of one type to another that is out of the range for the target type, the result will be a truncated number that has a different value. For example, `(byte) 300` is actually 44.

C++ NOTE: You cannot cast between `boolean` values and any numeric type. This convention prevents common errors. In the rare case that you want to convert a `boolean` value to a number, you can use a conditional expression such as `b ? 1 : 0`.

Parentheses and Operator Hierarchy

Table 3–4 shows the precedence of operators. If no parentheses are used, operations are performed in the hierarchical order indicated. Operators on the same level are processed from left to right, except for those that are right associative, as indicated in the table. For example, because `&&` has a higher precedence than `||`, the expression

```
a && b || c
```

means

```
(a && b) || c
```

Because `+=` associates right to left, the expression

```
a += b += c
```

means

```
a += (b += c)
```

That is, the value of `b += c` (which is the value of `b` after the addition) is added to `a`.

Table 3–4: Operator Precedence

Operators	Associativity
[] . () (method call)	Left to right
! ~ ++ -- + (unary) - (unary) () (cast) new	Right to left
* / %	Left to right
+ -	Left to right
<< >> >>>	Left to right
< <= > >= instanceof	Left to right
== !=	Left to right
&	Left to right
^	Left to right
|	Left to right
&&	Left to right
||	Left to right
?:	Right to left
= += -= *= /= %= &= |= ^= <<= >>= >>>=	Right to left

C++ NOTE: Unlike C or C++, Java does not have a comma operator. However, you can use a *comma-separated list of expressions* in the first and third slot of a `for` statement.

Enumerated Types

Sometimes, a variable should only hold a restricted set of values. For example, you may sell clothes or pizza in four sizes: small, medium, large, and extra large. Of course, you could encode these sizes as integers 1, 2, 3, 4, or characters `S`, `M`, `L`, and `X`. But that is an error-prone setup. It is too easy for a variable to hold a wrong value (such as 0 or `m`).

Starting with JDK 5.0, you can define your own *enumerated type* whenever such a situation arises. An enumerated type has a finite number of named values. For example,

```
enum Size { SMALL, MEDIUM, LARGE, EXTRA_LARGE };
```

Now you can declare variables of this type:

```
Size s = Size.MEDIUM;
```

A variable of type `Size` can hold only one of the values listed in the type declaration or the special value `null` that indicates that the variable is not set to any value at all.

We discuss enumerated types in greater detail in Chapter 5.

Strings

Conceptually, Java strings are sequences of Unicode characters. For example, the string `"Java\u2122"` consists of the five Unicode characters J, a, v, a, and ™. Java does not have a built-in string type. Instead, the standard Java library contains a predefined class called, naturally enough, `String`. Each quoted string is an instance of the `String` class:

```
String e = ""; // an empty string
String greeting = "Hello";
```

Code Points and Code Units

Java strings are implemented as sequences of `char` values. As we discussed on page 41, the `char` data type is a code unit for representing Unicode code points in the UTF-16 encoding. The most commonly used Unicode characters can be represented with a single code unit. The supplementary characters require a pair of code units.

The `length` method yields the number of code units required for a given string in the UTF-16 encoding. For example:

```
String greeting = "Hello";
int n = greeting.length(); // is 5.
```

To get the true length, that is, the number of code points, call

```
int cpCount = greeting.codePointCount(0, greeting.length());
```

The call `s.charAt(n)` returns the code unit at position `n`, where `n` is between 0 and `s.length() - 1`. For example,

```
char first = greeting.charAt(0); // first is 'H'
char last = greeting.charAt(4); // last is 'o'
```

To get at the `i`th code point, use the statements

```
int index = greeting.offsetByCodePoints(0, i);
int cp = greeting.codePointAt(index);
```

NOTE: Java counts the code units in strings in a peculiar fashion: the first code unit in a string has position 0. This convention originated in C, where there was a technical reason for counting positions starting at 0. That reason has long gone away and only the nuisance remains. However, so many programmers are used to this convention that the Java designers decided to keep it.

Why are we making a fuss about code units? Consider the sentence

```
ℤ is the set of integers
```

The ℤ character requires two code units in the UTF-16 encoding. Calling

```
char ch = sentence.charAt(1)
```

doesn't return a space but the second code unit of ℤ. To avoid this problem, you should not use the char type. It is too low-level.

If your code traverses a string, and you want to look at each code point in turn, use these statements:

```
int cp = sentence.codePointAt(i);
if (Character.isSupplementaryCodePoint(cp)) i += 2;
else i++;
```

Fortunately, the codePointAt method can tell whether a code unit is the first or second half of a supplementary character, and it returns the right result either way. That is, you can move backwards with the following statements:

```
i--;
int cp = sentence.codePointAt(i);
if (Character.isSupplementaryCodePoint(cp)) i--;
```

Substrings

You extract a substring from a larger string with the substring method of the String class. For example,

```
String greeting = "Hello";
String s = greeting.substring(0, 3);
```

creates a string consisting of the characters "Hel".

The second parameter of substring is the first code unit that you *do not* want to copy. In our case, we want to copy the code units in positions 0, 1, and 2 (from position 0 to position 2 inclusive). As substring counts it, this means from position 0 inclusive to position 3 *exclusive*.

There is one advantage to the way substring works: Computing the number of code units in the substring is easy. The string s.substring(a, b) always has b - a code units. For example, the substring "Hel" has 3 – 0 = 3 code units.

String Editing

The String class gives no methods that let you *change* a character in an existing string. If you want to turn greeting into "Help!", you cannot directly change the last positions of greeting into 'p' and '!'. If you are a C programmer, this will make you feel pretty helpless. How are you going to modify the string? In Java, it is quite easy: concatenate the substring that you want to keep with the characters that you want to replace.

```
greeting = greeting.substring(0, 3) + "p!";
```

This declaration changes the current value of the greeting variable to "Help!".

Because you cannot change the individual characters in a Java string, the documentation refers to the objects of the String class as being *immutable*. Just as the number 3 is always 3, the string "Hello" will always contain the code unit sequence describing the characters H, e, l, l, o. You cannot change these values. You can, as you just saw however, change the contents of the string *variable* greeting and make it refer to a different string, just as you can make a numeric variable currently holding the value 3 hold the value 4.

Isn't that a lot less efficient? It would seem simpler to change the code units than to build up a whole new string from scratch. Well, yes and no. Indeed, it isn't efficient to generate a new string that holds the concatenation of "Hel" and "p!". But immutable strings have one great advantage: the compiler can arrange that strings are *shared*.

To understand how this works, think of the various strings as sitting in a common pool. String variables then point to locations in the pool. If you copy a string variable, both the original and the copy share the same characters. Overall, the designers of Java decided that the efficiency of sharing outweighs the inefficiency of string editing by extracting substrings and concatenating.

Look at your own programs; we suspect that most of the time, you don't change strings—you just compare them. Of course, in some cases, direct manipulation of strings is more efficient. (One example is assembling strings from individual characters that come from a file or the keyboard.) For these situations, Java provides a separate StringBuilder class that we describe in Chapter 12. If you are not concerned with the efficiency of string handling, you can ignore StringBuilder and just use String.

C++ NOTE: C programmers generally are bewildered when they see Java strings for the first time because they think of strings as arrays of characters:

```
char greeting[] = "Hello";
```

That is the wrong analogy: a Java string is roughly analogous to a char* pointer,

```
char* greeting = "Hello";
```

When you replace greeting with another string, the Java code does roughly the following:

```
char* temp = malloc(6);
strncpy(temp, greeting, 3);
strncpy(temp + 3, "p!", 3);
greeting = temp;
```

Sure, now greeting points to the string "Help!". And even the most hardened C programmer must admit that the Java syntax is more pleasant than a sequence of strncpy calls. But what if we make another assignment to greeting?

```
greeting = "Howdy";
```

Don't we have a memory leak? After all, the original string was allocated on the heap. Fortunately, Java does automatic garbage collection. If a block of memory is no longer needed, it will eventually be recycled.

If you are a C++ programmer and use the string class defined by ANSI C++, you will be much more comfortable with the Java String type. C++ string objects also perform automatic allocation and deallocation of memory. The memory management is performed explicitly by constructors, assignment operators, and destructors. However, C++ strings are mutable—you can modify individual characters in a string.

Concatenation

Java, like most programming languages, allows you to use the + sign to join (concatenate) two strings.

```
String expletive = "Expletive";
String PG13 = "deleted";
String message = expletive + PG13;
```

The above code sets the variable message to the string "Expletivedeleted". (Note the lack of a space between the words: the + sign joins two strings in the order received, *exactly* as they are given.)

When you concatenate a string with a value that is not a string, the latter is converted to a string. (As you see in Chapter 5, every Java object can be converted to a string.) For example:

```
int age = 13;
String rating = "PG" + age;
```

sets `rating` to the string `"PG13"`.

This feature is commonly used in output statements. For example,

```
System.out.println("The answer is " + answer);
```

is perfectly acceptable and will print what one would want (and with the correct spacing because of the space after the word `is`).

Testing Strings for Equality

To test whether two strings are equal, use the `equals` method. The expression

```
s.equals(t)
```

returns `true` if the strings `s` and `t` are equal, `false` otherwise. Note that `s` and `t` can be string variables or string constants. For example, the expression

```
"Hello".equals(greeting)
```

is perfectly legal. To test whether two strings are identical except for the upper/lowercase letter distinction, use the `equalsIgnoreCase` method.

```
"Hello".equalsIgnoreCase("hello")
```

Do *not* use the `==` operator to test whether two strings are equal! It only determines whether or not the strings are stored in the same location. Sure, if strings are in the same location, they must be equal. But it is entirely possible to store multiple copies of identical strings in different places.

```
String greeting = "Hello"; //initialize greeting to a string
if (greeting == "Hello") . . .
   // probably true
if (greeting.substring(0, 3) == "Hel") . . .
   // probably false
```

If the virtual machine would always arrange for equal strings to be shared, then you could use the `==` operator for testing equality. But only string *constants* are shared, not strings that are the result of operations like `+` or `substring`. Therefore, *never* use `==` to compare strings lest you end up with a program with the worst kind of bug—an intermittent one that seems to occur randomly.

C++ NOTE: If you are used to the C++ `string` class, you have to be particularly careful about equality testing. The C++ `string` class does overload the `==` operator to test for equality of the string contents. It is perhaps unfortunate that Java goes out of its way to give strings the same "look and feel" as numeric values but then makes strings behave like pointers for equality testing. The language designers could have redefined `==` for strings, just as they made a special arrangement for `+`. Oh well, every language has its share of inconsistencies.

C programmers never use `==` to compare strings but use `strcmp` instead. The Java method `compareTo` is the exact analog to `strcmp`. You can use

```
if (greeting.compareTo("Hello") == 0) . . .
```

but it seems clearer to use `equals` instead.

The `String` class in Java contains more than 50 methods. A surprisingly large number of them are sufficiently useful so that we can imagine using them frequently. The following API note summarizes the ones we found most useful.

NOTE: You will find these API notes throughout the book to help you understand the Java Application Programming Interface (API). Each API note starts with the name of a class such as `java.lang.String`—the significance of the so-called *package* name `java.lang` is explained in Chapter 4. The class name is followed by the names, explanations, and parameter descriptions of one or more methods.

We typically do not list all methods of a particular class but instead select those that are most commonly used, and describe them in a concise form. For a full listing, consult the on-line documentation.

We also list the version number in which a particular class was introduced. If a method has been added later, it has a separate version number.

java.lang.String 1.0

- `char charAt(int index)`
  returns the code unit at the specified location. You probably don't want to call this method unless you are interested in low-level code units.
- `int codePointAt(int index)` 5.0
  returns the code point that starts or ends at the specified location.
- `int offsetByCodePoints(int startIndex, int cpCount)` 5.0
  returns the index of the code point that is `cpCount` code points away from the code point at `startIndex`.
- `int compareTo(String other)`
  returns a negative value if the string comes before `other` in dictionary order, a positive value if the string comes after `other` in dictionary order, or 0 if the strings are equal.
- `boolean endsWith(String suffix)`
  returns `true` if the string ends with `suffix`.
- `boolean equals(Object other)`
  returns `true` if the string equals `other`.
- `boolean equalsIgnoreCase(String other)`
  returns `true` if the string equals `other`, except for upper/lowercase distinction.
- `int indexOf(String str)`
- `int indexOf(String str, int fromIndex)`
- `int indexOf(int cp)`
- `int indexOf(int cp, int fromIndex)`
  return the start of the first substring equal to the string `str` or the code point `cp`, starting at index 0 or at `fromIndex`, or -1 if `str` does not occur in this string.
- `int lastIndexOf(String str)`
- `int lastIndexOf(String str, int fromIndex)`
- `int lastindexOf(int cp)`
- `int lastindexOf(int cp, int fromIndex)`
  return the start of the last substring equal to the string `str` or the code point `cp`, starting at the end of the string or at `fromIndex`.
- `int length()`
  returns the length of the string.
- `int codePointCount(int startIndex, int endIndex)` 5.0
  returns the number of code points between `startIndex` and `endIndex - 1`. Unpaired surrogates are counted as code points.

- `String replace(CharSequence oldString, CharSequence newString)`
  returns a new string that is obtained by replacing all substrings matching `oldString` in the string with the string `newString`. You can supply `String` or `StringBuilder` objects for the `CharSequence` parameters.
- `boolean startsWith(String prefix)`
  returns `true` if the string begins with `prefix`.
- `String substring(int beginIndex)`
- `String substring(int beginIndex, int endIndex)`
  return a new string consisting of all code units from `beginIndex` until the end of the string or until `endIndex - 1`.
- `String toLowerCase()`
  returns a new string containing all characters in the original string, with uppercase characters converted to lower case.
- `String toUpperCase()`
  returns a new string containing all characters in the original string, with lowercase characters converted to upper case.
- `String trim()`
  returns a new string by eliminating all leading and trailing spaces in the original string.

Reading the On-Line API Documentation

As you just saw, the `String` class has lots of methods. Furthermore, there are thousands of classes in the standard libraries, with many more methods. It is plainly impossible to remember all useful classes and methods. Therefore, it is essential that you become familiar with the on-line API documentation that lets you look up all classes and methods in the standard library. The API documentation is part of the JDK. It is in HTML format. Point your web browser to the `docs/api/index.html` subdirectory of your JDK installation. You will see a screen like that in Figure 3–2.

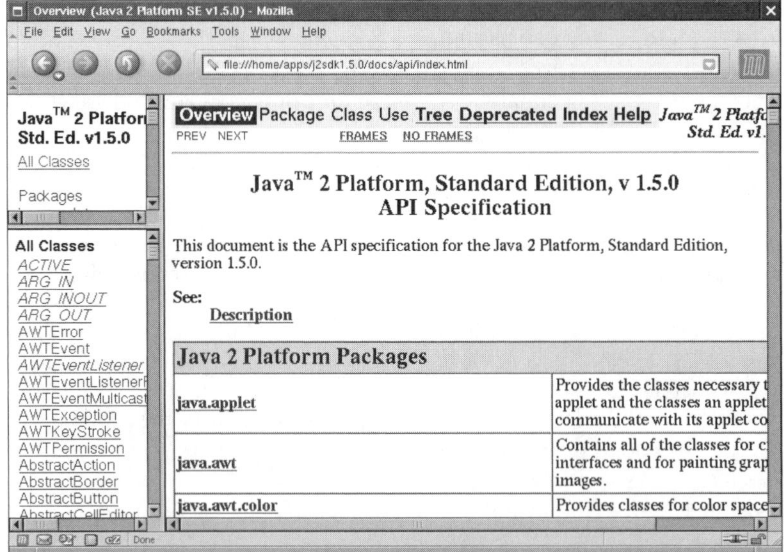

Figure 3–2: The three panes of the API documentation

The screen is organized into three frames. A small frame on the top left shows all available packages. Below it, a larger frame lists all classes. Click on any class name, and the API

documentation for the class is displayed in the large frame to the right (see Figure 3–3). For example, to get more information on the methods of the `String` class, scroll the second frame until you see the String link, then click on it.

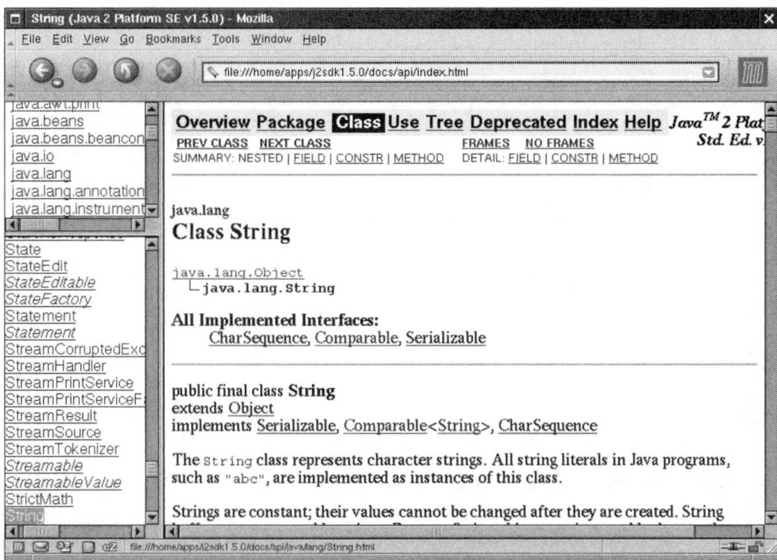

Figure 3–3: Class description for the `String` class

Then scroll the frame on the right until you reach a summary of all methods, sorted in alphabetical order (see Figure 3–4). Click on any method name for a detailed description of that method (see Figure 3–5). For example, if you click on the compareToIgnoreCase link, you get the description of the `compareToIgnoreCase` method.

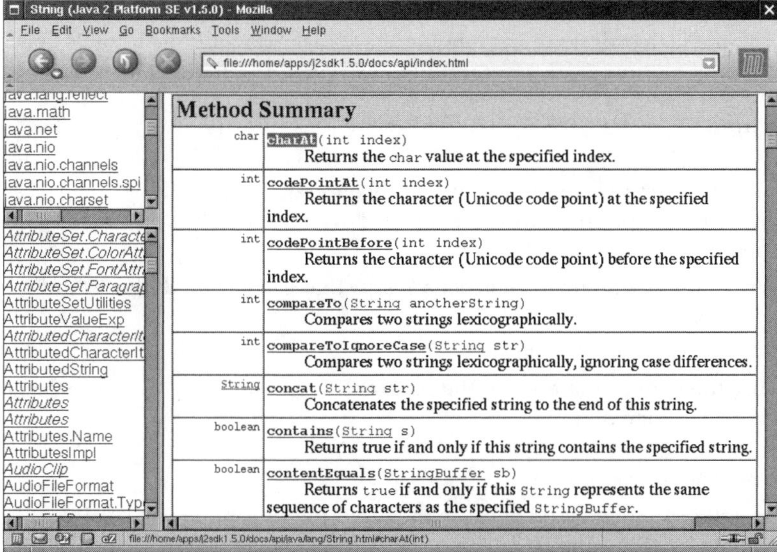

Figure 3–4: Method summary of the `String` class

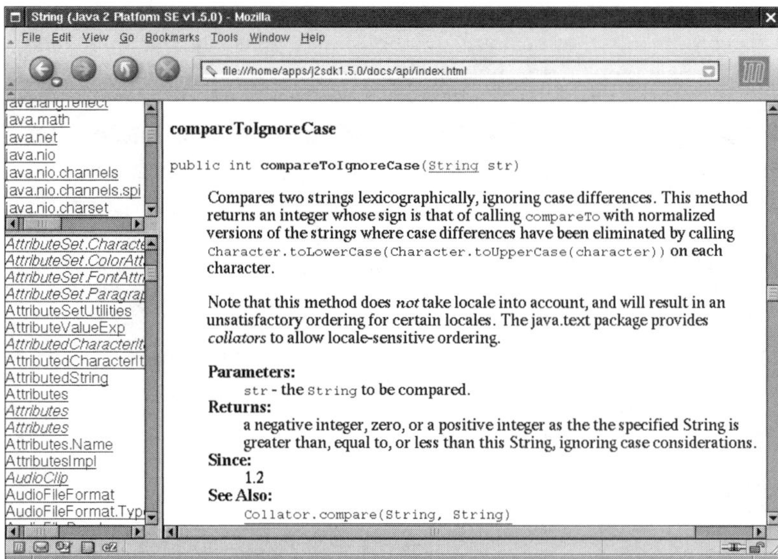

Figure 3–5: Detailed description of a `String` method

TIP: Bookmark the `docs/api/index.html` page in your browser right now.

Input and Output

To make our example programs more interesting, we want to accept input and properly format the program output. Of course, modern programs use a GUI for collecting user input. However, programming such an interface requires more tools and techniques than we have at our disposal at this time. Because the first order of business is to become more familiar with the Java programming language, we make do with the humble console for input and output for now. GUI programming is covered in Chapters 7 through 9.

Reading Input

You saw that it is easy to print output to the "standard output stream" (that is, the console window) just by calling `System.out.println`. Oddly enough, before JDK 5.0, there was no convenient way to read input from the console window. Fortunately, that situation has finally been rectified.

To read console input, you first construct a `Scanner` that is attached to the "standard input stream" `System.in`.

```
Scanner in = new Scanner(System.in);
```

Now you use the various methods of the `Scanner` class to read input. For example, the `nextLine` method reads a line of input.

```
System.out.print("What is your name? ");
String name = in.nextLine();
```

Here, we use the `nextLine` method because the input might contain spaces. To read a single word (delimited by whitespace), call

```
String firstName = in.next();
```

To read an integer, use the `nextInt` method.

```
System.out.print("How old are you? ");
int age = in.nextInt();
```

Similarly, the `nextDouble` method reads the next floating-point number.

The program in Example 3–2 asks for the user's name and age and then prints a message like

```
Hello, Cay. Next year, you'll be 46
```

Finally, add the line

```
import java.util.*;
```

at the beginning of the program. The `Scanner` class is defined in the `java.util` package. Whenever you use a class that is not defined in the basic `java.lang` package, you need to use an `import` directive. We look at packages and `import` directives in more detail in Chapter 4.

Example 3–2: InputTest.java

```
import java.util.*;

public class InputTest
{
   public static void main(String[] args)
   {
      Scanner in = new Scanner(System.in);

      // get first input
      System.out.print("What is your name? ");
      String name = in.nextLine();

      // get second input
      System.out.print("How old are you? ");
      int age = in.nextInt();

      // display output on console
      System.out.println("Hello, " + name + ". Next year, you'll be " + (age + 1));
   }
}
```

NOTE: If you do not have JDK 5.0 or above, you have to work harder to read user input. The simplest method is to use an input dialog (see Figure 3–6).

```
String input = JOptionPane.showInputDialog(promptString)
```

The return value is the string that the user typed.

For example, here is how you can query the name of the user of your program:

```
String name = JOptionPane.showInputDialog("What is your name?");
```

Reading numbers requires an additional step. The `JOptionPane.showInputDialog` method returns a string, not a number. You use the `Integer.parseInt` or `Double.parseDouble` method to convert the string to its numeric value. For example,

```
String input = JOptionPane.showInputDialog("How old are you?");
int age = Integer.parseInt(input);
```

If the user types `45`, then the string variable `input` is set to the string `"45"`. The `Integer.parseInt` method converts the string to its numeric value, the number 45.

The JOptionPane class is defined in the javax.swing package, so you need to add the statement

```
import javax.swing.*;
```

Finally, whenever your program calls JOptionPane.showInputDialog, you need to end it with a call to System.exit(0). The reason is a bit technical. Showing a dialog box starts a new thread of control. When the main method exits, the new thread does not automatically terminate. To end all threads, you call the System.exit method. (For more information on threads, see Chapter 1 of Volume 2.) The following program is the equivalent to Example 3–2 prior to JDK 5.0.

```
import javax.swing.*;
public class InputTest
{
   public static void main(String[] args)
   {
      String name = JOptionPane.showInputDialog("What is your name?");
      String input = JOptionPane.showInputDialog("How old are you?");
      int age = Integer.parseInt(input);
      System.out.println("Hello, " + name + ". Next year, you'll be " + (age + 1));
      System.exit(0);
   }
}
```

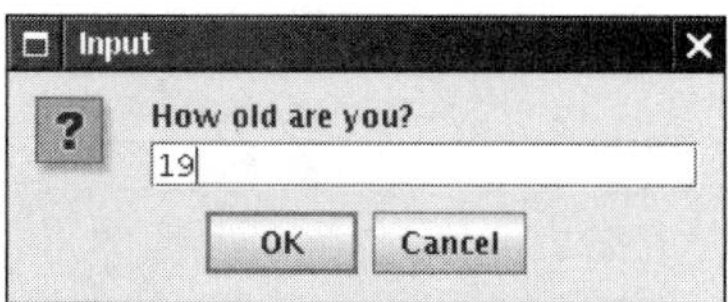

Figure 3–6: An input dialog

API java.util.Scanner 5.0

- `Scanner(InputStream in)`
  constructs a Scanner object from the given input stream.
- `String nextLine()`
  reads the next line of input.
- `String next()`
  reads the next word of input (delimited by whitespace).
- `int nextInt()`
- `double nextDouble()`
  read and convert the next character sequence that represents an integer or floating-point number.
- `boolean hasNext()`
  tests whether there is another word in the input.
- `boolean hasNextInt()`
- `boolean hasNextDouble()`
  test whether the next character sequence represents an integer or floating-point number.

javax.swing.JOptionPane 1.2

- `static String showInputDialog(Object message)`
  displays a dialog box with a message prompt, an input field, and "OK" and "Cancel" buttons. The method returns the string that the user typed.

java.lang.System 1.0

- `static void exit(int status)`
  terminates the virtual machine and passes the status code to the operating system. By convention, a non-zero status code indicates an error.

Formatting Output

You can print a number `x` to the console with the statement `System.out.print(x)`. That command will print `x` with the maximum number of non-zero digits for that type. For example,

```
double x = 10000.0 / 3.0;
System.out.print(x);
```

prints

```
3333.3333333333335
```

That is a problem if you want to display, for example, dollars and cents.

Before JDK 5.0, formatting numbers was a bit of a hassle. Fortunately, JDK 5.0 brought back the venerable `printf` method from the C library. For example, the call

```
System.out.printf("%8.2f", x);
```

prints `x` with a *field width* of 8 characters and a *precision* of 2 characters. That is, the printout contains a leading space and the seven characters

```
3333.33
```

You can supply multiple parameters to `printf`, for example:

```
System.out.printf("Hello, %s. Next year, you'll be %d", name, age);
```

Each of the *format specifiers* that start with a `%` character is replaced with the corresponding argument. The *conversion character* that ends a format specifier indicates the type of the value to be formatted: `f` is a floating-point number, `s` a string, and `d` a decimal integer. Table 3–5 shows all conversion characters.

Table 3–5: Conversions for `printf`

Conversion Character	Type	Example
`d`	Decimal integer	`159`
`x`	Hexadecimal integer	`9f`
`o`	Octal integer	`237`
`f`	Fixed-point floating-point	`15.9`
`e`	Exponential floating-point	`1.59e+01`
`g`	General floating-point (the shorter of `e` and `f`)	
`a`	Hexadecimal floating point	`0x1.fccdp3`
`s`	String	`Hello`
`c`	Character	`H`

Table 3–5: Conversions for `printf` (continued)

Conversion Character	Type	Example
`b`	Boolean	`true`
`h`	Hash code	`42628b2`
`t`*x*	Date and time	See Table 3–7
`%`	The percent symbol	`%`
`n`	The platform-dependent line separator	

In addition, you can specify *flags* that control the appearance of the formatted output. Table 3–6 shows all flags. For example, the comma flag adds group separators. That is,

```
System.out.printf("%,.2f", 10000.0 / 3.0);
```

prints

```
3,333.33
```

You can use multiple flags, for example, `"%,(.2f"`, to use group separators and enclose negative numbers in parentheses.

NOTE: You can use the `s` conversion to format arbitrary objects. If an arbitrary object implements the `Formattable` interface, the object's `formatTo` method is invoked. Otherwise, the `toString` method is invoked to turn the object into a string. We discuss the `toString` method in Chapter 5 and interfaces in Chapter 6.

Table 3–6: Flags for `printf`

Flag	Purpose	Example
`+`	Prints sign for positive and negative numbers	`+3333.33`
space	Adds a space before positive numbers	`| 3333.33|`
`0`	Adds leading zeroes	`003333.33`
`-`	Left-justifies field	`|3333.33 |`
`(`	Encloses negative number in parentheses	`(3333.33)`
`,`	Adds group separators	`3,333.33`
# (for `f` format)	Always includes a decimal point	`3,333.`
# (for `x` or `o` format)	Adds `0x` or `0` prefix	`0xcafe`
`^`	Converts to upper case	`0XCAFE`
`$`	Specifies the index of the argument to be formatted; for example, `%1$d %1$x` prints the first argument in decimal and hexadecimal	`159 9F`
`<`	Formats the same value as the previous specification; for example, `%d %<x` prints the same number in decimal and hexadecimal	`159 9F`

You can use the static `String.format` method to create a formatted string without printing it:

```
String message = String.format("Hello, %s. Next year, you'll be %d", name, age);
```

Although we do not describe the `Date` type in detail until Chapter 4, we do, in the interest of completeness, briefly discuss the date and time formatting options of the `printf` method. You use two a two-letter format, starting with `t` and ending in one of the letters of Table 3–7. For example,

```
System.out.printf("%tc", new Date());
```

prints the current date and time in the format

```
Mon Feb 09 18:05:19 PST 2004
```

Table 3–7: Date and Time Conversion Characters

Conversion Character	Type	Example
`c`	Complete date and time	`Mon Feb 09 18:05:19 PST 2004`
`F`	ISO 8601 date	`2004-02-09`
`D`	U.S. formatted date (month/day/year)	`02/09/2004`
`T`	24-hour time	`18:05:19`
`r`	12-hour time	`06:05:19 pm`
`R`	24-hour time, no seconds	`18:05`
`Y`	Four-digit year (with leading zeroes)	`2004`
`y`	Last two digits of the year (with leading zeroes)	`04`
`C`	First two digits of the year (with leading zeroes)	`20`
`B`	Full month name	`February`
`b` or `h`	Abbreviated month name	`Feb`
`m`	Two-digit month (with leading zeroes)	`02`
`d`	Two-digit day (with leading zeroes)	`09`
`e`	Two-digit day (without leading zeroes)	`9`
`A`	Full weekday name	`Monday`
`a`	Abbreviated weekday name	`Mon`
`j`	Three-digit day of year (with leading zeroes), between 001 and 366	`069`
`H`	Two-digit hour (with leading zeroes), between 00 and 23	`18`
`k`	Two-digit hour (without leading zeroes), between 0 and 23	`18`
`I`	Two-digit hour (with leading zeroes), between 01 and 12	`06`
`l`	Two-digit hour (without leading zeroes), between 1 and 12	`6`
`M`	Two-digit minutes (with leading zeroes)	`05`
`S`	Two-digit seconds (with leading zeroes)	`19`
`L`	Three-digit milliseconds (with leading zeroes)	`047`
`N`	Nine-digit nanoseconds (with leading zeroes)	`047000000`

Table 3–7: Date and Time Conversion Characters (continued)

Conversion Character	Type	Example
`P`	Uppercase morning or afternoon marker	`PM`
`p`	Lowercase morning or afternoon marker	`pm`
`z`	RFC 822 numeric offset from GMT	`-0800`
`Z`	Time zone	`PST`
`s`	Seconds since 1970-01-01 00:00:00 GMT	`1078884319`
`E`	Milliseconds since 1970-01-01 00:00:00 GMT	`1078884319047`

As you can see in Table 3–7, some of the formats yield only a part of a given date, for example, just the day or just the month. It would be a bit silly if you had to supply the date multiple times to format each part. For that reason, a format string can indicate the *index* of the argument to be formatted. The index must immediately follow the `%`, and it must be terminated by a `$`. For example,

```
System.out.printf("%1$s %2$tB %2$te, %2$tY", "Due date:", new Date());
```

prints

```
Due date: February 9, 2004
```

Alternatively, you can use the `<` flag. It indicates that the same argument as in the preceding format specification should be used again. That is, the statement

```
System.out.printf("%s %tB %<te, %<tY", "Due date:", new Date());
```

yields the same output as the preceding statement.

CAUTION: Argument index values start with 1, not with 0: `%1$...` formats the first argument. This avoids confusion with the `0` flag.

You have now seen all features of the `printf` method. Figure 3–7 shows a syntax diagram for format specifiers.

format-specifier:

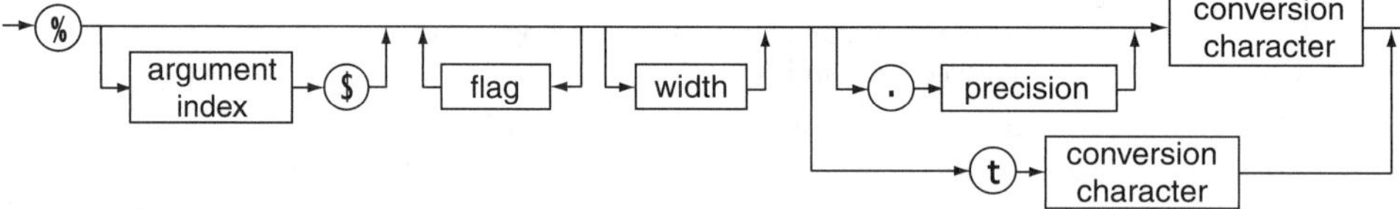

Figure 3–7: Format specifier syntax

NOTE: A number of the formatting rules are *locale specific*. For example, in Germany, the decimal separator is a period, not a comma, and Monday is formatted as Montag. You will see in Volume 2 how to control the international behavior of your applications.

TIP: If you use a version of Java prior to JDK 5.0, use the `NumberFormat` and `DateFormat` classes instead of `printf`.

Control Flow

Java, like any programming language, supports both conditional statements and loops to determine control flow. We start with the conditional statements and then move on to loops. We end with the somewhat cumbersome `switch` statement that you can use when you have to test for many values of a single expression.

C++ NOTE: The Java control flow constructs are identical to those in C and C++, with a few exceptions. There is no `goto`, but there is a "labeled" version of `break` that you can use to break out of a nested loop (where you perhaps would have used a `goto` in C). Finally. JDK 5.0 adds a variant of the `for` loop that has no analog in C or C++. It is similar to the `foreach` loop in C#.

Block Scope

Before we get into the actual control structures, you need to know more about *blocks.*

A block or compound statement is any number of simple Java statements that are surrounded by a pair of braces. Blocks define the scope of your variables. Blocks can be *nested* inside another block. Here is a block that is nested inside the block of the `main` method.

```
public static void main(String[] args)
{
   int n;
   . . .
   {
      int k;
      . . .
   } // k is only defined up to here
}
```

However, you may not declare identically named variables in two nested blocks. For example, the following is an error and will not compile:

```
public static void main(String[] args)
{
   int n;
   . . .
   {
      int k;
      int n; // error--can't redefine n in inner block
      . . .
   }
}
```

C++ NOTE: In C++, it is possible to redefine a variable inside a nested block. The inner definition then shadows the outer one. This can be a source of programming errors; hence, Java does not allow it.

Conditional Statements

The conditional statement in Java has the form

```
if (condition) statement
```

The condition must be surrounded by parentheses.

In Java, as in most programming languages, you will often want to execute multiple statements when a single condition is true. In this case, you use a *block statement* that takes the form

```
{
   statement1
   statement2
   . . .
}
```

For example:

```
if (yourSales >= target)
{
   performance = "Satisfactory";
   bonus = 100;
}
```

In this code all the statements surrounded by the braces will be executed when `yourSales` is greater than or equal to `target`. (See Figure 3–8.)

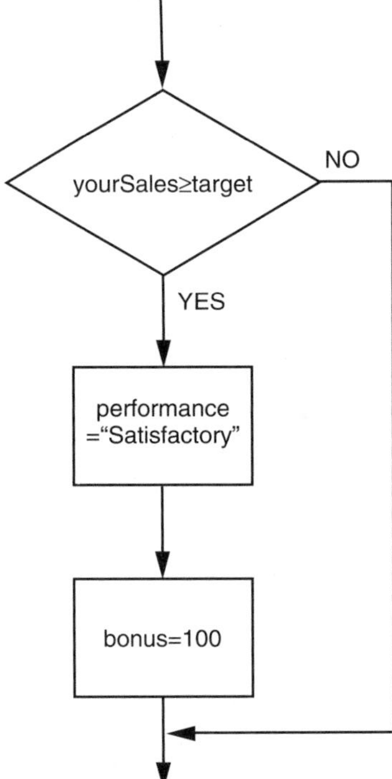

Figure 3–8: Flowchart for the `if` statement

NOTE: A block (sometimes called a *compound statement*) allows you to have more than one (simple) statement in any Java programming structure that might otherwise have a single (simple) statement.

The more general conditional in Java looks like this (see Figure 3–9):

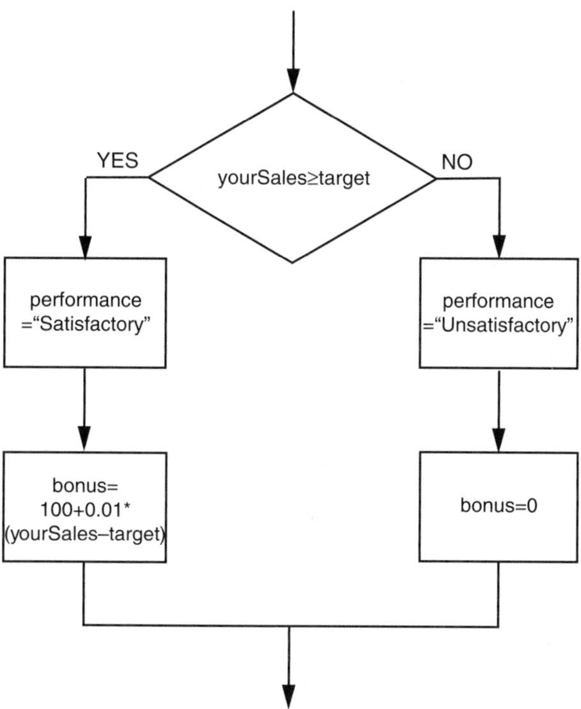

Figure 3–9: Flowchart for the if/else statement

`if (`*condition*`)` *statement*$_1$ `else` *statement*$_2$

For example:

```
if (yourSales >= target)
{
   performance = "Satisfactory";
   bonus = 100 + 0.01 * (yourSales - target);
}
else
{
   performance = "Unsatisfactory";
   bonus = 0;
}
```

The `else` part is always optional. An `else` groups with the closest `if`. Thus, in the statement

```
if (x <= 0) if (x == 0) sign = 0; else sign = -1;
```

the `else` belongs to the second `if`.

Repeated `if . . . else if . . .` alternatives are common (see Figure 3–10). For example:

```
if (yourSales >= 2 * target)
{
   performance = "Excellent";
   bonus = 1000;
}
else if (yourSales >= 1.5 * target)
{
   performance = "Fine";
```

```
   bonus = 500;
}
else if (yourSales >= target)
{
   performance = "Satisfactory";
   bonus = 100;
}
else
{
   System.out.println("You're fired");
}
```


Figure 3–10: Flowchart for the `if/else if` (multiple branches)

Loops

The `while` loop executes a statement (which may be a block statement) while a condition is `true`. The general form is

`while` (*condition*) *statement*

The `while` loop will never execute if the condition is `false` at the outset (see Figure 3–11).

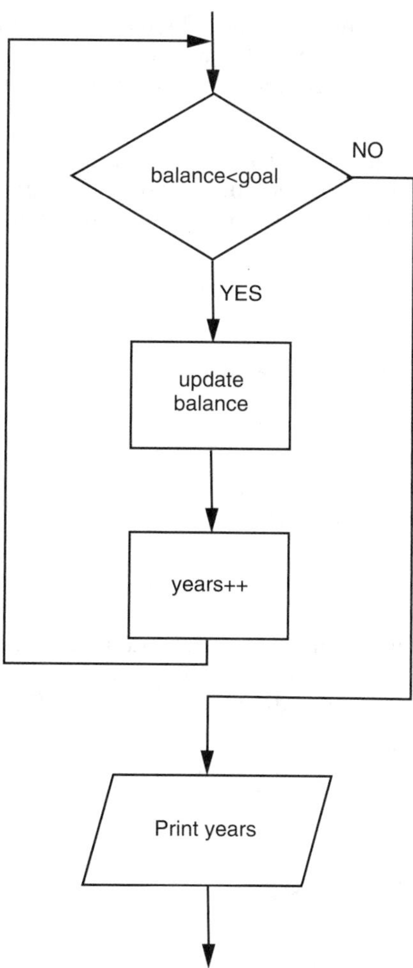

Figure 3–11: Flowchart for the `while` statement

The program in Example 3–3 determines how long it will take to save a specific amount of money for your well-earned retirement, assuming that you deposit the same amount of money per year and that the money earns a specified interest rate.

In the example, we are incrementing a counter and updating the amount currently accumulated in the body of the loop until the total exceeds the targeted amount.

```
while (balance < goal)
{
   balance += payment;
   double interest = balance * interestRate / 100;
   balance += interest;
   years++;
}
System.out.println(years + " years.");
```

(Don't rely on this program to plan for your retirement. We left out a few niceties such as inflation and your life expectancy.)

A `while` loop tests at the top. Therefore, the code in the block may never be executed. If you want to make sure a block is executed at least once, you will need to move the test to the bottom. You do that with the `do/while` loop. Its syntax looks like this:

```
do statement while (condition);
```

This loop executes the statement (which is typically a block) and only then tests the condition. It then repeats the statement and retests the condition, and so on. The code in Example 3–4 computes the new balance in your retirement account and then asks if you are ready to retire:

```
do
{
   balance += payment;
   double interest = balance * interestRate / 100;
   balance += interest;
   year++;
   // print current balance
   . . .
   // ask if ready to retire and get input
   . . .
}
while (input.equals("N"));
```

As long as the user answers `"N"`, the loop is repeated (see Figure 3–12). This program is a good example of a loop that needs to be entered at least once, because the user needs to see the balance before deciding whether it is sufficient for retirement.

Example 3–3: Retirement.java

```
import java.util.*;

public class Retirement
{
   public static void main(String[] args)
   {
      // read inputs
      Scanner in = new Scanner(System.in);

      System.out.print("How much money do you need to retire? ");
      double goal = in.nextDouble();

      System.out.print("How much money will you contribute every year? ");
      double payment = in.nextDouble();

      System.out.print("Interest rate in %: ");
      double interestRate = in.nextDouble();

      double balance = 0;
      int years = 0;

      // update account balance while goal isn't reached
      while (balance < goal)
      {
```

```
         // add this year's payment and interest
         balance += payment;
         double interest = balance * interestRate / 100;
         balance += interest;
         years++;
      }

      System.out.println("You can retire in " + years + " years.");
   }
}
```

Example 3–4: Retirement2.java

```
import java.util.*;

public class Retirement2
{
   public static void main(String[] args)
   {
      Scanner in = new Scanner(System.in);

      System.out.print("How much money will you contribute every year? ");
      double payment = in.nextDouble();

      System.out.print("Interest rate in %: ");
      double interestRate = in.nextDouble();

      double balance = 0;
      int year = 0;

      String input;

      // update account balance while user isn't ready to retire
      do
      {
         // add this year's payment and interest
         balance += payment;
         double interest = balance * interestRate / 100;
         balance += interest;

         year++;

         // print current balance
         System.out.printf("After year %d, your balance is %,.2f%n", year, balance);

         // ask if ready to retire and get input
         System.out.print("Ready to retire? (Y/N) ");
         input = in.next();
      }
      while (input.equals("N"));
   }
}
```

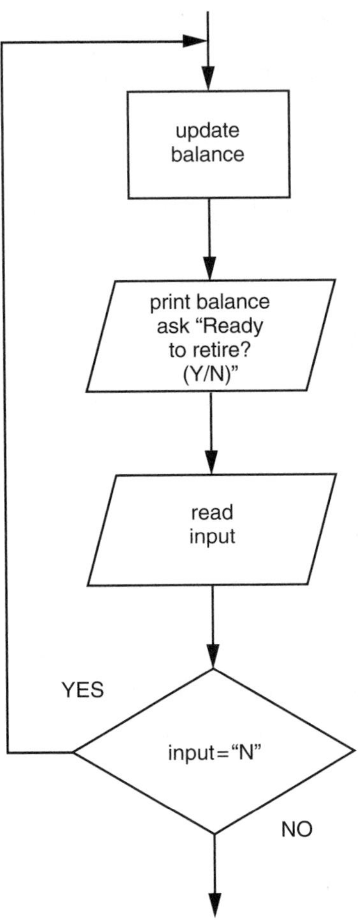

Figure 3–12: Flowchart for the `do/while` statement

Determinate Loops

The `for` loop is a general construct to support iteration that is controlled by a counter or similar variable that is updated after every iteration. As Figure 3–13 shows, the following loop prints the numbers from 1 to 10 on the screen.

```
for (int i = 1; i <= 10; i++)
     System.out.println(i);
```

The first slot of the `for` statement usually holds the counter initialization. The second slot gives the condition that will be tested before each new pass through the loop, and the third slot explains how to update the counter.

Although Java, like C++, allows almost any expression in the various slots of a `for` loop, it is an unwritten rule of good taste that the three slots of a `for` statement should only initialize, test, and update the same counter variable. One can write very obscure loops by disregarding this rule.

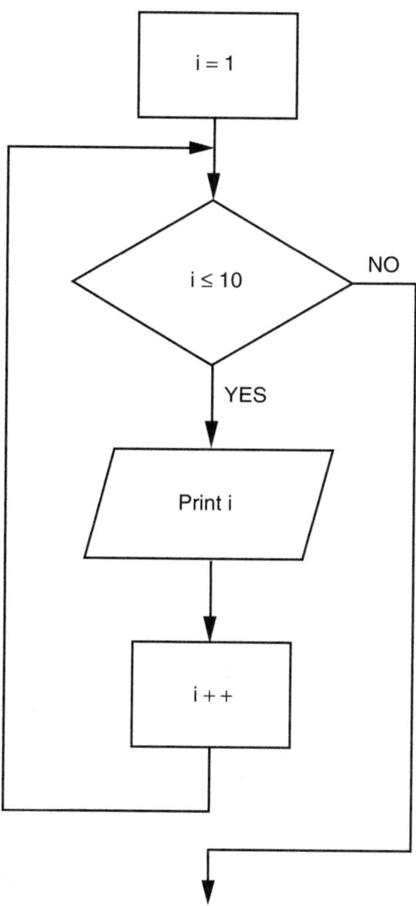

Figure 3–13: Flowchart for the for statement

Even within the bounds of good taste, much is possible. For example, you can have loops that count down:

```
for (int i = 10; i > 0; i--)
   System.out.println("Counting down . . . " + i);
System.out.println("Blastoff!");
```

CAUTION: Be careful about testing for equality of floating-point numbers in loops. A for loop that looks like this

```
for (double x = 0; x != 10; x += 0.1) . . .
```

may never end. Because of roundoff errors, the final value may not be reached exactly. For example, in the loop above, x jumps from 9.99999999999998 to 10.09999999999998 because there is no exact binary representation for 0.1.

When you declare a variable in the first slot of the for statement, the scope of that variable extends until the end of the body of the for loop.

```
for (int i = 1; i <= 10; i++)
{
   . . .
}
// i no longer defined here
```

In particular, if you define a variable inside a for statement, you cannot use the value of that variable outside the loop. Therefore, if you wish to use the final value of a loop counter outside the for loop, be sure to declare it outside the loop header!

```
int i;
for (i = 1; i <= 10; i++)
{
   . . .
}
// i still defined here
```

On the other hand, you can define variables with the same name in separate for loops:

```
for (int i = 1; i <= 10; i++)
{
   . . .
}
. . .
for (int i = 11; i <= 20; i++) // ok to define another variable named i
{
   . . .
}
```

A for loop is merely a convenient shortcut for a while loop. For example,

```
for (int i = 10; i > 0; i--)
   System.out.println("Counting down . . . " + i);
```

can be rewritten as

```
int i = 10;
while (i > 0)
{
   System.out.println("Counting down . . . " + i);
   i--;
}
```

Example 3–5 shows a typical example of a for loop.

The program computes the odds on winning a lottery. For example, if you must pick 6 numbers from the numbers 1 to 50 to win, then there are $(50 \times 49 \times 48 \times 47 \times 46 \times 45)/(1 \times 2 \times 3 \times 4 \times 5 \times 6)$ possible outcomes, so your chance is 1 in 15,890,700. Good luck!

In general, if you pick k numbers out of n, there are

$$\frac{n \times (n-1) \times (n-2) \times \ldots \times (n-k+1)}{1 \times 2 \times 3 \times \ldots \times k}$$

possible outcomes. The following for loop computes this value:

```
int lotteryOdds = 1;
for (int i = 1; i <= k; i++)
   lotteryOdds = lotteryOdds * (n - i + 1) / i;
```

NOTE: See page 82 for a description of the "generalized for loop" (also called "for each" loop) that was added to the Java language in JDK 5.0.

Example 3–5: LotteryOdds.java

```
import java.util.*;

public class LotteryOdds
{
   public static void main(String[] args)
   {
      Scanner in = new Scanner(System.in);

      System.out.print("How many numbers do you need to draw? ");
      int k = in.nextInt();

      System.out.print("What is the highest number you can draw? ");
      int n = in.nextInt();

      /*
         compute binomial coefficient
         n * (n - 1) * (n - 2) * . . . * (n - k + 1)
         -------------------------------------------
         1 * 2 * 3 * . . . * k
      */

      int lotteryOdds = 1;
      for (int i = 1; i <= k; i++)
         lotteryOdds = lotteryOdds * (n - i + 1) / i;

      System.out.println("Your odds are 1 in " + lotteryOdds + ". Good luck!");
   }
}
```

Multiple Selections—The switch Statement

The if/else construct can be cumbersome when you have to deal with multiple selections with many alternatives. Java has a switch statement that is exactly like the switch statement in C and C++, warts and all.

For example, if you set up a menuing system with four alternatives like that in Figure 3–14, you could use code that looks like this:

```
Scanner in = new Scanner(System.in);
System.out.print("Select an option (1, 2, 3, 4) ");
int choice = in.nextInt();
switch (choice)
{
   case 1:
      . . .
      break;
   case 2:
      . . .
      break;
   case 3:
      . . .
```

```
      break;
   case 4:
      . . .
      break;
   default:
      // bad input
      . . .
      break;
}
```

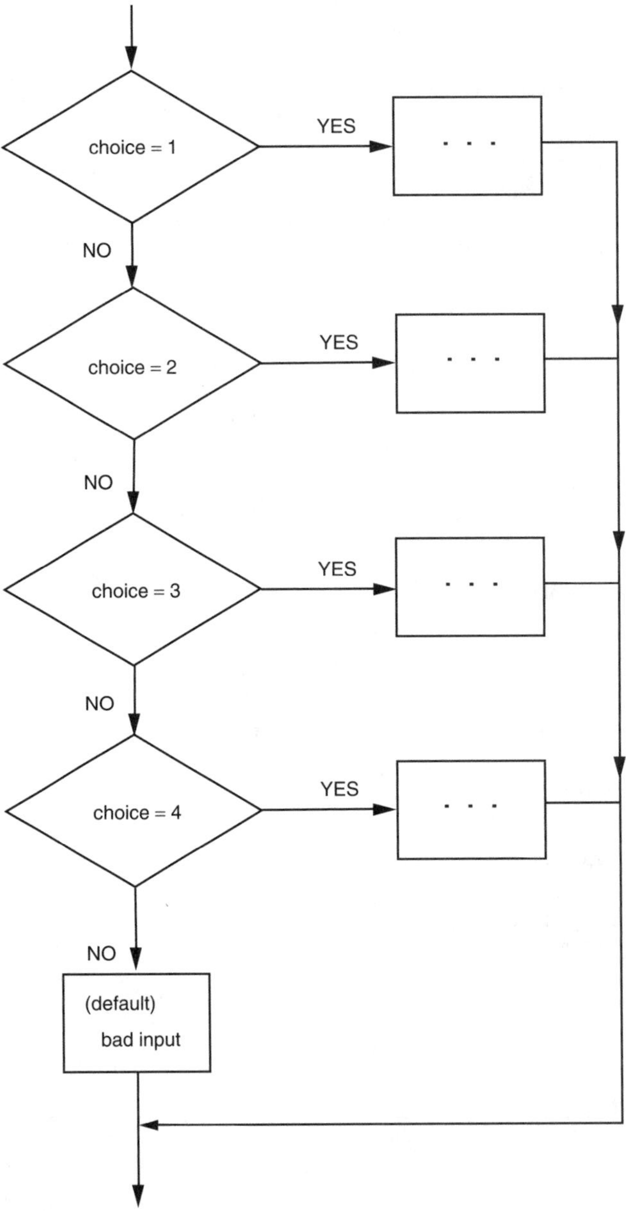

Figure 3–14: Flowchart for the `switch` statement

Execution starts at the case label that matches the value on which the selection is performed and continues until the next break or the end of the switch. If none of the case labels match, then the default clause is executed, if it is present.

Note that the case labels must be integers or enumerated constants. You cannot test strings. For example, the following is an error:

```
String input = . . .;
switch (input) // ERROR
{
   case "A": // ERROR
      . . .
      break;
   . . .
}
```

PITFALL: It is possible for multiple alternatives to be triggered. If you forget to add a break at the end of an alternative, then execution falls through to the next alternative! This behavior is plainly dangerous and a common cause for errors. For that reason, we never use the switch statement in our programs.

Statements That Break Control Flow

Although the designers of Java kept the goto as a reserved word, they decided not to include it in the language. In general, goto statements are considered poor style. Some programmers feel the anti-goto forces have gone too far (see, for example, the famous article of Donald Knuth called "Structured Programming with goto statements"). They argue that unrestricted use of goto is error prone but that an occasional jump *out of a loop* is beneficial. The Java designers agreed and even added a new statement, the labeled break, to support this programming style.

Let us first look at the unlabeled break statement. The same break statement that you use to exit a switch can also be used to break out of a loop. For example,

```
while (years <= 100)
{
   balance += payment;
   double interest = balance * interestRate / 100;
   balance += interest;
   if (balance >= goal) break;
   years++;
}
```

Now the loop is exited if either years > 100 occurs at the top of the loop or balance >= goal occurs in the middle of the loop. Of course, you could have computed the same value for years without a break, like this:

```
while (years <= 100 && balance < goal)
{
   balance += payment;
   double interest = balance * interestRate / 100;
   balance += interest;
   if (balance < goal)
      years++;
}
```

But note that the test balance < goal is repeated twice in this version. To avoid this repeated test, some programmers prefer the break statement.

Unlike C++, Java also offers a *labeled break* statement that lets you break out of multiple nested loops. Occasionally something weird happens inside a deeply nested loop. In that case, you may want to break completely out of all the nested loops. It is inconvenient to program that simply by adding extra conditions to the various loop tests.

Here's an example that shows the break statement at work. Notice that the label must precede the outermost loop out of which you want to break. It also must be followed by a colon.

```
Scanner in = new Scanner(System.in);
int n;
read_data:
while (. . .) // this loop statement is tagged with the label
{
   . . .
   for (. . .) // this inner loop is not labeled
   {
      System.out.print("Enter a number >= 0: ");
      n = in.nextInt();
      if (n < 0) // should never happen-can't go on
         break read_data;
         // break out of read_data loop
      . . .
   }
}
// this statement is executed immediately after the labeled break
if (n < 0) // check for bad situation
{
   // deal with bad situation
}
else
{
   // carry out normal processing
}
```

If there was a bad input, the labeled break moves past the end of the labeled block. As with any use of the `break` statement, you then need to test whether the loop exited normally or as a result of a break.

NOTE: Curiously, you can apply a label to any statement, even an `if` statement or a block statement, like this:

```
label:
{
   . . .
   if (condition) break label; // exits block
   . . .
}
// jumps here when the break statement executes
```

Thus, if you are lusting after a `goto` and if you can place a block that ends just before the place to which you want to jump, you can use a `break` statement! Naturally, we don't recommend this approach. Note, however, that you can only jump *out of* a block, never *into* a block.

Finally, there is a `continue` statement that, like the `break` statement, breaks the regular flow of control. The `continue` statement transfers control to the header of the innermost enclosing loop. Here is an example:

```
Scanner in = new Scanner(System.in);
while (sum < goal)
{
   System.out.print("Enter a number: ");
   n = in.nextInt();
   if (n < 0) continue;
   sum += n; // not executed if n < 0
}
```

If `n < 0`, then the `continue` statement jumps immediately to the loop header, skipping the remainder of the current iteration.

If the `continue` statement is used in a `for` loop, it jumps to the "update" part of the `for` loop. For example, consider this loop.

```
for (count = 1; count <= 100; count++)
{
   System.out.print("Enter a number, -1 to quit: ");
   n = in.nextInt();
   if (n < 0) continue;
   sum += n; // not executed if n < 0
}
```

If `n < 0`, then the `continue` statement jumps to the `count++` statement.

There is also a labeled form of the `continue` statement that jumps to the header of the loop with the matching label.

TIP: Many programmers find the `break` and `continue` statements confusing. These statements are entirely optional—you can always express the same logic without them. In this book, we never use `break` or `continue`.

Big Numbers

If the precision of the basic integer and floating-point types is not sufficient, you can turn to a couple of handy classes in the `java.math` package: `BigInteger` and `BigDecimal`. These are classes for manipulating numbers with an arbitrarily long sequence of digits. The `BigInteger` class implements arbitrary precision integer arithmetic, and `BigDecimal` does the same for floating-point numbers.

Use the static `valueOf` method to turn an ordinary number into a big number:

```
BigInteger a = BigInteger.valueOf(100);
```

Unfortunately, you cannot use the familiar mathematical operators such as + and * to combine big numbers. Instead, you must use methods such as `add` and `multiply` in the big number classes.

```
BigInteger c = a.add(b); // c = a + b
BigInteger d = c.multiply(b.add(BigInteger.valueOf(2))); // d = c * (b + 2)
```

C++ NOTE: Unlike C++, Java has no programmable operator overloading. There was no way for the programmer of the `BigInteger` class to redefine the + and * operators to give the `add` and `multiply` operations of the `BigInteger` classes. The language designers did overload the + operator to denote concatenation of strings. They chose not to overload other operators, and they did not give Java programmers the opportunity to overload operators themselves.

Example 3–6 shows a modification of the lottery odds program of Example 3–5, updated to work with big numbers. For example, if you are invited to participate in a lottery in which you need to pick 60 numbers out of a possible 490 numbers, then this program will tell you that your odds are 1 in 716395843461995557415116222540092933411717612789263493493351013459481104668848. Good luck!

The program in Example 3–5 computed the statement:

```
lotteryOdds = lotteryOdds * (n - i + 1) / i;
```

When big numbers are used, the equivalent statement becomes:

```
lotteryOdds = lotteryOdds.multiply(BigInteger.valueOf(n - i + 1)).divide(BigInteger.valueOf(i));
```

Example 3–6: BigIntegerTest.java

```
import java.math.*;
import java.util.*;

public class BigIntegerTest
{
   public static void main(String[] args)
   {
      Scanner in = new Scanner(System.in);

      System.out.print("How many numbers do you need to draw? ");
      int k = in.nextInt();

      System.out.print("What is the highest number you can draw? ");
      int n = in.nextInt();

      /*
         compute binomial coefficient
         n * (n - 1) * (n - 2) * . . . * (n - k + 1)
         -------------------------------------------
         1 * 2 * 3 * . . . * k
      */

      BigInteger lotteryOdds = BigInteger.valueOf(1);

      for (int i = 1; i <= k; i++)
         lotteryOdds = lotteryOdds
            .multiply(BigInteger.valueOf(n - i + 1))
            .divide(BigInteger.valueOf(i));

      System.out.println("Your odds are 1 in " + lotteryOdds +
        ". Good luck!");
   }
}
```

API **java.math.BigInteger 1.1**

- `BigInteger add(BigInteger other)`
- `BigInteger subtract(BigInteger other)`
- `BigInteger multiply(BigInteger other)`
- `BigInteger divide(BigInteger other)`
- `BigInteger mod(BigInteger other)`

  return the sum, difference, product, quotient, and remainder of this big integer and `other`.

- `int compareTo(BigInteger other)`
  returns 0 if this big integer equals `other`, a negative result if this big integer is less than `other`, and a positive result otherwise.
- `static BigInteger valueOf(long x)`
  returns a big integer whose value equals `x`.

java.math.BigDecimal 1.1

- `BigDecimal add(BigDecimal other)`
- `BigDecimal subtract(BigDecimal other)`
- `BigDecimal multiply(BigDecimal other)`
- `BigDecimal divide(BigDecimal other, RoundingMode mode)` **5.0**
  return the sum, difference, product, or quotient of this big decimal and `other`. To compute the quotient, you must supply a *rounding mode*. The mode `RoundingMode.HALF_UP` is the rounding mode that you learned in school (i.e., round down digits 0 . . . 4, round up digits 5 . . . 9). It is appropriate for routine calculations. See the API documentation for other rounding modes.
- `int compareTo(BigDecimal other)`
  returns 0 if this big decimal equals `other`, a negative result if this big decimal is less than `other`, and a positive result otherwise.
- `static BigDecimal valueOf(long x)`
- `static BigDecimal valueOf(long x, int scale)`
  return a big decimal whose value equals `x` or `x` / 10^{scale}.

Arrays

An array is a data structure that stores a collection of values of the same type. You access each individual value through an integer *index*. For example, if `a` is an array of integers, then `a[i]` is the `i`th integer in the array.

You declare an array variable by specifying the array type—which is the element type followed by `[]`—and the array variable name. For example, here is the declaration of an array `a` of integers:

```
int[] a;
```

However, this statement only declares the variable `a`. It does not yet initialize `a` with an actual array. You use the `new` operator to create the array.

```
int[] a = new int[100];
```

This statement sets up an array that can hold 100 integers.

NOTE: You can define an array variable either as

```
int[] a;
```

or as

```
int a[];
```

Most Java programmers prefer the former style because it neatly separates the type `int[]` (integer array) from the variable name.

The array entries are *numbered from 0 to 99* (and not 1 to 100). Once the array is created, you can fill the entries in an array, for example, by using a loop:

```
int[] a = new int[100];
for (int i = 0; i < 100; i++)
   a[i] = i;  // fills the array with 0 to 99
```

CAUTION: If you construct an array with 100 elements and then try to access the element `a[100]` (or any other index outside the range 0 . . . 99), then your program will terminate with an "array index out of bounds" exception.

To find the number of elements of an array, use *array*`.length`. For example,

```
for (int i = 0; i < a.length; i++)
   System.out.println(a[i]);
```

Once you create an array, you cannot change its size (although you can, of course, change an individual array element). If you frequently need to expand the size of an array while a program is running, you should use a different data structure called an *array list.* (See Chapter 5 for more on array lists.)

The "for each" Loop

JDK 5.0 introduces a powerful looping construct that allows you to loop through each element in an array (as well as other collections of elements) without having to fuss with index values.

The *enhanced* `for` *loop*

```
for (variable : collection) statement
```

sets the given variable to each element of the collection and then executes the statement (which, of course, may be a block). The *collection* expression must be an array or an object of a class that implements the `Iterable` interface, such as `ArrayList`. We discuss array lists in Chapter 5 and the `Iterable` interface in Chapter 2 of Volume 2.

For example,

```
for (int element : a)
   System.out.println(element);
```

prints each element of the array `a` on a separate line.

You should read this loop as "for each `element` in `a`". The designers of the Java language considered using keywords such as `foreach` and `in`. But this loop was a late addition to the Java language, and in the end nobody wanted to break old code that already contains methods or variables with the same names (such as `System.in`).

Of course, you could achieve the same effect with a traditional `for` loop:

```
for (int i = 0; i < a.length; i++)
   System.out.println(a[i]);
```

However, the "for each" loop is more concise and less error prone. (You don't have to worry about those pesky start and end index values.)

NOTE: The loop variable of the "for each" loop traverses the *elements* of the array, not the index values.

The "for each" loop is a pleasant improvement over the traditional loop if you need to process all elements in a collection. However, there are still plenty of opportunities to use the traditional `for` loop. For example, you may not want to traverse the entire collection, or you may need the index value inside the loop.

Array Initializers and Anonymous Arrays

Java has a shorthand to create an array object and supply initial values at the same time. Here's an example of the syntax at work:

```
int[] smallPrimes = { 2, 3, 5, 7, 11, 13 };
```

Notice that you do not call `new` when you use this syntax.

You can even initialize an *anonymous array:*

```
new int[] { 17, 19, 23, 29, 31, 37 }
```

This expression allocates a new array and fills it with the values inside the braces. It counts the number of initial values and sets the array size accordingly. You can use this syntax to reinitialize an array without creating a new variable. For example,

```
smallPrimes = new int[] { 17, 19, 23, 29, 31, 37 };
```

is shorthand for

```
int[] anonymous = { 17, 19, 23, 29, 31, 37 };
smallPrimes = anonymous;
```

NOTE: It is legal to have arrays of length 0. Such an array can be useful if you write a method that computes an array result and the result happens to be empty. You construct an array of length 0 as

```
new elementType[0]
```

Note that an array of length 0 is not the same as `null`. (See Chapter 4 for more information about `null`.)

Array Copying

You can copy one array variable into another, but then *both variables refer to the same array:*

```
int[] luckyNumbers = smallPrimes;
luckyNumbers[5] = 12; // now smallPrimes[5] is also 12
```

Figure 3–15 shows the result. If you actually want to copy all values of one array into another, you use the `arraycopy` method in the `System` class. The syntax for this call is

```
System.arraycopy(from, fromIndex, to, toIndex, count);
```

The `to` array must have sufficient space to hold the copied elements.

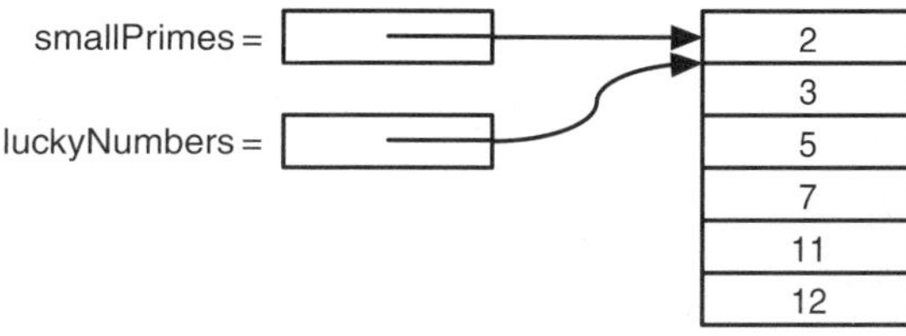

Figure 3–15: Copying an array variable

For example, the following statements, whose result is illustrated in Figure 3–16, set up two arrays and then copy the last four entries of the first array to the second array. The copy starts at position 2 in the source array and copies four entries, starting at position 3 of the target.

```
int[] smallPrimes = {2, 3, 5, 7, 11, 13};
int[] luckyNumbers = {1001, 1002, 1003, 1004, 1005, 1006, 1007};
System.arraycopy(smallPrimes, 2, luckyNumbers, 3, 4);
for (int i = 0; i < luckyNumbers.length; i++)
   System.out.println(i + ": " + luckyNumbers[i]);
```

The output is

```
0: 1001
1: 1002
2: 1003
3: 5
4: 7
5: 11
6: 13
```

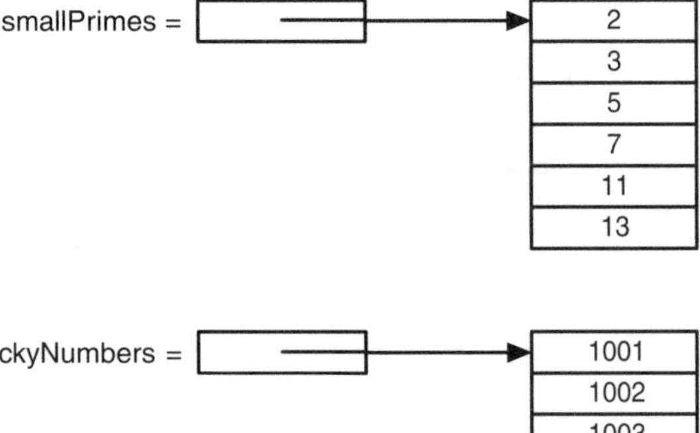

Figure 3–16: Copying values between arrays

C++ NOTE: A Java array is quite different from a C++ array on the stack. It is, however, essentially the same as a pointer to an array allocated on the *heap*. That is,

```
int[] a = new int[100]; // Java
```

is not the same as

```
int a[100]; // C++
```

but rather

```
int* a = new int[100]; // C++
```

In Java, the [] operator is predefined to perform *bounds checking*. Furthermore, there is no pointer arithmetic—you can't increment a to point to the next element in the array.

Command-Line Parameters

You have already seen one example of Java arrays repeated quite a few times. Every Java program has a `main` method with a `String[] args` parameter. This parameter indicates that the `main` method receives an array of strings, namely, the arguments specified on the command line.

For example, consider this program:

```
public class Message
{
   public static void main(String[] args)
   {
      if (args[0].equals("-h"))
```

```
            System.out.print("Hello,");
        else if (args[0].equals("-g"))
            System.out.print("Goodbye,");
        // print the other command-line arguments
        for (int i = 1; i < args.length; i++)
            System.out.print(" " + a[i]);
        System.out.println("!");
    }
}
```

If the program is called as

```
java Message -g cruel world
```

then the args array has the following contents:

```
args[0]: "-g"
args[1]: "cruel"
args[2]: "world"
```

The program prints the message

```
Goodbye, cruel world!
```

C++ NOTE: In the main method of a Java program, the name of the program is not stored in the args array. For example, when you start up a program as

```
java Message -h world
```

from the command line, then args[0] will be "-h" and not "Message" or "java".

Array Sorting

To sort an array of numbers, you can use one of the sort methods in the Arrays class:

```
int[] a = new int[10000];
. . .
Arrays.sort(a)
```

This method uses a tuned version of the QuickSort algorithm that is claimed to be very efficient on most data sets. The Arrays class provides several other convenience methods for arrays that are included in the API notes at the end of this section.

The program in Example 3–7 puts arrays to work. This program draws a random combination of numbers for a lottery game. For example, if you play a "choose 6 numbers from 49" lottery, then the program might print:

```
Bet the following combination. It'll make you rich!
   4
   7
   8
   19
   30
   44
```

To select such a random set of numbers, we first fill an array numbers with the values 1, 2, . . ., n:

```
int[] numbers = new int[n];
for (int i = 0; i < numbers.length; i++)
   numbers[i] = i + 1;
```

A second array holds the numbers to be drawn:

```
int[] result = new int[k];
```

Now we draw k numbers. The Math.random method returns a random floating-point number that is between 0 (inclusive) and 1 (exclusive). By multiplying the result with n, we obtain a random number between 0 and n – 1.

```
int r = (int) (Math.random() * n);
```

We set the ith result to be the number at that index. Initially, that is just r itself, but as you'll see presently, the contents of the numbers array are changed after each draw.

```
result[i] = numbers[r];
```

Now we must be sure never to draw that number again—all lottery numbers must be distinct. Therefore, we overwrite numbers[r] with the *last* number in the array and reduce n by 1.

```
numbers[r] = numbers[n - 1];
n--;
```

The point is that in each draw we pick an *index*, not the actual value. The index points into an array that contains the values that have not yet been drawn.

After drawing k lottery numbers, we sort the result array for a more pleasing output:

```
Arrays.sort(result);
for (int r : result)
   System.out.println(r);
```

Example 3–7: LotteryDrawing.java

```
import java.util.*;

public class LotteryDrawing
{
   public static void main(String[] args)
   {
      Scanner in = new Scanner(System.in);

      System.out.print("How many numbers do you need to draw? ");
      int k = in.nextInt();

      System.out.print("What is the highest number you can draw? ");
      int n = in.nextInt();

      // fill an array with numbers 1 2 3 . . . n
      int[] numbers = new int[n];
      for (int i = 0; i < numbers.length; i++)
         numbers[i] = i + 1;

      // draw k numbers and put them into a second array
      int[] result = new int[k];
      for (int i = 0; i < result.length; i++)
      {
         // make a random index between 0 and n - 1
         int r = (int) (Math.random() * n);

         // pick the element at the random location
         result[i] = numbers[r];

         // move the last element into the random location
         numbers[r] = numbers[n - 1];
         n--;
```

```
      }

      // print the sorted array
      Arrays.sort(result);
      System.out.println("Bet the following combination. It'll make you rich!");
      for (int r : result)
         System.out.println(r);
   }
}
```

java.lang.System 1.1

- `static void arraycopy(Object from, int fromIndex, Object to, int toIndex, int count)`
  copies elements from the first array to the second array.

Parameters:	`from`	an array of any type (Chapter 5 explains why this is a parameter of type `Object`)
	`fromIndex`	the starting index from which to copy elements
	`to`	an array of the same type as `from`
	`toIndex`	the starting index to which to copy elements
	`count`	the number of elements to copy

java.util.Arrays 1.2

- `static void sort(`*`type`*`[] a)`
  sorts the array, using a tuned QuickSort algorithm.

Parameters:	`a`	an array of type `int`, `long`, `short`, `char`, `byte`, `float` or `double`

- `static int binarySearch(`*`type`*`[] a, `*`type`*` v)`
  uses the BinarySearch algorithm to search for the value `v`. If it is found, its index is returned. Otherwise, a negative value `r` is returned; `-r - 1` is the spot at which `v` should be inserted to keep `a` sorted.

Parameters:	`a`	a *sorted* array of type `int`, `long`, `short`, `char`, `byte`, `float` or `double`
	`v`	a value of the same type as the elements of `a`

- `static void fill(`*`type`*`[] a, `*`type`*` v)`
  sets all elements of the array to `v`.

Parameters:	`a`	an array of type `int`, `long`, `short`, `char`, `byte`, `boolean`, `float` or `double`
	`v`	a value of the same type as the elements of `a`

- `static boolean equals(`*`type`*`[] a, `*`type`*`[] b)`
  returns `true` if the arrays have the same length, and if the elements in corresponding indexes match.

Parameters:	`a, b`	arrays of type `int`, `long`, `short`, `char`, `byte`, `boolean`, `float` or `double`

Multidimensional Arrays

Multidimensional arrays use more than one index to access array elements. They are used for tables and other more complex arrangements. You can safely skip this section until you have a need for this storage mechanism.

Suppose you want to make a table of numbers that shows how much an investment of $10,000 will grow under different interest rate scenarios in which interest is paid annually and reinvested. Table 3–8 illustrates this scenario.

Table 3–8: Growth of an Investment at Different Interest Rates

10%	11%	12%	13%	14%	15%
10,000.00	10,000.00	10,000.00	10,000.00	10,000.00	10,000.00
11,000.00	11,100.00	11,200.00	11,300.00	11,400.00	11,500.00
12,100.00	12,321.00	12,544.00	12,769.00	12,996.00	13,225.00
13,310.00	13,676.31	14,049.28	14,428.97	14,815.44	15,208.75
14,641.00	15,180.70	15,735.19	16,304.74	16,889.60	17,490.06
16,105.10	16,850.58	17,623.42	18,424.35	19,254.15	20,113.57
17,715.61	18,704.15	19,738.23	20,819.52	21,949.73	23,130.61
19,487.17	20,761.60	22,106.81	23,526.05	25,022.69	26,600.20
21,435.89	23,045.38	24,759.63	26,584.44	28,525.86	30,590.23
23,579.48	25,580.37	27,730.79	30,040.42	32,519.49	35,178.76

You can store this information in a two-dimensional array (or matrix), which we call `balances`.

Declaring a two-dimensional array in Java is simple enough. For example:

```
double[][] balances;
```

As always, you cannot use the array until you initialize it with a call to `new`. In this case, you can do the initialization as follows:

```
balances = new double[NYEARS][NRATES];
```

In other cases, if you know the array elements, you can use a shorthand notion for initializing multidimensional arrays without needing a call to `new`. For example:

```
int[][] magicSquare =
   {
      {16, 3, 2, 13},
      {5, 10, 11, 8},
      {9, 6, 7, 12},
      {4, 15, 14, 1}
   };
```

Once the array is initialized, you can access individual elements by supplying two brackets, for example, `balances[i][j]`.

The example program stores a one-dimensional array `interest` of interest rates and a two-dimensional array `balance` of account balances, one for each year and interest rate. We initialize the first row of the array with the initial balance:

```
for (int j = 0; j < balance[0].length; j++)
   balances[0][j] = 10000;
```

Then we compute the other rows, as follows:

```
for (int i = 1; i < balances.length; i++)
{
   for (int j = 0; j < balances[i].length; j++)
   {
      double oldBalance = balances[i - 1][j];
      double interest = . . .;
      balances[i][j] = oldBalance + interest;
   }
}
```

Example 3–8 shows the full program.

NOTE: A "for each" loop does not automatically loop through all entries in a two-dimensional array. Instead, it loops through the rows, which are themselves one-dimensional arrays. To visit all elements of a two-dimensional array, nest two loops, like this:

```
for (double[] row : balances)
   for (double b : row)
      do something with b
```

Example 3–8: CompoundInterest.java

```
public class CompoundInterest
{
   public static void main(String[] args)
   {
      final int STARTRATE = 10;
      final int NRATES = 6;
      final int NYEARS = 10;

      // set interest rates to 10 . . . 15%
      double[] interestRate = new double[NRATES];
      for (int j = 0; j < interestRate.length; j++)
         interestRate[j] = (STARTRATE + j) / 100.0;

      double[][] balances = new double[NYEARS][NRATES];

      // set initial balances to 10000
      for (int j = 0; j < balances[0].length; j++)
         balances[0][j] = 10000;

      // compute interest for future years
      for (int i = 1; i < balances.length; i++)
      {
         for (int j = 0; j < balances[i].length; j++)
         {
            // get last year's balances from previous row
            double oldBalance = balances[i - 1][j];

            // compute interest
            double interest = oldBalance * interestRate[j];

            // compute this year's balances
            balances[i][j] = oldBalance + interest;
         }
      }
```

```
      // print one row of interest rates
      for (int j = 0; j < interestRate.length; j++)
         System.out.printf("%9.0f%%", 100 * interestRate[j]);

      System.out.println();

      // print balance table
      for (double[] row : balances)
      {
         // print table row
         for (double b : row)
            System.out.printf("%10.2f", b);

         System.out.println();
      }
   }
}
```

Ragged Arrays

So far, what you have seen is not too different from other programming languages. But there is actually something subtle going on behind the scenes that you can sometimes turn to your advantage: Java has *no* multidimensional arrays at all, only one-dimensional arrays. Multidimensional arrays are faked as "arrays of arrays."

For example, the `balances` array in the preceding example is actually an array that contains 10 elements, each of which is an array of six floating-point numbers (see Figure 3–17).

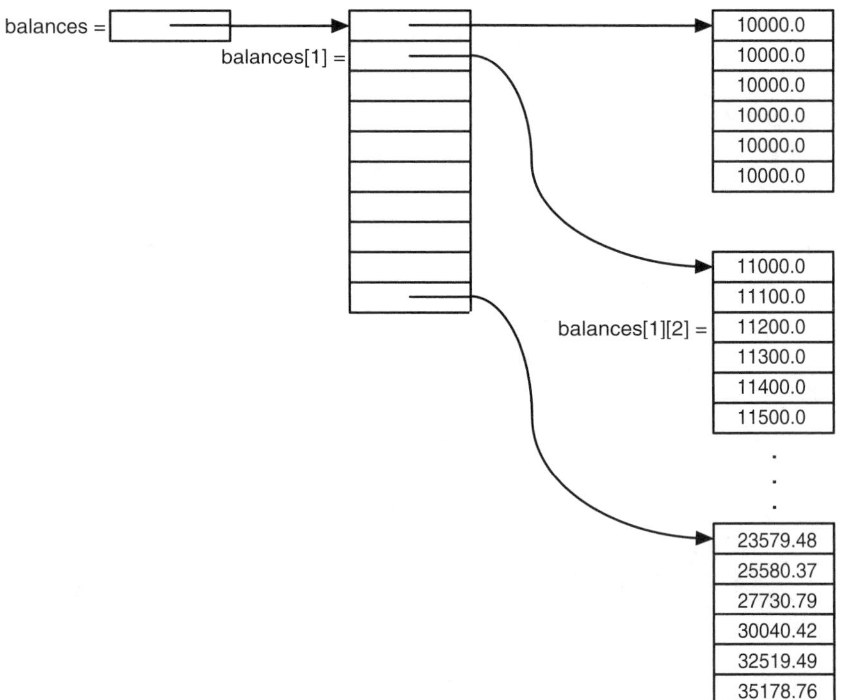

Figure 3–17: A two-dimensional array

The expression `balances[i]` refers to the `i`th subarray, that is, the `i`th row of the table. It is itself an array, and `balances[i][j]` refers to the `j`th entry of that array.

Because rows of arrays are individually accessible, you can actually swap them!

```
double[] temp = balances[i];
balances[i] = balances[i + 1];
balances[i + 1] = temp;
```

It is also easy to make "ragged" arrays, that is, arrays in which different rows have different lengths. Here is the standard example. Let us make an array in which the entry at row `i` and column `j` equals the number of possible outcomes of a "choose `j` numbers from `i` numbers" lottery.

```
1
1  1
1  2  1
1  3  3  1
1  4  6  4  1
1  5 10 10  5  1
1  6 15 20 15  6  1
```

Because `j` can never be larger than `i`, the matrix is triangular. The `i`th row has `i + 1` elements. (We allow choosing 0 elements; there is one way to make such a choice.) To build this ragged array, first allocate the array holding the rows.

```
int[][] odds = new int[NMAX + 1][];
```

Next, allocate the rows.

```
for (int n = 0; n <= NMAX; n++)
   odds[n] = new int[n + 1];
```

Now that the array is allocated, we can access the elements in the normal way, provided we do not overstep the bounds.

```
for (int n = 0; n < odds.length; n++)
   for (int k = 0; k < odds[n].length; k++)
   {
      // compute lotteryOdds
      . . .
      odds[n][k] = lotteryOdds;
   }
```

Example 3–9 gives the complete program.

C++ NOTE: In C++, the Java declaration

```
double[][] balances = new double[10][6]; // Java
```

is not the same as

```
double balances[10][6]; // C++
```

or even

```
double (*balances)[6] = new double[10][6]; // C++
```

Instead, an array of 10 pointers is allocated:

```
double** balances = new double*[10]; // C++
```

Then, each element in the pointer array is filled with an array of 6 numbers:

```
for (i = 0; i < 10; i++)
   balances[i] = new double[6];
```

Mercifully, this loop is automatic when you ask for a `new double[10][6]`. When you want ragged arrays, you allocate the row arrays separately.

Example 3–9: LotteryArray.java

```
public class LotteryArray
{
   public static void main(String[] args)
   {
      final int NMAX = 10;

      // allocate triangular array
      int[][] odds = new int[NMAX + 1][];
      for (int n = 0; n <= NMAX; n++)
         odds[n] = new int[n + 1];

      // fill triangular array
      for (int n = 0; n < odds.length; n++)
         for (int k = 0; k < odds[n].length; k++)
         {
            /*
               compute binomial coefficient
               n * (n - 1) * (n - 2) * . . . * (n - k + 1)
               -------------------------------------------
               1 * 2 * 3 * . . . * k
            */
            int lotteryOdds = 1;
            for (int i = 1; i <= k; i++)
               lotteryOdds = lotteryOdds * (n - i + 1) / i;

            odds[n][k] = lotteryOdds;
         }

      // print triangular array
      for (int[] row : odds)
      {
         for (int odd : row)
            System.out.printf("%4d", odd);
         System.out.println();
      }
   }
}
```

Chapter 4

Objects and Classes

In this chapter, we

- Introduce you to object-oriented programming;
- Show you how you can create objects that belong to classes in the standard Java library; and
- Show you how to write your own classes.

If you do not have a background in object-oriented programming, you will want to read this chapter carefully. Thinking about object-oriented programming requires a different way of thinking than for procedural languages. The transition is not always easy, but you do need some familiarity with object concepts to go further with Java.

For experienced C++ programmers, this chapter, like the previous chapter, presents familiar information; however, there are enough differences between the two languages that you should read the later sections of this chapter carefully. You'll find the C++ notes helpful for making the transition.

Introduction to Object-Oriented Programming

Object-oriented programming (or OOP for short) is the dominant programming paradigm these days, having replaced the "structured," procedural programming techniques that were developed in the early 1970s. Java is totally object oriented, and it is impossible to program it in the procedural style that you may be most comfortable with. We hope this section—especially when combined with the example code supplied in the text and on the companion web site—will give you enough information about OOP to become productive with Java.

Let's begin with a question that, on the surface, seems to have nothing to do with programming: How did companies like Compaq, Dell, Gateway, and the other major personal computer manufacturers get so big, so fast? Most people would probably say they made generally good computers and sold them at rock-bottom prices in an era when computer demand was skyrocketing. But go further—how were they able to manufacture so many models so fast and respond to the changes that were happening so quickly?

Well, a big part of the answer is that these companies farmed out a lot of the work. They bought components from reputable vendors and then assembled them. They often didn't invest time and money in designing and building power supplies, disk drives, motherboards, and other components. This made it possible for the companies to produce a product and make changes quickly for less money than if they had done the engineering themselves.

What the personal computer manufacturers were buying was "prepackaged functionality." For example, when they bought a power supply, they were buying something with certain properties (size, shape, and so on) and a certain functionality (smooth power output, amount of power available, and so on). Compaq provides a good example of how effective this operating procedure is. When Compaq moved from engineering most of the parts in its machines to buying many of the parts, it dramatically improved its bottom line.

OOP springs from the same idea. Your program is made of objects, with certain properties and operations that the objects can perform. Whether you build an object or buy it might depend on your budget or on time. But, basically, as long as objects satisfy your specifications, you don't care how the functionality was implemented. In OOP, you only care about what the objects *expose*. So, just as computer manufacturers don't care about the internals of a power supply as long as it does what they want, most Java programmers don't care how an object is implemented as long as it does what *they* want.

Traditional structured programming consists of designing a set of procedures (or *algorithms*) to solve a problem. After the procedures were determined, the traditional next step was to find appropriate ways to store the data. This is why the designer of the Pascal language, Niklaus Wirth, called his famous book on programming *Algorithms + Data Structures = Programs* (Prentice Hall, 1975). Notice that in Wirth's title, algorithms come first, and data structures come second. This mimics the way programmers worked at that time. First, you decided how to manipulate the data; then, you decided what structure to impose on the data to make the manipulations easier. OOP reverses the order and puts data first, then looks at the algorithms that operate on the data.

The key to being most productive in OOP is to make each object responsible for carrying out a set of related tasks. If an object relies on a task that isn't its responsibility, it needs to have access to another object whose responsibilities include that task. The first object then asks the second object to carry out the task. This is done with a more generalized version of the procedure call that you are familiar with in procedural programming. (Recall that in the Java programming language these procedure calls are usually called *method calls.*)

In particular, an object should never directly manipulate the internal data of another object, nor should it expose data for other objects to access directly. All communication should be through method calls. By *encapsulating* object data, you maximize reusability, reduce data dependency, and minimize debugging time.

Of course, just as with modules in a procedural language, you will not want an individual object to do *too* much. Both design and debugging are simplified when you build small objects that perform a few tasks, rather than building humongous objects with internal data that are extremely complex, with hundreds of procedures to manipulate the data.

The Vocabulary of OOP

You need to understand some of the terminology of OOP to go further. The most important term is the *class*, which you have already seen in the code examples of Chapter 3. A class is the template or blueprint from which objects are actually made. This leads to the standard way of thinking about classes: as cookie cutters. Objects are the cookies themselves. When you *construct* an object from a class, you are said to have created an *instance* of the class.

As you have seen, all code that you write in Java is inside a class. The standard Java library supplies several thousand classes for such diverse purposes as user interface design, dates and calendars, and network programming. Nonetheless, you still have to create your own classes in Java to describe the objects of the problem domains of your applications and to adapt the classes that are supplied by the standard library to your own purposes.

Encapsulation (sometimes called data hiding) is a key concept in working with objects. Formally, encapsulation is nothing more than combining data and behavior in one package and hiding the implementation of the data from the user of the object. The data in an object are called its *instance fields*, and the procedures that operate on the data are called its *methods*. A specific object that is an instance of a class will have specific values for its instance fields. The set of those values is the current *state* of the object. Whenever you invoke a message on an object, its state may change.

It cannot be stressed enough that the key to making encapsulation work is to have methods *never* directly access instance fields in a class other than their own. Programs should interact with object data *only* through the object's methods. Encapsulation is the way to give the object its "black box" behavior, which is the key to reuse and reliability. This means a class may totally change how it stores its data, but as long as it continues to use the same methods to manipulate the data, no other object will know or care.

When you do start writing your own classes in Java, another tenet of OOP makes this easier: classes can be built by *extending* other classes. Java, in fact, comes with a "cosmic superclass" called `Object`. All other classes extend this class. You will see more about the `Object` class in the next chapter.

When you extend an existing class, the new class has all the properties and methods of the class that you extend. You supply new methods and data fields that apply to your new class only. The concept of extending a class to obtain another class is called *inheritance*. See the next chapter for details on inheritance.

Objects

To work with OOP, you should be able to identify three key characteristics of objects:

- The object's *behavior*—what can you do with this object, or what methods can you apply to it?
- The object's *state*—how does the object react when you apply those methods?
- The object's *identity*—how is the object distinguished from others that may have the same behavior and state?

All objects that are instances of the same class share a family resemblance by supporting the same *behavior*. The behavior of an object is defined by the methods that you can call.

Next, each object stores information about what it currently looks like. This is the object's *state*. An object's state may change over time, but not spontaneously. A change in the state of an object must be a consequence of method calls. (If the object state changed without a method call on that object, someone broke encapsulation.)

However, the state of an object does not completely describe it, because each object has a distinct *identity*. For example, in an order-processing system, two orders are distinct even if they request identical items. Notice that the individual objects that are instances of a class *always* differ in their identity and *usually* differ in their state.

These key characteristics can influence each other. For example, the state of an object can influence its behavior. (If an order is "shipped" or "paid," it may reject a method call that asks it to add or remove items. Conversely, if an order is "empty," that is, no items have yet been ordered, it should not allow itself to be shipped.)

In a traditional procedural program, you start the process at the top, with the `main` function. When designing an object-oriented system, there is no "top," and newcomers to OOP often wonder where to begin. The answer is, you first find classes and then you add methods to each class.

TIP: A simple rule of thumb in identifying classes is to look for nouns in the problem analysis. Methods, on the other hand, correspond to verbs.

For example, in an order-processing system, some of these nouns are:

- Item
- Order
- Shipping address
- Payment
- Account

These nouns may lead to the classes `Item`, `Order`, and so on.

Next, look for verbs. Items are *added* to orders. Orders are *shipped* or *canceled*. Payments are *applied* to orders. With each verb, such as "add," "ship," "cancel," and "apply," you identify the one object that has the major responsibility for carrying it out. For example, when a new item is added to an order, the order object should be the one in charge because it knows how it stores and sorts items. That is, `add` should be a method of the `Order` class that takes an `Item` object as a parameter.

Of course, the "noun and verb" rule is only a rule of thumb, and only experience can help you decide which nouns and verbs are the important ones when building your classes.

Relationships Between Classes

The most common relationships between classes are

- *Dependence* ("uses–a")
- *Aggregation* ("has–a")
- *Inheritance* ("is–a")

The *dependence*, or "uses–a" relationship, is the most obvious and also the most general. For example, the `Order` class uses the `Account` class because `Order` objects need to access `Account` objects to check for credit status. But the `Item` class does not depend on the `Account` class, because `Item` objects never need to worry about customer accounts. Thus, a class depends on another class if its methods manipulate objects of that class.

TIP: Try to minimize the number of classes that depend on each other. The point is, if a class `A` is unaware of the existence of a class `B`, it is also unconcerned about any changes to `B`! (And this means that changes to `B` do not introduce bugs into `A`.) In software engineering terminology, you want to minimize the *coupling* between classes.

The *aggregation*, or "has-a" relationship, is easy to understand because it is concrete; for example, an Order object contains Item objects. Containment means that objects of class A contain objects of class B.

NOTE: Some methodologists view the concept of aggregation with disdain and prefer to use a more general "association" relationship. From the point of view of modeling, that is understandable. But for programmers, the "has-a" relationship makes a lot of sense. We like to use aggregation for a second reason—the standard notation for associations is less clear. See Table 4–1.

The *inheritance*, or "is-a" relationship, expresses a relationship between a more special and a more general class. For example, a RushOrder class inherits from an Order class. The specialized RushOrder class has special methods for priority handling and a different method for computing shipping charges, but its other methods, such as adding items and billing, are inherited from the Order class. In general, if class A extends class B, class A inherits methods from class B but has more capabilities. (We describe inheritance more fully in the next chapter, in which we discuss this important notion at some length.)

Many programmers use the UML (Unified Modeling Language) notation to draw *class diagrams* that describe the relationships between classes. You can see an example of such a diagram in Figure 4–1. You draw classes as rectangles, and relationships as arrows with various adornments. Table 4–1 shows the most common UML arrow styles.

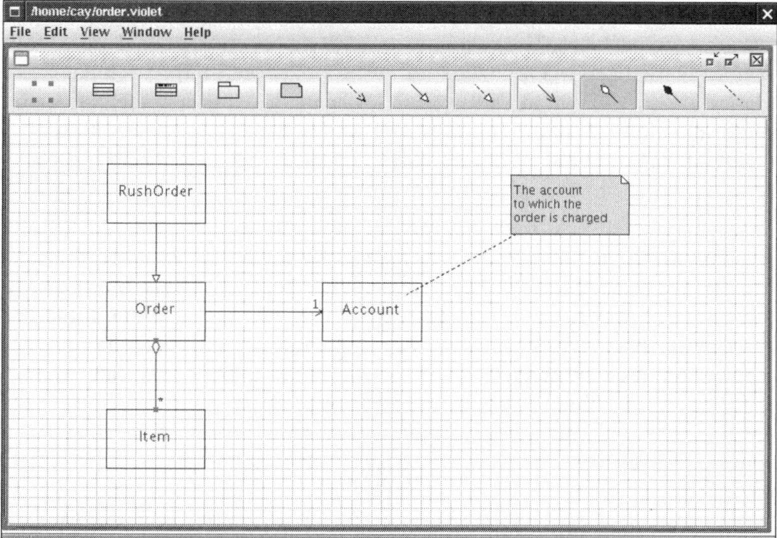

Figure 4–1: A class diagram

NOTE: A number of tools are available for drawing UML diagrams. Several vendors offer high-powered (and high-priced) tools that aim to be the focal point of your development process. Among them are Rational Rose (http://www.ibm.com/software/awdtools/developer/modeler) and Together (http://www.borland.com/together). Another choice is the open source program ArgoUML (http://argouml.tigris.org). A commercially supported version is available from GentleWare (http://gentleware.com). If you just want to draw a simple diagrams with a minimum of fuss, try out Violet (http://horstmann.com/violet).

Table 4–1: UML Notation for Class Relationships

Relationship	UML Connector
Inheritance	————————▷
Interface Inheritance	– – – – – – – –▷
Dependency	– – – – – – – –>
Aggregation	◇————————
Association	————————
Directed Association	————————>

OOP Contrasted with Traditional Procedural Programming Techniques

We want to end this short introduction to OOP by contrasting OOP with the procedural model that you may be more familiar with. In procedural programming, you identify the tasks to be performed and then you do the following:

- Use a stepwise refinement process: Break the task to be performed into subtasks, and these into smaller subtasks until the subtasks are simple enough to be implemented directly (this is the top-down approach).
- Write procedures to solve simple tasks and combine them into more sophisticated procedures until you have the functionality you want (this is the bottom-up approach).

Most programmers, of course, use a mixture of the top-down and bottom-up strategies to solve a programming problem. The rule of thumb for discovering procedures is the same as the rule for finding methods in OOP: look for verbs, or actions, in the problem description. The important difference is that in OOP, you *first* isolate the classes in the project. Only then do you look for the methods of the class. And there is another important difference between traditional procedures and OOP methods: each method is associated with the class that is responsible for carrying out the operation.

For small problems, the breakdown into procedures works very well. But for larger problems, classes and methods have two advantages. Classes provide a convenient clustering mechanism for methods. A simple web browser may require 2,000 procedures for its implementation, or it may require 100 classes with an average of 20 methods per class. The latter structure is much easier for a programmer to grasp. It is also much easier to distribute over a team of programmers. The encapsulation built into classes helps you here as well: classes hide their data representations from all code except their own methods. As Figure 4–2 shows, this means that if a programming bug messes up data, it is far easier to search for the culprit among the 20 methods that had access to that data item than among 2,000 procedures.

You may say that this doesn't sound much different from *modularization*. You have certainly written programs by breaking up the program into modules that communicate with each other through procedure calls only, not by sharing data. This (if well done) goes far in accomplishing encapsulation. However, in many programming languages, the slightest sloppiness in programming allows you to get at the data in another module—encapsulation is easy to defeat.

There is a more serious problem. While classes are factories for multiple objects with the same behavior, you cannot get multiple copies of a useful module. Suppose you have a module encapsulating a collection of orders, together with a spiffy balanced binary tree module to access them quickly. Now it turns out that you actually need *two* such collections, one for the pending orders and one for the completed orders. You cannot simply link

the order tree module twice. And you don't really want to make a copy and rename all procedures for the linker to work! Classes do not have this limitation. Once a class has been defined, it is easy to construct any number of instances of that class type (whereas a module can have only one instance).

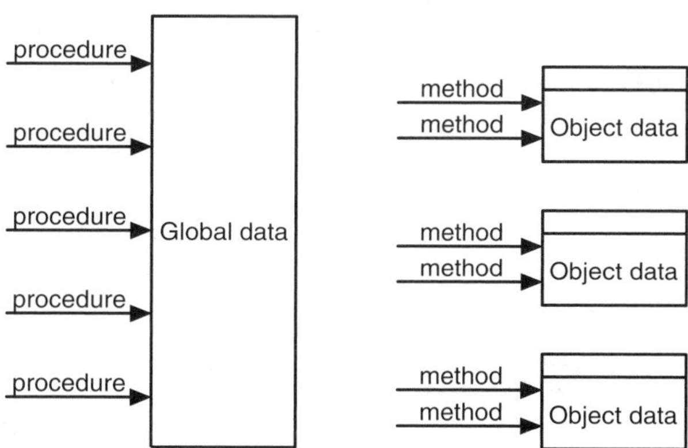

Figure 4–2: Procedural vs. OO programming

We have only scratched a very large surface. The end of this chapter has a short section on "Class Design Hints." For more information on understanding the OO design process, consult one of the many books on OO and UML. We like *The Unified Modeling Language User Guide* by Grady Booch, Ivar Jacobson, and James Rumbaugh (Addison-Wesley, 1999).

Using Predefined Classes

Because you can't do anything in Java without classes, you have already seen several classes at work. Unfortunately, many of these are quite anomalous in the Java scheme of things. Take, for example, the `Math` class. You have seen that you can use methods of the `Math` class, such as `Math.random`, without needing to know how they are implemented—all you need to know is the name and parameters (if any). That is the point of encapsulation and will certainly be true of all classes. Unfortunately, the `Math` class *only* encapsulates functionality; it neither needs nor hides data. Because there is no data, you do not need to worry about making objects and initializing their instance fields—there aren't any!

In the next section, we look at a more typical class, the `Date` class. You will see how to construct objects and call methods of this class.

Objects and Object Variables

To work with objects, you first construct them and specify their initial state. Then you apply methods to the objects.

In the Java programming language, you use *constructors* to construct new instances. A constructor is a special method whose purpose is to construct and initialize objects. Let us look at an example. The standard Java library contains a `Date` class. Its objects describe points in time, such as "December 31, 1999, 23:59:59 GMT".

NOTE: You may be wondering: Why use classes to represent dates rather than (as in some languages) a built-in type? For example, Visual Basic has a built-in date type and programmers can specify dates in the format `#6/1/1995#`. On the surface, this sounds convenient—programmers can simply use the built-in date type rather than worrying about classes. But actually, how

suitable is the Visual Basic design? In some locales, dates are specified as month/day/year, in others as day/month/year. Are the language designers really equipped to foresee these kinds of issues? If they do a poor job, the language becomes an unpleasant muddle, but unhappy programmers are powerless to do anything about it. With classes, the design task is offloaded to a library designer. If the class is not perfect, other programmers can easily write their own classes to enhance or replace the system classes.

Constructors always have the same name as the class name. Thus, the constructor for the `Date` class is called `Date`. To construct a `Date` object, you combine the constructor with the `new` operator, as follows:

```
new Date()
```

This expression constructs a new object. The object is initialized to the current date and time.

If you like, you can pass the object to a method:

```
System.out.println(new Date());
```

Alternatively, you can apply a method to the object that you just constructed. One of the methods of the `Date` class is the `toString` method. That method yields a string representation of the date. Here is how you would apply the `toString` method to a newly constructed `Date` object.

```
String s = new Date().toString();
```

In these two examples, the constructed object is used only once. Usually, you will want to hang on to the objects that you construct so that you can keep using them. Simply store the object in a variable:

```
Date birthday = new Date();
```

Figure 4–3 shows the object variable `birthday` that refers to the newly constructed object.

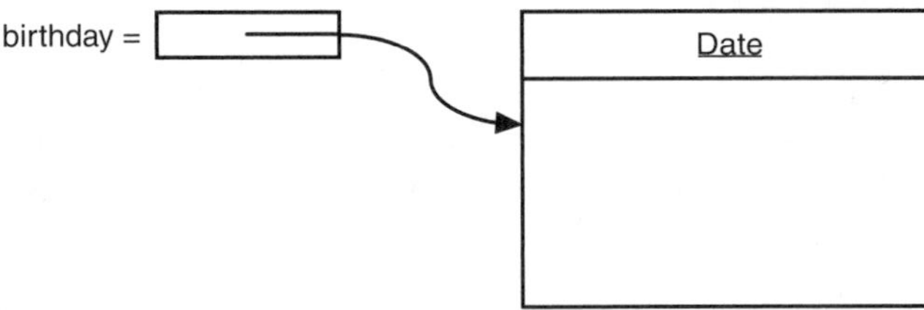

Figure 4–3: Creating a new object

There is an important difference between objects and object variables. For example, the statement

```
Date deadline; // deadline doesn't refer to any object
```

defines an object variable, `deadline`, that can refer to objects of type `Date`. It is important to realize that the variable `deadline` *is not an object* and, in fact, does not yet even refer to an object. You cannot use any `Date` methods on this variable at this time. The statement

```
s = deadline.toString(); // not yet
```

would cause a compile-time error.

You must first initialize the `deadline` variable. You have two choices. Of course, you can initialize the variable with a newly constructed object:

```
deadline = new Date();
```

Or you can set the variable to refer to an existing object:

```
deadline = birthday;
```

Now both variables refer to the *same* object (see Figure 4–4).

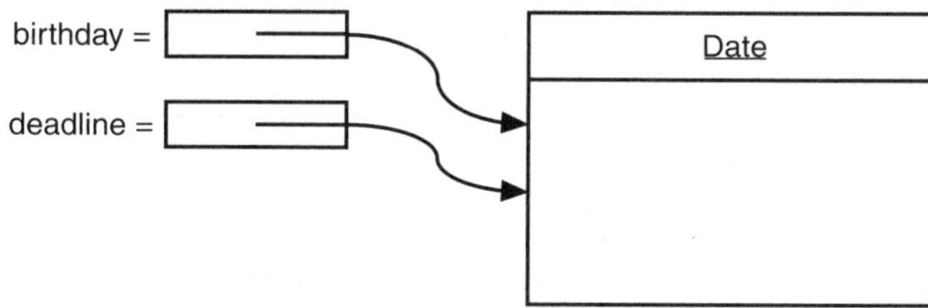

Figure 4–4: Object variables that refer to the same object

It is important to realize that an object variable doesn't actually contain an object. It only *refers* to an object.

In Java, the value of any object variable is a reference to an object that is stored elsewhere. The return value of the `new` operator is also a reference. A statement such as

```
Date deadline = new Date();
```

has two parts. The expression `new Date()` makes an object of type `Date`, and its value is a reference to that newly created object. That reference is then stored in the `deadline` variable.

You can explicitly set an object variable to `null` to indicate that it currently refers to no object.

```
deadline = null;
. . .
if (deadline != null)
   System.out.println(deadline);
```

If you apply a method to a variable that holds `null`, then a runtime error occurs.

```
birthday = null;
String s = birthday.toString(); // runtime error!
```

Variables are not automatically initialized to `null`. You must initialize them, either by calling `new` or by setting them to `null`.

C++ NOTE: Many people mistakenly believe that Java object variables behave like C++ references. But in C++ there are no null references, and references cannot be assigned. You should think of Java object variables as analogous to *object pointers* in C++. For example,

```
Date birthday; // Java
```

is really the same as

```
Date* birthday; // C++
```

Once you make this association, everything falls into place. Of course, a `Date*` pointer isn't initialized until you initialize it with a call to `new`. The syntax is almost the same in C++ and Java.

```
Date* birthday = new Date(); // C++
```

If you copy one variable to another, then both variables refer to the same date—they are pointers to the same object. The equivalent of the Java `null` reference is the C++ `NULL` pointer.

All Java objects live on the heap. When an object contains another object variable, that variable still contains just a pointer to yet another heap object.

In C++, pointers make you nervous because they are so error prone. It is easy to create bad pointers or to mess up memory management. In Java, these problems simply go away. If you use an uninitialized pointer, the runtime system will reliably generate a runtime error instead of producing random results. You don't worry about memory management, because the garbage collector takes care of it.

C++ makes quite an effort, with its support for copy constructors and assignment operators, to allow the implementation of objects that copy themselves automatically. For example, a copy of a linked list is a new linked list with the same contents but with an independent set of links. This makes it possible to design classes with the same copy behavior as the built-in types. In Java, you must use the `clone` method to get a complete copy of an object.

The `GregorianCalendar` Class of the Java Library

In the preceding examples, we used the `Date` class that is a part of the standard Java library. An instance of the `Date` class has a state, namely *a particular point in time.*

Although you don't need to know this when you use the `Date` class, the time is represented by the number of milliseconds (positive or negative) from a fixed point, the so-called *epoch,* which is 00:00:00 UTC, January 1, 1970. UTC is the Coordinated Universal Time, the scientific time standard that is, for practical purposes, the same as the more familiar GMT or Greenwich Mean Time.

But as it turns out, the `Date` class is not very useful for manipulating dates. The designers of the Java library take the point of view that a date description such as "December 31, 1999, 23:59:59" is an arbitrary convention, governed by a *calendar.* This particular description follows the Gregorian calendar, which is the calendar used in most places of the world. The same point in time would be described quite differently in the Chinese or Hebrew lunar calendars, not to mention the calendar used by your customers from Mars.

NOTE: Throughout human history, civilizations grappled with the design of calendars that attached names to dates and brought order to the solar and lunar cycles. For a fascinating explanation of calendars around the world, from the French Revolutionary calendar to the Mayan long count, see *Calendrical Calculations* by Nachum Dershowitz and Edward M. Reingold (Cambridge University Press, 2nd ed., 2001).

The library designers decided to separate the concerns of keeping time and attaching names to points in time. Therefore, the standard Java library contains two separate classes: the `Date` class, which represents a point in time, and the `GregorianCalendar` class, which expresses dates in the familiar calendar notation. In fact, the `GregorianCalendar` class extends a more generic `Calendar` class that describes the properties of calendars in general. In theory, you can extend the `Calendar` class and implement the Chinese lunar calendar or a Martian calendar. However, the standard library does not contain any calendar implementations besides the Gregorian calendar.

Separating time measurement from calendars is good object-oriented design. In general, it is a good idea to use separate classes to express different concepts.

The `Date` class has only a small number of methods that allow you to compare two points in time. For example, the `before` and `after` methods tell you if one point in time comes before or after another.

```
if (today.before(birthday))
   System.out.println("Still time to shop for a gift.");
```

NOTE: Actually, the `Date` class has methods such as `getDay`, `getMonth`, and `getYear`, but these methods are *deprecated.* A method is deprecated when a library designer realizes that the method should have never been introduced in the first place.

> These methods were a part of the Date class before the library designers realized that it makes more sense to supply separate calendar classes. When the calendar classes were introduced, the Date methods were tagged as deprecated. You can still use them in your programs, but you will get unsightly compiler warnings if you do. It is a good idea to stay away from using deprecated methods because they may be removed in a future version of the library.

The GregorianCalendar class has many more methods than the Date class. In particular, it has several useful constructors. The expression

```
new GregorianCalendar()
```

constructs a new object that represents the date and time at which the object was constructed.

You can construct a calendar object for midnight on a specific date by supplying year, month, and day:

```
new GregorianCalendar(1999, 11, 31)
```

Somewhat curiously, the months are counted from 0. Therefore, 11 is December. For greater clarity, there are constants like Calendar.DECEMBER.

```
new GregorianCalendar(1999, Calendar.DECEMBER, 31)
```

You can also set the time:

```
new GregorianCalendar(1999, Calendar.DECEMBER, 31, 23, 59, 59)
```

Of course, you will usually want to store the constructed object in an object variable:

```
GregorianCalendar deadline = new GregorianCalendar(. . .);
```

The GregorianCalendar has encapsulated instance fields to maintain the date to which it is set. Without looking at the source code, it is impossible to know the representation that the class uses internally. But, of course, the point of encapsulation is that this doesn't matter. What matters are the methods that a class exposes.

Mutator and Accessor Methods

At this point, you are probably asking yourself: How do I get at the current day or month or year for the date encapsulated in a specific GregorianCalendar object? And how do I change the values if I am unhappy with them? You can find out how to carry out these tasks by looking at the on-line documentation or the API notes at the end of this section. We go over the most important methods in this section.

The job of a calendar is to compute attributes, such as the date, weekday, month, or year, of a certain point in time. To query one of these settings, you use the get method of the GregorianCalendar class. To select the item that you want to get, you pass a constant defined in the Calendar class, such as Calendar.MONTH or Calendar.DAY_OF_WEEK:

```
GregorianCalendar now = new GregorianCalendar();
int month = now.get(Calendar.MONTH);
int weekday = now.get(Calendar.DAY_OF_WEEK);
```

The API notes list all the constants that you can use.

You change the state with a call to the set method:

```
deadline.set(Calendar.YEAR, 2001);
deadline.set(Calendar.MONTH, Calendar.APRIL);
deadline.set(Calendar.DAY_OF_MONTH, 15);
```

There is also a convenience method to set the year, month, and day with a single call:

```
deadline.set(2001, Calendar.APRIL, 15);
```

Finally, you can add a number of days, weeks, months, and so on, to a given calendar object.

```
deadline.add(Calendar.MONTH, 3); // move deadline by 3 months
```

If you add a negative number, then the calendar is moved backwards.

There is a conceptual difference between the `get` method on the one hand and the `set` and `add` methods on the other hand. The `get` method only looks up the state of the object and reports on it. The `set` and `add` methods modify the state of the object. Methods that change instance fields are called *mutator methods*, and those that only access instance fields without modifying them are called *accessor methods*.

C++ NOTE: In C++, the `const` suffix denotes accessor methods. A method that is not declared as `const` is assumed to be a mutator. However, in the Java programming language, no special syntax distinguishes between accessors and mutators.

A common convention is to prefix accessor methods with the prefix `get` and mutator methods with the prefix `set`. For example, the `GregorianCalendar` class has methods `getTime` and `setTime` that get and set the point in time that a calendar object represents.

```
Date time = calendar.getTime();
calendar.setTime(time);
```

These methods are particularly useful for converting between the `GregorianCalendar` and `Date` classes. Here is an example. Suppose you know the year, month, and day and you want to make a `Date` object with those settings. Because the `Date` class knows nothing about calendars, first construct a `GregorianCalendar` object and then call the `getTime` method to obtain a date:

```
GregorianCalendar calendar = new GregorianCalendar(year, month, day);
Date hireDay = calendar.getTime();
```

Conversely, if you want to find the year, month, or day of a `Date` object, you construct a `GregorianCalendar` object, set the time, and then call the `get` method:

```
GregorianCalendar calendar = new GregorianCalendar();
calendar.setTime(hireDay);
int year = calendar.get(Calendar.YEAR);
```

We finish this section with a program that puts the `GregorianCalendar` class to work. The program displays a calendar for the current month, like this:

```
Sun Mon Tue Wed Thu Fri Sat
                          1
  2   3   4   5   6   7   8
  9  10  11  12  13  14  15
 16  17  18  19* 20  21  22
 23  24  25  26  27  28  29
 30  31
```

The current day is marked with an `*`, and the program knows how to compute the days of the week.

Let us go through the key steps of the program. First, we construct a calendar object that is initialized with the current date and time. (We don't actually care about the time for this application.)

```
GregorianCalendar d = new GregorianCalendar();
```

We capture the current day and month by calling the `get` method twice.

```
int today = d.get(Calendar.DAY_OF_MONTH);
int month = d.get(Calendar.MONTH);
```

Then we set `d` to the first of the month and get the weekday of that date.

```
d.set(Calendar.DAY_OF_MONTH, 1);
int weekday = d.get(Calendar.DAY_OF_WEEK);
```

The variable weekday is set to 1 (or Calendar.SUNDAY) if the first day of the month is a Sunday, to 2 (or Calendar.MONDAY) if it is a Monday, and so on.

Next, we print the header and the spaces for indenting the first line of the calendar.

For each day, we print a space if the day is < 10, then the day, and then a * if the day equals the current day. Each Saturday, we print a new line.

Then we advance d to the next day:

```
d.add(Calendar.DAY_OF_MONTH, 1);
```

When do we stop? We don't know whether the month has 31, 30, 29, or 28 days. Instead, we keep iterating while d is still in the current month.

```
do
{
   . . .
}
while (d.get(Calendar.MONTH) == month);
```

Once d has moved into the next month, the program terminates.

Example 4–1 shows the complete program.

As you can see, the GregorianCalendar class makes it simple to write a calendar program that takes care of complexities such as weekdays and the varying month lengths. You don't need to know *how* the GregorianCalendar class computes months and weekdays. You just use the *interface* of the class—the get, set, and add methods.

The point of this example program is to show you how you can use the interface of a class to carry out fairly sophisticated tasks without ever having to know the implementation details.

Example 4–1: CalendarTest.java

```
import java.util.*;

public class CalendarTest
{
   public static void main(String[] args)
   {
      // construct d as current date
      GregorianCalendar d = new GregorianCalendar();

      int today = d.get(Calendar.DAY_OF_MONTH);
      int month = d.get(Calendar.MONTH);

      // set d to start date of the month
      d.set(Calendar.DAY_OF_MONTH, 1);

      int weekday = d.get(Calendar.DAY_OF_WEEK);

      // print heading
      System.out.println("Sun Mon Tue Wed Thu Fri Sat");

      // indent first line of calendar
      for (int i = Calendar.SUNDAY; i < weekday; i++ )
         System.out.print("    ");

      do
```

```
    {
       // print day
       int day = d.get(Calendar.DAY_OF_MONTH);
       System.out.printf("%3d", day);

       // mark current day with *
       if (day == today)
          System.out.print("*");
       else
          System.out.print(" ");

       // start a new line after every Saturday
       if (weekday == Calendar.SATURDAY)
          System.out.println();

       // advance d to the next day
       d.add(Calendar.DAY_OF_MONTH, 1);
       weekday = d.get(Calendar.DAY_OF_WEEK);
    }
    while (d.get(Calendar.MONTH) == month);
    // the loop exits when d is day 1 of the next month

    // print final end of line if necessary
    if (weekday != Calendar.SUNDAY)
       System.out.println();
  }
}
```

NOTE: In the interest of simplicity, the program in Example 4–1 prints a calendar with English names for the weekdays and the hard-wired assumption that the week starts on a Sunday. Look at the `DateFormatSymbols` class to get the weekday names for other languages. The `Calendar.getFirstDayOfWeek` method returns the weekday on which the week starts, for example Sunday in the USA and Monday in Germany.

API **java.util.GregorianCalendar** 1.1

- `GregorianCalendar()`
  constructs a calendar object that represents the current time in the default time zone with the default locale.
- `GregorianCalendar(int year, int month, int day)`
  constructs a Gregorian calendar with the given date.

Parameters:	`year`	the year of the date
	`month`	the month of the date. This value is 0-based; for example, 0 for January
	`day`	the day of the month

- `GregorianCalendar(int year, int month, int day, int hour, int minutes, int seconds)`
  constructs a Gregorian calendar with the given date and time.

Parameters:	`year`	the year of the date
	`month`	the month of the date. This value is 0-based; for example, 0 for January

`day`	the day of the month
`hour`	the hour (between 0 and 23)
`minutes`	the minutes (between 0 and 59)
`seconds`	the seconds (between 0 and 59)

- `int get(int field)`
  gets the value of a particular field.

  Parameters: `field` — one of `Calendar.ERA`, `Calendar.YEAR`, `Calendar.MONTH`, `Calendar.WEEK_OF_YEAR`, `Calendar.WEEK_OF_MONTH`, `Calendar.DAY_OF_MONTH`, `Calendar.DAY_OF_YEAR`, `Calendar.DAY_OF_WEEK`, `Calendar.DAY_OF_WEEK_IN_MONTH`, `Calendar.AM_PM`, `Calendar.HOUR`, `Calendar.HOUR_OF_DAY`, `Calendar.MINUTE`, `Calendar.SECOND`, `Calendar.MILLISECOND`, `Calendar.ZONE_OFFSET`, `Calendar.DST_OFFSET`

- `void set(int field, int value)`
  sets the value of a particular field.

Parameters:		
	`field`	one of the constants accepted by `get`
	`value`	the new value

- `void set(int year, int month, int day)`
  sets the date fields to a new date.

Parameters:		
	`year`	the year of the date
	`month`	the month of the date. This value is 0-based; for example, 0 for January
	`day`	the day of the month

- `void set(int year, int month, int day, int hour, int minutes, int seconds)`
  sets the date and time fields to new values.

Parameters:		
	`year`	the year of the date
	`month`	the month of the date. This value is 0-based; for example, 0 for January
	`day`	the day of the month
	`hour`	the hour (between 0 and 23)
	`minutes`	the minutes (between 0 and 59)
	`seconds`	the seconds (between 0 and 59)

- `void add(int field, int amount)`
  is a date arithmetic method. Adds the specified amount of time to the given time field. For example, to add 7 days to the current calendar date, call `c.add(Calendar.DAY_OF_MONTH, 7)`.

Parameters:		
	`field`	the field to modify (using one of the constants documented in the `get` method)
	`amount`	the amount by which the field should be changed (can be negative)

- `void setTime(Date time)`
  sets this calendar to the given point in time.

  Parameters: `time` a point in time

- `Date getTime()`
  gets the point in time that is represented by the current value of this calendar object.

Defining Your Own Classes

In Chapter 3, you started writing simple classes. However, all those classes had just a single `main` method. Now the time has come to show you how to write the kind of "workhorse classes" that are needed for more sophisticated applications. These classes typically do not have a `main` method. Instead, they have their own instance fields and methods. To build a complete program, you combine several classes, one of which has a `main` method.

An `Employee` Class

The simplest form for a class definition in Java is:

```
class ClassName
{
   constructor1
   constructor2
   . . .
   method1
   method2
   . . .
   field1
   field2
   . . .
}
```

NOTE: We adopt the style that the methods for the class come first and the fields come at the end. Perhaps this, in a small way, encourages the notion of looking at the interface first and paying less attention to the implementation.

Consider the following, very simplified, version of an `Employee` class that might be used by a business in writing a payroll system.

```
class Employee
{
   // constructor
   public Employee(String n, double s, int year, int month, int day)
   {
      name = n;
      salary = s;
      GregorianCalendar calendar = new GregorianCalendar(year, month - 1, day);
      hireDay = calendar.getTime();
   }

   // a method
   public String getName()
   {
      return name;
   }

   // more methods
```

```
   . . .

   // instance fields

   private String name;
   private double salary;
   private Date hireDay;
}
```

We break down the implementation of this class in some detail in the sections that follow. First, though, Example 4–2 shows a program code that shows the `Employee` class in action.

In the program, we construct an `Employee` array and fill it with three employee objects:

```
Employee[] staff = new Employee[3];

staff[0] = new Employee("Carl Cracker", . . .);
staff[1] = new Employee("Harry Hacker", . . .);
staff[2] = new Employee("Tony Tester", . . .);
```

Next, we use the `raiseSalary` method of the `Employee` class to raise each employee's salary by 5%:

```
for (Employee e : staff)
   e.raiseSalary(5);
```

Finally, we print out information about each employee, by calling the `getName`, `getSalary`, and `getHireDay` methods:

```
for (Employee e : staff)
   System.out.println("name=" + e.getName()
      + ",salary=" + e.getSalary()
      + ",hireDay=" + e.getHireDay());
```

Note that the example program consists of *two* classes: the `Employee` class and a class `EmployeeTest` with the `public` access specifier. The `main` method with the instructions that we just described is contained in the `EmployeeTest` class.

The name of the source file is `EmployeeTest.java` because the name of the file must match the name of the `public` class. You can have only one public class in a source file, but you can have any number of nonpublic classes.

Next, when you compile this source code, the compiler creates two class files in the directory: `EmployeeTest.class` and `Employee.class`.

You start the program by giving the bytecode interpreter the name of the class that contains the `main` method of your program:

```
java EmployeeTest
```

The bytecode interpreter starts running the code in the `main` method in the `EmployeeTest` class. This code in turn constructs three new `Employee` objects and shows you their state.

Example 4–2: EmployeeTest.java

```
import java.util.*;

public class EmployeeTest
{
   public static void main(String[] args)
   {
      // fill the staff array with three Employee objects
      Employee[] staff = new Employee[3];

```

```
      staff[0] = new Employee("Carl Cracker", 75000, 1987, 12, 15);
      staff[1] = new Employee("Harry Hacker", 50000, 1989, 10, 1);
      staff[2] = new Employee("Tony Tester", 40000, 1990, 3, 15);

      // raise everyone's salary by 5%
      for (Employee e : staff)
         e.raiseSalary(5);

      // print out information about all Employee objects
      for (Employee e : staff)
         System.out.println("name=" + e.getName()
            + ",salary=" + e.getSalary()
            + ",hireDay=" + e.getHireDay());
   }
}

class Employee
{
   public Employee(String n, double s, int year, int month, int day)
   {
      name = n;
      salary = s;
      GregorianCalendar calendar = new GregorianCalendar(year, month - 1, day);
         // GregorianCalendar uses 0 for January
      hireDay = calendar.getTime();
   }

   public String getName()
   {
      return name;
   }

   public double getSalary()
   {
      return salary;
   }

   public Date getHireDay()
   {
      return hireDay;
   }

   public void raiseSalary(double byPercent)
   {
      double raise = salary * byPercent / 100;
      salary += raise;
   }

   private String name;
   private double salary;
   private Date hireDay;
}
```

Use of Multiple Source Files

The program in Example 4–2 has two classes in a single source file. Many programmers prefer to put each class into its own source file. For example, you can place the `Employee` class into a file `Employee.java` and the `EmployeeTest` class into `EmployeeTest.java`.

If you like this arrangement, then you have two choices for compiling the program. You can invoke the Java compiler with a wildcard:

```
javac Employee*.java
```

Then, all source files matching the wildcard will be compiled into class files. Or, you can simply type:

```
javac EmployeeTest.java
```

You may find it surprising that the second choice works because the `Employee.java` file is never explicitly compiled. However, when the Java compiler sees the `Employee` class being used inside `EmployeeTest.java`, it will look for a file named `Employee.class`. If it does not find that file, it automatically searches for `Employee.java` and then compiles it. Even more is true: if the time stamp of the version of `Employee.java` that it finds is newer than that of the existing `Employee.class` file, the Java compiler will *automatically* recompile the file.

NOTE: If you are familiar with the “make” facility of UNIX (or one of its Windows cousins such as “nmake”), then you can think of the Java compiler as having the “make” functionality already built in.

Dissecting the `Employee` Class

In the sections that follow, we want to dissect the `Employee` class. Let’s start with the methods in this class. As you can see by examining the source code, this class has one constructor and four methods:

```
public Employee(String n, double s, int year, int month, int day)
public String getName()
public double getSalary()
public Date getHireDay()
public void raiseSalary(double byPercent)
```

All methods of this class are tagged as `public`. The keyword `public` means that any method in any class can call the method. (The four possible access levels are covered in this and the next chapter.)

Next, notice that three instance fields will hold the data we will manipulate inside an instance of the `Employee` class.

```
private String name;
private double salary;
private Date hireDay;
```

The `private` keyword makes sure that the *only* methods that can access these instance fields are the methods of the `Employee` class itself. No outside method can read or write to these fields.

NOTE: You could use the `public` keyword with your instance fields, but it would be a very bad idea. Having `public` data fields would allow any part of the program to read and modify the instance fields. That completely ruins encapsulation. Any method of any class can modify public fields—and, in our experience, some code usually will take advantage of that access privilege when you least expect it. We strongly recommend that you always make your instance fields `private`.

Finally, notice that two of the instance fields are themselves objects: the `name` and `hireDay` fields are references to `String` and `Date` objects. This is quite usual: classes will often contain instance fields of class type.

First Steps with Constructors

Let's look at the constructor listed in our `Employee` class.

```
public Employee(String n, double s, int year, int month, int day)
{
   name = n;
   salary = s;
   GregorianCalendar calendar = new GregorianCalendar(year, month - 1, day);
   hireDay = calendar.getTime();
}
```

As you can see, the name of the constructor is the same as the name of the class. This constructor runs when you construct objects of the `Employee` class—giving the instance fields the initial state you want them to have.

For example, when you create an instance of the `Employee` class with code like this

```
new Employee("James Bond", 100000, 1950, 1, 1);
```

you have set the instance fields as follows:

```
name = "James Bond";
salary = 100000;
hireDay = January 1, 1950;
```

There is an important difference between constructors and other methods. A constructor can only be called in conjunction with the `new` operator. You can't apply a constructor to an existing object to reset the instance fields. For example,

```
james.Employee("James Bond", 250000, 1950, 1, 1); // ERROR
```

is a compile-time error.

We have more to say about constructors later in this chapter. For now, keep the following in mind:

- A constructor has the same name as the class.
- A class can have more than one constructor.
- A constructor can take zero, one, or more parameters.
- A constructor has no return value.
- A constructor is always called with the `new` operator.

C++ NOTE: Constructors work the same way in Java as they do in C++. But keep in mind that all Java objects are constructed on the heap and that a constructor must be combined with `new`. It is a common C++ programmer error to forget the `new` operator:

```
Employee number007("James Bond", 100000, 1950, 1, 1);
   // C++, not Java
```

That works in C++ but does not work in Java.

CAUTION: Be careful not to introduce local variables with the same names as the instance fields. For example, the following constructor will not set the salary.

```
public Employee(String n, double s, . . .)
{
   String name = n; // ERROR
   double salary = s; // ERROR
   . . .
}
```

The constructor declares *local* variables `name` and `salary`. These variables are only accessible inside the constructor. They *shadow* the instance fields with the same name. Some programmers—such as the authors of this book—write this kind of code when they type faster than they think, because their fingers are used to adding the data type. This is a nasty error that can be hard to track down. You just have to be careful in all of your methods that you don't use variable names that equal the names of instance fields.

Implicit and Explicit Parameters

Methods operate on objects and access their instance fields. For example, the method

```
public void raiseSalary(double byPercent)
{
   double raise = salary * byPercent / 100;
   salary += raise;
}
```

sets a new value for the `salary` instance field in the object on which this method is invoked. Consider the call

```
number007.raiseSalary(5);
```

The effect is to increase the value of the `number007.salary` field by 5%. More specifically, the call executes the following instructions:

```
double raise = number007.salary * 5 / 100;
number007.salary += raise;
```

The `raiseSalary` method has two parameters. The first parameter, called the *implicit* parameter, is the object of type `Employee` that appears before the method name. The second parameter, the number inside the parentheses after the method name, is an *explicit* parameter.

As you can see, the explicit parameters are explicitly listed in the method declaration, for example, `double byPercent`. The implicit parameter does not appear in the method declaration.

In every method, the keyword `this` refers to the implicit parameter. If you like, you can write the `raiseSalary` method as follows:

```
public void raiseSalary(double byPercent)
{
   double raise = this.salary * byPercent / 100;
   this.salary += raise;
}
```

Some programmers prefer that style because it clearly distinguishes between instance fields and local variables.

C++ NOTE: In C++, you generally define methods outside the class:

```
void Employee::raiseSalary(double byPercent) // C++, not Java
{
   . . .
}
```

If you define a method inside a class, then it is automatically an inline method.

```
class Employee
{
   . . .
   int getName() { return name; } // inline in C++
}
```

In the Java programming language, all methods are defined inside the class itself. This does not make them inline. Finding opportunities for inline replacement is the job of the Java virtual machine. The just-in-time compiler watches for calls to methods that are short, commonly called, and not overridden, and optimizes them away.

Benefits of Encapsulation

Finally, let's look more closely at the rather simple getName, getSalary, and getHireDay methods.

```
public String getName()
{
   return name;
}

public double getSalary()
{
   return salary;
}

public Date getHireDay()
{
   return hireDay;
}
```

These are obvious examples of accessor methods. Because they simply return the values of instance fields, they are sometimes called *field accessors*.

Wouldn't it be easier to simply make the name, salary, and hireDay fields public, instead of having separate accessor methods?

The point is that the name field is a read-only field. Once you set it in the constructor, there is no method to change it. Thus, we have a guarantee that the name field will never be corrupted.

The salary field is not read-only, but it can only be changed by the raiseSalary method. In particular, should the value ever be wrong, only that method needs to be debugged. Had the salary field been public, the culprit for messing up the value could have been anywhere.

Sometimes, it happens that you want to get and set the value of an instance field. Then you need to supply *three* items:

- A private data field;
- A public field accessor method; and
- A public field mutator method.

This is a lot more tedious than supplying a single public data field, but there are considerable benefits:

1. You can change the internal implementation without affecting any code other than the methods of the class.

   For example, if the storage of the name is changed to

   ```
   String firstName;
   String lastName;
   ```

   then the getName method can be changed to return

   ```
   firstName + " " + lastName
   ```

   This change is completely invisible to the remainder of the program.

Of course, the accessor and mutator methods may need to do a lot of work and convert between the old and the new data representation. But that leads us to our second benefit.

2. Mutator methods can perform error-checking, whereas code that simply assigns to a field may not go to the trouble.

   For example, a setSalary method might check that the salary is never less than 0.

CAUTION: Be careful not to write accessor methods that return references to mutable objects. We violated that rule in our Employee class in which the getHireDay method returns an object of class Date:

```
class Employee
{
   . . .
   public Date getHireDay()
   {
      return hireDay;
   }
   . . .
   private Date hireDay;
}
```

This breaks the encapsulation! Consider the following rogue code:

```
Employee harry = . . .;
Date d = harry.getHireDay();
double tenYearsInMilliSeconds = 10 * 365.25 * 24 * 60 * 60 * 1000;
d.setTime(d.getTime() - (long) tenYearsInMilliSeconds);
// let's give Harry ten years added seniority
```

The reason is subtle. Both d and harry.hireDay refer to the same object (see Figure 4–5). Applying mutator methods to d automatically changes the private state of the employee object!

If you need to return a reference to a mutable object, you should *clone* it first. A clone is an exact copy of an object that is stored in a new location. We discuss cloning in detail in Chapter 6. Here is the corrected code:

```
class Employee
{
   . . .
   public Date getHireDay()
   {
      return (Date) hireDay.clone();
   }
   . . .
}
```

As a rule of thumb, always use clone whenever you need to return a copy of a mutable data field.

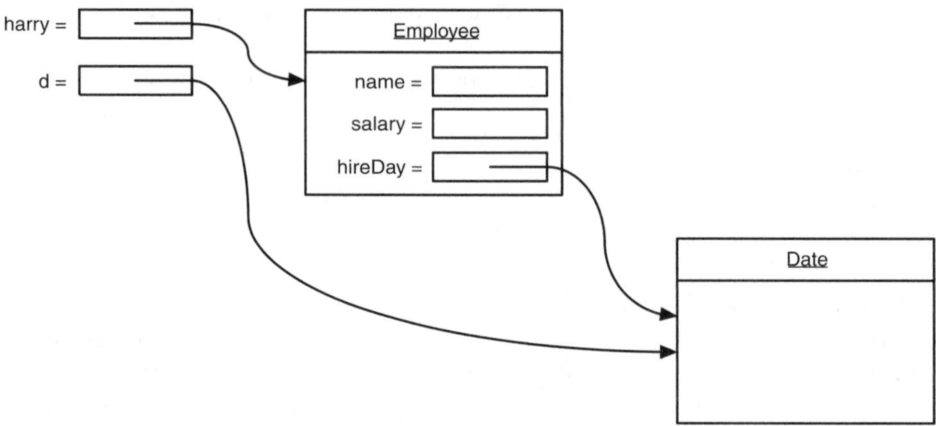

Figure 4–5: Returning a reference to a mutable data field

Class-Based Access Privileges

You know that a method can access the private data of the object on which it is invoked. What many people find surprising is that a method can access the private data of *all objects of its class*. For example, consider a method `equals` that compares two employees.

```
class Employee
{
   . . .
   boolean equals(Employee other)
   {
      return name.equals(other.name);
   }
}
```

A typical call is

```
if (harry.equals(boss)) . . .
```

This method accesses the private fields of `harry`, which is not surprising. It also accesses the private fields of `boss`. This is legal because `boss` is an object of type `Employee`, and a method of the `Employee` class is permitted to access the private fields of *any* object of type `Employee`.

C++ NOTE: C++ has the same rule. A method can access the private features of any object of its class, not just of the implicit parameter.

Private Methods

When implementing a class, we make all data fields private because public data are dangerous. But what about the methods? While most methods are public, private methods are used in certain circumstances. Sometimes, you may wish to break up the code for a computation into separate helper methods. Typically, these helper methods should not become part of the public interface—they may be too close to the current implementation or require a special protocol or calling order. Such methods are best implemented as `private`.

To implement a private method in Java, simply change the `public` keyword to `private`.

By making a method private, you are under no obligation to keep it available if you change to another implementation. The method may well be *harder* to implement or *unnecessary* if

the data representation changes: this is irrelevant. The point is that as long as the method is private, the designers of the class can be assured that it is never used outside the other class operations and can simply drop it. If a method is public, you cannot simply drop it because other code might rely on it.

Final Instance Fields

You can define an instance field as `final`. Such a field must be initialized when the object is constructed. That is, it must be guaranteed that the field value has been set after the end of every constructor. Afterwards, the field may not be modified again. For example, the `name` field of the `Employee` class may be declared as `final` because it never changes after the object is constructed—there is no `setName` method.

```
class Employee
{
   . . .
   private final String name;
}
```

The `final` modifier is particularly useful for fields whose type is primitive or an *immutable class.* (A class is immutable if none of its methods ever mutate its objects. For example, the `String` class is immutable.) For mutable classes, the `final` modifier is likely to confuse the reader. For example,

```
private final Date hiredate;
```

merely means that the object reference stored in the `hiredate` variable doesn't get changed after the object is constructed. That does not mean that the `hiredate` object is constant. Any method is free to invoke the `setTime` mutator on the object to which `hiredate` refers.

Static Fields and Methods

In all sample programs that you have seen, the `main` method is tagged with the `static` modifier. We are now ready to discuss the meaning of this modifier.

Static Fields

If you define a field as `static`, then there is only one such field per class. In contrast, each object has its own copy of all instance fields. For example, let's suppose we want to assign a unique identification number to each employee. We add an instance field `id` and a static field `nextId` to the `Employee` class:

```
class Employee
{
   . . .
   private int id;
   private static int nextId = 1;
}
```

Every employee object now has its own `id` field, but there is only one `nextId` field that is shared among all instances of the class. Let's put it another way. If there are 1000 objects of the `Employee` class, then there are 1000 instance fields `id`, one for each object. But there is a single static field `nextId`. Even if there are no employee objects, the static field `nextId` is present. It belongs to the class, not to any individual object.

NOTE: In most object-oriented programming languages, static fields are called *class fields.* The term "static" is a meaningless holdover from C++.

Let's implement a simple method:

```
public void setId()
{
   id = nextId;
   nextId++;
}
```

Suppose you set the employee identification number for harry:

```
harry.setId();
```

Then the id field of harry is set, and the value of the static field nextId is incremented:

```
harry.id = . . .;
Employee.nextId++;
```

Constants

Static variables are quite rare. However, static constants are more common. For example, the Math class defines a static constant:

```
public class Math
{
   . . .
   public static final double PI = 3.14159265358979323846;
   . . .
}
```

You can access this constant in your programs as Math.PI.

If the keyword static had been omitted, then PI would have been an instance field of the Math class. That is, you would need an object of the Math class to access PI, and every Math object would have its own copy of PI.

Another static constant that you have used many times is System.out. It is declared in the System class as:

```
public class System
{
   . . .
   public static final PrintStream out = . . .;
   . . .
}
```

As we mentioned several times, it is never a good idea to have public fields, because everyone can modify them. However, public constants (that is, final fields) are ok. Because out has been declared as final, you cannot reassign another print stream to it:

```
System.out = new PrintStream(. . .); // ERROR--out is final
```

NOTE: If you look at the System class, you will notice a method setOut that lets you set System.out to a different stream. You may wonder how that method can change the value of a final variable. However, the setOut method is a *native* method, not implemented in the Java programming language. Native methods can bypass the access control mechanisms of the Java language. This is a very unusual workaround that you should not emulate in your own programs.

Static Methods

Static methods are methods that do not operate on objects. For example, the pow method of the Math class is a static method. The expression:

```
Math.pow(x, a)
```

computes the power x^a. It does not use any Math object to carry out its task. In other words, it has no implicit parameter.

You can think of static methods as methods that don't have a `this` parameter. (In a non-static method, the `this` parameter refers to the implicit parameter of the method—see page 113.)

Because static methods don't operate on objects, you cannot access instance fields from a static method. But static methods can access the static fields in their class. Here is an example of such a static method:

```
public static int getNextId()
{
   return nextId; // returns static field
}
```

To call this method, you supply the name of the class:

```
int n = Employee.getNextId();
```

Could you have omitted the keyword `static` for this method? Yes, but then you would need to have an object reference of type `Employee` to invoke the method.

NOTE: It is legal to use an object to call a static method. For example, if `harry` is an `Employee` object, then you can call `harry.getNextId()` instead of `Employee.getnextId()`. However, we find that notation confusing. The `getNextId` method doesn't look at `harry` at all to compute the result. We recommend that you use class names, not objects, to invoke static methods.

You use static methods in two situations:

- When a method doesn't need to access the object state because all needed parameters are supplied as explicit parameters (example: `Math.pow`)
- When a method only needs to access static fields of the class (example: `Employee.getNextId`)

C++ NOTE: Static fields and methods have the same functionality in Java and C++. However, the syntax is slightly different. In C++, you use the `::` operator to access a static field or method outside its scope, such as `Math::PI`.

The term "static" has a curious history. At first, the keyword `static` was introduced in C to denote local variables that don't go away when a block is exited. In that context, the term "static" makes sense: the variable stays around and is still there when the block is entered again. Then `static` got a second meaning in C, to denote global variables and functions that cannot be accessed from other files. The keyword `static` was simply reused, to avoid introducing a new keyword. Finally, C++ reused the keyword for a third, unrelated, interpretation—to denote variables and functions that belong to a class but not to any particular object of the class. That is the same meaning that the keyword has in Java.

Factory Methods

Here is another common use for static methods. The `NumberFormat` class uses *factory methods* that yield formatter objects for various styles.

```
NumberFormat currencyFormatter = NumberFormat.getCurrencyInstance();
NumberFormat percentFormatter = NumberFormat.getPercentInstance();
double x = 0.1;
System.out.println(currencyFormatter.format(x)); // prints $0.10
System.out.println(percentFormatter.format(x)); // prints 10%
```

Why doesn't the `NumberFormat` class use a constructor instead? There are two reasons:

- You can't give names to constructors. The constructor name is always the same as the class name. But we want two different names to get the currency instance and the percent instance.
- When you use a constructor, you can't vary the type of the constructed object. But the factory methods actually return objects of the class `DecimalFormat`, a subclass that inherits from `NumberFormat`. (See Chapter 5 for more on inheritance.)

The `main` Method

Note that you can call static methods without having any objects. For example, you never construct any objects of the `Math` class to call `Math.pow`.

For the same reason, the `main` method is a static method.

```
public class Application
{
   public static void main(String[] args)
   {
      // construct objects here
      . . .
   }
}
```

The `main` method does not operate on any objects. In fact, when a program starts, there aren't any objects yet. The static `main` method executes, and constructs the objects that the program needs.

TIP: Every class can have a `main` method. That is a handy trick for unit testing of classes. For example, you can add a `main` method to the `Employee` class:

```
class Employee
{
   public Employee(String n, double s, int year, int month, int day)
   {
      name = n;
      salary = s;
      GregorianCalendar calendar = new GregorianCalendar(year, month - 1, day);
      hireDay = calendar.getTime();
   }
   . . .
   public static void main(String[] args) // unit test
   {
      Employee e = new Employee("Romeo", 50000, 2003, 3, 31);
      e.raiseSalary(10);
      System.out.println(e.getName() + " " + e.getSalary());
   }
   . . .
}
```

If you want to test the `Employee` class in isolation, you simply execute

```
java Employee
```

If the employee class is a part of a larger application, then you start the application with

```
java Application
```

and the `main` method of the `Employee` class is never executed.

The program in Example 4–3 contains a simple version of the `Employee` class with a static field `nextId` and a static method `getNextId`. We fill an array with three `Employee` objects and then print the employee information. Finally, we print the next available identification number, to demonstate the static method.

Note that the `Employee` class also has a static `main` method for unit testing. Try running both

```
java Employee
```

and

```
java StaticTest
```

to execute both `main` methods.

Example 4–3: StaticTest.java

```
public class StaticTest
{
   public static void main(String[] args)
   {
      // fill the staff array with three Employee objects
      Employee[] staff = new Employee[3];

      staff[0] = new Employee("Tom", 40000);
      staff[1] = new Employee("Dick", 60000);
      staff[2] = new Employee("Harry", 65000);

      // print out information about all Employee objects
      for (Employee e : staff)
      {
         e.setId();
         System.out.println("name=" + e.getName()
            + ",id=" + e.getId()
            + ",salary=" + e.getSalary());
      }

      int n = Employee.getNextId(); // calls static method
      System.out.println("Next available id=" + n);
   }
}

class Employee
{
   public Employee(String n, double s)
   {
      name = n;
      salary = s;
      id = 0;
   }

   public String getName()
   {
      return name;
   }

   public double getSalary()
   {
      return salary;
   }
```

```

   public int getId()
   {
      return id;
   }

   public void setId()
   {
      id = nextId; // set id to next available id
      nextId++;
   }

   public static int getNextId()
   {
      return nextId; // returns static field
   }

   public static void main(String[] args) // unit test
   {
      Employee e = new Employee("Harry", 50000);
      System.out.println(e.getName() + " " + e.getSalary());
   }

   private String name;
   private double salary;
   private int id;
   private static int nextId = 1;
}
```

Method Parameters

Let us review the computer science terms that describe how parameters can be passed to a method (or a function) in a programming language. The term *call by value* means that the method gets just the value that the caller provides. In contrast, *call by reference* means that the method gets the *location* of the variable that the caller provides. Thus, a method can *modify* the value stored in a variable that is passed by reference but not in one that is passed by value. These "call by . . . " terms are standard computer science terminology that describe the behavior of method parameters in various programming languages, not just Java. (In fact, there is also a *call by name* that is mainly of historical interest, being employed in the Algol programming language, one of the oldest high-level languages.)

The Java programming language *always* uses call by value. That means that the method gets a copy of all parameter values. In particular, the method cannot modify the contents of any parameter variables that are passed to it.

For example, consider the following call:

```
double percent = 10;
harry.raiseSalary(percent);
```

No matter how the method is implemented, we know that after the method call, the value of `percent` is still 10.

Let us look a little more closely at this situation. Suppose a method tried to triple the value of a method parameter:

```
public static void tripleValue(double x) // doesn't work
{
   x = 3 * x;
}
```

Let's call this method:

```
double percent = 10;
tripleValue(percent);
```

However, this does not work. After the method call, the value of percent is still 10. Here is what happens:

1. x is initialized with a copy of the value of percent (that is, 10).
2. x is tripled—it is now 30. But percent is still 10 (see Figure 4–6).
3. The method ends, and the parameter variable x is no longer in use.

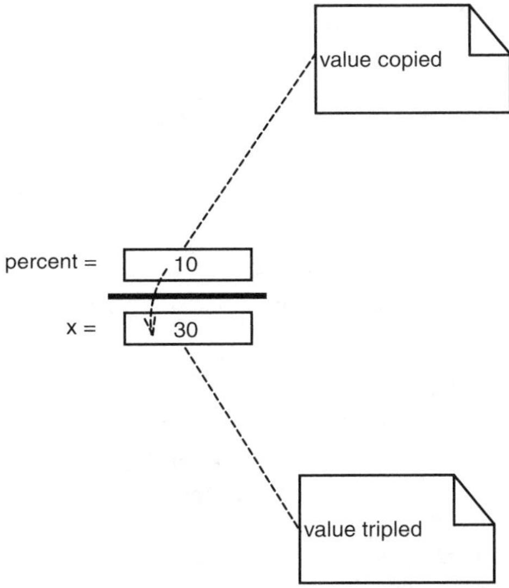

Figure 4–6: Modifying a numeric parameter has no lasting effect

There are, however, two kinds of method parameters:

- Primitive types (numbers, Boolean values)
- Object references

You have seen that it is impossible for a method to change a primitive type parameter. The situation is different for object parameters. You can easily implement a method that triples the salary of an employee:

```
public static void tripleSalary(Employee x) // works
{
   x.raiseSalary(200);
}
```

When you call

```
harry = new Employee(. . .);
tripleSalary(harry);
```

then the following happens:

1. x is initialized with a copy of the value of harry, that is, an object reference.
2. The raiseSalary method is applied to that object reference. The Employee object to which both x and harry refer gets its salary raised by 200 percent.

3. The method ends, and the parameter variable `x` is no longer in use. Of course, the object variable `harry` continues to refer to the object whose salary was tripled (see Figure 4–7).

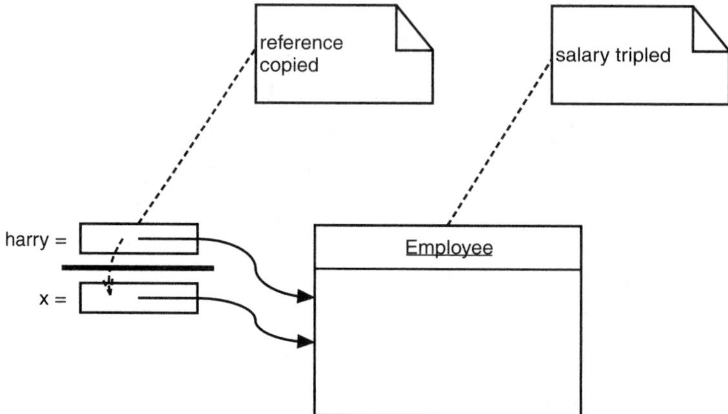

Figure 4–7: Modifying an object parameter has a lasting effect

As you have seen, it is easily possible—and in fact very common—to implement methods that change the state of an object parameter. The reason is simple. The method gets a copy of the object reference, and both the original and the copy refer to the same object.

Many programming languages (in particular, C++ and Pascal) have two methods for parameter passing: call by value and call by reference. Some programmers (and unfortunately even some book authors) claim that the Java programming language uses call by reference for objects. However, that is false. Because this is such a common misunderstanding, it is worth examining a counterexample in detail.

Let's try to write a method that swaps two employee objects:

```
public static void swap(Employee x, Employee y) // doesn't work
{
   Employee temp = x;
   x = y;
   y = temp;
}
```

If the Java programming language used call by reference for objects, this method would work:

```
Employee a = new Employee("Alice", . . .);
Employee b = new Employee("Bob", . . .);
swap(a, b);
// does a now refer to Bob, b to Alice?
```

However, the method does not actually change the object references that are stored in the variables `a` and `b`. The `x` and `y` parameters of the `swap` method are initialized with *copies* of these references. The method then proceeds to swap these copies.

```
// x refers to Alice, y to Bob
Employee temp = x;
x = y;
y = temp;
// now x refers to Bob, y to Alice
```

But ultimately, this is a wasted effort. When the method ends, the parameter variables x and y are abandoned. The original variables a and b still refer to the same objects as they did before the method call (see Figure 4–8).

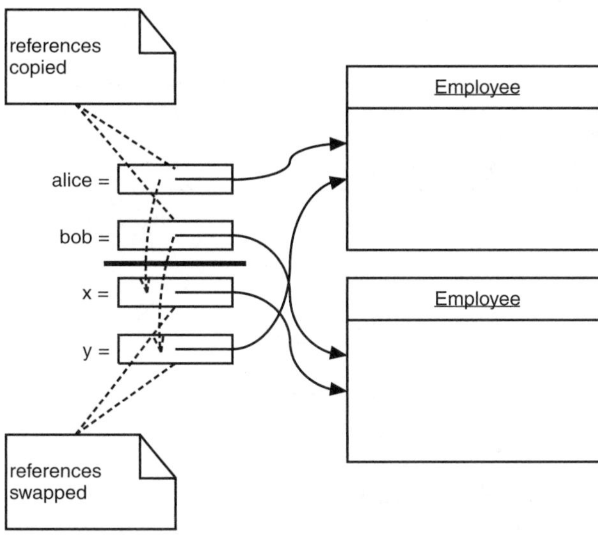

Figure 4–8: Swapping object parameters has no lasting effect

This discussion demonstrates that the Java programming language does not use call by reference for objects. Instead, *object references are passed by value.*

Here is a summary of what you can and cannot do with method parameters in the Java programming language:

- A method cannot modify a parameter of primitive type (that is, numbers or Boolean values).
- A method can change the *state* of an object parameter.
- A method cannot make an object parameter refer to a new object.

The program in Example 4–4 demonstrates these facts. The program first tries to triple the value of a number parameter and does not succeed:

```
Testing tripleValue:
Before: percent=10.0
End of method: x=30.0
After: percent=10.0
```

It then successfully triples the salary of an employee:

```
Testing tripleSalary:
Before: salary=50000.0
End of method: salary=150000.0
After: salary=150000.0
```

After the method, the state of the object to which harry refers has changed. This is possible because the method modified the state through a copy of the object reference.

Finally, the program demonstrates the failure of the swap method:

```
Testing swap:
Before: a=Alice
Before: b=Bob
```

```
End of method: x=Bob
End of method: y=Alice
After: a=Alice
After: b=Bob
```

As you can see, the parameter variables x and y are swapped, but the variables a and b are not affected.

C++ NOTE: C++ has both call by value and call by reference. You tag reference parameters with &. For example, you can easily implement methods `void tripleValue(double& x)` or `void swap(Employee& x, Employee& y)` that modify their reference parameters.

Example 4–4: ParamTest.java

```
public class ParamTest
{
   public static void main(String[] args)
   {
      /*
         Test 1: Methods can't modify numeric parameters
      */
      System.out.println("Testing tripleValue:");
      double percent = 10;
      System.out.println("Before: percent=" + percent);
      tripleValue(percent);
      System.out.println("After: percent=" + percent);

      /*
         Test 2: Methods can change the state of object
         parameters
      */
      System.out.println("\nTesting tripleSalary:");
      Employee harry = new Employee("Harry", 50000);
      System.out.println("Before: salary=" + harry.getSalary());
      tripleSalary(harry);
      System.out.println("After: salary=" + harry.getSalary());

      /*
         Test 3: Methods can't attach new objects to
         object parameters
      */
      System.out.println("\nTesting swap:");
      Employee a = new Employee("Alice", 70000);
      Employee b = new Employee("Bob", 60000);
      System.out.println("Before: a=" + a.getName());
      System.out.println("Before: b=" + b.getName());
      swap(a, b);
      System.out.println("After: a=" + a.getName());
      System.out.println("After: b=" + b.getName());
   }

   public static void tripleValue(double x) // doesn't work
   {
      x = 3 * x;
      System.out.println("End of method: x=" + x);
   }
```

```

   public static void tripleSalary(Employee x) // works
   {
      x.raiseSalary(200);
      System.out.println("End of method: salary="
         + x.getSalary());
   }

   public static void swap(Employee x, Employee y)
   {
      Employee temp = x;
      x = y;
      y = temp;
      System.out.println("End of method: x=" + x.getName());
      System.out.println("End of method: y=" + y.getName());
   }
}

class Employee // simplified Employee class
{
   public Employee(String n, double s)
   {
      name = n;
      salary = s;
   }

   public String getName()
   {
      return name;
   }

   public double getSalary()
   {
      return salary;
   }

   public void raiseSalary(double byPercent)
   {
      double raise = salary * byPercent / 100;
      salary += raise;
   }

   private String name;
   private double salary;
}
```

Object Construction

You have seen how to write simple constructors that define the initial state of your objects. However, because object construction is so important, Java offers quite a variety of mechanisms for writing constructors. We go over these mechanisms in the sections that follow.

Overloading

Recall that the `GregorianCalendar` class had more than one constructor. We could use:

```
GregorianCalendar today = new GregorianCalendar();
```

or:

```
GregorianCalendar deadline = new GregorianCalendar(2099, Calendar.DECEMBER, 31);
```

This capability is called *overloading*. Overloading occurs if several methods have the same name (in this case, the GregorianCalendar constructor method) but different parameters. The compiler must sort out which method to call. It picks the correct method by matching the parameter types in the headers of the various methods with the types of the values used in the specific method call. A compile-time error occurs if the compiler cannot match the parameters or if more than one match is possible. (This process is called *overloading resolution*.)

NOTE: Java allows you to overload any method—not just constructor methods. Thus, to completely describe a method, you need to specify the name of the method together with its parameter types. This is called the *signature* of the method. For example, the String class has four public methods called indexOf. They have signatures

```
indexOf(int)
indexOf(int, int)
indexOf(String)
indexOf(String, int)
```

The return type is not part of the method signature. That is, you cannot have two methods with the same names and parameter types but different return types.

Default Field Initialization

If you don't set a field explicitly in a constructor, it is automatically set to a default value: numbers to 0, Booleans to false, and object references to null. But it is considered poor programming practice to rely on this. Certainly, it makes it harder for someone to understand your code if fields are being initialized invisibly.

NOTE: This is an important difference between fields and local variables. You must always explicitly initialize local variables in a method. But if you don't initialize a field in a class, it is automatically initialized to a default (0, false, or null).

For example, consider the Employee class. Suppose you don't specify how to initialize some of the fields in a constructor. By default, the salary field would be initialized with 0 and the name and hireDay fields would be initialized with null.

However, that would not be a good idea. If anyone called the getName or getHireDay method, then they would get a null reference that they probably don't expect:

```
Date h = harry.getHireDay();
calendar.setTime(h); // throws exception if h is null
```

Default Constructors

A *default constructor* is a constructor with no parameters. For example, here is a default constructor for the Employee class:

```
public Employee()
{
   name = "";
   salary = 0;
   hireDay = new Date();
}
```

If you write a class with no constructors whatsoever, then a default constructor is provided for you. This default constructor sets *all* the instance fields to their default values. So, all

numeric data contained in the instance fields would be `0`, all Booleans would be `false`, and all object variables would be set to `null`.

If a class supplies at least one constructor but does not supply a default constructor, it is illegal to construct objects without construction parameters. For example, our original `Employee` class in Example 4–2 provided a single constructor:

```
Employee(String name, double salary, int y, int m, int d)
```

With that class, it was not legal to construct default employees. That is, the call

```
e = new Employee();
```

would have been an error.

CAUTION: Please keep in mind that you get a free default constructor *only* when your class has no other constructors. If you write your class with even a single constructor of your own and you want the users of your class to have the ability to create an instance by a call to

```
new ClassName()
```

then you must provide a default constructor (with no parameters). Of course, if you are happy with the default values for all fields, you can simply supply

```
public ClassName()
{
}
```

Explicit Field Initialization

Because you can overload the constructor methods in a class, you can obviously build in many ways to set the initial state of the instance fields of your classes. It is always a good idea to make sure that, regardless of the constructor call, every instance field is set to something meaningful.

You can simply assign a value to any field in the class definition. For example,

```
class Employee
{
   . . .
   private String name = "";
}
```

This assignment is carried out before the constructor executes. This syntax is particularly useful if all constructors of a class need to set a particular instance field to the same value.

The initialization value doesn't have to be a constant value. Here is an example in which a field is initialized with a method call. Consider an `Employee` class where each employee has an `id` field. You can initialize it as follows:

```
class Employee
{
   . . .
   static int assignId()
   {
      int r = nextId;
      nextId++;
      return r;
   }
   . . .
   private int id = assignId();
}
```

C++ NOTE: In C++, you cannot directly initialize instance fields of a class. All fields must be set in a constructor. However, C++ has a special initializer list syntax, such as:

```
Employee::Employee(String n, double s, int y, int m, int d) // C++
: name(n),
  salary(s),
  hireDay(y, m, d)
{
}
```

C++ uses this special syntax to call field constructors. In Java, there is no need for it because objects have no subobjects, only pointers to other objects.

Parameter Names

When you write very trivial constructors (and you'll write a lot of them), then it can be somewhat frustrating to come up with parameter names.

We have generally opted for single-letter parameter names:

```
public Employee(String n, double s)
{
   name = n;
   salary = s;
}
```

However, the drawback is that you need to read the code to tell what the `n` and `s` parameters mean.

Some programmers prefix each parameter with an "a":

```
public Employee(String aName, double aSalary)
{
   name = aName;
   salary = aSalary;
}
```

That is quite neat. Any reader can immediately figure out the meaning of the parameters.

Another commonly used trick relies on the fact that parameter variables *shadow* instance fields with the same name. For example, if you call a parameter `salary`, then `salary` refers to the parameter, not the instance field. But you can still access the instance field as `this.salary`. Recall that `this` denotes the implicit parameter, that is, the object that is being constructed. Here is an example:

```
public Employee(String name, double salary)
{
   this.name = name;
   this.salary = salary;
}
```

C++ NOTE: In C++, it is common to prefix instance fields with an underscore or a fixed letter. (The letters `m` and `x` are common choices.) For example, the salary field might be called `_salary`, `mSalary`, or `xSalary`. Java programmers don't usually do that.

Calling Another Constructor

The keyword `this` refers to the implicit parameter of a method. However, the keyword has a second meaning.

If *the first statement of a constructor* has the form `this(. . .)`, then the constructor calls another constructor of the same class. Here is a typical example:

```
public Employee(double s)
{
   // calls Employee(String, double)
   this("Employee #" + nextId, s);
   nextId++;
}
```

When you call `new Employee(60000)`, then the `Employee(double)` constructor calls the `Employee(String, double)` constructor.

Using the `this` keyword in this manner is useful—you only need to write common construction code once.

C++ NOTE: The `this` reference in Java is identical to the `this` pointer in C++. However, in C++ it is not possible for one constructor to call another. If you want to factor out common initialization code in C++, you must write a separate method.

Initialization Blocks

You have already seen two ways to initialize a data field:

- By setting a value in a constructor
- By assigning a value in the declaration

There is actually a *third* mechanism in Java; it's called an *initialization block*. Class declarations can contain arbitrary blocks of code. These blocks are executed whenever an object of that class is constructed. For example,

```
class Employee
{
   public Employee(String n, double s)
   {
      name = n;
      salary = s;
   }

   public Employee()
   {
      name = "";
      salary = 0;
   }
   . . .
   private static int nextId;

   private int id;
   private String name;
   private double salary;
   . . .
   // object initialization block
   {
      id = nextId;
      nextId++;
   }
}
```

In this example, the `id` field is initialized in the object initialization block, no matter which constructor is used to construct an object. The initialization block runs first, and then the body of the constructor is executed.

This mechanism is never necessary and is not common. It usually is more straightforward to place the initialization code inside a constructor.

NOTE: It is legal to set fields in initialization blocks even though they are only defined later in the class. Some versions of Sun's Java compiler handled this case incorrectly (bug # 4459133). This bug has been fixed in JDK 1.4.1. However, to avoid circular definitions, it is not legal to read from fields that are only initialized later. The exact rules are spelled out in section 8.3.2.3 of the Java Language Specification (`http://java.sun.com/docs/books/jls`). Because the rules are complex enough to baffle the compiler implementors, we suggest that you place initialization blocks after the field definitions.

With so many ways of initializing data fields, it can be quite confusing to give all possible pathways for the construction process. Here is what happens in detail when a constructor is called.

1. All data fields are initialized to their default value (`0`, `false`, or `null`).
2. All field initializers and initialization blocks are executed, in the order in which they occur in the class declaration.
3. If the first line of the constructor calls a second constructor, then the body of the second constructor is executed.
4. The body of the constructor is executed.

Naturally, it is always a good idea to organize your initialization code so that another programmer could easily understand it without having to be a language lawyer. For example, it would be quite strange and somewhat error prone to have a class whose constructors depend on the order in which the data fields are declared.

You initialize a static field either by supplying an initial value or by using a static initialization block. You have already seen the first mechanism:

```
static int nextId = 1;
```

If the static fields of your class require complex initialization code, use a static initialization block.

Place the code inside a block and tag it with the keyword `static`. Here is an example. We want the employee ID numbers to start at a random integer less than 10,000.

```
// static initialization block
static
{
   Random generator = new Random();
   nextId = generator.nextInt(10000);
}
```

Static initialization occurs when the class is first loaded. Like instance fields, static fields are `0`, `false`, or `null` unless you explicitly set them to another value. All static field initializers and static initialization blocks are executed in the order in which they occur in the class declaration.

NOTE: Here is a Java trivia fact to amaze your fellow Java coders: You can write a "Hello, World" program in Java without ever writing a `main` method.

```
public class Hello
{
   static
   {
      System.out.println("Hello, World");
   }
}
```

When you invoke the class with `java Hello`, the class is loaded, the static initialization block prints "Hello, World," and only then do you get an ugly error message that `main` is not defined. You can avoid that blemish by calling `System.exit(0)` at the end of the static initialization block.

The program in Example 4–5 shows many of the features that we discussed in this section:

- Overloaded constructors
- A call to another constructor with `this(...)`
- A default constructor
- An object initialization block
- A static initialization block
- An instance field initialization

Example 4–5: ConstructorTest.java

```
import java.util.*;

public class ConstructorTest
{
   public static void main(String[] args)
   {
      // fill the staff array with three Employee objects
      Employee[] staff = new Employee[3];

      staff[0] = new Employee("Harry", 40000);
      staff[1] = new Employee(60000);
      staff[2] = new Employee();

      // print out information about all Employee objects
      for (Employee e : staff)
         System.out.println("name=" + e.getName()
            + ",id=" + e.getId()
            + ",salary=" + e.getSalary());
   }
}

class Employee
{
   // three overloaded constructors
   public Employee(String n, double s)
   {
      name = n;
      salary = s;
   }

```

```
   public Employee(double s)
   {
      // calls the Employee(String, double) constructor
      this("Employee #" + nextId, s);
   }

   // the default constructor
   public Employee()
   {
      // name initialized to ""--see below
      // salary not explicitly set--initialized to 0
      // id initialized in initialization block
   }

   public String getName()
   {
      return name;
   }

   public double getSalary()
   {
      return salary;
   }

   public int getId()
   {
      return id;
   }

   private static int nextId;

   private int id;
   private String name = ""; // instance field initialization
   private double salary;

   // static initialization block
   static
   {
      Random generator = new Random();
      // set nextId to a random number between 0 and 9999
      nextId = generator.nextInt(10000);
   }

   // object initialization block
   {
      id = nextId;
      nextId++;
   }
}
```

API **java.util.Random 1.0**

- `Random()`
  constructs a new random number generator.

- `int nextInt(int n)` **1.2**
  returns a random number between 0 and `n` – 1.

Object Destruction and the `finalize` Method

Some object-oriented programming languages, notably C++, have explicit destructor methods for any cleanup code that may be needed when an object is no longer used. The most common activity in a destructor is reclaiming the memory set aside for objects. Because Java does automatic garbage collection, manual memory reclamation is not needed and so Java does not support destructors.

Of course, some objects utilize a resource other than memory, such as a file or a handle to another object that uses system resources. In this case, it is important that the resource be reclaimed and recycled when it is no longer needed.

You can add a `finalize` method to any class. The `finalize` method will be called before the garbage collector sweeps away the object. In practice, *do not rely on the* `finalize` *method* for recycling any resources that are in short supply—you simply cannot know when this method will be called.

NOTE: The method call `System.runFinalizersOnExit(true)` guarantees that finalizer methods are called before Java shuts down. However, this method is inherently unsafe and has been deprecated. An alternative is to add "shutdown hooks" with the method `Runtime.addShutdownHook`—see the API documentation for details.

If a resource needs to be closed as soon as you have finished using it, you need to manage it manually. Supply a method such as `dispose` or `close` that *you* call to clean up what needs cleaning. Just as importantly, if a class you use has such a method, you need to call it when you are done with the object.

Packages

Java allows you to group classes in a collection called a *package*. Packages are convenient for organizing your work and for separating your work from code libraries provided by others.

The standard Java library is distributed over a number of packages, including `java.lang`, `java.util`, `java.net`, and so on. The standard Java packages are examples of hierarchical packages. Just as you have nested subdirectories on your hard disk, you can organize packages by using levels of nesting. All standard Java packages are inside the `java` and `javax` package hierarchies.

The main reason for using packages is to guarantee the uniqueness of class names. Suppose two programmers come up with the bright idea of supplying an `Employee` class. As long as both of them place their class into different packages, there is no conflict. In fact, to absolutely guarantee a unique package name, Sun recommends that you use your company's Internet domain name (which is known to be unique) written in reverse. You then use subpackages for different projects. For example, `horstmann.com` is a domain that one of the authors registered. Written in reverse order, it turns into the package `com.horstmann`. That package can then be further subdivided into subpackages such as `com.horstmann.corejava`.

The sole purpose of package nesting is to manage unique names. From the point of view of the compiler, there is absolutely no relationship between nested packages. For example, the packages `java.util` and `java.util.jar` have nothing to do with each other. Each is its own independent collection of classes.

Class Importation

A class can use all classes from its own package and all *public* classes from other packages.

You can access the public classes in another package in two ways. The first is simply to add the full package name in front of *every* class name. For example:

```
java.util.Date today = new java.util.Date();
```

That is obviously tedious. The simpler, and more common, approach is to use the `import` statement. The point of the `import` statement is simply to give you a shorthand to refer to the classes in the package. Once you use `import`, you no longer have to give the classes their full names.

You can import a specific class or the whole package. You place `import` statements at the top of your source files (but below any `package` statements). For example, you can import all classes in the `java.util` package with the statement

```
import java.util.*;
```

Then you can use

```
Date today = new Date();
```

without a package prefix. You can also import a specific class inside a package:

```
import java.util.Date;
```

The `java.util.*` syntax is less tedious. It has no negative effect on code size. However, if you import classes explicitly, the reader of your code knows exactly which classes you use.

TIP: In Eclipse, you can select the menu option Source -> Organize Imports. Package statements such as `import java.util.*;` are automatically expanded into a list of specific imports such as

```
import java.util.ArrayList;
import java.util.Date;
```

This is an extremely convenient feature.

However, note that you can only use the `*` notation to import a single package. You cannot use `import java.*` or `import java.*.*` to import all packages with the `java` prefix.

Most of the time, you just import the packages that you need, without worrying too much about them. The only time that you need to pay attention to packages is when you have a name conflict. For example, both the `java.util` and `java.sql` packages have a `Date` class. Suppose you write a program that imports both packages.

```
import java.util.*;
import java.sql.*;
```

If you now use the `Date` class, then you get a compile-time error:

```
Date today; // ERROR--java.util.Date or java.sql.Date?
```

The compiler cannot figure out which `Date` class you want. You can solve this problem by adding a specific `import` statement:

```
import java.util.*;
import java.sql.*;
import java.util.Date;
```

What if you really need both `Date` classes? Then you need to use the full package name with every class name.

```
java.util.Date deadline = new java.util.Date();
java.sql.Date today = new java.sql.Date(...);
```

Locating classes in packages is an activity of the *compiler*. The bytecodes in class files always use full package names to refer to other classes.

C++ NOTE: C++ programmers usually confuse `import` with `#include`. The two have nothing in common. In C++, you must use `#include` to include the declarations of external features because the C++ compiler does not look inside any files except the one that it is compiling and explicitly included header files. The Java compiler will happily look inside other files provided you tell it where to look.

In Java, you can entirely avoid the `import` mechanism by explicitly naming all classes, such as `java.util.Date`. In C++, you cannot avoid the `#include` directives.

The only benefit of the `import` statement is convenience. You can refer to a class by a name shorter than the full package name. For example, after an `import java.util.*` (or `import java.util.Date`) statement, you can refer to the `java.util.Date` class simply as `Date`.

The analogous construction to the package mechanism in C++ is the namespace feature. Think of the `package` and `import` statements in Java as the analogs of the `namespace` and `using` directives in C++.

Static Imports

Starting with JDK 5.0, the `import` statement has been enhanced to permit the importing of static methods and fields, not just classes.

For example, if you add the directive

```
import static java.lang.System.*;
```

to the top of your source file, then you can use static methods and fields of the `System` class without the class name prefix:

```
out.println("Goodbye, World!"); // i.e., System.out
exit(0); // i.e., System.exit
```

You can also import a specific method or field:

```
import static java.lang.System.out;
```

In practice, it seems doubtful that many programmers will want to abbreviate `System.out` or `System.exit`. The resulting code seems less clear. But there are two practical uses for static imports.

1. Mathematical functions: If you use a static import for the `Math` class, you can use mathematical functions in a more natural way. For example,
   ```
   sqrt(pow(x, 2) + pow(y, 2))
   ```
   seems much clearer than
   ```
   Math.sqrt(Math.pow(x, 2) + Math.pow(y, 2))
   ```
2. Cumbersome constants: If you use lots of constants with tedious names, you will welcome static import. For example,
   ```
   if (d.get(DAY_OF_WEEK) == MONDAY)
   ```
   is easier on the eye than
   ```
   if (d.get(Calendar.DAY_OF_WEEK) == Calendar.MONDAY)
   ```

Addition of a Class into a Package

To place classes inside a package, you must put the name of the package at the top of your source file, *before* the code that defines the classes in the package. For example, the file `Employee.java` in Example 4–7 starts out like this:

```
package com.horstmann.corejava;

public class Employee
```

```
{
   . . .
}
```

If you don't put a package statement in the source file, then the classes in that source file belong to the *default package*. The default package has no package name. Up to now, all our example classes were located in the default package.

You place files in a package into a subdirectory that matches the full package name. For example, all class files in the package com.horstmann.corejava package should be in a subdirectory com/horstmann/corejava (com\horstmann\corejava on Windows).

The program in Examples 4–6 and 4–7 is distributed over two packages: the PackageTest class belongs to the default package and the Employee class belongs to the com.horstmann.corejava package. Therefore, the Employee.class file must be contained in a subdirectory com/horstmann/corejava. In other words, the directory structure is as follows:

```
. (base directory)
   ├─ PackageTest.java
   ├─ PackageTest.class
   └─ com/
        └─ horstmann/
             └─ corejava/
                  ├─ Employee.java
                  └─ Employee.class
```

To compile this program, simply change to the base directory and run the command

```
javac PackageTest.java
```

The compiler automatically finds the file com/horstmann/corejava/Employee.java and compiles it.

Let's look at a more realistic example, in which we don't use the default package but have classes distributed over several packages (com.horstmann.corejava and com.mycompany).

```
. (base directory)
   └─ com/
        ├─ horstmann/
        │    └─ corejava/
        │         ├─ Employee.java
        │         └─ Employee.class
        └─ mycompany/
             ├─ PayrollApp.java
             └─ PayrollApp.class
```

In this situation, you still must compile and run classes from the *base* directory, that is, the directory containing the com directory:

```
javac com/mycompany/PayrollApp.java
java com.mycompany.PayrollApp
```

Note again that the compiler operates on *files* (with file separators and an extension .java), whereas the Java interpreter loads a *class* (with dot separators).

CAUTION: The compiler does *not* check the directory structure when it compiles source files. For example, suppose you have a source file that starts with the directive

```
package com.mycompany;
```

You can compile the file even if it is not contained in a subdirectory com/mycompany. The source file will compile without errors *if it doesn't depend on other packages*. However, the resulting program will not run. The *virtual machine* won't find the resulting classes when you try to run the program.

Example 4–6: PackageTest.java

```
import com.horstmann.corejava.*;
   // the Employee class is defined in that package

import static java.lang.System.*;

public class PackageTest
{
   public static void main(String[] args)
   {
      // because of the import statement, we don't have to
      // use com.horstmann.corejava.Employee here
      Employee harry = new Employee("Harry Hacker", 50000, 1989, 10, 1);

      // raise salary by 5%
      harry.raiseSalary(5);

      // print out information about harry
      // use java.lang.System.out here
      out.println("name=" + harry.getName() + ",salary=" + harry.getSalary());
   }
}
```

Example 4–7: Employee.java

```
package com.horstmann.corejava;
   // the classes in this file are part of this package

import java.util.*;
   // import statements come after the package statement

public class Employee
{
   public Employee(String n, double s, int year, int month, int day)
   {
      name = n;
      salary = s;
      GregorianCalendar calendar = new GregorianCalendar(year, month - 1, day);
         // GregorianCalendar uses 0 for January
      hireDay = calendar.getTime();
   }

   public String getName()
   {
      return name;
   }

   public double getSalary()
   {
      return salary;
   }

   public Date getHireDay()
   {
      return hireDay;
```

```
    }

    public void raiseSalary(double byPercent)
    {
       double raise = salary * byPercent / 100;
       salary += raise;
    }

    private String name;
    private double salary;
    private Date hireDay;
}
```

How the Virtual Machine Locates Classes

As you have seen, classes are stored in subdirectories of the file system. The path to the class must match the package name. You can also use the JAR utility to add class files to an *archive*. An archive contains multiple class files and subdirectories inside a single file, saving space and improving performance. (We discuss JAR files in greater detail in Chapter 10.)

For example, the thousands of classes of the runtime library are all contained in the runtime library file `rt.jar`. You can find that file in the `jre/lib` subdirectory of the JDK.

TIP: JAR files use the ZIP format to organize files and subdirectories. You can use any ZIP utility to peek inside `rt.jar` and other JAR files.

In the preceding example program, the package directory `com/horstmann/corejava` was a subdirectory of the program directory. However, that arrangement is not very flexible. Generally, multiple programs need to access package files. To share your packages among programs, you need to do the following:

1. Place your classes inside one or more special directories, say, `/home/user/classdir`. Note that this directory is the *base* directory for the package tree. If you add the class `com.horstmann.corejava.Employee`, then the class file must be located in the subdirectory `/home/user/classdir/com/horstmann/corejava`.
2. Set the *class path*. The class path is the collection of all base directories whose subdirectories can contain class files.

How to set the class path depends on your compilation environment. If you use the JDK, then you have two choices: Specify the `-classpath` option for the compiler and bytecode interpreter, or set the `CLASSPATH` environment variable.

Details depend on your operating system. On UNIX, the elements on the class path are separated by colons.

```
/home/user/classdir:.:/home/user/archives/archive.jar
```

On Windows, they are separated by semicolons.

```
c:\classes;.;c:\archives\archive.jar
```

In both cases, the period denotes the current directory.

This class path contains

- The base directory `/home/user/classdir` or `c:\classes`;
- The current directory (.); and
- The JAR file `/home/user/archives/archive.jar` or `c:\archives\archive.jar`.

The runtime library files (`rt.jar` and the other JAR files in the `jre/lib` and `jre/lib/ext` directories) are always searched for classes; you don't include them explicitly in the class path.

NOTE: This is a change from version 1.0 and 1.1 of the Java Development Kit. In those versions, the system classes were stored in a file, `classes.zip`, which had to be part of the class path.

For example, here is how you set the class path for the compiler:

```
javac -classpath /home/user/classdir:.:/home/user/archives/archive.jar MyProg.java
```

(All instructions should be typed onto a single line. In Windows, use semicolons to separate the items of the class path.)

TIP: You can also use `-cp` instead of `-classpath`. However, before JDK 5.0, the `-cp` option only worked with the `java` bytecode interpreter, and you had to use `-classpath` with the `javac` compiler.

The class path lists all directories and archive files that are *starting points* for locating classes. Let's consider a sample class path:

```
/home/user/classdir:.:/home/user/archives/archive.jar
```

Suppose the interpreter searches for the class file of the `com.horstmann.corejava.Employee` class. It first looks in the system class files that are stored in archives in the `jre/lib` and `jre/lib/ext` directories. It won't find the class file there, so it turns to the class path. It then looks for the following files:

- `/home/user/classdir/com/horstmann/corejava/Employee.class`
- `com/horstmann/corejava/Employee.class` starting from the current directory
- `com/horstmann/corejava/Employee.class` inside `/home/user/archives/archive.jar`.

NOTE: The compiler has a harder time locating files than does the virtual machine. If you refer to a class without specifying its package, the compiler first needs to find out the package that contains the class. It consults all `import` directives as possible sources for the class. For example, suppose the source file contains directives

```
import java.util.*;
import com.horstmann.corejava.*;
```

and the source code refers to a class `Employee`. The compiler then tries to find `java.lang.Employee` (because the `java.lang` package is always imported by default), `java.util.Employee`, `com.horstmann.corejava.Employee`, and `Employee` in the current package. It searches for *each* of these classes in all of the locations of the class path. It is a compile-time error if more than one class is found. (Because classes must be unique, the order of the `import` statements doesn't matter.)

The compiler goes one step further. It looks at the *source files* to see if the source is newer than the class file. If so, the source file is recompiled automatically. Recall that you can import public classes only from other packages. A source file can only contain one public class, and the names of the file and the public class must match. Therefore, the compiler can easily locate source files for public classes. However, you can import nonpublic classes from the current packages. These classes may be defined in source files with different names. If you import a class from the current package, the compiler searches *all* source files of the current package to see which one defines the class.

CAUTION: The `javac` compiler always looks for files in the current directory, but the `java` interpreter only looks into the current directory if the "." directory is on the class path. If you have no class path set, this is not a problem—the default class path consists of the "." directory. But if you have set the class path and forgot to include the "." directory, then your programs will compile without error, but they won't run.

Setting the Class Path

As you just saw, you can set the class path with the `-classpath` option for the `javac` and `java` programs. We prefer this option, but some programmers find it tedious. Alternatively, you can set the `CLASSPATH` environment variable. Here are some tips for setting the `CLASSPATH` environment variable on UNIX/Linux and Windows.

- On UNIX/Linux, edit your shell's startup file.

  If you use the C shell, add a line such as the following to the `.cshrc` file in your home directory.

  ```
  setenv CLASSPATH /home/user/classdir:.
  ```

  If you use the Bourne Again shell or `bash`, add the following line to the `.bashrc` or `.bash_profile` file in your home directory.

  ```
  export CLASSPATH=/home/user/classdir:.
  ```

- On Windows 95/98/Me, edit the `autoexec.bat` file in the boot drive (usually the `C:` drive). Add a line:

  ```
  SET CLASSPATH=c:\user\classdir;.
  ```

  Make sure not to put any spaces around either side of the = character.

- On Windows NT/2000/XP, open the control panel. Then open the System icon and select the Environment tab. Add a new environment variable named `CLASSPATH`, or edit the variable if it exists already. In the value field, type the desired class path such as `c:\user\classdir;.`(see Figure 4–9).

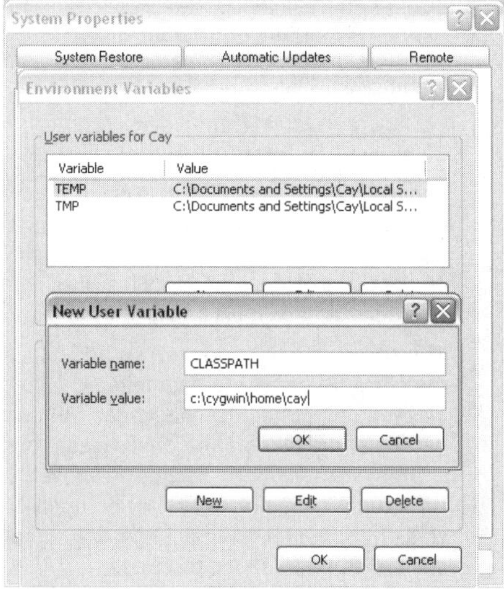

Figure 4–9: Setting the class path in Windows XP

Package Scope

You have already encountered the access modifiers public and private. Features tagged as public can be used by any class. Private features can be used only by the class that defines them. If you don't specify either public or private, then the feature (that is, the class, method, or variable) can be accessed by all methods in the same *package.*

Consider the program in Example 4–2 on page 109. The Employee class was not defined as a public class. Therefore, only other classes in the same package—the default package in this case—such as EmployeeTest can access it. For classes, this is a reasonable default. However, for variables, this default was an unfortunate choice. Variables must explicitly be marked private or they will default to being package-visible. This, of course, breaks encapsulation. The problem is that it is awfully easy to forget to type the private keyword. Here is an example from the Window class in the java.awt package, which is part of the source code supplied with the JDK:

```
public class Window extends Container
{
   String warningString;
   . . .
}
```

Note that the warningString variable is not private! That means the methods of all classes in the java.awt package can access this variable and set it to whatever they like (such as "Trust me!"). Actually, the only methods that access this variable are in the Window class, so it would have been entirely appropriate to make the variable private. We suspect that the programmer typed the code in a hurry and simply forgot the private modifier. (We won't mention the programmer's name to protect the guilty—you can look into the source file yourself.)

NOTE: Amazingly enough, this problem has never been fixed, even though we have pointed it out in seven editions of this book—apparently the library implementors don't read *Core Java.* Not only that—new fields have been added to the class over time, and about half of them aren't private either.

Is this really a problem? It depends. By default, packages are not closed entities. That is, anyone can add more classes to a package. Of course, hostile or clueless programmers can then add code that modifies variables with package visibility. For example, in earlier versions of the Java programming language, it was an easy matter to smuggle another class into the java.awt package—simply start out the class with

```
package java.awt;
```

Then place the resulting class file inside a subdirectory java/awt somewhere on the class path, and you have gained access to the internals of the java.awt package. Through this subterfuge, it was possible to set the warning border (see Figure 4–10).

Figure 4–10: Changing the warning string in an applet window

Starting with version 1.2, the JDK implementors rigged the class loader to explicitly disallow loading of user-defined classes whose package name starts with "`java.`"! Of course, your own classes won't benefit from that protection. Instead, you can use another mechanism, *package sealing*, to address the issue of promiscuous package access. If you seal a package, no further classes can be added to it. You will see in Chapter 10 how you can produce a JAR file that contains sealed packages.

Documentation Comments

The JDK contains a very useful tool, called `javadoc`, that generates HTML documentation from your source files. In fact, the on-line API documentation that we described in Chapter 3 is simply the result of running `javadoc` on the source code of the standard Java library.

If you add comments that start with the special delimiter `/**` to your source code, you too can easily produce professional-looking documentation. This is a very nice scheme because it lets you keep your code and documentation in one place. If you put your documentation into a separate file, then you probably know that the code and comments tend to diverge over time. But because the documentation comments are in the same file as the source code, it is an easy matter to update both and run `javadoc` again.

Comment Insertion

The `javadoc` utility extracts information for the following items:

- Packages
- Public classes and interfaces
- Public and protected methods
- Public and protected fields

Protected features are introduced in Chapter 5, interfaces in Chapter 6.

You can (and should) supply a comment for each of these features. Each comment is placed immediately *above* the feature it describes. A comment starts with a `/**` and ends with a `*/`.

Each `/** . . . */` documentation comment contains *free-form text* followed by *tags*. A tag starts with an `@`, such as `@author` or `@param`.

The *first sentence* of the free-form text should be a *summary statement*. The `javadoc` utility automatically generates summary pages that extract these sentences.

In the free-form text, you can use HTML modifiers such as `<em>...</em>` for emphasis, `<code>...</code>` for a monospaced "typewriter" font, `<strong>...</strong>` for strong emphasis, and even `<img ...>` to include an image. You should, however, stay away from headings `<h1>` or rules `<hr>` because they can interfere with the formatting of the document.

NOTE: If your comments contain links to other files such as images (for example, diagrams or images of user interface components), place those files into subdirectories named `doc-files`. The `javadoc` utility will copy these directories and the files in them from the source directory to the documentation directory.

Class Comments

The class comment must be placed *after* any `import` statements, directly before the `class` definition.

Here is an example of a class comment:

```
/**
   A <code>Card</code> object represents a playing card, such
   as "Queen of Hearts". A card has a suit (Diamond, Heart,
   Spade or Club) and a value (1 = Ace, 2 . . . 10, 11 = Jack,
   12 = Queen, 13 = King).
*/
public class Card
{
   . . .
}
```

NOTE: Many programmers start each line of a documentation with an asterisk, like this:

```
/**
 * A <code>Card</code> object represents a playing card, such
 * as "Queen of Hearts". A card has a suit (Diamond, Heart,
 * Spade or Club) and a value (1 = Ace, 2 . . . 10, 11 = Jack,
 * 12 = Queen, 13 = King)
 */
```

We don't do this because it *discourages* programmers from updating the comments. Nobody likes rearranging the * characters when the line breaks change. However, some text editors have a mode that takes care of this drudgery. If you know that all future maintainers of your code will use such a text editor, you may want to add the border to make the comment stand out.

Method Comments

Each method comment must immediately precede the method that it describes. In addition to the general-purpose tags, you can use the following tags:

`@param` *variable description*

This tag adds an entry to the "parameters" section of the current method. The description can span multiple lines and can use HTML tags. All `@param` tags for one method must be kept together.

`@return` *description*

This tag adds a "returns" section to the current method. The description can span multiple lines and can use HTML tags.

`@throws` *class description*

This tag adds a note that this method may throw an exception. Exceptions are the topic of Chapter 11.

Here is an example of a method comment:

```
/**
   Raises the salary of an employee.
   @param byPercent the percentage by which to raise the salary
      (e.g. 10 = 10%)
   @return the amount of the raise
*/
public double raiseSalary(double byPercent)
{
   double raise = salary * byPercent / 100;
   salary += raise;
   return raise;
}
```

Field Comments

You only need to document public fields—generally that means static constants. For example,

```
/**
   The "Hearts" card suit
*/
public static final int HEARTS = 1;
```

General Comments

The following tags can be used in class documentation comments.

`@author` *name*

This tag makes an "author" entry. You can have multiple `@author` tags, one for each author.

`@version` *text*

This tag makes a "version" entry. The `text` can be any description of the current version.

The following tags can be used in all documentation comments.

`@since` *text*

This tag makes a "since" entry. The `text` can be any description of the version that introduced this feature. For example, `@since version 1.7.1`

`@deprecated` *text*

This tag adds a comment that the class, method, or variable should no longer be used. The `text` should suggest a replacement. For example,

```
@deprecated Use <code>setVisible(true)</code> instead
```

You can use hyperlinks to other relevant parts of the `javadoc` documentation, or to external documents, with the `@see` and `@link` tags.

`@see` *reference*

This tag adds a hyperlink in the "see also" section. It can be used with both classes and methods. Here, *reference* can be one of the following:

- *package.class#feature label*
- `<a href="...">`*label*`</a>`
- `"`*text*`"`

The first case is the most useful. You supply the name of a class, method, or variable, and `javadoc` inserts a hyperlink to the documentation. For example,

```
@see com.horstmann.corejava.Employee#raiseSalary(double)
```

makes a link to the `raiseSalary(double)` method in the `com.horstmann.corejava.Employee` class. You can omit the name of the package or both the package and class name. Then, the feature will be located in the current package or class.

Note that you must use a `#`, not a period, to separate the class from the method or variable name. The Java compiler itself is highly skilled in guessing the various meanings of the period character, as separator between packages, subpackages, classes, inner classes, and methods and variables. But the `javadoc` utility isn't quite as clever, and you have to help it along.

If the `@see` tag is followed by a < character, then you need to specify a hyperlink. You can link to any URL you like. For example,

```
@see <a href="www.horstmann.com/corejava.html">The Core Java home page</a>
```

In each of these cases, you can specify an optional *label* that will appear as the link anchor. If you omit the label, then the user will see the target code name or URL as the anchor.

If the @see tag is followed by a " character, then the text is displayed in the "see also" section. For example,

```
@see "Core Java 2 volume 2"
```

You can add multiple @see tags for one feature, but you must keep them all together.

If you like, you can place hyperlinks to other classes or methods anywhere in any of your comments. You insert a special tag of the form {@link *package.class#feature label*} anywhere in a comment. The feature description follows the same rules as for the @see tag.

Package and Overview Comments

You place class, method, and variable comments directly into the Java source files, delimited by /** . . . */ documentation comments. However, to generate package comments, you need to add a file named package.html in each package directory. All text between the tags <BODY>...</BODY> is extracted.

You can also supply an overview comment for all source files. Place it in a file called overview.html, located in the parent directory that contains all the source files. All text between the tags <BODY>...</BODY> is extracted. This comment is displayed when the user selects "Overview" from the navigation bar.

Comment Extraction

Here, *docDirectory* is the name of the directory where you want the HTML files to go. Follow these steps:

1. Change to the directory that contains the source files you want to document. If you have nested packages to document, such as com.horstmann.corejava, you must be working in the directory that contains the subdirectory com. (This is the directory that contains the overview.html file if you supplied one.)
2. Run the command

   javadoc -d *docDirectory nameOfPackage*

   for a single package. Or run

   javadoc -d *docDirectory* $nameOfPackage_1$ $nameOfPackage_2$...

   to document multiple packages. If your files are in the default package, then instead run

   javadoc -d *docDirectory* *.java

If you omit the -d *docDirectory* option, then the HTML files are extracted to the current directory. That can get messy, and we don't recommend it.

The javadoc program can be fine-tuned by numerous command-line options. For example, you can use the -author and -version options to include the @author and @version tags in the documentation. (By default, they are omitted.) Another useful option is -link, to include hyperlinks to standard classes. For example, if you use the command

```
javadoc -link http://java.sun.com/j2se/5.0/docs/api *.java
```

then all standard library classes are automatically linked to the documentation on the Sun web site.

For additional options, we refer you to the on-line documentation of the javadoc utility at http://java.sun.com/j2se/javadoc.

NOTE: If you require further customization, for example, to produce documentation in a format other than HTML, then you can supply your own *doclet* to generate the output in any form you desire. Clearly, this is a specialized need, and we refer you to the on-line documentation for details on doclets at http://java.sun.com/j2se/javadoc.

TIP: A useful doclet is DocCheck, at `http://java.sun.com/j2se/javadoc/doccheck/`. It scans a set of source files for missing documentation comments.

Class Design Hints

Without trying to be comprehensive or tedious, we want to end this chapter with some hints that may make your classes more acceptable in well-mannered OOP circles.

1. *Always keep data private.*

   This is first and foremost: doing anything else violates encapsulation. You may need to write an accessor or mutator method occasionally, but you are still better off keeping the instance fields private. Bitter experience has shown that how the data are represented may change, but how they are used will change much less frequently. When data are kept private, changes in their representation do not affect the user of the class, and bugs are easier to detect.

2. *Always initialize data.*

   Java won't initialize local variables for you, but it will initialize instance fields of objects. Don't rely on the defaults, but initialize the variables explicitly, either by supplying a default or by setting defaults in all constructors.

3. *Don't use too many basic types in a class.*

   The idea is to replace multiple *related* uses of basic types with other classes. This keeps your classes easier to understand and to change. For example, replace the following instance fields in a `Customer` class

   ```
   private String street;
   private String city;
   private String state;
   private int zip;
   ```

   with a new class called `Address`. This way, you can easily cope with changes to addresses, such as the need to deal with international addresses.

4. *Not all fields need individual field accessors and mutators.*

   You may need to get and set an employee's salary. You certainly won't need to change the hiring date once the object is constructed. And, quite often, objects have instance fields that you don't want others to get or set, for example, an array of state abbreviations in an `Address` class.

5. *Use a standard form for class definitions.*

   We always list the contents of classes in the following order:

   public features
   package scope features
   private features

   Within each section, we list:

   instance methods
   static methods
   instance fields
   static fields

   After all, the users of your class are more interested in the public interface than in the details of the private implementation. And they are more interested in methods than in data.

However, there is no universal agreement on what is the best style. The Sun coding style guide for the Java programming language recommends listing fields first and then methods. Whatever style you use, the most important thing is to be consistent.

6. *Break up classes with too many responsibilities.*

   This hint is, of course, vague: "too many" is obviously in the eye of the beholder. However, if there is an obvious way to make one complicated class into two classes that are conceptually simpler, seize the opportunity. (On the other hand, don't go overboard; 10 classes, each with only one method, is usually overkill.)

   Here is an example of a bad design.

```
public class CardDeck // bad design
{
   public CardDeck() { . . . }
   public void shuffle() { . . . }
   public int getTopValue() { . . . }
   public int getTopSuit() { . . . }
   public void draw() { . . . }

   private int[] value;
   private int[] suit;
}
```

   This class really implements two separate concepts: a *deck of cards*, with its `shuffle` and `draw` methods, and a *card*, with the methods to inspect the value and suit of a card. It makes sense to introduce a `Card` class that represents an individual card. Now you have two classes, each with its own responsibilities:

```
public class CardDeck
{
   public CardDeck() { . . . }
   public void shuffle() { . . . }
   public Card getTop() { . . . }
   public void draw() { . . . }

   private Card[] cards;
}

public class Card
{
   public Card(int aValue, int aSuit) { . . . }
   public int getValue() { . . . }
   public int getSuit() { . . . }

   private int value;
   private int suit;
}
```

7. *Make the names of your classes and methods reflect their responsibilities.*

   Just as variables should have meaningful names that reflect what they represent, so should classes. (The standard library certainly contains some dubious examples, such as the `Date` class that describes time.)

   A good convention is that a class name should be a noun (`Order`) or a noun preceded by an adjective (`RushOrder`) or a gerund (an "-ing" word, like `BillingAddress`). As for methods, follow the standard convention that accessor methods begin with a lowercase `get` (`getSalary`), and that mutator methods use a lowercase `set` (`setSalary`).

Chapter 5

Inheritance

- ▼ CLASSES, SUPERCLASSES, AND SUBCLASSES
- ▼ `Object`: THE COSMIC SUPERCLASS
- ▼ GENERIC ARRAY LISTS
- ▼ OBJECT WRAPPERS AND AUTOBOXING
- ▼ REFLECTION
- ▼ ENUMERATION CLASSES
- ▼ DESIGN HINTS FOR INHERITANCE

Chapter 4 introduced you to classes and objects. In this chapter, you learn about *inheritance,* another fundamental concept of object-oriented programming. The idea behind inheritance is that you can create new classes that are built on existing classes. When you inherit from an existing class, you reuse (or inherit) its methods and fields and you add new methods and fields to adapt your new class to new situations. This technique is essential in Java programming.

As with the previous chapter, if you are coming from a procedure-oriented language like C, Visual Basic, or COBOL, you will want to read this chapter carefully. For experienced C++ programmers or those coming from another object-oriented language like Smalltalk, this chapter will seem largely familiar, but there are many differences between how inheritance is implemented in Java and how it is done in C++ or in other object-oriented languages.

This chapter also covers *reflection,* the ability to find out more about classes and their properties in a running program. Reflection is a powerful feature, but it is undeniably complex. Because reflection is of greater interest to tool builders than to application programmers, you can probably glance over that part of the chapter upon first reading and come back to it later.

Classes, Superclasses, and Subclasses

Let's return to the `Employee` class that we discussed in the previous chapter. Suppose (alas) you work for a company at which managers are treated differently from other employees. Managers are, of course, just like employees in many respects. Both employees and managers are paid a salary. However, while employees are expected to complete their assigned tasks in return for receiving their salary, managers get *bonuses* if they actually achieve what they are supposed to do. This is the kind of situation that cries out for inheritance. Why? Well, you need to define a new class, `Manager`, and add functionality. But you can retain some of what you have already programmed in the `Employee` class, and *all* the fields of the original class can be preserved. More abstractly, there is an obvious "is–a" relationship between `Manager` and `Employee`. Every manager *is an* employee: this "is–a" relationship is the hallmark of inheritance.

Here is how you define a `Manager` class that inherits from the `Employee` class. You use the Java keyword `extends` to denote inheritance.

```
class Manager extends Employee
{
   added methods and fields
}
```

C++ NOTE: Inheritance is similar in Java and C++. Java uses the `extends` keyword instead of the `:` token. All inheritance in Java is public inheritance; there is no analog to the C++ features of private and protected inheritance.

The keyword `extends` indicates that you are making a new class that derives from an existing class. The existing class is called the *superclass, base class,* or *parent class.* The new class is called the *subclass, derived class,* or *child class.* The terms superclass and subclass are those most commonly used by Java programmers, although some programmers prefer the parent/child analogy, which also ties in nicely with the "inheritance" theme.

The `Employee` class is a superclass, but not because it is superior to its subclass or contains more functionality. *In fact, the opposite is true:* subclasses have *more* functionality than their superclasses. For example, as you will see when we go over the rest of the `Manager` class code, the `Manager` class encapsulates more data and has more functionality than its superclass `Employee`.

NOTE: The prefixes *super* and *sub* come from the language of sets used in theoretical computer science and mathematics. The set of all employees contains the set of all managers, and this is described by saying it is a *superset* of the set of managers. Or, put it another way, the set of all managers is a *subset* of the set of all employees.

Our `Manager` class has a new field to store the bonus, and a new method to set it:

```
class Manager extends Employee
{
   . . .

   public void setBonus(double b)
   {
      bonus = b;
   }

   private double bonus;
}
```

There is nothing special about these methods and fields. If you have a `Manager` object, you can simply apply the `setBonus` method.

```
Manager boss = . . .;
boss.setBonus(5000);
```

Of course, if you have an Employee object, you cannot apply the setBonus method—it is not among the methods that are defined in the Employee class.

However, you *can* use methods such as getName and getHireDay with Manager objects. Even though these methods are not explicitly defined in the Manager class, they are automatically inherited from the Employee superclass.

Similarly, the fields name, salary, and hireDay are inherited from the superclass. Every Manager object has four fields: name, salary, hireDay, and bonus.

When defining a subclass by extending its superclass, you only need to indicate the *differences* between the subclass and the superclass. When designing classes, you place the most general methods into the superclass and more specialized methods in the subclass. Factoring out common functionality by moving it to a superclass is common in object-oriented programming.

However, some of the superclass methods are not appropriate for the Manager subclass. In particular, the getSalary method should return the sum of the base salary and the bonus. You need to supply a new method to *override* the superclass method:

```
class Manager extends Employee
{
   . . .
   public double getSalary()
   {
      . . .
   }
   . . .
}
```

How can you implement this method? At first glance, it appears to be simple: just return the sum of the salary and bonus fields:

```
public double getSalary()
{
   return salary + bonus; // won't work
}
```

However, that won't work. The getSalary method of the Manager class *has no direct access to the private fields of the superclass.* This means that the getSalary method of the Manager class cannot directly access the salary field, even though every Manager object has a field called salary. Only the methods of the Employee class have access to the private fields. If the Manager methods want to access those private fields, they have to do what every other method does—use the public interface, in this case, the public getSalary method of the Employee class.

So, let's try this again. You need to call getSalary instead of simply accessing the salary field.

```
public double getSalary()
{
   double baseSalary = getSalary(); // still won't work
   return baseSalary + bonus;
}
```

The problem is that the call to getSalary simply calls *itself,* because the Manager class has a getSalary method (namely, the method we are trying to implement). The consequence is an infinite set of calls to the same method, leading to a program crash.

We need to indicate that we want to call the getSalary method of the Employee superclass, not the current class. You use the special keyword super for this purpose. The call

```
super.getSalary()
```

calls the `getSalary` method of the `Employee` class. Here is the correct version of the `getSalary` method for the `Manager` class:

```
public double getSalary()
{
   double baseSalary = super.getSalary();
   return baseSalary + bonus;
}
```

NOTE: Some people think of `super` as being analogous to the `this` reference. However, that analogy is not quite accurate—`super` is not a reference to an object. For example, you cannot assign the value `super` to another object variable. Instead, `super` is a special keyword that directs the compiler to invoke the superclass method.

As you saw, a subclass can *add* fields, and it can *add* or *override* methods of the superclass. However, inheritance can never take away any fields or methods.

C++ NOTE: Java uses the keyword `super` to call a superclass method. In C++, you would use the name of the superclass with the `::` operator instead. For example, the `getSalary` method of the `Manager` class would call `Employee::getSalary` instead of `super.getSalary`.

Finally, let us supply a constructor.

```
public Manager(String n, double s, int year, int month, int day)
{
   super(n, s, year, month, day);
   bonus = 0;
}
```

Here, the keyword `super` has a different meaning. The instruction

```
super(n, s, year, month, day);
```

is shorthand for "call the constructor of the `Employee` superclass with `n`, `s`, `year`, `month`, and `day` as parameters."

Because the `Manager` constructor cannot access the private fields of the `Employee` class, it must initialize them through a constructor. The constructor is invoked with the special `super` syntax. The call using `super` must be the first statement in the constructor for the subclass.

If the subclass constructor does not call a superclass constructor explicitly, then the default (no-parameter) constructor of the superclass is invoked. If the superclass has no default constructor and the subclass constructor does not call another superclass constructor explicitly, then the Java compiler reports an error.

NOTE: Recall that the `this` keyword has two meanings: to denote a reference to the implicit parameter and to call another constructor of the same class. Likewise, the `super` keyword has two meanings: to invoke a superclass method and to invoke a superclass constructor. When used to invoke constructors, the `this` and `super` keywords are closely related. The constructor calls can only occur as the first statement in another constructor. The construction parameters are either passed to another constructor of the same class (`this`) or a constructor of the superclass (`super`).

C++ NOTE: In a C++ constructor, you do not call super, but you use the initializer list syntax to construct the superclass. The Manager constructor looks like this in C++:

```
Manager::Manager(String n, double s, int year, int month, int day) // C++
: Employee(n, s, year, month, day)
{
   bonus = 0;
}
```

Having redefined the getSalary method for Manager objects, managers will *automatically* have the bonus added to their salaries.

Here's an example of this at work: we make a new manager and set the manager's bonus:

```
Manager boss = new Manager("Carl Cracker", 80000, 1987, 12, 15);
boss.setBonus(5000);
```

We make an array of three employees:

```
Employee[] staff = new Employee[3];
```

We populate the array with a mix of managers and employees:

```
staff[0] = boss;
staff[1] = new Employee("Harry Hacker", 50000, 1989, 10, 1);
staff[2] = new Employee("Tony Tester", 40000, 1990, 3, 15);
```

We print out everyone's salary:

```
for (Employee e : staff)
   System.out.println(e.getName() + " " + e.getSalary());
```

This loop prints the following data:

```
Carl Cracker 85000.0
Harry Hacker 50000.0
Tommy Tester 40000.0
```

Now staff[1] and staff[2] each print their base salary because they are Employee objects. However, staff[0] is a Manager object and its getSalary method adds the bonus to the base salary.

What is remarkable is that the call

```
e.getSalary()
```

picks out the *correct* getSalary method. Note that the *declared* type of e is Employee, but the *actual* type of the object to which e refers can be either Employee (that is, when i is 1 or 2) or Manager (when i is 0).

When e refers to an Employee object, then the call e.getSalary() calls the getSalary method of the Employee class. However, when e refers to a Manager object, then the getSalary method of the Manager class is called instead. The virtual machine knows about the actual type of the object to which e refers, and therefore can invoke the correct method.

The fact that an object variable (such as the variable e) can refer to multiple actual types is called *polymorphism.* Automatically selecting the appropriate method at run time is called *dynamic binding.* We discuss both topics in more detail in this chapter.

C++ NOTE: In Java, you do not need to declare a method as virtual. Dynamic binding is the default behavior. If you do *not* want a method to be virtual, you tag it as final. (We discuss the final keyword later in this chapter.)

Example 5–1 contains a program that shows how the salary computation differs for `Employee` and `Manager` objects.

Example 5–1: ManagerTest.java

```
import java.util.*;

public class ManagerTest
{
   public static void main(String[] args)
   {
      // construct a Manager object
      Manager boss = new Manager("Carl Cracker", 80000, 1987, 12, 15);
      boss.setBonus(5000);

      Employee[] staff = new Employee[3];

      // fill the staff array with Manager and Employee objects

      staff[0] = boss;
      staff[1] = new Employee("Harry Hacker", 50000, 1989, 10, 1);
      staff[2] = new Employee("Tommy Tester", 40000, 1990, 3, 15);

      // print out information about all Employee objects
      for (Employee e : staff)
         System.out.println("name=" + e.getName()
            + ",salary=" + e.getSalary());
   }
}

class Employee
{
   public Employee(String n, double s, int year, int month, int day)
   {
      name = n;
      salary = s;
      GregorianCalendar calendar = new GregorianCalendar(year, month - 1, day);
      hireDay = calendar.getTime();
   }

   public String getName()
   {
      return name;
   }

   public double getSalary()
   {
      return salary;
   }

   public Date getHireDay()
   {
      return hireDay;
   }

   public void raiseSalary(double byPercent)
   {
```

```
      double raise = salary * byPercent / 100;
      salary += raise;
   }

   private String name;
   private double salary;
   private Date hireDay;
}

class Manager extends Employee
{
   /**
      @param n the employee's name
      @param s the salary
      @param year the hire year
      @param month the hire month
      @param day the hire day
   */
   public Manager(String n, double s, int year, int month, int day)
   {
      super(n, s, year, month, day);
      bonus = 0;
   }

   public double getSalary()
   {
      double baseSalary = super.getSalary();
      return baseSalary + bonus;
   }

   public void setBonus(double b)
   {
      bonus = b;
   }

   private double bonus;
}
```

Inheritance Hierarchies

Inheritance need not stop at deriving one layer of classes. We could have an `Executive` class that extends `Manager`, for example. The collection of all classes extending from a common superclass is called an *inheritance hierarchy,* as shown in Figure 5–1. The path from a particular class to its ancestors in the inheritance hierarchy is its *inheritance chain.*

There is usually more than one chain of descent from a distant ancestor class. You could form a subclass `Programmer` or `Secretary` that extends `Employee`, and they would have nothing to do with the `Manager` class (or with each other). This process can continue as long as is necessary.

C++ NOTE: Java does not support multiple inheritance. (For ways to recover much of the functionality of multiple inheritance, see the section on Interfaces in the next chapter.)

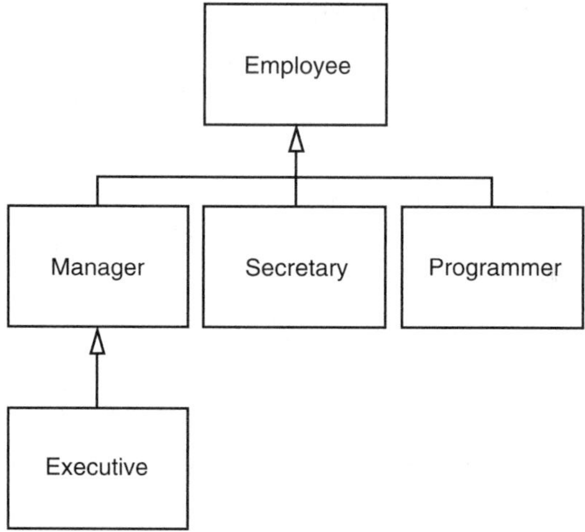

Figure 5–1: `Employee` inheritance hierarchy

Polymorphism

A simple rule enables you to know whether or not inheritance is the right design for your data. The "is-a" rule states that every object of the subclass is an object of the superclass. For example, every manager is an employee. Thus, it makes sense for the `Manager` class to be a subclass of the `Employee` class. Naturally, the opposite is not true—not every employee is a manager.

Another way of formulating the "is-a" rule is the *substitution principle.* That principle states that you can use a subclass object whenever the program expects a superclass object.

For example, you can assign a subclass object to a superclass variable.

```
Employee e;
e = new Employee(. . .);  // Employee object expected
e = new Manager(. . .); // OK, Manager can be used as well
```

In the Java programming language, object variables are *polymorphic.* A variable of type `Employee` can refer to an object of type `Employee` or to an object of any subclass of the `Employee` class (such as `Manager`, `Executive`, `Secretary`, and so on).

We took advantage of this principle in Example 5–1:

```
Manager boss = new Manager(. . .);
Employee[] staff = new Employee[3];
staff[0] = boss;
```

In this case, the variables `staff[0]` and `boss` refer to the same object. However, `staff[0]` is considered to be only an `Employee` object by the compiler.

That means, you can call

```
boss.setBonus(5000); // OK
```

but you can't call

```
staff[0].setBonus(5000); // ERROR
```

The declared type of `staff[0]` is `Employee`, and the `setBonus` method is not a method of the `Employee` class.

However, you cannot assign a superclass reference to a subclass variable. For example, it is not legal to make the assignment

```
Manager m = staff[i]; // ERROR
```

The reason is clear: Not all employees are managers. If this assignment were to succeed and `m` were to refer to an `Employee` object that is not a manager, then it would later be possible to call `m.setBonus(...)` and a runtime error would occur.

CAUTION: In Java, arrays of subclass references can be converted to arrays of superclass references without a cast. For example, consider an array of managers

```
Manager[] managers = new Manager[10];
```

It is legal to convert this array to an `Employee[]` array:

```
Employee[] staff = managers; // OK
```

Sure, why not, you may think. After all, if `manager[i]` is a `Manager`, it is also an `Employee`. But actually, something surprising is going on. Keep in mind that `managers` and `staff` are references to the same array. Now consider the statement

```
staff[0] = new Employee("Harry Hacker", ...);
```

The compiler will cheerfully allow this assignment. But `staff[0]` and `manager[0]` are the same reference, so it looks as if we managed to smuggle a mere employee into the management ranks. That would be very bad—calling `managers[0].setBonus(1000)` would try to access a nonexistent instance field and would corrupt neighboring memory.

To make sure no such corruption can occur, all arrays remember the element type with which they were created, and they monitor that only compatible references are stored into them. For example, the array created as `new Manager[10]` remembers that it is an array of managers. Attempting to store an `Employee` reference causes an `ArrayStoreException`.

Dynamic Binding

It is important to understand what happens when a method call is applied to an object. Here are the details:

1. The compiler looks at the declared type of the object and the method name. Let's say we call `x.f(param)`, and the implicit parameter `x` is declared to be an object of class `C`. Note that there may be multiple methods, all with the same name, `f`, but with different parameter types. For example, there may be a method `f(int)` and a method `f(String)`. The compiler enumerates all methods called `f` in the class `C` and all `public` methods called `f` in the superclasses of `C`.

   Now the compiler knows all possible candidates for the method to be called.
2. Next, the compiler determines the types of the parameters that are supplied in the method call. If among all the methods called `f` there is a unique method whose parameter types are a best match for the supplied parameters, then that method is chosen to be called. This process is called *overloading resolution*. For example, in a call `x.f("Hello")`, the compiler picks `f(String)` and not `f(int)`. The situation can get complex because of type conversions (`int` to `double`, `Manager` to `Employee`, and so on). If the compiler cannot find any method with matching parameter types or if multiple methods all match after applying conversions, then the compiler reports an error.

   Now the compiler knows the name and parameter types of the method that needs to be called.

NOTE: Recall that the name and parameter type list for a method is called the method's *signature*. For example, f(int) and f(String) are two methods with the same name but different signatures. If you define a method in a subclass that has the same signature as a superclass method, then you override that method.

The return type is not part of the signature. However, when you override a method, you need to keep the return type compatible. Prior to JDK 5.0, the return types had to be identical. However, it is now legal for the subclass to change the return type of an overridden method to a subtype of the original type. For example, suppose that the Employee class has a

```
public Employee getBuddy() { ... }
```

Then the Manager subclass can override this method as

```
public Manager getBuddy() { ... } // OK in JDK 5.0
```

We say that the two getBuddy methods have *covariant* return types.

3. If the method is private, static, final, or a constructor, then the compiler knows exactly which method to call. (The final modifier is explained in the next section.) This is called *static binding*. Otherwise, the method to be called depends on the actual type of the implicit parameter, and dynamic binding must be used at run time. In our example, the compiler would generate an instruction to call f(String) with dynamic binding.
4. When the program runs and uses dynamic binding to call a method, then the virtual machine must call the version of the method that is appropriate for the *actual* type of the object to which x refers. Let's say the actual type is D, a subclass of C. If the class D defines a method f(String), that method is called. If not, D's superclass is searched for a method f(String), and so on.

   It would be time consuming to carry out this search every time a method is called. Therefore, the virtual machine precomputes for each class a *method table* that lists all method signatures and the actual methods to be called. When a method is actually called, the virtual machine simply makes a table lookup. In our example, the virtual machine consults the method table for the class D and looks up the method to call for f(String). That method may be D.f(String) or X.f(String), where X is some superclass of D.

   There is one twist to this scenario. If the call is super.f(param), then the compiler consults the method table of the superclass of the implicit parameter.

Let's look at this process in detail in the call e.getSalary() in Example 5–1. The declared type of e is Employee. The Employee class has a single method, called getSalary, with no method parameters. Therefore, in this case, we don't worry about overloading resolution.

Because the getSalary method is not private, static, or final, it is dynamically bound. The virtual machine produces method tables for the Employee and Manager classes. The Employee table shows that all methods are defined in the Employee class itself:

```
Employee:
   getName() -> Employee.getName()
   getSalary() -> Employee.getSalary()
   getHireDay() -> Employee.getHireDay()
   raiseSalary(double) -> Employee.raiseSalary(double)
```

Actually, that isn't the whole story—as you will see later in this chapter, the Employee class has a superclass Object from which it inherits a number of methods. We ignore the Object methods for now.

The Manager method table is slightly different. Three methods are inherited, one method is redefined, and one method is added.

```
Manager:
   getName() -> Employee.getName()
   getSalary() -> Manager.getSalary()
   getHireDay() -> Employee.getHireDay()
   raiseSalary(double) -> Employee.raiseSalary(double)
   setBonus(double) -> Manager.setBonus(double)
```

At run time, the call `e.getSalary()` is resolved as follows.

1. First, the virtual machine fetches the method table for the actual type of `e`. That may be the table for `Employee`, `Manager`, or another subclass of `Employee`.
2. Then, the virtual machine looks up the defining class for the `getSalary()` signature. Now it knows which method to call.
3. Finally, the virtual machine calls the method.

Dynamic binding has a very important property: it makes programs *extensible* without the need for modifying existing code. Suppose a new class `Executive` is added and there is the possibility that the variable `e` refers to an object of that class. The code containing the call `e.getSalary()` need not be recompiled. The `Executive.getSalary()` method is called automatically if `e` happens to refer to an object of type `Executive`.

CAUTION: When you override a method, the subclass method must be *at least as visible* as the superclass method. In particular, if the superclass method is `public`, then the subclass method must also be declared as `public`. It is a common error to accidentally omit the `public` specifier for the subclass method. The compiler then complains that you try to supply a weaker access privilege.

Preventing Inheritance: Final Classes and Methods

Occasionally, you want to prevent someone from forming a subclass from one of your classes. Classes that cannot be extended are called *final* classes, and you use the `final` modifier in the definition of the class to indicate this. For example, let us suppose we want to prevent others from subclassing the `Executive` class. Then, we simply declare the class by using the `final` modifier as follows:

```
final class Executive extends Manager
{
   . . .
}
```

You can also make a specific method in a class `final`. If you do this, then no subclass can override that method. (All methods in a `final` class are automatically `final`.) For example,

```
class Employee
{
   . . .
   public final String getName()
   {
      return name;
   }
   . . .
}
```

NOTE: Recall that fields can also be declared as `final`. A final field cannot be changed after the object has been constructed. However, if a class is declared as `final`, only the methods, not the fields, are automatically `final`.

There is only one good reason to make a method or class `final`: to make sure that the semantics cannot be changed in a subclass. For example, the `getTime` and `setTime` methods of the `Calendar` class are `final`. This indicates that the designers of the `Calendar` class have taken over responsibility for the conversion between the `Date` class and the calendar state. No subclass should be allowed to mess up this arrangement. Similarly, the `String` class is a `final` class. That means nobody can define a subclass of `String`. In other words, if you have a `String` reference, then you know it refers to a `String` and nothing but a `String`.

Some programmers believe that you should declare all methods as `final` unless you have a good reason that you want polymorphism. In fact, in C++ and C#, methods do not use polymorphism unless you specifically request it. That may be a bit extreme, but we agree that it is a good idea to think carefully about final methods and classes when you design a class hierarchy.

In the early days of Java, some programmers used the `final` keyword in the hope of avoiding the overhead of dynamic binding. If a method is not overridden, and it is short, then a compiler can optimize the method call away—a process called *inlining*. For example, inlining the call `e.getName()` replaces it with the field access `e.name`. This is a worthwhile improvement—CPUs hate branching because it interferes with their strategy of prefetching instructions while processing the current one. However, if `getName` can be overridden in another class, then the compiler cannot inline it because it has no way of knowing what the overriding code may do.

Fortunately, the just-in-time compiler in the virtual machine can do a better job than a traditional compiler. It knows exactly which classes extend a given class, and it can check whether any class actually overrides a given method. If a method is short, frequently called, and not actually overridden, the just-in-time compiler can inline the method. What happens if the virtual machine loads another subclass that overrides an inlined method? Then the optimizer must undo the inlining. That's slow, but it happens rarely.

C++ NOTE: In C++, a method is not dynamically bound by default, and you can tag it as `inline` to have method calls replaced with the method source code. However, there is no mechanism that would prevent a subclass from overriding a superclass method. In C++, you can write classes from which no other class can derive, but doing so requires an obscure trick, and there are few reasons to write such a class. (The obscure trick is left as an exercise to the reader. Hint: Use a virtual base class.)

Casting

Recall from Chapter 3 that the process of forcing a conversion from one type to another is called casting. The Java programming language has a special notation for casts. For example:

```
double x = 3.405;
int nx = (int) x;
```

converts the value of the expression `x` into an integer, discarding the fractional part.

Just as you occasionally need to convert a floating-point number to an integer, you also need to convert an object reference from one class to another. To actually make a cast of an object reference, you use a syntax similar to what you use for casting a numeric expression. Surround the target class name with parentheses and place it before the object reference you want to cast. For example:

```
Manager boss = (Manager) staff[0];
```

There is only one reason why you would want to make a cast—to use an object in its full capacity after its actual type has been temporarily forgotten. For example, in the `ManagerTest` class, the `staff` array had to be an array of `Employee` objects because *some* of its entries were

regular employees. We would need to cast the managerial elements of the array back to Manager to access any of its new variables. (Note that in the sample code for the first section, we made a special effort to avoid the cast. We initialized the boss variable with a Manager object before storing it in the array. We needed the correct type to set the bonus of the manager.)

As you know, in Java every object variable has a type. The type describes the kind of object the variable refers to and what it can do. For example, staff[i] refers to an Employee object (so it can also refer to a Manager object).

The compiler checks that you do not promise too much when you store a value in a variable. If you assign a subclass reference to a superclass variable, you are promising less, and the compiler will simply let you do it. If you assign a superclass reference to a subclass variable, you are promising more. Then you must use a cast so that your promise can be checked at run time.

What happens if you try to cast down an inheritance chain and you are "lying" about what an object contains?

```
Manager boss = (Manager) staff[1]; // ERROR
```

When the program runs, the Java runtime system notices the broken promise and generates a ClassCastException. If you do not catch the exception, your program terminates. Thus, it is good programming practice to find out whether a cast will succeed before attempting it. Simply use the instanceof operator. For example:

```
if (staff[1] instanceof Manager)
{
   boss = (Manager) staff[1];
   . . .
}
```

Finally, the compiler will not let you make a cast if there is no chance for the cast to succeed. For example, the cast

```
Date c = (Date) staff[1];
```

is a compile-time error because Date is not a subclass of Employee.

To sum up:

- You can cast only within an inheritance hierarchy.
- Use instanceof to check before casting from a superclass to a subclass.

NOTE: The test

```
x instanceof C
```

does not generate an exception if x is null. It simply returns false. That makes sense. Because null refers to no object, it certainly doesn't refer to an object of type C.

Actually, converting the type of an object by performing a cast is not usually a good idea. In our example, you do not need to cast an Employee object to a Manager object for most purposes. The getSalary method will work correctly on both objects of both classes. The dynamic binding that makes polymorphism work locates the correct method automatically.

The only reason to make the cast is to use a method that is unique to managers, such as setBonus. If for some reason you find yourself wanting to call setBonus on Employee objects, ask yourself whether this is an indication of a design flaw in the superclass. It may make sense to redesign the superclass and add a setBonus method. Remember, it takes only one uncaught ClassCastException to terminate your program. In general, it is best to minimize the use of casts and the instanceof operator.

C++ NOTE: Java uses the cast syntax from the "bad old days" of C, but it works like the safe `dynamic_cast` operation of C++. For example,

```
Manager boss = (Manager) staff[1]; // Java
```

is the same as

```
Manager* boss = dynamic_cast<Manager*>(staff[1]); // C++
```

with one important difference. If the cast fails, it does not yield a null object but throws an exception. In this sense, it is like a C++ cast of *references*. This is a pain in the neck. In C++, you can take care of the type test and type conversion in one operation.

```
Manager* boss = dynamic_cast<Manager*>(staff[1]); // C++
if (boss != NULL) . . .
```

In Java, you use a combination of the `instanceof` operator and a cast.

```
if (staff[1] instanceof Manager)
{
   Manager boss = (Manager) staff[1];
   . . .
}
```

Abstract Classes

As you move up the inheritance hierarchy, classes become more general and probably more abstract. At some point, the ancestor class becomes *so* general that you think of it more as a basis for other classes than as a class with specific instances you want to use. Consider, for example, an extension of our `Employee` class hierarchy. An employee is a person, and so is a student. Let us extend our class hierarchy to include classes `Person` and `Student`. Figure 5–2 shows the inheritance relationships between these classes.

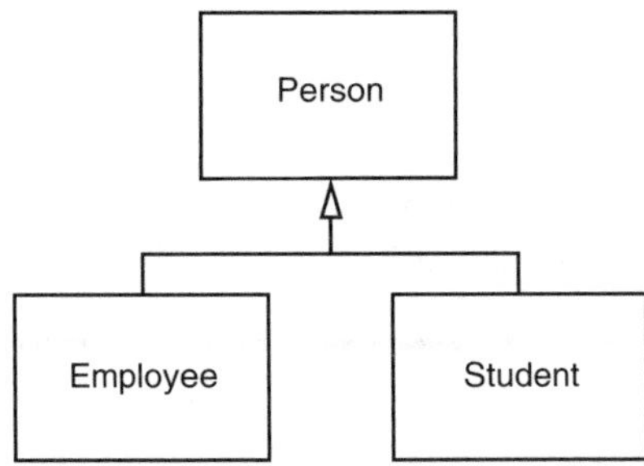

Figure 5–2: Inheritance diagram for `Person` and its subclasses

Why bother with so high a level of abstraction? There are some attributes that make sense for every person, such as the name. Both students and employees have names, and introducing a common superclass lets us factor out the `getName` method to a higher level in the inheritance hierarchy.

Now let's add another method, `getDescription`, whose purpose is to return a brief description of the person, such as

```
an employee with a salary of $50,000.00
a student majoring in computer science
```

It is easy to implement this method for the `Employee` and `Student` classes. But what information can you provide in the `Person` class? The `Person` class knows nothing about the person except

the name. Of course, you could implement `Person.getDescription()` to return an empty string. But there is a better way. If you use the `abstract` keyword, you do not need to implement the method at all.

```
public abstract String getDescription();
   // no implementation required
```

For added clarity, a class with one or more abstract methods must itself be declared abstract.

```
abstract class Person
{  . . .
   public abstract String getDescription();
}
```

In addition to abstract methods, abstract classes can have concrete data and methods. For example, the `Person` class stores the name of the person and has a concrete method that returns it.

```
abstract class Person
{
   public Person(String n)
   {
      name = n;
   }

   public abstract String getDescription();

   public String getName()
   {
       return name;
   }

   private String name;
}
```

TIP: Many programmers think that abstract classes should have only abstract methods. However, this is not true. It always makes sense to move as much functionality as possible into a superclass, whether or not it is abstract. In particular, move common fields and methods (whether abstract or not) to the abstract superclass.

Abstract methods act as placeholders for methods that are implemented in the subclasses. When you extend an abstract class, you have two choices. You can leave some or all of the abstract methods undefined. Then you must tag the subclass as abstract as well. Or you can define all methods. Then the subclass is no longer abstract.

For example, we will define a `Student` class that extends the abstract `Person` class and implements the `getDescription` method. Because none of the methods of the `Student` class are abstract, it does not need to be declared as an abstract class.

A class can even be declared as `abstract` even though it has no abstract methods.

Abstract classes cannot be instantiated. That is, if a class is declared as `abstract`, no objects of that class can be created. For example, the expression

```
new Person("Vince Vu")
```

is an error. However, you can create objects of concrete subclasses.

Note that you can still create *object variables* of an abstract class, but such a variable must refer to an object of a nonabstract subclass. For example,

```
Person p = new Student("Vince Vu", "Economics");
```

Here p is a variable of the abstract type Person that refers to an instance of the nonabstract subclass Student.

C++ NOTE: In C++, an abstract method is called a *pure virtual function* and is tagged with a trailing = 0, such as in

```
class Person // C++
{
public:
   virtual string getDescription() = 0;
   . . .
};
```

A C++ class is abstract if it has at least one pure virtual function. In C++, there is no special keyword to denote abstract classes.

Let us define a concrete subclass Student that extends the abstract Person class:

```
class Student extends Person
{
   public Student(String n, String m)
   {
      super(n);
      major = m;
   }

   public String getDescription()
   {
      return "a student majoring in " + major;
   }

   private String major;
}
```

The Student class defines the getDescription method. Therefore, all methods in the Student class are concrete, and the class is no longer an abstract class.

The program shown in Example 5–2 defines the abstract superclass Person and two concrete subclasses, Employee and Student. We fill an array of Person references with employee and student objects.

```
Person[] people = new Person[2];
people[0] = new Employee(. . .);
people[1] = new Student(. . .);
```

We then print the names and descriptions of these objects:

```
for (Person p : people)
   System.out.println(p.getName() + ", " + p.getDescription());
```

Some people are baffled by the call

```
p.getDescription()
```

Isn't this call an undefined method? Keep in mind that the variable p never refers to a Person object because it is impossible to construct an object of the abstract Person class. The variable p always refers to an object of a concrete subclass such as Employee or Student. For these objects, the getDescription method is defined.

Could you have omitted the abstract method altogether from the `Person` superclass and simply defined the `getDescription` methods in the `Employee` and `Student` subclasses? If you did that, then you wouldn't have been able to invoke the `getDescription` method on the variable `p`. The compiler ensures that you invoke only methods that are declared in the class.

Abstract methods are an important concept in the Java programming language. You will encounter them most commonly inside *interfaces*. For more information about interfaces, turn to Chapter 6.

Example 5–2: PersonTest.java

```
import java.text.*;
import java.util.*;

public class PersonTest
{
   public static void main(String[] args)
   {
      Person[] people = new Person[2];

      // fill the people array with Student and Employee objects
      people[0] = new Employee("Harry Hacker", 50000, 1989, 10, 1);
      people[1] = new Student("Maria Morris", "computer science");

      // print out names and descriptions of all Person objects
      for (Person p : people)
         System.out.println(p.getName() + ", " + p.getDescription());
   }
}

abstract class Person
{
   public Person(String n)
   {
      name = n;
   }

   public abstract String getDescription();

   public String getName()
   {
      return name;
   }

   private String name;
}

class Employee extends Person
{
   public Employee(String n, double s,
      int year, int month, int day)
   {
      super(n);
      salary = s;
      GregorianCalendar calendar = new GregorianCalendar(year, month - 1, day);
      hireDay = calendar.getTime();
   }
```

```

   public double getSalary()
   {
      return salary;
   }

   public Date getHireDay()
   {
      return hireDay;
   }

   public String getDescription()
   {
      return String.format("an employee with a salary of $%.2f", salary);
   }

   public void raiseSalary(double byPercent)
   {
      double raise = salary * byPercent / 100;
      salary += raise;
   }

   private double salary;
   private Date hireDay;
}


class Student extends Person
{
   /**
      @param n the student's name
      @param m the student's major
   */
   public Student(String n, String m)
   {
      // pass n to superclass constructor
      super(n);
      major = m;
   }

   public String getDescription()
   {
      return "a student majoring in " + major;
   }

   private String major;
}
```

Protected Access

As you know, fields in a class are best tagged as `private`, and methods are usually tagged as `public`. Any features declared `private` won't be visible to other classes. As we said at the beginning of this chapter, this is also true for subclasses: a subclass cannot access the private fields of its superclass.

There are times, however, when you want to restrict a method to subclasses only or, less commonly, to allow subclass methods to access a superclass field. In that case, you declare

a class feature as `protected`. For example, if the superclass `Employee` declares the `hireDay` field as `protected` instead of private, then the `Manager` methods can access it directly.

However, the `Manager` class methods can peek inside the `hireDay` field of `Manager` objects only, not of other `Employee` objects. This restriction is made so that you can't abuse the protected mechanism and form subclasses just to gain access to the protected fields.

In practice, use the `protected` attribute with caution. Suppose your class is used by other programmers and you designed it with protected fields. Unknown to you, other programmers may inherit classes from your class and then start accessing your protected fields. In this case, you can no longer change the implementation of your class without upsetting the other programmers. That is against the spirit of OOP, which encourages data encapsulation.

Protected methods make more sense. A class may declare a method as `protected` if it is tricky to use. This indicates that the subclasses (which, presumably, know their ancestors well) can be trusted to use the method correctly, but other classes cannot.

A good example of this kind of method is the `clone` method of the `Object` class—see Chapter 6 for more details.

C++ NOTE: As it happens, protected features in Java are visible to all subclasses as well as to all other classes in the same package. This is slightly different from the C++ meaning of protected, and it makes the notion of `protected` in Java even less safe than in C++.

Here is a summary of the four access modifiers in Java that control visibility:

1. Visible to the class only (`private`).
2. Visible to the world (`public`).
3. Visible to the package and all subclasses (`protected`).
4. Visible to the package—the (unfortunate) default. No modifiers are needed.

`Object`: The Cosmic Superclass

The `Object` class is the ultimate ancestor—every class in Java extends `Object`. However, you never have to write

```
class Employee extends Object
```

The ultimate superclass `Object` is taken for granted if no superclass is explicitly mentioned. Because *every* class in Java extends `Object`, it is important to be familiar with the services provided by the `Object` class. We go over the basic ones in this chapter and refer you to later chapters or to the on-line documentation for what is not covered here. (Several methods of `Object` come up only when dealing with threads—see Volume 2 for more on threads.)

You can use a variable of type `Object` to refer to objects of any type:

```
Object obj = new Employee("Harry Hacker", 35000);
```

Of course, a variable of type `Object` is only useful as a generic holder for arbitrary values. To do anything specific with the value, you need to have some knowledge about the original type and then apply a cast:

```
Employee e = (Employee) obj;
```

In Java, only the *primitive types* (numbers, characters, and `boolean` values) are not objects.

All array types, no matter whether they are arrays of objects or arrays of primitive types, are class types that extend the `Object` class.

```
Employee[] staff = new Employee[10];
obj = staff; // OK
obj = new int[10]; // OK
```

C++ NOTE: In C++, there is no cosmic root class. However, every pointer can be converted to a `void*` pointer.

The `equals` *Method*

The `equals` method in the `Object` class tests whether one object is considered equal to another. The `equals` method, as implemented in the `Object` class, determines whether two object references are identical. This is a pretty reasonable default—if two objects are identical, they should certainly be equal. For quite a few classes, nothing else is required. For example, it makes little sense to compare two `PrintStream` objects for equality. However, you will often want to implement state-based equality testing, in which two objects are considered equal when they have the same state.

For example, let us consider two employees equal if they have the same name, salary, and hire date. (In an actual employee database, it would be more sensible to compare IDs instead. We use this example to demonstrate the mechanics of implementing the `equals` method.)

```
class Employee
{  // . . .
   public boolean equals(Object otherObject)
   {
      // a quick test to see if the objects are identical
      if (this == otherObject) return true;

      // must return false if the explicit parameter is null
      if (otherObject == null) return false;

      // if the classes don't match, they can't be equal
      if (getClass() != otherObject.getClass())
         return false;

      // now we know otherObject is a non-null Employee
      Employee other = (Employee) otherObject;

      // test whether the fields have identical values
      return name.equals(other.name)
         && salary == other.salary
         && hireDay.equals(other.hireDay);
   }
}
```

The `getClass` method returns the class of an object—we discuss this method in detail later in this chapter. In our test, two objects can only be equal when they belong to the same class.

When you define the `equals` method for a subclass, first call `equals` on the superclass. If that test doesn't pass, then the objects can't be equal. If the superclass fields are equal, then you are ready to compare the instance fields of the subclass.

```
class Manager extends Employee
{
   . . .
   public boolean equals(Object otherObject)
```

```
    {
       if (!super.equals(otherObject)) return false;
       // super.equals checked that this and otherObject belong to the same class
       Manager other = (Manager) otherObject;
       return bonus == other.bonus;
    }
}
```

Equality Testing and Inheritance

How should the equals method behave if the implicit and explicit parameters don't belong to the same class? This has been an area of some controversy. In the preceding example, the equals method returns false if the classes don't match exactly. But many programmers use an instanceof test instead:

```
if (!(otherObject instanceof Employee)) return false;
```

This leaves open the possibility that otherObject can belong to a subclass. However, this approach can get you into trouble. Here is why. The Java Language Specification requires that the equals method has the following properties:

1. It is *reflexive*: for any non-null reference x, x.equals(x) should return true.
2. It is *symmetric*: for any references x and y, x.equals(y) should return true if and only if y.equals(x) returns true.
3. It is *transitive*: for any references x, y, and z, if x.equals(y) returns true and y.equals(z) returns true, then x.equals(z) should return true.
4. It is *consistent*: If the objects to which x and y refer haven't changed, then repeated calls to x.equals(y) return the same value.
5. For any non-null reference x, x.equals(null) should return false.

These rules are certainly reasonable. You wouldn't want a library implementor to ponder whether to call x.equals(y) or y.equals(x) when locating an element in a data structure.

However, the symmetry rule has subtle consequences when the parameters belong to different classes. Consider a call

```
e.equals(m)
```

where e is an Employee object and m is a Manager object, both of which happen to have the same name, salary, and hire date. If Employee.equals uses an instanceof test, the call returns true. But that means that the reverse call

```
m.equals(e)
```

also needs to return true—the symmetry rule does not allow it to return false or to throw an exception.

That leaves the Manager class in a bind. Its equals method must be willing to compare itself to any Employee, without taking manager-specific information into account! All of a sudden, the instanceof test looks less attractive!

Some authors have gone on record that the getClass test is wrong because it violates the substitution principle. A commonly cited example is the equals method in the AbstractSet class that tests whether two sets have the same elements, in the same order. The AbstractSet class has two concrete subclasses, TreeSet and HashSet, that use different algorithms for locating set elements. You really want to be able to compare any two sets, no matter how they are implemented.

However, the set example is rather specialized. It would make sense to declare AbstractSet.equals as final, because nobody should redefine the semantics of set equality. (The method is not actually `final`. This allows a subclass to implement a more efficient algorithm for the equality test.)

The way we see it, there are two distinct scenarios.

- If subclasses can have their own notion of equality, then the symmetry requirement forces you to use the `getClass` test.
- If the notion of equality is fixed in the superclass, then you can use the `instanceof` test and allow objects of different subclasses to be equal to another.

In the example of the employees and managers, we consider two objects to be equal when they have matching fields. If we have two `Manager` objects with the same name, salary, and hire date, but with different bonuses, we want them to be different. Therefore, we used the `getClass` test.

But suppose we used an employee ID for equality testing. This notion of equality makes sense for all subclasses. Then we could use the `instanceof` test, and we should declare `Employee.equals` as `final`.

Here is a recipe for writing the perfect `equals` method:

1. Name the explicit parameter `otherObject`—later, you need to cast it to another variable that you should call `other`.
2. Test whether `this` happens to be identical to `otherObject`:
   ```
   if (this == otherObject) return true;
   ```
   This statement is just an optimization. In practice, this is a common case. It is much cheaper to check for identity than to compare the fields.
3. Test whether `otherObject` is `null` and return `false` if it is. This test is required.
   ```
   if (otherObject == null) return false;
   ```
   Compare the classes of `this` and `otherObject`. If the semantics of `equals` can change in subclasses, use the `getClass` test:
   ```
   if (getClass() != otherObject.getClass()) return false;
   ```
   If the same semantics holds for *all* subclasses, you can use an `instanceof` test:
   ```
   if (!(otherObject instanceof ClassName)) return false;
   ```
4. Cast `otherObject` to a variable of your class type:
   ```
   ClassName other = (ClassName) otherObject
   ```
5. Now compare the fields, as required by your notion of equality. Use `==` for primitive type fields, `equals` for object fields. Return `true` if all fields match, `false` otherwise.
   ```
   return field1 == other.field1
      && field2.equals(other.field2)
      && . . .;
   ```
   If you redefine `equals` in a subclass, include a call to `super.equals(other)`.

NOTE: The standard Java library contains over 150 implementations of `equals` methods, with a mishmash of using `instanceof`, calling `getClass`, catching a `ClassCastException`, or doing nothing at all. Judging from this evidence, it does not appear as if all programmers have a clear understanding of the subtleties of the `equals` method. For example, `Rectangle` is a subclass of `Rectangle2D`. Both classes define an `equals` method with an `instanceof` test. Comparing a `Rectangle2D` with a `Rectangle` that has the same coordinates yields `true`, flipping the parameters yields `false`.

CAUTION: Here is a common mistake when implementing the `equals` method. Can you spot the problem?

```
public class Employee
{
   public boolean equals(Employee other)
   {
      return name.equals(other.name)
         && salary == other.salary
         && hireDay.equals(other.hireDay);
   }
   . . .
}
```

This method declares the explicit parameter type as `Employee`. As a result, it does not override the `equals` method of the `Object` class but defines a completely unrelated method.

Starting with JDK 5.0, you can protect yourself against this type of error by tagging methods that are intended to override superclass methods with `@Override`:

```
@Override public boolean equals(Object other)
```

If you made a mistake and you are defining a new method, the compiler reports an error. For example, suppose you add the following declaration to the `Employee` class.

```
@Override public boolean equals(Employee other)
```

An error is reported because this method doesn't override any method from the `Object` superclass.

The `@Override` tag is a *metadata* tag. The metadata mechanism is very general and extensible, allowing compilers and tools to carry out arbitrary actions. Time will tell whether tool builders take advantage of this mechanism. In JDK 5.0, the compiler implementors decided to blaze the trail with the `@Override` tag.

The `hashCode` *Method*

A hash code is an integer that is derived from an object. Hash codes should be scrambled—if `x` and `y` are two distinct objects, there should be a high probability that `x.hashCode()` and `y.hashCode()` are different. Table 5–1 lists a few examples of hash codes that result from the `hashCode` method of the `String` class.

Table 5–1: Hash Codes Resulting from the `hashCode` Function

String	Hash Code
`Hello`	140207504
`Harry`	140013338
`Hacker`	884756206

The `String` class uses the following algorithm to compute the hash code:

```
int hash = 0;
for (int i = 0; i < length(); i++)
   hash = 31 * hash + charAt(i);
```

The `hashCode` method is defined in the `Object` class. Therefore, every object has a default hash code. That hash code is derived from the object's memory address. Consider this example.

```
String s = "Ok";
StringBuffer sb = new StringBuffer(s);
System.out.println(s.hashCode() + " " + sb.hashCode());
```

```
String t = new String("Ok");
StringBuffer tb = new StringBuffer(t);
System.out.println(t.hashCode() + " " + tb.hashCode());
```

Table 5–2 shows the result.

Table 5–2: Hash Codes of Strings and String Buffers

Object	Hash Code
s	3030
sb	20526976
t	3030
tb	20527144

Note that the strings s and t have the same hash code because, for strings, the hash codes are derived from their *contents.* The string buffers sb and tb have different hash codes because no hashCode method has been defined for the StringBuffer class, and the default hashCode method in the Object class derives the hash code from the object's memory address.

If you redefine the equals method, you will also need to redefine the hashCode method for objects that users might insert into a hash table. (We discuss hash tables in Chapter 2 of Volume 2.)

The hashCode method should return an integer (which can be negative). Just combine the hash codes of the instance fields so that the hash codes for different objects are likely to be widely scattered.

For example, here is a hashCode method for the Employee class.

```
class Employee
{
   public int hashCode()
   {
      return 7 * name.hashCode()
         + 11 * new Double(salary).hashCode()
         + 13 * hireDay.hashCode();
   }
   . . .
}
```

Your definitions of equals and hashCode must be compatible: if x.equals(y) is true, then x.hashCode() must be the same value as y.hashCode(). For example, if you define Employee.equals to compare employee IDs, then the hashCode method needs to hash the IDs, not employee names or memory addresses.

java.lang.Object 1.0

- int hashCode()
  returns a hash code for this object. A hash code can be any integer, positive or negative. Equal objects need to return identical hash codes.

The toString Method

Another important method in Object is the toString method that returns a string representing the value of this object. Here is a typical example. The toString method of the Point class returns a string like this:

```
java.awt.Point[x=10,y=20]
```

Most (but not all) toString methods follow this format: the name of the class, followed by the field values enclosed in square brackets. Here is an implementation of the toString method for the Employee class:

```
public String toString()
{
   return "Employee[name=" + name
      + ",salary=" + salary
      + ",hireDay=" + hireDay
      + "]";
}
```

Actually, you can do a little better. Rather than hardwiring the class name into the toString method, call getClass().getName() to obtain a string with the class name.

```
public String toString()
{
   return getClass().getName()
      + "[name=" + name
      + ",salary=" + salary
      + ",hireDay=" + hireDay
      + "]";
}
```

The toString method then also works for subclasses.

Of course, the subclass programmer should define its own toString method and add the subclass fields. If the superclass uses getClass().getName(), then the subclass can simply call super.toString(). For example, here is a toString method for the Manager class:

```
class Manager extends Employee
{
   . . .
   public String toString()
   {
      return super.toString()
        + "[bonus=" + bonus
        + "]";
   }
}
```

Now a Manager object is printed as

```
Manager[name=...,salary=...,hireDay=...][bonus=...]
```

The toString method is ubiquitous for an important reason: whenever an object is concatenated with a string by the "+" operator, the Java compiler automatically invokes the toString method to obtain a string representation of the object. For example,

```
Point p = new Point(10, 20);
String message = "The current position is " + p;
   // automatically invokes p.toString()
```

TIP: Instead of writing x.toString(), you can write "" + x. This statement concatenates the empty string with the string representation of x that is exactly x.toString(). Unlike toString, this statement even works if x is of primitive type.

If x is any object and you call

```
System.out.println(x);
```

then the println method simply calls x.toString() and prints the resulting string.

The Object class defines the toString method to print the class name and the hash code of the object. For example, the call

```
System.out.println(System.out)
```

produces an output that looks like this:

```
java.io.PrintStream@2f6684
```

The reason is that the implementor of the PrintStream class didn't bother to override the toString method.

The toString method is a great tool for logging. Many classes in the standard class library define the toString method so that you can get useful information about the state of an object. This is particularly useful in logging messages like this:

```
System.out.println("Current position = " + position);
```

As we explain in Chapter 11, an even better solution is

```
Logger.global.info("Current position = " + position);
```

TIP: We strongly recommend that you add a toString method to each class that you write. You, as well as other programmers who use your classes, will be grateful for the logging support.

The program in Example 5–3 implements the equals, hashCode, and toString methods for the Employee and Manager classes.

Example 5–3: EqualsTest.java

```
import java.util.*;

public class EqualsTest
{
   public static void main(String[] args)
   {
      Employee alice1 = new Employee("Alice Adams", 75000, 1987, 12, 15);
      Employee alice2 = alice1;
      Employee alice3 = new Employee("Alice Adams", 75000, 1987, 12, 15);
      Employee bob = new Employee("Bob Brandson", 50000, 1989, 10, 1);

      System.out.println("alice1 == alice2: " + (alice1 == alice2));

      System.out.println("alice1 == alice3: " + (alice1 == alice3));

      System.out.println("alice1.equals(alice3): " + alice1.equals(alice3));

      System.out.println("alice1.equals(bob): " + alice1.equals(bob));

      System.out.println("bob.toString(): " + bob);

      Manager carl = new Manager("Carl Cracker", 80000, 1987, 12, 15);
      Manager boss = new Manager("Carl Cracker", 80000, 1987, 12, 15);
      boss.setBonus(5000);
      System.out.println("boss.toString(): " + boss);
      System.out.println("carl.equals(boss): "  + carl.equals(boss));
      System.out.println("alice1.hashCode(): " + alice1.hashCode());
      System.out.println("alice3.hashCode(): " + alice3.hashCode());
      System.out.println("bob.hashCode(): " + bob.hashCode());
      System.out.println("carl.hashCode(): " + carl.hashCode());
```

```
   }
}

class Employee
{
   public Employee(String n, double s,
      int year, int month, int day)
   {
      name = n;
      salary = s;
      GregorianCalendar calendar = new GregorianCalendar(year, month - 1, day);
      hireDay = calendar.getTime();
   }

   public String getName()
   {
      return name;
   }

   public double getSalary()
   {
      return salary;
   }

   public Date getHireDay()
   {
      return hireDay;
   }

   public void raiseSalary(double byPercent)
   {
      double raise = salary * byPercent / 100;
      salary += raise;
   }

   public boolean equals(Object otherObject)
   {
      // a quick test to see if the objects are identical
      if (this == otherObject) return true;

      // must return false if the explicit parameter is null
      if (otherObject == null) return false;

      // if the classes don't match, they can't be equal
      if (getClass() != otherObject.getClass())
         return false;

      // now we know otherObject is a non-null Employee
      Employee other = (Employee) otherObject;

      // test whether the fields have identical values
      return name.equals(other.name)
         && salary == other.salary
         && hireDay.equals(other.hireDay);
   }

```

```
   public int hashCode()
   {
      return 7 * name.hashCode()
         + 11 * new Double(salary).hashCode()
         + 13 * hireDay.hashCode();
   }

   public String toString()
   {
      return getClass().getName()
         + "[name=" + name
         + ",salary=" + salary
         + ",hireDay=" + hireDay
         + "]";
   }

   private String name;
   private double salary;
   private Date hireDay;
}

class Manager extends Employee
{
   public Manager(String n, double s,
      int year, int month, int day)
   {
      super(n, s, year, month, day);
      bonus = 0;
   }

   public double getSalary()
   {
      double baseSalary = super.getSalary();
      return baseSalary + bonus;
   }

   public void setBonus(double b)
   {
      bonus = b;
   }

   public boolean equals(Object otherObject)
   {
      if (!super.equals(otherObject)) return false;
      Manager other = (Manager) otherObject;
      // super.equals checked that this and other belong to the
      // same class
      return bonus == other.bonus;
   }

   public int hashCode()
   {
      return super.hashCode()
         + 17 * new Double(bonus).hashCode();
   }

```

```
    public String toString()
    {
       return super.toString()
         + "[bonus=" + bonus
         + "]";
    }

    private double bonus;
}
```

java.lang.Object 1.0

- `Class getClass()`
  returns a class object that contains information about the object. As you see later in this chapter, Java has a runtime representation for classes that is encapsulated in the `Class` class.
- `boolean equals(Object otherObject)`
  compares two objects for equality; returns `true` if the objects point to the same area of memory, and `false` otherwise. You should override this method in your own classes.
- `String toString()`
  returns a string that represents the value of this object. You should override this method in your own classes.
- `Object clone()`
  creates a clone of the object. The Java runtime system allocates memory for the new instance and copies the memory allocated for the current object.

NOTE: Cloning an object is important, but it also turns out to be a fairly subtle process filled with potential pitfalls for the unwary. We will have a lot more to say about the `clone` method in Chapter 6.

java.lang.Class 1.0

- `String getName()`
  returns the name of this class.
- `Class getSuperclass()`
  returns the superclass of this class as a `Class` object.

Generic Array Lists

In many programming languages—in particular, in C—you have to fix the sizes of all arrays at compile time. Programmers hate this because it forces them into uncomfortable trade-offs. How many employees will be in a department? Surely no more than 100. What if there is a humongous department with 150 employees? Do we want to waste 90 entries for every department with just 10 employees?

In Java, the situation is much better. You can set the size of an array at run time.

```
int actualSize = . . .;
Employee[] staff = new Employee[actualSize];
```

Of course, this code does not completely solve the problem of dynamically modifying arrays at run time. Once you set the array size, you cannot change it easily. Instead, the easiest way in Java to deal with this common situation is to use another Java class, classed

ArrayList. The ArrayList class is similar to an array, but it automatically adjusts its capacity as you add and remove elements, without your needing to write any code.

As of JDK 5.0, ArrayList is a *generic class* with a *type parameter*. To specify the type of the element objects that the array list holds, you append a class name enclosed in angle brackets, such as ArrayList<Employee>. You will see in Chapter 13 how to define your own generic class, but you don't need to know any of those technicalities to use the ArrayList type.

Here we declare and construct an array list that holds Employee objects:

```
ArrayList<Employee> staff = new ArrayList<Employee>();
```

NOTE: Before JDK 5.0, there were no generic classes. Instead, there was a single ArrayList class, a "one size fits all" collection that holds elements of type Object. If you must use an older version of Java, simply drop all <...> suffixes. You can still use ArrayList without a <...> suffix in JDK 5.0 and beyond. It is considered a "raw" type, with the type parameter erased.

NOTE: In even older versions of the Java programming language, programmers used the Vector class for dynamic arrays. However, the ArrayList class is more efficient, and there is no longer any good reason to use the Vector class.

You use the add method to add new elements to an array list. For example, here is how you populate an array list with employee objects:

```
staff.add(new Employee("Harry Hacker", . . .));
staff.add(new Employee("Tony Tester", . . .));
```

The array list manages an internal array of object references. Eventually, that array will run out of space. This is where array lists work their magic: If you call add and the internal array is full, the array list automatically creates a bigger array and copies all the objects from the smaller to the bigger array.

If you already know, or have a good guess, how many elements you want to store, then call the ensureCapacity method before filling the array list:

```
staff.ensureCapacity(100);
```

That call allocates an internal array of 100 objects. Then the first 100 calls to add do not involve any costly relocation.

You can also pass an initial capacity to the ArrayList constructor:

```
ArrayList<Employee> staff = new ArrayList<Employee>(100);
```

CAUTION: Allocating an array list as

```
new ArrayList<Employee>(100) // capacity is 100
```

is *not* the same as allocating a new array as

```
new Employee[100] // size is 100
```

There is an important distinction between the capacity of an array list and the size of an array. If you allocate an array with 100 entries, then the array has 100 slots, ready for use. An array list with a capacity of 100 elements has the *potential* of holding 100 elements (and, in fact, more than 100, at the cost of additional relocations), but at the beginning, even after its initial construction, an array list holds no elements at all.

The `size` method returns the actual number of elements in the array list. For example,

```
staff.size()
```

returns the current number of elements in the `staff` array list. This is the equivalent of

```
a.length
```

for an array `a`.

Once you are reasonably sure that the array list is at its permanent size, you can call the `trimToSize` method. This method adjusts the size of the memory block to use exactly as much storage space as is required to hold the current number of elements. The garbage collector will reclaim any excess memory.

Once you trim the size of an array list, adding new elements will move the block again, which takes time. You should only use `trimToSize` when you are sure you won't add any more elements to the array list.

C++ NOTE: The `ArrayList` class is similar to the C++ `vector` template. Both `ArrayList` and `vector` are generic types. But the C++ `vector` template overloads the `[]` operator for convenient element access. Because Java does not have operator overloading, it must use explicit method calls instead. Moreover, C++ vectors are copied by value. If `a` and `b` are two vectors, then the assignment `a = b` makes `a` into a new vector with the same length as `b`, and all elements are copied from `b` to `a`. The same assignment in Java makes both `a` and `b` refer to the same array list.

`java.util.ArrayList<T>` 1.2

- `ArrayList<T>()`
  constructs an empty array list.
- `ArrayList<T>(int initialCapacity)`
  constructs an empty array list with the specified capacity.

  Parameters: `initialCapacity` the initial storage capacity of the array list
- `boolean add(T obj)`
  appends an element at the end of the array list. Always returns `true`.

  Parameters: `obj` the element to be added
- `int size()`
  returns the number of elements currently stored in the array list. (This is different from, and, of course, never larger than, the array list's capacity.)
- `void ensureCapacity(int capacity)`
  ensures that the array list has the capacity to store the given number of elements without relocating its internal storage array.

  Parameters: `capacity` the desired storage capacity
- `void trimToSize()`
  reduces the storage capacity of the array list to its current size.

Accessing Array List Elements

Unfortunately, nothing comes for free. The automatic growth convenience that array lists give requires a more complicated syntax for accessing the elements. The reason is that the `ArrayList` class is not a part of the Java programming language; it is just a utility class programmed by someone and supplied in the standard library.

Instead of using the pleasant [] syntax to access or change the element of an array, you use the get and set methods.

For example, to set the ith element, you use

```
staff.set(i, harry);
```

This is equivalent to

```
a[i] = harry;
```

for an array a. (As with arrays, the index values are zero-based.)

To get an array list element, use

```
Employee e = staff.get(i);
```

This is equivalent to

```
Employee e = a[i];
```

As of JDK 5.0, you can use the "for each" loop for array lists:

```
for (Employee e : staff)
   // do something with e
```

In legacy code, the same loop would be written as

```
for (int i = 0; i < staff.size(); i++)
{
   Employee e = (Employee) staff.get(i);
   do something with e
}
```

NOTE: Before JDK 5.0, there were no generic classes, and the get method of the raw ArrayList class had no choice but to return an Object. Consequently, callers of get had to cast the returned value to the desired type:

```
Employee e = (Employee) staff.get(i);
```

The raw ArrayList is also a bit dangerous. Its add and set methods accept objects of any type. A call

```
staff.set(i, new Date());
```

compiles without so much as a warning, and you run into grief only when you retrieve the object and try to cast it. If you use an ArrayList<Employee> instead, the compiler will detect this error.

TIP: You can sometimes get the best of both worlds—flexible growth and convenient element access—with the following trick. First, make an array list and add all the elements.

```
ArrayList<X> list = new ArrayList<X>();
while (. . .)
{
   x = . . .;
   list.add(x);
}
```

When you are done, use the toArray method to copy the elements into an array.

```
X[] a = new X[list.size()];
list.toArray(a);
```

CAUTION: Do not call `list.set(i, x)` until the *size* of the array list is larger than `i`. For example, the following code is wrong:

```
ArrayList<Employee> list = new ArrayList<Employee>(100); // capacity 100, size 0
list.set(0, x); // no element 0 yet
```

Use the `add` method instead of `set` to fill up an array, and use `set` only to replace a previously added element.

Instead of appending elements at the end of an array list, you can also insert them in the middle.

```
int n = staff.size() / 2;
staff.add(n, e);
```

The elements at locations `n` and above are shifted up to make room for the new entry. If the new size of the array list after the insertion exceeds the capacity, then the array list reallocates its storage array.

Similarly, you can remove an element from the middle of an array list.

```
Employee e = staff.remove(n);
```

The elements located above it are copied down, and the size of the array is reduced by one.

Inserting and removing elements is not terribly efficient. It is probably not worth worrying about for small array lists. But if you store many elements and frequently insert and remove in the middle of a collection, consider using a linked list instead. We explain how to program with linked lists in Volume 2.

Example 5–4 is a modification of the `EmployeeTest` program of Chapter 4. The `Employee[]` array is replaced by an `ArrayList<Employee>`. Note the following changes:

- You don't have to specify the array size.
- You use `add` to add as many elements as you like.
- You use `size()` instead of `length` to count the number of elements.
- You use `a.get(i)` instead of `a[i]` to access an element.

Example 5–4: ArrayListTest.java

```
import java.util.*;

public class ArrayListTest
{
   public static void main(String[] args)
   {
      // fill the staff array list with three Employee objects
      ArrayList<Employee> staff = new ArrayList<Employee>();

      staff.add(new Employee("Carl Cracker", 75000, 1987, 12, 15));
      staff.add(new Employee("Harry Hacker", 50000, 1989, 10, 1));
      staff.add(new Employee("Tony Tester", 40000, 1990, 3, 15));

      // raise everyone's salary by 5%
      for (Employee e : staff)
         e.raiseSalary(5);

      // print out information about all Employee objects
      for (Employee e : staff)
         System.out.println("name=" + e.getName()
```

```
            + ",salary=" + e.getSalary()
            + ",hireDay=" + e.getHireDay());
   }
}

class Employee
{
   public Employee(String n, double s, int year, int month, int day)
   {
      name = n;
      salary = s;
      GregorianCalendar calendar = new GregorianCalendar(year, month - 1, day);
      hireDay = calendar.getTime();
   }

   public String getName()
   {
      return name;
   }

   public double getSalary()
   {
      return salary;
   }

   public Date getHireDay()
   {
      return hireDay;
   }

   public void raiseSalary(double byPercent)
   {
      double raise = salary * byPercent / 100;
      salary += raise;
   }

   private String name;
   private double salary;
   private Date hireDay;
}
```

API **java.util.ArrayList<T>** 1.2

- `void set(int index, T obj)`
  puts a value in the array list at the specified index, overwriting the previous contents.

Parameters:	`index`	the position (must be between `0` and `size()` − 1)
	`obj`	the new value

- `T get(int index)`
  gets the value stored at a specified index.

Parameters:	`index`	the index of the element to get (must be between `0` and `size()` − 1)

- `void add(int index, T obj)`
  shifts up elements to insert an element.

  Parameters: `index` the insertion position (must be between `0` and `size()`)
  `obj` the new element

- `T remove(int index)`
  removes an element and shifts down all elements above it. The removed element is returned.

  Parameters: `index` the position of the element to be removed (must be between `0` and `size() − 1`)

Compatibility Between Typed and Raw Array Lists

When you write new code with JDK 5.0 and beyond, you should use type parameters, such as `ArrayList<Employee>`, for array lists. However, you may need to interoperate with existing code that uses the raw `ArrayList` type.

Suppose that you have the following legacy class:

```
public class EmployeeDB
{
   public void update(ArrayList list) { ... }
   public ArrayList find(String query) { ... }
}
```

You can pass a typed array list to the `update` method without any casts.

```
ArrayList<Employee> staff = ...;
employeeDB.update(staff);
```

The `staff` object is simply passed to the `update` method.

CAUTION: Even though you get no error or warning from the compiler, this call is not completely safe. The `update` method might add elements into the array list that are not of type `Employee`. When these elements are retrieved, an exception occurs. This sounds scary, but if you think about it, the behavior is simply as it was before JDK 5.0. The integrity of the virtual machine is never jeopardized. In this situation, you do not lose security, but you also do not benefit from the compile-time checks.

Conversely, when you assign a raw `ArrayList` to a typed one, you get a warning.

```
ArrayList<Employee> result = employeeDB.find(query); // yields warning
```

NOTE: To see the text of the warning, compile with the option `-Xlint:unchecked`.

Using a cast does not make the warning go away.

```
ArrayList<Employee> result = (ArrayList<Employee>) employeeDB.find(query); // yields another warning
```

Instead, you get a different warning, telling you that the cast is misleading.

This is the consequence of a somewhat unfortunate limitation of parameterized types in Java. For compatibility, the compiler translates all typed array lists into raw `ArrayList` objects after checking that the type rules were not violated. In a running program, all array lists are the same—there are no type parameters in the virtual machine. Thus, the casts `(ArrayList)` and `(ArrayList<Employee>)` carry out identical runtime checks.

There isn't much you can do about that situation. When you interact with legacy code, study the compiler warnings and satisfy yourself that the warnings are not serious.

Object Wrappers and Autoboxing

Occasionally, you need to convert a primitive type like `int` to an object. All primitive types have class counterparts. For example, a class `Integer` corresponds to the primitive type `int`. These kinds of classes are usually called *wrappers*. The wrapper classes have obvious names: `Integer`, `Long`, `Float`, `Double`, `Short`, `Byte`, `Character`, `Void`, and `Boolean`. (The first six inherit from the common superclass `Number`.) The wrapper classes are immutable—you cannot change a wrapped value after the wrapper has been constructed. They are also `final`, so you cannot subclass them.

Suppose we want an array list of integers. Unfortunately, the type parameter inside the angle brackets cannot be a primitive type. It is not possible to form an `ArrayList<int>`. Here, the `Integer` wrapper class comes in. It is ok to declare an array list of `Integer` objects.

```
ArrayList<Integer> list = new ArrayList<Integer>();
```

CAUTION: An `ArrayList<Integer>` is far less efficient than an `int[]` array because each value is separately wrapped inside an object. You would only want to use this construct for small collections when programmer convenience is more important than efficiency.

Another JDK 5.0 innovation makes it easy to add and get array elements: The call

```
list.add(3);
```

is automatically translated to

```
list.add(new Integer(3));
```

This conversion is called *autoboxing*.

NOTE: You might think that *autowrapping* would be more consistent, but the "boxing" metaphor was taken from C#.

Conversely, when you assign an `Integer` object to an `int` value, it is automatically unboxed. That is, the compiler translates

```
int n = list.get(i);
```

into

```
int n = list.get(i).intValue();
```

Automatic boxing and unboxing even works with arithmetic expressions. For example, you can apply the increment operator to a wrapper reference:

```
Integer n = 3;
n++;
```

The compiler automatically inserts instructions to unbox the object, increment the resulting value, and box it back.

In most cases, you get the illusion that the primitive types and their wrappers are one and the same. There is just one point in which they differ considerably: identity. As you know, the `==` operator, applied to wrapper objects, only tests whether the objects have identical memory locations. The following comparison would therefore probably fail:

```
Integer a = 1000;
Integer b = 1000;
```

```
if (a == b) ...
```

However, a Java implementation *may,* if it chooses, wrap commonly occurring values into identical objects, and thus the comparison might succeed. This ambiguity is not what you want. The remedy is to call the `equals` method when comparing wrapper objects.

NOTE: The autoboxing specification requires that `boolean`, `byte`, `char` ≤ 127, and `short` and `int` between −128 and 127 are wrapped into fixed objects. For example, if `a` and `b` had been initialized with 100 in the preceding example, then the comparison would have had to succeed.

Finally, let us emphasize that boxing and unboxing is a courtesy of the *compiler,* not the virtual machine. The compiler inserts the necessary calls when it generates the bytecodes of a class. The virtual machine simply executes those bytecodes.

The wrapper classes exist since JDK 1.0, but before JDK 5.0, you had to insert the boxing and unboxing code by hand.

You will often see the number wrappers for another reason. The designers of Java found the wrappers a convenient place to put certain basic methods, like the ones for converting strings of digits to numbers.

To convert a string to an integer, you use the following statement:

```
int x = Integer.parseInt(s);
```

This has nothing to do with `Integer` objects—`parseInt` is a static method. But the `Integer` class was a good place to put it.

The API notes show some of the more important methods of the `Integer` class. The other number classes implement corresponding methods.

CAUTION: Some people think that the wrapper classes can be used to implement methods that can modify numeric parameters. However, that is not correct. Recall from Chapter 4 that it is impossible to write a Java method that increments an integer parameter because parameters to Java methods are always passed by value.

```
public static void triple(int x) // won't work
{
   x = 3 * x; // modifies local variable
}
```

Could we overcome this by using an `Integer` instead of an int?

```
public static void triple(Integer x) // won't work
{
   ...
}
```

The problem is that `Integer` objects are *immutable*: the information contained inside the wrapper can't change. You cannot use these wrapper classes to create a method that modifies numeric parameters.

NOTE: If you do want to write a method to change numeric parameters, you can use one of the *holder* types defined in the `org.omg.CORBA` package. There are types `IntHolder`, `BooleanHolder`, and so on. Each holder type has a public (!) field `value` through which you can access the stored value.

```
public static void triple(IntHolder x)
{
   x.value = 3 * x.value;
}
```

java.lang.Integer 1.0

- `int intValue()`
  returns the value of this `Integer` object as an `int` (overrides the `intValue` method in the `Number` class).
- `static String toString(int i)`
  returns a new `String` object representing the number `i` in base 10.
- `static String toString(int i, int radix)`
  lets you return a representation of the number `i` in the base specified by the `radix` parameter.
- `static int parseInt(String s)`
  returns the integer value of the string `s`, assuming it represents an integer in base 10.
- `static int parseInt(String s, int radix)`
  returns the integer value of the string `s`, assuming it represents an integer in the base specified by the `radix` parameter.
- `static Integer valueOf(String s)`
  returns a new `Integer` object initialized to the integer's value, assuming the specified `String` represents an integer in base 10.
- `static Integer valueOf(String s, int radix)`
  returns a new `Integer` object initialized to the integer's value, assuming the specified `String` represents an integer in the base specified by the `radix` parameter.

java.text.NumberFormat 1.1

- `Number parse(String s)`
  returns the numeric value, assuming the specified `String` represents a number.

Methods with a Variable Number of Parameters

Before JDK 5.0, every Java method had a fixed number of parameters. However, it is now possible to provide methods that can be called with a variable number of parameters. (These are sometimes called "varargs" methods.)

You have already seen such a method: `printf`. For example, the calls

```
System.out.printf("%d", n);
```

and

```
System.out.printf("%d %s", n, "widgets");
```

both call the same method, even though one call has two parameters and the other has three.

The `printf` method is defined like this:

```
public class PrintStream
{
   public PrintStream printf(String fmt, Object... args) { return format(fmt, args); }
}
```

Here, the ellipsis `...` is a part of the Java code. It denotes that the method can receive an arbitrary number of objects (in addition to the `fmt` parameter).

The `printf` method actually receives two parameters, the format string, and an `Object[]` array that holds all other parameters. (If the caller supplies integers or other primitive type values, autoboxing turns them into objects.) It now has the unenviable task of scanning the `fmt` string and matching up the `i`th format specifier with the value `args[i]`.

In other words, for the implementor of `printf`, the `Object...` parameter type is exactly the same as `Object[]`.

The compiler needs to transform each call to `printf`, bundling the parameters into an array and autoboxing as necessary:

```
System.out.printf("%d %d", new Object[] { new Integer(d), "widgets" } );
```

You can define your own methods with variable parameters, and you can specify any type for the parameters, even a primitive type. Here is a simple example: a function that computes the maximum of a variable number of values.

```
public static double max(double... values)
{
   double largest = Double.MIN_VALUE;
   for (double v : values) if (v > largest) largest = v;
   return largest;
}
```

Simply call the function like this:

```
double m = max(3.1, 40.4, -5);
```

The compiler passes a `new double[] { 3.1, 40.4, -5 }` to the `max` function.

NOTE: It is legal to pass an array as the last parameter of a method with variable parameters, for example

```
System.out.printf("%d %s", new Object[] { new Integer(1), "widgets" } );
```

Therefore, you can redefine an existing function whose last parameter is an array to a method with variable parameters, without breaking any existing code. For example, `MessageFormat.format` was enhanced in this way in JDK 5.0.

Reflection

The *reflection library* gives you a very rich and elaborate toolset to write programs that manipulate Java code dynamically. This feature is heavily used in *JavaBeans*, the component architecture for Java (see Volume 2 for more on JavaBeans). Using reflection, Java can support tools like the ones to which users of Visual Basic have grown accustomed. In particular, when new classes are added at design or run time, rapid application development tools can dynamically inquire about the capabilities of the classes that were added.

A program that can analyze the capabilities of classes is called *reflective*. The reflection mechanism is extremely powerful. As the next sections show, you can use it to

- Analyze the capabilities of classes at run time;
- Inspect objects at run time, for example, to write a single `toString` method that works for *all* classes;
- Implement generic array manipulation code; and
- Take advantage of `Method` objects that work just like function pointers in languages such as C++.

Reflection is a powerful and complex mechanism; however, it is of interest mainly to tool builders, not application programmers. If you are interested in programming applications rather than tools for other Java programmers, you can safely skip the remainder of this chapter and return to it later.

The `Class` Class

While your program is running, the Java runtime system always maintains what is called runtime type identification on all objects. This information keeps track of the class to which each object belongs. Runtime type information is used by the virtual machine to select the correct methods to execute.

However, you can also access this information by working with a special Java class. The class that holds this information is called, somewhat confusingly, `Class`. The `getClass()` method in the `Object` class returns an instance of `Class` type.

```
Employee e;
. . .
Class cl = e.getClass();
```

Just like an `Employee` object describes the properties of a particular employee, a `Class` object describes the properties of a particular class. Probably the most commonly used method of `Class` is `getName`. This returns the name of the class. For example, the statement

```
System.out.println(e.getClass().getName() + " " + e.getName());
```

prints

```
Employee Harry Hacker
```

if `e` is an employee, or

```
Manager Harry Hacker
```

if `e` is a manager.

You can also obtain a `Class` object corresponding to a string by using the static `forName` method.

```
String className = "java.util.Date";
Class cl = Class.forName(className);
```

You would use this method if the class name is stored in a string that varies at run time. This works if `className` is the name of a class or interface. Otherwise, the `forName` method throws a *checked exception*. See the sidebar "Catching Exceptions" on page 191 to see how to supply an *exception handler* whenever you use this method.

TIP: At startup, the class containing your `main` method is loaded. It loads all classes that it needs. Each of those loaded classes loads the classes that it needs, and so on. That can take a long time for a big application, frustrating the user. You can give users of your program the illusion of a faster start with the following trick. Make sure that the class containing the `main` method does not explicitly refer to other classes. First display a splash screen. Then manually force the loading of other classes by calling `Class.forName`.

A third method for obtaining an object of type `Class` is a convenient shorthand. If `T` is any Java type, then `T.class` is the matching class object. For example:

```
Class cl1 = Date.class; // if you import java.util.*;
Class cl2 = int.class;
Class cl3 = Double[].class;
```

Note that a `Class` object really describes a *type*, which may or may not be a class. For example, `int` is not a class, but `int.class` is nevertheless an object of type `Class`.

NOTE: As of JDK 5.0, the `Class` class is parameterized. For example, `Employee.class` is of type `Class<Employee>`. We are not dwelling on this issue because it would further complicate an already abstract concept. For most practical purposes, you can ignore the type parameter and work with the raw `Class` type. See Chapter 13 for more information on this issue.

CAUTION: For historical reasons, the `getName` method returns somewhat strange names for array types:

- `Double[].class.getName()` returns `"[Ljava.lang.Double;"`.
- `int[].class.getName()` returns `"[I"`.

The virtual machine manages a unique `Class` object for each type. Therefore, you can use the `==` operator to compare class objects, for example,

```
if (e.getClass() == Employee.class) . . .
```

Another example of a useful method is one that lets you create an instance of a class on the fly. This method is called, naturally enough, `newInstance()`. For example,

```
e.getClass().newInstance();
```

creates a new instance of the same class type as `e`. The `newInstance` method calls the default constructor (the one that takes no parameters) to initialize the newly created object. An exception is thrown if the class has no default constructor.

Using a combination of `forName` and `newInstance` lets you create an object from a class name stored in a string.

```
String s = "java.util.Date";
Object m = Class.forName(s).newInstance();
```

NOTE: If you need to provide parameters for the constructor of a class you want to create by name in this manner, then you can't use statements like the above. Instead, you must use the `newInstance` method in the `Constructor` class. (This is one of several classes in the `java.lang.reflect` package. We discuss reflection in the next section.)

C++ NOTE: The `newInstance` method corresponds to the idiom of a *virtual constructor* in C++. However, virtual constructors in C++ are not a language feature but just an idiom that needs to be supported by a specialized library. The `Class` class is similar to the `type_info` class in C++, and the `getClass` method is equivalent to the `typeid` operator. The Java `Class` is quite a bit more versatile than `type_info`, though. The C++ `type_info` can only reveal a string with the name of the type, not create new objects of that type.

Catching Exceptions

We cover exception handling fully in Chapter 11, but in the meantime you will occasionally encounter methods that threaten to throw exceptions.

When an error occurs at run time, a program can "throw an exception." Throwing an exception is more flexible than terminating the program because you can provide a *handler* that "catches" the exception and deals with it.

If you don't provide a handler, the program still terminates and prints a message to the console, giving the type of the exception. You may already have seen exception reports when you accidentally used a `null` reference or overstepped the bounds of an array.

There are two kinds of exceptions: *unchecked* exceptions and *checked* exceptions. With checked exceptions, the compiler checks that you provide a handler. However, many common exceptions, such as accessing a `null` reference, are unchecked. The compiler does not check whether you provide a handler for these errors—after all, you should spend your mental energy on avoiding these mistakes rather than coding handlers for them.

But not all errors are avoidable. If an exception can occur despite your best efforts, then the compiler insists that you provide a handler. The `Class.forName` method is an example of a method that throws a checked exception. In Chapter 11, you will see several exception handling strategies. For now, we just show you the simplest handler implementation.

Place one or more methods that might throw checked exceptions inside a `try` block. Then provide the handler code in the `catch` clause.

```
try
{
   statements that might throw exceptions
}
catch(Exception e)
{
   handler action
}
```

Here is an example:

```
try
{  String name = . . .; // get class name
   Class cl = Class.forName(name); // might throw exception
   . . . // do something with cl
}
catch(Exception e)
{
   e.printStackTrace();
}
```

If the class name doesn't exist, the remainder of the code in the `try` block is skipped and the program enters the `catch` clause. (Here, we print a stack trace by using the `printStackTrace` method of the `Throwable` class. `Throwable` is the superclass of the `Exception` class.) If none of the methods in the `try` block throws an exception, then the handler code in the `catch` clause is skipped.

You only need to supply an exception handler for checked exceptions. It is easy to find out which methods throw checked exceptions—the compiler will complain whenever you call a method that threatens to throw a checked exception and you don't supply a handler.

`java.lang.Class` 1.0

- `static Class forName(String className)`
  returns the `Class` object representing the class with name `className`.
- `Object newInstance()`
  returns a new instance of this class.

`java.lang.reflect.Constructor` 1.1

- `Object newInstance(Object[] args)`
  constructs a new instance of the constructor's declaring class.

Parameters:	`args`	the parameters supplied to the constructor. See the section on reflection for more information on how to supply parameters.

java.lang.Throwable 1.0

- `void printStackTrace()`
  prints the `Throwable` object and the stack trace to the standard error stream.

Using Reflection to Analyze the Capabilities of Classes

Here is a brief overview of the most important parts of the reflection mechanism for letting you examine the structure of a class.

The three classes `Field`, `Method`, and `Constructor` in the `java.lang.reflect` package describe the fields, methods, and constructors of a class, respectively. All three classes have a method called `getName` that returns the name of the item. The `Field` class has a method `getType` that returns an object, again of type `Class`, that describes the field type. The `Method` and `Constructor` classes have methods to report the types of the parameters, and the `Method` class also reports the return type. All three of these classes also have a method called `getModifiers` that returns an integer, with various bits turned on and off, that describes the modifiers used, such as `public` and `static`. You can then use the static methods in the `Modifier` class in the `java.lang.reflect` package to analyze the integer that `getModifiers` returns. Use methods like `isPublic`, `isPrivate`, or `isFinal` in the `Modifier` class to tell whether a method or constructor was `public`, `private`, or `final`. All you have to do is have the appropriate method in the `Modifier` class work on the integer that `getModifiers` returns. You can also use the `Modifier.toString` method to print the modifiers.

The `getFields`, `getMethods`, and `getConstructors` methods of the `Class` class return arrays of the *public* fields, methods, and constructors that the class supports. This includes public members of superclasses. The `getDeclaredFields`, `getDeclaredMethods`, and `getDeclaredConstructors` methods of the `Class` class return arrays consisting of all fields, operations, and constructors that are declared in the class. This includes private and protected members, but not members of superclasses.

Example 5–5 shows you how to print out all information about a class. The program prompts you for the name of a class and then writes out the signatures of all methods and constructors as well as the names of all data fields of a class. For example, if you enter

```
java.lang.Double
```

then the program prints:

```
class java.lang.Double extends java.lang.Number
{
   public java.lang.Double(java.lang.String);
   public java.lang.Double(double);

   public int hashCode();
   public int compareTo(java.lang.Object);
   public int compareTo(java.lang.Double);
   public boolean equals(java.lang.Object);
   public java.lang.String toString();
   public static java.lang.String toString(double);
   public static java.lang.Double valueOf(java.lang.String);
   public static boolean isNaN(double);
   public boolean isNaN();
   public static boolean isInfinite(double);
   public boolean isInfinite();
   public byte byteValue();
   public short shortValue();
   public int intValue();
   public long longValue();
   public float floatValue();
```

```
   public double doubleValue();
   public static double parseDouble(java.lang.String);
   public static native long doubleToLongBits(double);
   public static native long doubleToRawLongBits(double);
   public static native double longBitsToDouble(long);

   public static final double POSITIVE_INFINITY;
   public static final double NEGATIVE_INFINITY;
   public static final double NaN;
   public static final double MAX_VALUE;
   public static final double MIN_VALUE;
   public static final java.lang.Class TYPE;
   private double value;
   private static final long serialVersionUID;
}
```

What is remarkable about this program is that it can analyze any class that the Java interpreter can load, not just the classes that were available when the program was compiled. We use this program in the next chapter to peek inside the inner classes that the Java compiler generates automatically.

Example 5–5: ReflectionTest.java

```
import java.util.*;
import java.lang.reflect.*;

public class ReflectionTest
{
   public static void main(String[] args)
   {
      // read class name from command-line args or user input
      String name;
      if (args.length > 0)
         name = args[0];
      else
      {
         Scanner in = new Scanner(System.in);
         System.out.println("Enter class name (e.g. java.util.Date): ");
         name = in.next();
      }

      try
      {
         // print class name and superclass name (if != Object)
         Class cl = Class.forName(name);
         Class supercl = cl.getSuperclass();
         System.out.print("class " + name);
         if (supercl != null && supercl != Object.class)
            System.out.print(" extends " + supercl.getName());

         System.out.print("\n{\n");
         printConstructors(cl);
         System.out.println();
         printMethods(cl);
         System.out.println();
         printFields(cl);
         System.out.println("}");
      }
```

```
      catch(ClassNotFoundException e) { e.printStackTrace(); }
      System.exit(0);
   }

   /**
      Prints all constructors of a class
      @param cl a class
    */
   public static void printConstructors(Class cl)
   {
      Constructor[] constructors = cl.getDeclaredConstructors();

      for (Constructor c : constructors)
      {
         String name = c.getName();
         System.out.print("   " + Modifier.toString(c.getModifiers()));
         System.out.print(" " + name + "(");

         // print parameter types
         Class[] paramTypes = c.getParameterTypes();
         for (int j = 0; j < paramTypes.length; j++)
         {
            if (j > 0) System.out.print(", ");
            System.out.print(paramTypes[j].getName());
         }
         System.out.println(");");
      }
   }

   /**
      Prints all methods of a class
      @param cl a class
    */
   public static void printMethods(Class cl)
   {
      Method[] methods = cl.getDeclaredMethods();

      for (Method m : methods)
      {
         Class retType = m.getReturnType();
         String name = m.getName();

         // print modifiers, return type and method name
         System.out.print("   " + Modifier.toString(m.getModifiers()));
         System.out.print(" " + retType.getName() + " " + name + "(");

         // print parameter types
         Class[] paramTypes = m.getParameterTypes();
         for (int j = 0; j < paramTypes.length; j++)
         {
            if (j > 0) System.out.print(", ");
            System.out.print(paramTypes[j].getName());
         }
         System.out.println(");");
      }
   }
```

```
   /**
      Prints all fields of a class
      @param cl a class
    */
   public static void printFields(Class cl)
   {
      Field[] fields = cl.getDeclaredFields();

      for (Field f : fields)
      {
         Class type = f.getType();
         String name = f.getName();
         System.out.print("   " + Modifier.toString(f.getModifiers()));
         System.out.println(" " + type.getName() + " " + name + ";");
      }
   }
}
```

java.lang.Class 1.0

- `Field[] getFields()` **1.1**
- `Field[] getDeclaredFields()` **1.1**

  The `getFields` method returns an array containing `Field` objects for the public fields of this class or its superclasses. The `getDeclaredField` method returns an array of `Field` objects for all fields of this class. The methods return an array of length 0 if there are no such fields or if the `Class` object represents a primitive or array type.

- `Method[] getMethods()` **1.1**
- `Method[] getDeclaredMethods()` **1.1**

  return an array containing `Method` objects: `getMethods` returns public methods and includes inherited methods; `getDeclaredMethods` returns all methods of this class or interface but does not include inherited methods.

- `Constructor[] getConstructors()` **1.1**
- `Constructor[] getDeclaredConstructors()` **1.1**

  return an array containing `Constructor` objects that give you all the public constructors (for `getConstructors`) or all constructors (for `getDeclaredConstructors`) of the class represented by this `Class` object.

java.lang.reflect.Field 1.1

java.lang.reflect.Method 1.1

java.lang.reflect.Constructor 1.1

- `Class getDeclaringClass()`

  returns the `Class` object for the class that defines this constructor, method, or field.

- `Class[] getExceptionTypes()` (in `Constructor` and `Method` classes)

  returns an array of `Class` objects that represent the types of the exceptions thrown by the method.

- `int getModifiers()`

  returns an integer that describes the modifiers of this constructor, method, or field. Use the methods in the `Modifier` class to analyze the return value.

- `String getName()`
  returns a string that is the name of the constructor, method, or field.
- `Class[] getParameterTypes()` (in `Constructor` and `Method` classes)
  returns an array of `Class` objects that represent the types of the parameters.
- `Class getReturnType()` (in `Method` classes)
  returns a `Class` object that represents the return type.

API java.lang.reflect.Modifier 1.1

- `static String toString(int modifiers)`
  returns a string with the modifiers that correspond to the bits set in `modifiers`.
- `static boolean isAbstract(int modifiers)`
- `static boolean isFinal(int modifiers)`
- `static boolean isInterface(int modifiers)`
- `static boolean isNative(int modifiers)`
- `static boolean isPrivate(int modifiers)`
- `static boolean isProtected(int modifiers)`
- `static boolean isPublic(int modifiers)`
- `static boolean isStatic(int modifiers)`
- `static boolean isStrict(int modifiers)`
- `static boolean isSynchronized(int modifiers)`
- `static boolean isVolatile(int modifiers)`
  These methods test the bit in the `modifiers` value that corresponds to the modifier in the method name.

Using Reflection to Analyze Objects at Run Time

In the preceding section, we saw how we can find out the *names* and *types* of the data fields of any object:

- Get the corresponding `Class` object.
- Call `getDeclaredFields` on the `Class` object.

In this section, we go one step further and actually look at the *contents* of the data fields. Of course, it is easy to look at the contents of a specific field of an object whose name and type are known when you write a program. But reflection lets you look at fields of objects that were not known at compile time.

The key method to achieve this examination is the `get` method in the `Field` class. If `f` is an object of type `Field` (for example, one obtained from `getDeclaredFields`) and `obj` is an object of the class of which `f` is a field, then `f.get(obj)` returns an object whose value is the current value of the field of `obj`. This is all a bit abstract, so let's run through an example.

```
Employee harry = new Employee("Harry Hacker", 35000, 10, 1, 1989);
Class cl = harry.getClass();
   // the class object representing Employee
Field f = cl.getDeclaredField("name");
   // the name field of the Employee class
Object v = f.get(harry);
   // the value of the name field of the harry object
   // i.e., the String object "Harry Hacker"
```

Actually, there is a problem with this code. Because the `name` field is a private field, the `get` method will throw an `IllegalAccessException`. You can only use the `get` method to get the values of accessible fields. The security mechanism of Java lets you find out what fields any object has, but it won't let you read the values of those fields unless you have access permission.

The default behavior of the reflection mechanism is to respect Java access control. However, if a Java program is not controlled by a security manager that disallows it, you can override access control. To do this, invoke the setAccessible method on a Field, Method, or Constructor object, for example:

```
f.setAccessible(true); // now OK to call f.get(harry);
```

The setAccessible method is a method of the AccessibleObject class, the common superclass of the Field, Method, and Constructor classes. This feature is provided for debuggers, persistent storage, and similar mechanisms. We use it for a generic toString method later in this section.

There is another issue with the get method that we need to deal with. The name field is a String, and so it is not a problem to return the value as an Object. But suppose we want to look at the salary field. That is a double, and in Java, number types are not objects. To handle this, you can either use the getDouble method of the Field class, or you can call get, whereby the reflection mechanism automatically wraps the field value into the appropriate wrapper class, in this case, Double.

Of course, you can also set the values that you can get. The call f.set(obj, value) sets the field represented by f of the object obj to the new value.

Example 5–6 shows how to write a generic toString method that works for *any* class. It uses getDeclaredFields to obtain all data fields. It then uses the setAccessible convenience method to make all fields accessible. For each field, it obtains the name and the value. Example 5–6 turns each value into a string by recursively invoking toString.

```
class ObjectAnalyzer
{
  public String toString(Object obj)
  {
      Class cl = obj.getClass();
      . . .
      String r = cl.getName();
      // inspect the fields of this class and all superclasses
      do
      {
         r += "[";
         Field[] fields = cl.getDeclaredFields();
         AccessibleObject.setAccessible(fields, true);
         // get the names and values of all fields
         for (Field f : fields)
         {
            if (!Modifier.isStatic(f.getModifiers()))
            {
               if (!r.endsWith("[")) r += ","
               r += f.getName() + "=";
               try
               {
                  Object val = f.get(obj);
                  r += toString(val);
               }
               catch (Exception e) { e.printStackTrace(); }
            }
         }
         r += "]";
         cl = cl.getSuperclass();
      }
      while (cl != Object.class);
```

```
      return r;
   }
   . . .
}
```

The complete code in Example 5–6 needs to address a couple of complexities. Cycles of references could cause an infinite recursion. Therefore, the `ObjectAnalyzer` keeps track of objects that were already visited. Also, to peek inside arrays, you need a different approach. You'll learn about the details in the next section.

You can use this `toString` method to peek inside any object. For example, the call

```
ArrayList<Integer> squares = new ArrayList<Integer>();
for (int i = 1; i <= 5; i++) squares.add(i * i);
System.out.println(new ObjectAnalyzer().toString(squares));
```

yields the printout:

```
java.util.ArrayList[elementData=class java.lang.Object[]{java.lang.Integer[value=1][][],
java.lang.Integer[value=4][][],java.lang.Integer[value=9][][],java.lang.Integer[value=16][][],
java.lang.Integer[value=25][][],null,null,null,null,null},size=5][modCount=5][][]
```

You can use this generic `toString` method to implement the `toString` methods of your own classes, like this:

```
public String toString()
{
   return new ObjectAnalyzer().toString(this);
}
```

This is a hassle-free method for supplying a `toString` method that you may find useful in your own programs.

Example 5–6: ObjectAnalyzerTest.java

```
import java.lang.reflect.*;
import java.util.*;
import java.text.*;

public class ObjectAnalyzerTest
{
   public static void main(String[] args)
   {
      ArrayList<Integer> squares = new ArrayList<Integer>();
      for (int i = 1; i <= 5; i++) squares.add(i * i);
      System.out.println(new ObjectAnalyzer().toString(squares));
   }
}

class ObjectAnalyzer
{
   /**
      Converts an object to a string representation that lists
      all fields.
      @param obj an object
      @return a string with the object's class name and all
      field names and values
   */
   public String toString(Object obj)
   {
```

```
      if (obj == null) return "null";
      if (visited.contains(obj)) return "...";
      visited.add(obj);
      Class cl = obj.getClass();
      if (cl == String.class) return (String) obj;
      if (cl.isArray())
      {
         String r = cl.getComponentType() + "[]{";
         for (int i = 0; i < Array.getLength(obj); i++)
         {
            if (i > 0) r += ",";
            Object val = Array.get(obj, i);
            if (cl.getComponentType().isPrimitive()) r += val;
            else r += toString(val);
         }
         return r + "}";
      }

      String r = cl.getName();
      // inspect the fields of this class and all superclasses
      do
      {
         r += "[";
         Field[] fields = cl.getDeclaredFields();
         AccessibleObject.setAccessible(fields, true);
         // get the names and values of all fields
         for (Field f : fields)
         {
            if (!Modifier.isStatic(f.getModifiers()))
            {
               if (!r.endsWith("[")) r += ",";
               r += f.getName() + "=";
               try
               {
                  Class t = f.getType();
                  Object val = f.get(obj);
                  if (t.isPrimitive()) r += val;
                  else r += toString(val);
               }
               catch (Exception e) { e.printStackTrace(); }
            }
         }
         r += "]";
         cl = cl.getSuperclass();
      }
      while (cl != null);

      return r;
   }

   private ArrayList<Object> visited = new ArrayList<Object>();
}
```

java.lang.reflect.AccessibleObject 1.2

- `void setAccessible(boolean flag)`
  sets the accessibility flag for this reflection object. A value of `true` indicates that Java language access checking is suppressed and that the private properties of the object can be queried and set.
- `boolean isAccessible()`
  gets the value of the accessibility flag for this reflection object.
- `static void setAccessible(AccessibleObject[] array, boolean flag)`
  is a convenience method to set the accessibility flag for an array of objects.

java.lang.Class 1.1

- `Field getField(String name)`
- `Field[] getFields()`
  gets the public field with the given name, or an array of all fields.
- `Field getDeclaredField(String name)`
- `Field[] getDeclaredFields()`
  gets the field that is declared in this class with the given name, or an array of all fields.

java.lang.reflect.Field 1.1

- `Object get(Object obj)`
  gets the value of the field described by this `Field` object in the object `obj`.
- `void set(Object obj, Object newValue)`
  sets the field described by this `Field` object in the object `obj` to a new value.

Using Reflection to Write Generic Array Code

The `Array` class in the `java.lang.reflect` package allows you to create arrays dynamically. For example, when you use this feature with the `arrayCopy` method from Chapter 3, you can dynamically expand an existing array while preserving the current contents.

The problem we want to solve is pretty typical. Suppose you have an array of some type that is full and you want to grow it. And suppose you are sick of writing the grow-and-copy code by hand. You want to write a generic method to grow an array.

```
Employee[] a = new Employee[100];
. . .
// array is full
a = (Employee[]) arrayGrow(a);
```

How can we write such a generic method? It helps that an `Employee[]` array can be converted to an `Object[]` array. That sounds promising. Here is a first attempt to write a generic method. We simply grow the array by 10% + 10 elements (because the 10 percent growth is not substantial enough for small arrays).

```
static Object[] badArrayGrow(Object[] a) // not useful
{
   int newLength = a.length * 11 / 10 + 10;
   Object[] newArray = new Object[newLength];
   System.arraycopy(a, 0, newArray, 0, a.length);
   return newArray;
}
```

However, there is a problem with actually *using* the resulting array. The type of array that this code returns is an array of *objects* (`Object[]`) because we created the array using the line of code

```
new Object[newLength]
```

An array of objects *cannot* be cast to an array of employees (`Employee[]`). Java would generate a `ClassCastException` at run time. The point is, as we mentioned earlier, that a Java array remembers the type of its entries, that is, the element type used in the `new` expression that created it. It is legal to cast an `Employee[]` temporarily to an `Object[]` array and then cast it back, but an array that started its life as an `Object[]` array can never be cast into an `Employee[]` array. To write this kind of generic array code, we need to be able to make a new array of the *same* type as the original array. For this, we need the methods of the `Array` class in the `java.lang.reflect` package. The key is the static `newInstance` method of the `Array` class that constructs a new array. You must supply the type for the entries and the desired length as parameters to this method.

```
Object newArray = Array.newInstance(componentType, newLength);
```

To actually carry this out, we need to get the length and component type of the new array.

We obtain the length by calling `Array.getLength(a)`. The static `getLength` method of the `Array` class returns the length of any array. To get the component type of the new array:

1. First, get the class object of `a`.
2. Confirm that it is indeed an array.
3. Use the `getComponentType` method of the `Class` class (which is defined only for class objects that represent arrays) to find the right type for the array.

Why is `getLength` a method of `Array` but `getComponentType` a method of `Class`? We don't know—the distribution of the reflection methods seems a bit ad hoc at times.

Here's the code:

```
static Object goodArrayGrow(Object a) // useful
{
   Class cl = a.getClass();
   if (!cl.isArray()) return null;
   Class componentType = cl.getComponentType();
   int length = Array.getLength(a);
   int newLength = length * 11 / 10 + 10;
   Object newArray = Array.newInstance(componentType, newLength);
   System.arraycopy(a, 0, newArray, 0, length);
   return newArray;
}
```

Note that this `arrayGrow` method can be used to grow arrays of any type, not just arrays of objects.

```
int[] a = { 1, 2, 3, 4 };
a = (int[]) goodArrayGrow(a);
```

To make this possible, the parameter of `goodArrayGrow` is declared to be of type `Object`, *not an array of objects* (`Object[]`). The integer array type `int[]` can be converted to an `Object`, but not to an array of objects!

Example 5–7 shows both array grow methods in action. Note that the cast of the return value of `badArrayGrow` will throw an exception.

Example 5–7: ArrayGrowTest.java

```
import java.lang.reflect.*;
import java.util.*;

public class ArrayGrowTest
{
   public static void main(String[] args)
   {
      int[] a = { 1, 2, 3 };
      a = (int[]) goodArrayGrow(a);
      arrayPrint(a);

      String[] b = { "Tom", "Dick", "Harry" };
      b = (String[]) goodArrayGrow(b);
      arrayPrint(b);

      System.out.println("The following call will generate an exception.");
      b = (String[]) badArrayGrow(b);
   }

   /**
      This method attempts to grow an array by allocating a
      new array and copying all elements.
      @param a the array to grow
      @return a larger array that contains all elements of a.
      However, the returned array has type Object[], not
      the same type as a
   */
   static Object[] badArrayGrow(Object[] a)
   {
      int newLength = a.length * 11 / 10 + 10;
      Object[] newArray = new Object[newLength];
      System.arraycopy(a, 0, newArray, 0, a.length);
      return newArray;
   }

   /**
      This method grows an array by allocating a
      new array of the same type and copying all elements.
      @param a the array to grow. This can be an object array
      or a fundamental type array
      @return a larger array that contains all elements of a.

   */
   static Object goodArrayGrow(Object a)
   {
      Class cl = a.getClass();
      if (!cl.isArray()) return null;
      Class componentType = cl.getComponentType();
      int length = Array.getLength(a);
      int newLength = length * 11 / 10 + 10;

      Object newArray = Array.newInstance(componentType, newLength);
      System.arraycopy(a, 0, newArray, 0, length);
      return newArray;
```

```
    }

    /**
       A convenience method to print all elements in an array
       @param a the array to print. can be an object array
       or a fundamental type array
    */
    static void arrayPrint(Object a)
    {
       Class cl = a.getClass();
       if (!cl.isArray()) return;
       Class componentType = cl.getComponentType();
       int length = Array.getLength(a);
       System.out.print(componentType.getName()
          + "[" + length + "] = { ");
       for (int i = 0; i < Array.getLength(a); i++)
          System.out.print(Array.get(a, i) + " ");
       System.out.println("}");
    }
 }
```

java.lang.reflect.Array 1.1

- `static Object get(Object array, int index)`
- `static xxx getXxx(Object array, int index)`
  (*xxx* is one of the primitive types `boolean`, `byte`, `char`, `double`, `float`, `int`, `long`, `short`.) These methods return the value of the given array that is stored at the given index.
- `static void set(Object array, int index, Object newValue)`
- `static setXxx(Object array, int index, xxx newValue)`
  (*xxx* is one of the primitive types `boolean`, `byte`, `char`, `double`, `float`, `int`, `long`, `short`.) These methods store a new value into the given array at the given index.
- `static int getLength(Object array)`
  returns the length of the given array.
- `static Object newInstance(Class componentType, int length)`
- `static Object newInstance(Class componentType, int[] lengths)`
  return a new array of the given component type with the given dimensions.

Method Pointers!

On the surface, Java does not have method pointers—ways of giving the location of a method to another method so that the second method can invoke it later. In fact, the designers of Java have said that method pointers are dangerous and error prone and that Java *interfaces* (discussed in the next chapter) are a superior solution. However, it turns out that, as of JDK 1.1, Java does have method pointers, as a (perhaps accidental) by-product of the reflection package.

NOTE: Among the nonstandard language extensions that Microsoft added to its Java derivative J++ (and its successor, C#) is another method pointer type, called a *delegate*, that is different from the `Method` class that we discuss in this section. However, inner classes (which we will introduce in the next chapter) are a more useful construct than delegates.

To see method pointers at work, recall that you can inspect a field of an object with the get method of the Field class. Similarly, the Method class has an invoke method that lets you call the method that is wrapped in the current Method object. The signature for the invoke method is

```
Object invoke(Object obj, Object... args)
```

The first parameter is the implicit parameter, and the remaining objects provide the explicit parameters. (Before JDK 5.0, you had to pass an array of objects or null if the method has no explicit parameters.)

For a static method, the first parameter is ignored—you can set it to null.

For example, if m1 represents the getName method of the Employee class, the following code shows how you can call it:

```
String n = (String) m1.invoke(harry);
```

As with the get and set methods of the Field type, there's a problem if the parameter or return type is not a class but a primitive type. You either rely on autoboxing or, before JDK 5.0, wrap primitive types into their corresponding wrappers.

Conversely, if the return type is a primitive type, the invoke method will return the wrapper type instead. For example, suppose that m2 represents the getSalary method of the Employee class. Then, the returned object is actually a Double, and you must cast it accordingly. As of JDK 5.0, automatic unboxing takes care of the rest.

```
double s = (Double) m2.invoke(harry);
```

How do you obtain a Method object? You can, of course, call getDeclaredMethods and search through the returned array of Method objects until you find the method that you want. Or, you can call the getMethod method of the Class class. This is similar to the getField method that takes a string with the field name and returns a Field object. However, there may be several methods with the same name, so you need to be careful that you get the right one. For that reason, you must also supply the parameter types of the desired method. The signature of getMethod is

```
Method getMethod(String name, Class... parameterTypes)
```

For example, here is how you can get method pointers to the getName and raiseSalary methods of the Employee class.

```
Method m1 = Employee.class.getMethod("getName");
Method m2 = Employee.class.getMethod("raiseSalary", double.class);
```

(Before JDK 5.0, you had to package the Class objects into an array or to supply null if there were no parameters.)

Now that you have seen the rules for using Method objects, let's put them to work. Example 5–8 is a program that prints a table of values for a mathematical function such as Math.sqrt or Math.sin. The printout looks like this:

```
public static native double java.lang.Math.sqrt(double)
      1.0000 |      1.0000
      2.0000 |      1.4142
      3.0000 |      1.7321
      4.0000 |      2.0000
      5.0000 |      2.2361
      6.0000 |      2.4495
      7.0000 |      2.6458
      8.0000 |      2.8284
      9.0000 |      3.0000
     10.0000 |      3.1623
```

The code for printing a table is, of course, independent of the actual function that is being tabulated.

```
double dx = (to - from) / (n - 1);
for (double x = from; x <= to; x += dx)
{
   double y = (Double) f.invoke(null, x);
   System.out.printf("%10.4f | %10.4f%n" + y, x, y);
}
```

Here, `f` is an object of type `Method`. The first parameter of `invoke` is `null` because we are calling a static method.

To tabulate the `Math.sqrt` function, we set `f` to

```
Math.class.getMethod("sqrt", double.class)
```

That is the method of the `Math` class that has the name `sqrt` and a single parameter of type `double`.

Example 5–8 shows the complete code of the generic tabulator and a couple of test runs.

Example 5–8: MethodPointerTest.java

```
import java.lang.reflect.*;

public class MethodPointerTest
{
   public static void main(String[] args) throws Exception
   {
      // get method pointers to the square and sqrt methods
      Method square = MethodPointerTest.class.getMethod("square",
         double.class);
      Method sqrt = Math.class.getMethod("sqrt", double.class);

      // print tables of x- and y-values

      printTable(1, 10, 10, square);
      printTable(1, 10, 10, sqrt);
   }

   /**
      Returns the square of a number
      @param x a number
      @return x squared
   */
   public static double square(double x)
   {
      return x * x;
   }

   /**
      Prints a table with x- and y-values for a method
      @param from the lower bound for the x-values
      @param to the upper bound for the x-values
      @param n the number of rows in the table
      @param f a method with a double parameter and double
         return value
   */
   public static void printTable(double from, double to,
      int n, Method f)
```

```
   {
      // print out the method as table header
      System.out.println(f);

      // construct formatter to print with 4 digits precision

      double dx = (to - from) / (n - 1);

      for (double x = from; x <= to; x += dx)
      {
         try
         {
            double y = (Double) f.invoke(null, x);
            System.out.printf("%10.4f | %10.4f%n", x, y);
         }
         catch (Exception e) { e.printStackTrace(); }
      }
   }
}
```

As this example shows clearly, you can do anything with `Method` objects that you can do with function pointers in C (or delegates in C#). Just as in C, this style of programming is usually quite inconvenient and always error prone. What happens if you invoke a method with the wrong parameters? The `invoke` method throws an exception.

Also, the parameters and return values of `invoke` are necessarily of type `Object`. That means you must cast back and forth a lot. As a result, the compiler is deprived of the chance to check your code. Therefore, errors surface only during testing, when they are more tedious to find and fix. Moreover, code that uses reflection to get at method pointers is significantly slower than code that simply calls methods directly.

For that reason, we suggest that you use `Method` objects in your own programs only when absolutely necessary. Using interfaces and inner classes (the subject of the next chapter) is almost always a better idea. In particular, we echo the developers of Java and suggest not using `Method` objects for callback functions. Using interfaces for the callbacks (see the next chapter as well) leads to code that runs faster and is a lot more maintainable.

`java.lang.reflect.Method` 1.1

- `public Object invoke(Object implicitParameter, Object[] explicitParameters)`
  invokes the method described by this object, passing the given parameters and returning the value that the method returns. For static methods, pass `null` as the implicit parameter. Pass primitive type values by using wrappers. Primitive type return values must be unwrapped.

Enumeration Classes

You saw in Chapter 3 how to define enumerated types in JDK 5.0 and beyond. Here is a typical example:

```
public enum Size { SMALL, MEDIUM, LARGE, EXTRA_LARGE };
```

The type defined by this declaration is actually a class. The class has exactly four instances—it is not possible to construct new objects.

Therefore, you never need to use `equals` for values of enumerated types. Simply use `==` to compare them.

You can, if you like, add constructors, methods, and fields to an enumerated type. Of course, the constructors are only invoked when the enumerated constants are constructed. Here is an example.

```
enum Size
{
   SMALL("S"), MEDIUM("M"), LARGE("L"), EXTRA_LARGE("XL");

   private Size(String abbreviation) { this.abbreviation = abbreviation; }
   public String getAbbreviation() { return abbreviation; }

   private String abbreviation;
}
```

All enumerated types are subclasses of the class `Enum`. They inherit a number of methods from that class. The most useful one is `toString`, which returns the name of the enumerated constant. For example, `Size.SMALL.toString()` returns the string `"SMALL"`.

The converse of `toString` is the static `valueOf` method. For example, the statement

```
Size s = (Size) Enum.valueOf(Size.class, "SMALL");
```

sets `s` to `Size.SMALL`.

Each enumerated type has a static `values` method that returns an array of all values of the enumeration:

```
Size[] values = Size.values();
```

The short program in Example 5–9 demonstrates how to work with enumerated types.

NOTE: Just like `Class`, the `Enum` class has a type parameter that we have ignored for simplicity. For example, the enumerated type `Size` actually extends `Enum<Size>`.

Example 5–9: EnumTest.java

```
import java.util.*;

public class EnumTest
{
   public static void main(String[] args)
   {
      Scanner in = new Scanner(System.in);
      System.out.print("Enter a size: (SMALL, MEDIUM, LARGE, EXTRA_LARGE) ");
      String input = in.next().toUpperCase();
      Size size = Enum.valueOf(Size.class, input);
      System.out.println("size=" + size);
      System.out.println("abbreviation=" + size.getAbbreviation());
      if (size == Size.EXTRA_LARGE)
         System.out.println("Good job--you paid attention to the _.");
   }
}

enum Size
{
   SMALL("S"), MEDIUM("M"), LARGE("L"), EXTRA_LARGE("XL");

   private Size(String abbreviation) { this.abbreviation = abbreviation; }
   public String getAbbreviation() { return abbreviation; }
```

```
   private String abbreviation;
}
```

java.lang.Enum 5.0

- `static Enum valueOf(Class enumClass, String name)`
  returns the enumerated constant of the given class with the given name.
- `String toString()`
  returns the name of this enumerated constant.

Design Hints for Inheritance

We want to end this chapter with some hints that we have found useful when using inheritance.

1. *Place common operations and fields in the superclass.*

   This is why we put the name field into the `Person` class rather than replicating it in the `Employee` and `Student` classes.

2. *Don't use protected fields.*

   Some programmers think it is a good idea to define most instance fields as `protected`, "just in case," so that subclasses can access these fields if they need to. However, the `protected` mechanism doesn't give much protection, for two reasons. First, the set of subclasses is unbounded—anyone can form a subclass of your classes and then write code that directly accesses `protected` instance fields, thereby breaking encapsulation. And second, in the Java programming language, all classes in the same package have access to `protected` fields, whether or not they are subclasses.

   However, `protected` methods can be useful to indicate methods that are not ready for general use and should be redefined in subclasses. The `clone` method is a good example.

3. *Use inheritance to model the "is–a" relationship.*

   Inheritance is a handy code-saver, and sometimes people overuse it. For example, suppose we need a `Contractor` class. Contractors have names and hire dates, but they do not have salaries. Instead, they are paid by the hour, and they do not stay around long enough to get a raise. There is the temptation to form a subclass `Contractor` from `Employee` and add an `hourlyWage` field.

   ```
   class Contractor extends Employee
   {  . . .
      private double hourlyWage;
   }
   ```

   This is *not* a good idea, however, because now each contractor object has both a salary and hourly wage field. It will cause you no end of grief when you implement methods for printing paychecks or tax forms. You will end up writing more code than you would have by not inheriting in the first place.

   The contractor/employee relationship fails the "is–a" test. A contractor is not a special case of an employee.

4. *Don't use inheritance unless all inherited methods make sense.*

   Suppose we want to write a `Holiday` class. Surely every holiday is a day, and days can be expressed as instances of the `GregorianCalendar` class, so we can use inheritance.

   ```
   class Holiday extends GregorianCalendar { . . . }
   ```

Unfortunately, the set of holidays is not *closed* under the inherited operations. One of the public methods of GregorianCalendar is add. And add can turn holidays into nonholidays:

```
Holiday christmas;
christmas.add(Calendar.DAY_OF_MONTH, 12);
```

Therefore, inheritance is not appropriate in this example.

5. *Don't change the expected behavior when you override a method.*

   The substitution principle applies not just to syntax but, more important, to behavior. When you override a method, you should not unreasonably change its behavior. The compiler can't help you—it cannot check whether your redefinitions make sense. For example, you can "fix" the issue of the add method in the Holiday class by redefining add, perhaps to do nothing, or to throw an exception, or to move on to the next holiday.

   However, such a fix violates the substitution principle. The sequence of statements

   ```
   int d1 = x.get(Calendar.DAY_OF_MONTH);
   x.add(Calendar.DAY_OF_MONTH, 1);
   int d2 = x.get(Calendar.DAY_OF_MONTH);
   System.out.println(d2 - d1);
   ```

   should have the *expected behavior*, no matter whether x is of type GregorianCalendar or Holiday.

   Of course, therein lies the rub. Reasonable and unreasonable people can argue at length what the expected behavior is. For example, some authors argue that the substitution principle requires Manager.equals to ignore the bonus field because Employee.equals ignores it. These discussions are always pointless if they occur in a vacuum. Ultimately, what matters is that you do not circumvent the intent of the original design when you override methods in subclasses.

6. *Use polymorphism, not type information.*

   Whenever you find code of the form

   ```
   if (x is of type 1)
      action1(x);
   else if (x is of type 2)
      action2(x);
   ```

   think polymorphism.

   Do action1 and action2 represent a common concept? If so, make the concept a method of a common superclass or interface of both types. Then, you can simply call

   ```
   x.action();
   ```

   and have the dynamic dispatch mechanism inherent in polymorphism launch the correct action.

   Code using polymorphic methods or interface implementations is much easier to maintain and extend than code that uses multiple type tests.

7. *Don't overuse reflection.*

   The reflection mechanism lets you write programs with amazing generality, by detecting fields and methods at run time. This capability can be extremely useful for systems programming, but it is usually not appropriate in applications. Reflection is fragile—the compiler cannot help you find programming errors. Any errors are found at run time and result in exceptions.

Chapter 6

Interfaces and Inner Classes

- Interfaces
- Object Cloning
- Interfaces and Callbacks
- Inner Classes
- Proxies

You have now seen all the basic tools for object-oriented programming in Java. This chapter shows you several advanced techniques that are commonly used. Despite their less obvious nature, you will need to master them to complete your Java tool chest.

The first, called an *interface,* is a way of describing *what* classes should do, without specifying *how* they should do it. A class can *implement* one or more interfaces. You can then use objects of these implementing classes anytime that conformance to the interface is required. After we cover interfaces, we take up cloning an object (or deep copying, as it is sometimes called). A clone of an object is a new object that has the same state as the original. In particular, you can modify the clone without affecting the original.

Next, we move on to the mechanism of *inner classes.* Inner classes are technically somewhat complex—they are defined inside other classes, and their methods can access the fields of the surrounding class. Inner classes are useful when you design collections of cooperating classes. In particular, inner classes enable you to write concise, professional-looking code to handle GUI events.

This chapter concludes with a discussion of *proxies*, objects that implement arbitrary interfaces. A proxy is a very specialized construct that is useful for building system-level tools. You can safely skip that section on first reading.

Interfaces

In the Java programming language, an interface is not a class but a set of *requirements* for classes that want to conform to the interface.

Typically, the supplier of some service states: "If your class conforms to a particular interface, then I'll perform the service." Let's look at a concrete example. The `sort` method of the `Arrays` class promises to sort an array of objects, but under one condition: The objects must belong to classes that implement the `Comparable` interface.

Here is what the `Comparable` interface looks like:

```
public interface Comparable
{
   int compareTo(Object other);
}
```

This means that any class that implements the `Comparable` interface is required to have a `compareTo` method, and the method must take an `Object` parameter and return an integer.

NOTE: As of JDK 5.0, the `Comparable` interface has been enhanced to be a generic type.

```
public interface Comparable<T>
{
   int compareTo(T other); // parameter has type T
}
```

For example, a class that implements `Comparable<Employee>` must supply a method

```
int compareTo(Employee other)
```

You can still use the "raw" `Comparable` type without a type parameter, but then you have to manually cast the parameter of the `compareTo` method to the desired type.

All methods of an interface are automatically `public`. For that reason, it is not necessary to supply the keyword `public` when declaring a method in an interface.

Of course, there is an additional requirement that the interface cannot spell out: When calling `x.compareTo(y)`, the `compareTo` method must actually be able to compare two objects and return an indication whether `x` or `y` is larger. The method is supposed to return a negative number if `x` is smaller than `y`, zero if they are equal, and a positive number otherwise.

This particular interface has a single method. Some interfaces have more than one method. As you will see later, interfaces can also define constants. What is more important, however, is what interfaces *cannot* supply. Interfaces never have instance fields, and the methods are never implemented in the interface. Supplying instance fields and method implementations is the job of the classes that implement the interface. You can think of an interface as being similar to an abstract class with no instance fields. However, there are some differences between these two concepts—we look at them later in some detail.

Now suppose we want to use the `sort` method of the `Arrays` class to sort an array of `Employee` objects. Then the `Employee` class must *implement* the `Comparable` interface.

To make a class implement an interface, you carry out two steps:

1. You declare that your class intends to implement the given interface.
2. You supply definitions for all methods in the interface.

To declare that a class implements an interface, use the `implements` keyword:

```
class Employee implements Comparable
```

Of course, now the `Employee` class needs to supply the `compareTo` method. Let's suppose that we want to compare employees by their salary. Here is a `compareTo` method that returns –1 if the first employee's salary is less than the second employee's salary, 0 if they are equal, and 1 otherwise.

```
public int compareTo(Object otherObject)
{
   Employee other = (Employee) otherObject;
   if (salary < other.salary) return -1;
   if (salary > other.salary) return 1;
   return 0;
}
```

CAUTION: In the interface declaration, the `compareTo` method was not declared `public` because all methods in an *interface* are automatically public. However, when implementing the interface, you must declare the method as `public`. Otherwise, the compiler assumes that the method has package visibility—the default for a *class*. Then the compiler complains that you try to supply a weaker access privilege.

As of JDK 5.0, we can do a little better. We'll decide to implement the `Comparable<Employee>` interface type instead.

```
class Employee implements Comparable<Employee>
{
   public int compareTo(Employee other)
   {
      if (salary < other.salary) return -1;
      if (salary > other.salary) return 1;
      return 0;
   }
    . . .
}
```

Note that the unsightly cast of the `Object` parameter has gone away.

TIP: The `compareTo` method of the `Comparable` interface returns an integer. If the objects are not equal, it does not matter what negative or positive value you return. This flexibility can be useful when you are comparing integer fields. For example, suppose each employee has a unique integer `id` and you want to sort by employee ID number. Then you can simply return `id - other.id`. That value will be some negative value if the first ID number is less than the other, 0 if they are the same ID, and some positive value otherwise. However, there is one caveat: The range of the integers must be small enough that the subtraction does not overflow. If you know that the IDs are not negative or that their absolute value is at most `(Integer.MAX_VALUE - 1) / 2`, you are safe.

Of course, the subtraction trick doesn't work for floating-point numbers. The difference `salary - other.salary` can round to 0 if the salaries are close together but not identical.

Now you saw what a class must do to avail itself of the sorting service—it must implement a `compareTo` method. That's eminently reasonable. There needs to be some way for the `sort` method to compare objects. But why can't the `Employee` class simply provide a `compareTo` method without implementing the `Comparable` interface?

The reason for interfaces is that the Java programming language is *strongly typed*. When making a method call, the compiler needs to be able to check that the method actually exists. Somewhere in the `sort` method will be statements like this:

```
if (a[i].compareTo(a[j]) > 0)
{
   // rearrange a[i] and a[j]
   . . .
}
```

The compiler must know that `a[i]` actually has a `compareTo` method. If `a` is an array of `Comparable` objects, then the existence of the method is assured because every class that implements the `Comparable` interface must supply the method.

NOTE: You would expect that the `sort` method in the `Arrays` class is defined to accept a `Comparable[]` array so that the compiler can complain if anyone ever calls `sort` with an array whose element type doesn't implement the `Comparable` interface. Sadly, that is not the case. Instead, the `sort` method accepts an `Object[]` array and uses a clumsy cast:

```
// from the standard library--not recommended
if (((Comparable) a[i]).compareTo(a[j]) > 0)
{
   // rearrange a[i] and a[j]
   . . .
}
```

If `a[i]` does not belong to a class that implements the `Comparable` interface, then the virtual machine throws an exception.

Example 6–1 presents the full code for sorting an employee array.

Example 6–1: EmployeeSortTest.java

```
import java.util.*;

public class EmployeeSortTest
{
   public static void main(String[] args)
   {
      Employee[] staff = new Employee[3];

      staff[0] = new Employee("Harry Hacker", 35000);
      staff[1] = new Employee("Carl Cracker", 75000);
      staff[2] = new Employee("Tony Tester", 38000);

      Arrays.sort(staff);

      // print out information about all Employee objects
      for (Employee e : staff)
         System.out.println("name=" + e.getName() + ",salary=" + e.getSalary());
   }
}

class Employee implements Comparable<Employee>
{
   public Employee(String n, double s)
   {
      name = n;
      salary = s;
   }

   public String getName()
   {
      return name;
   }

```

```
   public double getSalary()
   {
      return salary;
   }

   public void raiseSalary(double byPercent)
   {
      double raise = salary * byPercent / 100;
      salary += raise;
   }

   /**
      Compares employees by salary
      @param other another Employee object
      @return a negative value if this employee has a lower
      salary than otherObject, 0 if the salaries are the same,
      a positive value otherwise
   */
   public int compareTo(Employee other)
   {
      if (salary < other.salary) return -1;
      if (salary > other.salary) return 1;
      return 0;
   }

   private String name;
   private double salary;
}
```

java.lang.Comparable 1.0

- `int compareTo(Object otherObject)`
  compares this object with `otherObject` and returns a negative integer if this object is less than `otherObject`, zero if they are equal, and a positive integer otherwise.

java.lang.Comparable<T> 5.0

- `int compareTo(T other)`
  compares this object with `other` and returns a negative integer if this object is less than `other`, zero if they are equal, and a positive integer otherwise.

java.util.Arrays 1.2

- `static void sort(Object[] a)`
  sorts the elements in the array `a`, using a tuned `mergesort` algorithm. All elements in the array must belong to classes that implement the `Comparable` interface, and they must all be comparable to each other.

NOTE: According to the language standard: "The implementor must ensure sgn(`x.compareTo(y)`) = –sgn(`y.compareTo(x)`) for all `x` and `y`. (This implies that `x.compareTo(y)` must throw an exception if `y.compareTo(x)` throws an exception.)" Here, "sgn" is the *sign* of a number: sgn(n) is –1 if n is negative, 0 if n equals 0, and 1 if n is positive. In plain English, if you flip the parameters of `compareTo`, the sign (but not necessarily the actual value) of the result must also flip.

As with the equals method, problems can arise when inheritance comes into play.

Because Manager extends Employee, it implements Comparable<Employee> and not Comparable<Manager>. If Manager chooses to override compareTo, it must be prepared to compare managers to employees. It can't simply cast the employee to a manager:

```
class Manager extends Employee
{
   public int compareTo(Employee other)
   {
      Manager otherManager = (Manager) other; // NO
      . . .
   }
   . . .
}
```

That violates the "antisymmetry" rule. If x is an Employee and y is a Manager, then the call x.compareTo(y) doesn't throw an exception—it simply compares x and y as employees. But the reverse, y.compareTo(x), throws a ClassCastException.

This is the same situation as with the equals method that we discussed in Chapter 5, and the remedy is the same. There are two distinct scenarios.

If subclasses have different notions of comparison, then you should outlaw comparison of objects that belong to different classes. Each compareTo method should start out with the test

```
if (getClass() != other.getClass()) throw new ClassCastException();
```

If there is a common algorithm for comparing subclass objects, simply provide a single compareTo method in the superclass and declare it as final.

For example, suppose that you want managers to be better than regular employees, regardless of the salary. What about other subclasses such as Executive and Secretary? If you need to establish a pecking order, supply a method such as rank in the Employee class. Have each subclass override rank, and implement a single compareTo method that takes the rank values into account.

Properties of Interfaces

Interfaces are not classes. In particular, you can never use the new operator to instantiate an interface:

```
x = new Comparable(. . .); // ERROR
```

However, even though you can't construct interface objects, you can still declare interface variables.

```
Comparable x; // OK
```

An interface variable must refer to an object of a class that implements the interface:

```
x = new Employee(. . .); // OK provided Employee implements Comparable
```

Next, just as you use instanceof to check whether an object is of a specific class, you can use instanceof to check whether an object implements an interface:

```
if (anObject instanceof Comparable) { . . . }
```

Just as you can build hierarchies of classes, you can extend interfaces. This allows for multiple chains of interfaces that go from a greater degree of generality to a greater degree of specialization. For example, suppose you had an interface called Moveable.

```
public interface Moveable
{
   void move(double x, double y);
}
```

Then, you could imagine an interface called Powered that extends it:

```
public interface Powered extends Moveable
{
   double milesPerGallon();
}
```

Although you cannot put instance fields or static methods in an interface, you can supply constants in them. For example:

```
public interface Powered extends Moveable
{
   double milesPerGallon();
   double SPEED_LIMIT = 95; // a public static final constant
}
```

Just as methods in an interface are automatically `public`, fields are always `public static final`.

NOTE: It is legal to tag interface methods as `public`, and fields as `public static final`. Some programmers do that, either out of habit or for greater clarity. However, the Java Language Specification recommends that the redundant keywords not be supplied, and we follow that recommendation.

Some interfaces define just constants and no methods. For example, the standard library contains an interface `SwingConstants` that defines constants `NORTH`, `SOUTH`, `HORIZONTAL`, and so on. Any class that chooses to implement the `SwingConstants` interface automatically inherits these constants. Its methods can simply refer to `NORTH` rather than the more cumbersome `SwingConstants.NORTH`. However, this use of interfaces seems rather degenerate, and we do not recommend it.

While each class can have only one superclass, classes can implement *multiple* interfaces. This gives you the maximum amount of flexibility in defining a class's behavior. For example, the Java programming language has an important interface built into it, called `Cloneable`. (We discuss this interface in detail in the next section.) If your class implements `Cloneable`, the `clone` method in the `Object` class will make an exact copy of your class's objects. Suppose, therefore, you want cloneability and comparability. Then you simply implement both interfaces.

```
class Employee implements Cloneable, Comparable
```

Use commas to separate the interfaces that describe the characteristics that you want to supply.

Interfaces and Abstract Classes

If you read the section about abstract classes in Chapter 5, you may wonder why the designers of the Java programming language bothered with introducing the concept of interfaces. Why can't `Comparable` simply be an abstract class:

```
abstract class Comparable // why not?
{
   public abstract int compareTo(Object other);
}
```

The `Employee` class would then simply extend this abstract class and supply the `compareTo` method:

```
class Employee extends Comparable // why not?
{
   public int compareTo(Object other) { . . . }
}
```

There is, unfortunately, a major problem with using an abstract base class to express a generic property. A class can only extend a single class. Suppose that the Employee class already extends a different class, say, Person. Then it can't extend a second class.

```
class Employee extends Person, Comparable // ERROR
```

But each class can implement as many interfaces as it likes:

```
class Employee extends Person implements Comparable // OK
```

Other programming languages, in particular C++, allow a class to have more than one superclass. This feature is called *multiple inheritance.* The designers of Java chose not to support multiple inheritance, because it makes the language either very complex (as in C++) or less efficient (as in Eiffel).

Instead, interfaces afford most of the benefits of multiple inheritance while avoiding the complexities and inefficiencies.

C++ NOTE: C++ has multiple inheritance and all the complications that come with it, such as virtual base classes, dominance rules, and transverse pointer casts. Few C++ programmers use multiple inheritance, and some say it should never be used. Other programmers recommend using multiple inheritance only for "mix in" style inheritance. In the mix-in style, a primary base class describes the parent object, and additional base classes (the so-called mix-ins) may supply auxiliary characteristics. That style is similar to a Java class with a single base class and additional interfaces. However, in C++, mix-ins can add default behavior, whereas Java interfaces cannot.

Object Cloning

When you make a copy of a variable, the original and the copy are references to the same object. (See Figure 6–1.) This means a change to either variable also affects the other.

```
Employee original = new Employee("John Public", 50000);
Employee copy = original;
copy.raiseSalary(10); // oops--also changed original
```

If you would like copy to be a new object that begins its life being identical to original but whose state can diverge over time, then you use the clone method.

```
Employee copy = original.clone();
copy.raiseSalary(10); // OK--original unchanged
```

But it isn't quite so simple. The clone method is a protected method of Object, which means that your code cannot simply call it. Only the Employee class can clone Employee objects. There is a reason for this restriction. Think about the way in which the Object class can implement clone. It knows nothing about the object at all, so it can make only a field-by-field copy. If all data fields in the object are numbers or other basic types, copying the fields is just fine. But if the object contains references to subobjects, then copying the field gives you another reference to the subobject, so the original and the cloned objects still share some information.

To visualize that phenomenon, let's consider the Employee class that was introduced in Chapter 4. Figure 6–2 shows what happens when you use the clone method of the Object class to clone such an Employee object. As you can see, the default cloning operation is "shallow"—it doesn't clone objects that are referenced inside other objects.

Does it matter if the copy is shallow? It depends. If the subobject that is shared between the original and the shallow clone is *immutable*, then the sharing is safe. This certainly happens if the subobject belongs to an immutable class, such as String. Alternatively, the subobject may simply remain constant throughout the lifetime of the object, with no mutators touching it and no methods yielding a reference to it.

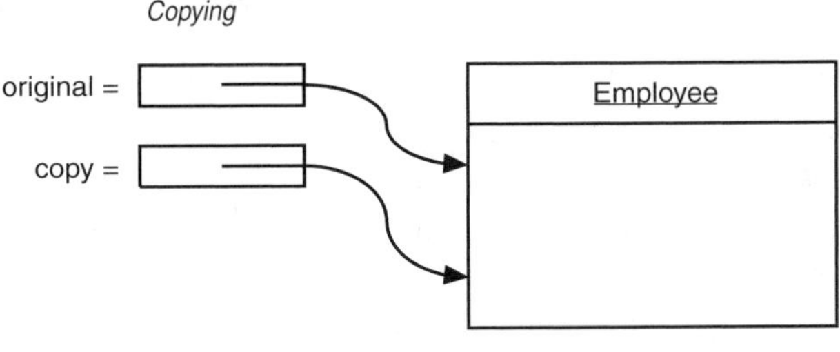

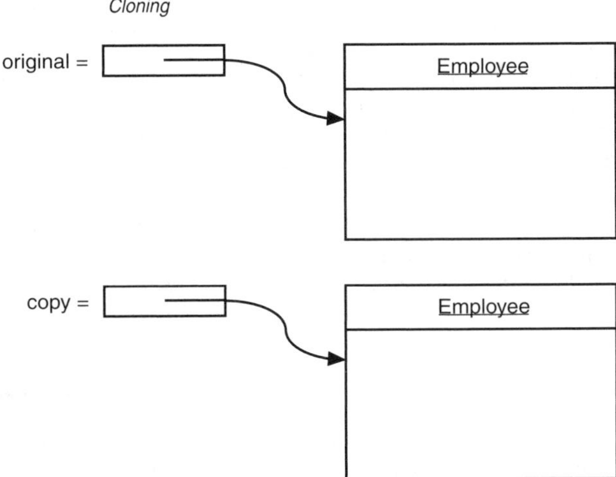

Figure 6–1: Copying and cloning

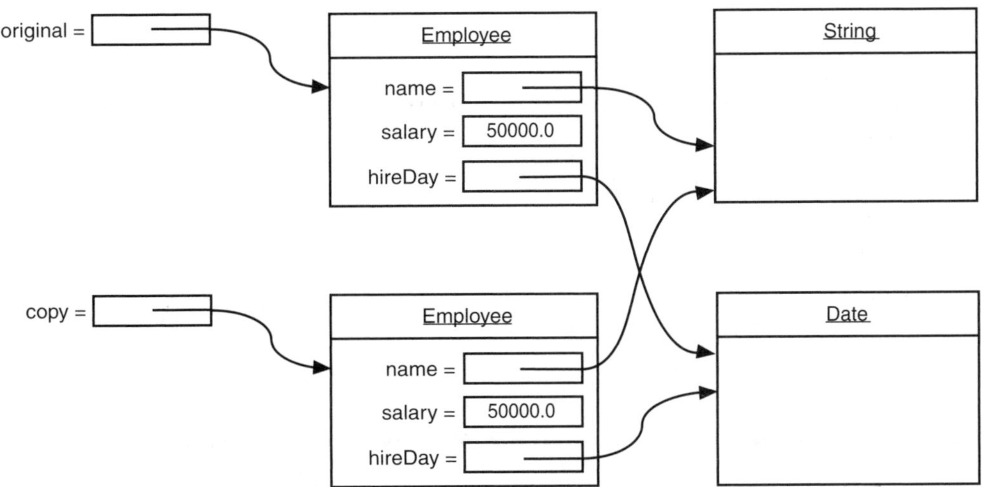

Figure 6–2: A shallow copy

Quite frequently, however, subobjects are mutable, and you must redefine the `clone` method to make a *deep copy* that clones the subobjects as well. In our example, the `hireDay` field is a `Date`, which is mutable.

For every class, you need to decide whether

1. The default `clone` method is good enough;
2. The default `clone` method can be patched up by calling `clone` on the mutable subobjects;
3. `clone` should not be attempted.

The third option is actually the default. To choose either the first or the second option, a class must

1. Implement the `Cloneable` interface, and
2. Redefine the `clone` method with the `public` access modifier.

NOTE: The `clone` method is declared `protected` in the `Object` class so that your code can't simply call `anObject.clone()`. But aren't protected methods accessible from any subclass, and isn't every class a subclass of `Object`? Fortunately, the rules for protected access are more subtle (see Chapter 5). A subclass can call a protected `clone` method only to clone *its own* objects. You must redefine `clone` to be public to allow objects to be cloned by any method.

In this case, the appearance of the `Cloneable` interface has nothing to do with the normal use of interfaces. In particular, it does *not* specify the `clone` method—that method is inherited from the `Object` class. The interface merely serves as a tag, indicating that the class designer understands the cloning process. Objects are so paranoid about cloning that they generate a checked exception if an object requests cloning but does not implement that interface.

NOTE: The `Cloneable` interface is one of a handful of *tagging interfaces* that Java provides. (Some programmers call them *marker interfaces*.) Recall that the usual purpose of an interface such as `Comparable` is to ensure that a class implements a particular method or set of methods. A tagging interface has no methods; its only purpose is to allow the use of `instanceof` in a type inquiry:

```
if (obj instanceof Cloneable) . . .
```

We recommend that you do not use this technique in your own programs.

Even if the default (shallow copy) implementation of `clone` is adequate, you still need to implement the `Cloneable` interface, redefine `clone` to be public, and call `super.clone()`. Here is an example:

```
class Employee implements Cloneable
{
   // raise visibility level to public, change return type
   public Employee clone() throws CloneNotSupportedException
   {
      return super.clone();
   }
   . . .
}
```

NOTE: Before JDK 5.0, the `clone` method always had return type `Object`. The covariant return types of JDK 5.0 let you specify the correct return type for your `clone` methods.

The clone method that you just saw adds no functionality to the shallow copy provided by Object.clone. It merely makes the method public. To make a deep copy, you have to work harder and clone the mutable instance fields.

Here is an example of a clone method that creates a deep copy:

```
class Employee implements Cloneable
{
   . . .
   public Object clone() throws CloneNotSupportedException
   {
      // call Object.clone()
      Employee cloned = (Employee) super.clone();

      // clone mutable fields
      cloned.hireDay = (Date) hireDay.clone()

      return cloned;
   }
}
```

The clone method of the Object class threatens to throw a CloneNotSupportedException—it does that whenever clone is invoked on an object whose class does not implement the Cloneable interface. Of course, the Employee and Date class implements the Cloneable interface, so the exception won't be thrown. However, the compiler does not know that. Therefore, we declared the exception:

```
public Employee clone() throws CloneNotSupportedException
```

Would it be better to catch the exception instead?

```
public Employee clone()
{
   try
   {
      return super.clone();
   }
   catch (CloneNotSupportedException e) { return null; }
   // this won't happen, since we are Cloneable
}
```

This is appropriate for final classes. Otherwise, it is a good idea to leave the throws specifier in place. That gives subclasses the option of throwing a CloneNotSupportedException if they can't support cloning.

You have to be careful about cloning of subclasses. For example, once you have defined the clone method for the Employee class, anyone can use it to clone Manager objects. Can the Employee clone method do the job? It depends on the fields of the Manager class. In our case, there is no problem because the bonus field has primitive type. But Manager might have acquired fields that require a deep copy or that are not cloneable. There is no guarantee that the implementor of the subclass has fixed clone to do the right thing. For that reason, the clone method is declared as protected in the Object class. But you don't have that luxury if you want users of your classes to invoke clone.

Should you implement clone in your own classes? If your clients need to make deep copies, then you probably should. Some authors feel that you should avoid clone altogether and instead implement another method for the same purpose. We agree that clone is rather awkward, but you'll run into the same issues if you shift the responsibility to another method.

At any rate, cloning is less common than you may think. Less than 5 percent of the classes in the standard library implement `clone`.

The program in Example 6–2 clones an `Employee` object, then invokes two mutators. The `raiseSalary` method changes the value of the `salary` field, whereas the `setHireDay` method changes the state of the `hireDay` field. Neither mutation affects the original object because `clone` has been defined to make a deep copy.

NOTE: Chapter 12 shows an alternate mechanism for cloning objects, using the object serialization feature of Java. That mechanism is easy to implement and safe, but it is not very efficient.

Example 6–2: CloneTest.java

```
import java.util.*;

public class CloneTest
{
   public static void main(String[] args)
   {
      try
      {
         Employee original = new Employee("John Q. Public", 50000);
         original.setHireDay(2000, 1, 1);
         Employee copy = original.clone();
         copy.raiseSalary(10);
         copy.setHireDay(2002, 12, 31);
         System.out.println("original=" + original);
         System.out.println("copy=" + copy);
      }
      catch (CloneNotSupportedException e)
      {
         e.printStackTrace();
      }
   }
}

class Employee implements Cloneable
{
   public Employee(String n, double s)
   {
      name = n;
      salary = s;
   }

   public Employee clone() throws CloneNotSupportedException
   {
      // call Object.clone()
      Employee cloned = (Employee)super.clone();

      // clone mutable fields
      cloned.hireDay = (Date)hireDay.clone();

      return cloned;
   }
```

```

   /**
      Set the hire day to a given date
      @param year the year of the hire day
      @param month the month of the hire day
      @param day the day of the hire day
   */
   public void setHireDay(int year, int month, int day)
   {
      hireDay = new GregorianCalendar(year, month - 1, day).getTime();
   }

   public void raiseSalary(double byPercent)
   {
      double raise = salary * byPercent / 100;
      salary += raise;
   }

   public String toString()
   {
      return "Employee[name=" + name
         + ",salary=" + salary
         + ",hireDay=" + hireDay
         + "]";
   }

   private String name;
   private double salary;
   private Date hireDay;
}
```

Interfaces and Callbacks

A common pattern in programming is the *callback* pattern. In this pattern, you want to specify the action that should occur whenever a particular event happens. For example, you may want a particular action to occur when a button is clicked or a menu item is selected. However, because you have not yet seen how to implement user interfaces, we consider a similar but simpler situation.

The `javax.swing` package contains a `Timer` class that is useful if you want to be notified whenever a time interval has elapsed. For example, if a part of your program contains a clock, then you can ask to be notified every second so that you can update the clock face.

When you construct a timer, you set the time interval and you tell it what it should do whenever the time interval has elapsed.

How do you tell the timer what it should do? In many programming languages, you supply the name of a function that the timer should call periodically. However, the classes in the Java standard library take an object-oriented approach. You pass an object of some class. The timer then calls one of the methods on that object. Passing an object is more flexible than passing a function because the object can carry additional information.

Of course, the timer needs to know what method to call. The timer requires that you specify an object of a class that implements the `ActionListener` interface of the `java.awt.event` package. Here is that interface:

```
public interface ActionListener
{
   void actionPerformed(ActionEvent event);
}
```

The timer calls the actionPerformed method when the time interval has expired.

C++ NOTE: As you saw in Chapter 5, Java does have the equivalent of function pointers, namely, Method objects. However, they are difficult to use, slower, and cannot be checked for type safety at compile time. Whenever you would use a function pointer in C++, you should consider using an interface in Java.

Suppose you want to print a message "At the tone, the time is . . .", followed by a beep, once every 10 seconds. You would define a class that implements the ActionListener interface. You would then place whatever statements you want to have executed inside the actionPerformed method.

```
class TimePrinter implements ActionListener
{
   public void actionPerformed(ActionEvent event)
   {
      Date now = new Date();
      System.out.println("At the tone, the time is " + now);
      Toolkit.getDefaultToolkit().beep();
   }
}
```

Note the ActionEvent parameter of the actionPerformed method. This parameter gives information about the event, such as the source object that generated it—see Chapter 8 for more information. However, detailed information about the event is not important in this program, and you can safely ignore the parameter.

Next, you construct an object of this class and pass it to the Timer constructor.

```
ActionListener listener = new TimePrinter();
Timer t = new Timer(10000, listener);
```

The first parameter of the Timer constructor is the time interval that must elapse between notifications, measured in milliseconds. We want to be notified every 10 seconds. The second parameter is the listener object.

Finally, you start the timer.

```
t.start();
```

Every 10 seconds, a message like

```
At the tone, the time is Thu Apr 13 23:29:08 PDT 2000
```

is displayed, followed by a beep.

Example 6–3 puts the timer and its action listener to work. After the timer is started, the program puts up a message dialog and waits for the user to click the Ok button to stop. While the program waits for the user, the current time is displayed in 10-second intervals.

Be patient when running the program. The "Quit program?" dialog box appears right away, but the first timer message is displayed after 10 seconds.

Note that the program imports the javax.swing.Timer class by name, in addition to importing javax.swing.* and java.util.*. This breaks the ambiguity between javax.swing.Timer and java.util.Timer, an unrelated class for scheduling background tasks.

Example 6–3: TimerTest.java

```
import java.awt.*;
import java.awt.event.*;
import java.util.*;
import javax.swing.*;
import javax.swing.Timer;
// to resolve conflict with java.util.Timer

public class TimerTest
{
   public static void main(String[] args)
   {
      ActionListener listener = new TimePrinter();

      // construct a timer that calls the listener
      // once every 10 seconds
      Timer t = new Timer(10000, listener);
      t.start();

      JOptionPane.showMessageDialog(null, "Quit program?");
      System.exit(0);
   }
}

class TimePrinter implements ActionListener
{
   public void actionPerformed(ActionEvent event)
   {
      Date now = new Date();
      System.out.println("At the tone, the time is " + now);
      Toolkit.getDefaultToolkit().beep();
   }
}
```

`javax.swing.JOptionPane` 1.2

- `static void showMessageDialog(Component parent, Object message)`
  displays a dialog box with a message prompt and an OK button. The dialog is centered over the `parent` component. If `parent` is `null`, the dialog is centered on the screen.

`javax.swing.Timer` 1.2

- `Timer(int interval, ActionListener listener)`
  constructs a timer that notifies `listener` whenever `interval` milliseconds have elapsed.
- `void start()`
  starts the timer. Once started, the timer calls `actionPerformed` on its listeners.
- `void stop()`
  stops the timer. Once stopped, the timer no longer calls `actionPerformed` on its listeners.

`javax.awt.Toolkit` 1.0

- `static Toolkit getDefaultToolkit()`
  gets the default toolkit. A toolkit contains information about the GUI environment.

- `void beep()`
  emits a beep sound.

Inner Classes

An *inner class* is a class that is defined inside another class. Why would you want to do that? There are three reasons:

- Inner class methods can access the data from the scope in which they are defined—including data that would otherwise be private.
- Inner classes can be hidden from other classes in the same package.
- *Anonymous* inner classes are handy when you want to define callbacks without writing a lot of code.

We will break up this rather complex topic into several steps.

- Starting on page 227, you will see a simple inner class that accesses an instance field of its outer class.
- On page 230, we cover the special syntax rules for inner classes.
- Starting on page 230, we peek inside inner classes to see how they are translated into regular classes. Squeamish readers may want to skip that section.
- Starting on page 232, we discuss *local inner classes* that can access local variables of the enclosing scope.
- Starting on page 234, we introduce *anonymous inner classes* and show how they are commonly used to implement callbacks.
- Finally, starting on page 237, you will see how *static inner classes* can be used for nested helper classes.

C++ NOTE: C++ has *nested classes.* A nested class is contained inside the scope of the enclosing class. Here is a typical example: a linked list class defines a class to hold the links, and a class to define an iterator position.

```
class LinkedList
{
public:
   class Iterator // a nested class
   {
   public:
      void insert(int x);
      int erase();
      . . .
   };
   . . .
private:
   class Link // a nested class
   {
   public:
      Link* next;
      int data;
   };
   . . .
};
```

The nesting is a relationship between *classes,* not *objects.* A `LinkedList` object does *not* have subobjects of type `Iterator` or `Link`.

There are two benefits: *name control* and *access control.* Because the name `Iterator` is nested inside the `LinkedList` class, it is externally known as `LinkedList::Iterator` and cannot conflict with another class called `Iterator`. In Java, this benefit is not as important because Java *packages* give the same kind of name control. Note that the `Link` class is in the *private* part of the `LinkedList` class. It is completely hidden from all other code. For that reason, it is safe to make its data fields public. They can be accessed by the methods of the `LinkedList` class (which has a legitimate need to access them), and they are not visible elsewhere. In Java, this kind of control was not possible until inner classes were introduced.

However, the Java inner classes have an additional feature that makes them richer and more useful than nested classes in C++. An object that comes from an inner class has an implicit reference to the outer class object that instantiated it. Through this pointer, it gains access to the total state of the outer object. You will see the details of the Java mechanism later in this chapter.

In Java, `static` inner classes do not have this added pointer. They are the Java analog to nested classes in C++.

Use of an Inner Class to Access Object State

The syntax for inner classes is rather complex. For that reason, we use a simple but somewhat artificial example to demonstrate the use of inner classes. We refactor the `TimerTest` example and extract a `TalkingClock` class. A talking clock is constructed with two parameters: the interval between announcements and a flag to turn beeps on or off.

```
class TalkingClock
{
   public TalkingClock(int interval, boolean beep) { . . . }
   public void start() { . . . }

   private int interval;
   private boolean beep;

   private class TimePrinter implements ActionListener
      // an inner class
   {
      . . .
   }
}
```

Note that the `TimePrinter` class is now located inside the `TalkingClock` class. This does *not* mean that every `TalkingClock` has a `TimePrinter` instance field. As you will see, the `TimePrinter` objects are constructed by methods of the `TalkingClock` class.

The `TimePrinter` class is a *private inner class* inside `TalkingClock`. This is a safety mechanism. Only `TalkingClock` methods can generate `TimePrinter` objects.

Only inner classes can be private. Regular classes always have either package or public visibility.

Here is the `TimePrinter` class in greater detail. Note that the `actionPerformed` method checks the `beep` flag before emitting a beep.

```
private class TimePrinter implements ActionListener
{
   public void actionPerformed(ActionEvent event)
   {
      Date now = new Date();
      System.out.println("At the tone, the time is " + now);
      if (beep) Toolkit.getDefaultToolkit().beep();
   }
}
```

Something surprising is going on. The TimePrinter class has no instance field or variable named beep. Instead, beep refers to the field of the TalkingClock object that created this TimePrinter. This is quite innovative. Traditionally, a method could refer to the data fields of the object invoking the method. An inner class method gets to access both its own data fields *and* those of the outer object creating it.

For this to work, an object of an inner class always gets an implicit reference to the object that created it. (See Figure 6–3.)

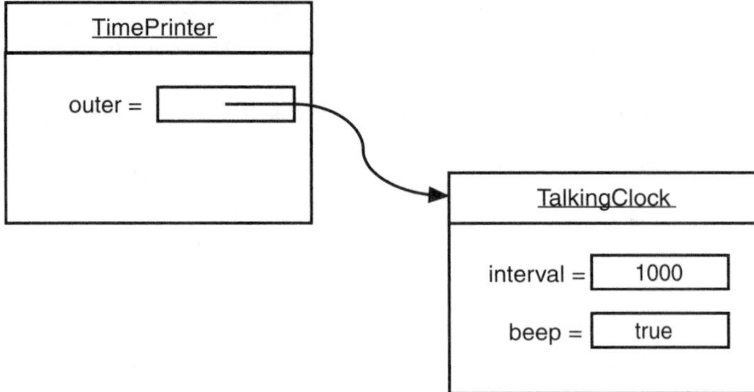

Figure 6–3: An inner class object has a reference to an outer class object

This reference is invisible in the definition of the inner class. However, to illuminate the concept, let us call the reference to the outer object *outer*. Then, the actionPerformed method is equivalent to the following:

```
public void actionPerformed(ActionEvent event)
{
   Date now = new Date();
   System.out.println("At the tone, the time is " + now);
   if (outer.beep) Toolkit.getDefaultToolkit().beep();
}
```

The outer class reference is set in the constructor. Because the TalkingClock defines no constructors, the compiler synthesizes a constructor, generating code like this:

```
public TimePrinter(TalkingClock clock) // automatically generated code
{
    outer = clock;
}
```

Again, please note, *outer* is not a Java keyword. We just use it to illustrate the mechanism involved in an inner class.

NOTE: If an inner class has constructors, the compiler modifies them, adding a parameter for the outer class reference.

When a TimePrinter object is constructed in the start method, the compiler passes the this reference to the current talking clock into the constructor:

```
ActionListener listener = new TimePrinter(this); // parameter automatically added
```

Example 6–4 shows the complete program that tests the inner class. Have another look at the access control. Had the TimePrinter class been a regular class, then it would have needed

to access the beep flag through a public method of the TalkingClock class. Using an inner class is an improvement. There is no need to provide accessors that are of interest only to one other class.

Example 6–4: InnerClassTest.java

```
import java.awt.*;
import java.awt.event.*;
import java.util.*;
import javax.swing.*;
import javax.swing.Timer;

public class InnerClassTest
{
   public static void main(String[] args)
   {
      TalkingClock clock = new TalkingClock(1000, true);
      clock.start();

      // keep program running until user selects "Ok"
      JOptionPane.showMessageDialog(null, "Quit program?");
      System.exit(0);
   }
}

/**
   A clock that prints the time in regular intervals.
*/
class TalkingClock
{
   /**
      Constructs a talking clock
      @param interval the interval between messages (in milliseconds)
      @param beep true if the clock should beep
   */
   public TalkingClock(int interval, boolean beep)
   {
      this.interval = interval;
      this.beep = beep;
   }

   /**
      Starts the clock.
   */
   public void start()
   {
      ActionListener listener = new TimePrinter();
      Timer t = new Timer(interval, listener);
      t.start();
   }

   private int interval;
   private boolean beep;

   private class TimePrinter implements ActionListener
   {
```

```
      public void actionPerformed(ActionEvent event)
      {
         Date now = new Date();
         System.out.println("At the tone, the time is " + now);
         if (beep) Toolkit.getDefaultToolkit().beep();
      }
   }
}
```

Special Syntax Rules for Inner Classes

In the preceding section, we explained the outer class reference of an inner class by calling it `outer`. Actually, the proper syntax for the outer reference is a bit more complex. The expression

OuterClass`.this`

denotes the outer class reference. For example, you can write the `actionPerformed` method of the `TimePrinter` inner class as

```
public void actionPerformed(ActionEvent event)
{
   . . .
   if (TalkingClock.this.beep) Toolkit.getDefaultToolkit().beep();
}
```

Conversely, you can write the inner object constructor more explicitly, using the syntax

outerObject`.new` *InnerClass*(*construction parameters*)

For example,

```
ActionListener listener = this.new TimePrinter();
```

Here, the outer class reference of the newly constructed `TimePrinter` object is set to the `this` reference of the method that creates the inner class object. This is the most common case. As always, the `this.` qualifier is redundant. However, it is also possible to set the outer class reference to another object by explicitly naming it. For example, if `TimePrinter` were a public inner class, you could construct a `TimePrinter` for any talking clock:

```
TalkingClock jabberer = new TalkingClock(1000, true);
TalkingClock.TimePrinter listener = jabberer.new TimePrinter();
```

Note that you refer to an inner class as

OuterClass.*InnerClass*

when it occurs outside the scope of the outer class. For example, if `TimePrinter` had been a public class, you could have referred to it as `TalkingClock.TimePrinter` elsewhere in your program.

Are Inner Classes Useful? Actually Necessary? Secure?

When inner classes were added to the Java language in JDK 1.1, many programmers considered them a major new feature that was out of character with the Java philosophy of being simpler than C++. The inner class syntax is undeniably complex. (It gets more complex as we study anonymous inner classes later in this chapter.) It is not obvious how inner classes interact with other features of the language, such as access control and security.

By adding a feature that was elegant and interesting rather than needed, has Java started down the road to ruin that has afflicted so many other languages?

While we won't try to answer this question completely, it is worth noting that inner classes are a phenomenon of the *compiler,* not the virtual machine. Inner classes are translated into regular class files with `$` (dollar signs) delimiting outer and inner class names, and the virtual machine does not have any special knowledge about them.

For example, the TimePrinter class inside the TalkingClock class is translated to a class file TalkingClock$TimePrinter.class. To see this at work, try the following experiment: run the ReflectionTest program of Chapter 5, and give it the class TalkingClock$TimePrinter to reflect upon. You will get the following printout:

```
class TalkingClock$TimePrinter
{
   private TalkingClock$TimePrinter(TalkingClock);
   TalkingClock$TimePrinter(TalkingClock, TalkingClock$1);

   public void actionPerformed(java.awt.event.ActionEvent);

   final TalkingClock this$0;
}
```

NOTE: If you use UNIX, remember to escape the $ character if you supply the class name on the command line. That is, run the ReflectionTest program as

```
java ReflectionTest 'TalkingClock$TimePrinter'
```

You can plainly see that the compiler has generated an additional instance field, this$0, for the reference to the outer class. (The name this$0 is synthesized by the compiler—you cannot refer to it in your code.) You can also see the added parameter for the constructor. Actually, the construction sequence is somewhat mysterious. A private constructor sets the this$0 field, and a package-visible constructor has a second parameter of type TalkingClock$1, a package-visible class with no fields or methods. That class is never instantiated. The TalkingClock class calls

```
new TalkingClock$TimePrinter(this, null)
```

If the compiler can automatically do this transformation, couldn't you simply program the same mechanism by hand? Let's try it. We would make TimePrinter a regular class, outside the TalkingClock class. When constructing a TimePrinter object, we pass it the this reference of the object that is creating it.

```
class TalkingClock
{
   . . .

   public void start()
   {
      ActionListener listener = new TimePrinter(this);
      Timer t = new Timer(interval, listener);
      t.start();
   }
}

class TimePrinter implements ActionListener
{
   public TimePrinter(TalkingClock clock)
   {
      outer = clock;
   }
   . . .
   private TalkingClock outer;
}
```

Now let us look at the actionPerformed method. It needs to access outer.beep.

```
if (outer.beep) . . . // ERROR
```

Here we run into a problem. The inner class can access the private data of the outer class, but our external TimePrinter class cannot.

Thus, inner classes are genuinely more powerful than regular classes because they have more access privileges.

You may well wonder how inner classes manage to acquire those added access privileges, because inner classes are translated to regular classes with funny names—the virtual machine knows nothing at all about them. To solve this mystery, let's again use the ReflectionTest program to spy on the TalkingClock class:

```
class TalkingClock
{
   public TalkingClock(int, boolean);

   static boolean access$100(TalkingClock);
   public void start();

   private int interval;
   private boolean beep;
}
```

Notice the static access$100 method that the compiler added to the outer class. It returns the beep field of the object that is passed as a parameter.

The inner class methods call that method. The statement

```
if (beep)
```

in the actionPerformed method of the TimePrinter class effectively makes the following call:

```
if (access$100(outer));
```

Is this a security risk? You bet it is. It is an easy matter for someone else to invoke the access$100 method to read the private beep field. Of course, access$100 is not a legal name for a Java method. However, hackers who are familiar with the structure of class files can easily produce a class file with virtual machine instructions to call that method, for example, by using a hex editor. Because the secret access methods have package visibility, the attack code would need to be placed inside the same package as the class under attack.

To summarize, if an inner class accesses a private data field, then it is possible to access that data field through other classes that are added to the package of the outer class, but to do so requires skill and determination. A programmer cannot accidentally obtain access but must intentionally build or modify a class file for that purpose.

Local Inner Classes

If you look carefully at the code of the TalkingClock example, you will find that you need the name of the type TimePrinter only once: when you create an object of that type in the start method.

When you have a situation like this, you can define the class *locally in a single method.*

```
public void start()
{
   class TimePrinter implements ActionListener
   {
      public void actionPerformed(ActionEvent event)
      {
         Date now = new Date();
```

```
            System.out.println("At the tone, the time is " + now);
            if (beep) Toolkit.getDefaultToolkit().beep();
         }
      }

      ActionListener listener = new TimePrinter();
      Timer t = new Timer(1000, listener);
      t.start();
   }
```

Local classes are never declared with an access specifier (that is, `public` or `private`). Their scope is always restricted to the block in which they are declared.

Local classes have a great advantage: they are completely hidden from the outside world—not even other code in the `TalkingClock` class can access them. No method except `start` has any knowledge of the `TimePrinter` class.

Local classes have another advantage over other inner classes. Not only can they access the fields of their outer classes, they can even access local variables! However, those local variables must be declared `final`. Here is a typical example. Let's move the `interval` and `beep` parameters from the `TalkingClock` constructor to the `start` method.

```
public void start(int interval, final boolean beep)
{
   class TimePrinter implements ActionListener
   {
      public void actionPerformed(ActionEvent event)
      {
          Date now = new Date();
          System.out.println("At the tone, the time is " + now);
          if (beep) Toolkit.getDefaultToolkit().beep();
      }
   }

   ActionListener listener = new TimePrinter();
   Timer t = new Timer(1000, listener);
   t.start();
}
```

Note that the `TimePrinter` class no longer needs to store a `beep` instance variable. It simply refers to the parameter variable of the method that contains the class definition.

Maybe this should not be so surprising. The line

```
if (beep) . . .
```

is, after all, ultimately inside the `start` method, so why shouldn't it have access to the value of the `beep` variable?

To see why there is a subtle issue here, let's consider the flow of control more closely.

1. The `start` method is called.
2. The object variable `listener` is initialized by a call to the constructor of the inner class `TimePrinter`.
3. The `listener` reference is passed to the `Timer` constructor, the timer is started, and the `start` method exits. At this point, the `beep` parameter variable of the `start` method no longer exists.
4. A second later, the `actionPerformed` method executes `if (beep) . . .`.

For the code in the actionPerformed method to work, the TimePrinter class must have copied the beep field, as a local variable of the start method, before the beep field went away. That is indeed exactly what happens. In our example, the compiler synthesizes the name TalkingClock$1TimePrinter for the local inner class. If you use the ReflectionTest program again to spy on the TalkingClock$1TimePrinter class, you get the following output:

```
class TalkingClock$1TimePrinter
{
   TalkingClock$1TimePrinter(TalkingClock, boolean);

   public void actionPerformed(java.awt.event.ActionEvent);

   final boolean val$beep;
   final TalkingClock this$0;
}
```

Note the boolean parameter to the constructor and the val$beep instance variable. When an object is created, the value beep is passed into the constructor and stored in the val$beep field. This sounds like an extraordinary amount of trouble for the implementors of the compiler. The compiler must detect access of local variables, make matching data fields for each one of them, and copy the local variables into the constructor so that the data fields can be initialized as copies of them.

From the programmer's point of view, however, local variable access is quite pleasant. It makes your inner classes simpler by reducing the instance fields that you need to program explicitly.

As we already mentioned, the methods of a local class can refer only to local variables that are declared final. For that reason, the beep parameter was declared final in our example. A local variable that is declared final cannot be modified after it has been initialized. Thus, it is guaranteed that the local variable and the copy that is made inside the local class always have the same value.

NOTE: You have seen final variables used for constants, such as

```
public static final double SPEED_LIMIT = 55;
```

The final keyword can be applied to local variables, instance variables, and static variables. In all cases it means the same thing: You can assign to this variable *once* after it has been created. Afterwards, you cannot change the value—it is final.

However, you don't have to initialize a final variable when you define it. For example, the final parameter variable beep is initialized once after its creation, when the start method is called. (If the method is called multiple times, each call has its own newly created beep parameter.) The val$beep instance variable that you can see in the TalkingClock$1TimePrinter inner class is set once, in the inner class constructor. A final variable that isn't initialized when it is defined is often called a *blank final* variable.

Anonymous Inner Classes

When using local inner classes, you can often go a step further. If you want to make only a single object of this class, you don't even need to give the class a name. Such a class is called an *anonymous inner class.*

```
public void start(int interval, final boolean beep)
{
   ActionListener listener = new
      ActionListener()
```

```
      {
         public void actionPerformed(ActionEvent event)
         {
            Date now = new Date();
            System.out.println("At the tone, the time is " + now);
            if (beep) Toolkit.getDefaultToolkit().beep();
         }
      };
   Timer t = new Timer(1000, listener);
   t.start();
}
```

This syntax is very cryptic indeed. What it means is this:

Create a new object of a class that implements the `ActionListener` interface, where the required method `actionPerformed` is the one defined inside the braces { }.

Any parameters used to construct the object are given inside the parentheses ( ) following the supertype name. In general, the syntax is

```
new SuperType(construction parameters)
{
   inner class methods and data
}
```

Here, *SuperType* can be an interface, such as `ActionListener`; then, the inner class implements that interface. Or *SuperType* can be a class; then, the inner class extends that class.

An anonymous inner class cannot have constructors because the name of a constructor must be the same as the name of a class, and the class has no name. Instead, the construction parameters are given to the *superclass* constructor. In particular, whenever an inner class implements an interface, it cannot have any construction parameters. Nevertheless, you must supply a set of parentheses as in

```
new InterfaceType() { methods and data }
```

You have to look carefully to see the difference between the construction of a new object of a class and the construction of an object of an anonymous inner class extending that class. If the closing parenthesis of the construction parameter list is followed by an opening brace, then an anonymous inner class is being defined.

```
Person queen = new Person("Mary");
   // a Person object
Person count = new Person("Dracula") { . . .};
   // an object of an inner class extending Person
```

Are anonymous inner classes a great idea or are they a great way of writing obfuscated code? Probably a bit of both. When the code for an inner class is short, just a few lines of simple code, then anonymous inner classes can save typing time, but it is exactly time-saving features like this that lead you down the slippery slope to "Obfuscated Java Code Contests."

It is a shame that the designers of Java did not try to improve the syntax of anonymous inner classes, because generally, Java syntax is a great improvement over C++. The designers of the inner class feature could have helped the human reader with a syntax such as

```
Person count = new class extends Person("Dracula") { . . . };
   // not the actual Java syntax
```

But they didn't. Because many programmers find code with too many anonymous inner classes hard to read, we recommend restraint when using them.

Example 6–5 contains the complete source code for the talking clock program with an anonymous inner class. If you compare this program with Example 6–4, you will find that in this case the solution with the anonymous inner class is quite a bit shorter, and, hopefully, with a bit of practice, as easy to comprehend.

Example 6–5: AnonymousInnerClassTest.java

```
import java.awt.*;
import java.awt.event.*;
import java.util.*;
import javax.swing.*;
import javax.swing.Timer;

public class AnonymousInnerClassTest
{
   public static void main(String[] args)
   {
      TalkingClock clock = new TalkingClock();
      clock.start(1000, true);

      // keep program running until user selects "Ok"
      JOptionPane.showMessageDialog(null, "Quit program?");
      System.exit(0);
   }
}

/**
   A clock that prints the time in regular intervals.
*/
class TalkingClock
{
   /**
      Starts the clock.
      @param interval the interval between messages (in milliseconds)
      @param beep true if the clock should beep
   */
   public void start(int interval, final boolean beep)
   {
      ActionListener listener = new
         ActionListener()
         {
            public void actionPerformed(ActionEvent event)
            {
               Date now = new Date();
               System.out.println("At the tone, the time is " + now);
               if (beep) Toolkit.getDefaultToolkit().beep();
            }
         };
      Timer t = new Timer(interval, listener);
      t.start();
   }
}
```

Static Inner Classes

Occasionally, you want to use an inner class simply to hide one class inside another, but you don't need the inner class to have a reference to the outer class object. You can suppress the generation of that reference by declaring the inner class static.

Here is a typical example of where you would want to do this. Consider the task of computing the minimum and maximum value in an array. Of course, you write one method to compute the minimum and another method to compute the maximum. When you call both methods, then the array is traversed twice. It would be more efficient to traverse the array only once, computing both the minimum and the maximum simultaneously.

```
double min = Double.MAX_VALUE;
double max = Double.MIN_VALUE;
for (double v : values)
{
   if (min > v) min = v;
   if (max < v) max = v;
}
```

However, the method must return two numbers. We can achieve that by defining a class Pair that holds two values:

```
class Pair
{
   public Pair(double f, double s)
   {
      first = f;
      second = s;
   }
   public double getFirst() { return first; }
   public double getSecond() {  return second; }

   private double first;
   private double second;
}
```

The minmax function can then return an object of type Pair.

```
class ArrayAlg
{
   public static Pair minmax(double[] values)
   {
      . . .
      return new Pair(min, max);
   }
}
```

The caller of the function uses the getFirst and getSecond methods to retrieve the answers:

```
Pair p = ArrayAlg.minmax(d);
System.out.println("min = " + p.getFirst());
System.out.println("max = " + p.getSecond());
```

Of course, the name Pair is an exceedingly common name, and in a large project, it is quite possible that some other programmer had the same bright idea, except that the other programmer made a Pair class that contains a pair of strings. We can solve this potential name clash by making Pair a public inner class inside ArrayAlg. Then the class will be known to the public as ArrayAlg.Pair:

```
ArrayAlg.Pair p = ArrayAlg.minmax(d);
```

However, unlike the inner classes that we used in previous examples, we do not want to have a reference to any other object inside a Pair object. That reference can be suppressed by declaring the inner class static:

```
class ArrayAlg
{
   public static class Pair
   {
      . . .
   }
   . . .
}
```

Of course, only inner classes can be declared static. A static inner class is exactly like any other inner class, except that an object of a static inner class does not have a reference to the outer class object that generated it. In our example, we must use a static inner class because the inner class object is constructed inside a static method:

```
public static Pair minmax(double[] d)
{
    . . .
    return new Pair(min, max);
}
```

Had the Pair class not been declared as static, the compiler would have complained that there was no implicit object of type ArrayAlg available to initialize the inner class object.

NOTE: You use a static inner class whenever the inner class does not need to access an outer class object. Some programmers use the term *nested class* to describe static inner classes.

NOTE: Inner classes that are declared inside an interface are automatically static and public.

Example 6–6 contains the complete source code of the ArrayAlg class and the nested Pair class.

Example 6–6: StaticInnerClassTest.java

```
public class StaticInnerClassTest
{
   public static void main(String[] args)
   {
      double[] d = new double[20];
      for (int i = 0; i < d.length; i++)
         d[i] = 100 * Math.random();
      ArrayAlg.Pair p = ArrayAlg.minmax(d);
      System.out.println("min = " + p.getFirst());
      System.out.println("max = " + p.getSecond());
   }
}

class ArrayAlg
{
   /**
      A pair of floating-point numbers
   */
   public static class Pair
   {
```

```
      /**
          Constructs a pair from two floating-point numbers
          @param f the first number
          @param s the second number
      */
      public Pair(double f, double s)
      {
         first = f;
         second = s;
      }

      /**
         Returns the first number of the pair
         @return the first number
      */
      public double getFirst()
      {
         return first;
      }

      /**
         Returns the second number of the pair
         @return the second number
      */
      public double getSecond()
      {
         return second;
      }

      private double first;
      private double second;
   }

   /**
      Computes both the minimum and the maximum of an array
      @param values an array of floating-point numbers
      @return a pair whose first element is the minimum and whose
      second element is the maximum
   */
   public static Pair minmax(double[] values)
   {
      double min = Double.MAX_VALUE;
      double max = Double.MIN_VALUE;
      for (double v : values)
      {
         if (min > v) min = v;
         if (max < v) max = v;
      }
      return new Pair(min, max);
   }
}
```

Proxies

In the final section of this chapter, we discuss *proxies,* a feature that became available with version 1.3 of the JDK. You use a proxy to create at run time new classes that implement a given set of interfaces. Proxies are only necessary when you don't yet know at compile time which interfaces you need to implement. This is not a common situation for application programmers. However, for certain system programming applications, the flexibility that proxies offer can be very important. By using proxies, you can often avoid the mechanical generation and compilation of "stub" code.

NOTE: Stub classes have been used in a number of specialized situations. When you use *remote method invocation* (RMI), a special utility called `rmic` produces stub classes that you need to add to your program. (See Chapter 5 of Volume 2 for more information on RMI.) And when you use the *bean box*, stub classes are produced and compiled on the fly when you connect beans to each other. (See Chapter 8 of Volume 2 for more information on Java beans.) As of JDK 5.0, the proxy facility is used to generate RMI stubs without having to run a utility.

Suppose you have an array of `Class` objects representing interfaces (maybe only containing a single interface), whose exact nature you may not know at compile time. Now you want to construct an object of a class that implements these interfaces. This is a difficult problem. If a `Class` object represents an actual class, then you can simply use the `newInstance` method or use reflection to find a constructor of that class. But you can't instantiate an interface. And you can't define new classes in a running program.

To overcome this problem, some programs—such as the `BeanBox` in early versions of the Bean Development Kit—generate code, place it into a file, invoke the compiler, and then load the resulting class file. Naturally, this is slow, and it also requires deployment of the compiler together with the program. The *proxy* mechanism is a better solution. The proxy class can create brand-new classes at run time. Such a proxy class implements the interfaces that you specify. In particular, the proxy class has the following methods:

- All methods required by the specified interfaces; and
- All methods defined in the `Object` class (`toString`, `equals`, and so on).

However, you cannot define new code for these methods at run time. Instead, you must supply an *invocation handler.* An invocation handler is an object of any class that implements the `InvocationHandler` interface. That interface has a single method:

```
Object invoke(Object proxy, Method method, Object[] args)
```

Whenever a method is called on the proxy object, the `invoke` method of the invocation handler gets called, with the `Method` object and parameters of the original call. The invocation handler must then figure out how to handle the call.

To create a proxy object, you use the `newProxyInstance` method of the `Proxy` class. The method has three parameters:

- A *class loader.* As part of the Java security model, different class loaders for system classes, classes that are downloaded from the Internet, and so on, can be used. We discuss class loaders in Volume 2. For now, we specify `null` to use the default class loader.
- An array of `Class` objects, one for each interface to be implemented.
- An invocation handler.

There are two remaining questions. How do we define the handler? And what can we do with the resulting proxy object? The answers depend, of course, on the problem that we want to solve with the proxy mechanism. Proxies can be used for many purposes, such as

- Routing method calls to remote servers;
- Associating user interface events with actions in a running program; and
- Tracing method calls for debugging purposes.

In our example program, we use proxies and invocation handlers to trace method calls. We define a TraceHandler wrapper class that stores a wrapped object. Its invoke method simply prints the name and parameters of the method to be called and then calls the method with the wrapped object as the implicit parameter.

```
class TraceHandler implements InvocationHandler
{
   public TraceHandler(Object t)
   {
      target = t;
   }

   public Object invoke(Object proxy, Method m, Object[] args)
      throws Throwable
   {
      // print method name and parameters
      . . .
      // invoke actual method
      return m.invoke(target, args);
   }

   private Object target;
}
```

Here is how you construct a proxy object that causes the tracing behavior whenever one of its methods is called.

```
Object value = . . .;
// construct wrapper
InvocationHandler handler = new TraceHandler(value);
// construct proxy for all interfaces
Class[] interfaces = value.getClass().getInterfaces();
Object proxy = Proxy.newProxyInstance(null, interfaces, handler);
```

Now, whenever a method is called on proxy, the method name and parameters are printed out and the method is then invoked on value.

In the program shown in Example 6–7, we use proxy objects to trace a binary search. We fill an array with proxies to the integers 1 . . . 1000. Then we invoke the binarySearch method of the Arrays class to search for a random integer in the array. Finally, we print the matching element.

```
Object[] elements = new Object[1000];
// fill elements with proxies for the integers 1 . . . 1000
for (int i = 0; i < elements.length; i++)
{
   Integer value = i + 1;
   elements[i] = . . .; // proxy for value;
}

// construct a random integer
Integer key = new Random().nextInt(elements.length) + 1;

// search for the key
int result = Arrays.binarySearch(elements, key);

// print match if found
if (result >= 0) System.out.println(elements[result]);
```

The Integer class implements the Comparable interface. The proxy objects belong to a class that is defined at run time. (It has a name such as $Proxy0.) That class also implements the Comparable interface. However, its compareTo method calls the invoke method of the proxy object's handler.

NOTE: As you saw earlier in this chapter, as of JDK 5.0, the Integer class actually implements Comparable<Integer>. However, at run time, all generic types are erased and the proxy is constructed with the class object for the raw Comparable class.

The binarySearch method makes calls like this:

```
if (elements[i].compareTo(key) < 0) . . .
```

Because we filled the array with proxy objects, the compareTo calls call the invoke method of the TraceHandler class. That method prints the method name and parameters and then invokes compareTo on the wrapped Integer object.

Finally, at the end of the sample program, we call

```
System.out.println(elements[result]);
```

The println method calls toString on the proxy object, and that call is also redirected to the invocation handler.

Here is the complete trace of a program run:

```
500.compareTo(288)
250.compareTo(288)
375.compareTo(288)
312.compareTo(288)
281.compareTo(288)
296.compareTo(288)
288.compareTo(288)
288.toString()
```

You can see how the binary search algorithm homes in on the key by cutting the search interval in half in every step.

Example 6–7: ProxyTest.java

```
import java.lang.reflect.*;
import java.util.*;

public class ProxyTest
{
   public static void main(String[] args)
   {
      Object[] elements = new Object[1000];

      // fill elements with proxies for the integers 1 ... 1000
      for (int i = 0; i < elements.length; i++)
      {
         Integer value = i + 1;
         Class[] interfaces = value.getClass().getInterfaces();
         InvocationHandler handler = new TraceHandler(value);
         Object proxy = Proxy.newProxyInstance(null,
            interfaces, handler);
         elements[i] = proxy;
      }

      // construct a random integer
```

```
      Integer key = new Random().nextInt(elements.length) + 1;

      // search for the key
      int result = Arrays.binarySearch(elements, key);

      // print match if found
      if (result >= 0) System.out.println(elements[result]);
   }
}

/**
   An invocation handler that prints out the method name
   and parameters, then invokes the original method
*/
class TraceHandler implements InvocationHandler
{
   /**
      Constructs a TraceHandler
      @param t the implicit parameter of the method call
   */
   public TraceHandler(Object t)
   {
      target = t;
   }

   public Object invoke(Object proxy, Method m, Object[] args) throws Throwable
   {
      // print implicit argument
      System.out.print(target);
      // print method name
      System.out.print("." + m.getName() + "(");
      // print explicit arguments
      if (args != null)
      {
         for (int i = 0; i < args.length; i++)
         {
            System.out.print(args[i]);
            if (i < args.length - 1)
               System.out.print(", ");
         }
      }
      System.out.println(")");

      // invoke actual method
      return m.invoke(target, args);
   }

   private Object target;
}
```

Properties of Proxy Classes

Now that you have seen proxy classes in action, we want to go over some of their properties. Remember that proxy classes are created on the fly in a running program. However, once they are created, they are regular classes, just like any other classes in the virtual machine.

All proxy classes extend the class `Proxy`. A proxy class has only one instance variable—the invocation handler, which is defined in the `Proxy` superclass. Any additional data that are required to carry out the proxy objects' tasks must be stored in the invocation handler. For example, when we proxied `Comparable` objects in the program shown in Example 6–7, the `TraceHandler` wrapped the actual objects.

All proxy classes override the `toString`, `equals`, and `hashCode` methods of the `Object` class. Like all proxy methods, these methods simply call `invoke` on the invocation handler. The other methods of the `Object` class (such as `clone` and `getClass`) are not redefined.

The names of proxy classes are not defined. The `Proxy` class in Sun's virtual machine generates class names that begin with the string `$Proxy`.

There is only one proxy class for a particular class loader and ordered set of interfaces. That is, if you call the `newProxyInstance` method twice with the same class loader and interface array, then you get two objects of the same class. You can also obtain that class with the `getProxyClass` method:

```
Class proxyClass = Proxy.getProxyClass(null, interfaces);
```

A proxy class is always `public` and `final`. If all interfaces that the proxy class implements are `public`, then the proxy class does not belong to any particular package. Otherwise, all non-public interfaces must belong to the same package, and then the proxy class also belongs to that package.

You can test whether a particular `Class` object represents a proxy class by calling the `isProxyClass` method of the `Proxy` class.

`java.lang.reflect.InvocationHandler` 1.3

- `Object invoke(Object proxy, Method method, Object[] args)`
  define this method to contain the action that you want carried out whenever a method was invoked on the proxy object.

`java.lang.reflect.Proxy` 1.3

- `static Class getProxyClass(ClassLoader loader, Class[] interfaces)`
  returns the proxy class that implements the given interfaces.
- `static Object newProxyInstance(ClassLoader loader, Class[] interfaces, InvocationHandler handler)`
  constructs a new instance of the proxy class that implements the given interfaces. All methods call the `invoke` method of the given handler object.
- `static boolean isProxyClass(Class c)`
  returns `true` if `c` is a proxy class.

This ends our final chapter on the fundamentals of the Java programming language. Interfaces and inner classes are concepts that you will encounter frequently. However, as we already mentioned, proxies are an advanced technique that is of interest mainly to tool builders, not application programmers. You are now ready to go on to learn about graphics and user interfaces, starting with Chapter 7.

Chapter 7

Graphics Programming

- INTRODUCING SWING
- CREATING A FRAME
- POSITIONING A FRAME
- DISPLAYING INFORMATION IN A PANEL
- WORKING WITH 2D SHAPES
- USING COLOR
- USING SPECIAL FONTS FOR TEXT
- DOING MORE WITH IMAGES

To this point, you have seen only how to write programs that take input from the keyboard, fuss with it, and then display the results on a console screen. This is not what most users want now. Modern programs don't work this way and neither do web pages. This chapter starts you on the road to writing Java programs that use a graphical user interface (GUI). In particular, you learn how to write programs that size and locate windows on the screen, display text with multiple fonts in a window, display images, and so on. This gives you a useful, valuable repertoire of skills that you will put to good use in subsequent chapters as you write interesting programs.

The next two chapters show you how to process events, such as keystrokes and mouse clicks, and how to add interface elements, such as menus and buttons, to your applications. When you finish these three chapters, you will know the essentials for writing *stand-alone* graphical applications. Chapter 10 shows how to program applets that use these features and are embedded in web pages. For more sophisticated graphics programming techniques, we refer you to Volume 2.

Introducing Swing

When Java 1.0 was introduced, it contained a class library, which Sun called the Abstract Window Toolkit (AWT), for basic GUI programming. The basic AWT library deals with user interface elements by delegating their creation and behavior to the native GUI toolkit on each target platform (Windows, Solaris, Macintosh, and so on). For example, if you used the original AWT to put a text box on a Java window, an underlying "peer" text box actually handled the text input. The resulting program could then, in theory, run on any of these platforms, with the "look and feel" of the target platform—hence Sun's trademarked slogan "Write Once, Run Anywhere."

The peer-based approach worked well for simple applications, but it soon became apparent that it was fiendishly difficult to write a high-quality portable graphics library that depended on native user interface elements. User interface elements such as menus, scrollbars, and text fields can have subtle differences in behavior on different platforms. It was hard, therefore, to give users a consistent and predictable experience with this approach. Moreover, some graphical environments (such as X11/Motif) do not have as rich a collection of user interface components as does Windows or the Macintosh. This in turn further limits a portable library based on peers to a "lowest common denominator" approach. As a result, GUI applications built with the AWT simply did not look as nice as native Windows or Macintosh applications, nor did they have the kind of functionality that users of those platforms had come to expect. More depressingly, there were *different* bugs in the AWT user interface library on the different platforms. Developers complained that they needed to test their applications on each platform, a practice derisively called "write once, debug everywhere."

In 1996, Netscape created a GUI library they called the IFC (Internet Foundation Classes) that used an entirely different approach. User interface elements, such as buttons, menus, and so on, were *painted* onto blank windows. The only peer functionality needed was a way to put up windows and to paint on the window. Thus, Netscape's IFC widgets looked and behaved the same no matter which platform the program ran on. Sun worked with Netscape to perfect this approach, creating a user interface library with the code name "Swing" (sometimes called the "Swing set"). Swing was available as an extension to Java 1.1 and became a part of the standard library in JDK 1.2.

Since, as Duke Ellington said, "It Don't Mean a Thing If It Ain't Got That Swing," Swing is now the official name for the non-peer-based GUI toolkit. Swing is part of the Java Foundation Classes (JFC). The full JFC is vast and contains far more than the Swing GUI toolkit. JFC features not only include the Swing components but also an accessibility API, a 2D API, and a drag-and-drop API.

NOTE: Swing is not a complete replacement for the AWT—it is built on top of the AWT architecture. Swing simply gives you more capable user interface components. You use the foundations of the AWT, in particular, event handling, whenever you write a Swing program. From now on, we say "Swing" when we mean the "painted" non-peer-based user interface classes, and we say "AWT" when we mean the underlying mechanisms of the windowing toolkit, such as event handling.

Of course, Swing-based user interface elements will be somewhat slower to appear on the user's screen than the peer-based components used by the AWT. Our experience is that on any reasonably modern machine, the speed difference shouldn't be a problem. On the other hand, the reasons to choose Swing are overwhelming:

- Swing has a rich and convenient set of user interface elements.
- Swing has few dependencies on the underlying platform; it is therefore less prone to platform-specific bugs.
- Swing gives a consistent user experience across platforms.

All this means Swing has the potential of fulfilling the promise of Sun's "Write Once, Run Anywhere" slogan.

Still, the third plus is also a potential drawback: if the user interface elements look the same on all platforms, then they will look *different* from the native controls and thus users will be less familiar with them.

Swing solves this problem in a very elegant way. Programmers writing Swing programs can give the program a specific "look and feel." For example, Figure 7–1 and 7–2 show the same program running with the Windows[1] and the Motif look and feel.

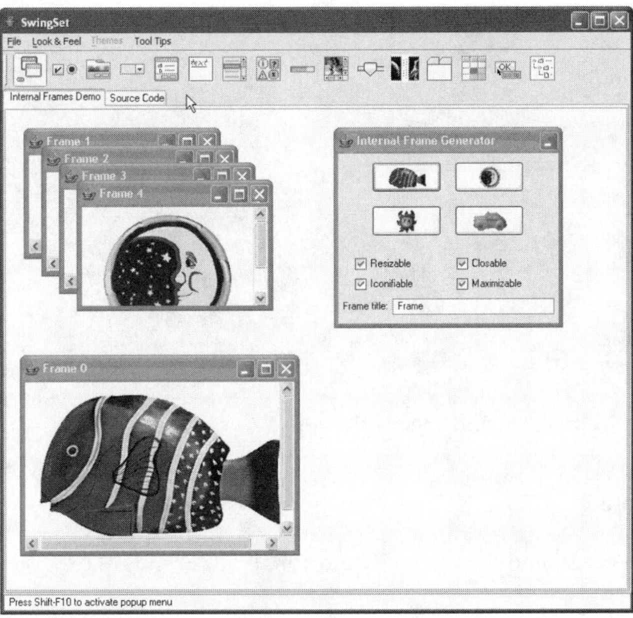

Figure 7–1: The Windows look and feel of Swing

NOTE: Although we won't have space in this book to tell you how to do it, Java programmers can extend an existing look and feel or even design a totally new look and feel. This is a tedious process that involves specifying how each Swing component is painted. Some developers have done just that, especially when porting Java to nontraditional platforms such as kiosk terminals or handheld devices. See `http://www.javootoo.com` for a collection of interesting look-and-feel implementations.

JDK 5.0 introduces a new look and feel, called Synth, that makes this process easier. In Synth, you can define a new look and feel by providing image files and XML descriptors, without doing any programming.

Furthermore, Sun developed a platform-independent look and feel that was called "Metal" until the marketing folks renamed it as the "Java look and feel." However, most programmers continue to use the term "Metal," and we will do the same in this book.

1. For what are apparently copyright reasons, the Windows and Macintosh look and feel are available only with the Java runtime environments for those platforms.

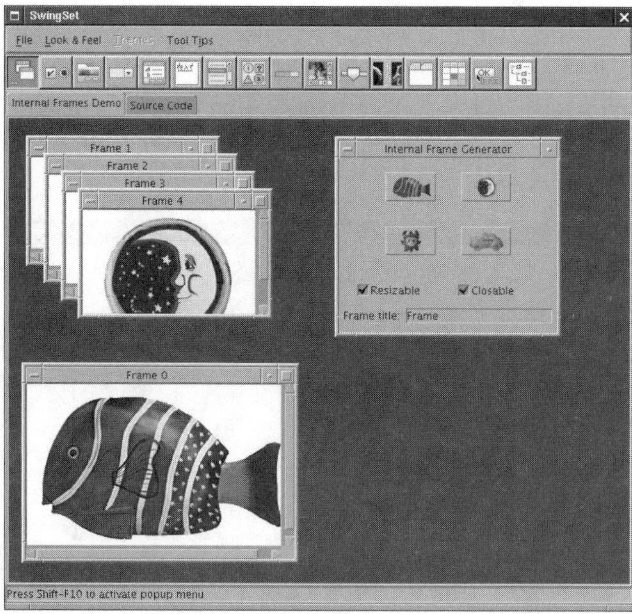

Figure 7–2: The Motif look and feel of Swing

Some people criticized Metal as being stodgy, and the look was freshened up for the 5.0 release (see Figure 7–3). Now the Metal look supports multiple themes—minor variations in colors and fonts. The default theme is called "Ocean." In this book, we use Swing, with the Metal look and feel and the Ocean theme, for all our graphical programs.

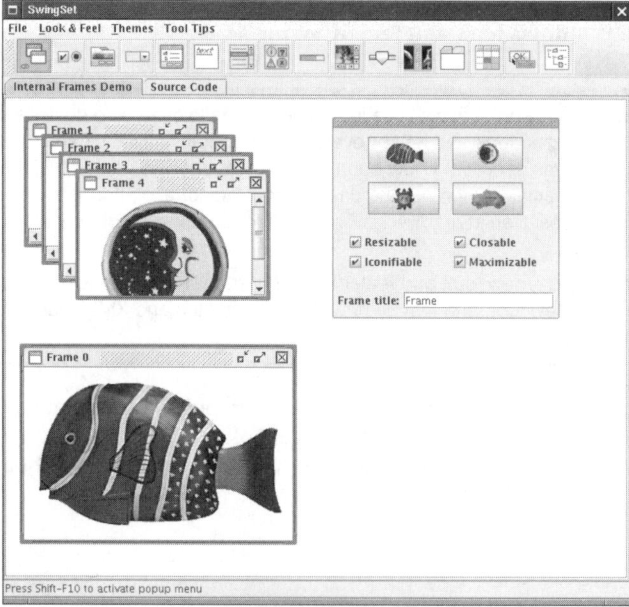

Figure 7–3: The Ocean theme of the Metal look and feel

NOTE: Most Java user interface programming is nowadays done in Swing, with one notable exception. The Eclipse integrated development environment uses a graphics toolkit called SWT that is similar to the AWT, mapping to native components on various platforms. You can find articles describing SWT at `http://www.eclipse.org/articles/`.

Finally, we do have to warn you that if you have programmed Microsoft Windows applications with Visual Basic or C#, you know about the ease of use that comes with the graphical layout tools and resource editors these products provide. These tools let you design the visual appearance of your application, and then they generate much (often all) of the GUI code for you. Although GUI builders are available for Java programming, these products are not as mature as the corresponding tools for Windows. In any case, to fully understand graphical user interface programming (or even, we feel, to use these tools effectively), you need to know how to build a user interface manually. Naturally, this often requires writing *a lot of code.*

Creating a Frame

A top-level window (that is, a window that is not contained inside another window) is called a *frame* in Java. The AWT library has a class, called `Frame`, for this top level. The Swing version of this class is called `JFrame` and extends the `Frame` class. The `JFrame` is one of the few Swing components that is not painted on a canvas. Thus, the decorations (buttons, title bar, icons, and so on) are drawn by the user's windowing system, not by Swing.

CAUTION: Most Swing component classes start with a "J": `JButton`, `JFrame`, and so on. There are classes such as `Button` and `Frame`, but they are AWT components. If you accidentally omit a "J", your program may still compile and run, but the mixture of Swing and AWT components can lead to visual and behavioral inconsistencies.

In this section, we go over the most common methods for working with a Swing *JFrame.* Example 7–1 lists a simple program that displays an empty frame on the screen, as illustrated in Figure 7–4.

Figure 7–4: The simplest visible frame

Example 7–1: SimpleFrameTest.java

```
import javax.swing.*;

public class SimpleFrameTest
{
   public static void main(String[] args)
   {
      SimpleFrame frame = new SimpleFrame();
      frame.setDefaultCloseOperation(JFrame.EXIT_ON_CLOSE);
      frame.setVisible(true);
```

```
    }
}

class SimpleFrame extends JFrame
{
   public SimpleFrame()
   {
      setSize(DEFAULT_WIDTH, DEFAULT_HEIGHT);
   }

   public static final int DEFAULT_WIDTH = 300;
   public static final int DEFAULT_HEIGHT = 200;
}
```

Let's work through this program, line by line.

The Swing classes are placed in the `javax.swing` package. The package name `javax` indicates a Java extension package, not a core package. The Swing classes are indeed an extension to Java 1.1. Because the Swing classes were not made a part of the core hierarchy, it is possible to load the Swing classes into a Java 1.1-compatible browser. (The security manager of the browser does not allow adding any packages that start with "`java.`".) On the Java 2 platform, the Swing package is no longer an extension but is instead part of the core hierarchy. Any Java implementation that is compatible with Java 2 must supply the Swing classes. Nevertheless, the `javax` name remains, for compatibility with Java 1.1 code. (Actually, the Swing package started out as `com.sun.java.swing`, then was briefly moved to `java.awt.swing` during early Java 2 beta versions, then went back to `com.sun.java.swing` in late Java 2 beta versions, and after howls of protest by Java programmers, found its final resting place in `javax.swing`.)

By default, a frame has a rather useless size of 0×0 pixels. We define a subclass `SimpleFrame` whose constructor sets the size to 300×200 pixels. In the `main` method of the `SimpleFrameTest` class, we start out by constructing a `SimpleFrame` object.

Next, we define what should happen when the user closes this frame. For this particular program, we want the program to exit. To select this behavior, we use the statement

```
frame.setDefaultCloseOperation(JFrame.EXIT_ON_CLOSE);
```

In other programs with multiple frames, you would not want the program to exit just because the user closes one of the frames. By default, a frame is hidden when the user closes it, but the program does not terminate.

Simply constructing a frame does not automatically display it. Frames start their life invisible. That gives the programmer the chance to add components into the frame before showing it for the first time. To show the frame, the `main` method calls the `setVisible` method of the frame.

Afterwards, the `main` method exits. Note that exiting `main` does not terminate the program, just the main thread. Showing the frame activates a user interface thread that keeps the program alive.

NOTE: Before JDK 5.0, it was possible to use the `show` method that the `JFrame` class inherits from the superclass `Window`. The `Window` class has a superclass `Component` that also has a `show` method. The `Component.show` method was deprecated in JDK 1.2. You are supposed to call `setVisible(true)` instead if you want to show a component. However, until JDK 1.4, the `Window.show` method was *not* deprecated. In fact, it was quite useful, making the window visible *and* bringing it to the front. Sadly, that benefit was lost on the deprecation police, and JDK 5.0 deprecates the `show` method for windows as well.

The running program is shown in Figure 7–4 on page 249—it is a truly boring top-level window. As you can see in the figure, the title bar and surrounding decorations, such as resize corners, are drawn by the operating system and not the Swing library. If you run the same program in X Windows, the frame decorations are different. The Swing library draws everything inside the frame. In this program, it just fills the frame with a default background color.

NOTE: As of JDK 1.4, you can turn off all frame decorations by calling `frame.setUndecorated(true)`.

NOTE: In the preceding example we wrote two classes, one to define a frame class and one that contains a `main` method that creates and shows a frame object. You will frequently see programs in which the `main` method is opportunistically tossed into a convenient class, like this:

```
class SimpleFrame extends JFrame
{
   public static void main(String[] args)
   {
      SimpleFrame frame = new SimpleFrame();
      frame.setDefaultCloseOperation(JFrame.EXIT_ON_CLOSE);
      frame.show();
   }

   public SimpleFrame()
   {
      setSize(DEFAULT_WIDTH, DEFAULT_HEIGHT);
   }

   public static final int DEFAULT_WIDTH = 300;
   public static final int DEFAULT_HEIGHT = 200;
}
```

Using the `main` method of the frame class for the code that launches the program is simpler in one sense. You do not have to introduce another auxiliary class. However, quite a few programmers find this code style a bit confusing. Therefore, we prefer to separate out the class that launches the program from the classes that define the user interface.

Positioning a Frame

The `JFrame` class itself has only a few methods for changing how frames look. Of course, through the magic of inheritance, most of the methods for working with the size and position of a frame come from the various superclasses of `JFrame`. Among the most important methods are the following ones:

- The `dispose` method that closes the window and reclaims any system resources used in creating it;
- The `setIconImage` method, which takes an `Image` object to use as the icon when the window is minimized (often called *iconized* in Java terminology);
- The `setTitle` method for changing the text in the title bar;
- The `setResizable` method, which takes a `boolean` to determine if a frame will be resizeable by the user.

Figure 7–5 illustrates the inheritance hierarchy for the `JFrame` class.

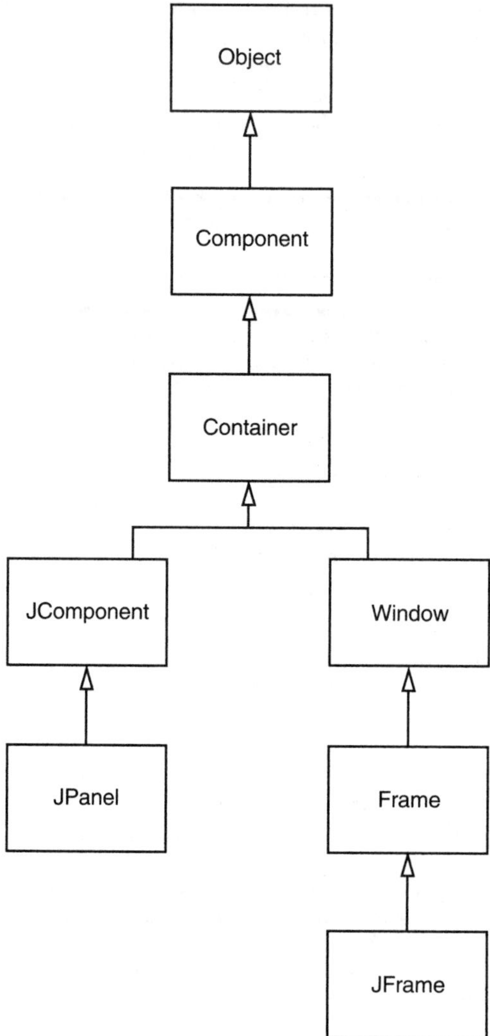

Figure 7–5: Inheritance hierarchy for the `JFrame` and `JPanel` classes

As the API notes indicate, the `Component` class (which is the ancestor of all GUI objects) and the `Window` class (which is the superclass of the `Frame` class) are where you need to look to find the methods to resize and reshape frames. For example, the `setLocation` method in the `Component` class is one way to reposition a component. If you make the call

```
setLocation(x, y)
```

the top-left corner is located `x` pixels across and `y` pixels down, where (0, 0) is the top-left corner of the screen. Similarly, the `setBounds` method in `Component` lets you resize and relocate a component (in particular, a `JFrame`) in one step, as

```
setBounds(x, y, width, height)
```

NOTE: For a frame, the coordinates of the `setLocation` and `setBounds` are taken relative to the whole screen. As you will see in Chapter 9, for other components inside a container, the measurements are taken relative to the container.

Remember: if you don't explicitly size a frame, all frames will default to being 0 by 0 pixels. To keep our example programs simple, we resize the frames to a size that we hope works acceptably on most displays. However, in a professional application, you should check the resolution of the user's screen and write code that resizes the frames accordingly: a window that looks nice on a laptop screen will look like a postage stamp on a high-resolution screen. As you will soon see, you can obtain the screen dimensions in pixels on the user's system. You can then use this information to compute the optimal window size for your program.

TIP: The API notes for this section give what we think are the most important methods for giving frames the proper look and feel. Some of these methods are defined in the `JFrame` class. Others come from the various superclasses of `JFrame`. At some point, you may need to search the API docs to see if there are methods for some special purpose. Unfortunately, that is a bit tedious to do with the JDK documentation. For subclasses, the API documentation only explains *overridden* methods. For example, the `toFront` method is applicable to objects of type `JFrame`, but because it is simply inherited from the `Window` class, the `JFrame` documentation doesn't explain it. If you feel that there should be a method to do something and it isn't explained in the documentation for the class you are working with, try looking at the API documentation for the methods of the *superclasses* of that class. The top of each API page has hyperlinks to the superclasses, and inherited methods are listed below the method summary for the new and overridden methods.

To give you an idea of what you can do with a window, we end this section by showing you a sample program that positions one of our closable frames so that

- Its area is one-fourth that of the whole screen;
- It is centered in the middle of the screen.

For example, if the screen was 800 × 600 pixels, we need a frame that is 400 × 300 pixels and we need to move it so the top left-hand corner is at (200,150).

To find out the screen size, use the following steps. Call the static `getDefaultToolkit` method of the `Toolkit` class to get the `Toolkit` object. (The `Toolkit` class is a dumping ground for a variety of methods that interface with the native windowing system.) Then call the `getScreenSize` method, which returns the screen size as a `Dimension` object. A `Dimension` object simultaneously stores a width and a height, in public (!) instance variables `width` and `height`. Here is the code:

```
Toolkit kit = Toolkit.getDefaultToolkit();
Dimension screenSize = kit.getScreenSize();
int screenWidth = screenSize.width;
int screenHeight = screenSize.height;
```

We also supply an icon. Because the representation of images is also system dependent, we again use the toolkit to load an image. Then, we set the image as the icon for the frame.

```
Image img = kit.getImage("icon.gif");
setIconImage(img);
```

Depending on your operating system, you can see the icon in various places. For example, in Windows, the icon is displayed in the top-left corner of the window, and you can see it in the list of active tasks when you press ALT+TAB.

Example 7–2 is the complete program. When you run the program, pay attention to the "Core Java" icon.

TIP: It is quite common to set the main frame of a program to the maximum size. As of JDK 1.4, you can simply maximize a frame by calling

```
frame.setExtendedState(Frame.MAXIMIZED_BOTH);
```

NOTE: If you write an application that takes advantage of multiple display screens, you should use the `GraphicsEnvironment` and `GraphicsDevice` classes to find the dimensions of the display screens. As of JDK 1.4, the `GraphicsDevice` class also lets you execute your application in full-screen mode.

Example 7–2: CenteredFrameTest.java

```
/**import java.awt.*;
import java.awt.event.*;
import javax.swing.*;

public class CenteredFrameTest
{
   public static void main(String[] args)
   {
      CenteredFrame frame = new CenteredFrame();
      frame.setDefaultCloseOperation(JFrame.EXIT_ON_CLOSE);
      frame.setVisible(true);
   }
}

class CenteredFrame extends JFrame
{
   public CenteredFrame()
   {
      // get screen dimensions

      Toolkit kit = Toolkit.getDefaultToolkit();
      Dimension screenSize = kit.getScreenSize();
      int screenHeight = screenSize.height;
      int screenWidth = screenSize.width;

      // center frame in screen

      setSize(screenWidth / 2, screenHeight / 2);
      setLocation(screenWidth / 4, screenHeight / 4);

      // set frame icon and title

      Image img = kit.getImage("icon.gif");
      setIconImage(img);
      setTitle("CenteredFrame");
   }
}
```

java.awt.Component 1.0

- `boolean isVisible()`
  checks whether this component is set to be visible. Components are initially visible, with the exception of top-level components such as `JFrame`.
- `void setVisible(boolean b)`
  shows or hides the component depending on whether `b` is `true` or `false`.
- `boolean isShowing()`
  checks whether this component is showing on the screen. For this, it must be visible and be inside a container that is showing.
- `boolean isEnabled()`
  checks whether this component is enabled. An enabled component can receive keyboard input. Components are initially enabled.
- `void setEnabled(boolean b)`
  enables or disables a component.
- `Point getLocation()` 1.1
  returns the location of the top-left corner of this component, relative to the top-left corner of the surrounding container. (A `Point` object `p` encapsulates an *x*- and a *y*-coordinate which are accessible by `p.x` and `p.y`.)
- `Point getLocationOnScreen()` 1.1
  returns the location of the top-left corner of this component, using the screen's coordinates.
- `void setBounds(int x, int y, int width, int height)` 1.1
  moves and resizes this component. The location of the top-left corner is given by `x` and `y`, and the new size is given by the `width` and `height` parameters.
- `void setLocation(int x, int y)` 1.1
- `void setLocation(Point p)` 1.1
  move the component to a new location. The *x*- and *y*-coordinates (or `p.x` and `p.y`) use the coordinates of the container if the component is not a top-level component, or the coordinates of the screen if the component is top level (for example, a `JFrame`).
- `Dimension getSize()` 1.1
  gets the current size of this component.
- `void setSize(int width, int height)` 1.1
- `void setSize(Dimension d)` 1.1
  resize the component to the specified width and height.

java.awt.Window 1.0

- `void toFront()`
  shows this window on top of any other windows.
- `void toBack()`
  moves this window to the back of the stack of windows on the desktop and rearranges all other visible windows accordingly.

java.awt.Frame 1.0

- `void setResizable(boolean b)`
  determines whether the user can resize the frame.

- `void setTitle(String s)`
  sets the text in the title bar for the frame to the string `s`.
- `void setIconImage(Image image)`

  Parameters: `image` The image you want to appear as the icon for the frame
- `void setUndecorated(boolean b)` **1.4**
  removes the frame decorations if `b` is `true`.
- `boolean isUndecorated()` **1.4**
  returns `true` if this frame is undecorated.
- `int getExtendedState()` **1.4**
- `void setExtendedState(int state)` **1.4**
  get or set the window state. The state is one of

  ```
  Frame.NORMAL
  Frame.ICONIFIED
  Frame.MAXIMIZED_HORIZ
  Frame.MAXIMIZED_VERT
  Frame.MAXIMIZED_BOTH
  ```

`java.awt.Toolkit` **1.0**

- `static Toolkit getDefaultToolkit()`
  returns the default toolkit.
- `Dimension getScreenSize()`
  gets the size of the user's screen.
- `Image getImage(String filename)`
  loads an image from the file with name `filename`.

Displaying Information in a Panel

In this section, we show you how to display information inside a frame. For example, rather than displaying "Not a Hello, World program" in text mode in a console window as we did in Chapter 3, we display the message in a frame, as shown in Figure 7–6.

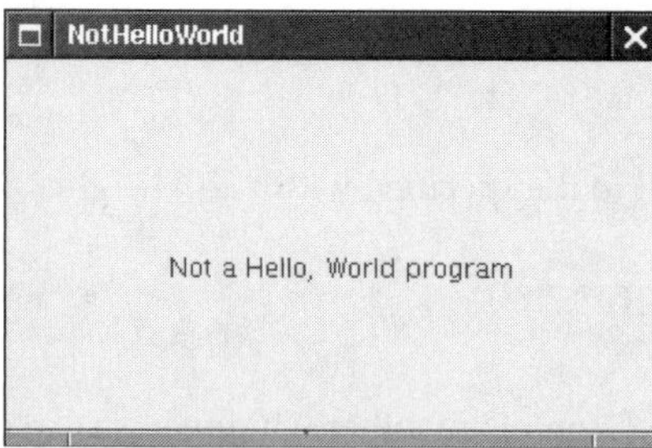

Figure 7–6: A simple graphical program

You could draw the message string directly onto a frame, but that is not considered good programming practice. In Java, frames are really designed to be containers for components such as a menu bar and other user interface elements. You normally draw on another component, called a *panel,* which you add to the frame.

The structure of a `JFrame` is surprisingly complex. Look at Figure 7–7, which shows the makeup of a `JFrame`. As you can see, four panes are layered in a `JFrame`. The root pane, layered

pane, and glass pane are of no interest to us; they are required to organize the menu bar and content pane and to implement the look and feel. The part that most concerns Swing programmers is the *content pane*. When designing a frame, you add components into the content pane, using code such as the following:

```
Container contentPane = frame.getContentPane();
Component c = . . .;
contentPane.add(c);
```

Up to JDK 1.4, the `add` method of the `JFrame` class was defined to throw an exception with the message "Do not use `JFrame.add()`. Use `JFrame.getContentPane().add()` instead". As of JDK 5.0, the `JFrame.add` method has given up trying to reeducate programmers, and it simply calls `add` on the content pane.

Thus, as of JDK 5.0, you can simply use the call

```
frame.add(c);
```

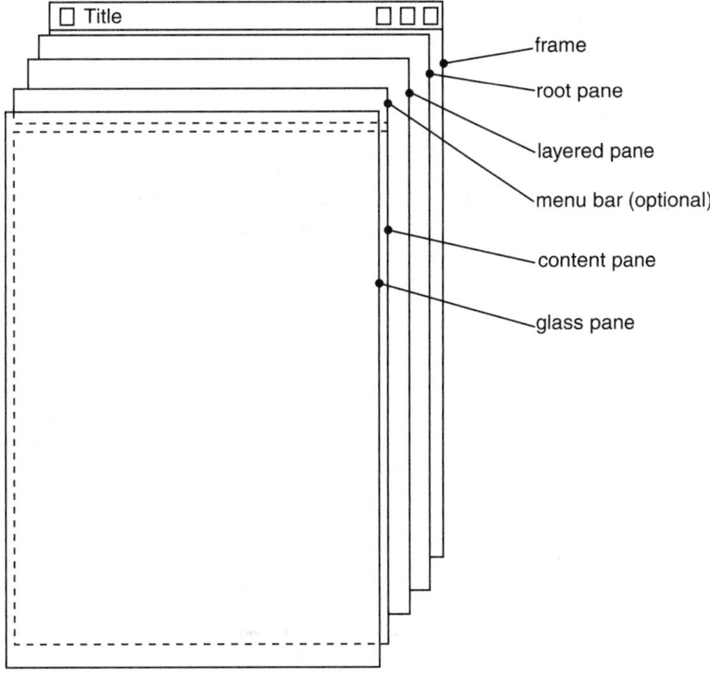

Figure 7–7: Internal structure of a `JFrame`

In our case, we want to add a single *panel* to the frame onto which we will draw our message. Panels are implemented by the `JPanel` class. They are user interface elements with two useful properties:

- They have a surface onto which you can draw.
- They themselves are containers.

Thus, they can hold other user interface components such as buttons, sliders, and so on.

To make a panel more interesting, you use inheritance to create a new class, and then override or add methods to get the extra functionality you want.

In particular, to draw on a panel, you

- Define a class that extends `JPanel`; and
- Override the `paintComponent` method in that class.

The `paintComponent` method is actually in `JComponent`—the superclass for all nonwindow Swing components. It takes one parameter of type `Graphics`. A `Graphics` object remembers a collection of settings for drawing images and text, such as the font you set or the current color. All drawing in Java must go through a `Graphics` object. It has methods that draw patterns, images, and text.

NOTE: The Graphics parameter is similar to a device context in Windows or a graphics context in X11 programming.

Here's how to make a panel onto which you can draw:

```
class MyPanel extends JPanel
{
   public void paintComponent(Graphics g)
   {
      . . . // code for drawing will go here
   }
}
```

Each time a window needs to be redrawn, no matter what the reason, the event handler notifies the component. This causes the `paintComponent` methods of all components to be executed.

Never call the `paintComponent` method yourself. It is called automatically whenever a part of your application needs to be redrawn, and you should not interfere with this automatic process.

What sorts of actions trigger this automatic response? For example, painting occurs because the user increased the size of the window or minimized and then restored the window. If the user popped up another window and it covered an existing window and then made the overlaid window disappear, the application window that was covered is now corrupted and will need to be repainted. (The graphics system does not save the pixels underneath.) And, of course, when the window is displayed for the first time, it needs to process the code that specifies how and where it should draw the initial elements.

TIP: If you need to force repainting of the screen, call the `repaint` method instead of `paintComponent`. The `repaint` method will cause `paintComponent` to be called for all components, with a properly configured `Graphics` object.

As you saw in the code fragment above, the `paintComponent` method takes a single parameter of type `Graphics`. Measurement on a `Graphics` object for screen display is done in pixels. The (0, 0) coordinate denotes the top-left corner of the component on whose surface you are drawing.

Displaying text is considered a special kind of drawing. The `Graphics` class has a `drawString` method that has the following syntax:

```
g.drawString(text, x, y)
```

In our case, we want to draw the string `"Not a Hello, World Program"` in our original window, roughly one-quarter of the way across and halfway down. Although we don't yet know

how to measure the size of the string, we'll start the string at coordinates (75, 100). This means the first character in the string will start at a position 75 pixels to the right and 100 pixels down. (Actually, it is the baseline for the text that is 100 pixels down—see below for more on how text is measured.) Thus, our `paintComponent` method looks like this:

```
class NotHelloWorldPanel extends JPanel
{
   public void paintComponent(Graphics g)
   {
      . . . // see below

      g.drawString("Not a Hello, World program", MESSAGE_X, MESSAGE_Y);
   }

   public static final int MESSAGE_X = 75;
   public static final int MESSAGE_Y = 100;
}
```

However, this `paintComponent` method is not complete. The `NotHelloWorldPanel` class extends the `JPanel` class, which has its own idea of how to paint the panel, namely, to fill it with the background color. To make sure that the superclass does its part of the job, we must call `super.paintComponent` before doing any painting on our own.

```
class NotHelloWorldPanel extends JPanel
{
   public void paintComponent(Graphics g)
   {
      super.paintComponent(g);

      . . . // code for drawing will go here
   }
}
```

Example 7–3 shows the complete code. If you use JDK 1.4 or below, remember to change the call `add(panel)` to `getContentPane().add(panel)`.

Example 7–3: NotHelloWorld.java

```
import javax.swing.*;
import java.awt.*;

public class NotHelloWorld
{
   public static void main(String[] args)
   {
      NotHelloWorldFrame frame = new NotHelloWorldFrame();
      frame.setDefaultCloseOperation(JFrame.EXIT_ON_CLOSE);
      frame.setVisible(true);
   }
}

/**
   A frame that contains a message panel
*/
class NotHelloWorldFrame extends JFrame
{
   public NotHelloWorldFrame()
   {
      setTitle("NotHelloWorld");
```

```
      setSize(DEFAULT_WIDTH, DEFAULT_HEIGHT);

      // add panel to frame

      NotHelloWorldPanel panel = new NotHelloWorldPanel();
      add(panel);
   }

   public static final int DEFAULT_WIDTH = 300;
   public static final int DEFAULT_HEIGHT = 200;
}

/**
   A panel that displays a message.
*/
class NotHelloWorldPanel extends JPanel
{
   public void paintComponent(Graphics g)
   {
      super.paintComponent(g);

      g.drawString("Not a Hello, World program", MESSAGE_X, MESSAGE_Y);
   }

   public static final int MESSAGE_X = 75;
   public static final int MESSAGE_Y = 100;
}
```

javax.swing.JFrame 1.2

- `Container getContentPane()`
  returns the content pane object for this `JFrame`.
- `void add(Component c)`
  adds the given component to the content pane of this frame. (Before JDK 5.0, this method threw an exception.)

java.awt.Component 1.0

- `void repaint()`
  causes a repaint of the component "as soon as possible."
- `public void repaint(int x, int y, int width, int height)`
  causes a repaint of a part of the component "as soon as possible."

javax.swing.JComponent 1.2

- `void paintComponent(Graphics g)`
  override this method to describe how your component needs to be painted.

Working with 2D Shapes

Since JDK version 1.0, the `Graphics` class had methods to draw lines, rectangles, ellipses, and so on. But those drawing operations are very limited. For example, you cannot vary the line thickness and you cannot rotate the shapes.

JDK 1.2 introduced the *Java 2D* library, which implements a powerful set of graphical operations. In this chapter, we only look at the basics of the Java 2D library—see the Advanced AWT chapter in Volume 2 for more information on the advanced features.

To draw shapes in the Java 2D library, you need to obtain an object of the `Graphics2D` class. This class is a subclass of the `Graphics` class. If you use a version of the JDK that is Java 2D enabled, methods such as `paintComponent` automatically receive an object of the `Graphics2D` class. Simply use a cast, as follows:

```
public void paintComponent(Graphics g)
{
   Graphics2D g2 = (Graphics2D) g;
   . . .
}
```

The Java 2D library organizes geometric shapes in an object-oriented fashion. In particular, there are classes to represent lines, rectangles, and ellipses:

```
Line2D
Rectangle2D
Ellipse2D
```

These classes all implement the `Shape` interface.

NOTE: The Java 2D library supports more complex shapes—in particular, arcs, quadratic and cubic curves, and general paths. See Volume 2 for more information.

To draw a shape, you first create an object of a class that implements the `Shape` interface and then call the `draw` method of the `Graphics2D` class. For example,

```
Rectangle2D rect = . . .;
g2.draw(rect);
```

NOTE: Before the Java 2D library appeared, programmers used methods of the `Graphics` class such as `drawRectangle` to draw shapes. Superficially, the old-style method calls look a bit simpler. However, by using the Java 2D library, you keep your options open—you can later enhance your drawings with some of the many tools that the Java 2D library supplies.

Using the Java 2D shape classes introduces some complexity. Unlike the 1.0 draw methods, which used integer pixel coordinates, the Java 2D shapes use floating-point coordinates. In many cases, that is a great convenience because it allows you to specify your shapes in coordinates that are meaningful to you (such as millimeters or inches) and then translate to pixels. The Java 2D library uses single-precision `float` quantities for many of its internal floating-point calculations. Single precision is sufficient—after all, the ultimate purpose of the geometric computations is to set pixels on the screen or printer. As long as any roundoff errors stay within one pixel, the visual outcome is not affected. Furthermore, `float` computations are faster on some platforms, and `float` values require half the storage of `double` values.

However, manipulating `float` values is sometimes inconvenient for the programmer because the Java programming language is adamant about requiring casts when converting `double` values into `float` values. For example, consider the following statement:

```
float f = 1.2; // Error
```

This statement does not compile because the constant `1.2` has type `double`, and the compiler is nervous about loss of precision. The remedy is to add an `F` suffix to the floating-point constant:

```
float f = 1.2F; // Ok
```

Now consider this statement:

```
Rectangle2D r = . . .
float f = r.getWidth(); // Error
```

This statement does not compile either, for the same reason. The `getWidth` method returns a `double`. This time, the remedy is to provide a cast:

```
float f = (float) r.getWidth(); // Ok
```

Because the suffixes and casts are a bit of a pain, the designers of the 2D library decided to supply *two versions* of each shape class: one with `float` coordinates for frugal programmers, and one with `double` coordinates for the lazy ones. (In this book, we fall into the second camp and use `double` coordinates whenever we can.)

The library designers chose a curious, and initially confusing, method for packaging these choices. Consider the `Rectangle2D` class. This is an abstract class with two concrete subclasses, which are also static inner classes:

```
Rectangle2D.Float
Rectangle2D.Double
```

Figure 7–8 shows the inheritance diagram.

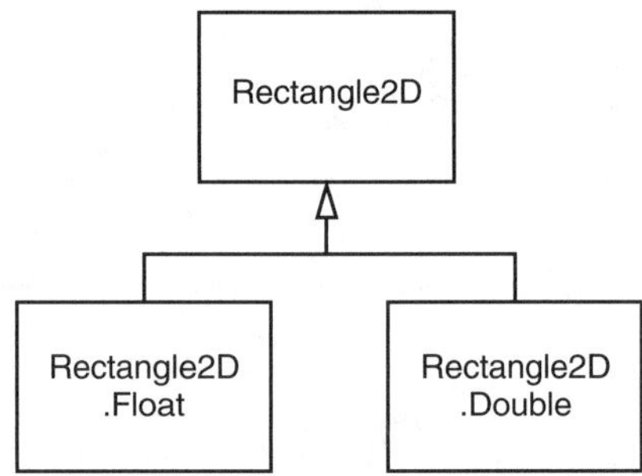

Figure 7–8: 2D rectangle classes

It is best to try to ignore the fact that the two concrete classes are static inner classes—that is just a gimmick to avoid names such as `FloatRectangle2D` and `DoubleRectangle2D`. (For more information on static inner classes, see Chapter 6.)

When you construct a `Rectangle2D.Float` object, you supply the coordinates as `float` numbers. For a `Rectangle2D.Double` object, you supply them as `double` numbers.

```
Rectangle2D.Float floatRect = new Rectangle2D.Float(10.0F, 25.0F, 22.5F, 20.0F);
Rectangle2D.Double doubleRect = new Rectangle2D.Double(10.0, 25.0, 22.5, 20.0);
```

Actually, because both `Rectangle2D.Float` and `Rectangle2D.Double` extend the common `Rectangle2D` class and the methods in the subclasses simply override methods in the `Rectangle2D` superclass, there is no benefit in remembering the exact shape type. You can simply use `Rectangle2D` variables to hold the rectangle references.

```
Rectangle2D floatRect = new Rectangle2D.Float(10.0F, 25.0F, 22.5F, 20.0F);
Rectangle2D doubleRect = new Rectangle2D.Double(10.0, 25.0, 22.5, 20.0);
```

That is, you only need to use the pesky inner classes when you construct the shape objects.

The construction parameters denote the top-left corner, width, and height of the rectangle.

NOTE: Actually, the `Rectangle2D.Float` class has one additional method that is not inherited from `Rectangle2D`, namely, `setRect(float x, float y, float h, float w)`. You lose that method if you store the `Rectangle2D.Float` reference in a `Rectangle2D` variable. But it is not a big loss—the `Rectangle2D` class has a `setRect` method with `double` parameters.

The `Rectangle2D` methods use `double` parameters and return values. For example, the `getWidth` method returns a `double` value, even if the width is stored as a `float` in a `Rectangle2D.Float` object.

TIP: Simply use the `Double` shape classes to avoid dealing with `float` values altogether. However, if you are constructing thousands of shape objects, then you can consider using the `Float` classes to conserve memory.

What we just discussed for the `Rectangle2D` classes holds for the other shape classes as well. Furthermore, there is a `Point2D` class with subclasses `Point2D.Float` and `Point2D.Double`. Here is how to make a point object.

```
Point2D p = new Point2D.Double(10, 20);
```

TIP: The `Point2D` class is very useful—it is more object oriented to work with `Point2D` objects than with separate *x*- and *y*- values. Many constructors and methods accept `Point2D` parameters. We suggest that you use `Point2D` objects when you can—they usually make geometric computations easier to understand.

The classes `Rectangle2D` and `Ellipse2D` both inherit from the common superclass `RectangularShape`. Admittedly, ellipses are not rectangular, but they have a *bounding rectangle* (see Figure 7–9).

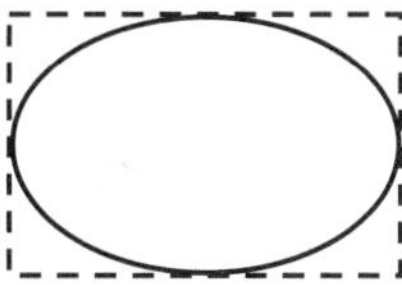

Figure 7–9: The bounding rectangle of an ellipse

The `RectangularShape` class defines over 20 methods that are common to these shapes, among them such useful methods as `getWidth`, `getHeight`, `getCenterX`, and `getCenterY` (but sadly, at the time of this writing, not a `getCenter` method that returns the center as a `Point2D` object).

Finally, a couple of legacy classes from JDK 1.0 have been fitted into the shape class hierarchy. The `Rectangle` and `Point` classes, which store a rectangle and a point with integer coordinates, extend the `Rectangle2D` and `Point2D` classes.

Figure 7–10 shows the relationships between the shape classes. However, the `Double` and `Float` subclasses are omitted. Legacy classes are marked with a gray fill.

`Rectangle2D` and `Ellipse2D` objects are simple to construct. You need to specify

- The *x*- and *y*-coordinates of the top-left corner; and
- The width and height.

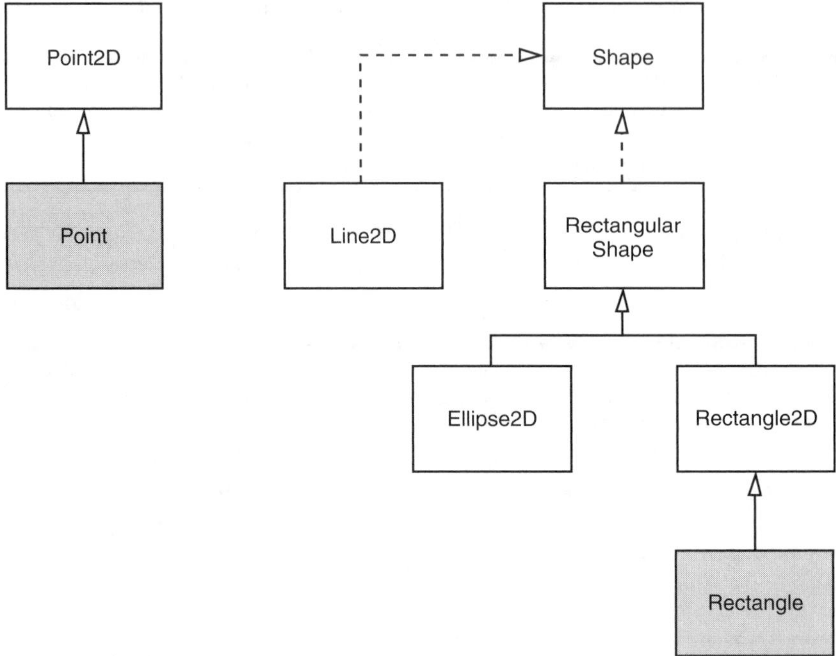

Figure 7–10: Relationships between the shape classes

For ellipses, these refer to the bounding rectangle.

For example,

```
Ellipse2D e = new Ellipse2D.Double(150, 200, 100, 50);
```

constructs an ellipse that is bounded by a rectangle with the top-left corner at (150, 200), width 100, and height 50.

However, sometimes you don't have the top-left corner readily available. It is quite common to have two diagonal corner points of a rectangle, but perhaps they aren't the top-left and bottom-right corners. You can't simply construct a rectangle as

```
Rectangle2D rect = new Rectangle2D.Double(px, py,
   qx - px, qy - py); // Error
```

If `p` isn't the top-left corner, one or both of the coordinate differences will be negative and the rectangle will come out empty. In that case, first create a blank rectangle and use the `setFrameFromDiagonal` method.

```
Rectangle2D rect = new Rectangle2D.Double();
rect.setFrameFromDiagonal(px, py, qx, qy);
```

Or, even better, if you know the corner points as `Point2D` objects `p` and `q`,

```
rect.setFrameFromDiagonal(p, q);
```

When constructing an ellipse, you usually know the center, width, and height, and not the corner points of the bounding rectangle (which don't even lie on the ellipse). The `setFrameFromCenter` method uses the center point, but it still requires one of the four corner points. Thus, you will usually end up constructing an ellipse as follows:

```
Ellipse2D ellipse = new Ellipse2D.Double(centerX - width / 2, centerY - height / 2, width, height);
```

To construct a line, you supply the start and end points, either as `Point2D` objects or as pairs of numbers:

```
Line2D line = new Line2D.Double(start, end);
```

or

```
Line2D line = new Line2D.Double(startX, startY, endX, endY);
```

The program in Example 7–4 draws

- A rectangle;
- The ellipse that is enclosed in the rectangle;
- A diagonal of the rectangle; and
- A circle that has the same center as the rectangle.

Figure 7–11 shows the result.

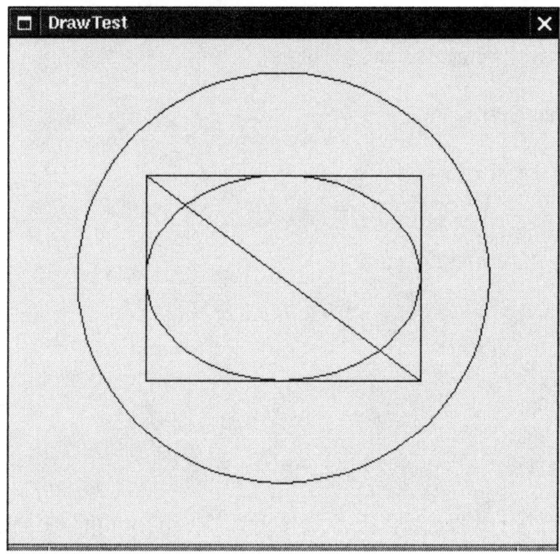

Figure 7–11: Rectangles and ellipses

Example 7–4: DrawTest.java

```
import java.awt.*;
import java.awt.geom.*;
import javax.swing.*;

public class DrawTest
{
   public static void main(String[] args)
   {
      DrawFrame frame = new DrawFrame();
      frame.setDefaultCloseOperation(JFrame.EXIT_ON_CLOSE);
      frame.setVisible(true);
   }
}

/**
   A frame that contains a panel with drawings
*/
class DrawFrame extends JFrame
{
```

```
   public DrawFrame()
   {
      setTitle("DrawTest");
      setSize(DEFAULT_WIDTH, DEFAULT_HEIGHT);

      // add panel to frame

      DrawPanel panel = new DrawPanel();
      add(panel);
   }

   public static final int DEFAULT_WIDTH = 400;
   public static final int DEFAULT_HEIGHT = 400;
}

/**
   A panel that displays rectangles and ellipses.
*/
class DrawPanel extends JPanel
{
   public void paintComponent(Graphics g)
   {
      super.paintComponent(g);
      Graphics2D g2 = (Graphics2D) g;

      // draw a rectangle

      double leftX = 100;
      double topY = 100;
      double width = 200;
      double height = 150;

      Rectangle2D rect = new Rectangle2D.Double(leftX, topY, width, height);
      g2.draw(rect);

      // draw the enclosed ellipse

      Ellipse2D ellipse = new Ellipse2D.Double();
      ellipse.setFrame(rect);
      g2.draw(ellipse);

      // draw a diagonal line

      g2.draw(new Line2D.Double(leftX, topY, leftX + width, topY + height));

      // draw a circle with the same center

      double centerX = rect.getCenterX();
      double centerY = rect.getCenterY();
      double radius = 150;

      Ellipse2D circle = new Ellipse2D.Double();
      circle.setFrameFromCenter(centerX, centerY, centerX + radius, centerY + radius);
      g2.draw(circle);
   }
}
```

java.awt.geom.RectangularShape 1.2

- `double getCenterX()`
- `double getCenterY()`
- `double getMinX()`
- `double getMinY()`
- `double getMaxX()`
- `double getMaxY()`

  return the center, minimum, or maximum *x*- or *y*-value of the enclosing rectangle.
- `double getWidth()`
- `double getHeight()`

  return the width or height of the enclosing rectangle.
- `double getX()`
- `double getY()`

  return the *x*- or *y*-coordinate of the top-left corner of the enclosing rectangle.

java.awt.geom.Rectangle2D.Double 1.2

- `Rectangle2D.Double(double x, double y, double w, double h)`

  constructs a rectangle with the given top-left corner, width, and height.

java.awt.geom.Rectangle2D.Float 1.2

- `Rectangle2D.Float(float x, float y, float w, float h)`

  constructs a rectangle with the given top-left corner, width, and height.

java.awt.geom.Ellipse2D.Double 1.2

- `Ellipse2D.Double(double x, double y, double w, double h)`

  constructs an ellipse whose bounding rectangle has the given top-left corner, width, and height.

java.awt.geom.Point2D.Double 1.2

- `Point2D.Double(double x, double y)`

  constructs a point with the given coordinates.

java.awt.geom.Line2D.Double 1.2

- `Line2D.Double(Point2D start, Point2D end)`
- `Line2D.Double(double startX, double startY, double endX, double endY)`

  construct a line with the given start and end points.

Using Color

The `setPaint` method of the `Graphics2D` class lets you select a color that is used for all subsequent drawing operations on the graphics context. To draw in multiple colors, you select a color, draw, then select another color, and draw again.

You define colors with the `Color` class. The `java.awt.Color` class offers predefined constants for the 13 standard colors listed in Table 7–1.

For example,

```
g2.setPaint(Color.RED);
g2.drawString("Warning!", 100, 100);
```

Table 7–1: Standard Colors

BLACK	GREEN	RED
BLUE	LIGHT_GRAY	WHITE
CYAN	MAGENTA	YELLOW
DARK_GRAY	ORANGE	
GRAY	PINK	

NOTE: Before JDK 1.4, color constant names were lower case, such as `Color.red`. This is odd because the standard coding convention is to write constants in upper case. Starting with JDK 1.4, you can write the standard color names in upper case or, for backward compatibility, in lower case.

You can specify a custom color by creating a `Color` object by its red, green, and blue components. Using a scale of 0–255 (that is, one byte) for the redness, blueness, and greenness, call the `Color` constructor like this:

```
Color(int redness, int  greenness, int blueness)
```

Here is an example of setting a custom color:

```
g2.setPaint(new Color(0, 128, 128)); // a dull blue-green
g2.drawString("Welcome!", 75, 125);
```

NOTE: In addition to solid colors, you can select more complex "paint" settings, such as varying hues or images. See the Advanced AWT chapter in Volume 2 for more details. If you use a `Graphics` object instead of a `Graphics2D` object, you need to use the `setColor` method to set colors.

To set the *background color,* you use the `setBackground` method of the `Component` class, an ancestor of `JPanel`.

```
MyPanel p = new MyPanel();
p.setBackground(Color.PINK);
```

There is also a `setForeground` method. It specifies the default color that is used for drawing on the component.

TIP: The `brighter()` and `darker()` methods of the `Color` class produce, as their names suggest, either brighter or darker versions of the current color. Using the `brighter` method is also a good way to highlight an item. Actually, `brighter()` is just a little bit brighter. To make a color really stand out, apply it three times: `c.brighter().brighter().brighter()`.

Java gives you predefined names for many more colors in its `SystemColor` class. The constants in this class encapsulate the colors used for various elements of the user's system. For example,

```
p.setBackground(SystemColor.window)
```

sets the background color of the panel to the default used by all windows on the user's desktop. (The background is filled in whenever the window is repainted.) Using the colors in the `SystemColor` class is particularly useful when you want to draw user interface elements so that the colors match those already found on the user's desktop. Table 7–2 lists the system color names and their meanings.

Table 7–2: System Colors

`desktop`	Background color of desktop
`activeCaption`	Background color for captions
`activeCaptionText`	Text color for captions
`activeCaptionBorder`	Border color for caption text
`inactiveCaption`	Background color for inactive captions
`inactiveCaptionText`	Text color for inactive captions
`inactiveCaptionBorder`	Border color for inactive captions
`window`	Background for windows
`windowBorder`	Color of window border frame
`windowText`	Text color inside windows
`menu`	Background for menus
`menuText`	Text color for menus
`text`	Background color for text
`textText`	Text color for text
`textInactiveText`	Text color for inactive controls
`textHighlight`	Background color for highlighted text
`textHighlightText`	Text color for highlighted text
`control`	Background color for controls
`controlText`	Text color for controls
`controlLtHighlight`	Light highlight color for controls
`controlHighlight`	Highlight color for controls
`controlShadow`	Shadow color for controls
`controlDkShadow`	Dark shadow color for controls
`scrollbar`	Background color for scrollbars
`info`	Background color for spot-help text
`infoText`	Text color for spot-help text

`java.awt.Color` 1.0

- `Color(int r, int g, int b)`
  creates a color object.

Parameters:	`r`	The red value (0–255)
	`g`	The green value (0–255)
	`b`	The blue value (0–255)

java.awt.Graphics 1.0

- `void setColor(Color c)`
  changes the current color. All subsequent graphics operations will use the new color.
  Parameters: `c` The new color

java.awt.Graphics2D 1.2

- `void setPaint(Paint p)`
  sets the paint attribute of this graphics context. The `Color` class implements the `Paint` interface. Therefore, you can use this method to set the paint attribute to a solid color.

java.awt.Component 1.0

- `void setBackground(Color c)`
  sets the background color.
  Parameters: c The new background color
- `void setForeground(Color c)`
  sets the foreground color.
  Parameters: `c` The new foreground color

Filling Shapes

You can fill the interiors of closed shapes (such as rectangles or ellipses) with a color (or, more generally, the current paint setting). Simply call `fill` instead of `draw`:

```
Rectangle2D rect = . . .;
g2.setPaint(Color.RED);
g2.fill(rect); // fills rect with red color
```

The program in Example 7–5 fills a rectangle in red, then an ellipse with the same boundary in a dull green (see Figure 7–12).

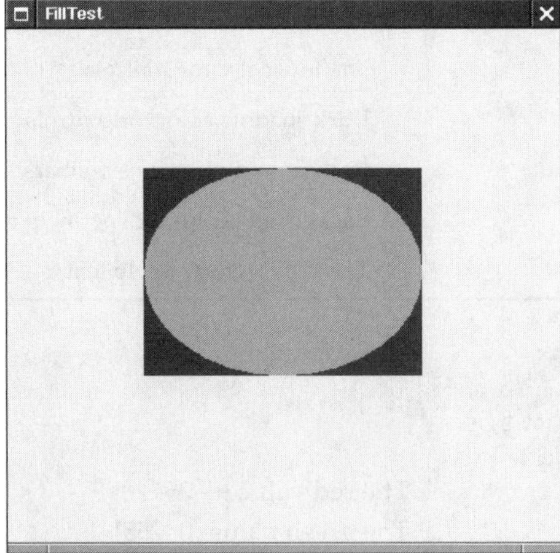

Figure 7–12: Filled rectangles and ellipses

Example 7–5: FillTest.java

```
import java.awt.*;
import java.awt.geom.*;
import javax.swing.*;

public class FillTest
{
   public static void main(String[] args)
   {
      FillFrame frame = new FillFrame();
      frame.setDefaultCloseOperation(JFrame.EXIT_ON_CLOSE);
      frame.setVisible(true);
   }
}

/**
   A frame that contains a panel with drawings
*/
class FillFrame extends JFrame
{
   public FillFrame()
   {
      setTitle("FillTest");
      setSize(DEFAULT_WIDTH, DEFAULT_HEIGHT);

      // add panel to frame

      FillPanel panel = new FillPanel();
      add(panel);
   }

   public static final int DEFAULT_WIDTH = 400;
   public static final int DEFAULT_HEIGHT = 400;
}

/**
   A panel that displays filled rectangles and ellipses
*/
class FillPanel extends JPanel
{
   public void paintComponent(Graphics g)
   {
      super.paintComponent(g);
      Graphics2D g2 = (Graphics2D) g;

      // draw a rectangle

      double leftX = 100;
      double topY = 100;
      double width = 200;
      double height = 150;

      Rectangle2D rect = new Rectangle2D.Double(leftX, topY, width, height);
      g2.setPaint(Color.RED);
      g2.fill(rect);
```

```

      // draw the enclosed ellipse

      Ellipse2D ellipse = new Ellipse2D.Double();
      ellipse.setFrame(rect);
      g2.setPaint(new Color(0,  128, 128)); // a dull blue-green
      g2.fill(ellipse);
   }
}
```

Using Special Fonts for Text

The "Not a Hello, World" program at the beginning of this chapter displayed a string in the default font. Often, you want to show text in a different font. You specify a font by its *font face name*. A font face name is composed of a *font family name*, such as "Helvetica," and an optional suffix such as "Bold." For example, the font faces "Helvetica" and "Helvetica Bold" are both considered to be part of the family named "Helvetica."

To find out which fonts are available on a particular computer, call the `getAvailableFontFamilyNames` method of the `GraphicsEnvironment` class. The method returns an array of strings that contains the names of all available fonts. To obtain an instance of the `GraphicsEnvironment` class that describes the graphics environment of the user's system, use the static `getLocalGraphicsEnvironment` method. Thus, the following program prints the names of all fonts on your system:

```
import java.awt.*;

public class ListFonts
{
   public static void main(String[] args)
   {
      String[] fontNames = GraphicsEnvironment
         .getLocalGraphicsEnvironment()
         .getAvailableFontFamilyNames();
      for (String fontName : fontNames)
         System.out.println(fontName);
   }
}
```

On one system, the list starts out like this:

```
Abadi MT Condensed Light
Arial
Arial Black
Arial Narrow
Arioso
Baskerville
Binner Gothic
. . .
```

and goes on for another 70 fonts or so.

NOTE: The JDK documentation claims that suffixes such as "heavy," "medium," "oblique," or "gothic" are variations inside a single family. In our experience, that is not the case. The "Bold," "Italic," and "Bold Italic" suffixes are recognized as family variations, but other suffixes aren't.

Unfortunately, there is no absolute way of knowing whether a user has a font with a particular "look" installed. Font face names can be trademarked, and font designs can be copyrighted in some jurisdictions. Thus, the distribution of fonts often involves royalty payments to a font foundry. Of course, just as there are inexpensive imitations of famous perfumes, there are lookalikes for name-brand fonts. For example, the Helvetica imitation that is shipped with Windows is called Arial.

To establish a common baseline, the AWT defines five *logical* font names:

SansSerif
Serif
Monospaced
Dialog
DialogInput

These names are always mapped to fonts that actually exist on the client machine. For example, on a Windows system, SansSerif is mapped to Arial.

NOTE: The font mapping is defined in the `fontconfig.properties` file in the `jre/lib` subdirectory of the Java installation. See `http://java.sun.com/j2se/5.0/docs/guide/intl/fontconfig.html` for information on this file. Earlier versions of the JDK used a `font.properties` file that is now obsolete.

To draw characters in a font, you must first create an object of the class `Font`. You specify the font face name, the font style, and the point size. Here is an example of how you construct a `Font` object:

```
Font helvb14 = new Font("Helvetica", Font.BOLD, 14);
```

The third argument is the point size. Points are commonly used in typography to indicate the size of a font. There are 72 points per inch. This sentence uses a 9-point font.

You can use a logical font name in the place of a font face name in the `Font` constructor. You specify the style (plain, **bold**, *italic*, or ***bold italic***) by setting the second `Font` constructor argument to one of the following values:

```
Font.PLAIN
Font.BOLD
Font.ITALIC
Font.BOLD + Font.ITALIC
```

Here is an example:

```
Font sansbold14 = new Font("SansSerif", Font.BOLD, 14)
```

NOTE: Prior versions of Java used the names Helvetica, TimesRoman, Courier, and ZapfDingbats as logical font names. For backward compatibility, these font names are still treated as logical font names even though Helvetica is really a font face name and TimesRoman and ZapfDingbats are not font names at all—the actual font face names are "Times Roman" and "Zapf Dingbats."

TIP: Starting with JDK version 1.3, you can read TrueType fonts. You need an input stream for the font—typically from a disk file or URL. (See Chapter 12 for more information on streams.) Then call the static `Font.createFont` method:

```
URL url = new URL("http://www.fonts.com/Wingbats.ttf");
InputStream in = url.openStream();
Font f = Font.createFont(Font.TRUETYPE_FONT, in);
```

The font is plain with a font size of 1 point. Use the deriveFont method to get a font of the desired size:

```
Font df = f.deriveFont(14.0F);
```

CAUTION: There are two overloaded versions of the deriveFont method. One of them (with a float parameter) sets the font size, the other (with an int parameter) sets the font style. Thus, f.deriveFont(14) sets the style and not the size! (The result is an italic font because it happens that the binary representation of 14 sets the ITALIC bit but not the BOLD bit.)

The Java fonts contain the usual ASCII characters as well as symbols. For example, if you print the character '\u2297' in the Dialog font, then you get a ⊗ character. Only those symbols that are defined in the Unicode character set are available.

Here's the code that displays the string "Hello, World!" in the standard sans serif font on your system, using 14-point bold type:

```
Font sansbold14 = new Font("SansSerif", Font.BOLD, 14);
g2.setFont(sansbold14);
String message = "Hello, World!";
g2.drawString(message, 75, 100);
```

Next, let's *center* the string in its panel rather than drawing it at an arbitrary position. We need to know the width and height of the string in pixels. These dimensions depend on three factors:

- The font used (in our case, sans serif, bold, 14 point);
- The string (in our case, "Hello, World!"); and
- The device on which the font is drawn (in our case, the user's screen).

To obtain an object that represents the font characteristics of the screen device, you call the getFontRenderContext method of the Graphics2D class. It returns an object of the FontRenderContext class. You simply pass that object to the getStringBounds method of the Font class:

```
FontRenderContext context = g2.getFontRenderContext();
Rectangle2D bounds = f.getStringBounds(message, context);
```

The getStringBounds method returns a rectangle that encloses the string.

To interpret the dimensions of that rectangle, you should know some basic typesetting terms (see Figure 7–13). The *baseline* is the imaginary line where, for example, the bottom of a character like "e" rests. The *ascent* is the distance from the baseline to the top of an *ascender,* which is the upper part of a letter like "b" or "k," or an uppercase character. The *descent* is the distance from the baseline to a *descender,* which is the lower portion of a letter like "p" or "g."

Figure 7–13: Typesetting terms illustrated

Leading is the space between the descent of one line and the ascent of the next line. (The term has its origin from the strips of lead that typesetters used to separate lines.) The *height* of a font is the distance between successive baselines, which is the same as descent + leading + ascent.

The width of the rectangle that the `getStringBounds` method returns is the horizontal extent of the string. The height of the rectangle is the sum of ascent, descent, and leading. The rectangle has its origin at the baseline of the string. The top *y*-coordinate of the rectangle is negative. Thus, you can obtain string width, height, and ascent as follows:

```
double stringWidth = bounds.getWidth();
double stringHeight = bounds.getHeight();
double ascent = -bounds.getY();
```

If you need to know the descent or leading, you need to use the `getLineMetrics` method of the `Font` class. That method returns an object of the `LineMetrics` class, which has methods to obtain the descent and leading:

```
LineMetrics metrics = f.getLineMetrics(message, context);
float descent = metrics.getDescent();
float leading = metrics.getLeading();
```

The following code uses all this information to center a string in its surrounding panel:

```
FontRenderContext context = g2.getFontRenderContext();
Rectangle2D bounds = f.getStringBounds(message, context);

// (x,y) = top left corner of text
double x = (getWidth() - bounds.getWidth()) / 2;
double y = (getHeight() - bounds.getHeight()) / 2;

// add ascent to y to reach the baseline
double ascent = -bounds.getY();
double baseY = y + ascent;
g2.drawString(message, (int) x, (int) baseY);
```

To understand the centering, consider that `getWidth()` returns the width of the panel. A portion of that width, namely, `bounds.getWidth()`, is occupied by the message string. The remainder should be equally distributed on both sides. Therefore, the blank space on each side is half the difference. The same reasoning applies to the height.

Finally, the program draws the baseline and the bounding rectangle.

Figure 7–14 shows the screen display; Example 7–6 is the program listing.

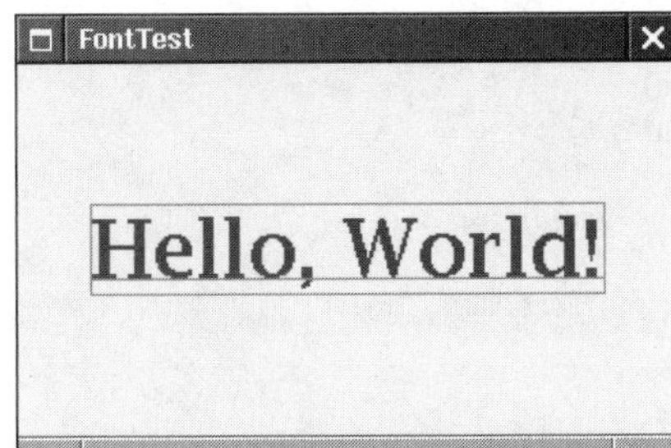

Figure 7–14: Drawing the baseline and string bounds

Example 7–6: FontTest.java

```
import java.awt.*;
import java.awt.font.*;
import java.awt.geom.*;
import javax.swing.*;

public class FontTest
{
   public static void main(String[] args)
   {
      FontFrame frame = new FontFrame();
      frame.setDefaultCloseOperation(JFrame.EXIT_ON_CLOSE);
      frame.setVisible(true);
   }
}

/**
   A frame with a text message panel
*/
class FontFrame extends JFrame
{
   public FontFrame()
   {
      setTitle("FontTest");
      setSize(DEFAULT_WIDTH, DEFAULT_HEIGHT);

      // add panel to frame

      FontPanel panel = new FontPanel();
      add(panel);
   }

   public static final int DEFAULT_WIDTH = 300;
   public static final int DEFAULT_HEIGHT = 200;
}

/**
   A panel that shows a centered message in a box.
*/
class FontPanel extends JPanel
{
   public void paintComponent(Graphics g)
   {
      super.paintComponent(g);
      Graphics2D g2 = (Graphics2D) g;

      String message = "Hello, World!";

      Font f = new Font("Serif", Font.BOLD, 36);
      g2.setFont(f);

      // measure the size of the message

      FontRenderContext context = g2.getFontRenderContext();
      Rectangle2D bounds = f.getStringBounds(message, context);
```

```
    // set (x,y) = top left corner of text

    double x = (getWidth() - bounds.getWidth()) / 2;
    double y = (getHeight() - bounds.getHeight()) / 2;

    // add ascent to y to reach the baseline

    double ascent = -bounds.getY();
    double baseY = y + ascent;

    // draw the message

    g2.drawString(message, (int) x, (int) baseY);

    g2.setPaint(Color.GRAY);

    // draw the baseline

    g2.draw(new Line2D.Double(x, baseY, x + bounds.getWidth(), baseY));

    // draw the enclosing rectangle

    Rectangle2D rect = new Rectangle2D.Double(x, y, bounds.getWidth(), bounds.getHeight());
    g2.draw(rect);
  }
}
```

API **java.awt.Font 1.0**

- `Font(String name, int style, int size)`
  creates a new font object.

Parameters:	`name`	The font name. This is either a font face name (such as "Helvetica Bold") or a logical font name (such as "Serif", "SansSerif")
	`style`	The style (`Font.PLAIN`, `Font.BOLD`, `Font.ITALIC`, or `Font.BOLD + Font.ITALIC`)
	`size`	The point size (for example, 12)

- `String getFontName()`
  gets the font face name (such as "Helvetica Bold").
- `String getFamily()`
  gets the font family name (such as "Helvetica").
- `String getName()`
  gets the logical name (such as "SansSerif") if the font was created with a logical font name; otherwise, gets the font face name.
- `Rectangle2D getStringBounds(String s, FontRenderContext context)` **1.2**
  returns a rectangle that encloses the string. The origin of the rectangle falls on the baseline. The top *y*-coordinate of the rectangle equals the negative of the ascent. The height of the rectangle equals the sum of ascent, descent, and leading. The width equals the string width.

- `LineMetrics getLineMetrics(String s, FontRenderContext context)` **1.2**
  returns a line metrics object to determine the extent of the string.
- `Font deriveFont(int style)` **1.2**
- `Font deriveFont(float size)` **1.2**
- `Font deriveFont(int style, float size)` **1.2**
  return a new font that equals this font, except that it has the given size and style.

`java.awt.font.LineMetrics` 1.2

- `float getAscent()`
  gets the font ascent—the distance from the baseline to the tops of uppercase characters.
- `float getDescent()`
  gets the font descent—the distance from the baseline to the bottoms of descenders.
- `float getLeading()`
  gets the font leading—the space between the bottom of one line of text and the top of the next line.
- `float getHeight()`
  gets the total height of the font—the distance between the two baselines of text (descent + leading + ascent).

`java.awt.Graphics` 1.0

- `void setFont(Font font)`
  selects a font for the graphics context. That font will be used for subsequent text-drawing operations.

Parameters:	`font`	A font

- `void drawString(String str, int x, int y)`
  draws a string in the current font and color.

Parameters:	`str`	The string to be drawn
	`x`	The x-coordinate of the start of the string
	`y`	The y-coordinate of the baseline of the string

`java.awt.Graphics2D` 1.2

- `FontRenderContext getFontRenderContext()`
  gets a font render context that specifies font characteristics in this graphics context.
- `void drawString(String str, float x, float y)`
  draws a string in the current font and color.

Parameters:	`str`	The string to be drawn
	`x`	The x-coordinate of the start of the string
	`y`	The y-coordinate of the baseline of the string

Doing More with Images

You have already seen how to build up simple images by drawing lines and shapes. Complex images, such as photographs, are usually generated externally, for example, with a scanner or special image-manipulation software. (As you will see in Volume 2, it is also possible to produce an image, pixel by pixel, and store the result in an array. This procedure is common for fractal images, for example.)

Once images are stored in local files or someplace on the Internet, you can read them into a Java application and display them on Graphics objects. As of JDK 1.4, reading an image is very simple. If the image is stored in a local file, call

```
String filename = "...";
Image image = ImageIO.read(new File(filename));
```

Otherwise, you can supply a URL:

```
String urlname = "...";
Image image = ImageIO.read(new URL(urlname));
```

The read method throws an IOException if the image is not available. We discuss the general topic of exception handling in Chapter 11. For now, our sample program just catches that exception and prints a stack trace if it occurs.

Now the variable image contains a reference to an object that encapsulates the image data. You can display the image with the drawImage method of the Graphics class.

```
public void paintComponent(Graphics g)
{
   . . .
   g.drawImage(image, x, y, null);
}
```

Example 7–7 takes this a little bit further and *tiles* the window with the graphics image. The result looks like the screen shown in Figure 7–15. We do the tiling in the paintComponent method. We first draw one copy of the image in the top-left corner and then use the copyArea call to copy it into the entire window:

```
for (int i = 0; i * imageWidth <= getWidth(); i++)
  for (int j = 0; j * imageHeight <= getHeight(); j++)
     if (i + j > 0)
        g.copyArea(0, 0, imageWidth, imageHeight, i * imageWidth, j * imageHeight);
```

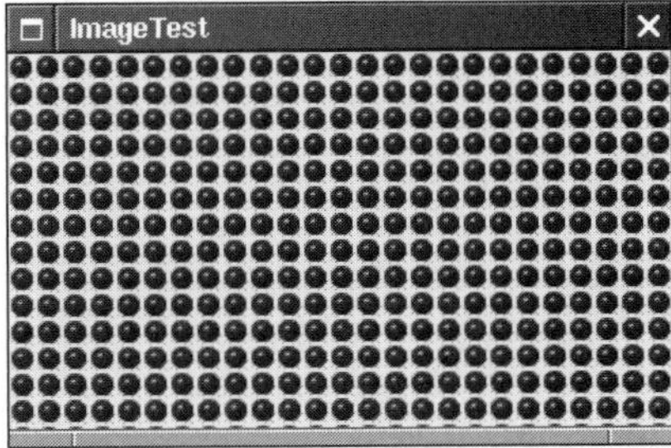

Figure 7–15: Window with tiled graphics image

NOTE: To load an image with JDK 1.3 or earlier, you should use the MediaTracker class instead. A media tracker can track the acquisition of one or more images. (The name "media" suggests that the class should also be able to track audio files or other media. While such an extension may have been envisioned for the future, the current implementation tracks images only.)

You add an image to a tracker object with the following command:

```
MediaTracker tracker = new MediaTracker(component);
Image img = Toolkit.getDefaultToolkit().getImage(name);
int id = 1; // the ID used to track the image loading process
tracker.addImage(img, id);
```

You can add as many images as you like to a single media tracker. Each of the images should have a different ID number, but you can choose any numbering that is convenient. To wait for an image to be loaded completely, you use code like this:

```
try { tracker.waitForID(id); }
catch (InterruptedException e) {}
```

If you want to acquire multiple images, then you can add them all to the media tracker object and wait until they are all loaded. You can achieve this with the following code:

```
try { tracker.waitForAll(); }
catch (InterruptedException e) {}
```

Example 7–7 shows the full source code of the image display program. This concludes our introduction to Java graphics programming. For more advanced techniques, you can turn to the discussion about 2D graphics and image manipulation in Volume 2.

Example 7–7: ImageTest.java

```
import java.awt.*;
import java.awt.event.*;
import java.io.*;
import javax.imageio.*;
import javax.swing.*;

public class ImageTest
{
   public static void main(String[] args)
   {
      ImageFrame frame = new ImageFrame();
      frame.setDefaultCloseOperation(JFrame.EXIT_ON_CLOSE);
      frame.setVisible(true);
   }
}

/**
    A frame with an image panel
*/
class ImageFrame extends JFrame
{
   public ImageFrame()
   {
      setTitle("ImageTest");
      setSize(DEFAULT_WIDTH, DEFAULT_HEIGHT);

      // add panel to frame

      ImagePanel panel = new ImagePanel();
      add(panel);
   }

   public static final int DEFAULT_WIDTH = 300;
   public static final int DEFAULT_HEIGHT = 200;
}

/**
   A panel that displays a tiled image
*/
```

```
class ImagePanel extends JPanel
{
   public ImagePanel()
   {
      // acquire the image
      try
      {
         image = ImageIO.read(new File("blue-ball.gif"));
      }
      catch (IOException e)
      {
         e.printStackTrace();
      }
   }

   public void paintComponent(Graphics g)
   {
      super.paintComponent(g);
      if (image == null) return;

      int imageWidth = image.getWidth(this);
      int imageHeight = image.getHeight(this);

      // draw the image in the upper-left corner

      g.drawImage(image, 0, 0, null);
      // tile the image across the panel

      for (int i = 0; i * imageWidth <= getWidth(); i++)
         for (int j = 0; j * imageHeight <= getHeight(); j++)
            if (i + j > 0)
               g.copyArea(0, 0, imageWidth, imageHeight,
                  i * imageWidth, j * imageHeight);
   }

   private Image image;
}
```

API **javax.swing.ImageIO 1.4**

- `static BufferedImage read(File f)`
- `static BufferedImage read(URL u)`

  read an image from the given file or URL.

API **java.awt.Image 1.0**

- `Graphics getGraphics()`

  gets a graphics context to draw into this image buffer.
- `void flush()`

  releases all resources held by this image object.

API **java.awt.Graphics 1.0**

- `boolean drawImage(Image img, int x, int y, ImageObserver observer)`

  draws an unscaled image. Note: This call may return before the image is drawn.

Parameters:	`img`	The image to be drawn
	`x`	The *x*-coordinate of the upper-left corner
	`y`	The *y*-coordinate of the upper-left corner
	`observer`	The object to notify of the progress of the rendering process (may be `null`)

- `boolean drawImage(Image img, int x, int y, int width, int height, ImageObserver observer)`
  draws a scaled image. The system scales the image to fit into a region with the given width and height. Note: This call may return before the image is drawn.

Parameters:	`img`	The image to be drawn
	`x`	The *x*-coordinate of the upper-left corner
	`y`	The *y*-coordinate of the upper-left corner
	`width`	The desired width of image
	`height`	The desired height of image
	`observer`	The object to notify of the progress of the rendering process (may be `null`)

- `void copyArea(int x, int y, int width, int height, int dx, int dy)`
  copies an area of the screen.

Parameters:	`x`	The *x*-coordinate of the upper-left corner of the source area
	`y`	The *y*-coordinate of the upper-left corner of the source area
	`width`	The width of the source area
	`height`	The height of the source area
	`dx`	The horizontal distance from the source area to the target area
	`dy`	The vertical distance from the source area to the target area

- `void dispose()`
  disposes of this graphics context and releases operating system resources. You should always dispose of the graphics contexts that you receive from calls to methods such as `Image.getGraphics`, but not the ones handed to you by `paintComponent`.

`java.awt.Component` 1.0

- `Image createImage(int width, int height)`
  creates an off-screen image buffer to be used for double buffering.

Parameters:	`width`	The width of the image
	`height`	The height of the image

`java.awt.MediaTracker` 1.0

- `MediaTracker(Component c)`
  tracks images that are displayed in the given component.

- `void addImage(Image image, int id)`
  adds an image to the list of images being tracked. When the image is added, the image loading process is started.

Parameters:	`image`	The image to be tracked
	`id`	The identifier used to later refer to this image

- `void waitForID(int id)`
  waits until all images with the specified ID are loaded.
- `void waitForAll()`
  waits until all images that are being tracked are loaded.

Chapter 8

Event Handling

Event handling is of fundamental importance to programs with a graphical user interface. To implement user interfaces, you must master the way in which Java handles events. This chapter explains how the Java AWT event model works. You will see how to capture events from the mouse and the keyboard. This chapter also shows you how to use the simplest GUI elements, such as buttons. In particular, this chapter discusses how to work with the basic events generated by these components. The next chapter shows you how to put together the most common of the components that Swing offers, along with a detailed coverage of the events they generate.

NOTE: Java 1.1 introduced a much improved event model for GUI programming. We do not cover the deprecated 1.0 event model in this chapter.

Basics of Event Handling

Any operating environment that supports GUIs constantly monitors events such as keystrokes or mouse clicks. The operating environment reports these events to the programs that are running. Each program then decides what, if anything, to do in response to these events. In languages like Visual Basic, the correspondence between events and code is obvious. One writes code for each specific event of interest and places the code in what is usually called an *event procedure*. For example, a Visual Basic button named HelpButton would have a `HelpButton_Click` event procedure associated with it. The code in this procedure executes whenever that button is clicked. Each Visual Basic GUI component

responds to a fixed set of events, and it is impossible to change the events to which a Visual Basic component responds.

On the other hand, if you use a language like raw C to do event-driven programming, you need to write the code that constantly checks the event queue for what the operating environment is reporting. (You usually do this by encasing your code in a giant loop with a massive switch statement!) This technique is obviously rather ugly, and, in any case, it is much more difficult to code. The advantage is that the events you can respond to are not as limited as in languages, like Visual Basic, that go to great lengths to hide the event queue from the programmer.

The Java programming environment takes an approach somewhat between the Visual Basic approach and the raw C approach in terms of power and, therefore, in resulting complexity. Within the limits of the events that the AWT knows about, you completely control how events are transmitted from the *event sources* (such as buttons or scrollbars) to *event listeners*. You can designate *any* object to be an event listener—in practice, you pick an object that can conveniently carry out the desired response to the event. This *event delegation model* gives you much more flexibility than is possible with Visual Basic, in which the listener is predetermined, but it requires more code and is more difficult to untangle (at least until you get used to it).

Event sources have methods that allow you to register event listeners with them. When an event happens to the source, the source sends a notification of that event to all the listener objects that were registered for that event.

As one would expect in an object-oriented language like Java, the information about the event is encapsulated in an *event* object. In Java, all event objects ultimately derive from the class `java.util.EventObject`. Of course, there are subclasses for each event type, such as `ActionEvent` and `WindowEvent`.

Different event sources can produce different kinds of events. For example, a button can send `ActionEvent` objects, whereas a window can send `WindowEvent` objects.

To sum up, here's an overview of how event handling in the AWT works.

- A listener object is an instance of a class that implements a special interface called (naturally enough) a *listener interface*.
- An event source is an object that can register listener objects and send them event objects.
- The event source sends out event objects to all registered listeners when that event occurs.
- The listener objects will then use the information in the event object to determine their reaction to the event.

You register the listener object with the source object by using lines of code that follow the model

```
eventSourceObject.addEventListener(eventListenerObject);
```

Here is an example:

```
ActionListener listener = . . .;
JButton button = new JButton("Ok");
button.addActionListener(listener);
```

Now the `listener` object is notified whenever an "action event" occurs in the button. For buttons, as you might expect, an action event is a button click.

Code like the above requires that the class to which the listener object belongs implements the appropriate interface (which in this case is the `ActionListener` interface). As with all interfaces in Java, implementing an interface means supplying methods with the right signatures. To implement the `ActionListener` interface, the listener class must have a method called `actionPerformed` that receives an `ActionEvent` object as a parameter.

```
class MyListener implements ActionListener
{
   . . .
   public void actionPerformed(ActionEvent event)
   {
      // reaction to button click goes here
      . . .
   }
}
```

Whenever the user clicks the button, the `JButton` object creates an `ActionEvent` object and calls `listener.actionPerformed(event)`, passing that event object. It is possible for multiple objects to be added as listeners to an event source such as a button. In that case, the button calls the `actionPerformed` methods of all listeners whenever the user clicks the button.

Figure 8–1 shows the interaction between the event source, event listener, and event object.

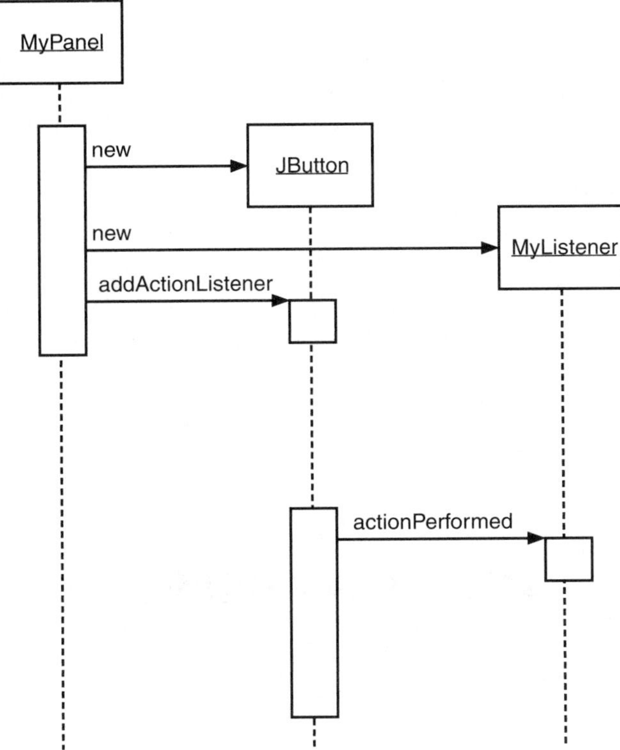

Figure 8–1: Event notification

NOTE: In this chapter, we put particular emphasis on event handling for *user interface* events such as button clicks and mouse moves. However, the basic event handling architecture is not limited to user interfaces. As you will see in the next chapter, objects that are not user interface components can also send event notifications to listeners—usually to tell them that a property of the object has changed.

Example: Handling a Button Click

As a way of getting comfortable with the event delegation model, let's work through all details needed for the simple example of responding to a button click. For this example, we will want

- A panel populated with three buttons; and
- Three listener objects that are added as action listeners to the buttons.

With this scenario, each time a user clicks on any of the buttons on the panel, the associated listener object then receives an `ActionEvent` that indicates a button click. In our sample program, the listener object will then change the background color of the panel.

Before we can show you the program that listens to button clicks, we first need to explain how to create buttons and how to add them to a panel. (For more on GUI elements, see Chapter 9.)

You create a button by specifying a label string, an icon, or both in the button constructor. Here are two examples:

```
JButton yellowButton = new JButton("Yellow");
JButton blueButton = new JButton(new ImageIcon("blue-ball.gif"));
```

Adding buttons to a panel occurs through a call to a method named (quite mnemonically) `add`. The `add` method takes as a parameter the specific component to be added to the container. For example,

```
class ButtonPanel extends JPanel
{
   public ButtonPanel()
   {
      JButton yellowButton = new JButton("Yellow");
      JButton blueButton = new JButton("Blue");
      JButton redButton = new JButton("Red");

      add(yellowButton);
      add(blueButton);
      add(redButton);
   }
}
```

Figure 8–2 shows the result.

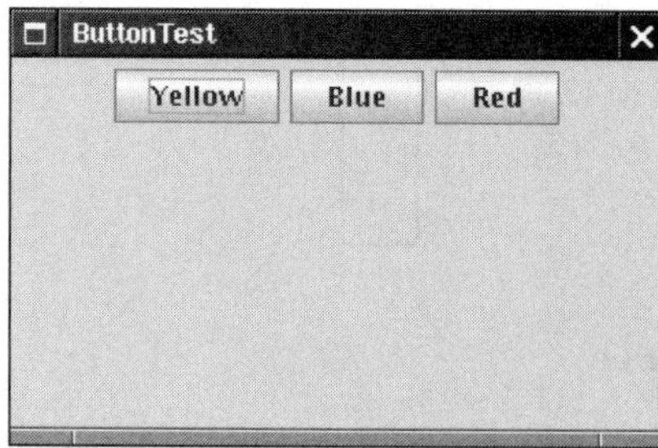

Figure 8–2: A panel filled with buttons

Now that you know how to add buttons to a panel, you'll need to add code that lets the panel listen to these buttons. This requires classes that implement the `ActionListener` interface, which, as we just mentioned, has one method: `actionPerformed`, whose signature looks like this:

```
public void actionPerformed(ActionEvent event)
```

NOTE: The `ActionListener` interface we used in the button example is not restricted to button clicks. It is used in many separate situations:

- When an item is selected from a list box with a double click;
- When a menu item is selected;
- When the ENTER key is clicked in a text field;
- When a certain amount of time has elapsed for a `Timer` component.

You will see more details in this chapter and the next.

The way to use the `ActionListener` interface is the same in all situations: the `actionPerformed` method (which is the only method in `ActionListener`) takes an object of type `ActionEvent` as a parameter. This event object gives you information about the event that happened.

When a button is clicked, then we want to set the background color of the panel to a particular color. We store the desired color in our listener class.

```
class ColorAction implements ActionListener
{
   public ColorAction(Color c)
   {
      backgroundColor = c;
   }

   public void actionPerformed(ActionEvent event)
   {
      // set panel background color
      . . .
   }

   private Color backgroundColor;
}
```

We then construct one object for each color and set the objects as the button listeners.

```
ColorAction yellowAction = new ColorAction(Color.YELLOW);
ColorAction blueAction = new ColorAction(Color.BLUE);
ColorAction redAction = new ColorAction(Color.RED);

yellowButton.addActionListener(yellowAction);
blueButton.addActionListener(blueAction);
redButton.addActionListener(redAction);
```

For example, if a user clicks on the button marked "Yellow," then the `actionPerformed` method of the `yellowAction` object is called. Its `backgroundColor` instance field is set to `Color.YELLOW`, and it can now proceed to set the panel's background color.

Just one issue remains. The `ColorAction` object doesn't have access to the `panel` variable. You can solve this problem in two ways. You can store the panel in the `ColorAction` object and set it in the `ColorAction` constructor. Or, more conveniently, you can make `ColorAction` into an inner class of the `ButtonPanel` class. Its methods can then access the outer panel automatically. (For more information on inner classes, see Chapter 6.)

We follow the latter approach. Here is how you place the `ColorAction` class inside the `ButtonPanel` class.

```
class ButtonPanel extends JPanel
{
   . . .
```

```
private class ColorAction implements ActionListener
{
   . . .

   public void actionPerformed(ActionEvent event)
   {
      setBackground(backgroundColor);
      // i.e., outer.setBackground(...)
   }

   private Color backgroundColor;
}
}
```

Look closely at the `actionPerformed` method. The `ColorAction` class doesn't have a `setBackground` method. But the outer `ButtonPanel` class does. The methods are invoked on the `ButtonPanel` object that constructed the inner class objects. (Note again that *outer* is not a keyword in the Java programming language. We just use it as an intuitive symbol for the invisible outer class reference in the inner class object.)

This situation is very common. Event listener objects usually need to carry out some action that affects other objects. You can often strategically place the listener class inside the class whose state the listener should modify.

Example 8–1 contains the complete program. Whenever you click one of the buttons, the appropriate action listener changes the background color of the panel.

Example 8–1: ButtonTest.java

```
import java.awt.*;
import java.awt.event.*;
import javax.swing.*;

public class ButtonTest
{
   public static void main(String[] args)
   {
      ButtonFrame frame = new ButtonFrame();
      frame.setDefaultCloseOperation(JFrame.EXIT_ON_CLOSE);
      frame.setVisible(true);
   }
}

/**
   A frame with a button panel
*/
class ButtonFrame extends JFrame
{
   public ButtonFrame()
   {
      setTitle("ButtonTest");
      setSize(DEFAULT_WIDTH, DEFAULT_HEIGHT);

      // add panel to frame

      ButtonPanel panel = new ButtonPanel();
      add(panel);
   }
```

```

   public static final int DEFAULT_WIDTH = 300;
   public static final int DEFAULT_HEIGHT = 200;
}

/**
   A panel with three buttons.
*/
class ButtonPanel extends JPanel
{
   public ButtonPanel()
   {
      // create buttons

      JButton yellowButton = new JButton("Yellow");
      JButton blueButton = new JButton("Blue");
      JButton redButton = new JButton("Red");

      // add buttons to panel

      add(yellowButton);
      add(blueButton);
      add(redButton);

      // create button actions

      ColorAction yellowAction = new ColorAction(Color.YELLOW);
      ColorAction blueAction = new ColorAction(Color.BLUE);
      ColorAction redAction = new ColorAction(Color.RED);

      // associate actions with buttons

      yellowButton.addActionListener(yellowAction);
      blueButton.addActionListener(blueAction);
      redButton.addActionListener(redAction);
   }

   /**
      An action listener that sets the panel's background color.
   */
   private class ColorAction implements ActionListener
   {
      public ColorAction(Color c)
      {
         backgroundColor = c;
      }

      public void actionPerformed(ActionEvent event)
      {
         setBackground(backgroundColor);
      }

      private Color backgroundColor;
   }
}
```

javax.swing.JButton 1.2

- `JButton(String label)`
  constructs a button. The label string can be plain text, or, starting with JDK 1.3, HTML; for example, `"<html><b>Ok</b></html>"`.

Parameters:	`label`	The text you want on the face of the button

- `JButton(Icon icon)`
  constructs a button.

Parameters:	`icon`	The icon you want on the face of the button

- `JButton(String label, Icon icon)`
  constructs a button.

Parameters:	`label`	The text you want on the face of the button
	`icon`	The icon you want on the face of the button

java.awt.Container 1.0

- `Component add(Component c)`
  adds the component `c` to this container.

javax.swing.ImageIcon 1.2

- `ImageIcon(String filename)`
  constructs an icon whose image is stored in a file. The image is automatically loaded with a media tracker (see Chapter 7).

Becoming Comfortable with Inner Classes

Some people dislike inner classes because they feel that a proliferation of classes and objects makes their programs slower. Let's have a look at that claim. You don't need a new class for every user interface component. In our example, all three buttons share the same listener class. Of course, each of them has a separate listener object. But these objects aren't large. They each contain a color value and a reference to the panel. And the traditional solution, with `if . . . else` statements, also references the same color objects that the action listeners store, just as local variables and not as instance fields.

We believe the time has come to get used to inner classes. We recommend that you use dedicated inner classes for event handlers rather than turning existing classes into listeners. We think that even anonymous inner classes have their place.

Here is a good example of how anonymous inner classes can actually simplify your code. If you look at the code of Example 8–1, you will note that each button requires the same treatment:

1. Construct the button with a label string.
2. Add the button to the panel.
3. Construct an action listener with the appropriate color.
4. Add that action listener.

Let's implement a helper method to simplify these tasks:

```
void makeButton(String name, Color backgroundColor)
{
   JButton button = new JButton(name);
   add(button);
```

```
      ColorAction action = new ColorAction(backgroundColor);
      button.addActionListener(action);
   }
```

Then the `ButtonPanel` constructor simply becomes

```
   public ButtonPanel()
   {
      makeButton("yellow", Color.YELLOW);
      makeButton("blue", Color.BLUE);
      makeButton("red", Color.RED);
   }
```

Now you can make a further simplification. Note that the `ColorAction` class is only needed *once*: in the `makeButton` method. Therefore, you can make it into an anonymous class:

```
   void makeButton(String name, final Color backgroundColor)
   {
      JButton button = new JButton(name);
      add(button);
      button.addActionListener(new
         ActionListener()
         {
            public void actionPerformed(ActionEvent event)
            {
               setBackground(backgroundColor);
            }
         });
   }
```

The action listener code has become quite a bit simpler. The `actionPerformed` method simply refers to the parameter variable `backgroundColor`. (As with all local variables that are accessed in the inner class, the parameter needs to be declared as `final`.)

No explicit constructor is needed. As you saw in Chapter 6, the inner class mechanism automatically generates a constructor that stores all local `final` variables that are used in one of the methods of the inner class.

TIP: Anonymous inner classes can look confusing. But you can get used to deciphering them if you train your eyes to glaze over the routine code, like this:

```
   button.addActionListener(new
      ActionListener()
      {
         public void actionPerformed(ActionEvent event)
         {
            setBackground(backgroundColor);
         }
      });
```

That is, the button action sets the background color. As long as the event handler consists of just a few statements, we think this can be quite readable, particularly if you don't worry about the inner class mechanics.

TIP: JDK 1.4 introduces a mechanism that lets you specify simple event listeners without programming inner classes. For example, suppose you have a button labeled Load whose event handler contains a single method call:

```
   frame.loadData();
```

Of course, you can use an anonymous inner class:

```
loadButton.addActionListener(new
   ActionListener()
   {
      public void actionPerformed(ActionEvent event)
      {
         frame.loadData();
      }
   });
```

But the EventHandler class can create such a listener automatically, with the call

```
EventHandler.create(ActionListener.class, frame, "loadData")
```

Of course, you still need to install the handler:

```
loadButton.addActionListener((ActionListener)
   EventHandler.create(ActionListener.class, frame, "loadData"));
```

The cast is necessary because the create method returns an Object. Perhaps a future version of the JDK will make use of generic types to make this method even more convenient.

If the event listener calls a method with a single parameter that is derived from the event handler, then you can use another form of the create method. For example, the call

```
EventHandler.create(ActionListener.class, frame, "loadData", "source.text")
```

is equivalent to

```
new ActionListener()
{
   public void actionPerformed(ActionEvent event)
   {
      frame.loadData(((JTextField) event.getSource()).getText());
   }
}
```

Note that the event handler turns the names of the *properties* source and text into method calls getSource and getText, using the *JavaBeans* convention. (For more information on properties and JavaBeans components, please turn to Volume 2.)

However, in practice, this situation is not all that common, and there is no mechanism for supplying parameters that aren't derived from the event object.

Turning Components into Event Listeners

You are completely free to designate *any* object of a class that implements the ActionListener interface as a button listener. We prefer to use objects of a new class that was expressly created for carrying out the desired button actions. However, some programmers are not comfortable with inner classes and choose a different strategy. They locate the component that changes as a result of the event, make that component implement the ActionListener interface, and add an actionPerformed method. In our example, you can turn the ButtonPanel into an action listener:

```
class ButtonPanel extends JPanel implements ActionListener
{
   . . .
   public void actionPerformed(ActionEvent event)
   {
      // set background color
      . . .
   }
}
```

Then the panel sets *itself* as the listener to all three buttons:

```
yellowButton.addActionListener(this);
blueButton.addActionListener(this);
redButton.addActionListener(this);
```

Note that now the three buttons no longer have individual listeners. They share a single listener object, namely, the button panel. Therefore, the actionPerformed method must figure out *which* button was clicked.

The getSource method of the EventObject class, the superclass of all other event classes, will tell you the *source* of every event. The event source is the object that generated the event and notified the listener:

```
Object source = event.getSource();
```

The actionPerformed method can then check which of the buttons was the source:

```
if (source == yellowButton) . . .
else if (source == blueButton) . . .
else if (source == redButton ) . . .
```

Of course, this approach requires that you keep references to the buttons as instance fields in the surrounding panel.

As you can see, turning the button panel into the action listener isn't really any simpler than defining an inner class. It also becomes *really* messy when the panel contains multiple user interface elements.

CAUTION: Some programmers use a different way to find out the event source in a listener object that is shared among multiple sources. The ActionEvent class has a getActionCommand method that returns the *command string* associated with this action. For buttons, it turns out that the command string defaults to being the button label. If you take this approach, an actionPerformed method contains code like this:

```
String command = event.getActionCommand();
if (command.equals("Yellow")) . . .;
else if (command.equals("Blue")) . . .;
else if (command.equals("Red")) . . .;
```

We suggest that you do not follow this approach. Relying on the button strings is dangerous. It is an easy mistake to label a button "Gray" and then spell the string slightly differently in the test:

```
if (command.equals("Grey")) . . .
```

Button strings give you grief when the time comes to internationalize your application. To make the German version with button labels “Gelb,” “Blau,” and “Rot,” you have to change *both* the button labels and the strings in the actionPerformed method.

java.util.EventObject 1.1

- Object getSource()
  returns a reference to the object where the event occurred.

java.awt.event.ActionEvent 1.1

- String getActionCommand()
  returns the command string associated with this action event. If the action event originated from a button, the command string equals the button label, unless it has been changed with the setActionCommand method.

java.beans.EventHandler 1.4

- `static Object create(Class listenerInterface, Object target, String action)`
- `static Object create(Class listenerInterface, Object target, String action, String eventProperty)`
- `static Object create(Class listenerInterface, Object target, String action, String eventProperty, String listenerMethod)`

  construct an object of a proxy class that implements the given interface. Either the named method or all methods of the interface carry out the given action on the target object.

  The action can be a method name or a property of the target. If it is a property, its setter method is executed. For example, an action "text" is turned into a call of the setText method.

  The event property consists of one or more dot-separated property names. The first property is read from the parameter of the listener method. The second property is read from the resulting object, and so on. The final result becomes the parameter of the action. For example, the property "source.text" is turned into calls to the getSource and getText methods.

Example: Changing the Look and Feel

By default, Swing programs use the Metal look and feel. There are two ways to change to a different look and feel. The first way is to supply a file swing.properties in the jre/lib subdirectory of your Java installation. In that file, set the property swing.defaultlaf to the class name of the look and feel that you want. For example,

```
swing.defaultlaf=com.sun.java.swing.plaf.motif.MotifLookAndFeel
```

Note that the Metal look and feel is located in the javax.swing package. The other look-and-feel packages are located in the com.sun.java package and need not be present in every Java implementation. Currently, for copyright reasons, the Windows and Mac look-and-feel packages are only shipped with the Windows and Mac versions of the Java runtime environment.

TIP: Here is a useful tip for testing. Because lines starting with a # character are ignored in property files, you can supply several look and feel selections in the swing.properties file and move around the # to select one of them:

```
#swing.defaultlaf=javax.swing.plaf.metal.MetalLookAndFeel
swing.defaultlaf=com.sun.java.swing.plaf.motif.MotifLookAndFeel
#swing.defaultlaf=com.sun.java.swing.plaf.windows.WindowsLookAndFeel
```

You must restart your program to switch the look and feel in this way. A Swing program reads the swing.properties file only once, at startup.

The second way is to change the look and feel dynamically. Call the static UIManager.setLookAndFeel method and give it the name of the look-and-feel class that you want. Then call the static method SwingUtilities.updateComponentTreeUI to refresh the entire set of components. You need to supply one component to that method; it will find all others. The UIManager.setLookAndFeel method may throw a number of exceptions when it can't find the look and feel that you request, or when there is an error loading it. As always, we ask you to gloss over the exception handling code and wait until Chapter 11 for a full explanation.

Here is an example showing how you can switch to the Motif look and feel in your program:

```
String plaf = "com.sun.java.swing.plaf.motif.MotifLookAndFeel";
try
{
   UIManager.setLookAndFeel(plaf);
   SwingUtilities.updateComponentTreeUI(panel);
}
catch(Exception e) { e.printStackTrace(); }
```

To enumerate all installed look and feel implementations, call

```
UIManager.LookAndFeelInfo[] infos = UIManager.getInstalledLookAndFeels();
```

Then you can get the name and class name for each look and feel as

```
String name = infos[i].getName();
String className = infos[i].getClassName();
```

Example 8–2 is a complete program that demonstrates how to switch the look and feel (see Figure 8–3). The program is similar to Example 8–1. Following the advice of the preceding section, we use a helper method `makeButton` and an anonymous inner class to specify the button action, namely, to switch the look and feel.

There is one fine point to this program. The `actionPerformed` method of the inner action listener class needs to pass the `this` reference of the outer `PlafPanel` class to the `updateComponentTreeUI` method. Recall from Chapter 6 that the outer object's `this` pointer must be prefixed by the outer class name:

```
SwingUtilities.updateComponentTreeUI(PlafPanel.this);
```

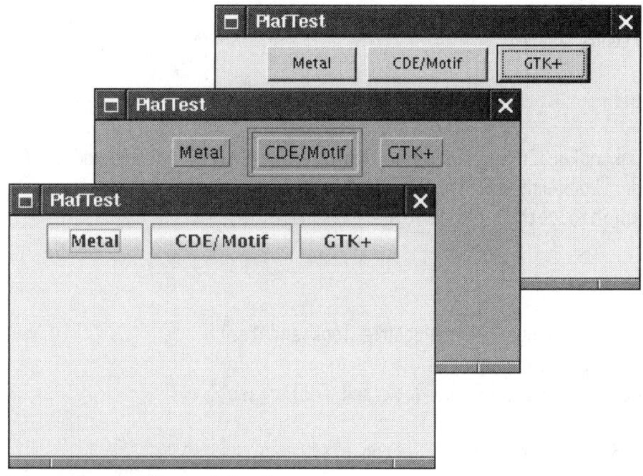

Figure 8–3: Switching the look and feel

Example 8–2: PlafTest.java

```
import java.awt.*;
import java.awt.event.*;
import javax.swing.*;

public class PlafTest
{
   public static void main(String[] args)
   {
      PlafFrame frame = new PlafFrame();
      frame.setDefaultCloseOperation(JFrame.EXIT_ON_CLOSE);
      frame.setVisible(true);
```

```
   }
}

/**
   A frame with a button panel for changing look and feel
*/
class PlafFrame extends JFrame
{
   public PlafFrame()
   {
      setTitle("PlafTest");
      setSize(DEFAULT_WIDTH, DEFAULT_HEIGHT);

      // add panel to frame

      PlafPanel panel = new PlafPanel();
      add(panel);
   }

   public static final int DEFAULT_WIDTH = 300;
   public static final int DEFAULT_HEIGHT = 200;
}

/**
   A panel with buttons to change the pluggable look and feel
*/
class PlafPanel extends JPanel
{
   public PlafPanel()
   {
      UIManager.LookAndFeelInfo[] infos = UIManager.getInstalledLookAndFeels();
      for (UIManager.LookAndFeelInfo info : infos)
         makeButton(info.getName(), info.getClassName());
   }

   /**
      Makes a button to change the pluggable look and feel.
      @param name the button name
      @param plafName the name of the look and feel class
    */
   void makeButton(String name, final String plafName)
   {
      // add button to panel

      JButton button = new JButton(name);
      add(button);

      // set button action

      button.addActionListener(new
         ActionListener()
         {
            public void actionPerformed(ActionEvent event)
            {
               // button action: switch to the new look and feel
               try
```

```
                {
                    UIManager.setLookAndFeel(plafName);
                    SwingUtilities.updateComponentTreeUI(PlafPanel.this);
                }
                catch(Exception e) { e.printStackTrace(); }
            }
        });
    }
}
```

javax.swing.UIManager 1.2

- `static UIManager.LookAndFeelInfo[] getInstalledLookAndFeels()`
  gets an array of objects that describe the installed look-and-feel implementations.
- `static setLookAndFeel(String className)`
  sets the current look and feel.

  Parameters: `className` the name of the look-and-feel implementation class

javax.swing.UIManager.LookAndFeelInfo 1.2

- `String getName()`
  returns the display name for the look and feel.
- `String getClassName()`
  returns the name of the implementation class for the look and feel.

Example: Capturing Window Events

Not all events are as simple to handle as button clicks. Here is an example of a more complex case that we already briefly noted in Chapter 7. Before the appearance of the `EXIT_ON_CLOSE` option in the JDK 1.3, programmers had to manually exit the program when the main frame was closed. In a non-toy program, you will want to do that as well because you want to close the program only after you check that the user won't lose work. For example, when the user closes the frame, you may want to put up a dialog to warn the user if unsaved work is about to be lost and to exit the program only when the user agrees.

When the program user tries to close a frame window, the `JFrame` object is the source of a `WindowEvent`. If you want to catch that event, you must have an appropriate listener object and add it to the list of window listeners.

```
WindowListener listener = . . .;
frame.addWindowListener(listener);
```

The window listener must be an object of a class that implements the `WindowListener` interface. There are actually seven methods in the `WindowListener` interface. The frame calls them as the responses to seven distinct events that could happen to a window. The names are self-explanatory, except that "iconified" is usually called "minimized" under Windows. Here is the complete `WindowListener` interface:

```
public interface WindowListener
{
   void windowOpened(WindowEvent e);
   void windowClosing(WindowEvent e);
   void windowClosed(WindowEvent e);
   void windowIconified(WindowEvent e);
   void windowDeiconified(WindowEvent e);
   void windowActivated(WindowEvent e);
   void windowDeactivated(WindowEvent e);
}
```

NOTE: To find out whether a window has been maximized, install a WindowStateListener. See the following API notes on page 302 for details.

As is always the case in Java, any class that implements an interface must implement all its methods; in this case, that means implementing *seven* methods. Recall that we are only interested in one of these seven methods, namely, the windowClosing method.

Of course, we can define a class that implements the interface, add a call to System.exit(0) in the windowClosing method, and write do-nothing functions for the other six methods:

```
class Terminator implements WindowListener
{
   public void windowClosing(WindowEvent e)
   {
      System.exit(0);
   }

   public void windowOpened(WindowEvent e) {}
   public void windowClosed(WindowEvent e) {}
   public void windowIconified(WindowEvent e) {}
   public void windowDeiconified(WindowEvent e) {}
   public void windowActivated(WindowEvent e) {}
   public void windowDeactivated(WindowEvent e) {}
}
```

Adapter Classes

Typing code for six methods that don't do anything is the kind of tedious busywork that nobody likes. To simplify this task, each of the AWT listener interfaces that has more than one method comes with a companion *adapter* class that implements all the methods in the interface but does nothing with them. For example, the WindowAdapter class has seven do-nothing methods. This means the adapter class automatically satisfies the technical requirements that Java imposes for implementing the associated listener interface. You can extend the adapter class to specify the desired reactions to some, but not all, of the event types in the interface. (An interface such as ActionListener that has only a single method does not need an adapter class.)

Let us make use of the window adapter. We can extend the WindowAdapter class, inherit six of the do-nothing methods, and override the windowClosing method:

```
class Terminator extends WindowAdapter
{
   public void windowClosing(WindowEvent e)
   {
      System.exit(0);
   }
}
```

Now you can register an object of type Terminator as the event listener:

```
WindowListener listener = new Terminator();
frame.addWindowListener(listener);
```

Whenever the frame generates a window event, it passes it to the listener object by calling one of its seven methods (see Figure 8–4). Six of those methods do nothing; the windowClosing method calls System.exit(0), terminating the application.

CAUTION: If you misspell the name of a method when extending an adapter class, then the compiler won't catch your error. For example, if you define a method windowIsClosing in a WindowAdapter class, then you get a class with eight methods, and the windowClosing method does nothing.

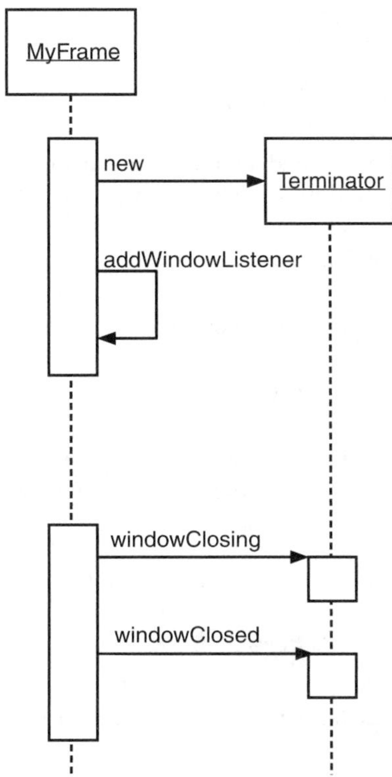

Figure 8–4: A window listener

Creating a listener class that extends the `WindowAdapter` is an improvement, but we can go even further. There is no need to give a name to the `listener` object. Simply write

```
frame.addWindowListener(new Terminator());
```

But why stop there? We can make the listener class into an anonymous inner class of the frame.

```
frame.addWindowListener(new
   WindowAdapter()
   {
      public void windowClosing(WindowEvent e)
      {
         System.exit(0);
      }
   });
```

This code does the following:

- Defines a class without a name that extends the `WindowAdapter` class;
- Adds a `windowClosing` method to that anonymous class (as before, this method exits the program);
- Inherits the remaining six do-nothing methods from `WindowAdapter`;
- Creates an object of this class; that object does not have a name, either;
- Passes that object to the `addWindowListener` method.

We say again that the syntax for using anonymous inner classes takes some getting used to. The payoff is that the resulting code is as short as possible.

java.awt.event.WindowListener 1.1

- `void windowOpened(WindowEvent e)`
  is called after the window has been opened.
- `void windowClosing(WindowEvent e)`
  is called when the user has issued a window manager command to close the window. Note that the window will close only if its `hide` or `dispose` method is called.
- `void windowClosed(WindowEvent e)`
  is called after the window has closed.
- `void windowIconified(WindowEvent e)`
  is called after the window has been iconified.
- `void windowDeiconified(WindowEvent e)`
  is called after the window has been deiconified.
- `void windowActivated(WindowEvent e)`
  is called after the window has become active. Only a frame or dialog can be active. Typically, the window manager decorates the active window, for example, by highlighting the title bar.
- `void windowDeactivated(WindowEvent e)`
  is called after the window has become deactivated.

java.awt.event.WindowStateListener 1.4

- `void windowStateChanged(WindowEvent event)`
  is called after the window has been maximized, iconified, or restored to its normal size.

java.awt.event.WindowEvent 1.1

- `int getNewState()` 1.4
- `int getOldState()` 1.4
  return the new and old state of a window in a window state change event. The returned integer is one of the following values:

```
Frame.NORMAL
Frame.ICONIFIED
Frame.MAXIMIZED_HORIZ
Frame.MAXIMIZED_VERT
Frame.MAXIMIZED_BOTH
```

The AWT Event Hierarchy

Having given you a taste of how event handling works, we want to turn to a more general discussion of event handling in Java. As we briefly mentioned earlier, event handling in Java is object oriented, with all events descending from the `EventObject` class in the `java.util` package. (The common superclass is not called `Event` because that is the name of the event class in the old event model. Although the old model is now deprecated, its classes are still a part of the Java library.)

The `EventObject` class has a subclass `AWTEvent`, which is the parent of all AWT event classes. Figure 8–5 shows the inheritance diagram of the AWT events.

Some of the Swing components generate event objects of yet more event types; these directly extend `EventObject`, not `AWTEvent`.

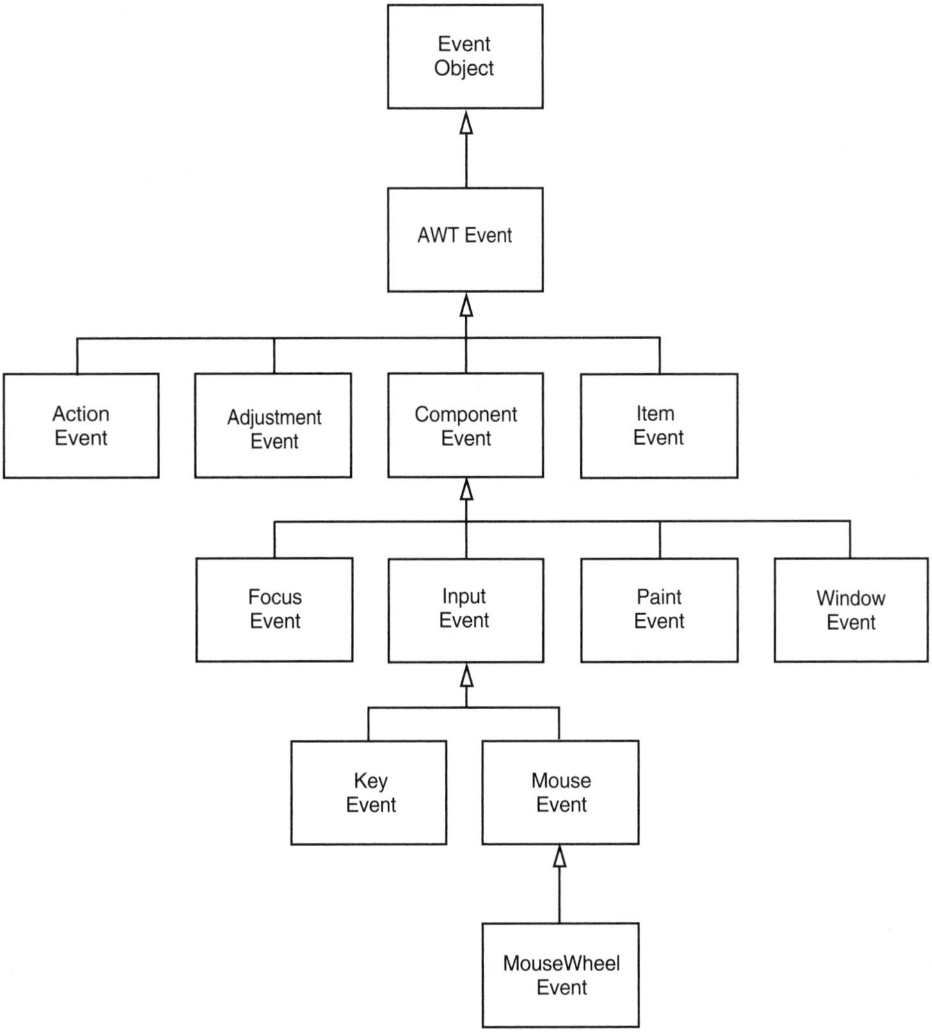

Event Object

AWT Event

Action Event
Adjustment Event
Component Event
Item Event

Focus Event
Input Event
Paint Event
Window Event

Key Event
Mouse Event

MouseWheel Event

Figure 8–5: Inheritance diagram of AWT event classes

The event objects encapsulate information about the event that the event source communicates to its listeners. When necessary, you can then analyze the event objects that were passed to the listener object, as we did in the button example with the `getSource` and `getActionCommand` methods.

Some of the AWT event classes are of no practical use for the Java programmer. For example, the AWT inserts `PaintEvent` objects into the event queue, but these objects are not delivered to listeners. Java programmers don't listen to paint events; they override the `paintComponent` method to control repainting. The AWT also generates a number of events that are needed only by system programmers, to provide input systems for ideographic languages, automated testing robots, and so on. We do not discuss these specialized event types. Finally, we omit events that are associated with obsolete AWT components.

Here is a list of the commonly used AWT event types.

```
ActionEvent              KeyEvent
AdjustmentEvent          MouseEvent
FocusEvent               MouseWheelEvent
ItemEvent                WindowEvent
```

You will see examples of these event types in this chapter and the next.

The `javax.swing.event` package contains additional events that are specific to Swing components. We cover some of them in the next chapter.

The following interfaces listen to these events.

```
ActionListener           MouseMotionListener
AdjustmentListener       MouseWheelListener
FocusListener            WindowListener
ItemListener             WindowFocusListener
KeyListener              WindowStateListener
MouseListener
```

You have already seen the `ActionListener` and `WindowListener` interface.

Although the `javax.swing.event` package contains many more listener interfaces that are specific to Swing user interface components, it still uses the basic AWT listener interfaces extensively for general event processing.

Several of the AWT listener interfaces, namely, those that have more than one method, come with a companion adapter class that implements all the methods in the interface to do nothing. (The other interfaces have only a single method each, so there is no benefit in having adapter classes for these interfaces.) Here are the commonly used adapter classes:

```
FocusAdapter             MouseMotionAdapter
KeyAdapter               WindowAdapter
MouseAdapter
```

Obviously, there are a lot of classes and interfaces to keep track of—it can all be a bit overwhelming. Fortunately, the principle is simple. A class that is interested in receiving events must implement a listener interface. It registers itself with the event source. It then gets the events that it asked for and processes them through the methods of the listener interface.

C++ NOTE: People coming from a C/C++ background may be wondering: Why the proliferation of objects, methods, and interfaces needed for event handling? C++ programmers are accustomed to doing GUI programming by writing callbacks with generic pointers or handles. This won't work in Java. The Java event model is strongly typed: the compiler watches out that events are sent only to objects that are capable of handling them.

Semantic and Low-Level Events in the AWT

The AWT makes a useful distinction between *low-level* and *semantic* events. A semantic event is one that expresses what the user is doing, such as "clicking that button"; hence, an `ActionEvent` is a semantic event. Low-level events are those events that make this possible. In the case of a button click, this is a mouse down, a series of mouse moves, and a mouse up (but only if the mouse up is inside the button area). Or it might be a keystroke, which happens if the user selects the button with the TAB key and then activates it with the space bar. Similarly, adjusting a scrollbar is a semantic event, but dragging the mouse is a low-level event.

Here are the most commonly used semantic event classes in the `java.awt.event` package:

- `ActionEvent` (for a button click, a menu selection, selecting a list item, or ENTER typed in a text field)
- `AdjustmentEvent` (the user adjusted a scrollbar)
- `ItemEvent` (the user made a selection from a set of checkbox or list items)

Five low-level event classes are commonly used:

- `KeyEvent` (a key was pressed or released)
- `MouseEvent` (the mouse button was pressed, released, moved, or dragged)
- `MouseWheelEvent` (the mouse wheel was rotated)
- `FocusEvent` (a component got focus, or lost focus). See page 320 for more information about the focus concept.
- `WindowEvent` (the window state changed)

Table 8–1 shows the most important AWT listener interfaces, events, and event sources.

Event Handling Summary

Let's go over the event delegation mechanism one more time to make sure that you understand the relationship between event classes, listener interfaces, and adapter classes.

Event *sources* are user interface components, windows, and menus. The operating system notifies an event source about interesting activities, such as mouse moves and keystrokes. The event source describes the nature of the event in an *event object*. It also keeps a set of *listeners*—objects that want to be called when the event happens (see Figure 8–6). The event source then calls the appropriate method of the *listener interface* to deliver information about the event to the various listeners. The source does this by passing the appropriate event object to the method in the listener class. The listener analyzes the event object to find out more about the event. For example, you can use the `getSource` method to find out the source, or the `getX` and `getY` methods of the `MouseEvent` class to find out the current location of the mouse.

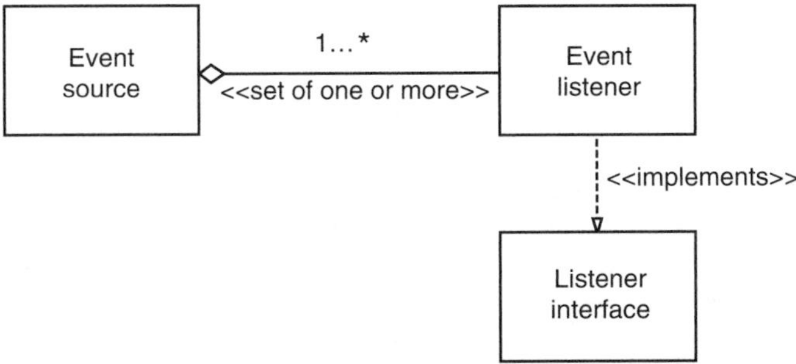

Figure 8–6: Relationship between event sources and listeners

Note that there are separate `MouseListener` and `MouseMotionListener` interfaces. This is done for efficiency—there are a lot of mouse events as the user moves the mouse around, and a listener that just cares about mouse *clicks* will not be bothered with unwanted mouse *moves*.

All low-level events inherit from `ComponentEvent`. This class has a method, called `getComponent`, which reports the component that originated the event; you can use `getComponent` instead of `getSource`. The `getComponent` method returns the same value as `getSource`, but already cast as a `Component`. For example, if a key event was fired because of an input into a text field, then `getComponent` returns a reference to that text field.

Table 8–1: Event Handling Summary

Interface	Methods	Parameter/Accessors	Events Generated By
ActionListener	actionPerformed	ActionEvent • getActionCommand • getModifiers	AbstractButton JComboBox JTextField Timer
AdjustmentListener	adjustmentValueChanged	AdjustmentEvent • getAdjustable • getAdjustmentType • getValue	JScrollbar
ItemListener	itemStateChanged	ItemEvent • getItem • getItemSelectable • getStateChange	AbstractButton JComboBox
FocusListener	focusGained focusLost	FocusEvent • isTemporary	Component
KeyListener	keyPressed keyReleased keyTyped	KeyEvent • getKeyChar • getKeyCode • getKeyModifiersText • getKeyText • isActionKey	Component
MouseListener	mousePressed mouseReleased mouseEntered mouseExited mouseClicked	MouseEvent • getClickCount • getX • getY • getPoint • translatePoint	Component
MouseMotionListener	mouseDragged mouseMoved	MouseEvent	Component
MouseWheelListener	mouseWheelMoved	MouseWheelEvent • getWheelRotation • getScrollAmount	Component
WindowListener	windowClosing windowOpened windowIconified windowDeiconified windowClosed windowActivated windowDeactivated	WindowEvent • getWindow	Window
WindowFocusListener	windowGainedFocus windowLostFocus	WindowEvent • getOppositeWindow	Window
WindowStateListener	windowStateChanged	WindowEvent • getOldState • getNewState	Window

java.awt.event.ComponentEvent 1.0

- `Component getComponent()`
  returns a reference to the component that is the source for the event. This is the same as `(Component) getSource()`.

Low-Level Event Types

In the sections that follow, we discuss in more detail the events that are not linked to specific user interface components, in particular, events related to keystrokes and mouse activity. You can find a detailed discussion of semantic events generated by user interface components in the next chapter.

Keyboard Events

When the user pushes a key, a `KeyEvent` with ID `KEY_PRESSED` is generated. When the user releases the key, a `KEY_RELEASED` `KeyEvent` is triggered. You trap these events in the `keyPressed` and `keyReleased` methods of any class that implements the `KeyListener` interface. Use these methods to trap raw keystrokes. A third method, `keyTyped`, combines the two: it reports on the *characters* that were generated by the user's keystrokes.

The best way to see what happens is with an example. But before we can do that, we have to add a little more terminology. Java makes a distinction between characters and *virtual key codes*. Virtual key codes are indicated with a prefix of `VK_`, such as `VK_A` or `VK_SHIFT`. Virtual key codes correspond to keys on the keyboard. For example, `VK_A` denotes the key marked A. There is no separate lowercase virtual key code—the keyboard does not have separate lowercase keys.

NOTE: Virtual key codes are related to the "scan codes" that the keyboard sends to the computer whenever a physical key is pressed or released.

So, suppose that the user types an uppercase "A" in the usual way, by pressing the SHIFT key along with the A key. Java reports *five* events in response to this user action. Here are the actions and the associated events:

1. Pressed the SHIFT key (`keyPressed` called for `VK_SHIFT`)
2. Pressed the A key (`keyPressed` called for `VK_A`)
3. Typed "A" (`keyTyped` called for an "A")
4. Released the A key (`keyReleased` called for `VK_A`)
5. Released the SHIFT key (`keyReleased` called for `VK_SHIFT`)

On the other hand, if the user typed a lowercase "a" by simply pressing the A key, then only three events occur:

1. Pressed the A key (`keyPressed` called for `VK_A`)
2. Typed "a" (`keyTyped` called for an "a")
3. Released the A key (`keyReleased` called for `VK_A`)

Thus, the `keyTyped` procedure reports the *character* that was typed ("A" or "a"), whereas the `keyPressed` and `keyReleased` methods report on the actual *keys* that the user pressed.

To work with the `keyPressed` and `keyReleased` methods, you should first check the *key code.*

```
public void keyPressed(KeyEvent event)
{
   int keyCode = event.getKeyCode();
   . . .
}
```

The key code will equal one of the following (reasonably mnemonic) constants. They are defined in the KeyEvent class.

```
VK_A . . . VK_Z
VK_0 . . . VK_9
VK_COMMA, VK_PERIOD, VK_SLASH, VK_SEMICOLON, VK_EQUALS
VK_OPEN_BRACKET, VK_BACK_SLASH, VK_CLOSE_BRACKET
VK_BACK_QUOTE, VK_QUOTE
VK_GREATER, VK_LESS, VK_UNDERSCORE, VK_MINUS
VK_AMPERSAND, VK_ASTERISK, VK_AT, VK_BRACELEFT, VK_BRACERIGHT
VK_LEFT_PARENTHESIS, VK_RIGHT_PARENTHESIS
VK_CIRCUMFLEX, VK_COLON, VK_NUMBER_SIGN, VK_QUOTEDBL
VK_EXCLAMATION_MARK, VK_INVERTED_EXCLAMATION_MARK
VK_DEAD_ABOVEDOT, VK_DEAD_ABOVERING, VK_DEAD_ACUTE
VK_DEAD_BREVE
VK_DEAD_CARON, VK_DEAD_CEDILLA, VK_DEAD_CIRCUMFLEX
VK_DEAD_DIAERESIS
VK_DEAD_DOUBLEACUTE, VK_DEAD_GRAVE, VK_DEAD_IOTA, VK_DEAD_MACRON
VK_DEAD_OGONEK, VK_DEAD_SEMIVOICED_SOUND, VK_DEAD_TILDE VK_DEAD_VOICED_SOUND
VK_DOLLAR, VK_EURO_SIGN
VK_SPACE, VK_ENTER, VK_BACK_SPACE, VK_TAB, VK_ESCAPE
VK_SHIFT, VK_CONTROL, VK_ALT, VK_ALT_GRAPH, VK_META
VK_NUM_LOCK, VK_SCROLL_LOCK, VK_CAPS_LOCK
VK_PAUSE, VK_PRINTSCREEN
VK_PAGE_UP, VK_PAGE_DOWN, VK_END, VK_HOME, VK_LEFT, VK_UP, VK_RIGHT, VK_DOWN
VK_F1 . . .VK_F24
VK_NUMPAD0 . . . VK_NUMPAD9
VK_KP_DOWN, VK_KP_LEFT, VK_KP_RIGHT, VK_KP_UP
VK_MULTIPLY, VK_ADD, VK_SEPARATER [sic], VK_SUBTRACT, VK_DECIMAL, VK_DIVIDE
VK_DELETE, VK_INSERT
VK_HELP, VK_CANCEL, VK_CLEAR, VK_FINAL
VK_CONVERT, VK_NONCONVERT, VK_ACCEPT, VK_MODECHANGE
VK_AGAIN, VK_ALPHANUMERIC, VK_CODE_INPUT, VK_COMPOSE, VK_PROPS
VK_STOP
VK_ALL_CANDIDATES, VK_PREVIOUS_CANDIDATE
VK_COPY, VK_CUT, VK_PASTE, VK_UNDO
VK_FULL_WIDTH, VK_HALF_WIDTH
VK_HIRAGANA, VK_KATAKANA, VK_ROMAN_CHARACTERS
VK_KANA, VK_KANJI
VK_JAPANESE_HIRAGANA, VK_JAPANESE_KATAKANA, VK_JAPANESE_ROMAN
VK_WINDOWS, VK_CONTEXT_MENU
VK_UNDEFINED
```

To find the current state of the SHIFT, CONTROL, ALT, and META keys, you can, of course, track the VK_SHIFT, VK_CONTROL, VK_ALT, and VK_META key presses, but that is tedious. Instead, simply use the isShiftDown, isControlDown, isAltDown, and isMetaDown methods. (Sun and Macintosh keyboards have a special META key. On a Sun keyboard, the key is marked a diamond. On a Macintosh, the key is marked with an apple and a cloverleaf.)

For example, the following code tests whether the user presses SHIFT + RIGHT ARROW:

```
public void keyPressed(KeyEvent event)
{
   int keyCode = event.getKeyCode();
   if (keyCode == KeyEvent.VK_RIGHT && event.isShiftDown())
   {
      . . .
   }
}
```

In the keyTyped method, you call the getKeyChar method to obtain the actual character that was typed.

NOTE: Not all keystrokes result in a call to keyTyped. Only those keystrokes that generate a Unicode character can be captured in the keyTyped method. You use the keyPressed method to check for cursor keys and other command keys.

Example 8–3 shows how to handle keystrokes. The program (shown in Figure 8–7) is a simple implementation of the Etch-A-Sketch™ toy.

You move a pen up, down, left, and right with the cursor keys. If you hold down the SHIFT key, the pen moves by a larger increment. Or, if you are experienced in using the vi editor, you can bypass the cursor keys and use the lowercase h, j, k, and l keys to move the pen. The uppercase H, J, K, and L move the pen by a larger increment. We trap the cursor keys in the keyPressed method and the characters in the keyTyped method.

Figure 8–7: A sketch program

There is one technicality: Normally, a panel does not receive any key events. To override this default, we call the setFocusable method. We discuss the concept of keyboard focus later in this chapter.

Example 8–3: Sketch.java

```
import java.awt.*;
import java.awt.geom.*;
import java.util.*;
import java.awt.event.*;
import javax.swing.*;

public class Sketch
{
   public static void main(String[] args)
   {
      SketchFrame frame = new SketchFrame();
      frame.setDefaultCloseOperation(JFrame.EXIT_ON_CLOSE);
      frame.setVisible(true);
   }
}

/**
   A frame with a panel for sketching a figure
*/
class SketchFrame extends JFrame
{
```

```
   public SketchFrame()
   {
      setTitle("Sketch");
      setSize(DEFAULT_WIDTH, DEFAULT_HEIGHT);

      // add panel to frame

      SketchPanel panel = new SketchPanel();
      add(panel);
   }

   public static final int DEFAULT_WIDTH = 300;
   public static final int DEFAULT_HEIGHT = 200;
}

/**
   A panel for sketching with the keyboard.
*/
class SketchPanel extends JPanel
{
   public SketchPanel()
   {
      last = new Point2D.Double(100, 100);
      lines = new ArrayList<Line2D>();
      KeyHandler listener = new KeyHandler();
      addKeyListener(listener);
      setFocusable(true);
   }

   /**
      Add a new line segment to the sketch.
      @param dx the movement in x direction
      @param dy the movement in y direction
   */
   public void add(int dx, int dy)
   {
      // compute new end point
      Point2D end = new Point2D.Double(last.getX() + dx, last.getY() + dy);

      // add line segment
      Line2D line = new Line2D.Double(last, end);
      lines.add(line);
      repaint();

      // remember new end point
      last = end;
   }

   public void paintComponent(Graphics g)
   {
      super.paintComponent(g);
      Graphics2D g2 = (Graphics2D) g;

      // draw all lines
      for (Line2D l : lines)
         g2.draw(l);
```

```
   }

   private Point2D last;
   private ArrayList<Line2D> lines;

   private static final int SMALL_INCREMENT = 1;
   private static final int LARGE_INCREMENT = 5;

   private class KeyHandler implements KeyListener
   {
      public void keyPressed(KeyEvent event)
      {
         int keyCode = event.getKeyCode();

         // set distance
         int d;
         if (event.isShiftDown())
            d = LARGE_INCREMENT;
         else
            d = SMALL_INCREMENT;

         // add line segment
         if (keyCode == KeyEvent.VK_LEFT) add(-d, 0);
         else if (keyCode == KeyEvent.VK_RIGHT) add(d, 0);
         else if (keyCode == KeyEvent.VK_UP) add(0, -d);
         else if (keyCode == KeyEvent.VK_DOWN) add(0, d);
      }

      public void keyReleased(KeyEvent event) {}

      public void keyTyped(KeyEvent event)
      {
         char keyChar = event.getKeyChar();

         // set distance
         int d;
         if (Character.isUpperCase(keyChar))
         {
            d = LARGE_INCREMENT;
            keyChar = Character.toLowerCase(keyChar);
         }
         else
            d = SMALL_INCREMENT;

         // add line segment
         if (keyChar == 'h') add(-d, 0);
         else if (keyChar == 'l') add(d, 0);
         else if (keyChar == 'k') add(0, -d);
         else if (keyChar == 'j') add(0, d);
      }
   }
}
```

java.awt.event.KeyEvent 1.1

- `char getKeyChar()`
  returns the character that the user typed.
- `int getKeyCode()`
  returns the virtual key code of this key event.
- `boolean isActionKey()`
  returns `true` if the key in this event is an "action" key. The following keys are action keys: HOME, END, PAGE UP, PAGE DOWN, UP, DOWN, LEFT, RIGHT, F1 ... F24, PRINT SCREEN, SCROLL LOCK, CAPS LOCK, NUM LOCK, PAUSE, INSERT, DELETE, ENTER, BACKSPACE, DELETE, and TAB.
- `static String getKeyText(int keyCode)`
  returns a string describing the key code. For example, `getKeyText(KeyEvent.VK_END)` is the string `"End"`.
- `static String getKeyModifiersText(int modifiers)`
  returns a string describing the modifier keys, such as SHIFT or CTRL + SHIFT.

  Parameters: `modifiers` The modifier state, as reported by `getModifiers`

java.awt.event.InputEvent 1.1

- `int getModifiers()`
  returns an integer whose bits describe the state of the modifiers SHIFT, CONTROL, ALT, and META. This method applies to both keyboard and mouse events. To see if a bit is set, test the return value against one of the bit masks `SHIFT_MASK`, `CTRL_MASK`, `ALT_MASK`, `ALT_GRAPH_MASK`, `META_MASK`, or use one of the following methods.
- `boolean isShiftDown()`
- `boolean isControlDown()`
- `boolean isAltDown()`
- `boolean isAltGraphDown()` 1.2
- `boolean isMetaDown()`
  return `true` if the modifier key was held down when this event was generated.

Mouse Events

You do not need to handle mouse events explicitly if you just want the user to be able to click on a button or menu. These mouse operations are handled internally by the various components in the user interface and then translated into the appropriate semantic event. However, if you want to enable the user to draw with the mouse, you will need to trap mouse move, click, and drag events.

In this section, we show you a simple graphics editor application that allows the user to place, move, and erase squares on a canvas (see Figure 8–8).

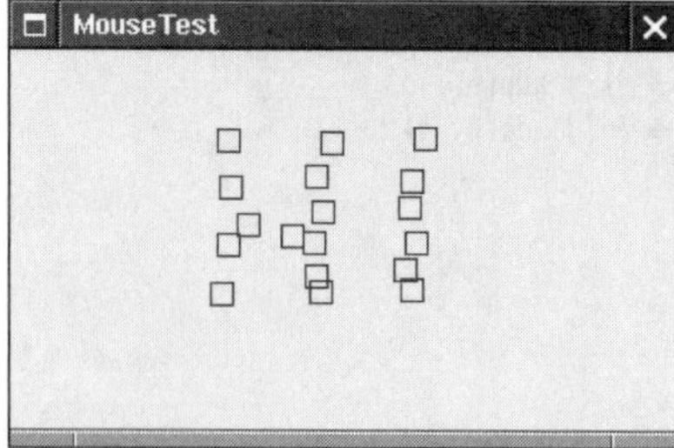

Figure 8–8: A mouse test program

When the user clicks a mouse button, three listener methods are called: `mousePressed` when the mouse is first pressed, `mouseReleased` when the mouse is released, and, finally, `mouseClicked`. If you are only interested in complete clicks, you can ignore the first two methods. By using the `getX` and `getY` methods on the `MouseEvent` argument, you can obtain the *x*- and *y*-coordinates of the mouse pointer when the mouse was clicked. To distinguish between single, double, and triple (!) clicks, use the `getClickCount` method.

Some user interface designers inflict mouse click and keyboard modifier combinations, such as CONTROL + SHIFT + CLICK, on their users. We find this practice reprehensible, but if you disagree, you will find that checking for mouse buttons and keyboard modifiers is a mess. In the original API, two of the button masks equal two keyboard modifier masks, namely:

```
BUTTON2_MASK == ALT_MASK
BUTTON3_MASK == META_MASK
```

This was done so that users with a one-button mouse could simulate the other mouse buttons by holding down modifier keys instead. However, as of JDK 1.4, a different approach is recommended. There are now masks

```
BUTTON1_DOWN_MASK
BUTTON2_DOWN_MASK
BUTTON3_DOWN_MASK
SHIFT_DOWN_MASK
CTRL_DOWN_MASK
ALT_DOWN_MASK
ALT_GRAPH_DOWN_MASK
META_DOWN_MASK
```

The `getModifiersEx` method accurately reports the mouse buttons and keyboard modifiers of a mouse event.

Note that `BUTTON3_DOWN_MASK` tests for the right (nonprimary) mouse button under Windows. For example, you can use code like this to detect whether the right mouse button is down:

```
if ((event.getModifiersEx() & InputEvent.BUTTON3_DOWN_MASK) != 0)
   . . . // code for right click
```

In our sample program, we supply both a `mousePressed` and a `mouseClicked` method. When you click onto a pixel that is not inside any of the squares that have been drawn, a new square is added. We implemented this in the `mousePressed` method so that the user receives immediate feedback and does not have to wait until the mouse button is released. When a user double-clicks inside an existing square, it is erased. We implemented this in the `mouseClicked` method because we need the click count.

```
public void mousePressed(MouseEvent event)
{
   current = find(event.getPoint());
   if (current == null) // not inside a square
      add(event.getPoint());
}

public void mouseClicked(MouseEvent event)
{
   current = find(event.getPoint());
   if (current != null && event.getClickCount() >= 2)
      remove(current);
}
```

As the mouse moves over a window, the window receives a steady stream of mouse movement events. These are ignored by most applications. However, our test application traps the events to change the cursor to a different shape (a cross hair) when it is over a square. This is done with the `getPredefinedCursor` method of the `Cursor` class. Table 8–2 lists the constants to use with this method along with what the cursors look like under Windows. (Note that several of these cursors look the same, but you should check how they look on your platform.)

Table 8–2: Sample Cursor Shapes

Icon	Constant
	`DEFAULT_CURSOR`
	`CROSSHAIR_CURSOR`
	`HAND_CURSOR`
	`MOVE_CURSOR`
	`TEXT_CURSOR`
	`WAIT_CURSOR`
	`N_RESIZE_CURSOR`
	`NE_RESIZE_CURSOR`
	`E_RESIZE_CURSOR`
	`SE_RESIZE_CURSOR`
	`S_RESIZE_CURSOR`
	`SW_RESIZE_CURSOR`
	`W_RESIZE_CURSOR`
	`NW_RESIZE_CURSOR`

TIP: You can find cursor images in the `jre/lib/images/cursors` directory. The file `cursors.properties` defines the cursor "hot spots." This is the point that the user associates with the pointing action of the cursor. For example, if the cursor has the shape of a magnifying glass, the hot spot would be the center of the lens.

Here is the `mouseMoved` method of the `MouseMotionListener` in our example program:

```
public void mouseMoved(MouseEvent event)
{
   if (find(event.getPoint()) == null)
      setCursor(Cursor.getDefaultCursor());
   else
      setCursor(Cursor.getPredefinedCursor(Cursor.CROSSHAIR_CURSOR));
}
```

NOTE: You can also define your own cursor types through the use of the `createCustomCursor` method in the `Toolkit` class:

```
Toolkit tk = Toolkit.getDefaultToolkit();
Image img = tk.getImage("dynamite.gif");
Cursor dynamiteCursor = tk.createCustomCursor(img, new Point(10, 10), "dynamite stick");
```

The first parameter of the `createCustomCursor` points to the cursor image. The second parameter gives the offset of the "hot spot" of the cursor. The third parameter is a string that describes the cursor. This string can be used for accessibility support, for example, to read the cursor shape to a user who is visually impaired or who simply is not facing the screen.

If the user presses a mouse button while the mouse is in motion, `mouseDragged` calls are generated instead of `mouseMoved` calls. Our test application lets a user drag the square under the cursor. We simply update the currently dragged rectangle to be centered under the mouse position. Then, we repaint the canvas to show the new mouse position.

```
public void mouseDragged(MouseEvent event)
{
   if (current != null)
   {
      int x = event.getX();
      int y = event.getY();

      current.setFrame(
         x - SIDELENGTH / 2,
         y - SIDELENGTH / 2,
         SIDELENGTH,
         SIDELENGTH);
      repaint();

}
```

NOTE: The `mouseMoved` method is only called as long as the mouse stays inside the component. However, the `mouseDragged` method keeps getting called even when the mouse is being dragged outside the component.

There are two other mouse event methods: `mouseEntered` and `mouseExited`. These methods are called when the mouse enters or exits a component.

Finally, we explain how to listen to mouse events. Mouse clicks are reported through the `mouseClicked` procedure, which is part of the `MouseListener` interface. Because many applications are interested only in mouse clicks and not in mouse moves and because mouse move events occur so frequently, the mouse move and drag events are defined in a separate interface called `MouseMotionListener`.

In our program we are interested in both types of mouse events. We define two inner classes: `MouseHandler` and `MouseMotionHandler`. The `MouseHandler` class extends the `MouseAdapter` class because it defines only two of the five `MouseListener` methods. The `MouseMotionHandler` implements the `MouseMotionListener` and defines both methods of that interface.
Example 8–4 is the program listing.

Example 8–4: MouseTest.java

```
import java.awt.*;
import java.awt.event.*;
import java.util.*;
import java.awt.geom.*;
import javax.swing.*;

public class MouseTest
{
   public static void main(String[] args)
   {
      MouseFrame frame = new MouseFrame();
      frame.setDefaultCloseOperation(JFrame.EXIT_ON_CLOSE);
      frame.setVisible(true);
   }
}

/**
   A frame containing a panel for testing mouse operations
*/
class MouseFrame extends JFrame
{
   public MouseFrame()
   {
      setTitle("MouseTest");
      setSize(DEFAULT_WIDTH, DEFAULT_HEIGHT);

      // add panel to frame

      MousePanel panel = new MousePanel();
      add(panel);
   }

   public static final int DEFAULT_WIDTH = 300;
   public static final int DEFAULT_HEIGHT = 200;
}

/**
   A panel with mouse operations for adding and removing squares.
*/
class MousePanel extends JPanel
```

```
{
   public MousePanel()
   {
      squares = new ArrayList<Rectangle2D>();
      current = null;

      addMouseListener(new MouseHandler());
      addMouseMotionListener(new MouseMotionHandler());
   }

   public void paintComponent(Graphics g)
   {
      super.paintComponent(g);
      Graphics2D g2 = (Graphics2D) g;

      // draw all squares
      for (Rectangle2D r : squares)
         g2.draw(r);
   }

   /**
      Finds the first square containing a point.
      @param p a point
      @return the first square that contains p
   */
   public Rectangle2D find(Point2D p)
   {
      for (Rectangle2D r : squares)
      {
         if (r.contains(p)) return r;
      }
      return null;
   }

   /**
      Adds a square to the collection.
      @param p the center of the square
   */
   public void add(Point2D p)
   {
      double x = p.getX();
      double y = p.getY();

      current = new Rectangle2D.Double(
         x - SIDELENGTH / 2,
         y - SIDELENGTH / 2,
         SIDELENGTH,
         SIDELENGTH);
      squares.add(current);
      repaint();
   }

   /**
      Removes a square from the collection.
      @param s the square to remove
   */
```

```
   public void remove(Rectangle2D s)
   {
      if (s == null) return;
      if (s == current) current = null;
      squares.remove(s);
      repaint();
   }


   private static final int SIDELENGTH = 10;
   private ArrayList<Rectangle2D> squares;
   private Rectangle2D current;
   // the square containing the mouse cursor

   private class MouseHandler extends MouseAdapter
   {
      public void mousePressed(MouseEvent event)
      {
         // add a new square if the cursor isn't inside a square
         current = find(event.getPoint());
         if (current == null)
            add(event.getPoint());
      }

      public void mouseClicked(MouseEvent event)
      {
         // remove the current square if double clicked
         current = find(event.getPoint());
         if (current != null && event.getClickCount() >= 2)
            remove(current);
      }
   }

   private class MouseMotionHandler
      implements MouseMotionListener
   {
      public void mouseMoved(MouseEvent event)
      {
         // set the mouse cursor to cross hairs if it is inside
         // a rectangle

         if (find(event.getPoint()) == null)
            setCursor(Cursor.getDefaultCursor());
         else
            setCursor(Cursor.getPredefinedCursor(Cursor.CROSSHAIR_CURSOR));
      }

      public void mouseDragged(MouseEvent event)
      {
         if (current != null)
         {
            int x = event.getX();
            int y = event.getY();

            // drag the current rectangle to center it at (x, y)
            current.setFrame(
```

```
                x - SIDELENGTH / 2,
                y - SIDELENGTH / 2,
                SIDELENGTH,
                SIDELENGTH);
            repaint();
         }
      }
   }
}
```

java.awt.event.MouseEvent 1.1

- `int getX()`
- `int getY()`
- `Point getPoint()`
  return the *x*- (horizontal) and *y*- (vertical) coordinate, or point where the event happened, measured from the top-left corner of the component that is the event source.
- `void translatePoint(int x, int y)`
  translates the coordinates of the event by moving `x` units horizontally and `y` units vertically.
- `int getClickCount()`
  returns the number of consecutive mouse clicks associated with this event. (The time interval for what constitutes "consecutive" is system dependent.)

java.awt.event.InputEvent 1.1

- `int getModifiersEx()` 1.4
  returns the extended or "down" modifiers for this event. Use the following mask values to test the returned value:

```
BUTTON1_DOWN_MASK
BUTTON2_DOWN_MASK
BUTTON3_DOWN_MASK
SHIFT_DOWN_MASK
CTRL_DOWN_MASK
ALT_DOWN_MASK
ALT_GRAPH_DOWN_MASK
META_DOWN_MASK
```

- `static String getModifiersExText(int modifiers)` 1.4
  returns a string such as "Shift+Button1" describing the extended or "down" modifiers in the given flag set.

java.awt.Toolkit 1.0

- `public Cursor createCustomCursor(Image image, Point hotSpot, String name)` 1.2
  creates a new custom cursor object.

Parameters:	`image`	The image to display when the cursor is active
	`hotSpot`	The cursor's hot spot (such as the tip of an arrow or the center of cross hairs)
	`name`	A description of the cursor, to support special accessibility environments

java.awt.Component 1.0

- `public void setCursor(Cursor cursor)` **1.1**
  sets the cursor image to the specified cursor.

Focus Events

When you use a mouse, you can point to any object on the screen. But when you type, your keystrokes must go to a specific screen object. The *window manager* (such as Windows or X Windows) directs all keystrokes to the *active window*. Often, the active window is distinguished by a highlighted title bar. Only one window can be active at any one time.

Now suppose the active window is controlled by a Java program. The Java window receives the keystrokes, and it in turn directs them toward a particular *component*. That component is said to have *focus*. Just like the active window is usually distinguished in some way, most Swing components give a visual cue if they currently have focus. A text field has a blinking caret, a button has a rectangle around the label, and so on. When a text field has focus, you can enter text into the text field. When a button has focus, you can "click" it by pressing the space bar.

Only one component in a window can have focus. A component *loses focus* if the user clicks on another component, which then *gains focus*. The user can also use the TAB key to give focus to each component in turn. This traverses all components that are able to receive input focus. By default, Swing components are traversed from left to right, then top to bottom, as they are laid out in the container. You can change the focus traversal order; see the next chapter for more on this subject.

NOTE: Unfortunately, focus handling in older versions of the JDK had quite a few problems, with over 100 separate bugs reported. The reasons for focus flakiness were twofold. Component focus interacts with window focus, which is the responsibility of the windowing system. Therefore, some focus behavior showed platform-dependent variations. Moreover, the implementation code had apparently mushroomed out of control, particularly with the addition of an unsatisfactory focus traversal architecture in JDK 1.3.

Winston Churchill once said "The Americans will always do the right thing... after they've exhausted all the alternatives." Apparently, the same is true for the Java team, and they decided to do the right thing in JDK 1.4. They completely reimplemented the focus handling code, and they provided a complete description of the expected behavior, including an explanation of unavoidable platform dependencies.

You can find the focus specification at `http://java.sun.com/j2se/1.4/docs/api/java/awt/doc-files/FocusSpec.html`.

Fortunately, most application programmers don't need to worry too much about focus handling. Before JDK 1.4, a common use for trapping component focus events was error checking or data validation. Suppose you have a text field that contains a credit card number. When the user is done editing the field and moves to another field, you trap the lost focus event. If the credit card format was not formatted properly, you can display an error message and give the focus back to the credit card field. However, JDK 1.4 has robust validation mechanisms that are easier to program. We discuss validation in Chapter 9.

Some components, such as labels or panels, do not get focus by default because it is assumed that they are just used for decoration or grouping. You need to override this default if you implement a drawing program with panels that paint something in reaction to keystrokes. As of JDK 1.4, you can simply call

```
panel.setFocusable(true);
```

NOTE: In older versions of the JDK, you had to override the `isFocusTraversable` method of the component to achieve the same effect. However, the old focus implementation had separate concepts for the ability to gain focus and participation in focus traversal. That distinction led to confusing behavior and has now been removed. The `isFocusTraversable` method has been deprecated.

In the remainder of this section, we discuss focus event details that you can safely skip until you have a special need that requires fine-grained control of focus handling.

In JDK 1.4, you can easily find out

- The *focus owner*, that is, the component that has focus;
- The *focused window*, that is, the window that contains the focus owner;
- The *active window*, that is, the frame or dialog that contains the focus owner.

The focused window is usually the same as the active window. You get a different result only when the focus owner is contained in a top-level window with no frame decorations, such as a pop-up menu.

To obtain that information, first get the keyboard focus manager:

```
KeyboardFocusManager manager = KeyboardFocusManager.getCurrentKeyboardFocusManager();
```

Then call

```
Component owner = manager.getFocusOwner();
Window focused = manager.getFocusedWindow();
Window active = manager.getActiveWindow(); // a frame or dialog
```

For notification of focus changes, you need to install focus listeners into components or windows. A component focus listener must implement the `FocusListener` interface with two methods, `focusGained` and `focusLost`. These methods are triggered when the component gains or loses the focus. Each of these methods has a `FocusEvent` parameter. There are several useful methods for this class. The `getComponent` method reports the component that gained or lost the focus, and the `isTemporary` method returns `true` if the focus change was *temporary*. A temporary focus change occurs when a component loses control temporarily but will automatically get it back. This happens, for example, when the user selects a different active window. As soon as the user selects the current window again, the same component regains focus.

JDK 1.4 introduces the delivery of window focus events. You add a `WindowFocusListener` to a window and implement the `windowGainedFocus` and `windowLostFocus` methods.

As of JDK 1.4, you can find out the "opposite" component or window when focus is transferred. When a component or window has lost focus, the opposite is the component or window that gains focus. Conversely, when a component or window gains focus, then its opposite is the one that lost focus. The `getOppositeComponent` method of the `FocusEvent` class reports the opposite component, and the `getOppositeWindow` of the `WindowEvent` class reports the opposite window.

You can programmatically move the focus to another component by calling the `requestFocus` method of the `Component` class. However, the behavior is intrinsically platform dependent if the component is not contained in the currently focused window. To enable programmers to develop platform-independent code, JDK 1.4 adds a method `requestFocusInWindow` to the `Component` class. That method succeeds only if the component is contained in the focused window.

NOTE: You should not assume that your component has focus if `requestFocus` or `requestFocusInWindow` returns `true`. Wait for the `FOCUS_GAINED` event to be delivered to be sure.

NOTE: Some programmers are confused about the FOCUS_LOST event and try to stop another component from gaining focus by requesting the focus in the focusLost handler. However, at that time, the focus is already lost. If you must trap the focus in a particular component, install a "vetoable change listener" in the KeyboardFocusManager and veto the focusOwner property. See Chapter 8 of Volume 2 for details on property vetoes.

java.awt.Component 1.0

- void requestFocus()
  requests that this component gets the focus.
- boolean requestFocusInWindow() 1.4
  requests that this component gets the focus. Returns false if this component is not contained in the focused window or if the request cannot be fulfilled for another reason. Returns true if it is likely that the request will be fulfilled.
- void setFocusable(boolean b) 1.4
- boolean isFocusable() 1.4
  set or get the "focusable" state of this component. If b is true, then this component can gain focus.
- boolean isFocusOwner() 1.4
  returns true if this component currently owns the focus.

java.awt.KeyboardFocusManager 1.4

- static KeyboardFocusManager getCurrentKeyboardFocusManager()
  gets the current focus manager.
- Component getFocusOwner()
  gets the component that owns the focus, or null if this focus manager does not manage the component that has focus.
- Window getFocusedWindow()
  gets the window that contains the component that owns the focus, or null if this focus manager does not manage the component that has focus.
- Window getActiveWindow()
  gets the dialog or frame that contains the focused window, or null if this focus manager does not manage the focused window.

java.awt.Window() 1.0

- boolean isFocused() 1.4
  returns true if this window is currently the focused window.
- boolean isActive() 1.4
  returns true if this frame or dialog is currently the active window. The title bars of active frames and dialogs are usually marked by the window manager.

java.awt.event.FocusEvent 1.1

- Component getOppositeComponent() 1.4
  returns the component that lost focus in the focusGained handler, or the component that gained focus in the focusLost handler.

java.awt.event.WindowEvent 1.4

- `Window getOppositeWindow()` 1.4
  returns the window that lost focus in the `windowGainedFocus` handler, the window that gained focus in the `windowLostFocus` handler, the window that was deactivated in the `windowActivated` handler, or the window that was activated in the `windowDeactivated` handler.

***java.awt.event.WindowFocusListener* 1.4**

- `void windowGainedFocus(WindowEvent event)`
  is called when the event source window gained focus.
- `void windowLostFocus(WindowEvent event)`
  is called when the event source window lost focus.

Actions

It is common to have multiple ways to activate the same command. The user can choose a certain function through a menu, a keystroke, or a button on a toolbar. This is easy to achieve in the AWT event model: link all events to the same listener. For example, suppose `blueAction` is an action listener whose `actionPerformed` method changes the background color to blue. You can attach the same object as a listener to several event sources:

- A toolbar button labeled "Blue"
- A menu item labeled "Blue"
- A keystroke CTRL+B

Then the color change command is handled in a uniform way, no matter whether it was caused by a button click, a menu selection, or a key press.

The Swing package provides a very useful mechanism to encapsulate commands and to attach them to multiple event sources: the `Action` interface. An *action* is an object that encapsulates

- A description of the command (as a text string and an optional icon); and
- Parameters that are necessary to carry out the command (such as the requested color in our example).

The `Action` interface has the following methods:

```
void actionPerformed(ActionEvent event)
void setEnabled(boolean b)
boolean isEnabled()
void putValue(String key, Object value)
Object getValue(String key)
void addPropertyChangeListener(PropertyChangeListener listener)
void removePropertyChangeListener(PropertyChangeListener listener)
```

The first method is the familiar method in the `ActionListener` interface: in fact, the `Action` interface extends the `ActionListener` interface. Therefore, you can use an `Action` object whenever an `ActionListener` object is expected.

The next two methods let you enable or disable the action and check whether the action is currently enabled. When an action is attached to a menu or toolbar and the action is disabled, then the option is grayed out.

The `putValue` and `getValue` methods let you store and retrieve arbitrary name/value pairs in the action object. A couple of important predefined strings, namely, `Action.NAME` and `Action.SMALL_ICON`, store action names and icons into an action object:

```
action.putValue(Action.NAME, "Blue");
action.putValue(Action.SMALL_ICON, new ImageIcon("blue-ball.gif"));
```

Table 8–3 shows all predefined action table names.

Table 8–3: Predefined Action Table Names

Name	Value
NAME	The name of the action; displayed on buttons and menu items.
SMALL_ICON	A place to store a small icon; for display in a button, menu item, or toolbar.
SHORT_DESCRIPTION	A short description of the icon; for display in a tooltip.
LONG_DESCRIPTION	A long description of the icon; for potential use in online help. No Swing component uses this value.
MNEMONIC_KEY	A mnemonic abbreviation; for display in menu items (see Chapter 9).
ACCELERATOR_KEY	A place to store an accelerator keystroke. No Swing component uses this value.
ACTION_COMMAND_KEY	Historically, used in the now obsolete registerKeyboardAction method.
DEFAULT	Potentially useful catch-all property. No Swing component uses this value.

If the action object is added to a menu or toolbar, then the name and icon are automatically retrieved and displayed in the menu item or toolbar button. The SHORT_DESCRIPTION value turns into a tooltip.

The final two methods of the Action interface allow other objects, in particular menus or toolbars that trigger the action, to be notified when the properties of the action object change. For example, if a menu is added as a property change listener of an action object and the action object is subsequently disabled, then the menu is called and can gray out the action name. Property change listeners are a general construct that is a part of the "JavaBeans" component model. You can find out more about beans and their properties in Volume 2.

Note that Action is an *interface*, not a class. Any class implementing this interface must implement the seven methods we just discussed. Fortunately, a friendly soul has provided a class AbstractAction that implements all methods except for actionPerformed. That class takes care of storing all name/value pairs and managing the property change listeners. You simply extend AbstractAction and supply an actionPerformed method.

Let's build an action object that can execute color change commands. We store the name of the command, an icon, and the desired color. We store the color in the table of name/value pairs that the AbstractAction class provides. Here is the code for the ColorAction class. The constructor sets the name/value pairs, and the actionPerformed method carries out the color change action.

```
public class ColorAction extends AbstractAction
{
   public ColorAction(String name, Icon icon, Color c)
   {
      putValue(Action.NAME, name);
      putValue(Action.SMALL_ICON, icon);
      putValue("color", c);
      putValue(Action.SHORT_DESCRIPTION, "Set panel color to " + name.toLowerCase());
   }

   public void actionPerformed(ActionEvent event)
   {
      Color c = (Color) getValue("color");
```

```
        setBackground(c);
    }
}
```

Our test program creates three objects of this class, such as

```
Action blueAction = new ColorAction("Blue", new ImageIcon("blue-ball.gif"), Color.BLUE);
```

Next, let's associate this action with a button. That is easy because we can use a `JButton` constructor that takes an `Action` object.

```
JButton blueButton = new JButton(blueAction);
```

That constructor reads the name and icon from the action, sets the short description as the tooltip, and sets the action as the listener. You can see the icons and a tooltip in Figure 8–9.

As we demonstrate in the next chapter, it is just as easy to add the same action to a menu.

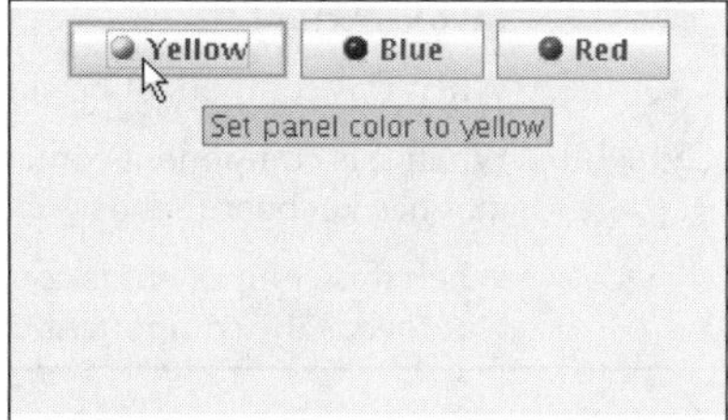

Figure 8–9: Buttons display the icons from the action objects

Finally, we want to add the action objects to keystrokes so that the actions are carried out when the user types keyboard commands. Now we run into a technical complexity. Keystrokes are delivered to the component that has focus. Our sample application is made up of several components, namely, three buttons inside a panel. Therefore, at any time, any one of the three buttons may have focus. *Each* of the buttons would need to handle key events and listen to the CTRL+Y, CTRL+B, and CTRL+R keys.

This is a common problem, and the Swing designers came up with a convenient solution for solving it.

NOTE: In fact, in JDK version 1.2, there were two different solutions for binding keys to actions: the `registerKeyboardAction` method of the `JComponent` class and the `KeyMap` concept for `JTextComponent` commands. As of JDK version 1.3, these two mechanisms are unified. This section describes the unified approach.

To associate actions with keystrokes, you first need to generate objects of the `KeyStroke` class. This is a convenience class that encapsulates the description of a key. To generate a `KeyStroke` object, you don't call a constructor but instead use the static `getKeyStroke` method of the `KeyStroke` class. You specify the virtual key code and the flags (such as SHIFT and CONTROL key combinations):

```
KeyStroke ctrlBKey = KeyStroke.getKeyStroke(KeyEvent.VK_B, InputEvent.CTRL_MASK);
```

Alternatively, you can describe the keystroke as a string:

```
KeyStroke ctrlBKey = KeyStroke.getKeyStroke("ctrl B");
```

Every `JComponent` has three *input maps*, each mapping `KeyStroke` objects to associated actions. The three input maps correspond to three different conditions (see Table 8–4).

Keystroke processing checks these maps in the following order:

1. Check the WHEN_FOCUSED map of the component with input focus. If the keystroke exists, execute the corresponding action. If the action is enabled, stop processing.
2. Starting from the component with input focus, check the WHEN_ANCESTOR_OF_FOCUSED_COMPONENT maps of its parent components. As soon as a map with the keystroke is found, execute the corresponding action. If the action is enabled, stop processing.
3. Look at all *visible* and *enabled* components in the window with input focus that have this keystroke registered in a WHEN_IN_FOCUSED_WINDOW map. Give these components (in the order of their keystroke registration) a chance to execute the corresponding action. As soon as the first enabled action is executed, stop processing. This part of the process is somewhat fragile if a keystroke appears in more than one WHEN_IN_FOCUSED_WINDOW map.

Table 8–4: Input Map Conditions

Flag	Invoke Action
WHEN_FOCUSED	When this component has keyboard focus
WHEN_ANCESTOR_OF_FOCUSED_COMPONENT	When this component contains the component that has keyboard focus
WHEN_IN_FOCUSED_WINDOW	When this component is contained in the same window as the component that has keyboard focus

You obtain an input map from the component with the getInputMap method, for example:

```
InputMap imap = panel.getInputMap(JComponent.WHEN_FOCUSED);
```

The WHEN_FOCUSED condition means that this map is consulted when the current component has the keyboard focus. In our situation, that isn't the map we want. One of the buttons, not the panel, has the input focus. Either of the other two map choices works fine for inserting the color change keystrokes. We use WHEN_ANCESTOR_OF_FOCUSED_COMPONENT in our example program.

The InputMap doesn't directly map KeyStroke objects to Action objects. Instead, it maps to arbitrary objects, and a second map, implemented by the ActionMap class, maps objects to actions. That makes it easier to share the same actions among keystrokes that come from different input maps.

Thus, each component has three input maps and one action map. To tie them together, you need to come up with names for the actions. Here is how you can tie a key to an action:

```
imap.put(KeyStroke.getKeyStroke("ctrl Y"), "panel.yellow");
ActionMap amap = panel.getActionMap();
amap.put("panel.yellow", yellowAction);
```

It is customary to use the string "none" for a do-nothing action. That makes it easy to deactivate a key:

```
imap.put(KeyStroke.getKeyStroke("ctrl C"), "none");
```

CAUTION: The JDK documentation suggests using the action name as the action's key. We don't think that is a good idea. The action name is displayed on buttons and menu items; thus, it can change at the whim of the UI designer and it may be translated into multiple languages. Such unstable strings are poor choices for lookup keys. Instead, we recommend that you come up with action names that are independent of the displayed names.

To summarize, here is what you do to carry out the same action in response to a button, a menu item, or a keystroke:

1. Implement a class that extends the AbstractAction class. You may be able to use the same class for multiple related actions.
2. Construct an object of the action class.
3. Construct a button or menu item from the action object. The constructor will read the label text and icon from the action object.
4. For actions that can be triggered by keystrokes, you have to carry out additional steps. First locate the top-level component of the window, such as a panel that contains all other components.
5. Then get the WHEN_ANCESTOR_OF_FOCUSED_COMPONENT input map of the top-level component. Make a KeyStroke object for the desired keystroke. Make an action key object, such as a string that describes your action. Add the pair (keystroke, action key) into the input map.
6. Finally, get the action map of the top-level component. Add the pair (action key, action object) into the map.

Example 8–5 shows the complete code of the program that maps both buttons and keystrokes to action objects. Try it out—clicking either the buttons or pressing CTRL+Y, CTRL+B, or CTRL+R changes the panel color.

Example 8–5: ActionTest.java

```
import java.awt.*;
import java.awt.event.*;
import javax.swing.*;

public class ActionTest
{
   public static void main(String[] args)
   {
      ActionFrame frame = new ActionFrame();
      frame.setDefaultCloseOperation(JFrame.EXIT_ON_CLOSE);
      frame.setVisible(true);
   }
}

/**
   A frame with a panel that demonstrates color change actions.
*/
class ActionFrame extends JFrame
{
   public ActionFrame()
   {
      setTitle("ActionTest");
      setSize(DEFAULT_WIDTH, DEFAULT_HEIGHT);

      // add panel to frame

      ActionPanel panel = new ActionPanel();
      add(panel);
   }

   public static final int DEFAULT_WIDTH = 300;
   public static final int DEFAULT_HEIGHT = 200;
}
```

```

/**
   A panel with buttons and keyboard shortcuts to change
   the background color.
*/
class ActionPanel extends JPanel
{
   public ActionPanel()
   {
      // define actions

      Action yellowAction = new ColorAction("Yellow",
         new ImageIcon("yellow-ball.gif"),
         Color.YELLOW);
      Action blueAction = new ColorAction("Blue",
         new ImageIcon("blue-ball.gif"),
         Color.BLUE);
      Action redAction = new ColorAction("Red",
         new ImageIcon("red-ball.gif"),
         Color.RED);

      // add buttons for these actions

      add(new JButton(yellowAction));
      add(new JButton(blueAction));
      add(new JButton(redAction));

      // associate the Y, B, and R keys with names

      InputMap imap = getInputMap(JComponent.WHEN_ANCESTOR_OF_FOCUSED_COMPONENT);

      imap.put(KeyStroke.getKeyStroke("ctrl Y"), "panel.yellow");
      imap.put(KeyStroke.getKeyStroke("ctrl B"), "panel.blue");
      imap.put(KeyStroke.getKeyStroke("ctrl R"), "panel.red");

      // associate the names with actions

      ActionMap amap = getActionMap();
      amap.put("panel.yellow", yellowAction);
      amap.put("panel.blue", blueAction);
      amap.put("panel.red", redAction);
   }

   public class ColorAction extends AbstractAction
   {
      /**
         Constructs a color action.
         @param name the name to show on the button
         @param icon the icon to display on the button
         @param c the background color
      */
      public ColorAction(String name, Icon icon, Color c)
      {
         putValue(Action.NAME, name);
         putValue(Action.SMALL_ICON, icon);
```

```
            putValue(Action.SHORT_DESCRIPTION, "Set panel color to " + name.toLowerCase());
            putValue("color", c);
         }

         public void actionPerformed(ActionEvent event)
         {
            Color c = (Color) getValue("color");
            setBackground(c);
         }
      }
}
```

javax.swing.Action 1.2

- `void setEnabled(boolean b)`
  enables or disables this action.
- `boolean isEnabled()`
  returns `true` if this action is enabled.
- `void putValue(String key, Object value)`
  places a name/value pair inside the action object.

Parameters:	`key`	The name of the feature to store with the action object. This can be any string, but several names have predefined meanings—see Table 8–3 on page 324.
	`value`	The object associated with the name.

- `Object getValue(String key)`
  returns the value of a stored name/value pair.

javax.swing.JMenu 1.2

- `JMenuItem add(Action a)`
  adds a menu item to the menu that invokes the action `a` when selected; returns the added menu item.

javax.swing.KeyStroke 1.2

- `static KeyStroke getKeyStroke(char keyChar)`
  creates a `KeyStroke` object that encapsulates a keystroke corresponding to a `KEY_TYPED` event.
- `static KeyStroke getKeyStroke(int keyCode, int modifiers)`
- `static KeyStroke getKeyStroke(int keyCode, int modifiers, boolean onRelease)`
  create a `KeyStroke` object that encapsulates a keystroke corresponding to a `KEY_PRESSED` or `KEY_RELEASED` event.

Parameters:	`keyCode`	The virtual key code
	`modifiers`	Any combination of `InputEvent.SHIFT_MASK`, `InputEvent.CTRL_MASK`, `InputEvent.ALT_MASK`, `InputEvent.META_MASK`
	`onRelease`	`true` if the keystroke is to be recognized when the key is released

- `static KeyStroke getKeyStroke(String description)`
  constructs a keystroke from a humanly readable description. The description is a sequence of whitespace-delimited strings in the following format:

1. The strings `shift control ctrl meta alt button1 button2 button3` are translated to the appropriate mask bits.
2. The string `typed` must be followed by a one-character string, for example, `"typed a"`.
3. The string `pressed` or `released` indicates a key press or release. (Key press is the default.)
4. Otherwise, the string, when prefixed with `VK_`, should correspond to a `KeyEvent` constant, for example, `"INSERT"` corresponds to `KeyEvent.VK_INSERT`.

For example, `"released ctrl Y"` corresponds to: `getKeyStroke(KeyEvent.VK_Y, Event.CTRL_MASK, true)`

`javax.swing.JComponent` 1.2

- `ActionMap getActionMap()` 1.3
  returns the action map that maps keystrokes to action keys.
- `InputMap getInputMap(int flag)` 1.3
  gets the input map that maps action keys to action objects.

  Parameters: `flag` A condition on the keyboard focus to trigger the action, one of the values in Table 8–4 on page 326

Multicasting

In the preceding section, we had several event sources report to the same event listener. In this section, we do the opposite. All AWT event sources support a *multicast* model for listeners. This means that the same event can be sent to more than one listener object. Multicasting is useful if an event is *potentially* of interest to many parties. Simply add multiple listeners to an event source to give all registered listeners a chance to react to the events.

CAUTION: According to the JDK documentation, "The API makes no guarantees about the order in which the events are delivered to a set of registered listeners for a given event on a given source." Therefore, don't implement program logic that depends on the delivery order.

Here we show a simple application of multicasting. We will have a frame that can spawn multiple windows with the New button, and it can close all windows with the Close all button—see Figure 8–10.

The listener to the New button of the `MulticastPanel` is the `newListener` object constructed in the `MulticastPanel` constructor—it makes a new frame whenever the button is clicked.

But the Close all button of the `MulticastPanel` has *multiple listeners.* Each time the `BlankFrame` constructor executes, it adds another action listener to the Close all button. Each of those listeners is responsible for closing a single frame in its `actionPerformed` method. When the user clicks the Close all button, each of the listeners is activated and each of them closes its frame.

Furthermore, the `actionPerformed` method removes the listener from the Close all button because it is no longer needed once the frame is closed.

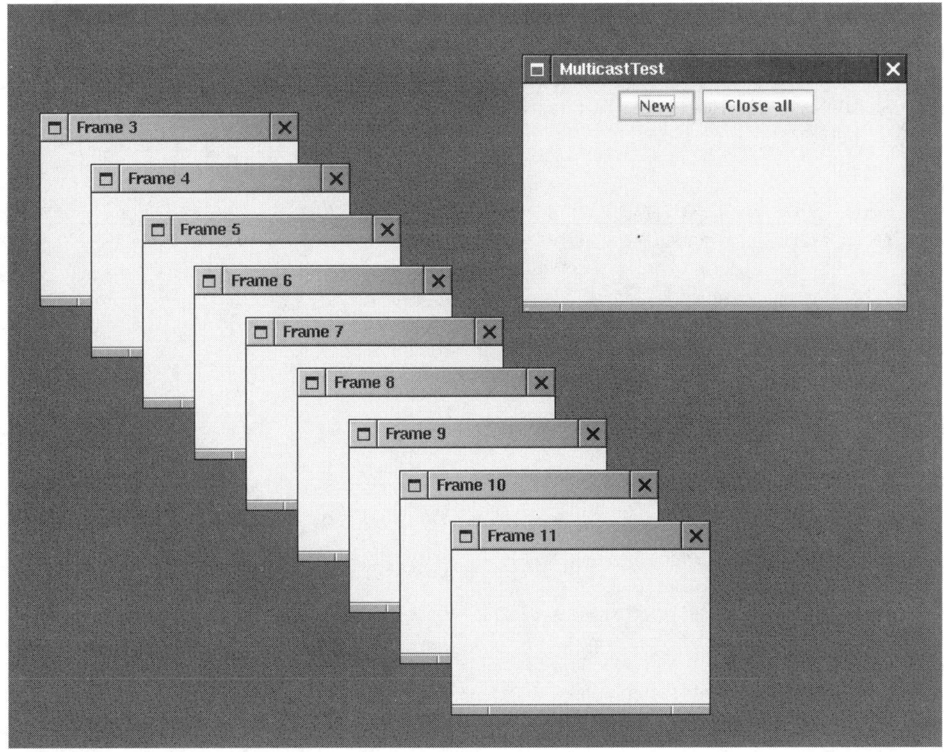

Figure 8–10: All frames listen to the Close all command

Example 8–6 shows the source code.

Example 8–6: MulticastTest.java

```
import java.awt.*;
import java.awt.event.*;
import javax.swing.*;

public class MulticastTest
{
   public static void main(String[] args)
   {
      MulticastFrame frame = new MulticastFrame();
      frame.setDefaultCloseOperation(JFrame.EXIT_ON_CLOSE);
      frame.setVisible(true);
   }
}

/**
   A frame with buttons to make and close secondary frames
*/
class MulticastFrame extends JFrame
{
   public MulticastFrame()
   {
      setTitle("MulticastTest");
```

```
      setSize(DEFAULT_WIDTH, DEFAULT_HEIGHT);

      // add panel to frame

      MulticastPanel panel = new MulticastPanel();
      add(panel);
   }

   public static final int DEFAULT_WIDTH = 300;
   public static final int DEFAULT_HEIGHT = 200;
}

/**
   A panel with buttons to create and close sample frames.
*/
class MulticastPanel extends JPanel
{
   public MulticastPanel()
   {
      // add "New" button

      JButton newButton = new JButton("New");
      add(newButton);
      final JButton closeAllButton = new JButton("Close all");
      add(closeAllButton);

      ActionListener newListener = new
         ActionListener()
         {
            public void actionPerformed(ActionEvent event)
            {
               BlankFrame frame = new BlankFrame(closeAllButton);
               frame.setVisible(true);
            }
         };

      newButton.addActionListener(newListener);
   }
}

/**
   A blank frame that can be closed by clicking a button.
*/
class BlankFrame extends JFrame
{
   /**
      Constructs a blank frame
      @param closeButton the button to close this frame
   */
   public BlankFrame(final JButton closeButton)
   {
      counter++;
      setTitle("Frame " + counter);
      setSize(DEFAULT_WIDTH, DEFAULT_HEIGHT);
      setLocation(SPACING * counter, SPACING * counter);
```

```
      closeListener = new
         ActionListener()
         {
            public void actionPerformed(ActionEvent event)
            {
               closeButton.removeActionListener(closeListener);
               dispose();
            }
         };
      closeButton.addActionListener(closeListener);
   }

   private ActionListener closeListener;
   public static final int DEFAULT_WIDTH = 200;
   public static final int DEFAULT_HEIGHT = 150;
   public static final int SPACING = 40;
   private static int counter = 0;
}
```

Implementing Event Sources

In the last section of this chapter, we show you how to implement a class that generates its own events and notifies interested listeners. This is occasionally necessary when you use advanced Swing components. It is also interesting to see what goes on behind the scenes when you add a listener to a component.

Our event source will be a `PaintCountPanel` that counts how often the `paintComponent` method was called. Every time the count is incremented, the `PaintCountPanel` notifies all listeners. In our sample program, we will attach just one listener that updates the frame title—see Figure 8–11.

Whenever you define an event source, you need three ingredients:

- an *event type*. We could define our own event class, but we will simply use the existing `PropertyChangeEvent` class.
- an *event listener interface*. Again, we could define our own interface, but we will use the existing `PropertyChangeListener` interface. That interface has a single method.

  `public void propertyChange(PropertyChangeEvent event)`
- methods for adding and removing listeners. We will supply two methods in the `PaintCountPanel` class:

  `public void addPropertyChangeListener(PropertyChangeListener listener)`

  `public void removePropertyChangeListener(PropertyChangeListener listener)`

How do we make sure that events are sent to interested parties? This is the responsibility of the event source. It must construct an event object and pass it to the registered listeners whenever an event occurs.

Event management is a common task, and the Swing designers provide a convenience class, `EventListenerList`, to make it easy to implement the methods for adding and removing listeners and for firing events. The class takes care of the tricky details that can arise when multiple threads attempt to add, remove, or dispatch events at the same time.

Because some event sources accept listeners of multiple types, each listener in the event listener list is associated with a particular class. The `add` and `remove` methods are intended for the implementation of `add`*Xxx*`Listener` methods. For example,

```
public void addPropertyChangeListener(PropertyChangeListener listener)
{
   listenerList.add(PropertyChangeListener.class, listener);
}

public void removePropertyChangeListener(PropertyChangeListener listener)
{
   listenerList.remove(PropertyChangeListener.class, listener);
}
```

NOTE: You may wonder why the EventListenerList doesn't simply check which interface the listener object implements. But an object can implement multiple interfaces. For example, it is possible that listener happens to implement both the PropertyChangeListener and the ActionListener interface, but a programmer may choose only to add it as a PropertyChangeListener by calling the addPropertyChangeListener. The EventListenerList must respect that choice.

Whenever the paintComponent method is called, the PaintCountPanel class constructs a PropertyChangeEvent object, specifying the event source, the property name, and the old and new property values. It then calls the firePropertyChangeEvent helper method.

```
public void paintComponent(Graphics g)
{
   int oldPaintCount = paintCount;
   paintCount++;
   firePropertyChangeEvent(new PropertyChangeEvent(this,
      "paintCount", oldPaintCount, paintCount));
   super.paintComponent(g);
}
```

The firePropertyChangeEvent method locates all registered listeners and calls their propertyChange methods.

```
public void firePropertyChangeEvent(PropertyChangeEvent event)
{
   EventListener[] listeners = listenerList.getListeners(PropertyChangeListener.class);
   for (EventListener l : listeners)
      ((PropertyChangeListener) l).propertyChange(event);
}
```

Example 8–7 shows the source code of a sample program that listens to a PaintCountPanel. The frame constructor adds a property change listener to the panel that updates the frame title:

```
panel.addPropertyChangeListener(new
   PropertyChangeListener()
   {
      public void propertyChange(PropertyChangeEvent event)
      {
         setTitle("EventSourceTest - " + event.getNewValue());
      }
   });
```

This ends our discussion of event handling. In the next chapter, you will learn more about user interface components. Of course, to program user interfaces, you will put your knowledge of event handling to work by capturing the events that the user interface components generate.

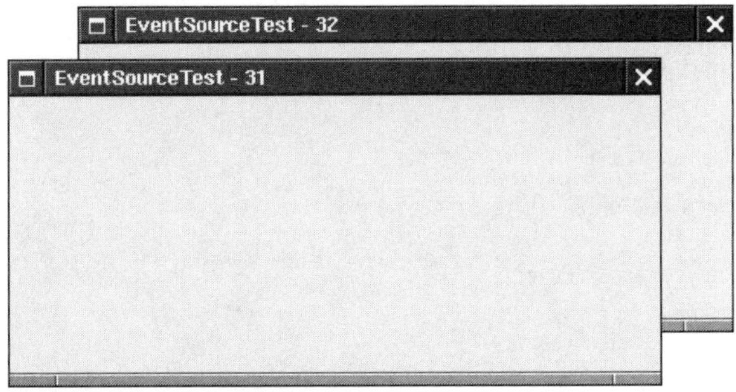

Figure 8–11: Counting how often the panel is painted

Example 8–7: EventSourceTest.java

```
import java.awt.*;
import java.awt.event.*;
import java.util.*;
import javax.swing.*;
import java.beans.*;

public class EventSourceTest
{
   public static void main(String[] args)
   {
      EventSourceFrame frame = new EventSourceFrame();
      frame.setDefaultCloseOperation(JFrame.EXIT_ON_CLOSE);
      frame.setVisible(true);
   }
}

/**
   A frame that contains a panel with drawings
*/
class EventSourceFrame extends JFrame
{
   public EventSourceFrame()
   {
      setTitle("EventSourceTest");
      setSize(DEFAULT_WIDTH, DEFAULT_HEIGHT);

      // add panel to frame

      final PaintCountPanel panel = new PaintCountPanel();
      add(panel);

      panel.addPropertyChangeListener(new
         PropertyChangeListener()
         {
            public void propertyChange(PropertyChangeEvent event)
            {
               setTitle("EventSourceTest - " + event.getNewValue());
            }
         });
   }
```

```
   public static final int DEFAULT_WIDTH = 400;
   public static final int DEFAULT_HEIGHT = 200;
}

/**
   A panel that counts how often it is painted.
*/
class PaintCountPanel extends JPanel
{
   public void paintComponent(Graphics g)
   {
      int oldPaintCount = paintCount;
      paintCount++;
      firePropertyChangeEvent(new PropertyChangeEvent(this,
         "paintCount", oldPaintCount, paintCount));
      super.paintComponent(g);
   }

   /**
      Adds a change listener
      @param listener the listener to add
   */
   public void addPropertyChangeListener(PropertyChangeListener listener)
   {
      listenerList.add(PropertyChangeListener.class, listener);
   }

   /**
      Removes a change listener
      @param listener the listener to remove
   */
   public void removePropertyChangeListener(PropertyChangeListener listener)
   {
      listenerList.remove(PropertyChangeListener.class, listener);
   }

   public void firePropertyChangeEvent(PropertyChangeEvent event)
   {
      EventListener[] listeners = listenerList.getListeners(PropertyChangeListener.class);
      for (EventListener l : listeners)
         ((PropertyChangeListener) l).propertyChange(event);
   }

   public int getPaintCount()
   {
      return paintCount;
   }

   private int paintCount;
}
```

javax.swing.event.EventListenerList 1.2

- `void add(Class t, EventListener l)`
  adds an event listener and its class to the list. The class is stored so that event firing methods can selectively call events. Typical usage is in an `addXxxListener` method:

```
public void addXxxListener(XxxListener l)
{
   listenerList.add(XxxListener.class, l);
}
```

  Parameters: `t` The listener type
  `l` The listener

- `void remove(Class t, EventListener l)`
  removes an event listener and its class from the list. Typical usage is in a `removeXxxListener` method:

```
public void removeXxxListener(XxxListener l)
{
   listenerList.remove(XxxListener.class, l);
}
```

  Parameters: `t` The listener type
  `l` The listener

- `EventListener[] getListeners(Class t)` 1.3
  returns an array of all the listeners of the given type. The array is guaranteed to be non-`null`.
- `Object[] getListenerList()`
  returns an array whose elements with an even-numbered index are listener classes and whose elements with an odd-numbered index are listener objects. The array is guaranteed to be non-`null`.

java.beans.PropertyChangeEvent 1.1

- `PropertyChangeEvent(Object source, String name, Object oldValue, Object newValue)`
  constructs a property change event.

  Parameters: `source` The event source, that is, the object that reports a property change
  `name` The name of the property
  `oldValue` The value of the property before the change
  `newValue` The value of the property after the change

***java.beans.PropertyChangeListener* 1.1**

- `void propertyChange(PropertyChangeEvent event)`
  called when a property value has changed.

Chapter 9

User Interface Components with Swing

- ▼ The Model-View-Controller Design Pattern
- ▼ Introduction to Layout Management
- ▼ Text Input
- ▼ Choice Components
- ▼ Menus
- ▼ Sophisticated Layout Management
- ▼ Dialog Boxes

The last chapter was primarily designed to show you how to use the event model in Java. In the process you took the first steps toward learning how to build a graphical user interface. This chapter shows you the most important tools you'll need to build more full-featured GUIs.

We start out with a tour of the architectural underpinnings of Swing. Knowing what goes on "under the hood" is important in understanding how to use some of the more advanced components effectively. We then show you how to use the most common user interface components in Swing such as text fields, radio buttons, and menus. Next, you will learn how to use the nifty layout manager features of Java to arrange these components in a window, regardless of the look and feel of a particular user interface. Finally, you'll see how to implement dialog boxes in Swing.

This chapter covers basic Swing components such as text components, buttons, and sliders. These are the essential user interface components that you will need most frequently. We cover advanced Swing components in Volume 2. For an even more comprehensive look into all details of the Swing framework, we recommend the books *Core JFC* and *Core Swing: Advanced Topics* by Kim Topley (both published by Prentice Hall PTR).

The Model-View-Controller Design Pattern

As promised, we start this chapter with a section describing the architecture of Swing components. Before we explain just what the title of this section means, let's step back for a minute and think about the pieces that make up a user interface component such as a button, a checkbox, a text field, or a sophisticated tree control. Every component has three characteristics:

- Its *content*, such as the state of a button (pushed in or not), or the text in a text field;
- Its *visual appearance* (color, size, and so on);
- Its *behavior* (reaction to events).

Even a seemingly simple component such as a button exhibits some moderately complex interaction among these characteristics. Obviously, the visual appearance of a button depends on the look and feel. A Metal button looks different from a Windows button or a Motif button. In addition, the appearance depends on the button state: when a button is pushed in, it needs to be redrawn to look different. The state depends on the events that the button receives. When the user depresses the mouse inside the button, the button is pushed in.

Of course, when you use a button in your programs, you simply consider it as a *button*, and you don't think too much about the inner workings and characteristics. That, after all, is the job of the programmer who implemented the button. However, those programmers who implement buttons are motivated to think a little harder about them. After all, they have to implement buttons, and all other user interface components, so that they work well no matter what look and feel is installed.

To do this, the Swing designers turned to a well-known *design pattern*: the *model-view-controller* pattern. This pattern, like many other design patterns, goes back to one of the principles of object-oriented design that we mentioned way back in Chapter 5: don't make one object responsible for too much. Don't have a single button class do everything. Instead, have the look and feel of the component associated with one object and store the content in *another* object. The model-view-controller (MVC) design pattern teaches how to accomplish this. Implement three separate classes:

- The *model,* which stores the content
- The *view,* which displays the content
- The *controller,* which handles user input

The pattern specifies precisely how these three objects interact. The model stores the content and has *no user interface*. For a button, the content is pretty trivial—it is just a small set of flags that tells whether the button is currently pushed in or out, whether it is active or inactive, and so on. For a text field, the content is a bit more interesting. It is a string object that holds the current text. This is *not the same* as the view of the content—if the content is larger than the text field, the user sees only a portion of the text displayed (see Figure 9–1).

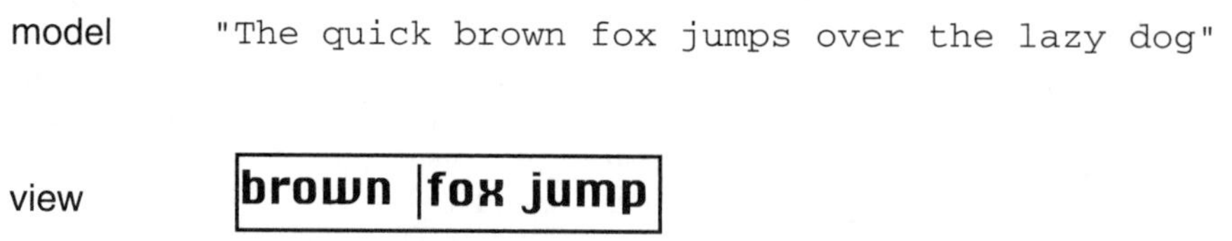

Figure 9–1: Model and view of a text field

The model must implement methods to change the content and to discover what the content is. For example, a text model has methods to add or remove characters in the current text and to return the current text as a string. Again, keep in mind that the model is completely nonvisual. It is the job of a view to draw the data that is stored in the model.

NOTE: The term "model" is perhaps unfortunate because we often think of a model as a representation of an abstract concept. Car and airplane designers build models to simulate real cars and planes. But that analogy really leads you astray when thinking about the model-view-controller pattern. In the design pattern, the model stores the complete content, and the view gives a (complete or incomplete) visual representation of the content. A better analogy might be the model who poses for an artist. It is up to the artist to look at the model and create a view. Depending on the artist, that view might be a formal portrait, an impressionist painting, or a cubist drawing that shows the limbs in strange contortions.

One of the advantages of the model-view-controller pattern is that a model can have multiple views, each showing a different part or aspect of the full content. For example, an HTML editor can offer two *simultaneous* views of the same content: a WYSIWYG view and a "raw tag" view (see Figure 9–2). When the model is updated through the controller of one of the views, it tells both attached views about the change. When the views are notified, they refresh themselves automatically. Of course, for a simple user interface component such as a button, you won't have multiple views of the same model.

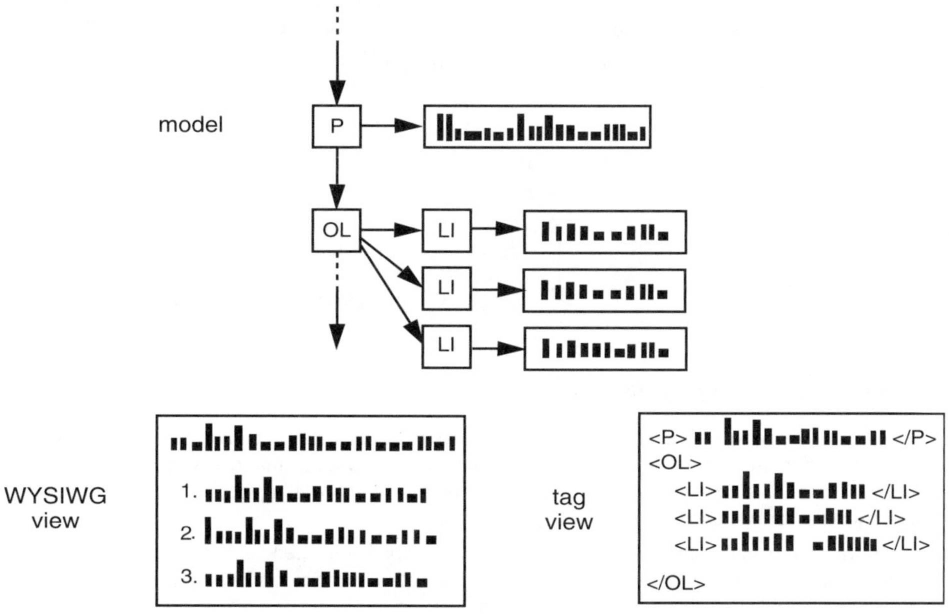

Figure 9–2: Two separate views of the same model

The controller handles the user-input events such as mouse clicks and keystrokes. It then decides whether to translate these events into changes in the model or the view. For example, if the user presses a character key in a text box, the controller calls the "insert character" command of the model. The model then tells the view to update itself. The view never knows why the text changed. But if the user presses a cursor key, then the controller may tell the view to scroll. Scrolling the view has no effect on the underlying text, so the model never knows that this event happened.

Design Patterns

When solving a problem, you don't usually figure out a solution from first principles. Instead, you are likely to be guided by past experience, or you may ask other experts for advice on what has worked for them. Design patterns are a method for presenting this expertise in a structured way.

In recent years, software engineers have begun to assemble catalogs of such patterns. The pioneers in this area were inspired by the architectural design patterns of the architect Christopher Alexander. In his book *The Timeless Way of Building* (Oxford University Press, 1979), Alexander gives a catalog of patterns for designing public and private living spaces. Here is a typical example:

> Window Place
>
> Everybody loves window seats, bay windows, and big windows with low sills and comfortable chairs drawn up to them . . . A room which does not have a place like this seldom allows you to feel comfortable or perfectly at ease . . .
>
> If the room contains no window which is a "place," a person in the room will be torn between two forces:
>
> 1. He wants to sit down and be comfortable.
> 2. He is drawn toward the light.
>
> Obviously, if the comfortable places—those places in the room where you most want to sit—are away from the windows, there is no way of overcoming this conflict . . .
>
> Therefore: In every room where you spend any length of time during the day, make at least one window into a "window place."

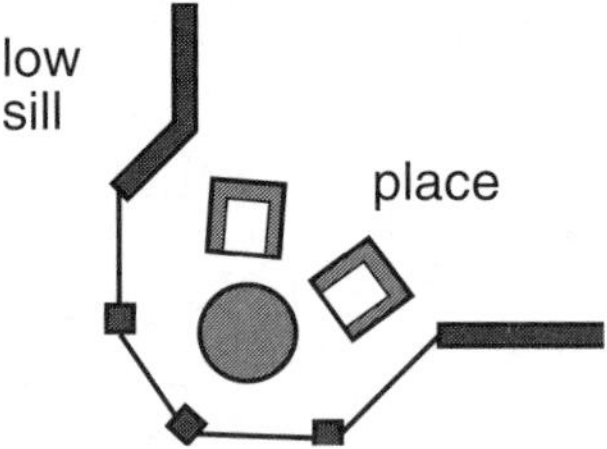

Figure 9–3: A window place

Each pattern in Alexander's catalog, as well as those in the catalogs of software patterns, follows a particular format. The pattern first describes a context, a situation that gives rise to a design problem. Then, the problem is explained, usually as a set of conflicting forces. Finally, the solution shows a configuration that balances these forces.

In the "window place" pattern, the context is a room in which you spend any length of time during the day. The conflicting forces are that you want to sit down and be comfortable and that you are drawn to the light. The solution is to make a "window place."

In the model-view-controller pattern, the context is a user interface system that presents information and receives user input. There are several forces. There may be multiple visual representations of the same data that need to be updated together. The visual representation may change, for example, to accommodate various look-and-feel standards. The interaction mechanisms may change, for example, to support voice commands. The solution is to distribute responsibilities into three separate interacting components: the model, view, and controller.

Of course, the model-view-controller pattern is more complex than the "window place" pattern, and it needs to teach in some detail how to make this distribution of responsibilities work.

You will find a formal description of the model-view-controller pattern, as well as numerous other useful software patterns, in the seminal book of the pattern movement, *Design Patterns—Elements of Reusable Object-Oriented Software*, by Erich Gamma et al. (Addison-Wesley, 1995).

We also highly recommend the excellent book *A System of Patterns* by Frank Buschmann et al. (John Wiley & Sons, 1996), which we find less seminal and more approachable.

The model-view-controller pattern is not the only pattern used in the design of Java. For example, the AWT event handling mechanism follows the "observer" pattern.

One important aspect of design patterns is that they become part of the culture. Programmers all over the world know what you mean when you talk about the model-view-controller pattern or the "observer" pattern. Thus, patterns become an efficient way of talking about design problems.

Figure 9–4 shows the interactions among model, view, and controller objects.

As a programmer using Swing components, you generally don't need to think about the model-view-controller architecture. Each user interface has a wrapper class (such as `JButton` or `JTextField`) that stores the model and the view. When you want to inquire about the content (for example, the text in a text field), the wrapper class asks the model and returns the answer to you. When you want to change the view (for example, move the caret position in a text field), the wrapper class forwards that request to the view. However, occasionally the wrapper class doesn't work hard enough on forwarding commands. Then, you have to ask it to retrieve the model and work directly with the model. (You don't have to work directly with the view—that is the job of the look-and-feel code.)

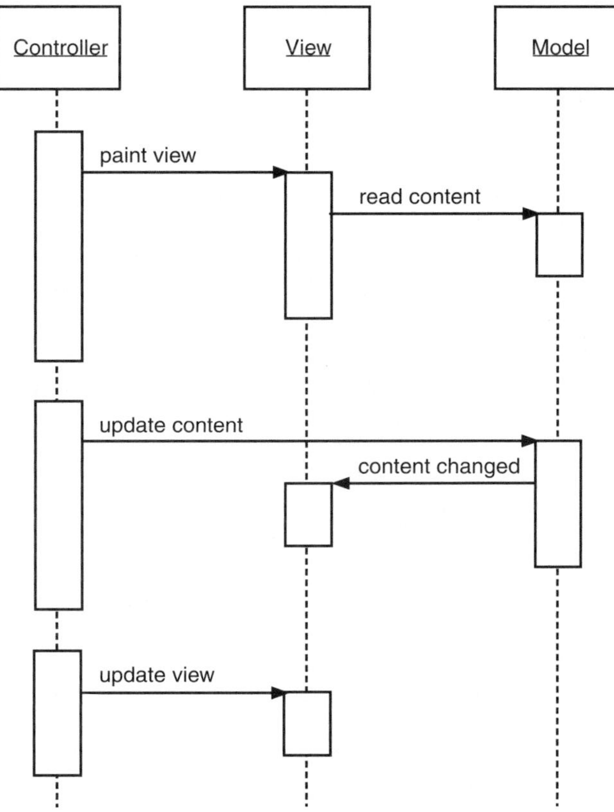

Figure 9–4: Interactions among model, view, and controller objects

Besides being "the right thing to do," the model-view-controller pattern was attractive for the Swing designers because it allowed them to implement pluggable look and feel. The model of a button or text field is independent of the look and feel. But of course the visual representation is completely dependent on the user interface design of a particular look and feel. The controller can vary as well. For example, in a voice-controlled device, the controller must cope with an entirely different set of events than in a standard computer with a keyboard and a mouse. By separating out the underlying model from the user interface, the Swing designers can reuse the code for the models and can even switch the look and feel in a running program.

Of course, patterns are only intended as guidance, not as religion. No pattern is applicable in all situations. For example, you may find it difficult to follow the "window places" pattern (see the sidebar on design patterns) to rearrange your cubicle. Similarly, the Swing designers found that the harsh reality of pluggable look-and-feel implementation does not always allow for a neat realization of the model-view-controller pattern. Models are easy to separate, and each user interface component has a model class. But the responsibilities of the view and controller are not always clearly separated and are distributed over a number of different classes. Of course, as a user of these classes, you won't be concerned about this. In fact, as we pointed out before, you often won't have to worry about the models either—you can just use the component wrapper classes.

A Model-View-Controller Analysis of Swing Buttons

You already learned how to use buttons in the previous chapter, without having to worry about the controller, model, or view for them. Still, buttons are about the simplest user interface elements, so they are a good place to become comfortable with the model-view-controller pattern. You will encounter similar kinds of classes and interfaces for the more sophisticated Swing components.

For most components, the model class implements an interface whose name ends in `Model`; thus the interface called `ButtonModel`. Classes implementing that interface can define the state of the various kinds of buttons. Actually, buttons aren't all that complicated, and the Swing library contains a single class, called `DefaultButtonModel`, that implements this interface.

You can get a sense of what sort of data are maintained by a button model by looking at the methods of the `ButtonModel` interface. Table 9–1 shows the accessor methods.

Table 9–1: Accessor Methods of the `ButtonModel` Interface

`getActionCommand()`	The action command string associated with this button
`getMnemonic()`	The keyboard mnemonic for this button
`isArmed()`	`true` if the button was pressed and the mouse is still over the button
`isEnabled()`	`true` if the button is selectable
`isPressed()`	`true` if the button was pressed but the mouse button hasn't yet been released
`isRollover()`	`true` if the mouse is over the button
`isSelected()`	`true` if the button has been toggled on (used for checkboxes and radio buttons)

Each `JButton` object stores a button model object, which you can retrieve.

```
JButton button = new JButton("Blue");
ButtonModel model = button.getModel();
```

In practice, you won't care—the minutiae of the button state are only of interest to the view that draws it. And the important information—such as whether a button is enabled—is available from the `JButton` class. (The `JButton` then asks its model, of course, to retrieve that information.)

Have another look at the `ButtonModel` interface to see what *isn't* there. The model does *not* store the button label or icon. There is no way to find out what's on the face of a button just by looking at its model. (Actually, as you will see in the section on radio button groups, that purity of design is the source of some grief for the programmer.)

It is also worth noting that the *same* model (namely, `DefaultButtonModel`) is used for push buttons, radio buttons, checkboxes, and even menu items. Of course, each of these button types has different views and controllers. When using the Metal look and feel, the `JButton` uses a class called `BasicButtonUI` for the view and a class called `ButtonUIListener` as controller. In general, each Swing component has an associated view object that ends in `UI`. But not all Swing components have dedicated controller objects.

So, having read this short introduction to what is going on under the hood in a `JButton`, you may be wondering: Just what is a `JButton` really? It is simply a wrapper class inheriting from `JComponent` that holds the `DefaultButtonModel` object, some view data (such as the button label and icons), and a `BasicButtonUI` object that is responsible for the button view.

Introduction to Layout Management

Before we go on to discussing individual Swing components, such as text fields and radio buttons, we briefly cover how to arrange these components inside a frame. Unlike Visual Basic, the JDK has no form designer. You need to write code to position (lay out) the user interface components where you want them to be.

Of course, if you have a Java-enabled development environment, it will probably have a layout tool that automates some or all of these tasks. Nevertheless, it is important to know exactly what goes on "under the hood" because even the best of these tools will usually require hand-tweaking.

Let's start by reviewing the program from the last chapter that used buttons to change the background color of a frame (see Figure 9–5).

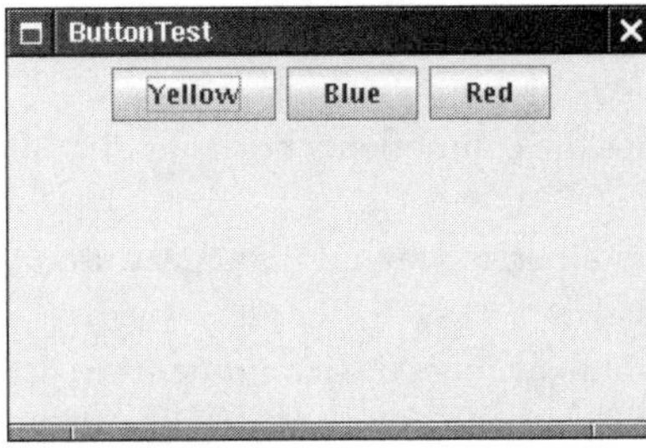

Figure 9–5: A panel with three buttons

Let us quickly recall how we built this program:

1. We defined the appearance of each button by setting the label string in the constructor, for example:
   ```
   JButton yellowButton = new JButton("Yellow")
   ```
2. We then added the individual buttons to a panel, for example, with
   ```
   panel.add(yellowButton);
   ```

3. We then added the needed event handlers, for example:

```
yellowButton.addActionListener(listener);
```

What happens if we add more buttons? Figure 9–6 shows what happens when you add six buttons to the panel. As you can see, they are centered in a row, and when there is no more room, a new row is started.

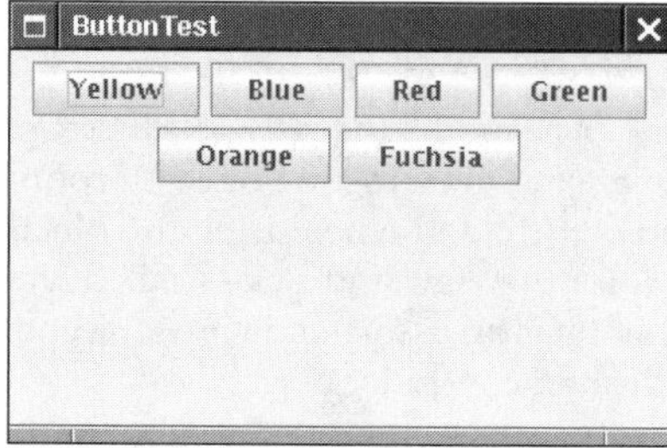

Figure 9–6: A panel with six buttons managed by a flow layout

Moreover, the buttons stay centered in the panel, even when the user resizes the frame (see Figure 9–7).

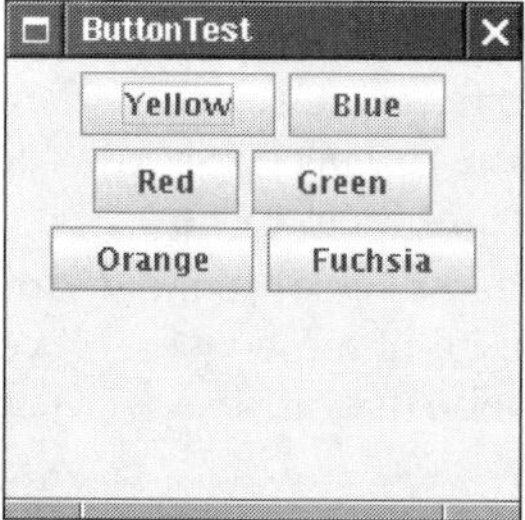

Figure 9–7: Changing the panel size rearranges the buttons automatically

An elegant concept enables this dynamic layout: all components in a container are positioned by a *layout manager*. In our example, the buttons are managed by the *flow layout manager*, the default layout manager for a panel.

The flow layout manager lines the components horizontally until there is no more room and then starts a new row of components.

When the user resizes the container, the layout manager automatically reflows the components to fill the available space.

You can choose how you want to arrange the components in each row. The default is to center them in the container. The other choices are to align them to the left or to the right of the container. To use one of these alignments, specify `LEFT` or `RIGHT` in the constructor of the `FlowLayout` object.

```
panel.setLayout(new FlowLayout(FlowLayout.LEFT));
```

NOTE: Normally, you just let the flow layout manager control the vertical and horizontal gaps between the components. You can, however, force a specific horizontal or vertical gap by using another version of the flow layout constructor. (See the API notes.)

java.awt.Container 1.0

- `setLayout(LayoutManager m)`
  sets the layout manager for this container.

java.awt.FlowLayout 1.0

- `FlowLayout(int align)`
  constructs a new `FlowLayout` with the specified alignment.

  Parameters: `align` One of `LEFT`, `CENTER`, or `RIGHT`

- `FlowLayout(int align, int hgap, int vgap)`
  constructs a new `FlowLayout` with the specified alignment and the specified horizontal and vertical gaps between components.

Parameters:	`align`	One of `LEFT`, `CENTER`, or `RIGHT`
	`hgap`	The horizontal gap to use in pixels (negative values force an overlap)
	`vgap`	The vertical gap to use in pixels (negative values force an overlap)

Border Layout

Java comes with several layout managers, and you can also make your own layout managers. We cover all of them later in this chapter. However, to enable us to give you more interesting examples right away, we briefly describe another layout manager called the *border layout manager*. This is the default layout manager of the content pane of every `JFrame`. Unlike the flow layout manager, which completely controls the position of each component, the border layout manager lets you choose where you want to place each component. You can choose to place the component in the center, north, south, east, or west of the content pane (see Figure 9–8).

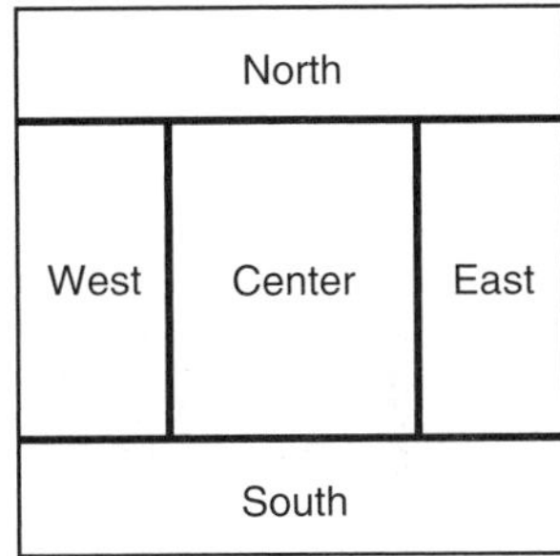

Figure 9–8: Border layout

For example:

```
panel.setLayout(new BorderLayout());
panel.add(yellowButton, BorderLayout.SOUTH);
```

The edge components are laid out first, and the remaining available space is occupied by the center. When the container is resized, the dimensions of the edge components are unchanged, but the center component changes its size. You add components by specifying a constant `CENTER`, `NORTH`, `SOUTH`, `EAST`, or `WEST` of the `BorderLayout` class. Not all of the positions need to be occupied. If you don't supply any value, `CENTER` is assumed.

NOTE: The `BorderLayout` constants are defined as strings. For example, `BorderLayout.SOUTH` is defined as the string `"South"`. Many programmers prefer to use the strings directly because they are shorter, for example, `frame.add(component, "South")`. However, if you accidentally misspell a string, the compiler won't catch that error.

Unlike the flow layout, the border layout grows all components to fill the available space. (The flow layout leaves each component at its preferred size.)

As with flow layouts, if you want to specify a gap between the regions, you can do so in the constructor of the `BorderLayout`.

As previously noted, the content pane of a `JFrame` uses a border layout. Up to now, we never took advantage of this—we simply added panels into the default (center) area. But you can add components into the other areas as well:

```
frame.add(yellowButton, BorderLayout.SOUTH);
```

However, this code fragment has a problem, which we take up in the next section.

java.awt.Container 1.0

- `void add(Component c, Object constraints)` **1.1**
  adds a component to this container.

Parameters:	`c`	The component to add
	`constraints`	An identifier understood by the layout manager

java.awt.Borderlayout 1.0

- `BorderLayout(int hgap, int vgap)`
  constructs a new `BorderLayout` with the specified horizontal and vertical gaps between components.

Parameters:	`hgap`	The horizontal gap to use in pixels (negative values force an overlap)
	`vgap`	The vertical gap to use in pixels (negative values force an overlap)

Panels

A `BorderLayout` is not very useful by itself. Figure 9–9 shows what happens when you use the code fragment above. The button has grown to fill the entire southern region of the frame. And, if you were to add another button to the southern region, it would just displace the first button.

One common method to overcome this problem is to use additional *panels.* Panels act as (smaller) containers for interface elements and can themselves be arranged inside a larger panel under the control of a layout manager. For example, you can have one panel in the southern area for the buttons and another in the center for text. By nesting panels and using a mixture of border layouts and flow layouts, you can achieve fairly precise positioning of components. This approach to layout is certainly enough for prototyping, and it is the approach that we use for the example programs in the first part of this chapter. See the section on the `GridBagLayout` later in this chapter for the most precise way to position components.

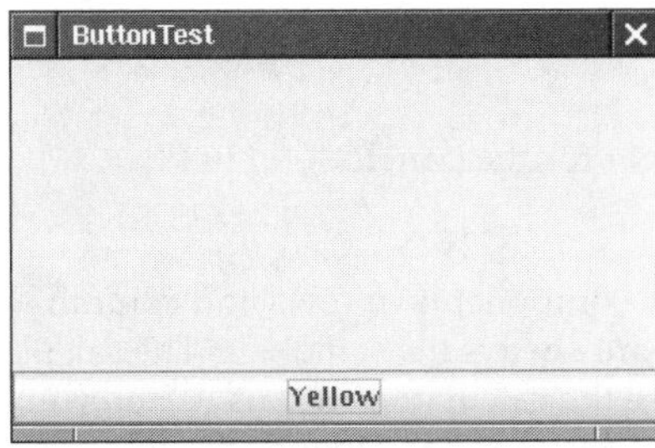

Figure 9–9: A single button managed by a border layout

For example, look at Figure 9–10. The three buttons at the bottom of the screen are all contained in a panel. The panel is put into the southern region of the content pane.

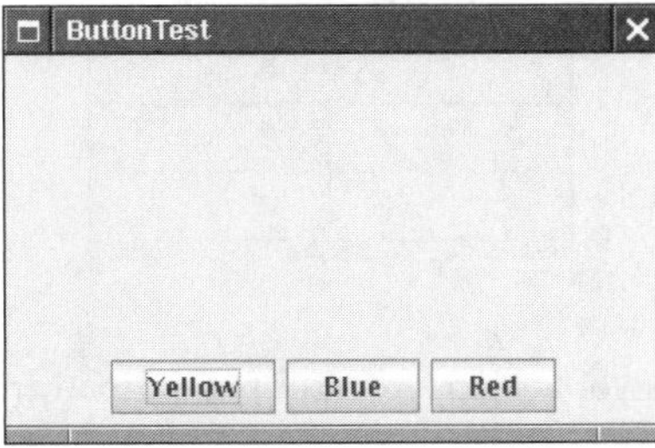

Figure 9–10: Panel placed at the southern region of the frame

So, suppose you want to add a panel with three buttons as in Figure 9–10. First create a new `JPanel` object, then add the individual buttons to the panel. The default layout manager for a panel is a `FlowLayout`, which is a good choice for this situation. Finally, you add the individual buttons, using the `add` method you have seen before. Because you are adding buttons to a panel and haven't changed the default layout manager, the position and size of the buttons is under the control of the `FlowLayout` manager. This means the buttons stay centered within the panel, and they do not expand to fill the entire panel area.

Here's a code fragment that adds a panel containing three buttons in the southern region of a frame.

```
JPanel panel = new JPanel();
panel.add(yellowButton);
panel.add(blueButton);
panel.add(redButton);
frame.add(panel, BorderLayout.SOUTH);
```

NOTE: The panel boundaries are not visible to the user. Panels are just an organizing mechanism for the user interface designer.

As you just saw, the `JPanel` class uses a `FlowLayout` as the default layout manager. For a `JPanel`, you can supply a different layout manager object in the constructor. However, most other containers do not have such a constructor. But all containers have a `setLayout` method to set the layout manager to something other than the default for the container.

javax.swing.JPanel 1.2

- `JPanel(LayoutManager m)`
  sets the layout manager for the panel.

Grid Layout

The grid layout arranges all components in rows and columns like a spreadsheet. However, for a grid layout, cells are always the same size. The calculator program in Figure 9–11 uses a grid layout to arrange the calculator buttons. When you resize the window, the buttons grow and shrink, but all buttons have identical sizes.

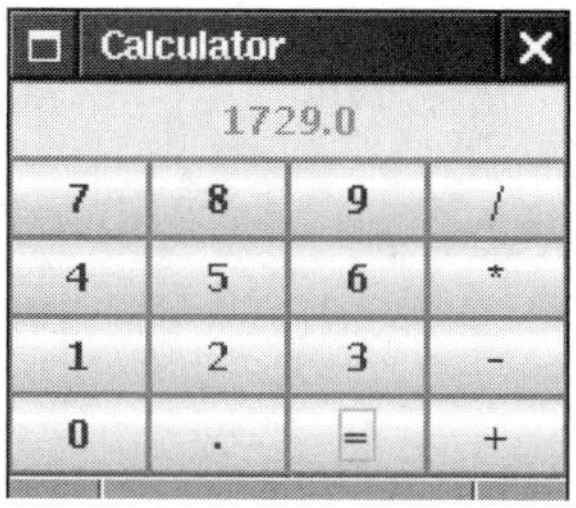

Figure 9–11: A calculator

In the constructor of the grid layout object, you specify how many rows and columns you need.

```
panel.setLayout(new GridLayout(5, 4));
```

As with the border layout and flow layout managers, you can also specify the vertical and horizontal gaps you want.

```
panel.setLayout(new GridLayout(5, 4, 3, 3));
```

The last two parameters of this constructor specify the size of the horizontal and vertical gaps (in pixels) between the components.

You add the components, starting with the first entry in the first row, then the second entry in the first row, and so on.

```
panel.add(new JButton("1"));
panel.add(new JButton("2"));
```

Example 9–1 is the source listing for the calculator program. This is a regular calculator, not the "reverse Polish" variety that is so oddly popular in Java tutorials. In this program, we call the `pack` method after adding the component to the frame. This method uses the preferred sizes of all components to compute the width and height of the frame.

Of course, few applications have as rigid a layout as the face of a calculator. In practice, small grids (usually with just one row or one column) can be useful to organize partial areas of a window. For example, if you want to have a row of buttons with identical size, then you can put the buttons inside a panel that is governed by a grid layout with a single row.

Example 9–1: Calculator.java

```
import java.awt.*;
import java.awt.event.*;
import javax.swing.*;

public class Calculator
{
```

```
   public static void main(String[] args)
   {
      CalculatorFrame frame = new CalculatorFrame();
      frame.setDefaultCloseOperation(JFrame.EXIT_ON_CLOSE);
      frame.setVisible(true);
   }
}

/**
   A frame with a calculator panel.
*/
class CalculatorFrame extends JFrame
{
   public CalculatorFrame()
   {
      setTitle("Calculator");
      CalculatorPanel panel = new CalculatorPanel();
      add(panel);
      pack();
   }
}

/**
   A panel with calculator buttons and a result display.
*/
class CalculatorPanel extends JPanel
{
   public CalculatorPanel()
   {
      setLayout(new BorderLayout());

      result = 0;
      lastCommand = "=";
      start = true;

      // add the display

      display = new JButton("0");
      display.setEnabled(false);
      add(display, BorderLayout.NORTH);

      ActionListener insert = new InsertAction();
      ActionListener command = new CommandAction();

      // add the buttons in a 4 x 4 grid

      panel = new JPanel();
      panel.setLayout(new GridLayout(4, 4));

      addButton("7", insert);
      addButton("8", insert);
      addButton("9", insert);
      addButton("/", command);

      addButton("4", insert);
```

```
      addButton("5", insert);
      addButton("6", insert);
      addButton("*", command);

      addButton("1", insert);
      addButton("2", insert);
      addButton("3", insert);
      addButton("-", command);

      addButton("0", insert);
      addButton(".", insert);
      addButton("=", command);
      addButton("+", command);

      add(panel, BorderLayout.CENTER);
   }

   /**
      Adds a button to the center panel.
      @param label the button label
      @param listener the button listener
   */
   private void addButton(String label, ActionListener listener)
   {
      JButton button = new JButton(label);
      button.addActionListener(listener);
      panel.add(button);
   }

   /**
      This action inserts the button action string to the
      end of the display text.
   */
   private class InsertAction implements ActionListener
   {
      public void actionPerformed(ActionEvent event)
      {
         String input = event.getActionCommand();
         if (start)
         {
            display.setText("");
            start = false;
         }
         display.setText(display.getText() + input);
      }
   }

   /**
      This action executes the command that the button
      action string denotes.
   */
   private class CommandAction implements ActionListener
   {
      public void actionPerformed(ActionEvent event)
      {
```

```
         String command = event.getActionCommand();

         if (start)
         {
            if (command.equals("-"))
            {
               display.setText(command);
               start = false;
            }
            else
               lastCommand = command;
         }
         else
         {
            calculate(Double.parseDouble(display.getText()));
            lastCommand = command;
            start = true;
         }
      }
   }

   /**
      Carries out the pending calculation.
      @param x the value to be accumulated with the prior result.
   */
   public void calculate(double x)
   {
      if (lastCommand.equals("+")) result += x;
      else if (lastCommand.equals("-")) result -= x;
      else if (lastCommand.equals("*")) result *= x;
      else if (lastCommand.equals("/")) result /= x;
      else if (lastCommand.equals("=")) result = x;
      display.setText("" + result);
   }

   private JButton display;
   private JPanel panel;
   private double result;
   private String lastCommand;
   private boolean start;
}
```

API **java.awt.GridLayout 1.0**

- `GridLayout(int rows, int cols)`
  constructs a new `GridLayout`.

Parameters:	`rows`	The number of rows in the grid
	`columns`	The number of columns in the grid

- `GridLayout(int rows, int columns, int hgap, int vgap)`
  constructs a new `GridLayout` with horizontal and vertical gaps between components.

Parameters:	`rows`	The number of rows in the grid
	`columns`	The number of columns in the grid

`hgap`	The horizontal gap to use in pixels (negative values force an overlap)
`vgap`	The vertical gap to use in pixels (negative values force an overlap)

 **java.awt.Window 1.0**

- `void pack()`
  resizes this window, taking into account the preferred sizes of its components.

Text Input

We are finally ready to start introducing the Swing user interface components. We start with components that let a user input and edit text. You can use the `JTextField` and `JTextArea` components for gathering text input. A text field can accept only one line of text; a text area can accept multiple lines of text.

Both of these classes inherit from a class called `JTextComponent`. You will not be able to construct a `JTextComponent` yourself because it is an abstract class. On the other hand, as is so often the case in Java, when you go searching through the API documentation, you may find that the methods you are looking for are actually in the parent class `JTextComponent` rather than in the derived class. For example, the methods that get or set the text in a text field or text area are actually methods in `JTextComponent`.

 **javax.swing.text.JTextComponent 1.2**

- `void setText(String t)`
  changes the text of a text component.

  Parameters: `t` The new text

- `String getText()`
  returns the text contained in this text component.
- `void setEditable(boolean b)`
  determines whether the user can edit the content of the `JTextComponent`.

Text Fields

The usual way to add a text field to a window is to add it to a panel or other container—just as you would a button:

```
JPanel panel = new JPanel();
JTextField textField = new JTextField("Default input", 20);
panel.add(textField);
```

This code adds a text field and initializes the text field by placing the string `"Default input"` inside it. The second parameter of this constructor sets the width. In this case, the width is 20 "columns." Unfortunately, a column is a rather imprecise measurement. One column is the expected width of one character in the font you are using for the text. The idea is that if you expect the inputs to be *n* characters or less, you are supposed to specify *n* as the column width. In practice, this measurement doesn't work out too well, and you should add 1 or 2 to the maximum input length to be on the safe side. Also, keep in mind that the number of columns is only a hint to the AWT that gives the *preferred* size. If the layout manager needs to grow or shrink the text field, it can adjust its size. The column width that you set in the `JTextField` constructor is not an upper limit on the number of characters the user can enter. The user can still type in longer strings, but the input scrolls when the text exceeds the

length of the field. Users tend to find scrolling text fields irritating, so you should size the fields generously. If you need to reset the number of columns at run time, you can do that with the `setColumns` method.

TIP: After changing the size of a text box with the `setColumns` method, call the `revalidate` method of the surrounding container.

```
textField.setColumns(10);
panel.revalidate();
```

The `revalidate` method recomputes the size and layout of all components in a container. After you use the `revalidate` method, the layout manager resizes the container, and the changed size of the text field will be visible.

The `revalidate` method belongs to the `JComponent` class. It doesn't immediately resize the component but merely marks it for resizing. This approach avoids repetitive calculations if multiple components request to be resized. However, if you want to recompute all components inside a `JFrame`, you have to call the `validate` method—`JFrame` doesn't extend `JComponent`.

In general, you want to let the user add text (or edit the existing text) in a text field. Quite often these text fields start out blank. To make a blank text field, just leave out the string as a parameter for the `JTextField` constructor:

```
JTextField textField = new JTextField(20);
```

You can change the content of the text field at any time by using the `setText` method from the `JTextComponent` parent class mentioned in the previous section. For example:

```
textField.setText("Hello!");
```

And, as was also mentioned in the previous section, you can find out what the user typed by calling the `getText` method. This method returns the exact text that the user typed. To trim any extraneous leading and trailing spaces from the data in a text field, apply the `trim` method to the return value of `getText`:

```
String text = textField.getText().trim();
```

To change the font in which the user text appears, use the `setFont` method.

`javax.swing.JTextField` 1.2

- `JTextField(int cols)`
  constructs an empty `JTextField` with a specified number of columns.

  Parameters: `cols` The number of columns in the field

- `JTextField(String text, int cols)`
  constructs a new `JTextField` with an initial string and the specified number of columns.

  Parameters: `text` The text to display
  `cols` The number of columns

- `void setColumns(int cols)`
  tells the text field the number of columns it should use.

  Parameters: `cols` The number of columns

`javax.swing.JComponent` 1.2

- `void revalidate()`
  causes the position and size of a component to be recomputed.

java.awt.Component 1.0

- `void validate()`
  recomputes the position and size of a component. If the component is a container, the positions and sizes of its components are recomputed.

Labels and Labeling Components

Labels are components that hold text. They have no decorations (for example, no boundaries). They also do not react to user input. You can use a label to identify components. For example, unlike buttons, text fields have no label to identify them. To label a component that does not itself come with an identifier:

1. Construct a `JLabel` component with the correct text.
2. Place it close enough to the component you want to identify so that the user can see that the label identifies the correct component.

The constructor for a `JLabel` lets you specify the initial text or icon, and optionally, the alignment of the content. You use constants from the `SwingConstants` interface to specify alignment. That interface defines a number of useful constants such as `LEFT`, `RIGHT`, `CENTER`, `NORTH`, `EAST`, and so on. The `JLabel` class is one of several Swing classes that implement this interface. Therefore, you can specify a right-aligned label either as

```
JLabel label = new JLabel("Minutes", SwingConstants.RIGHT);
```

or

```
JLabel label = new JLabel("Minutes", JLabel.RIGHT);
```

The `setText` and `setIcon` methods let you set the text and icon of the label at run time.

TIP: Beginning with JDK 1.3, you can use both plain and HTML text in buttons, labels, and menu items. We don't recommend HTML in buttons—it interferes with the look and feel. But HTML in labels can be very effective. Simply surround the label string with `<html>. . .</html>`, like this:

```
label = new JLabel("<html><b>Required</b> entry:</html>");
```

Fair warning—the first component with an HTML label takes some time to be displayed because the rather complex HTML rendering code must be loaded.

Labels can be positioned inside a container like any other component. This means you can use the techniques you have seen before to place labels where you need them.

javax.swing.JLabel 1.2

- `JLabel(String text)`
  constructs a label with left-aligned text.

Parameters:	`text`	The text in the label

- `JLabel(Icon icon)`
  constructs a label with a left-aligned icon.

Parameters:	`icon`	The icon in the label

- `JLabel(String text, int align)`
  constructs a label with the given text and alignment

Parameters:	`text`	The text in the label
	`align`	One of the `SwingConstants` constants `LEFT`, `CENTER`, or `RIGHT`

- `JLabel(String text, Icon icon, int align)`
  constructs a label with both text and an icon. The icon is to the left of the text.

Parameters:	`text`	The text in the label
	`icon`	The icon in the label
	`align`	One of the `SwingConstants` constants `LEFT`, `CENTER`, or `RIGHT`

- `void setText(String text)`
  sets the text of this label.

Parameters:	`text`	The text in the label

- `void setIcon(Icon icon)`
  sets the icon of this label.

Parameters:	`icon`	The icon in the label

Change Tracking in Text Fields

Let us put a few text fields to work. Figure 9–12 shows the running application listed in Example 9–2. The program shows a clock and two text fields that enter the hours and minutes. Whenever the content of the text fields changes, the clock is updated.

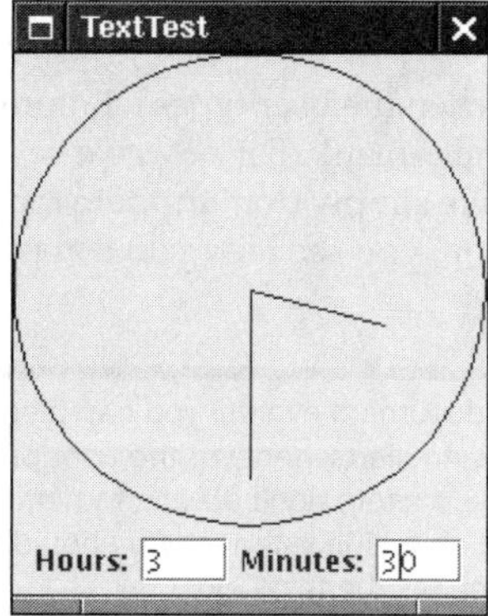

Figure 9–12: Text field example

To track every change in the text field requires a bit of an effort. First of all, note that it is not a good idea to monitor keystrokes. Some keystrokes (such as the arrow keys) don't change the text. And, depending on the look and feel, there may be mouse actions that result in text changes. As you saw in the beginning of this chapter, the Swing text field is implemented in a rather general way: the string that you see in the text field is just a visible manifestation (the *view*) of an underlying data structure (the *model*). Of course, for a humble text field, there is no great difference between the two. The view is a displayed string, and the model is a string object. But the same architecture is used in more advanced editing components to present formatted text, with fonts, paragraphs, and other attributes that are internally represented by a more complex data structure. The model for all text components is described by the `Document` interface, which covers both plain text and formatted text (such as HTML). The point is that you can ask the *document* (and not the text component) to notify you whenever the data has changed, by installing a *document listener:*

```
textField.getDocument().addDocumentListener(listener);
```

When the text has changed, one of the following `DocumentListener` methods is called:

```
void insertUpdate(DocumentEvent event)
void removeUpdate(DocumentEvent event)
void changedUpdate(DocumentEvent event)
```

The first two methods are called when characters have been inserted or removed. The third method is not called at all for text fields. For more complex document types, it would be called when some other change, such as a change in formatting, has occurred. Unfortunately, there is no single callback to tell you that the text has changed—usually you don't much care how it has changed. And there is no adapter class either. Thus, your document listener must implement all three methods. Here is what we do in our sample program:

```
private class ClockFieldListener implements DocumentListener
{
   public void insertUpdate(DocumentEvent event) { setClock(); }
   public void removeUpdate(DocumentEvent event) { setClock(); }
   public void changedUpdate(DocumentEvent event) {}
}
```

The `setClock` method uses the `getText` method to obtain the current user-input strings from the text fields. Unfortunately, that is what we get: strings. We need to convert the strings to integers by using the familiar, if cumbersome, incantation:

```
int hours = Integer.parseInt(hourField.getText().trim());
int minutes = Integer.parseInt(minuteField.getText().trim());
```

But this code won't work right when the user types a noninteger string, such as `"two"`, into the text field or even leaves the field blank. For now, we catch the `NumberFormatException` that the `parseInt` method throws, and we simply don't update the clock when the text field entry is not a number. In the next section, you see how you can prevent the user from entering invalid input in the first place.

NOTE: Instead of listening to document events, you can also add an action event listener to a text field. The action listener is notified whenever the user presses the ENTER key. We don't recommend this approach, because users don't always remember to press ENTER when they are done entering data. If you use an action listener, you should also install a focus listener so that you can track when the user leaves the text field.

Finally, note how the `ClockPanel` constructor sets the preferred size:

```
public ClockPanel()
{
   setPreferredSize(new Dimension(2 * RADIUS + 1, 2 * RADIUS + 1));
}
```

When the frame's `pack` method computes the frame size, it uses the panel's preferred size.

Example 9–2: TextTest.java

```
import java.awt.*;
import java.awt.event.*;
import java.awt.geom.*;
import javax.swing.*;
import javax.swing.event.*;

public class TextTest
{
   public static void main(String[] args)
```

```
   {
      TextTestFrame frame = new TextTestFrame();
      frame.setDefaultCloseOperation(JFrame.EXIT_ON_CLOSE);
      frame.setVisible(true);
   }
}

/**
   A frame with two text fields to set a clock.
*/
class TextTestFrame extends JFrame
{
   public TextTestFrame()
   {
      setTitle("TextTest");

      DocumentListener listener = new ClockFieldListener();

      // add a panel with text fields

      JPanel panel = new JPanel();

      panel.add(new JLabel("Hours:"));
      hourField = new JTextField("12", 3);
      panel.add(hourField);
      hourField.getDocument().addDocumentListener(listener);

      panel.add(new JLabel("Minutes:"));
      minuteField = new JTextField("00", 3);
      panel.add(minuteField);
      minuteField.getDocument().addDocumentListener(listener);

      add(panel, BorderLayout.SOUTH);

      // add the clock

      clock = new ClockPanel();
      add(clock, BorderLayout.CENTER);
      pack();
   }

   /**
      Set the clock to the values stored in the text fields.
   */
   public void setClock()
   {
      try
      {
         int hours = Integer.parseInt(hourField.getText().trim());
         int minutes = Integer.parseInt(minuteField.getText().trim());
         clock.setTime(hours, minutes);
      }
      catch (NumberFormatException e) {}
      // don't set the clock if the input can't be parsed
   }
```

```

   public static final int DEFAULT_WIDTH = 300;
   public static final int DEFAULT_HEIGHT = 300;

   private JTextField hourField;
   private JTextField minuteField;
   private ClockPanel clock;

   private class ClockFieldListener implements DocumentListener
   {
      public void insertUpdate(DocumentEvent event) { setClock(); }
      public void removeUpdate(DocumentEvent event) { setClock(); }
      public void changedUpdate(DocumentEvent event) {}
   }
}

/**
   A panel that draws a clock.
*/
class ClockPanel extends JPanel
{
   public ClockPanel()
   {
      setPreferredSize(new Dimension(2 * RADIUS + 1, 2 * RADIUS + 1));
   }

   public void paintComponent(Graphics g)
   {
      // draw the circular boundary

      super.paintComponent(g);
      Graphics2D g2 = (Graphics2D) g;
      Ellipse2D circle = new Ellipse2D.Double(0, 0, 2 * RADIUS, 2 * RADIUS);
      g2.draw(circle);

      // draw the hour hand

      double hourAngle = Math.toRadians(90 - 360 * minutes / (12 * 60));
      drawHand(g2, hourAngle, HOUR_HAND_LENGTH);

      // draw the minute hand

      double minuteAngle = Math.toRadians(90 - 360 * minutes / 60);
      drawHand(g2, minuteAngle, MINUTE_HAND_LENGTH);
   }

   public void drawHand(Graphics2D g2, double angle, double handLength)
   {
      Point2D end = new Point2D.Double(
         RADIUS + handLength * Math.cos(angle),
         RADIUS - handLength * Math.sin(angle));
      Point2D center = new Point2D.Double(RADIUS, RADIUS);
      g2.draw(new Line2D.Double(center, end));
   }

```

```
   /**
      Set the time to be displayed on the clock
      @param h hours
      @param m minutes
   */
   public void setTime(int h, int m)
   {
      minutes = h * 60 + m;
      repaint();
   }

   private double minutes = 0;
   private int RADIUS = 100;
   private double MINUTE_HAND_LENGTH = 0.8 * RADIUS;
   private double HOUR_HAND_LENGTH = 0.6 * RADIUS;
}
```

javax.swing.JComponent 1.2

- `void setPreferredSize(Dimension d)`
  sets the preferred size of this component.

javax.swing.text.Document 1.2

- `int getLength()`
  returns the number of characters currently in the document.
- `String getText(int offset, int length)`
  returns the text contained within the given portion of the document.

Parameters:	`offset`	The start of the text
	`length`	The length of the desired string

- `void addDocumentListener(DocumentListener listener)`
  registers the listener to be notified when the document changes.

javax.swing.event.DocumentEvent 1.2

- `Document getDocument()`
  gets the document that is the source of the event.

javax.swing.event.DocumentListener 1.2

- `void changedUpdate(DocumentEvent event)`
  is called whenever an attribute or set of attributes changes.
- `void insertUpdate(DocumentEvent event)`
  is called whenever an insertion into the document occurs.
- `void removeUpdate(DocumentEvent event)`
  is called whenever a portion of the document has been removed.

Password Fields

Password fields are a special kind of text field. To avoid nosy bystanders being able to glance at a password, the characters that the user entered are not actually displayed. Instead, each typed character is represented by an *echo character,* typically an asterisk (*). Swing supplies a `JPasswordField` class that implements such a text field.

The password field is another example of the power of the model-view-controller architecture pattern. The password field uses the same model to store the data as a regular text field, but its view has been changed to display all characters as echo characters.

javax.swing.JPasswordField 1.2

- `JPasswordField(String text, int columns)`
  constructs a new password field.

Parameters:	`text`	The text to be displayed, `null` if none
	`columns`	The number of columns

- `void setEchoChar(char echo)`
  sets the echo character for this password field. This is advisory; a particular look and feel may insist on its own choice of echo character. A value of 0 resets the echo character to the default.

Parameters:	`echo`	The echo character to display instead of the text characters

- `char[] getPassword()`
  returns the text contained in this password field. For stronger security, you should overwrite the content of the returned array after use. (The password is not returned as a `String` because a string would stay in the virtual machine until it is garbage-collected.)

Formatted Input Fields

In the last example program, we wanted the program user to type numbers, not arbitrary strings. That is, the user is allowed to enter only digits 0 through 9 and a hyphen (–). The hyphen, if present at all, must be the *first* symbol of the input string.

On the surface, this input validation task sounds simple. We can install a key listener to the text field and then consume all key events that aren't digits or a hyphen. Unfortunately, this simple approach, although commonly recommended as a method for input validation, does not work well in practice. First, not every combination of the valid input characters is a valid number. For example, `--3` and `3-3` aren't valid, even though they are made up from valid input characters. But, more important, there are other ways of changing the text that don't involve typing character keys. Depending on the look and feel, certain key combinations can be used to cut, copy, and paste text. For example, in the Metal look and feel, the CTRL+V key combination pastes the content of the paste buffer into the text field. That is, we also need to monitor that the user doesn't paste in an invalid character. Clearly, trying to filter keystrokes to ensure that the content of the text field is always valid begins to look like a real chore. This is certainly not something that an application programmer should have to worry about.

Perhaps surprisingly, before JDK 1.4, there were no components for entering numeric values. Starting with the first edition of Core Java, we supplied an implementation for an `IntTextField`, a text field for entering a properly formatted integer. In every new edition, we changed the implementation to take whatever limited advantage we could from the various half-baked validation schemes that were added to each version of the JDK. Finally, in JDK 1.4, the Swing designers faced the issues head-on and supplied a versatile `JFormattedTextField` class that can be used not just for numeric input but also for dates and for even more esoteric formatted values such as IP addresses.

Integer Input

Let's get started with an easy case first: a text field for integer input.

```
JFormattedTextField intField = new JFormattedTextField(NumberFormat.getIntegerInstance());
```

The `NumberFormat.getIntegerInstance` returns a formatter object that formats integers, using the current locale. In the US locale, commas are used as decimal separators, allowing users to enter values such as 1,729. The internationalization chapter in Volume 2 explains in detail how you can select other locales.

As with any text field, you can set the number of columns:

```
intField.setColumns(6);
```

You can set a default value with the `setValue` method. That method takes an `Object` parameter, so you'll need to wrap the default `int` value in an `Integer` object:

```
intField.setValue(new Integer(100));
```

Typically, users will supply inputs in multiple text fields and then click a button to read all values. When the button is clicked, you can get the user-supplied value with the `getValue` method. That method returns an `Object` result, and you need to cast it into the appropriate type. The `JFormattedTextField` returns an object of type `Long` if the user edited the value. However, if the user made no changes, the original `Integer` object is returned. Therefore, you should cast the return value to the common superclass `Number`:

```
Number value = (Number) intField.getValue();
int v = value.intValue();
```

The formatted text field is not very interesting until you consider what happens when a user provides illegal input. That is the topic of the next section.

Behavior on Loss of Focus

Consider what happens when a user supplies input to a text field. The user types input and eventually decides to leave the field, perhaps by clicking on another component with the mouse. Then the text field *loses focus*. The I-beam cursor is no longer visible in the text field, and keystrokes are directed toward a different component.

When the formatted text field loses focus, the formatter looks at the text string that the user produced. If the formatter knows how to convert the text string to an object, the text is valid. Otherwise it is invalid. You can use the `isEditValid` method to check whether the current content of the text field is valid.

The default behavior on loss of focus is called "commit or revert." If the text string is valid, it is *committed*. The formatter converts it to an object. That object becomes the current value of the field (that is, the return value of the `getValue` method that you saw in the preceding section). The value is then converted back to a string, which becomes the text string that is visible in the field. For example, the integer formatter recognizes the input `1729` as valid, sets the current value to `new Long(1729)` and then converts it back into a string with a decimal comma: `1,729`.

Conversely, if the text string is invalid, then the current value is not changed and the text field *reverts* to the string that represents the old value. For example, if the user enters a bad value, such as `x1`, then the old value is restored when the text field loses focus.

NOTE: The integer formatter regards a text string as valid if it starts with an integer. For example, `1729x` is a valid string. It is converted to the number 1729, which is then formatted as the string `1,729`.

You can set other behaviors with the `setFocusLostBehavior` method. The "commit" behavior is subtly different from the default. If the text string is invalid, then both the text string and the field value stay unchanged—they are now out of sync. The "persist" behavior is even more conservative. Even if the text string is valid, neither the text field nor the current value are changed. You would need to call `commitEdit`, `setValue`, or `setText` to bring them back in sync. Finally, there is a "revert" behavior that doesn't ever seem to be useful. Whenever focus is lost, the user input is disregarded, and the text string reverts to the old value.

NOTE: Generally, the "commit or revert" default behavior is reasonable. There is just one potential problem. Suppose a dialog box contains a text field for an integer value. A user enters a string `" 1729"`, with a leading space and then clicks the OK button. The leading space makes the number invalid, and the field value reverts to the old value. The action listener of the OK button retrieves the field value and closes the dialog. The user never knows that the new value has been rejected. In this situation, it is appropriate to select the "commit" behavior and have the OK button listener check that all field edits are valid before closing the dialog.

Filters

This basic functionality of formatted text fields is straightforward and sufficient for most uses. However, you can add a couple of refinements. Perhaps you want to prevent the user from entering nondigits altogether. You achieve that behavior with a *document filter*. Recall that in the model-view-controller architecture, the controller translates input events into commands that modify the underlying document of the text field, that is, the text string that is stored in a `PlainDocument` object. For example, whenever the controller processes a command that causes text to be inserted into the document, it calls the "insert string" command. The string to be inserted can be either a single character or the content of the paste buffer. A document filter can intercept this command and modify the string or cancel the insertion altogether. Here is the code for the `insertString` method of a filter that analyzes the string to be inserted and inserts only the characters that are digits or a - sign. (The code handles supplementary Unicode characters, as explained in Chapter 3. See Chapter 12 for the `StringBuilder` class.)

```
public void insertString(FilterBypass fb, int offset, String string, AttributeSet attr)
   throws BadLocationException
{
   StringBuilder builder = new StringBuilder(string);
   for (int i = builder.length() - 1; i >= 0; i--)
   {
      int cp = builder.codePointAt(i);
      if (!Character.isDigit(cp) && cp != '-')
      {
         builder.deleteCharAt(i);
         if (Character.isSupplementaryCodePoint(cp))
         {
            i--;
            builder.deleteCharAt(i);
         }
      }
   }
   super.insertString(fb, offset, builder.toString(), attr);
}
```

You should also override the `replace` method of the `DocumentFilter` class—it is called when text is selected and then replaced. The implementation of the `replace` method is straightforward—see the program at the end of this section.

Now you need to install the document filter. Unfortunately, there is no straightforward method to do that. You need to override the `getDocumentFilter` method of a formatter class, and pass an object of that formatter class to the `JFormattedTextField`. The integer text field uses

an InternationalFormatter that is initialized with NumberFormat.getIntegerInstance(). Here is how you install a formatter to yield the desired filter:

```
JFormattedTextField intField = new JFormattedTextField(new
      InternationalFormatter(NumberFormat.getIntegerInstance())
      {
         protected DocumentFilter getDocumentFilter()
         {
            return filter;
         }
         private DocumentFilter filter = new IntFilter();
      });
```

NOTE: The JDK documentation states that the DocumentFilter class was invented to avoid subclassing. Until JDK 1.3, filtering in a text field was achieved by extending the PlainDocument class and overriding the insertString and replace methods. Now the PlainDocument class has a pluggable filter instead. That is a splendid improvement. It would have been even more splendid if the filter had also been made pluggable in the formatter class. Alas, it was not, and we must subclass the formatter.

Try out the FormatTest example program at the end of this section. The third text field has a filter installed. You can insert only digits or the minus ('-') character. Note that you can still enter invalid strings such as "1-2-3". In general, it is impossible to avoid all invalid strings through filtering. For example, the string "-" is invalid, but a filter can't reject it because it is a prefix of a legal string "-1". Even though filters can't give perfect protection, it makes sense to use them to reject inputs that are obviously invalid.

TIP: Another use for filtering is to turn all characters of a string to upper case. Such a filter is easy to write. In the insertString and replace methods of the filter, convert the string to be inserted to upper case and then invoke the superclass method.

Verifiers

There is another potentially useful mechanism to alert users to invalid inputs. You can attach a *verifier* to any JComponent. If the component loses focus, then the verifier is queried. If the verifier reports the content of the component to be invalid, the component immediately regains focus. The user is thus forced to fix the content before supplying other inputs.

A verifier must extend the abstract InputVerifier class and define a verify method. It is particularly easy to define a verifier that checks formatted text fields. The isEditValid method of the JFormattedTextField class calls the formatter and returns true if the formatter can turn the text string into an object. Here is the verifier.

```
class FormattedTextFieldVerifier extends InputVerifier
{
   public boolean verify(JComponent component)
   {
      JFormattedTextField field = (JFormattedTextField) component;
      return field.isEditValid();
   }
}
```

You can attach it to any JFormattedTextField:

```
intField.setInputVerifier(new FormattedTextFieldVerifier());
```

However, a verifier is not entirely foolproof. If you click on a button, then the button notifies its action listeners before an invalid component regains focus. The action listeners can then get an invalid result from the component that failed verification. There is a reason for this behavior: users may want to press a Cancel button without first having to fix an invalid input.

The fourth text field in the example program has a verifier attached. Try entering an invalid number (such as `x1729`) and press the TAB key or click with the mouse on another text field. Note that the field immediately regains focus. However, if you press the OK button, the action listener calls `getValue`, which reports the last good value.

Other Standard Formatters

Besides the integer formatter, the `JFormattedTextField` supports several other formatters. The `NumberFormat` class has static methods

```
getNumberInstance
getCurrencyInstance
getPercentInstance
```

that yield formatters of floating-point numbers, currency values, and percentages. For example, you can obtain a text field for the input of currency values by calling

```
JFormattedTextField currencyField = new JFormattedTextField(NumberFormat.getCurrencyInstance());
```

To edit dates and times, call one of the static methods of the `DateFormat` class:

```
getDateInstance
getTimeInstance
getDateTimeInstance
```

For example,

```
JFormattedTextField dateField = new JFormattedTextField(DateFormat.getDateInstance());
```

This field edits a date in the default or "medium" format such as

```
Feb 24, 2002
```

You can instead choose a "short" format such as

```
2/24/02
```

by calling

```
DateFormat.getDateInstance(DateFormat.SHORT)
```

NOTE: By default, the date format is "lenient." That is, an invalid date such as February 31, 2002, is rolled over to the next valid date, March 3, 2002. That behavior may be surprising to your users. In that case, call `setLenient(false)` on the `DateFormat` object.

The `DefaultFormatter` can format objects of any class that has a constructor with a string parameter and a matching `toString` method. For example, the `URL` class has a `URL(String)` constructor that can be used to construct a URL from a string, such as

```
URL url = new URL("http://java.sun.com");
```

Therefore, you can use the `DefaultFormatter` to format `URL` objects. The formatter calls `toString` on the field value to initialize the field text. When the field loses focus, the formatter constructs a new object of the same class as the current value, using the constructor with a `String` parameter. If that constructor throws an exception, then the edit is not valid. You can try that out in the example program by entering a URL that does not start with a prefix such as `"http:"`.

NOTE: By default, the `DefaultFormatter` is in *overwrite mode.* That is different from the other formatters and not very useful. Call `setOverwriteMode(false)` to turn off overwrite mode.

Finally, the `MaskFormatter` is useful for fixed-size patterns that contain some constant and some variable characters. For example, social security numbers (such as 078-05-1120) can be formatted with a

```
new MaskFormatter("###-##-####")
```

The `#` symbol denotes a single digit. Table 9–2 shows the symbols that you can use in a mask formatter.

Table 9–2: `MaskFormatter` Symbols

`#`	A digit
`?`	A letter
`U`	A letter, converted to upper case
`L`	A letter, converted to lower case
`A`	A letter or digit
`H`	A hexadecimal digit `[0-9A-Fa-f]`
`*`	Any character
`'`	Escape character to include a symbol in the pattern

You can restrict the characters that can be typed into the field by calling one of the methods of the `MaskFormatter` class:

```
setValidCharacters
setInvalidCharacters
```

For example, to read in a letter grade (such as A+ or F), you could use

```
MaskFormatter formatter = new MaskFormatter("U*");
formatter.setValidCharacters("ABCDF+- ");
```

However, there is no way of specifying that the second character cannot be a letter.

Note that the string that is formatted by the mask formatter has exactly the same length as the mask. If the user erases characters during editing, then they are replaced with the *placeholder character.* The default placeholder character is a space, but you can change it with the `setPlaceholderCharacter` method, for example,

```
formatter.setPlaceholderCharacter('0');
```

By default, a mask formatter is in overtype mode, which is quite intuitive—try it out in the example program. Also note that the caret position jumps over the fixed characters in the mask.

The mask formatter is very effective for rigid patterns such as social security numbers or American telephone numbers. However, note that no variation at all is permitted in the mask pattern. For example, you cannot use a mask formatter for international telephone numbers that have a variable number of digits.

Custom Formatters

If none of the standard formatters is appropriate, it is fairly easy to define your own formatter. Consider 4-byte IP addresses such as

```
130.65.86.66
```

You can't use a MaskFormatter because each byte might be represented by one, two, or three digits. Also, we want to check in the formatter that each byte's value is at most 255.

To define your own formatter, extend the DefaultFormatter class and override the methods

```
String valueToString(Object value)
Object stringToValue(String text)
```

The first method turns the field value into the string that is displayed in the text field. The second method parses the text that the user typed and turns it back into an object. If either method detects an error, it should throw a ParseException.

In our example program, we store an IP address in a byte[] array of length 4. The valueToString method forms a string that separates the bytes with periods. Note that byte values are signed quantities between –128 and 127. To turn negative byte values into unsigned integer values, you add 256.

```
public String valueToString(Object value) throws ParseException
{
   if (!(value instanceof byte[]))
      throw new ParseException("Not a byte[]", 0);
   byte[] a = (byte[]) value;
   if (a.length != 4)
       throw new ParseException("Length != 4", 0);
   StringBuilder builder = new StringBuilder();
   for (int i = 0; i < 4; i++)
   {
      int b = a[i];
      if (b < 0) b += 256;
      builder.append(String.valueOf(b));
      if (i < 3) builder.append('.');
   }
   return builder.toString();
}
```

Conversely, the stringToValue method parses the string and produces a byte[] object if the string is valid. If not, it throws a ParseException.

```
public Object stringToValue(String text) throws ParseException
{
   StringTokenizer tokenizer = new StringTokenizer(text, ".");
   byte[] a = new byte[4];
   for (int i = 0; i < 4; i++)
   {
      int b = 0;
      try
      {
         b = Integer.parseInt(tokenizer.nextToken());
      }
      catch (NumberFormatException e)
      {
         throw new ParseException("Not an integer", 0);
      }
      if (b < 0 || b >= 256)
         throw new ParseException("Byte out of range", 0);
      a[i] = (byte) b;
   }
   return a;
}
```

Try out the IP address field in the sample program. If you enter an invalid address, the field reverts to the last valid address.

The program in Example 9–3 shows various formatted text fields in action (see Figure 9–13). Click the Ok button to retrieve the current values from the fields.

NOTE: The "Swing Connection" online newsletter has a short article describing a formatter that matches any regular expression. See `http://java.sun.com/products/jfc/tsc/articles/reftf/`.

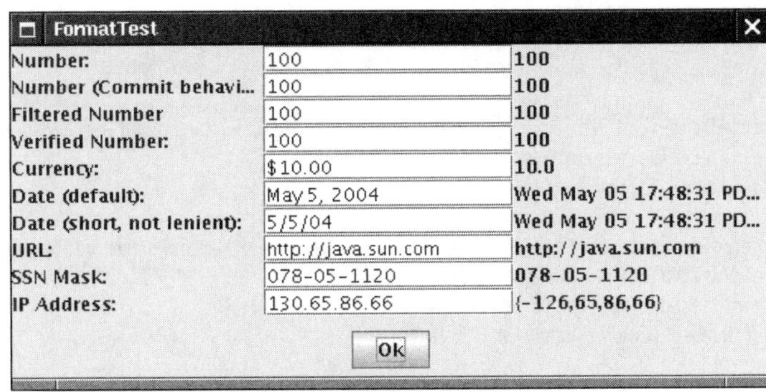

Figure 9–13: The FormatTest program

Example 9–3: FormatTest.java

```
import java.awt.*;
import java.awt.event.*;
import java.lang.reflect.*;
import java.net.*;
import java.text.*;
import java.util.*;
import javax.swing.*;
import javax.swing.text.*;

/**
   A program to test formatted text fields
*/
public class FormatTest
{
   public static void main(String[] args)
   {
      FormatTestFrame frame = new FormatTestFrame();
      frame.setDefaultCloseOperation(JFrame.EXIT_ON_CLOSE);
      frame.setVisible(true);
   }
}

/**
   A frame with a collection of formatted text fields and
   a button that displays the field values.
*/
class FormatTestFrame extends JFrame
{
```

```
   public FormatTestFrame()
   {
      setTitle("FormatTest");
      setSize(WIDTH, HEIGHT);

      JPanel buttonPanel = new JPanel();
      okButton = new JButton("Ok");
      buttonPanel.add(okButton);
      add(buttonPanel, BorderLayout.SOUTH);

      mainPanel = new JPanel();
      mainPanel.setLayout(new GridLayout(0, 3));
      add(mainPanel, BorderLayout.CENTER);

      JFormattedTextField intField = new JFormattedTextField(NumberFormat.getIntegerInstance());
      intField.setValue(new Integer(100));
      addRow("Number:", intField);

      JFormattedTextField intField2 = new JFormattedTextField(NumberFormat.getIntegerInstance());
      intField2.setValue(new Integer(100));
      intField2.setFocusLostBehavior(JFormattedTextField.COMMIT);
      addRow("Number (Commit behavior):", intField2);

      JFormattedTextField intField3
         = new JFormattedTextField(new
            InternationalFormatter(NumberFormat.getIntegerInstance())
            {
               protected DocumentFilter getDocumentFilter()
               {
                  return filter;
               }
               private DocumentFilter filter = new IntFilter();
            });
      intField3.setValue(new Integer(100));
      addRow("Filtered Number", intField3);

      JFormattedTextField intField4 = new JFormattedTextField(NumberFormat.getIntegerInstance());
      intField4.setValue(new Integer(100));
      intField4.setInputVerifier(new FormattedTextFieldVerifier());
      addRow("Verified Number:", intField4);

      JFormattedTextField currencyField
         = new JFormattedTextField(NumberFormat.getCurrencyInstance());
      currencyField.setValue(new Double(10));
      addRow("Currency:", currencyField);

      JFormattedTextField dateField = new JFormattedTextField(DateFormat.getDateInstance());
      dateField.setValue(new Date());
      addRow("Date (default):", dateField);

      DateFormat format = DateFormat.getDateInstance(DateFormat.SHORT);
      format.setLenient(false);
      JFormattedTextField dateField2 = new JFormattedTextField(format);
      dateField2.setValue(new Date());
      addRow("Date (short, not lenient):", dateField2);
```

```

      try
      {
         DefaultFormatter formatter = new DefaultFormatter();
         formatter.setOverwriteMode(false);
         JFormattedTextField urlField = new JFormattedTextField(formatter);
         urlField.setValue(new URL("http://java.sun.com"));
         addRow("URL:", urlField);
      }
      catch (MalformedURLException e)
      {
         e.printStackTrace();
      }

      try
      {
         MaskFormatter formatter = new MaskFormatter("###-##-####");
         formatter.setPlaceholderCharacter('0');
         JFormattedTextField ssnField = new JFormattedTextField(formatter);
         ssnField.setValue("078-05-1120");
         addRow("SSN Mask:", ssnField);
      }
      catch (ParseException exception)
      {
         exception.printStackTrace();
      }

      JFormattedTextField ipField = new JFormattedTextField(new IPAddressFormatter());
      ipField.setValue(new byte[] { (byte) 130, 65, 86, 66 });
      addRow("IP Address:", ipField);
   }

   /**
      Adds a row to the main panel.
      @param labelText the label of the field
      @param field the sample field
   */
   public void addRow(String labelText, final JFormattedTextField field)
   {
      mainPanel.add(new JLabel(labelText));
      mainPanel.add(field);
      final JLabel valueLabel = new JLabel();
      mainPanel.add(valueLabel);
      okButton.addActionListener(new
         ActionListener()
         {
            public void actionPerformed(ActionEvent event)
            {
               Object value = field.getValue();
               if (value.getClass().isArray())
               {
                  StringBuilder builder = new StringBuilder();
                  builder.append('{');
                  for (int i = 0; i < Array.getLength(value); i++)
                  {
```

```
                  if (i > 0) builder.append(',');
                  builder.append(Array.get(value, i).toString());
               }
               builder.append('}');
               valueLabel.setText(builder.toString());
            }
            else
               valueLabel.setText(value.toString());
         }
      });
   }

   public static final int WIDTH = 500;
   public static final int HEIGHT = 250;

   private JButton okButton;
   private JPanel mainPanel;
}

/**
   A filter that restricts input to digits and a '-' sign.
*/
class IntFilter extends DocumentFilter
{
   public void insertString(FilterBypass fb, int offset, String string, AttributeSet attr)
      throws BadLocationException
   {
      StringBuilder builder = new StringBuilder(string);
      for (int i = builder.length() - 1; i >= 0; i--)
      {
         int cp = builder.codePointAt(i);
         if (!Character.isDigit(cp) && cp != '-')
         {
            builder.deleteCharAt(i);
            if (Character.isSupplementaryCodePoint(cp))
            {
               i--;
               builder.deleteCharAt(i);
            }
         }
      }
      super.insertString(fb, offset, builder.toString(), attr);
   }

   public void replace(FilterBypass fb, int offset, int length, String string, AttributeSet attr)
      throws BadLocationException
   {
      if (string != null)
      {
         StringBuilder builder = new StringBuilder(string);
         for (int i = builder.length() - 1; i >= 0; i--)
         {
            int cp = builder.codePointAt(i);
            if (!Character.isDigit(cp) && cp != '-')
            {
```

```
               builder.deleteCharAt(i);
               if (Character.isSupplementaryCodePoint(cp))
               {
                  i--;
                  builder.deleteCharAt(i);
               }
            }
         }
         string = builder.toString();
      }
      super.replace(fb, offset, length, string, attr);
   }
}

/**
   A verifier that checks whether the content of
   a formatted text field is valid.
*/
class FormattedTextFieldVerifier extends InputVerifier
{
   public boolean verify(JComponent component)
   {
      JFormattedTextField field = (JFormattedTextField) component;
      return field.isEditValid();
   }
}

/**
   A formatter for 4-byte IP addresses of the form a.b.c.d
*/
class IPAddressFormatter extends DefaultFormatter
{
   public String valueToString(Object value)
      throws ParseException
   {
      if (!(value instanceof byte[]))
         throw new ParseException("Not a byte[]", 0);
      byte[] a = (byte[]) value;
      if (a.length != 4)
         throw new ParseException("Length != 4", 0);
      StringBuilder builder = new StringBuilder();
      for (int i = 0; i < 4; i++)
      {
         int b = a[i];
         if (b < 0) b += 256;
         builder.append(String.valueOf(b));
         if (i < 3) builder.append('.');
      }
      return builder.toString();
   }

   public Object stringToValue(String text) throws ParseException
   {
      StringTokenizer tokenizer = new StringTokenizer(text, ".");
      byte[] a = new byte[4];
```

```
      for (int i = 0; i < 4; i++)
      {
         int b = 0;
         if (!tokenizer.hasMoreTokens())
            throw new ParseException("Too few bytes", 0);
         try
         {
            b = Integer.parseInt(tokenizer.nextToken());
         }
         catch (NumberFormatException e)
         {
            throw new ParseException("Not an integer", 0);
         }
         if (b < 0 || b >= 256)
            throw new ParseException("Byte out of range", 0);
         a[i] = (byte) b;
      }
      if (tokenizer.hasMoreTokens())
         throw new ParseException("Too many bytes", 0);
      return a;
   }
}
```

API **javax.swing.JFormattedTextField 1.4**

- `JFormattedTextField(Format fmt)`
  constructs a text field that uses the specified format.
- `JFormattedTextField(JFormattedTextField.AbstractFormatter formatter)`
  constructs a text field that uses the specified formatter. Note that `DefaultFormatter` and `InternationalFormatter` are subclasses of `JFormattedTextField.AbstractFormatter`.
- `Object getValue()`
  returns the current valid value of the field. Note that this may not correspond to the string that is being edited.
- `void setValue(Object value)`
  attempts to set the value of the given object. The attempt fails if the formatter cannot convert the object to a string.
- `void commitEdit()`
  attempts to set the valid value of the field from the edited string. The attempt may fail if the formatter cannot convert the string.
- `boolean isEditValid()`
  checks whether the edited string represents a valid value.
- `void setFocusLostBehavior(int behavior)`
- `int getFocusLostBehavior()`
  set or get the "focus lost" behavior. Legal values for `behavior` are the constants `COMMIT_OR_REVERT`, `REVERT`, `COMMIT`, and `PERSIST` of the `JFormattedTextField` class.

API **java.text.DateFormat 1.1**

- `static DateFormat getDateInstance()`
- `static DateFormat getDateInstance(int dateStyle)`
- `static DateFormat getTimeInstance()`
- `static DateFormat getTimeInstance(int timeStyle)`
- `static DateFormat getDateTimeInstance()`

- `static DateFormat getDateTimeInstance(int dateStyle, int timeStyle)`
  return formatters that yield the date, time, or both date and time of `Date` objects. Legal values for `dateStyle` and `timeStyle` are the constants `SHORT`, `MEDIUM`, `LONG`, `FULL`, and `DEFAULT` of the `DateFormat` class.

`javax.swing.JFormattedTextField.AbstractFormatter` 1.4

- `abstract String valueToString(Object value)`
  converts a value to an editable string. Throws a `ParseException` if `value` is not appropriate for this formatter.
- `abstract Object stringToValue(String s)`
  converts a string to a value. Throws a `ParseException` if `s` is not in the appropriate format.
- `DocumentFilter getDocumentFilter()`
  override this method to provide a document filter that restricts inputs into the text field. A return value of `null` indicates that no filtering is needed.

`javax.swing.text.DefaultFormatter` 1.3

- `void setOverwriteMode(boolean mode)`
- `boolean getOverwriteMode()`
  set or get the overwrite mode. If `mode` is `true`, then new characters overwrite existing characters when editing text.

`javax.swing.text.DocumentFilter` 1.4

- `void insertString(DocumentFilter.FilterBypass bypass, int offset, String text, AttributeSet attrib)`
  is invoked before a string is inserted into a document. You can override the method and modify the string. You can disable insertion by not calling `super.insertString` or by calling `bypass` methods to modify the document without filtering.

Parameters:	`bypass`	An object that allows you to execute edit commands that bypass the filter
	`offset`	The offset at which to insert the text
	`text`	The characters to insert
	`attrib`	The formatting attributes of the inserted text

- `void replace(DocumentFilter.FilterBypass bypass, int offset, int length, String text, AttributeSet attrib)`
  is invoked before a part of a document is replaced with a new string. You can override the method and modify the string. You can disable replacement by not calling `super.replace` or by calling `bypass` methods to modify the document without filtering.

Parameters:	`bypass`	An object that allows you to execute edit commands that bypass the filter
	`offset`	The offset at which to insert the text
	`length`	The length of the part to be replaced
	`text`	The characters to insert
	`attrib`	The formatting attributes of the inserted text

- `void remove(DocumentFilter.FilterBypass bypass, int offset, int length)`
  is invoked before a part of a document is removed. Get the document by calling `bypass.getDocument()` if you need to analyze the effect of the removal.

Parameters:	`bypass`	An object that allows you to execute edit commands that bypass the filter
	`offset`	The offset of the part to be removed
	`length`	The length of the part to be removed

javax.swing.text.MaskFormatter 1.4

- `MaskFormatter(String mask)`
  constructs a mask formatter with the given mask. See Table 9–2 on page 367 for the symbols in a mask.
- `void setValidCharacters(String characters)`
- `String getValidCharacters()`
  set or get the valid editing characters. Only the characters in the given string are accepted for the variable parts of the mask.
- `void setInvalidCharacters(String characters)`
- `String getInvalidCharacters()`
  set or get the invalid editing characters. None of the characters in the given string are accepted as input.
- `void setPlaceholderCharacter(char ch)`
- `char getPlaceholderCharacter()`
  set or get the placeholder character that is used for variable characters in the mask that the user has not yet supplied. The default placeholder character is a space.
- `void setPlaceholder(String s)`
- `String getPlaceholder()`
  set or get the placeholder string. Its tail end is used if the user has not supplied all variable characters in the mask. If it is `null` or shorter than the mask, then the placeholder character fills remaining inputs.
- `void setValueContainsLiteralCharacters(boolean b)`
- `boolean getValueContainsLiteralCharacters()`
  set or get the "value contains literal characters" flag. If this flag is `true`, then the field value contains the literal (nonvariable) parts of the mask. If it is `false`, then the literal characters are removed. The default is `true`.

Text Areas

Sometimes, you need to collect user input that is more than one line long. As mentioned earlier, you use the `JTextArea` component for this collection. When you place a text area component in your program, a user can enter any number of lines of text, using the ENTER key to separate them. Each line ends with a `'\n'`. If you need to break up the user's entry into separate lines, you can use the `StringTokenizer` class (see Chapter 12). Figure 9–14 shows a text area at work.

In the constructor for the `JTextArea` component, you specify the number of rows and columns for the text area. For example:

```
textArea = new JTextArea(8, 40); // 8 lines of 40 columns each
```

where the `columns` parameter works as before—and you still need to add a few more columns for safety's sake. Also, as before, the user is not restricted to the number of rows and columns; the text simply scrolls when the user inputs too much. You can also use the

setColumns method to change the number of columns, and the setRows method to change the number of rows. These numbers only indicate the preferred size—the layout manager can still grow or shrink the text area.

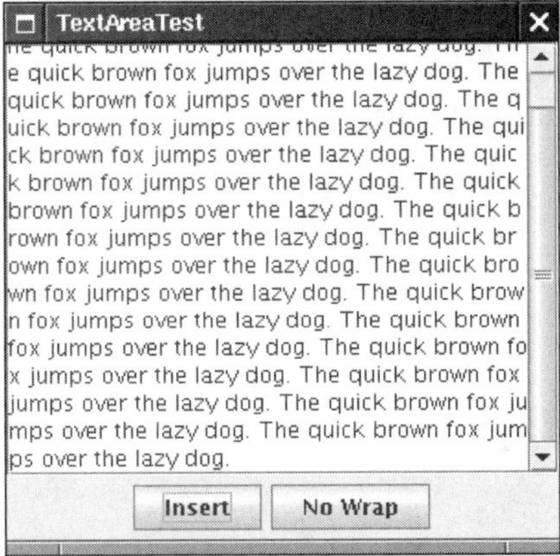

Figure 9–14: A text area

If there is more text than the text area can display, then the remaining text is simply clipped. You can avoid clipping long lines by turning on line wrapping:

```
textArea.setLineWrap(true); // long lines are wrapped
```

This wrapping is a visual effect only; the text in the document is not changed—no '\n' characters are inserted into the text.

In Swing, a text area does not have scrollbars. If you want scrollbars, you have to insert the text area inside a *scroll pane.*

```
textArea = new JTextArea(8, 40);
JScrollPane scrollPane = new JScrollPane(textArea);
```

The scroll pane now manages the view of the text area. Scrollbars automatically appear if there is more text than the text area can display, and they vanish again if text is deleted and the remaining text fits inside the area. The scrolling is handled internally in the scroll pane—your program does not need to process scroll events.

TIP: This is a general mechanism that you will encounter many times when working with Swing—to add scrollbars to a component, put them inside a scroll pane.

Example 9–4 is the complete code for the text area demo. This program simply lets you edit text in a text area. Click on "Insert" to insert a sentence at the end of the text. Click the second button to turn line wrapping on and off. (Its name toggles between "Wrap" and "No wrap".) Of course, you can simply use the keyboard to edit the text in the text area. Note how you can highlight a section of text, and how you can cut, copy, and paste with the CTRL+X, CTRL+C, and CTRL+V keys. (Keyboard shortcuts are specific to the look and feel. These particular key combinations work for the Metal and Windows look and feel.)

NOTE: The JTextArea component displays plain text only, without special fonts or formatting. To display formatted text (such as HTML or RTF), you can use the JEditorPane and JTextPane classes. These classes are discussed in Volume 2.

Example 9–4: TextAreaTest.java

```
import java.awt.*;
import java.awt.event.*;
import javax.swing.*;

public class TextAreaTest
{
   public static void main(String[] args)
   {
      TextAreaFrame frame = new TextAreaFrame();
      frame.setDefaultCloseOperation(JFrame.EXIT_ON_CLOSE);
      frame.setVisible(true);
   }
}

/**
   A frame with a text area and buttons for text editing
*/
class TextAreaFrame extends JFrame
{
   public TextAreaFrame()
   {
      setTitle("TextAreaTest");
      setSize(DEFAULT_WIDTH, DEFAULT_HEIGHT);

      buttonPanel = new JPanel();

      // add button to append text into the text area

      JButton insertButton = new JButton("Insert");
      buttonPanel.add(insertButton);
      insertButton.addActionListener(new
         ActionListener()
         {
            public void actionPerformed(ActionEvent event)
            {
               textArea.append("The quick brown fox jumps over the lazy dog. ");
            }
         });

      // add button to turn line wrapping on and off

      wrapButton = new JButton("Wrap");
      buttonPanel.add(wrapButton);
      wrapButton.addActionListener(new
         ActionListener()
         {
            public void actionPerformed(ActionEvent event)
            {
               boolean wrap = !textArea.getLineWrap();
               textArea.setLineWrap(wrap);
               scrollPane.revalidate();
               wrapButton.setText(wrap ? "No Wrap" : "Wrap");
            }
         });
```

```
      add(buttonPanel, BorderLayout.SOUTH);

      // add a text area with scrollbars

      textArea = new JTextArea(8, 40);
      scrollPane = new JScrollPane(textArea);

      add(scrollPane, BorderLayout.CENTER);
   }

   public static final int DEFAULT_WIDTH = 300;
   public static final int DEFAULT_HEIGHT = 300;

   private JTextArea textArea;
   private JScrollPane scrollPane;
   private JPanel buttonPanel;
   private JButton wrapButton;
}
```

API javax.swing.JTextArea 1.2

- `JTextArea(int rows, int cols)`
  constructs a new text area.

  Parameters: `rows` The number of rows
  `cols` The number of columns

- `JTextArea(String text, int rows, int cols)`
  constructs a new text area with an initial text.

  Parameters: `text` The initial text
  `rows` The number of rows
  `cols` The number of columns

- `void setColumns(int cols)`
  tells the text area the preferred number of columns it should use.

  Parameters: `cols` The number of columns

- `void setRows(int rows)`
  tells the text area the preferred number of rows it should use.

  Parameters: `rows` The number of rows

- `void append(String newText)`
  appends the given text to the end of the text already in the text area.

  Parameters: `newText` The text to append

- `void setLineWrap(boolean wrap)`
  turns line wrapping on or off.

  Parameters: `wrap` `true` if lines should be wrapped

- `void setWrapStyleWord(boolean word)`
  If `word` is `true`, then long lines are wrapped at word boundaries. If it is `false`, then long lines are broken without taking word boundaries into account.

- `void setTabSize(int c)`
  sets tab stops every `c` columns. Note that the tabs aren't converted to spaces but cause alignment with the next tab stop.

  Parameters: `c` The number of columns for a tab stop

javax.swing.JScrollPane 1.2

- `JScrollPane(Component c)`
  creates a scroll pane that displays the content of the specified component. Scrollbars are supplied when the component is larger than the view.

  Parameters: `c` The component to scroll

Choice Components

You now know how to collect text input from users, but there are many occasions for which you would rather give users a finite set of choices than have them enter the data in a text component. Using a set of buttons or a list of items tells your users what choices they have. (It also saves you the trouble of error checking.) In this section, you learn how to program checkboxes, radio buttons, lists of choices, and sliders.

Checkboxes

If you want to collect just a "yes" or "no" input, use a checkbox component. Checkboxes automatically come with labels that identify them. The user usually checks the box by clicking inside it and turns off the check mark by clicking inside the box again. To toggle the check mark, the user can also press the space bar when the focus is in the checkbox.

Figure 9–15 shows a simple program with two checkboxes, one to turn on or off the italic attribute of a font, and the other for boldface. Note that the second checkbox has focus, as indicated by the rectangle around the label. Each time the user clicks one of the checkboxes, we refresh the screen, using the new font attributes.

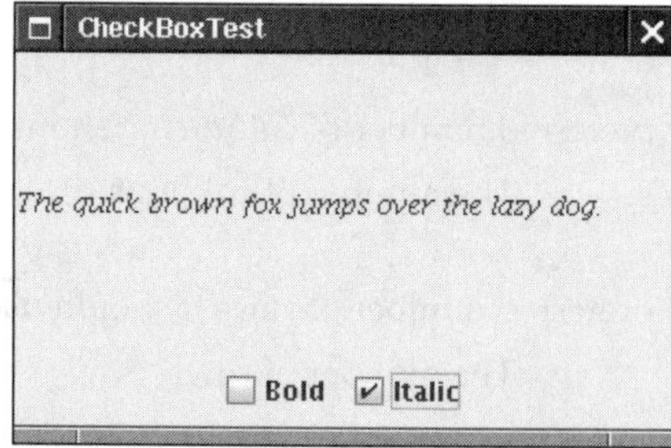

Figure 9–15: Checkboxes

Checkboxes need a label next to them to identify their purpose. You give the label text in the constructor.

```
bold = new JCheckBox("Bold");
```

You use the `setSelected` method to turn a checkbox on or off. For example,

```
bold.setSelected(true);
```

The `isSelected` method then retrieves the current state of each checkbox. It is `false` if unchecked; `true` if checked.

When the user clicks on a checkbox, this triggers an action event. As always, you attach an action listener to the checkbox. In our program, the two checkboxes share the same action listener.

```
ActionListener listener = . . .
bold.addActionListener(listener);
italic.addActionListener(listener);
```

The `actionPerformed` method queries the state of the `bold` and `italic` checkboxes and sets the font of the panel to plain, bold, italic, or both bold and italic.

```
public void actionPerformed(ActionEvent event)
{
   int mode = 0;
   if (bold.isSelected()) mode += Font.BOLD;
   if (italic.isSelected()) mode += Font.ITALIC;
   label.setFont(new Font("Serif", mode, FONTSIZE));
}
```

Example 9–5 is the complete program listing for the checkbox example.

Example 9–5: CheckBoxTest.java

```
import java.awt.*;
import java.awt.event.*;
import javax.swing.*;

public class CheckBoxTest
{
   public static void main(String[] args)
   {
      CheckBoxFrame frame = new CheckBoxFrame();
      frame.setDefaultCloseOperation(JFrame.EXIT_ON_CLOSE);
      frame.setVisible(true);
   }
}

/**
   A frame with a sample text label and checkboxes for
   selecting font attributes.
*/
class CheckBoxFrame extends JFrame
{
   public CheckBoxFrame()
   {
      setTitle("CheckBoxTest");
      setSize(DEFAULT_WIDTH, DEFAULT_HEIGHT);

      // add the sample text label

      label = new JLabel("The quick brown fox jumps over the lazy dog.");
      label.setFont(new Font("Serif", Font.PLAIN, FONTSIZE));
      add(label, BorderLayout.CENTER);

      // this listener sets the font attribute of
      // the label to the checkbox state

      ActionListener listener = new
         ActionListener()
```

```
         {
            public void actionPerformed(ActionEvent event)
            {
               int mode = 0;
               if (bold.isSelected()) mode += Font.BOLD;
               if (italic.isSelected()) mode += Font.ITALIC;
               label.setFont(new Font("Serif", mode, FONTSIZE));
            }
         };

      // add the checkboxes

      JPanel buttonPanel = new JPanel();

      bold = new JCheckBox("Bold");
      bold.addActionListener(listener);
      buttonPanel.add(bold);

      italic = new JCheckBox("Italic");
      italic.addActionListener(listener);
      buttonPanel.add(italic);

      add(buttonPanel, BorderLayout.SOUTH);
   }

   public static final int DEFAULT_WIDTH = 300;
   public static final int DEFAULT_HEIGHT = 200;

   private JLabel label;
   private JCheckBox bold;
   private JCheckBox italic;

   private static final int FONTSIZE = 12;
}
```

API **javax.swing.JCheckBox 1.2**

- `JCheckBox(String label)`
  constructs a checkbox with the given label that is initially unselected.
- `JCheckBox(String label, boolean state)`
  constructs a checkbox with the given label and initial state.
- `JCheckBox(String label, Icon icon)`
  constructs a checkbox with the given label and icon that is initially unselected.
- `boolean isSelected ()`
  returns the state of the checkbox.
- `void setSelected(boolean state)`
  sets the checkbox to a new state.

Radio Buttons

In the previous example, the user could check either, both, or neither of the two checkboxes. In many cases, we want to require the user to check only one of several boxes. When another box is checked, the previous box is automatically unchecked. Such a group of boxes is often called a *radio button group* because the buttons work like the station selector buttons on a radio. When you push in one button, the previously depressed button pops

out. Figure 9–16 shows a typical example. We allow the user to select a font size from among the choices—Small, Medium, Large, and Extra large—but, of course, we will allow the user to select only one size at a time.

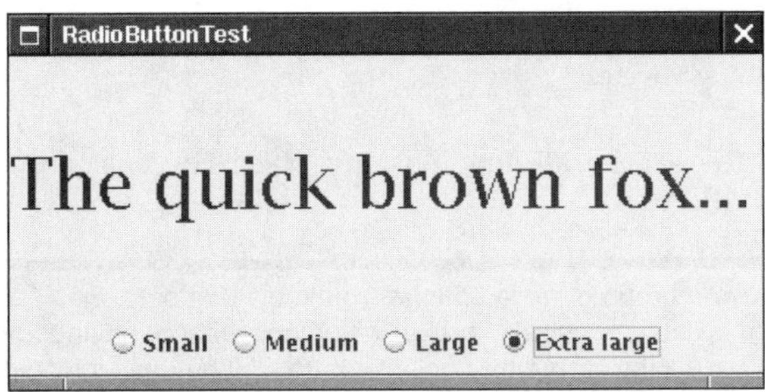

Figure 9–16: A radio button group

Implementing radio button groups is easy in Swing. You construct one object of type ButtonGroup for every group of buttons. Then, you add objects of type JRadioButton to the button group. The button group object is responsible for turning off the previously set button when a new button is clicked.

```
ButtonGroup group = new ButtonGroup();

JRadioButton smallButton = new JRadioButton("Small", false);
group.add(smallButton);

JRadioButton mediumButton = new JRadioButton("Medium", true);
group.add(mediumButton);
. . .
```

The second argument of the constructor is true for the button that should be checked initially and false for all others. Note that the button group controls only the *behavior* of the buttons; if you want to group the buttons for layout purposes, you also need to add them to a container such as a JPanel.

If you look again at Figures 9–15 and 9–16, you will note that the appearance of the radio buttons is different from that of checkboxes. Checkboxes are square and contain a check mark when selected. Radio buttons are round and contain a dot when selected.

The event notification mechanism for radio buttons is the same as for any other buttons. When the user checks a radio button, the radio button generates an action event. In our example program, we define an action listener that sets the font size to a particular value:

```
ActionListener listener = new
   ActionListener()
   {
      public void actionPerformed(ActionEvent event)
      {
         // size refers to the final parameter of the addRadioButton method
         label.setFont(new Font("Serif", Font.PLAIN, size));
      }
   };
```

Compare this listener setup with that of the checkbox example. Each radio button gets a different listener object. Each listener object knows exactly what it needs to do—set the font size to a particular value. In the case of the checkboxes, we used a different approach. Both

checkboxes have the same action listener. It called a method that looked at the current state of both checkboxes.

Could we follow the same approach here? We could have a single listener that computes the size as follows:

```
if (smallButton.isSelected()) size = 8;
else if (mediumButton.isSelected()) size = 12;
. . .
```

However, we prefer to use separate action listener objects because they tie the size values more closely to the buttons.

NOTE: If you have a group of radio buttons, you know that only one of them is selected. It would be nice to be able to quickly find out which one without having to query all the buttons in the group. Because the `ButtonGroup` object controls all buttons, it would be convenient if this object could give us a reference to the selected button. Indeed, the `ButtonGroup` class has a `getSelection` method, but that method doesn't return the radio button that is selected. Instead, it returns a `ButtonModel` reference to the model attached to the button. Unfortunately, none of the `ButtonModel` methods are very helpful. The `ButtonModel` interface inherits a method `getSelectedObjects` from the `ItemSelectable` interface that, rather uselessly, returns `null`. The `getActionCommand` method looks promising because the "action command" of a radio button is its text label. But the action command of its model is `null`. Only if you explicitly set the action commands of all radio buttons with the `setActionCommand` method do the models' action command values also get set. Then you can retrieve the action command of the currently selected button with `buttonGroup.getSelection().getActionCommand()`.

Example 9–6 is the complete program for font size selection that puts a set of radio buttons to work.

Example 9–6: RadioButtonTest.java

```
import java.awt.*;
import java.awt.event.*;
import javax.swing.*;

public class RadioButtonTest
{
   public static void main(String[] args)
   {
      RadioButtonFrame frame = new RadioButtonFrame();
      frame.setDefaultCloseOperation(JFrame.EXIT_ON_CLOSE);
      frame.setVisible(true);
   }
}

/**
   A frame with a sample text label and radio buttons for
   selecting font sizes.
*/
class RadioButtonFrame extends JFrame
{
   public RadioButtonFrame()
   {
      setTitle("RadioButtonTest");
      setSize(DEFAULT_WIDTH, DEFAULT_HEIGHT);

```

```
      // add the sample text label

      label = new JLabel("The quick brown fox jumps over the lazy dog.");
      label.setFont(new Font("Serif", Font.PLAIN, DEFAULT_SIZE));
      add(label, BorderLayout.CENTER);

      // add the radio buttons

      buttonPanel = new JPanel();
      group = new ButtonGroup();

      addRadioButton("Small", 8);
      addRadioButton("Medium", 12);
      addRadioButton("Large", 18);
      addRadioButton("Extra large", 36);

      add(buttonPanel, BorderLayout.SOUTH);
   }

   /**
      Adds a radio button that sets the font size of the
      sample text.
      @param name the string to appear on the button
      @param size the font size that this button sets
   */
   public void addRadioButton(String name, final int size)
   {
      boolean selected = size == DEFAULT_SIZE;
      JRadioButton button = new JRadioButton(name, selected);
      group.add(button);
      buttonPanel.add(button);

      // this listener sets the label font size

      ActionListener listener = new
         ActionListener()
         {
            public void actionPerformed(ActionEvent event)
            {
               // size refers to the final parameter of the addRadioButton method
               label.setFont(new Font("Serif", Font.PLAIN, size));
            }
         };

      button.addActionListener(listener);
   }

   public static final int DEFAULT_WIDTH = 400;
   public static final int DEFAULT_HEIGHT = 200;

   private JPanel buttonPanel;
   private ButtonGroup group;
   private JLabel label;

   private static final int DEFAULT_SIZE = 12;
}
```

javax.swing.JRadioButton 1.2

- `JRadioButton(String label, boolean state)`
  constructs a radio button with the given label and initial state.
- `JRadioButton(String label, Icon icon)`
  constructs a radio button with the given label and icon that is initially unselected.

javax.swing.ButtonGroup 1.2

- `void add(AbstractButton b)`
  adds the button to the group.
- `ButtonModel getSelection()`
  returns the button model of the selected button.

***javax.swing.ButtonModel* 1.2**

- `String getActionCommand()`
  returns the action command for this button model.

javax.swing.AbstractButton 1.2

- `void setActionCommand(String s)`
  sets the action command for this button and its model.

Borders

If you have multiple groups of radio buttons in a window, you will want to visually indicate which buttons are grouped. Swing provides a set of useful *borders* for this purpose. You can apply a border to any component that extends `JComponent`. The most common usage is to place a border around a panel and fill that panel with other user interface elements such as radio buttons.

You can choose from quite a few borders, but you follow the same steps for all of them.

1. Call a static method of the `BorderFactory` to create a border. You can choose among the following styles (see Figure 9–17):
   - Lowered bevel
   - Raised bevel
   - Etched
   - Line
   - Matte
   - Empty (just to create some blank space around the component)
2. If you like, add a title to your border by passing your border to `BorderFactory.createTitledBorder`.
3. If you really want to go all out, combine several borders with a call to `BorderFactory.createCompoundBorder`.
4. Add the resulting border to your component by calling the `setBorder` method of the `JComponent` class.

For example, here is how you add an etched border with a title to a panel:

```
Border etched = BorderFactory.createEtchedBorder()
Border titled = BorderFactory.createTitledBorder(etched, "A Title");
panel.setBorder(titled);
```

Run the program in Example 9–7 to get an idea what the various borders look like.

The various borders have different options for setting border widths and colors. See the API notes for details. True border enthusiasts will appreciate that there is also a `SoftBevelBorder` class for beveled borders with softened corners and that a `LineBorder` can have rounded corners as well. You can construct these borders only by using one of the class constructors—there is no `BorderFactory` method for them.

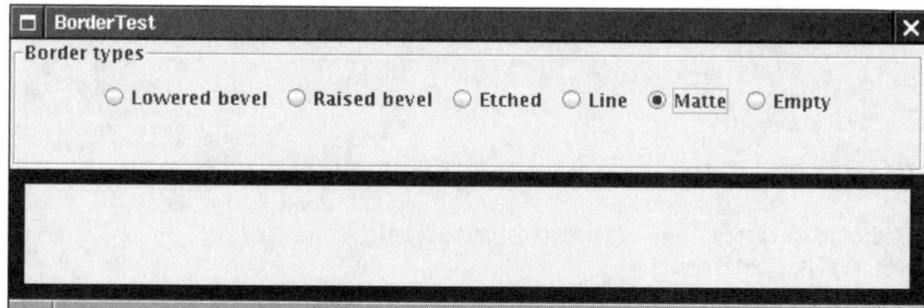

Figure 9–17: Testing border types

Example 9–7: BorderTest.java

```
import java.awt.*;
import java.awt.event.*;
import javax.swing.*;
import javax.swing.border.*;

public class BorderTest
{
   public static void main(String[] args)
   {
      BorderFrame frame = new BorderFrame();
      frame.setDefaultCloseOperation(JFrame.EXIT_ON_CLOSE);
      frame.setVisible(true);
   }
}

/**
   A frame with radio buttons to pick a border style.
*/
class BorderFrame extends JFrame
{
   public BorderFrame()
   {
      setTitle("BorderTest");
      setSize(DEFAULT_WIDTH, DEFAULT_HEIGHT);

      demoPanel = new JPanel();
      buttonPanel = new JPanel();
      group = new ButtonGroup();

      addRadioButton("Lowered bevel", BorderFactory.createLoweredBevelBorder());
      addRadioButton("Raised bevel", BorderFactory.createRaisedBevelBorder());
      addRadioButton("Etched", BorderFactory.createEtchedBorder());
```

```
      addRadioButton("Line", BorderFactory.createLineBorder(Color.BLUE));
      addRadioButton("Matte", BorderFactory.createMatteBorder(10, 10, 10, 10, Color.BLUE));
      addRadioButton("Empty", BorderFactory.createEmptyBorder());

      Border etched = BorderFactory.createEtchedBorder();
      Border titled = BorderFactory.createTitledBorder(etched, "Border types");
      buttonPanel.setBorder(titled);

      setLayout(new GridLayout(2, 1));
      add(buttonPanel);
      add(demoPanel);
   }

   public void addRadioButton(String buttonName, final Border b)
   {
      JRadioButton button = new JRadioButton(buttonName);
      button.addActionListener(new
         ActionListener()
         {
            public void actionPerformed(ActionEvent event)
            {
               demoPanel.setBorder(b);
               validate();
            }
         });
      group.add(button);
      buttonPanel.add(button);
   }

   public static final int DEFAULT_WIDTH = 600;
   public static final int DEFAULT_HEIGHT = 200;

   private JPanel demoPanel;
   private JPanel buttonPanel;
   private ButtonGroup group;
}
```

API **javax.swing.BorderFactory 1.2**

- `static Border createLineBorder(Color color)`
- `static Border createLineBorder(Color color, int thickness)`
  create a simple line border.
- `static MatteBorder createMatteBorder(int top, int left, int bottom, int right, Color color)`
- `static MatteBorder createMatteBorder(int top, int left, int bottom, int right, Icon tileIcon)`
  create a thick border that is filled with a color or a repeating icon.
- `static Border createEmptyBorder()`
- `static Border createEmptyBorder(int top, int left, int bottom, int right)`
  create an empty border.
- `static Border createEtchedBorder()`
- `static Border createEtchedBorder(Color highlight, Color shadow)`
- `static Border createEtchedBorder(int type)`

- `static Border createEtchedBorder(int type, Color highlight, Color shadow)`
  create a line border with a 3D effect.

Parameters:	`highlight, shadow`	Colors for 3D effect
	`type`	One of `EtchedBorder.RAISED`, `EtchedBorder.LOWERED`

- `static Border createBevelBorder(int type)`
- `static Border createBevelBorder(int type, Color highlight, Color shadow)`
- `static Border createLoweredBevelBorder()`
- `static Border createRaisedBevelBorder()`
  create a border that gives the effect of a lowered or raised surface.

Parameters:	`type`	One of `BevelBorder.LOWERED`, `BevelBorder.RAISED`
	`highlight, shadow`	Colors for 3D effect

- `static TitledBorder createTitledBorder(String title)`
- `static TitledBorder createTitledBorder(Border border)`
- `static TitledBorder createTitledBorder(Border border, String title)`
- `static TitledBorder createTitledBorder(Border border, String title, int justification, int position)`
- `static TitledBorder createTitledBorder(Border border, String title, int justification, int position, Font font)`
- `static TitledBorder createTitledBorder(Border border, String title, int justification, int position, Font font, Color color)`
  Creates a titled border with the specified properties.

Parameters:	`title`	The title string
	`border`	The border to decorate with the title
	`justification`	One of the `TitledBorder` constants `LEFT`, `CENTER`, `RIGHT`, `LEADING`, `TRAILING`, or `DEFAULT_JUSTIFICATION` (left)
	`position`	One of the `TitledBorder` constants `ABOVE_TOP`, `TOP`, `BELOW_TOP`, `ABOVE_BOTTOM`, `BOTTOM`, `BELOW_BOTTOM`, or `DEFAULT_POSITION` (top)
	`font`	The font for the title
	`color`	The color of the title

- `static CompoundBorder createCompoundBorder(Border outsideBorder, Border insideBorder)`
  combines two borders to a new border.

API `javax.swing.border.SoftBevelBorder` 1.2

- `SoftBevelBorder(int type)`
- `SoftBevelBorder(int type, Color highlight, Color shadow)`
  create a bevel border with softened corners.

Parameters:	`type`	One of `BevelBorder.LOWERED`, `BevelBorder.RAISED`
	`highlight, shadow`	Colors for 3D effect

API `javax.swing.border.LineBorder` 1.2

- `public LineBorder(Color color, int thickness, boolean roundedCorners)`
  creates a line border with the given color and thickness. If `roundedCorners` is `true`, the border has rounded corners.

javax.swing.JComponent 1.2

- `void setBorder(Border border)`
  sets the border of this component.

Combo Boxes

If you have more than a handful of alternatives, radio buttons are not a good choice because they take up too much screen space. Instead, you can use a combo box. When the user clicks on the component, a list of choices drops down, and the user can then select one of them (see Figure 9–18).

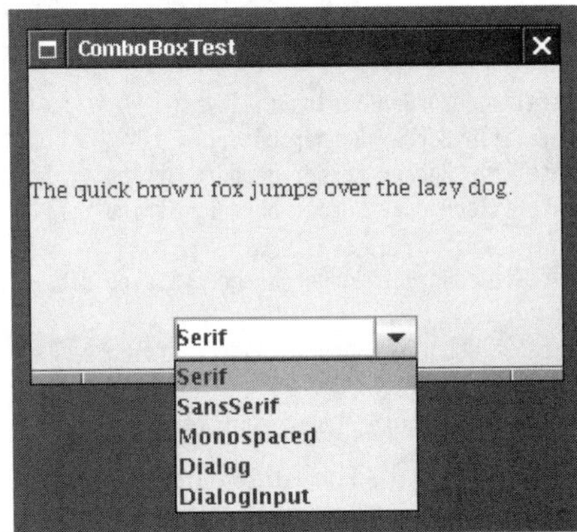

Figure 9–18: A combo box

If the drop-down list box is set to be *editable*, then you can edit the current selection as if it were a text field. For that reason, this component is called a *combo box*—it combines the flexibility of a text field with a set of predefined choices. The `JComboBox` class provides a combo box component.

You call the `setEditable` method to make the combo box editable. Note that editing affects only the current item. It does not change the content of the list.

You can obtain the current selection or edited text by calling the `getSelectedItem` method.

In the example program, the user can choose a font style from a list of styles (Serif, SansSerif, Monospaced, etc.). The user can also type in another font.

You add the choice items with the `addItem` method. In our program, `addItem` is called only in the constructor, but you can call it any time.

```
faceCombo = new JComboBox();
faceCombo.setEditable(true);
faceCombo.addItem("Serif");
faceCombo.addItem("SansSerif");
. . .
```

This method adds the string at the end of the list. You can add new items anywhere in the list with the `insertItemAt` method:

```
faceCombo.insertItemAt("Monospaced", 0); // add at the beginning
```

You can add items of any type—the combo box invokes each item's `toString` method to display it.

If you need to remove items at run time, you use the `removeItem` or `removeItemAt` method, depending on whether you supply the item to be removed or its position.

```
faceCombo.removeItem("Monospaced");
faceCombo.removeItemAt(0); // remove first item
```

The `removeAllItems` method removes all items at once.

TIP: If you need to add a large number of items to a combo box, the `addItem` method will perform poorly. Instead, construct a `DefaultComboBoxModel`, populate it by calling `addElement`, and then call the `setModel` method of the `JComboBox` class.

When the user selects an item from a combo box, the combo box generates an action event. To find out which item was selected, call `getSource` on the event parameter to get a reference to the combo box that sent the event. Then call the `getSelectedItem` method to retrieve the currently selected item. You need to cast the returned value to the appropriate type, usually `String`.

```
public void actionPerformed(ActionEvent event)
{
   label.setFont(new Font(
      (String) faceCombo.getSelectedItem(),
      Font.PLAIN,
      DEFAULT_SIZE));
}
```

Example 9–8 shows the complete program.

NOTE: If you want to show a permanently displayed list instead of a dropdown list, use the `JList` component. We cover `JList` in Chapter 6 of Volume 2.

Example 9–8: ComboBoxTest.java

```
import java.awt.*;
import java.awt.event.*;
import javax.swing.*;

public class ComboBoxTest
{
   public static void main(String[] args)
   {
      ComboBoxFrame frame = new ComboBoxFrame();
      frame.setDefaultCloseOperation(JFrame.EXIT_ON_CLOSE);
      frame.setVisible(true);
   }
}

/**
   A frame with a sample text label and a combo box for
   selecting font faces.
*/
class ComboBoxFrame extends JFrame
{
   public ComboBoxFrame()
```

```
   {
      setTitle("ComboBoxTest");
      setSize(DEFAULT_WIDTH, DEFAULT_HEIGHT);

      // add the sample text label

      label = new JLabel("The quick brown fox jumps over the lazy dog.");
      label.setFont(new Font("Serif", Font.PLAIN, DEFAULT_SIZE));
      add(label, BorderLayout.CENTER);

      // make a combo box and add face names

      faceCombo = new JComboBox();
      faceCombo.setEditable(true);
      faceCombo.addItem("Serif");
      faceCombo.addItem("SansSerif");
      faceCombo.addItem("Monospaced");
      faceCombo.addItem("Dialog");
      faceCombo.addItem("DialogInput");

      // the combo box listener changes the label font to the selected face name

      faceCombo.addActionListener(new
         ActionListener()
         {
            public void actionPerformed(ActionEvent event)
            {
               label.setFont(new Font(
                  (String) faceCombo.getSelectedItem(),
                  Font.PLAIN,
                  DEFAULT_SIZE));
            }
         });

      // add combo box to a panel at the frame's southern border

      JPanel comboPanel = new JPanel();
      comboPanel.add(faceCombo);
      add(comboPanel, BorderLayout.SOUTH);
   }

   public static final int DEFAULT_WIDTH = 300;
   public static final int DEFAULT_HEIGHT = 200;

   private JComboBox faceCombo;
   private JLabel label;
   private static final int DEFAULT_SIZE = 12;
}
```

javax.swing.JComboBox 1.2

- `void setEditable(boolean b)`

  Parameters: `b` — `true` if the combo box field can be edited by the user, `false` otherwise

- `void addItem(Object item)`
  adds an item to the item list.
- `void insertItemAt(Object item, int index)`
  inserts an item into the item list at a given index.
- `void removeItem(Object item)`
  removes an item from the item list.
- `void removeItemAt(int index)`
  removes the item at an index.
- `void removeAllItems()`
  removes all items from the item list.
- `Object getSelectedItem()`
  returns the currently selected item.

Sliders

Combo boxes let users choose from a discrete set of values. Sliders offer a choice from a continuum of values, for example, any number between 1 and 100.

The most common way of constructing a slider is as follows:

```
JSlider slider = new JSlider(min, max, initialValue);
```

If you omit the minimum, maximum, and initial values, they are initialized with 0, 100, and 50, respectively.

Or if you want the slider to be vertical, then use the following constructor call:

```
JSlider slider = new JSlider(SwingConstants.VERTICAL, min, max, initialValue);
```

These constructors create a plain slider, such as the top slider in Figure 9–19. You will see presently how to add decorations to a slider.

As the user slides the slider bar, the *value* of the slider moves between the minimum and the maximum values. When the value changes, a `ChangeEvent` is sent to all change listeners. To be notified of the change, you call the `addChangeListener` method and install an object that implements the `ChangeListener` interface. That interface has a single method, `stateChanged`. In that method, you should retrieve the slider value:

```
public void stateChanged(ChangeEvent event)
{
   JSlider slider = (JSlider) event.getSource();
   int value = slider.getValue();
   . . .
}
```

You can embellish the slider by showing *ticks*. For example, in the sample program, the second slider uses the following settings:

```
slider.setMajorTickSpacing(20);
slider.setMinorTickSpacing(5);
```

The slider is decorated with large tick marks every 20 units and small tick marks every 5 units. The units refer to slider values, not pixels.

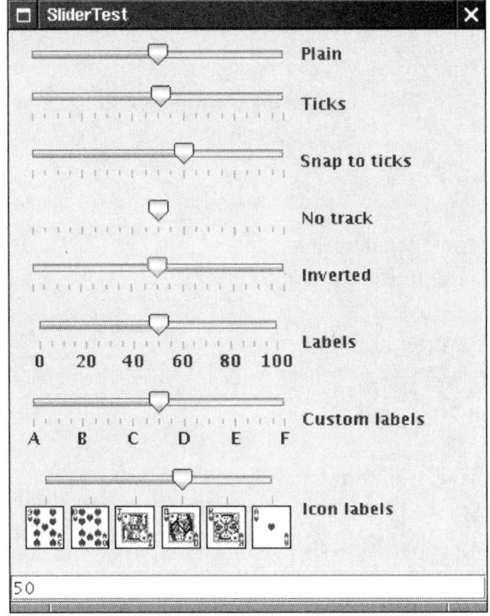

Figure 9–19: Sliders

These instructions only set the units for the tick marks. To actually have the tick marks appear, you also call

```
slider.setPaintTicks(true);
```

The major and minor tick marks are independent. For example, you can set major tick marks every 20 units and minor tick marks every 7 units, but you'll get a very messy scale.

You can force the slider to *snap to ticks.* Whenever the user has finished dragging a slider in snap mode, it is immediately moved to the closest tick. You activate this mode with the call

```
slider.setSnapToTicks(true);
```

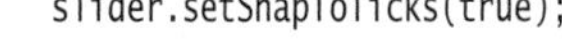

NOTE: The "snap to ticks" behavior doesn't work as well as you might imagine. Until the slider has actually snapped, the change listener still reports slider values that don't correspond to ticks. And if you click next to the slider—an action that normally advances the slider a bit in the direction of the click—a slider with "snap to ticks" does not move to the next tick.

You can ask for *tick mark labels* for the major tick marks by calling

```
slider.setPaintLabels(true);
```

For example, with a slider ranging from 0 to 100 and major tick spacing of 20, the ticks are labeled 0, 20, 40, 60, 80, and 100.

You can also supply other tick marks, such as strings or icons (see Figure 9–19). The process is a bit convoluted. You need to fill a hash table with keys of type `Integer` and values of type `Component`. (Autoboxing makes this simple in JDK 5.0 and beyond.) You then call the `setLabelTable` method. The components are placed under the tick marks. Usually, you use `JLabel` objects. Here is how you can label ticks as A, B, C, D, E, and F.

```
Hashtable<Integer, Component> labelTable = new Hashtable<Integer, Component>();
labelTable.put(0, new JLabel("A"));
labelTable.put(20, new JLabel("B"));
. . .
```

```
labelTable.put(100, new JLabel("F"));
slider.setLabelTable(labelTable);
```

See Chapter 2 of Volume 2 for more information about hash tables.

Example 9–9 also shows a slider with icons as tick labels.

TIP: If your tick marks or labels don't show, double-check that you called `setPaintTicks(true)` and `setPaintLabels(true)`.

To suppress the "track" in which the slider moves, call

```
slider.setPaintTrack(false);
```

The fourth slider in Figure 9–19 has no track.

The fifth slider has its direction reversed by a call to

```
slider.setInverted(true);
```

The example program shows all these visual effects with a collection of sliders. Each slider has a change event listener installed that places the current slider value into the text field at the bottom of the frame.

Example 9–9: SliderTest.java

```
import java.awt.*;
import java.awt.event.*;
import java.util.*;
import javax.swing.*;
import javax.swing.event.*;

public class SliderTest
{
   public static void main(String[] args)
   {
      SliderTestFrame frame = new SliderTestFrame();
      frame.setDefaultCloseOperation(JFrame.EXIT_ON_CLOSE);
      frame.setVisible(true);
   }
}

/**
   A frame with many sliders and a text field to show slider
   values.
*/
class SliderTestFrame extends JFrame
{
   public SliderTestFrame()
   {
      setTitle("SliderTest");
      setSize(DEFAULT_WIDTH, DEFAULT_HEIGHT);

      sliderPanel = new JPanel();
      sliderPanel.setLayout(new FlowLayout(FlowLayout.LEFT));

      // common listener for all sliders
      listener = new
         ChangeListener()
         {
```

```
         public void stateChanged(ChangeEvent event)
         {
            // update text field when the slider value changes
            JSlider source = (JSlider) event.getSource();
            textField.setText("" + source.getValue());
         }
      };

   // add a plain slider

   JSlider slider = new JSlider();
   addSlider(slider, "Plain");

   // add a slider with major and minor ticks

   slider = new JSlider();
   slider.setPaintTicks(true);
   slider.setMajorTickSpacing(20);
   slider.setMinorTickSpacing(5);
   addSlider(slider, "Ticks");

   // add a slider that snaps to ticks

   slider = new JSlider();
   slider.setPaintTicks(true);
   slider.setSnapToTicks(true);
   slider.setMajorTickSpacing(20);
   slider.setMinorTickSpacing(5);
   addSlider(slider, "Snap to ticks");

   // add a slider with no track

   slider = new JSlider();
   slider.setPaintTicks(true);
   slider.setMajorTickSpacing(20);
   slider.setMinorTickSpacing(5);
   slider.setPaintTrack(false);
   addSlider(slider, "No track");

   // add an inverted slider

   slider = new JSlider();
   slider.setPaintTicks(true);
   slider.setMajorTickSpacing(20);
   slider.setMinorTickSpacing(5);
   slider.setInverted(true);
   addSlider(slider, "Inverted");

   // add a slider with numeric labels

   slider = new JSlider();
   slider.setPaintTicks(true);
   slider.setPaintLabels(true);
   slider.setMajorTickSpacing(20);
   slider.setMinorTickSpacing(5);
   addSlider(slider, "Labels");
```

```

      // add a slider with alphabetic labels

      slider = new JSlider();
      slider.setPaintLabels(true);
      slider.setPaintTicks(true);
      slider.setMajorTickSpacing(20);
      slider.setMinorTickSpacing(5);

      Dictionary<Integer, Component> labelTable = new Hashtable<Integer, Component>();
      labelTable.put(0, new JLabel("A"));
      labelTable.put(20, new JLabel("B"));
      labelTable.put(40, new JLabel("C"));
      labelTable.put(60, new JLabel("D"));
      labelTable.put(80, new JLabel("E"));
      labelTable.put(100, new JLabel("F"));

      slider.setLabelTable(labelTable);
      addSlider(slider, "Custom labels");

      // add a slider with icon labels

      slider = new JSlider();
      slider.setPaintTicks(true);
      slider.setPaintLabels(true);
      slider.setSnapToTicks(true);
      slider.setMajorTickSpacing(20);
      slider.setMinorTickSpacing(20);

      labelTable = new Hashtable<Integer, Component>();

      // add card images

      labelTable.put(0, new JLabel(new ImageIcon("nine.gif")));
      labelTable.put(20, new JLabel(new ImageIcon("ten.gif")));
      labelTable.put(40, new JLabel(new ImageIcon("jack.gif")));
      labelTable.put(60, new JLabel(new ImageIcon("queen.gif")));
      labelTable.put(80, new JLabel(new ImageIcon("king.gif")));
      labelTable.put(100, new JLabel(new ImageIcon("ace.gif")));

      slider.setLabelTable(labelTable);
      addSlider(slider, "Icon labels");

      // add the text field that displays the slider value

      textField = new JTextField();
      add(sliderPanel, BorderLayout.CENTER);
      add(textField, BorderLayout.SOUTH);
   }

   /**
      Adds a slider to the slider panel and hooks up the listener
      @param s the slider
      @param description the slider description
   */
   public void addSlider(JSlider s, String description)
```

```
   {
      s.addChangeListener(listener);
      JPanel panel = new JPanel();
      panel.add(s);
      panel.add(new JLabel(description));
      sliderPanel.add(panel);
   }

   public static final int DEFAULT_WIDTH = 350;
   public static final int DEFAULT_HEIGHT = 450;

   private JPanel sliderPanel;
   private JTextField textField;
   private ChangeListener listener;
}
```

API **javax.swing.JSlider 1.2**

- `JSlider()`
- `JSlider(int direction)`
- `JSlider(int min, int max)`
- `JSlider(int min, int max, int initialValue)`
- `JSlider(int direction, int min, int max, int initialValue)`

  construct a horizontal slider with the given direction and minimum, maximum, and initial values.

Parameters:	`direction`	One of `SwingConstants.HORIZONTAL` or `SwingConstants.VERTICAL`. The default is horizontal.
	`min, max`	The minimum and maximum for the slider values. Defaults are 0 and 100.
	`initialValue`	The initial value for the slider. The default is 50.

- `void setPaintTicks(boolean b)`

  displays ticks if `b` is `true`.

- `void setMajorTickSpacing(int units)`
- `void setMinorTickSpacing(int units)`

  set major or minor ticks at multiples of the given slider units.

- `void setPaintLabels(boolean b)`

  displays tick labels if `b` is `true`.

- `void setLabelTable(Dictionary table)`

  sets the components to use for the tick labels. Each key/value pair in the table has the form `new Integer(`*value*`)`/*component*.

- `void setSnapToTicks(boolean b)`

  if `b` is `true`, then the slider snaps to the closest tick after each adjustment.

- `void setPaintTrack(boolean b)`

  if `b` is `true`, then a track is displayed in which the slider runs.

The `JSpinner` *Component*

A `JSpinner` is a text field with two small buttons on the side. When the buttons are clicked, the text field value is incremented or decremented (see Figure 9–20).

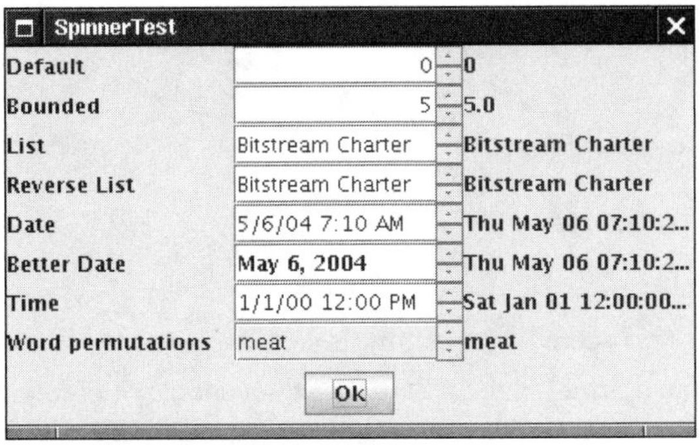

Figure 9–20: Several variations of the JSpinner component

The values in the spinner can be numbers, dates, values from a list, or, in the most general case, any sequence of values for which predecessors and successors can be determined. The JSpinner class defines standard data models for the first three cases. You can define your own data model to describe arbitrary sequences.

By default, a spinner manages an integer, and the buttons increment or decrement it by 1. You can get the current value by calling the getValue method. That method returns an Object. Cast it to an Integer and retrieve the wrapped value.

```
JSpinner defaultSpinner = new JSpinner();
. . .
int value = (Integer) defaultSpinner.getValue();
```

You can change the increment to a value other than 1, and you can also supply lower and upper bounds. Here is a spinner with starting value 5, bounded between 0 and 10, and an increment of 0.5:

```
JSpinner boundedSpinner = new JSpinner(new SpinnerNumberModel(5, 0, 10, 0.5));
```

There are two SpinnerNumberModel constructors, one with only int parameters and one with double parameters. If any of the parameters is a floating-point number, then the second constructor is used. It sets the spinner value to a Double object.

Spinners aren't restricted to numeric values. You can have a spinner iterate through any collection of values. Simply pass a SpinnerListModel to the JSpinner constructor. You can construct a SpinnerListModel from an array or a class implementing the List interface (such as an ArrayList). In our sample program, we display a spinner control with all available font names.

```
String[] fonts = GraphicsEnvironment.getLocalGraphicsEnvironment().getAvailableFontFamilyNames();
JSpinner listSpinner = new JSpinner(new SpinnerListModel(fonts));
```

However, we found that the direction of the iteration was mildly confusing because it is opposite from the user experience with a combo box. In a combo box, higher values are *below* lower values, so you would expect the downward arrow to navigate toward higher values. But the spinner increments the array index so that the upward arrow yields higher values. There is no provision for reversing the traversal order in the SpinnerListModel, but an impromptu anonymous subclass yields the desired result:

```
JSpinner reverseListSpinner = new JSpinner(
   new SpinnerListModel(fonts)
   {
      public Object getNextValue()
```

```
        {
           return super.getPreviousValue();

        }
        public Object getPreviousValue()
        {
            return super.getNextValue();
        }
    });
```

Try out both versions and see which you find more intuitive.

Another good use for a spinner is for a date that the user can increment or decrement. You get such a spinner, initialized with today's date, with the call

```
JSpinner dateSpinner = new JSpinner(new SpinnerDateModel());
```

However, if you look carefully at Figure 9–20, you will see that the spinner text shows both date and time, such as

```
3/12/02 7:23 PM
```

The time doesn't make any sense for a date picker. It turns out to be somewhat difficult to make the spinner show just the date. Here is the magic incantation:

```
JSpinner betterDateSpinner = new JSpinner(new SpinnerDateModel());
String pattern = ((SimpleDateFormat) DateFormat.getDateInstance()).toPattern();
betterDateSpinner.setEditor(new JSpinner.DateEditor(betterDateSpinner, pattern));
```

Using the same approach, you can also make a time picker. Then use the `SpinnerDateModel` constructor that lets you specify a `Date`, the lower and upper bounds (or `null` if there are no bounds), and the `Calendar` field (such as `Calendar.HOUR`) to be modified.

```
JSpinner timeSpinner = new JSpinner(
   new SpinnerDateModel(
      new GregorianCalendar(2000, Calendar.JANUARY, 1, 12, 0, 0).getTime(),
         null, null, Calendar.HOUR));
```

However, if you want to update the minutes in 15-minute increments, then you exceed the capabilities of the standard `SpinnerDateModel` class.

You can display arbitrary sequences in a spinner by defining your own spinner model. In our sample program, we have a spinner that iterates through all permutations of the string "meat". You can get to "mate", "meta", "team", and another 20 permutations by clicking the spinner buttons.

When you define your own model, you should extend the `AbstractSpinnerModel` class and define the following four methods:

```
Object getValue()
void setValue(Object value)
Object getNextValue()
Object getPreviousValue()
```

The `getValue` method returns the value stored by the model. The `setValue` method sets a new value. It should throw an `IllegalArgumentException` if the new value is not appropriate.

CAUTION: The `setValue` method must call the `fireStateChanged` method after setting the new value. Otherwise, the spinner field won't be updated.

The `getNextValue` and `getPreviousValue` methods return the values that should come after or before the current value, or `null` if the end of the traversal has been reached.

CAUTION: The getNextValue and getPreviousValue methods should *not* change the current value. When a user clicks on the upward arrow of the spinner, the getNextValue method is called. If the return value is not null, it is set by a call to setValue.

In the sample program, we use a standard algorithm to determine the next and previous permutations. The details of the algorithm are not important.

Example 9–10 shows how to generate the various spinner types. Click on the Ok button to see the spinner values.

Example 9–10: SpinnerTest.java

```
import java.awt.*;
import java.awt.event.*;
import java.text.*;
import java.util.*;
import javax.swing.*;

/**
   A program to test spinners.
*/
public class SpinnerTest
{
   public static void main(String[] args)
   {
      SpinnerFrame frame = new SpinnerFrame();
      frame.setDefaultCloseOperation(JFrame.EXIT_ON_CLOSE);
      frame.setVisible(true);
   }
}

/**
   A frame with a panel that contains several spinners and
   a button that displays the spinner values.
*/
class SpinnerFrame extends JFrame
{
   public SpinnerFrame()
   {
      setTitle("SpinnerTest");
      setSize(DEFAULT_WIDTH, DEFAULT_HEIGHT);
      JPanel buttonPanel = new JPanel();
      okButton = new JButton("Ok");
      buttonPanel.add(okButton);
      add(buttonPanel, BorderLayout.SOUTH);

      mainPanel = new JPanel();
      mainPanel.setLayout(new GridLayout(0, 3));
      add(mainPanel, BorderLayout.CENTER);

      JSpinner defaultSpinner = new JSpinner();
      addRow("Default", defaultSpinner);

      JSpinner boundedSpinner = new JSpinner(new SpinnerNumberModel(5, 0, 10, 0.5));
      addRow("Bounded", boundedSpinner);

```

```
      String[] fonts = GraphicsEnvironment
         .getLocalGraphicsEnvironment()
         .getAvailableFontFamilyNames();

      JSpinner listSpinner = new JSpinner(new SpinnerListModel(fonts));
      addRow("List", listSpinner);

      JSpinner reverseListSpinner = new JSpinner(
         new
            SpinnerListModel(fonts)
            {
               public Object getNextValue()
               {
                  return super.getPreviousValue();
               }
               public Object getPreviousValue()
               {
                  return super.getNextValue();
               }
            });
      addRow("Reverse List", reverseListSpinner);

      JSpinner dateSpinner = new JSpinner(new SpinnerDateModel());
      addRow("Date", dateSpinner);

      JSpinner betterDateSpinner = new JSpinner(new SpinnerDateModel());
      String pattern = ((SimpleDateFormat) DateFormat.getDateInstance()).toPattern();
      betterDateSpinner.setEditor(new JSpinner.DateEditor(betterDateSpinner, pattern));
      addRow("Better Date", betterDateSpinner);

      JSpinner timeSpinner = new JSpinner(
         new SpinnerDateModel(
            new GregorianCalendar(2000, Calendar.JANUARY, 1, 12, 0, 0).getTime(),
               null, null, Calendar.HOUR));
      addRow("Time", timeSpinner);

      JSpinner permSpinner = new JSpinner(new PermutationSpinnerModel("meat"));
      addRow("Word permutations", permSpinner);
   }

   /**
      Adds a row to the main panel.
      @param labelText the label of the spinner
      @param spinner the sample spinner
   */
   public void addRow(String labelText, final JSpinner spinner)
   {
      mainPanel.add(new JLabel(labelText));
      mainPanel.add(spinner);
      final JLabel valueLabel = new JLabel();
      mainPanel.add(valueLabel);
      okButton.addActionListener(new
         ActionListener()
         {
            public void actionPerformed(ActionEvent event)
            {
```

```
                Object value = spinner.getValue();
                valueLabel.setText(value.toString());
             }
          });
    }

    public static final int DEFAULT_WIDTH = 400;
    public static final int DEFAULT_HEIGHT = 250;

    private JPanel mainPanel;
    private JButton okButton;
}

/**
   A model that dynamically generates word permutations
*/
class PermutationSpinnerModel extends AbstractSpinnerModel
{
   /**
      Constructs the model.
      @param w the word to permute
   */
   public PermutationSpinnerModel(String w)
   {
      word = w;
   }

   public Object getValue()
   {
      return word;
   }

   public void setValue(Object value)
   {
      if (!(value instanceof String))
         throw new IllegalArgumentException();
      word = (String) value;
      fireStateChanged();
   }

   public Object getNextValue()
   {
      int[] codePoints = toCodePointArray(word);
      for (int i = codePoints.length - 1; i > 0; i--)
      {
         if (codePoints[i - 1] < codePoints[i])
         {
            int j = codePoints.length - 1;
            while (codePoints[i - 1] > codePoints[j]) j--;
            swap(codePoints, i - 1, j);
            reverse(codePoints, i, codePoints.length - 1);
            return new String(codePoints, 0, codePoints.length);
         }
      }
      reverse(codePoints, 0, codePoints.length - 1);
      return new String(codePoints, 0, codePoints.length);
   }
```

```
   public Object getPreviousValue()
   {
      int[] codePoints = toCodePointArray(word);
      for (int i = codePoints.length - 1; i > 0; i--)
      {
         if (codePoints[i - 1] > codePoints[i])
         {
            int j = codePoints.length - 1;
            while (codePoints[i - 1] < codePoints[j]) j--;
            swap(codePoints, i - 1, j);
            reverse(codePoints, i, codePoints.length - 1);
            return new String(codePoints, 0, codePoints.length);
         }
      }
      reverse(codePoints, 0, codePoints.length - 1);
      return new String(codePoints, 0, codePoints.length);
   }

   private static int[] toCodePointArray(String str)
   {
      int[] codePoints = new int[str.codePointCount(0, str.length())];
      for (int i = 0, j = 0; i < str.length(); i++, j++)
      {
         int cp = str.codePointAt(i);
         if (Character.isSupplementaryCodePoint(cp)) i++;
         codePoints[j] = cp;
      }
      return codePoints;
   }

   private static void swap(int[] a, int i, int j)
   {
      int temp = a[i];
      a[i] = a[j];
      a[j] = temp;
   }

   private static void reverse(int[] a, int i, int j)
   {
      while (i < j) { swap(a, i, j); i++; j--; }
   }

   private String word;
}
```

API `javax.swing.JSpinner` 1.4

- `JSpinner()`
  constructs a spinner that edits an integer with starting value 0, increment 1, and no bounds.
- `JSpinner(SpinnerModel model)`
  constructs a spinner that uses the given data model.
- `Object getValue()`
  gets the current value of the spinner.

- `void setValue(Object value)`
  attempts to set the value of the spinner. Throws an `IllegalArgumentException` if the model does not accept the value.
- `void setEditor(JComponent editor)`
  sets the component that is used for editing the spinner value.

`javax.swing.SpinnerNumberModel` 1.4

- `SpinnerNumberModel(int initval, int minimum, int maximum, int stepSize)`
- `SpinnerNumberModel(double initval, double minimum, double maximum, double stepSize)`
  these constructors yield number models that manage an `Integer` or `Double` value. Use the `MIN_VALUE` and `MAX_VALUE` constants of the `Integer` and `Double` classes for unbounded values.

Parameters:	`initval`	The initial value
	`minimum`	The minimum valid value
	`maximum`	The maximum valid value
	`stepSize`	The increment or decrement of each spin

`javax.swing.SpinnerListModel` 1.4

- `SpinnerListModel(Object[] values)`
- `SpinnerListModel(List values)`
  these constructors yield models that select a value from among the given values.

`javax.swing.SpinnerDateModel` 1.4

- `SpinnerDateModel()`
  constructs a date model with today's date as the initial value, no lower or upper bounds, and an increment of `Calendar.DAY_OF_MONTH`.
- `SpinnerDateModel(Date initval, Comparable minimum, Comparable maximum, int step)`

Parameters:	`initval`	The initial value
	`minimum`	The minimum valid value, or `null` if no lower bound is desired
	`maximum`	The maximum valid value, or `null` if no lower bound is desired
	`step`	The date field to increment or decrement of each spin. One of the constants `ERA`, `YEAR`, `MONTH`, `WEEK_OF_YEAR`, `WEEK_OF_MONTH`, `DAY_OF_MONTH`, `DAY_OF_YEAR`, `DAY_OF_WEEK`, `DAY_OF_WEEK_IN_MONTH`, `AM_PM`, `HOUR`, `HOUR_OF_DAY`, `MINUTE`, `SECOND`, or `MILLISECOND` of the `Calendar` class

`java.text.SimpleDateFormat` 1.1

- `String toPattern()` 1.2
  gets the editing pattern for this date formatter. A typical pattern is `"yyyy-MM-dd"`. See the JDK documentation for more details about the pattern.

javax.swing.JSpinner.DateEditor 1.4

- `DateEditor(JSpinner spinner, String pattern)`
  constructs a date editor for a spinner.

Parameters:	`spinner`	The spinner to which this editor belongs
	`pattern`	The format pattern for the associated `SimpleDateFormat`

javax.swing.AbstractSpinnerModel 1.4

- `Object getValue()`
  gets the current value of the model.
- `void setValue(Object value)`
  attempts to set a new value for the model. Throws an `IllegalArgumentException` if the value is not acceptable. When overriding this method, you should call `fireStateChanged` after setting the new value.
- `Object getNextValue()`
- `Object getPreviousValue()`
  compute (but do not set) the next or previous value in the sequence that this model defines.

Menus

We started this chapter by introducing the most common components that you might want to place into a window, such as various kinds of buttons, text fields, and combo boxes. Swing also supports another type of user interface element, the pull-down menus that are familiar from GUI applications.

A *menu bar* on top of the window contains the names of the pull-down menus. Clicking on a name opens the menu containing *menu items* and *submenus.* When the user clicks on a menu item, all menus are closed and a message is sent to the program. Figure 9–21 shows a typical menu with a submenu.

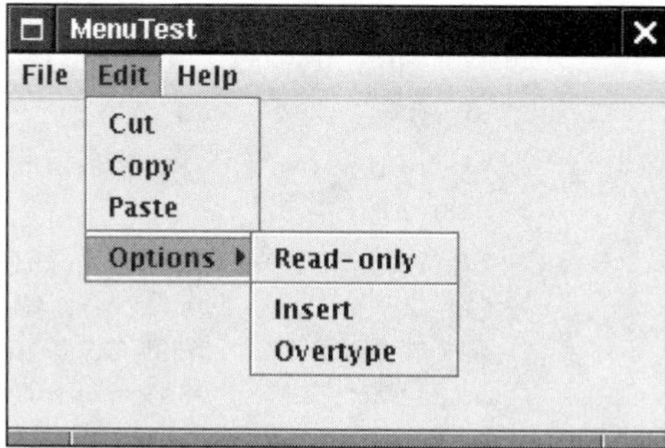

Figure 9–21: A menu with a submenu

Menu Building

Building menus is straightforward. You create a menu bar:

```
JMenuBar menuBar = new JMenuBar();
```

A menu bar is just a component that you can add anywhere you like. Normally, you want it to appear at the top of a frame. You can add it there with the `setJMenuBar` method:

```
frame.setJMenuBar(menuBar);
```

For each menu, you create a menu object:

```
JMenu editMenu = new JMenu("Edit");
```

You add the top-level menus to the menu bar:

```
menuBar.add(editMenu);
```

You add menu items, separators, and submenus to the menu object:

```
JMenuItem pasteItem = new JMenuItem("Paste");
editMenu.add(pasteItem);
editMenu.addSeparator();
JMenu optionsMenu = . . .; // a submenu
editMenu.add(optionsMenu);
```

You can see separators in Figure 9–21 below the "Paste" and "Read-only" menu items.

When the user selects a menu, an action event is triggered. You need to install an action listener for each menu item.

```
ActionListener listener = . . .;
pasteItem.addActionListener(listener);
```

The method `JMenu.add(String s)` conveniently adds a menu item to the end of a menu, for example:

```
editMenu.add("Paste");
```

The `add` method returns the created menu item, so you can capture it and then add the listener, as follows:

```
JMenuItem pasteItem = editMenu.add("Paste");
pasteItem.addActionListener(listener);
```

It often happens that menu items trigger commands that can also be activated through other user interface elements such as toolbar buttons. In Chapter 8, you saw how to specify commands through `Action` objects. You define a class that implements the `Action` interface, usually by extending the `AbstractAction` convenience class. You specify the menu item label in the constructor of the `AbstractAction` object, and you override the `actionPerformed` method to hold the menu action handler. For example,

```
Action exitAction = new
   AbstractAction("Exit") // menu item text goes here
   {
      public void actionPerformed(ActionEvent event)
      {
         // action code goes here
         System.exit(0);
      }
   };
```

You can then add the action to the menu:

```
JMenuItem exitItem = fileMenu.add(exitAction);
```

This command adds a menu item to the menu, using the action name. The action object becomes its listener. This is just a convenient shortcut for

```
JMenuItem exitItem = new JMenuItem(exitAction);
fileMenu.add(exitItem);
```

NOTE: In Windows and Macintosh programs, menus are generally defined in an external resource file and tied to the application with resource identifiers. It is possible to build menus programmatically, but it is not commonly done. In Java, menus are still usually built inside the program because the mechanism for dealing with external resources is far more limited than it is in Windows or Mac OS.

javax.swing.JMenu 1.2

- `JMenu(String label)`
  constructs a menu.

  Parameters: `label` The label for the menu in the menu bar or parent menu

- `JMenuItem add(JMenuItem item)`
  adds a menu item (or a menu).

  Parameters: `item` The item or menu to add

- `JMenuItem add(String label)`
  adds a menu item to this menu.

  Parameters: `label` The label for the menu items

- `JMenuItem add(Action a)`
  adds a menu item and associates an action with it.

  Parameters: `a` An action encapsulating a name, optional icon, and listener (see Chapter 8)

- `void addSeparator()`
  adds a separator line to the menu.
- `JMenuItem insert(JMenuItem menu, int index)`
  adds a new menu item (or submenu) to the menu at a specific index.

  Parameters: `menu` The menu to be added
  `index` Where to add the item

- `JMenuItem insert(Action a, int index)`
  adds a new menu item at a specific index and associates an action with it.

  Parameters: `a` An action encapsulating a name, optional icon, and listener
  `index` Where to add the item

- `void insertSeparator(int index)`
  adds a separator to the menu.

  Parameters: `index` Where to add the separator

- `void remove(int index)`
  removes a specific item from the menu.

  Parameters: `index` The position of the item to remove

- `void remove(JMenuItem item)`
  removes a specific item from the menu.

  Parameters: `item` The item to remove

javax.swing.JMenuItem 1.2

- `JMenuItem(String label)`
  constructs a menu item with a given label.

- `JMenuItem(Action a)` 1.3
  constructs a menu item for the given action.

  Parameters: `a` An action encapsulating a name, optional icon, and listener

`javax.swing.AbstractButton` 1.2

- `void setAction(Action a)` 1.3
  sets the action for this button or menu item.

  Parameters: `a` An action encapsulating a name, optional icon, and listener

`javax.swing.JFrame` 1.2

- `void setJMenuBar(JMenuBar menubar)`
  sets the menu bar for this frame.

Icons in Menu Items

Menu items are very similar to buttons. In fact, the `JMenuItem` class extends the `AbstractButton` class. Just like buttons, menus can have just a text label, just an icon, or both. You can specify the icon with the `JMenuItem(String, Icon)` or `JMenuItem(Icon)` constructor, or you can set it with the `setIcon` method that the `JMenuItem` class inherits from the `AbstractButton` class. Here is an example:

```
JMenuItem cutItem = new JMenuItem("Cut", new ImageIcon("cut.gif"));
```

Figure 9–22 shows a menu with icons next to several menu items. As you can see, by default, the menu item text is placed to the right of the icon. If you prefer the text to be placed on the left, call the `setHorizontalTextPosition` method that the `JMenuItem` class inherits from the `AbstractButton` class. For example, the call

```
cutItem.setHorizontalTextPosition(SwingConstants.LEFT);
```

moves the menu item text to the left of the icon.

You can also add an icon to an action:

```
cutAction.putValue(Action.SMALL_ICON, new ImageIcon("cut.gif"));
```

Whenever you construct a menu item out of an action, the `Action.NAME` value becomes the text of the menu item and the `Action.SMALL_ICON` value becomes the icon.

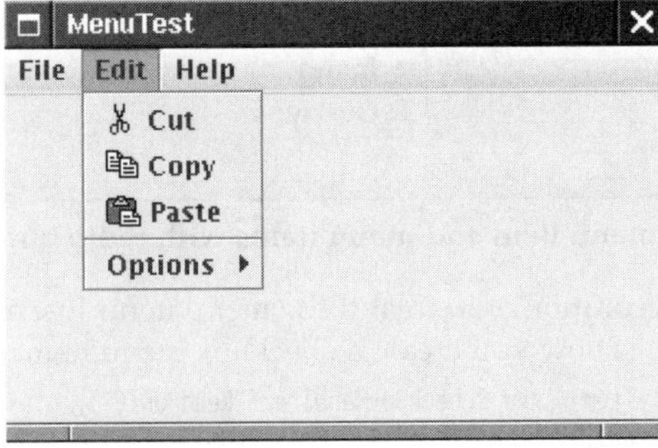

Figure 9–22: Icons in menu items

Alternatively, you can set the icon in the AbstractAction constructor:

```
cutAction = new
   AbstractAction("Cut", new ImageIcon("cut.gif"))
   {
      public void actionPerformed(ActionEvent event)
      {
         // action code goes here
      }
   };
```

API **javax.swing.JMenuItem 1.2**

- JMenuItem(String label, Icon icon)
  constructs a menu item with the given label and icon.

API **javax.swing.AbstractButton 1.2**

- void setHorizontalTextPosition(int pos)
  sets the horizontal position of the text relative to the icon.

Parameters:	pos	SwingConstants.RIGHT (text is to the right of icon) or SwingConstants.LEFT

API **javax.swing.AbstractAction 1.2**

- AbstractAction(String name, Icon smallIcon)
  constructs an abstract action with the given name and icon.

Checkbox and Radio Button Menu Items

Checkbox and *radio button* menu items display a checkbox or radio button next to the name (see Figure 9–23). When the user selects the menu item, the item automatically toggles between checked and unchecked.

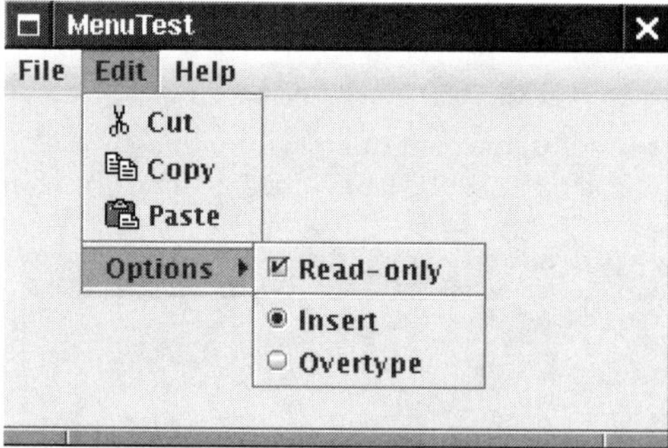

Figure 9–23: A checked menu item and menu items with radio buttons

Apart from the button decoration, you treat these menu items just as you would any others. For example, here is how you create a checkbox menu item.

```
JCheckBoxMenuItem readonlyItem = new JCheckBoxMenuItem("Read-only");
optionsMenu.add(readonlyItem);
```

The radio button menu items work just like regular radio buttons. You must add them to a button group. When one of the buttons in a group is selected, all others are automatically deselected.

```
ButtonGroup group = new ButtonGroup();
JRadioButtonMenuItem insertItem = new JRadioButtonMenuItem("Insert");
insertItem.setSelected(true);
JRadioButtonMenuItem overtypeItem = new JRadioButtonMenuItem("Overtype");
group.add(insertItem);
group.add(overtypeItem);
optionsMenu.add(insertItem);
optionsMenu.add(overtypeItem);
```

With these menu items, you don't necessarily want to be notified at the exact moment the user selects the item. Instead, you can simply use the `isSelected` method to test the current state of the menu item. (Of course, that means that you should keep a reference to the menu item stored in an instance field.) Use the `setSelected` method to set the state.

`javax.swing.JCheckBoxMenuItem` 1.2

- `JCheckBoxMenuItem(String label)`
  constructs the checkbox menu item with the given label.
- `JCheckBoxMenuItem(String label, boolean state)`
  constructs the checkbox menu item with the given label and the given initial state (`true` is checked).

`javax.swing.JRadioButtonMenuItem` 1.2

- `JRadioButtonMenuItem(String label)`
  constructs the radio button menu item with the given label.
- `JRadioButtonMenuItem(String label, boolean state)`
  constructs the radio button menu item with the given label and the given initial state (`true` is checked).

`javax.swing.AbstractButton` 1.2

- `boolean isSelected()`
  returns the check state of this item (`true` is checked).
- `void setSelected(boolean state)`
  sets the check state of this item.

Pop-Up Menus

A *pop-up menu* is a menu that is not attached to a menu bar but that floats somewhere (see Figure 9–24).

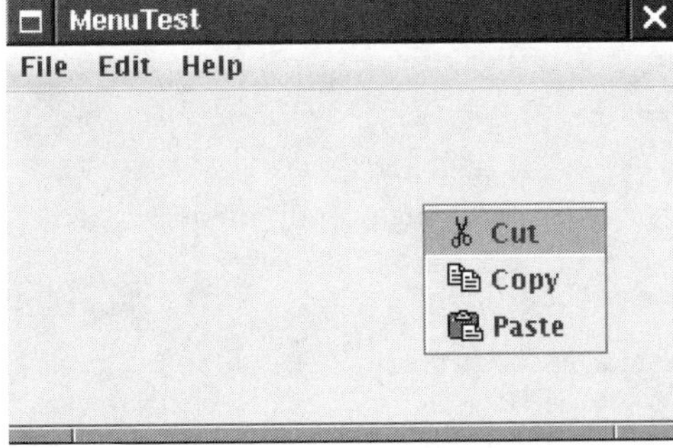

Figure 9–24: A pop-up menu

You create a pop-up menu similarly to the way you create a regular menu, but a pop-up menu has no title.

```
JPopupMenu popup = new JPopupMenu();
```

You then add menu items in the usual way:

```
JMenuItem item = new JMenuItem("Cut");
item.addActionListener(listener);
popup.add(item);
```

Unlike the regular menu bar that is always shown at the top of the frame, you must explicitly display a pop-up menu by using the `show` method. You specify the parent component and the location of the pop-up, using the coordinate system of the parent. For example:

```
popup.show(panel, x, y);
```

Usually you write code to pop up a menu when the user clicks a particular mouse button, the so-called *pop-up trigger.* In Windows and Linux, the pop-up trigger is the nonprimary (usually, the right) mouse button. To pop up a menu when the user clicks on a component, using the pop-up trigger, simply call the method

```
component.setComponentPopupMenu(popup);
```

Very occasionally, you may place a component inside another component that has a pop-up menu. The child component can inherit the parent component's pop-up menu by calling

```
child.setInheritsPopupMenu(true);
```

These methods were added in JDK 5.0 to insulate programmers from system dependencies with pop-up menus. Before JDK 5.0, you had to install a mouse listener and add the following code to *both* the `mousePressed` and the `mouseReleased` listener methods:

```
if (popup.isPopupTrigger(event))
   popup.show(event.getComponent(), event.getX(), event.getY());
```

Some systems trigger pop-ups when the mouse button goes down, others when the mouse button goes up.

javax.swing.JPopupMenu 1.2

- `void show(Component c, int x, int y)`
  shows the pop-up menu.

Parameters:	`c`	The component over which the pop-up menu is to appear
	`x, y`	The coordinates (in the coordinate space of `c`) of the top-left corner of the pop-up menu

- `boolean isPopupTrigger(MouseEvent event)` 1.3
  returns `true` if the mouse event is the pop-up menu trigger.

java.awt.event.MouseEvent 1.1

- `boolean isPopupTrigger()`
  returns `true` if this mouse event is the pop-up menu trigger.

API

javax.swing.JComponent 1.2

- `void setComponentPopupMenu(JPopupMenu popup)` 5.0
- `JPopup getComponentPopupMenu()` 5.0
  set or get the pop-up menu for this component.

- `void setInheritsPopupMenu(boolean b)` **5.0**
- `boolean getInheritsPopupMenu()` **5.0**

  set or get the `inheritsPopupMenu` property. If the property is set and this component's pop-up menu is `null`, it uses its parent's pop-up menu.

Keyboard Mnemonics and Accelerators

It is a real convenience for the experienced user to select menu items by *keyboard mnemonics.* You can specify keyboard mnemonics for menu items by specifying a mnemonic letter in the menu item constructor:

```
JMenuItem cutItem = new JMenuItem("Cut", 'T');
```

The keyboard mnemonic is displayed automatically in the menu, with the mnemonic letter underlined (see Figure 9–25). For example, in the item defined in the last example, the label will be displayed as "Cut" with an underlined letter 't'. When the menu is displayed, the user just needs to press the T key, and the menu item is selected. (If the mnemonic letter is not part of the menu string, then typing it still selects the item, but the mnemonic is not displayed in the menu. Naturally, such invisible mnemonics are of dubious utility.)

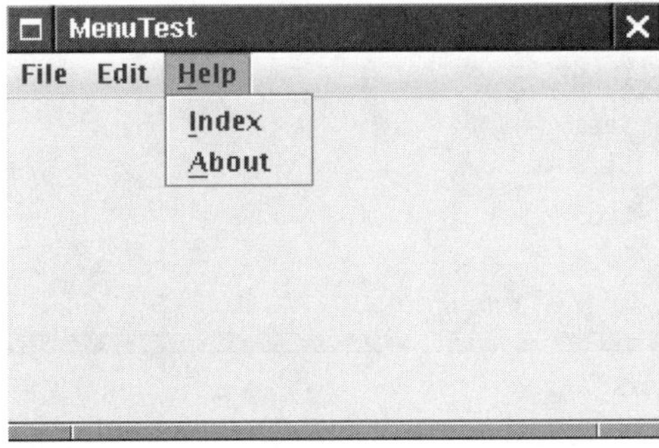

Figure 9–25: Keyboard mnemonics

Sometimes, you don't want to underline the first letter of the menu item that matches the mnemonic. For example, if you have a mnemonic "A" for the menu item "Save As," then it makes more sense to underline the second "A" (Save As). As of JDK 1.4, you can specify which character you want to have underlined; call the `setDisplayedMnemonicIndex` method.

If you have an `Action` object, you can add the mnemonic as the value of the `Action.MNEMONIC_KEY` key, as follows:

```
cutAction.putValue(Action.MNEMONIC_KEY, new Integer('T'));
```

You can supply a mnemonic letter only in the constructor of a menu item, not in the constructor for a menu. Instead, to attach a mnemonic to a menu, you call the `setMnemonic` method:

```
JMenu helpMenu = new JMenu("Help");
helpMenu.setMnemonic('H');
```

To select a top-level menu from the menu bar, you press the ALT key together with the mnemonic letter. For example, you press ALT+H to select the Help menu from the menu bar.

Keyboard mnemonics let you select a submenu or menu item from the currently open menu. In contrast, *accelerators* are keyboard shortcuts that let you select menu items without ever opening a menu. For example, many programs attach the accelerators CTRL+O and

CTRL+S to the Open and Save items in the File menu. You use the `setAccelerator` method to attach an accelerator key to a menu item. The `setAccelerator` method takes an object of type `Keystroke`. For example, the following call attaches the accelerator CTRL+O to the `openItem` menu item.

```
openItem.setAccelerator(KeyStroke.getKeyStroke(KeyEvent.VK_O, InputEvent.CTRL_MASK));
```

When the user presses the accelerator key combination, this automatically selects the menu option and fires an action event, as if the user had selected the menu option manually.

You can attach accelerators only to menu items, not to menus. Accelerator keys don't actually open the menu. Instead, they directly fire the action event that is associated with a menu.

Conceptually, adding an accelerator to a menu item is similar to the technique of adding an accelerator to a Swing component. (We discussed that technique in Chapter 8.) However, when the accelerator is added to a menu item, the key combination is automatically displayed in the menu (see Figure 9–26).

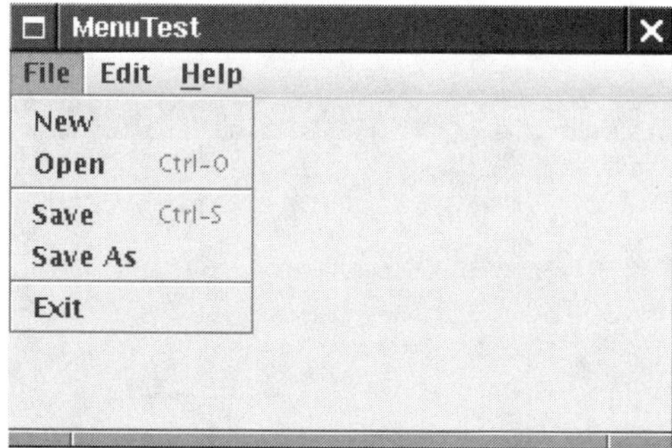

Figure 9–26: Accelerators

NOTE: Under Windows, ALT+F4 closes a window. But this is not an accelerator that was programmed in Java. It is a shortcut defined by the operating system. This key combination will always trigger the `WindowClosing` event for the active window regardless of whether there is a Close item on the menu.

`javax.swing.JMenuItem` 1.2

- `JMenuItem(String label, int mnemonic)`
  constructs a menu item with a given label and mnemonic.

  Parameters:

`label`	The label for this menu item
`mnemonic`	The mnemonic character for the item; this character will be underlined in the label

- `void setAccelerator(KeyStroke k)`
  sets the keystroke `k` as accelerator for this menu item. The accelerator key is displayed next to the label.

`javax.swing.AbstractButton` 1.2

- `void setMnemonic(int mnemonic)`
  sets the mnemonic character for the button. This character will be underlined in the label.

Parameters: `mnemonic` The mnemonic character for the button

- `void setDisplayedMnemonicIndex(int index)` **1.4**
  sets the index of the character to be underlined in the button text. Use this method if you don't want the first occurrence of the mnemonic character to be underlined.

  Parameters: `index` The index of the button text character to be underlined

Enabling and Disabling Menu Items

Occasionally, a particular menu item should be selected only in certain contexts. For example, when a document is opened for reading only, then the Save menu item is not meaningful. Of course, we could remove the item from the menu with the `JMenu.remove` method, but users would react with some surprise to menus whose content keeps changing. Instead, it is better to deactivate the menu items that lead to temporarily inappropriate commands. A deactivated menu item is shown in gray, and it cannot be selected (see Figure 9–27).

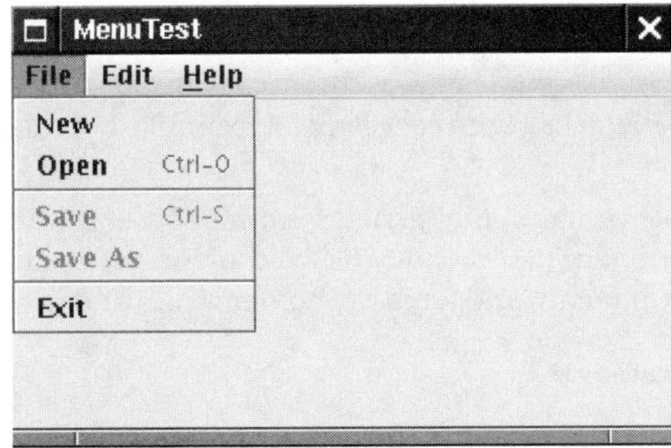

Figure 9–27: Disabled menu items

To enable or disable a menu item, use the `setEnabled` method:

```
saveItem.setEnabled(false);
```

There are two strategies for enabling and disabling menu items. Each time circumstances change, you can call `setEnabled` on the relevant menu items or actions. For example, as soon as a document has been set to read-only mode, you can locate the Save and Save As menu items and disable them. Alternatively, you can disable items just before displaying the menu. To do this, you must register a listener for the "menu selected" event. The `javax.swing.event` package defines a `MenuListener` interface with three methods:

```
void menuSelected(MenuEvent event)
void menuDeselected(MenuEvent event)
void menuCanceled(MenuEvent event)
```

The `menuSelected` method is called *before* the menu is displayed. It can therefore be used to disable or enable menu items. The following code shows how to disable the Save and Save As actions whenever the Read Only checkbox menu item is selected:

```
public void menuSelected(MenuEvent event)
{
   saveAction.setEnabled(!readonlyItem.isSelected());
   saveAsAction.setEnabled(!readonlyItem.isSelected());
}
```

CAUTION: Disabling menu items just before displaying the menu is a clever idea, but it does not work for menu items that also have accelerator keys. Because the menu is never opened when the accelerator key is pressed, the action is never disabled, and it is still triggered by the accelerator key.

javax.swing.JMenuItem 1.2

- `void setEnabled(boolean b)`
  enables or disables the menu item.

javax.swing.event.MenuListener 1.2

- `void menuSelected(MenuEvent e)`
  is called when the menu has been selected, before it is opened.
- `void menuDeselected(MenuEvent e)`
  is called when the menu has been deselected, after it has been closed.
- `void menuCanceled(MenuEvent e)`
  is called when the menu has been canceled, for example, by a user clicking outside the menu.

Example 9–11 is a sample program that generates a set of menus. It shows all the features that you saw in this section: nested menus, disabled menu items, checkbox and radio button menu items, a pop-up menu, and keyboard mnemonics and accelerators.

Example 9–11: MenuTest.java

```
import java.awt.*;
import java.awt.event.*;
import javax.swing.*;
import javax.swing.event.*;

public class MenuTest
{
   public static void main(String[] args)
   {
      MenuFrame frame = new MenuFrame();
      frame.setDefaultCloseOperation(JFrame.EXIT_ON_CLOSE);
      frame.setVisible(true);
   }
}

/**
   A frame with a sample menu bar.
*/
class MenuFrame extends JFrame
{
   public MenuFrame()
   {
      setTitle("MenuTest");
      setSize(DEFAULT_WIDTH, DEFAULT_HEIGHT);

      JMenu fileMenu = new JMenu("File");
      JMenuItem newItem = fileMenu.add(new TestAction("New"));
```

```
      // demonstrate accelerators

      JMenuItem openItem = fileMenu.add(new TestAction("Open"));
      openItem.setAccelerator(KeyStroke.getKeyStroke(KeyEvent.VK_O, InputEvent.CTRL_MASK));

      fileMenu.addSeparator();

      saveAction = new TestAction("Save");
      JMenuItem saveItem = fileMenu.add(saveAction);
      saveItem.setAccelerator(KeyStroke.getKeyStroke(KeyEvent.VK_S, InputEvent.CTRL_MASK));

      saveAsAction = new TestAction("Save As");
      JMenuItem saveAsItem = fileMenu.add(saveAsAction);
      fileMenu.addSeparator();

      fileMenu.add(new
         AbstractAction("Exit")
         {
            public void actionPerformed(ActionEvent event)
            {
               System.exit(0);
            }
         });

      // demonstrate checkbox and radio button menus

      readonlyItem = new JCheckBoxMenuItem("Read-only");
      readonlyItem.addActionListener(new
         ActionListener()
         {
            public void actionPerformed(ActionEvent event)
            {
               boolean saveOk = !readonlyItem.isSelected();
               saveAction.setEnabled(saveOk);
               saveAsAction.setEnabled(saveOk);
            }
         });

      ButtonGroup group = new ButtonGroup();

      JRadioButtonMenuItem insertItem = new JRadioButtonMenuItem("Insert");
      insertItem.setSelected(true);
      JRadioButtonMenuItem overtypeItem = new JRadioButtonMenuItem("Overtype");

      group.add(insertItem);
      group.add(overtypeItem);

      // demonstrate icons

      Action cutAction = new TestAction("Cut");
      cutAction.putValue(Action.SMALL_ICON, new ImageIcon("cut.gif"));
      Action copyAction = new TestAction("Copy");
      copyAction.putValue(Action.SMALL_ICON, new ImageIcon("copy.gif"));
```

```
        Action pasteAction = new TestAction("Paste");
        pasteAction.putValue(Action.SMALL_ICON, new ImageIcon("paste.gif"));

        JMenu editMenu = new JMenu("Edit");
        editMenu.add(cutAction);
        editMenu.add(copyAction);
        editMenu.add(pasteAction);

        // demonstrate nested menus

        JMenu optionMenu = new JMenu("Options");

        optionMenu.add(readonlyItem);
        optionMenu.addSeparator();
        optionMenu.add(insertItem);
        optionMenu.add(overtypeItem);

        editMenu.addSeparator();
        editMenu.add(optionMenu);

        // demonstrate mnemonics

        JMenu helpMenu = new JMenu("Help");
        helpMenu.setMnemonic('H');

        JMenuItem indexItem = new JMenuItem("Index");
        indexItem.setMnemonic('I');
        helpMenu.add(indexItem);

        // you can also add the mnemonic key to an action
        Action aboutAction = new TestAction("About");
        aboutAction.putValue(Action.MNEMONIC_KEY, new Integer('A'));
        helpMenu.add(aboutAction);

        // add all top-level menus to menu bar

        JMenuBar menuBar = new JMenuBar();
        setJMenuBar(menuBar);

        menuBar.add(fileMenu);
        menuBar.add(editMenu);
        menuBar.add(helpMenu);

        // demonstrate pop-ups

        popup = new JPopupMenu();
        popup.add(cutAction);
        popup.add(copyAction);
        popup.add(pasteAction);

        JPanel panel = new JPanel();
        panel.setComponentPopupMenu(popup);
        add(panel);

```

```
      // the following line is a workaround for bug 4966109
      panel.addMouseListener(new MouseAdapter() {});
   }

   public static final int DEFAULT_WIDTH = 300;
   public static final int DEFAULT_HEIGHT = 200;

   private Action saveAction;
   private Action saveAsAction;
   private JCheckBoxMenuItem readonlyItem;
   private JPopupMenu popup;
}

/**
   A sample action that prints the action name to System.out
*/
class TestAction extends AbstractAction
{
   public TestAction(String name) { super(name); }

   public void actionPerformed(ActionEvent event)
   {
      System.out.println(getValue(Action.NAME) + " selected.");
   }
}
```

Toolbars

A toolbar is a button bar that gives quick access to the most commonly used commands in a program (see Figure 9–28).

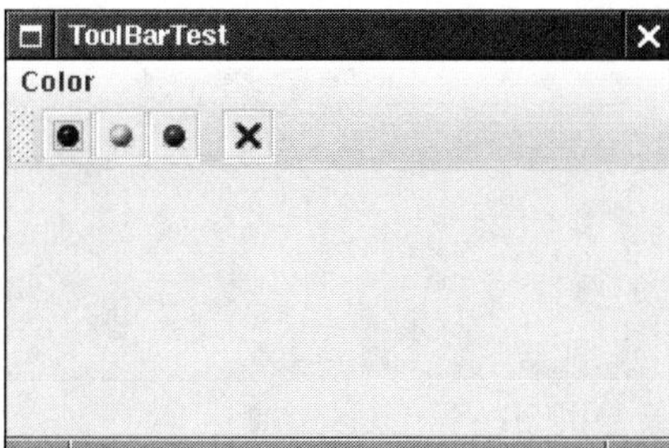

Figure 9–28: A toolbar

What makes toolbars special is that you can move them elsewhere. You can drag the toolbar to one of the four borders of the frame (see Figure 9–29). When you release the mouse button, the toolbar is dropped into the new location (see Figure 9–30).

NOTE: Toolbar dragging works if the toolbar is inside a container with a border layout, or any other layout manager that supports the `North`, `East`, `South`, and `West` constraints.

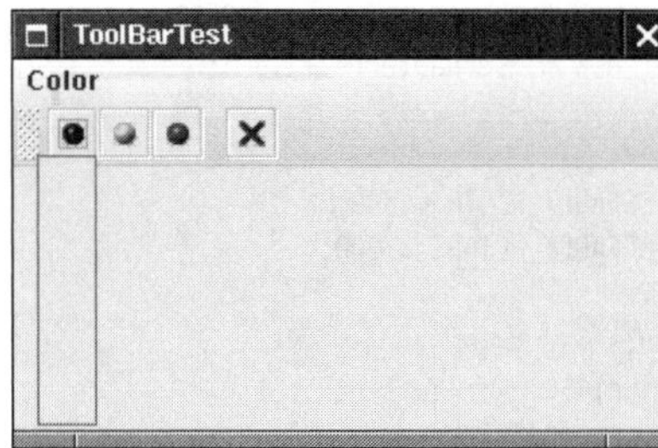

Figure 9–29: Dragging the toolbar

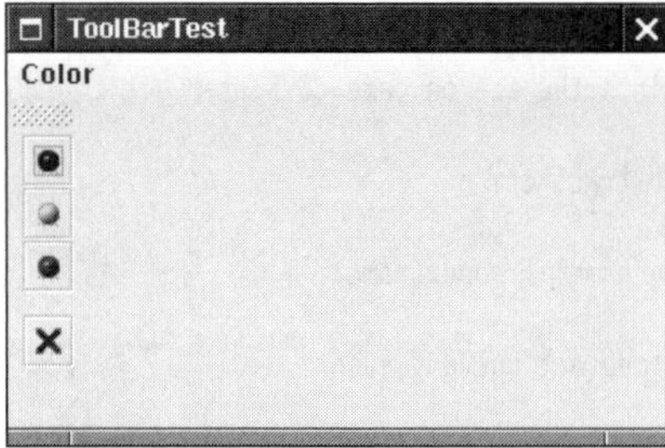

Figure 9–30: Dragging the toolbar to another border

The toolbar can even be completely detached from the frame. A detached toolbar is contained in its own frame (see Figure 9–31). When you close the frame containing a detached toolbar, the toolbar jumps back into the original frame.

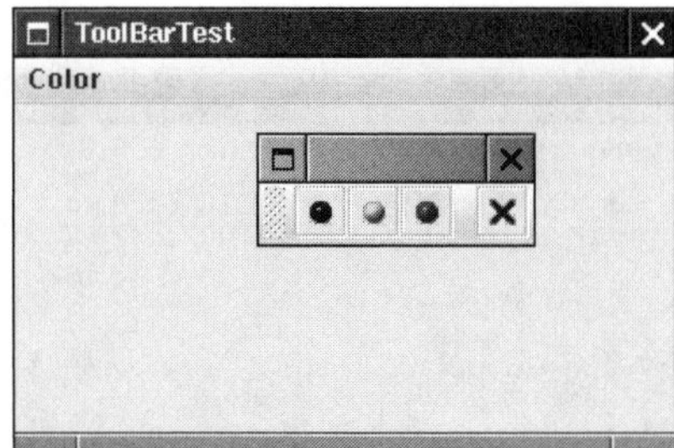

Figure 9–31: Detaching the toolbar

Toolbars are straightforward to program. You add components into the toolbar:

```
JToolBar bar = new JToolBar();
bar.add(blueButton);
```

The `JToolBar` class also has a method to add an `Action` object. Simply populate the toolbar with `Action` objects, like this:

```
bar.add(blueAction);
```

The small icon of the action is displayed in the toolbar.

You can separate groups of buttons with a separator:

```
bar.addSeparator();
```

For example, the toolbar in Figure 9–28 has a separator between the third and fourth button.

Then, you add the toolbar to the frame.

```
add(bar, BorderLayout.NORTH);
```

You can also specify a title for the toolbar that appears when the toolbar is undocked:

```
bar = new JToolBar(titleString);
```

By default, toolbars are initially horizontal. To have a toolbar start out as vertical, use

```
bar = new JToolBar(SwingConstants.VERTICAL)
```

or

```
bar = new JToolBar(titleString, SwingConstants.VERTICAL)
```

Buttons are the most common components inside toolbars. But there is no restriction on the components that you can add to a toolbar. For example, you can add a combo box to a toolbar.

TIP: You can find nice toolbar buttons at `http://developer.java.sun.com/developer/techDocs/hi/repository`.

Tooltips

A disadvantage of toolbars is that users are often mystified by the meanings of the tiny icons in toolbars. To solve this problem, user interface designers invented *tooltips*. A tooltip is activated when the cursor rests for a moment over a button. The tooltip text is displayed inside a colored rectangle. When the user moves the mouse away, the tooltip is removed. (See Figure 9–32.)

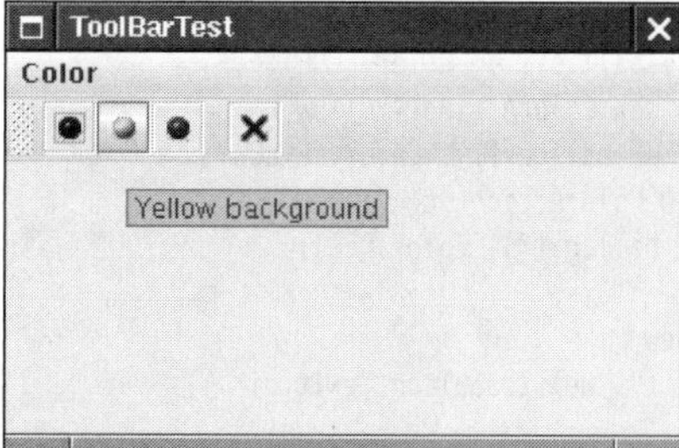

Figure 9–32: A tooltip

In Swing, you can add tooltips to any `JComponent` simply by calling the `setToolTipText` method:

```
exitButton.setToolTipText("Exit");
```

Alternatively, if you use `Action` objects, you associate the tooltip with the `SHORT_DESCRIPTION` key:

```
exitAction.putValue(Action.SHORT_DESCRIPTION, "Exit");
```

Example 9–12 shows how the same `Action` objects can be added to a menu and a toolbar. Note that the action names show up as the menu item names in the menu, and the short descriptions as the tooltips in the toolbar.

Example 9–12: ToolBarTest.java

```
import java.awt.*;
import java.awt.event.*;
import java.beans.*;
import javax.swing.*;
```

```
public class ToolBarTest
{
   public static void main(String[] args)
   {
      ToolBarFrame frame = new ToolBarFrame();
      frame.setDefaultCloseOperation(JFrame.EXIT_ON_CLOSE);
      frame.setVisible(true);
   }
}

/**
   A frame with a toolbar and menu for color changes.
*/
class ToolBarFrame extends JFrame
{
   public ToolBarFrame()
   {
      setTitle("ToolBarTest");
      setSize(DEFAULT_WIDTH, DEFAULT_HEIGHT);

      // add a panel for color change

      panel = new JPanel();

      // set up actions

      Action blueAction = new ColorAction("Blue",
         new ImageIcon("blue-ball.gif"), Color.BLUE);
      Action yellowAction = new ColorAction("Yellow",
         new ImageIcon("yellow-ball.gif"), Color.YELLOW);
      Action redAction = new ColorAction("Red",
         new ImageIcon("red-ball.gif"), Color.RED);

      Action exitAction = new
         AbstractAction("Exit", new ImageIcon("exit.gif"))
         {
            public void actionPerformed(ActionEvent event)
            {
               System.exit(0);
            }
         };
      exitAction.putValue(Action.SHORT_DESCRIPTION, "Exit");

      // populate toolbar

      JToolBar bar = new JToolBar();
      bar.add(blueAction);
      bar.add(yellowAction);
      bar.add(redAction);
      bar.addSeparator();
      bar.add(exitAction);
      add(bar, BorderLayout.NORTH);

```

```
      // populate menu

      JMenu menu = new JMenu("Color");
      menu.add(yellowAction);
      menu.add(blueAction);
      menu.add(redAction);
      menu.add(exitAction);
      JMenuBar menuBar = new JMenuBar();
      menuBar.add(menu);
      setJMenuBar(menuBar);
   }

   public static final int DEFAULT_WIDTH = 300;
   public static final int DEFAULT_HEIGHT = 200;

   private JPanel panel;

   /**
      The color action sets the background of the frame to a
      given color.
   */
   class ColorAction extends AbstractAction
   {
      public ColorAction(String name, Icon icon, Color c)
      {
         putValue(Action.NAME, name);
         putValue(Action.SMALL_ICON, icon);
         putValue(Action.SHORT_DESCRIPTION, name + " background");
         putValue("Color", c);
      }

      public void actionPerformed(ActionEvent event)
      {
         Color c = (Color) getValue("Color");
         panel.setBackground(c);
      }
   }
}
```

API **javax.swing.JToolBar 1.2**

- `JToolBar()`
- `JToolBar(String titleString)`
- `JToolBar(int orientation)`
- `JToolBar(String titleString, int orientation)`
  construct a toolbar with the given title string and orientation. `orientation` is one of `SwingConstants.HORIZONTAL` (the default) and `SwingConstants.VERTICAL`.
- `JButton add(Action a)`
  constructs a new button inside the toolbar with name, icon, short description, and action callback from the given action, and adds the button to the end of the toolbar.
- `void addSeparator()`
  adds a separator to the end of the toolbar.

javax.swing.JComponent 1.2

- `void setToolTipText(String text)`
  sets the text that should be displayed as a tooltip when the mouse hovers over the component.

Sophisticated Layout Management

We have managed to lay out the user interface components of our sample applications so far by using only the border layout, flow layout, and grid layout. For more complex tasks, this is not going to be enough. In this section, we give you a detailed discussion of the advanced layout managers that the standard Java library provides to organize components.

Windows programmers may well wonder why Java makes so much fuss about layout managers. After all, in Windows, layout management is not a big deal: First, you use a dialog editor to drag and drop your components onto the surface of the dialog, and then you use editor tools to line up components, to space them equally, to center them, and so on. If you are working on a big project, you probably don't have to worry about component layout at all—a skilled user interface designer does all this for you.

The problem with this approach is that the resulting layout must be manually updated if the size of the components changes. Why would the component size change? There are two common cases. First, a user may choose a larger font for button labels and other dialog text. If you try this out for yourself in Windows, you will find that many applications deal with this exceedingly poorly. The buttons do not grow, and the larger font is simply crammed into the same space as before. The same problem can occur when the strings in an application are translated to a foreign language. For example, the German word for "Cancel" is "Abbrechen." If a button has been designed with just enough room for the string "Cancel", then the German version will look broken, with a clipped command string.

Why don't Windows buttons simply grow to accommodate the labels? Because the designer of the user interface gave no instructions in which direction they should grow. After the dragging and dropping and arranging, the dialog editor merely remembers the pixel position and size of each component. It does not remember *why* the components were arranged in this fashion.

The Java layout managers are a much better approach to component layout. With a layout manager, the layout comes with instructions about the relationships among the components. This was particularly important in the original AWT, which used native user interface elements. The size of a button or list box in Motif, Windows, and the Macintosh could vary widely, and an application or applet would not know *a priori* on which platform it would display its user interface. To some extent, that degree of variability has gone away with Swing. If your application forces a particular look and feel, such as the Metal look and feel, then it looks identical on all platforms. However, if you let users of your application choose their favorite look and feel, then you again need to rely on the flexibility of layout managers to arrange the components.

Of course, to achieve complex layouts, you will need to have more control over the layout than the border layout, flow layout, and grid layout give you. In this section, we discuss the layout managers that the standard Java library has to offer. Using a sophisticated layout manager combined with the appropriate use of multiple panels will give you complete control over how your application will look.

TIP: If none of the layout schemes fit your needs, break the surface of your window into separate panels and lay out each panel separately. Then, use another layout manager to organize the panels.

First, let's review a few basic principles. As you know, in the AWT, *components* are laid out inside *containers*. Buttons, text fields, and other user interface elements are components and can be placed inside containers. Therefore, these classes extend the class `Component`. Containers such as panels can themselves be put inside other containers. Therefore, the class `Container` derives from `Component`. Figure 9–33 shows the inheritance hierarchy for `Component`.

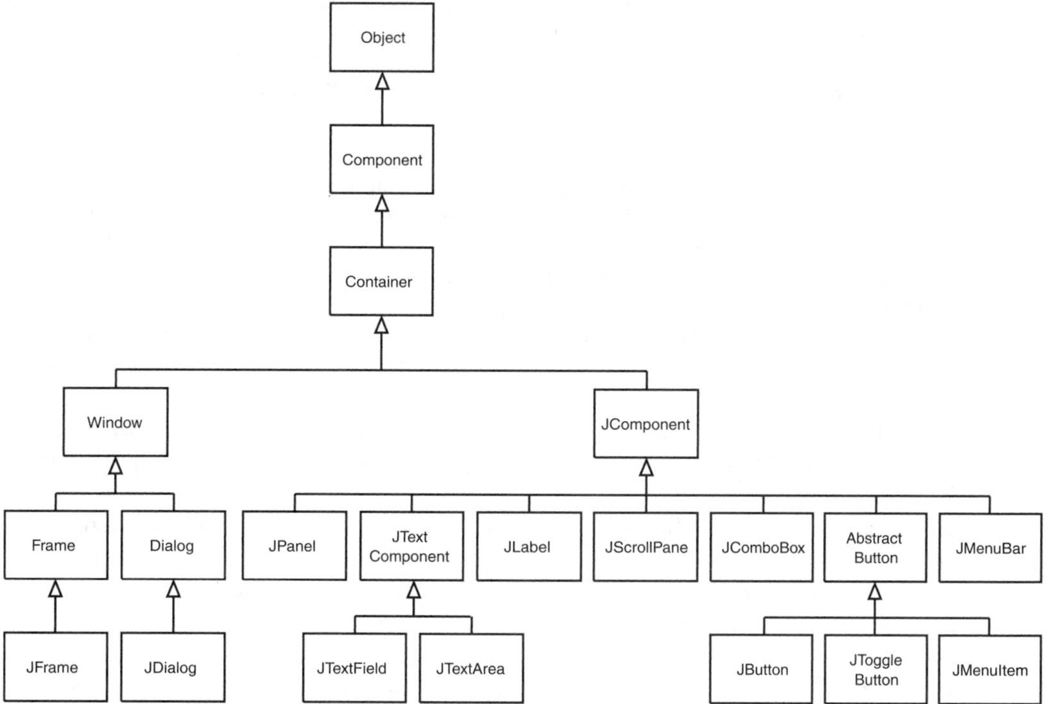

Figure 9–33: Inheritance hierarchy for the `Component` class

NOTE: Some objects belong to classes extending `Component` even though they are not user interface components and cannot be inserted into containers. Top-level windows such as `JFrame` and `JApplet` cannot be contained inside another window or panel.

As you have seen, to organize the components in a container, you first specify a layout manager. For example, the statement

```
panel.setLayout(new GridLayout(4, 4));
```

will use the `GridLayout` class to lay out the panels. After you set the layout manager, you add components to the container. The `add` method of the container passes the component and any placement directions to the layout manager.

With the border layout manager, you give a string to specify component placement:

```
panel.add(new JTextField(), BorderLayout.SOUTH);
```

With the grid layout, you need to add components sequentially:

```
panel.add(new JCheckBox("italic"));
panel.add(new JCheckBox("bold"));
```

The grid layout is useful for arranging components in a grid, somewhat like the rows and columns of a spreadsheet. However, all rows and columns of the grid have *identical* size, which is not all that useful in practice.

To overcome the limitations of the grid layout, the AWT supplies the *grid bag layout*. It, too, lays out components in rows and columns, but the row and column sizes are flexible and components can span multiple rows and columns. This layout manager is very flexible, but it is also very complex. The mere mention of the words "grid bag layout" has been known to strike fear in the hearts of Java programmers. Actually, in most common situations, the grid bag layout is not that hard to use, and we tell you a strategy that should make grid bag layouts relatively painless.

In an (unsuccessful) attempt to design a layout manager that would free programmers from the tyranny of the grid bag layout, the Swing designers came up with the *box layout*. The box layout simply arranges a sequence of components horizontally or vertically. When arranging components horizontally, the box layout is similar to the flow layout; however, components do not "wrap" to a new row when one row is full. By placing a number of horizontal box layouts inside a vertical box layout (or the other way around), you can give some order to a set of components in a two-dimensional area. However, because each box is laid out independently, you cannot use box layouts to arrange neighboring components both horizontally and vertically.

JDK 1.4 saw yet another attempt to design a replacement for the grid bag layout—the *spring layout*. We discuss the spring layout on page 440, and we leave it to you to decide whether it succeeds in its goal.

Swing also contains an *overlay layout* that lets you place components on top of each other. This layout manager is not generally useful, and we don't discuss it.

Finally, there is a *card layout* that was used in the original AWT to produce tabbed dialogs. Because Swing has a much better tabbed dialog container (called `JTabbedPane`—see Volume 2), we do not cover the card layout here.

We end the discussion of layout managers by showing you how you can bypass layout management altogether and place components manually and by showing you how you can write your own layout manager.

Box Layout

The box layout lets you lay out a single row or column of components with more flexibility than the grid layout affords. There is even a container—the `Box` class—whose default layout manager is the `BoxLayout` (unlike the `JPanel` class whose default layout manager is the `FlowLayout`). Of course, you can also set the layout manager of a `JPanel` to the box layout, but it is simpler to just start with a `Box` container. The `Box` class also contains a number of static methods that are useful for managing box layouts.

To create a new container with a box layout, you can simply call

```
Box b = Box.createHorizontalBox();
```

or

```
Box b = Box.createVerticalBox();
```

You then add components in the usual way:

```
b.add(okButton);
b.add(cancelButton);
```

In a horizontal box, the components are arranged left to right. In a vertical box, the components are arranged top to bottom. Let us look at the horizontal layout more closely.

Each component has three sizes:

- The *preferred size*—the width and height at which the component would like to be displayed
- The *maximum size*—the largest width and height at which the component is willing to be displayed
- The *minimum size*—the smallest width and height at which the component is willing to be displayed

Here are details about what the box layout manager does:

1. It computes the maximum (!) height of the tallest component.
2. It tries to grow all components vertically to that height.
3. If a component does not actually grow to that height when requested, then its *y*-alignment is queried by a call to its `getAlignmentY` method. That method returns a floating-point number between 0 (align on top) and 1 (align on bottom). The default in the `Component` class is 0.5 (center). The value is used to align the component vertically.
4. The preferred width of each component is obtained. All preferred widths are added up.
5. If the total preferred width is less than the box width, then the components are expanded by being allowed to grow to their maximum width. Components are then placed, from left to right, with no additional space between them. If the total preferred width is greater than the box width, the components are shrunk, potentially down to their minimum width but no further. If the components don't all fit at their minimum width, some of them will not be shown.

For vertical layouts, the process is analogous.

TIP: It is unfortunate that `BoxLayout` tries to grow components beyond the preferred size. In particular, text fields have maximum width and height set to `Integer.MAX_VALUE`; that is, they are willing to grow as much as necessary. If you put a text field into a box layout, it will grow to monstrous proportions. Remedy: set the maximum size to the preferred size with

```
textField.setMaximumSize(textField.getPreferredSize());
```

Fillers

By default, there is no space between the components in a box layout. (Unlike the flow layout, the box layout does not have a notion of gaps between components.) To space the components out, you add invisible *fillers*. There are three kinds of fillers:

- Struts
- Rigid areas
- Glue

A strut simply adds some space between components. For example, here is how you can add 10 pixels of space between two components in a horizontal box:

```
b.add(label);
b.add(Box.createHorizontalStrut(10));
b.add(textField);
```

You add a horizontal strut into a horizontal box, or a vertical strut into a vertical box, to add space between components. You can also add a vertical strut into a horizontal box, but that does not affect the horizontal layout. Instead, it sets the minimum height of the box.

The rigid area filler is similar to a pair of struts. It separates adjacent components but also adds a height or width minimum in the other direction. For example,

```
b.add(Box.createRigidArea(new Dimension(5, 20));
```

adds an invisible area with minimum, preferred, and maximum width of 5 pixels and height of 20 pixels, and centered alignment. If added into a horizontal box, it acts like a strut of width 5 and also forces the minimum height of the box to be 20 pixels.

By adding struts, you separate adjacent components by a fixed amount. Adding glue separates components *as much as possible*. The (invisible) glue expands to consume all available empty space, pushing the components away from each other. (We don't know why the designers of the box layout came up with the name "glue"—"spring" would have been a more appropriate name.)

For example, here is how you space two buttons in a box as far apart as possible:

```
b.add(button1);
b.add(Box.createGlue());
b.add(button2);
```

If the box contains no other components, then `button1` is moved all the way to the left and `button2` is moved all the way to the right.

The program in Example 9–13 arranges a set of labels, text fields, and buttons, using a set of horizontal and vertical box layouts. Each row is placed in a horizontal box. Struts separate the labels from the text fields. Glue pushes the two buttons away from each other. The three horizontal boxes are placed in a vertical box, with glue pushing the button box to the bottom (see Figure 9–34).

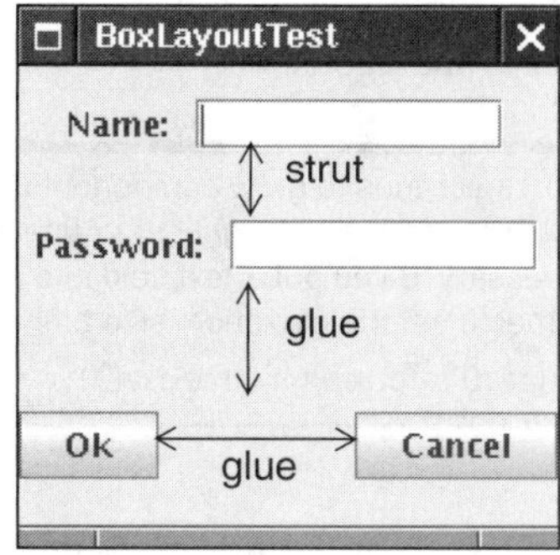

Figure 9–34: Box layouts

Example 9–13: BoxLayoutTest.java

```
import java.awt.*;
import java.awt.event.*;
import javax.swing.*;

public class BoxLayoutTest
{
   public static void main(String[] args)
   {
      BoxLayoutFrame frame = new BoxLayoutFrame();
```

```
      frame.setDefaultCloseOperation(JFrame.EXIT_ON_CLOSE);
      frame.setVisible(true);
   }
}

/**
   A frame that uses box layouts to organize various components.
*/
class BoxLayoutFrame extends JFrame
{
   public BoxLayoutFrame()
   {
      setTitle("BoxLayoutTest");
      setSize(DEFAULT_WIDTH, DEFAULT_HEIGHT);

      // construct the top horizontal box

      JLabel label1 = new JLabel("Name:");
      JTextField textField1 = new JTextField(10);
      textField1.setMaximumSize(textField1.getPreferredSize());

      Box hbox1 = Box.createHorizontalBox();
      hbox1.add(label1);
      // separate with a 10-pixel strut
      hbox1.add(Box.createHorizontalStrut(10));
      hbox1.add(textField1);

      // construct the middle horizontal box

      JLabel label2 = new JLabel("Password:");
      JTextField textField2 = new JTextField(10);
      textField2.setMaximumSize(textField2.getPreferredSize());


      Box hbox2 = Box.createHorizontalBox();
      hbox2.add(label2);
      // separate with a 10-pixel strut
      hbox2.add(Box.createHorizontalStrut(10));
      hbox2.add(textField2);

      // construct the bottom horizontal box

      JButton button1 = new JButton("Ok");
      JButton button2 = new JButton("Cancel");

      Box hbox3 = Box.createHorizontalBox();
      hbox3.add(button1);
      // use "glue" to push the two buttons apart
      hbox3.add(Box.createGlue());
      hbox3.add(button2);

      // add the three horizontal boxes inside a vertical box

      Box vbox = Box.createVerticalBox();
      vbox.add(hbox1);
      vbox.add(hbox2);
```

```
        vbox.add(Box.createGlue());
        vbox.add(hbox3);

        add(vbox, BorderLayout.CENTER);
    }

    public static final int DEFAULT_WIDTH = 200;
    public static final int DEFAULT_HEIGHT = 200;
}
```

javax.swing.Box 1.2

- `static Box createHorizontalBox()`
- `static Box createVerticalBox()`

  create a container that arranges its content horizontally or vertically.
- `static Component createHorizontalGlue()`
- `static Component createVerticalGlue()`
- `static Component createGlue()`

  create an invisible component that can expand infinitely horizontally, vertically, or in both directions.
- `static Component createHorizontalStrut(int width)`
- `static Component createVerticalStrut(int height)`
- `static Component createRigidArea(Dimension d)`

  create an invisible component with fixed width, fixed height, or fixed width and height.

java.awt.Component 1.0

- `float getAlignmentX()` 1.1
- `float getAlignmentY()` 1.1

  return the alignment along the *x*- or *y*-axis, a value between 0 and 1. The value 0 denotes alignment on top or left, 0.5 is centered, 1 is aligned on bottom or right.

The Grid Bag Layout

The grid bag layout is the mother of all layout managers. You can think of a grid bag layout as a grid layout without the limitations. In a grid bag layout, the rows and columns can have variable sizes. You can join adjacent cells to make room for larger components. (Many word processors, as well as HTML, have the same capability when tables are edited: you start out with a grid and then merge adjacent cells if need be.) The components need not fill the entire cell area, and you can specify their alignment within cells.

Fair warning: using grid bag layouts can be incredibly complex. The payoff is that they have the most flexibility and will work in the widest variety of situations. Keep in mind that the purpose of layout managers is to keep the arrangement of the components reasonable under different font sizes and operating systems, so it is not surprising that you need to work somewhat harder than when you design a layout just for one environment.

NOTE: According to the JDK documentation of the `BoxLayout` class: "Nesting multiple panels with different combinations of horizontal and vertical [*sic*] gives an effect similar to GridBagLayout, without the complexity." However, as you can see from Figure 9–34, the effect that you can achieve from multiple box layouts is plainly not useful in practice. No amount of fussing with boxes, struts, and glue will ensure that the components line up. When you need to arrange components so that they line up horizontally and vertically, you should consider the `GridBagLayout` class.

Consider the font selection dialog of Figure 9–35. It consists of the following components:

- Two combo boxes to specify the font face and size
- Labels for these two combo boxes
- Two check boxes to select bold and italic
- A text area for the sample string

Figure 9–35: Font dialog box

Now, chop up the dialog box into a grid of cells, as shown in Figure 9–36. (The rows and columns need not have equal size.) Each checkbox spans two columns, and the text area spans four rows.

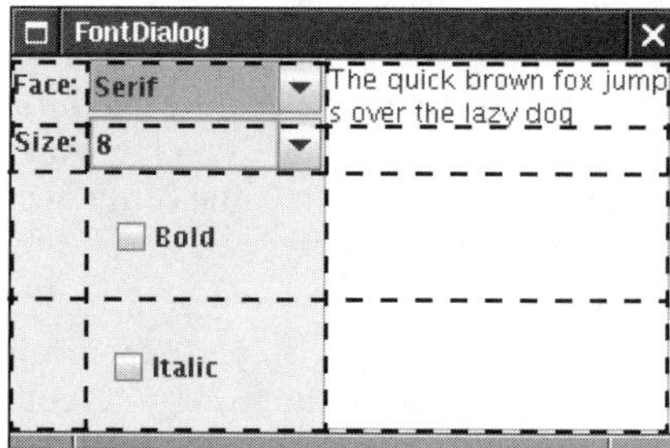

Figure 9–36: Dialog box grid used in design

To describe the layout to the grid bag manager, you must go through the following convoluted procedure.

1. Create an object of type `GridBagLayout`. You don't tell it how many rows and columns the underlying grid has. Instead, the layout manager will try to guess it from the information you give it later.
2. Set this `GridBagLayout` object to be the layout manager for the component.
3. For *each component,* create an object of type `GridBagConstraints`. Set field values of the `GridBagConstraints` object to specify how the components are laid out within the grid bag.
4. Then (finally), add the component with the constraints by using the call:
   ```
   add(component, constraints);
   ```

Here's an example of the code needed. (We go over the various constraints in more detail in the sections that follow—so don't worry if you don't know what some of the constraints do.)

```
GridBagLayout layout = new GridBagLayout();
panel.setLayout(layout);
```

```
GridBagConstraints constraints = new GridBagConstraints();
constraints.weightx = 100;
constraints.weighty = 100;
constraints.gridx = 0;
constraints.gridy = 2;
constraints.gridwidth = 2;
constraints.gridheight = 1;
panel.add(style, bold);
```

The trick is knowing how to set the state of the `GridBagConstraints` object. We go over the most important constraints for using this object in the sections that follow.

The `gridx`, `gridy`, `gridwidth`, and `gridheight` Parameters

These constraints define where the component is located in the grid. The `gridx` and `gridy` values specify the column and row positions of the upper-left corner of the component to be added. The `gridwidth` and `gridheight` values determine how many columns and rows the component occupies.

The grid coordinates start with 0. In particular, `gridx` = 0 and `gridy` = 0 denotes the top-left corner.

For example, the text area in our example has `gridx` = 2, `gridy` = 0 because it starts in column 2 (that is, the third column) of row 0. It has `gridwidth` = 1 and `gridheight` = 4 because it spans one column and four rows.

Weight Fields

You always need to set the *weight* fields (`weightx` and `weighty`) for each area in a grid bag layout. If you set the weight to 0, then the area never grows or shrinks beyond its initial size in that direction. In the grid bag layout for Figure 9–35, we set the `weightx` field of the labels to be 0. This allows the labels to remain a constant width when you resize the window. On the other hand, if you set the weights for all areas to 0, the container will huddle in the center of its allotted area rather than stretching to fill it.

Conceptually, the problem with the weight parameters is that weights are properties of rows and columns, not individual cells. But you need to specify them in terms of cells because the grid bag layout does not expose the rows and columns. The row and column weights are computed as the maxima of the cell weights in each row or column. Thus, if you want a row or column to stay at a fixed size, you need to set the weights of all components in it to zero.

Note that the weights don't actually give the relative sizes of the columns. They tell what proportion of the "slack" space should be allocated to each area if the container exceeds its preferred size. This isn't particularly intuitive. We recommend that you set all weights at 100. Then, run the program and see how the layout looks. Resize the dialog to see how the rows and columns adjust. If you find that a particular row or column should not grow, set the weights of all components in it to zero. You can tinker with other weight values, but it is usually not worth the effort.

The `fill` and `anchor` Parameters

If you don't want a component to stretch out and fill the entire area, you set the `fill` constraint. You have four possibilities for this parameter: the valid values are used in the forms `GridBagConstraints.NONE`, `GridBagConstraints.HORIZONTAL`, `GridBagConstraints.VERTICAL`, and `GridBagConstraints.BOTH`.

If the component does not fill the entire area, you can specify where in the area you want it by setting the `anchor` field. The valid values are `GridBagConstraints.CENTER` (the default), `GridBagConstraints.NORTH`, `GridBagConstraints.NORTHEAST`, `GridBagConstraints.EAST`, and so on.

Padding

You can surround a component with additional blank space by setting the `insets` field of `GridBagConstraints`. Set the `left`, `top`, `right` and `bottom` values of the `Insets` object to the amount of space that you want to have around the component. This is called the *external padding*.

The `ipadx` and `ipady` values set the *internal padding*. These values are added to the minimum width and height of the component. This ensures that the component does not shrink down to its minimum size.

Alternative Method to Specify the `gridx`, `gridy`, `gridwidth`, and `gridheight` Parameters

The AWT documentation recommends that instead of setting the `gridx` and `gridy` values to absolute positions, you set them to the constant `GridBagConstraints.RELATIVE`. Then, add the components to the grid bag layout in a standardized order, going from left to right in the first row, then moving along the next row, and so on.

You still specify the number of rows and columns spanned, by giving the appropriate `gridheight` and `gridwidth` fields. Except, if the component extends to the *last* row or column, you aren't supposed to specify the actual number, but the constant `GridBag-Constraints.REMAINDER`. This tells the layout manager that the component is the last one in its row.

This scheme does seem to work. But it sounds really goofy to hide the actual placement information from the layout manager and hope that it will rediscover it.

All this sounds like a lot of trouble and complexity. But in practice, the strategy in the following recipe makes grid bag layouts relatively trouble-free.

Recipe for Making a Grid Bag Layout

Step 1. Sketch out the component layout on a piece of paper.

Step 2. Find a grid such that the small components are each contained in a cell and the larger components span multiple cells.

Step 3. Label the rows and columns of your grid with 0, 1, 2, 3, . . . You can now read off the `gridx`, `gridy`, `gridwidth`, and `gridheight` values.

Step 4. For each component, ask yourself whether it needs to fill its cell horizontally or vertically. If not, how do you want it aligned? This tells you the `fill` and `anchor` parameters.

Step 5. Set all weights to 100. However, if you want a particular row or column to always stay at its default size, set the `weightx` or `weighty` to 0 in all components that belong to that row or column.

Step 6. Write the code. Carefully double-check your settings for the `GridBagConstraints`. One wrong constraint can ruin your whole layout.

Step 7. Compile, run, and enjoy.

A Helper Class to Tame the Grid Bag Constraints

The most tedious aspect of the grid bag layout is writing the code that sets the constraints. Most programmers write helper functions or a small helper class for this purpose. We present such a class after the complete code for the font dialog example. This class has the following features:

- Its name is short: `GBC` instead of `GridBagConstraints`
- It extends `GridBagConstraints`, so you can use shorter names such as `GBC.EAST` for the constants.
- Use a `GBC` object when adding a component, such as

```
add(component, new GBC(1, 2));
```

- There are two constructors to set the most common parameters: `gridx` and `gridy`, or `gridx`, `gridy`, `gridwidth`, and `gridheight`.

  `add(component, new GBC(1, 2, 1, 4));`

- There are convenient setters for the fields that come in `x/y` pairs:

  `add(component, new GBC(1, 2).setWeight(100, 100));`

- The setter methods return `this`, so you can chain them:

  `add(component, new GBC(1, 2).setAnchor(GBC.EAST).setWeight(100, 100));`

- The `setInsets` methods construct the `Insets` object for you. To get one-pixel insets, simply call

  `add(component, new GBC(1, 2).setAnchor(GBC.EAST).setInsets(1));`

Example 9–14 shows the complete code for the font dialog example. Here is the code that adds the components to the grid bag:

```
add(faceLabel, new GBC(0, 0).setAnchor(GBC.EAST));
add(face, new GBC(1, 0).setFill(GBC.HORIZONTAL).setWeight(100, 0).setInsets(1));
add(sizeLabel, new GBC(0, 1).setAnchor(GBC.EAST));
add(size, new GBC(1, 1).setFill(GBC.HORIZONTAL).setWeight(100, 0).setInsets(1));
add(bold, new GBC(0, 2, 2, 1).setAnchor(GBC.CENTER).setWeight(100, 100));
add(italic, new GBC(0, 3, 2, 1).setAnchor(GBC.CENTER).setWeight(100, 100));
add(sample, new GBC(2, 0, 1, 4).setFill(GBC.BOTH).setWeight(100, 100));
```

Once you understand the grid bag constraints, this kind of code is fairly easy to read and debug.

NOTE: The Sun tutorial at `http://java.sun.com/docs/books/tutorial/uiswing/layout/gridbag.html` suggests that you reuse the same `GridBagConstraints` object for all components. We find the resulting code hard to read and error prone. For example, look at the demo at `http://java.sun.com/docs/books/tutorial/uiswing/events/containerlistener.html`. Was it really intended that the buttons are stretched horizontally, or did the programmer just forget to turn off the `BOTH` setting for the `fill` constraint?

Example 9–14: FontDialog.java

```
import java.awt.*;
import java.awt.event.*;
import javax.swing.*;
import javax.swing.event.*;

public class FontDialog
{
   public static void main(String[] args)
   {
      FontDialogFrame frame = new FontDialogFrame();
      frame.setDefaultCloseOperation(JFrame.EXIT_ON_CLOSE);
      frame.setVisible(true);
   }
}

/**
   A frame that uses a grid bag layout to arrange font
   selection components.
*/
class FontDialogFrame extends JFrame
```

```
{
   public FontDialogFrame()
   {
      setTitle("FontDialog");
      setSize(DEFAULT_WIDTH, DEFAULT_HEIGHT);

      GridBagLayout layout = new GridBagLayout();
      setLayout(layout);

      ActionListener listener = new FontAction();

      // construct components

      JLabel faceLabel = new JLabel("Face: ");

      face = new JComboBox(new String[]
         {
            "Serif", "SansSerif", "Monospaced",
            "Dialog", "DialogInput"
         });

      face.addActionListener(listener);

      JLabel sizeLabel = new JLabel("Size: ");

      size = new JComboBox(new String[]
         {
            "8", "10", "12", "15", "18", "24", "36", "48"
         });

      size.addActionListener(listener);

      bold = new JCheckBox("Bold");
      bold.addActionListener(listener);

      italic = new JCheckBox("Italic");
      italic.addActionListener(listener);

      sample = new JTextArea();
      sample.setText("The quick brown fox jumps over the lazy dog");
      sample.setEditable(false);
      sample.setLineWrap(true);
      sample.setBorder(BorderFactory.createEtchedBorder());

      // add components to grid, using GBC convenience class

      add(faceLabel, new GBC(0, 0).setAnchor(GBC.EAST));
      add(face, new GBC(1, 0).setFill(GBC.HORIZONTAL).setWeight(100, 0).setInsets(1));
      add(sizeLabel, new GBC(0, 1).setAnchor(GBC.EAST));
      add(size, new GBC(1, 1).setFill(GBC.HORIZONTAL).setWeight(100, 0).setInsets(1));
      add(bold, new GBC(0, 2, 2, 1).setAnchor(GBC.CENTER).setWeight(100, 100));
      add(italic, new GBC(0, 3, 2, 1).setAnchor(GBC.CENTER).setWeight(100, 100));
      add(sample, new GBC(2, 0, 1, 4).setFill(GBC.BOTH).setWeight(100, 100));
   }
```

```
   public static final int DEFAULT_WIDTH = 300;
   public static final int DEFAULT_HEIGHT = 200;

   private JComboBox face;
   private JComboBox size;
   private JCheckBox bold;
   private JCheckBox italic;
   private JTextArea sample;

   /**
      An action listener that changes the font of the
      sample text.
   */
   private class FontAction implements ActionListener
   {
      public void actionPerformed(ActionEvent event)
      {
         String fontFace = (String) face.getSelectedItem();
         int fontStyle = (bold.isSelected() ? Font.BOLD : 0)
            + (italic.isSelected() ? Font.ITALIC : 0);
         int fontSize = Integer.parseInt((String) size.getSelectedItem());
         Font font = new Font(fontFace, fontStyle, fontSize);
         sample.setFont(font);
         sample.repaint();
      }
   }
}
```

Example 9–15 shows the code of the GBC helper class.

Example 9–15: GBC.java

```
/*
GBC - A convenience class to tame the GridBagLayout

Copyright (C) 2002 Cay S. Horstmann (http://horstmann.com)

This program is free software; you can redistribute it and/or modify
it under the terms of the GNU General Public License as published by
the Free Software Foundation; either version 2 of the License, or
(at your option) any later version.

This program is distributed in the hope that it will be useful,
but WITHOUT ANY WARRANTY; without even the implied warranty of
MERCHANTABILITY or FITNESS FOR A PARTICULAR PURPOSE.  See the
GNU General Public License for more details.

You should have received a copy of the GNU General Public License
along with this program; if not, write to the Free Software
Foundation, Inc., 59 Temple Place, Suite 330, Boston, MA  02111-1307  USA
*/

import java.awt.*;

/**
```

```
   This class simplifies the use of the GridBagConstraints
   class.
*/
public class GBC extends GridBagConstraints
{
   /**
      Constructs a GBC with a given gridx and gridy position and
      all other grid bag constraint values set to the default.
      @param gridx the gridx position
      @param gridy the gridy position
   */
   public GBC(int gridx, int gridy)
   {
      this.gridx = gridx;
      this.gridy = gridy;
   }

   /**
      Constructs a GBC with given gridx, gridy, gridwidth, gridheight
      and all other grid bag constraint values set to the default.
      @param gridx the gridx position
      @param gridy the gridy position
      @param gridwidth the cell span in x-direction
      @param gridheight the cell span in y-direction
   */
   public GBC(int gridx, int gridy, int gridwidth, int gridheight)
   {
      this.gridx = gridx;
      this.gridy = gridy;
      this.gridwidth = gridwidth;
      this.gridheight = gridheight;
   }

   /**
      Sets the anchor.
      @param anchor the anchor value
      @return this object for further modification
   */
   public GBC setAnchor(int anchor)
   {
      this.anchor = anchor;
      return this;
   }

   /**
      Sets the fill direction.
      @param fill the fill direction
      @return this object for further modification
   */
   public GBC setFill(int fill)
   {
      this.fill = fill;
      return this;
   }
```

```

   /**
      Sets the cell weights.
      @param weightx the cell weight in x-direction
      @param weighty the cell weight in y-direction
      @return this object for further modification
   */
   public GBC setWeight(double weightx, double weighty)
   {
      this.weightx = weightx;
      this.weighty = weighty;
      return this;
   }

   /**
      Sets the insets of this cell.
      @param distance the spacing to use in all directions
      @return this object for further modification
   */
   public GBC setInsets(int distance)
   {
      this.insets = new Insets(distance, distance, distance, distance);
      return this;
   }

   /**
      Sets the insets of this cell.
      @param top the spacing to use on top
      @param left the spacing to use to the left
      @param bottom the spacing to use on the bottom
      @param right the spacing to use to the right
      @return this object for further modification
   */
   public GBC setInsets(int top, int left, int bottom, int right)
   {
      this.insets = new Insets(top, left, bottom, right);
      return this;
   }

   /**
      Sets the internal padding
      @param ipadx the internal padding in x-direction
      @param ipady the internal padding in y-direction
      @return this object for further modification
   */
   public GBC setIpad(int ipadx, int ipady)
   {
      this.ipadx = ipadx;
      this.ipady = ipady;
      return this;
   }
}
```

TIP: Some GUI builders have tools for specifying the constraints visually—see Figure 9–37 for the configuration dialog in NetBeans.

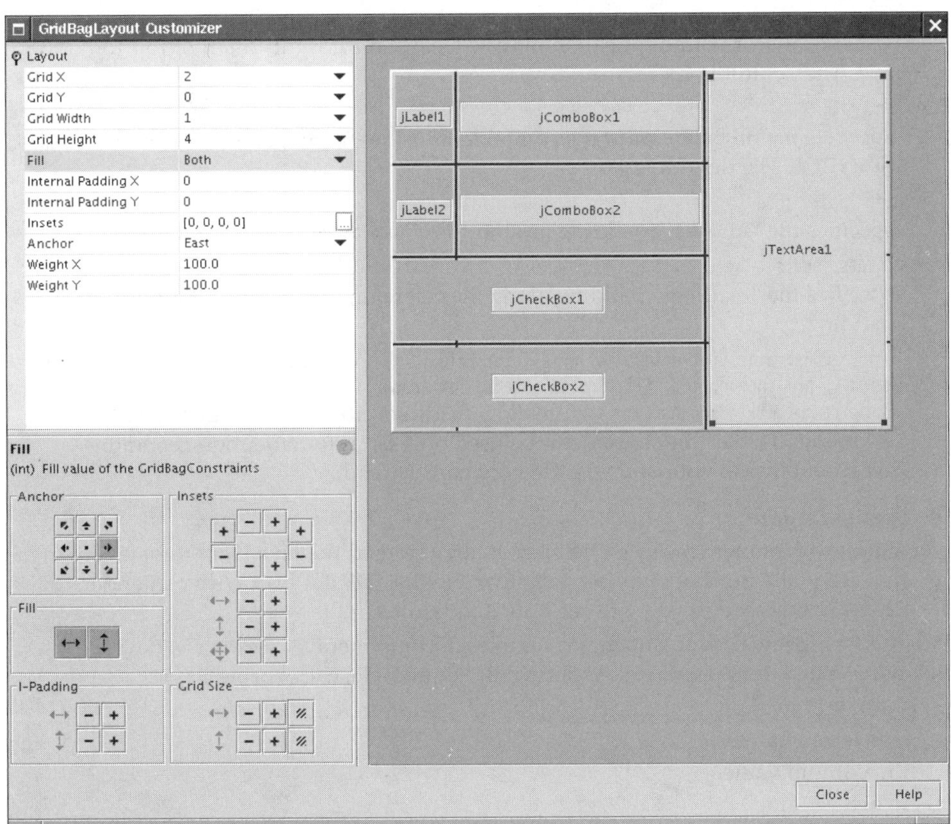

Figure 9–37: Specifying grid bag constraints in NetBeans

API **`java.awt.GridBagConstraints`** 1.0

- `int gridx, gridy`
  specifies the starting column and row of the cell. The default is 0.
- `int gridwidth, gridheight`
  specifies the column and row extent of the cell. The default is 1.
- `double weightx, weighty`
  specifies the capacity of the cell to grow. The default is 0.
- `int anchor`
  indicates the alignment of the component inside the cell. You can choose between absolute positions—

`NORTHWEST`	`NORTH`	`NORTHEAST`
`WEST`	`CENTER`	`EAST`
`SOUTHWEST`	`SOUTH`	`SOUTHEAST`

—or their orientation-independent counterparts

FIRST_LINE_START	LINE_START	FIRST_LINE_END
PAGE_START	CENTER	PAGE_END
LAST_LINE_START	LINE_END	LAST_LINE_END

Use the latter if your application may be localized for right-to-left or top-to-bottom text. The default is CENTER.

- `int fill`
  specifies the fill behavior of the component inside the cell, one of NONE, BOTH, HORIZONTAL, or VERTICAL. The default is NONE.
- `int ipadx, ipady`
  specifies the "internal" padding around the component. The default is 0.
- `Insets insets`
  specifies the "external" padding along the cell boundaries. The default is no padding.
- `GridBagConstraints(int gridx, int gridy, int gridwidth, int gridheight, double weightx, double weighty, int anchor, int fill, Insets insets, int ipadx, int ipady)` **1.2**
  constructs a GridBagConstraints with all its fields specified in the arguments. Sun recommends that this constructor be used only by automatic code generators because it makes your source code very hard to read.

The Spring Layout

Ever since programmers met the GridBagLayout, they begged the Java team for a layout manager that is equally flexible but more intuitive. Finally, JDK 1.4 features a contender, the SpringLayout. In this section you will see how it measures up.

With the spring layout, you attach *springs* to each component. A spring is a device for specifying component positions. As shown in Figure 9–38, each spring has

- A minimum value
- A preferred value
- A maximum value
- An actual value

When the spring is compressed or expanded in the layout phase, the actual value is fixed; it falls between the minimum and maximum value and is as close to the preferred value as the other springs allow. Then the actual value determines the position of the component to which it has been attached.

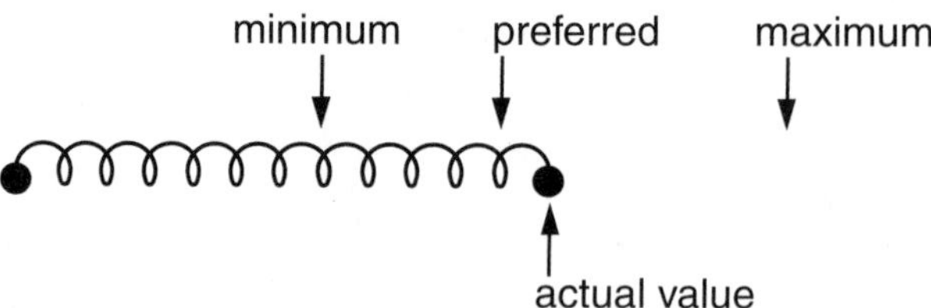

Figure 9–38: A spring

The spring class defines a *sum* operation that takes two springs and produces a new spring that combines the characteristics of the individual springs. When you lay out a number of components in a row, you attach several springs so that their sum spans the entire container—see Figure 9–39. That sum spring is now compressed or expanded so that its value

equals the dimension of the container. This operation exerts a strain on the individual springs. Each spring value is set so that the strain of each spring equals the strain of the sum. Thus, the values of the individual springs are determined, and the layout is fixed. (If you are interested in the details of the strain computations, check the API documentation of the `Spring` class for more information.)

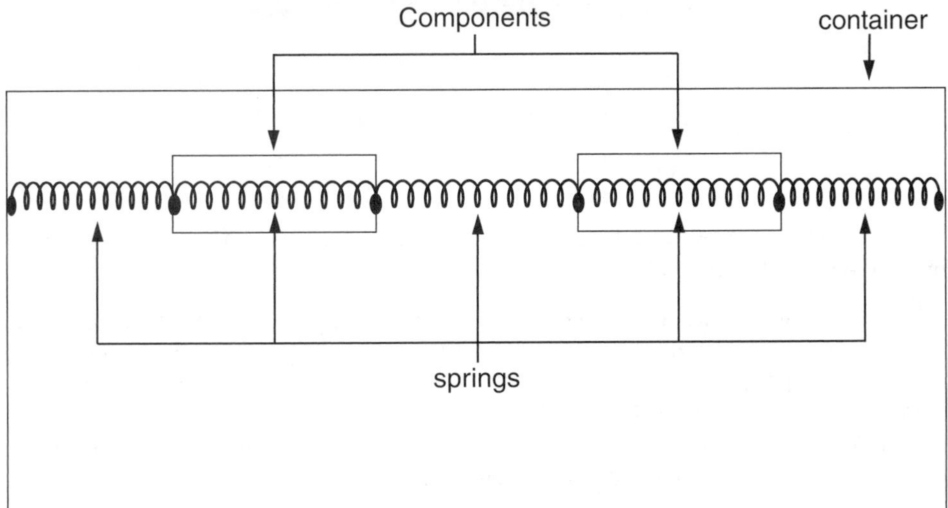

Figure 9–39: Summing springs

Let's run through a simple example. Suppose you want to lay out three buttons horizontally.

```
JButton b1 = new JButton("Yellow");
JButton b2 = new JButton("Blue");
JButton b3 = new JButton("Red");
```

You first set the layout manager of the frame to a `SpringLayout` and add the components.

```
SpringLayout layout = new SpringLayout();
panel.setLayout(layout);
panel.add(b1);
panel.add(b2);
panel.add(b3);
```

Now construct a spring with a good amount of compressibility. The static `Spring.constant` method produces a spring with given minimum, preferred, and maximum values. (The spring isn't actually constant—it can be compressed or expanded.)

```
Spring s = Spring.constant(0, 10000, 10000);
```

Next, attach one copy of the spring from the west side of the container to the west side of `b1`:

```
layout.putConstraint(SpringLayout.WEST, b1, s, SpringLayout.WEST, panel);
```

The `putConstraint` method adds the given spring so that it ends at the first parameter set (the west side of `b1` in our case) and starts from the second parameter set (the west side of the content pane).

Next, you link up the other springs:

```
layout.putConstraint(SpringLayout.WEST, b2, s, SpringLayout.EAST, b1);
layout.putConstraint(SpringLayout.WEST, b3, s, SpringLayout.EAST, b2);
```

Finally, you hook up a spring with the east wall of the container:

```
layout.putConstraint(SpringLayout.EAST, panel, s, SpringLayout.EAST, b3);
```

The result is that the four springs are compressed to the same size, and the buttons are equally spaced (see Figure 9–40).

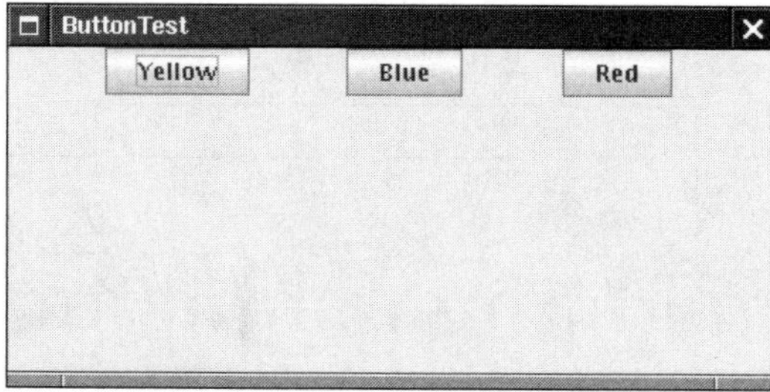

Figure 9–40: Equally spaced buttons

Alternatively, you may want to vary the distances. Let's suppose you want to have a fixed distance between the buttons. Use a *strut*—a spring that can't be expanded or compressed. You get such a spring with the single-parameter version of the `Spring.constant` method:

```
Spring strut = Spring.constant(10);
```

If you add two struts between the buttons, but leave the springs at the ends, the result is a button group that is centered in the container (see Figure 9–41).

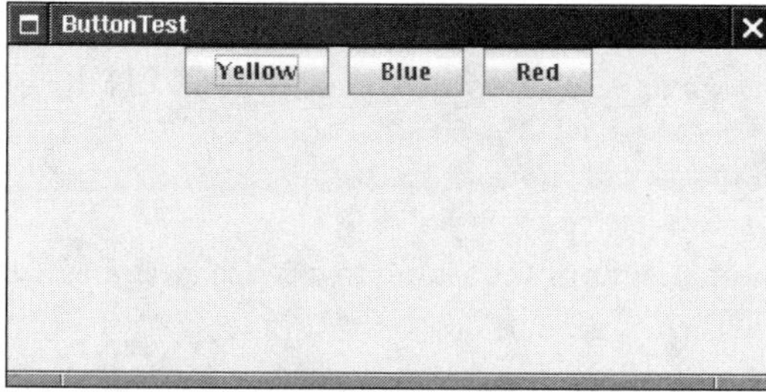

Figure 9–41: Springs and struts

Of course, you don't really need the spring layout for such a simple arrangement. Let's look at something more complex, a portion of the font dialog of the preceding example. We have two combo boxes with labels, and we want to have the west sides of both combo boxes start after the *longer* label (see Figure 9–42).

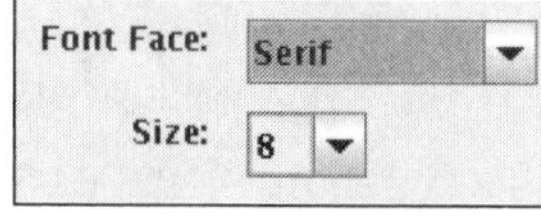

Figure 9–42: Lining up columns

This calls for another spring operation. You can form the *maximum* of two springs with the static `Spring.max` method. The result is a spring that is as long as the longer of the two inputs.

We get the maximum of the two east sides like this:

```
Spring labelsEast = Spring.max(
   layout.getConstraint(SpringLayout.EAST, faceLabel),
   layout.getConstraint(SpringLayout.EAST, sizeLabel));
```

Note that the `getConstraint` method yields a spring that reaches all the way from the west side of the container to the given sides of the component

Let's add a strut so that there is some space between the labels and the combo boxes:

```
Spring combosWest = Spring.sum(labelsEast, strut);
```

Now we attach this spring to the west side of both combo boxes. The starting point is the start of the container because the `labelsEast` spring starts there.

```
layout.putConstraint(SpringLayout.WEST, face, combosWest,SpringLayout.WEST, panel);
layout.putConstraint(SpringLayout.WEST, size, combosWest,SpringLayout.WEST, panel);
```

Now the two combo boxes line up because they are held by the same spring.

However, there is a slight blemish. We'd prefer the labels to be right-aligned. It is possible to achieve this effect as well, but it requires a more precise understanding of spring attachments.

Let's look at the horizontal springs in detail. Vertical springs follow the same logic. Figure 9–43 shows the three ways in which horizontal springs can be attached:

- Connecting the west side of the component with the west side of the component;
- Traversing the width of the component;
- Connecting the west side of the component with the east side of the component.

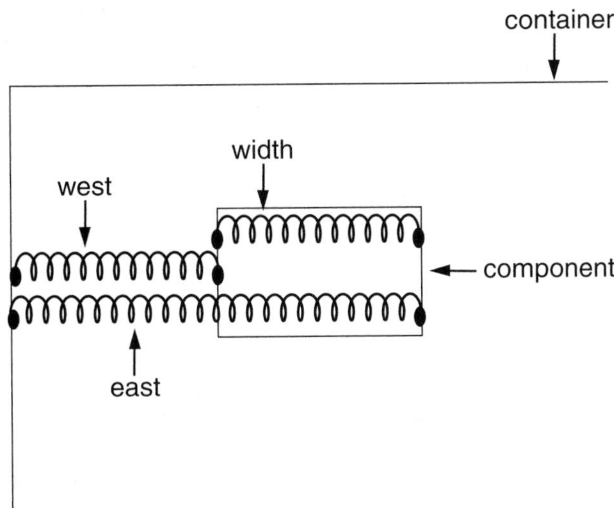

Figure 9–43: Horizontal springs attached to a component

You get these springs as follows:

```
Spring west = layout.getConstraints(component).getX();
Spring width = layout.getConstraints(component).getWidth();
Spring east = layout.getConstraint(SpringLayout.EAST, component);
```

The `getConstraints` method yields an object of type `SpringLayout.Constraints`. You can think of such an object as a rectangle, except that the x, y, width, and height values are springs, not numbers. The `getConstraint` method yields a single spring that reaches to one of the four component boundaries. You can also get the west spring as

```
Spring west = layout.getConstraint(SpringLayout.WEST, component);
```

Of course, the three springs are related: The spring sum of `west` and `width` must equal `east`.

When the component constraints are first set, the width is set to a spring whose parameters are the minimum, preferred, and maximum width of the component. The west is set to 0.

CAUTION: If you don't set the west (and north) spring of a component, then the component stays at offset 0 in the container.

If a component has two springs set and you add a third one, then it becomes *over-constrained*. One of the existing springs is removed and its value is computed as the sum or difference of the other springs. Table 9–3 shows which spring is recomputed.

Table 9–3: Adding a Spring to an Overconstrained Component

Added Spring	Removed Spring	Replaced By
west	width	east - west
width	east	west + width
east	west	east - width

NOTE: The difference between two springs may not be intuitive, but it makes sense in the spring algebra. There is no Java method for spring subtraction. If you need to compute the difference of two springs, use

```
Spring.sum(s, Spring.minus(t))
```

Now you know enough about springs to solve the "right alignment" problem. Compute the maximum of the widths of the two labels. Then set the *east* spring of both labels to that maximum. As you can see from Table 9–3, the label widths don't change, the west springs are recomputed, and the labels become aligned at the eastern boundary.

```
Spring labelsEast = Spring.sum(strut,
   Spring.max(layout.getConstraints(faceLabel).getWidth(),
   Spring.max(layout.getConstraints(sizeLabel).getWidth()));
layout.putConstraint(SpringLayout.EAST, faceLabel, labelsEast, SpringLayout.WEST, panel);
layout.putConstraint(SpringLayout.EAST, sizeLabel, labelsEast, SpringLayout.WEST, panel);
```

Example 9–16 shows how to lay out the font dialog with springs. If you look at the code, you will probably agree that the spring layout is quite a bit less intuitive than the grid bag layout. We hope to someday see tools that make the spring layout more approachable. However, in the meantime we recommend that you stick with the grid bag layout for complex layouts.

Example 9–16: SpringLayoutTest.java

```
import java.awt.*;
import java.awt.event.*;
import javax.swing.*;
import javax.swing.event.*;

```

```
public class SpringLayoutTest
{
   public static void main(String[] args)
   {
      FontDialogFrame frame = new FontDialogFrame();
      frame.setDefaultCloseOperation(JFrame.EXIT_ON_CLOSE);
      frame.setVisible(true);
   }
}

/**
   A frame that uses a spring layout to arrange font
   selection components.
*/
class FontDialogFrame extends JFrame
{
   public FontDialogFrame()
   {
      setTitle("FontDialog");
      setSize(DEFAULT_WIDTH, DEFAULT_HEIGHT);

      JPanel panel = new JPanel();
      SpringLayout layout = new SpringLayout();
      panel.setLayout(layout);

      ActionListener listener = new FontAction();

      // construct components

      JLabel faceLabel = new JLabel("Font Face: ");

      face = new JComboBox(new String[]
         {
            "Serif", "SansSerif", "Monospaced",
            "Dialog", "DialogInput"
         });

      face.addActionListener(listener);

      JLabel sizeLabel = new JLabel("Size: ");

      size = new JComboBox(new String[]
         {
            "8", "10", "12", "15", "18", "24", "36", "48"
         });

      size.addActionListener(listener);

      bold = new JCheckBox("Bold");
      bold.addActionListener(listener);

      italic = new JCheckBox("Italic");
      italic.addActionListener(listener);

      sample = new JTextArea();
```

```
      sample.setText("The quick brown fox jumps over the lazy dog");
      sample.setEditable(false);
      sample.setLineWrap(true);
      sample.setBorder(BorderFactory.createEtchedBorder());

      panel.add(faceLabel);
      panel.add(sizeLabel);
      panel.add(face);
      panel.add(size);
      panel.add(bold);
      panel.add(italic);
      panel.add(sample);

      // add springs to lay out components
      Spring strut = Spring.constant(10);

      Spring labelsEast = Spring.sum(strut,
         Spring.max(
            layout.getConstraints(faceLabel).getWidth(),
            layout.getConstraints(sizeLabel).getWidth()));

      layout.putConstraint(SpringLayout.EAST, faceLabel, labelsEast, SpringLayout.WEST, panel);
      layout.putConstraint(SpringLayout.EAST, sizeLabel, labelsEast, SpringLayout.WEST, panel);

      layout.putConstraint(SpringLayout.NORTH, faceLabel, strut, SpringLayout.NORTH, panel);
      layout.putConstraint(SpringLayout.NORTH, face, strut, SpringLayout.NORTH, panel);

      Spring secondRowNorth = Spring.sum(strut,
         Spring.max(
            layout.getConstraint(SpringLayout.SOUTH, faceLabel),
            layout.getConstraint(SpringLayout.SOUTH, face)));

      layout.putConstraint(SpringLayout.NORTH, sizeLabel, secondRowNorth, SpringLayout.NORTH,
         panel);
      layout.putConstraint(SpringLayout.NORTH, size, secondRowNorth, SpringLayout.NORTH, panel);

      layout.putConstraint(SpringLayout.WEST, face, strut, SpringLayout.EAST, faceLabel);
      layout.putConstraint(SpringLayout.WEST, size, strut, SpringLayout.EAST, sizeLabel);

      layout.putConstraint(SpringLayout.WEST, bold, strut, SpringLayout.WEST, panel);
      layout.putConstraint(SpringLayout.WEST, italic, strut, SpringLayout.WEST, panel);

      Spring s = Spring.constant(10, 10000, 10000);

      Spring thirdRowNorth = Spring.sum(s,
         Spring.max(
            layout.getConstraint(SpringLayout.SOUTH, sizeLabel),
            layout.getConstraint(SpringLayout.SOUTH, size)));

      layout.putConstraint(SpringLayout.NORTH, bold, thirdRowNorth, SpringLayout.NORTH, panel);
      layout.putConstraint(SpringLayout.NORTH, italic, s, SpringLayout.SOUTH, bold);
      layout.putConstraint(SpringLayout.SOUTH, panel, s, SpringLayout.SOUTH, italic);

      Spring secondColumnWest = Spring.sum(strut,
```

```
            Spring.max(
               layout.getConstraint(SpringLayout.EAST, face),
               layout.getConstraint(SpringLayout.EAST, size)));

      layout.putConstraint(SpringLayout.WEST, sample, secondColumnWest, SpringLayout.WEST, panel);
      layout.putConstraint(SpringLayout.SOUTH, sample, Spring.minus(strut), SpringLayout.SOUTH,
         panel);
      layout.putConstraint(SpringLayout.NORTH, sample, strut, SpringLayout.NORTH, panel);
      layout.putConstraint(SpringLayout.EAST, panel, strut, SpringLayout.EAST, sample);

      add(panel);
   }

   public static final int DEFAULT_WIDTH = 400;
   public static final int DEFAULT_HEIGHT = 200;

   private JComboBox face;
   private JComboBox size;
   private JCheckBox bold;
   private JCheckBox italic;
   private JTextArea sample;

   /**
      An action listener that changes the font of the
      sample text.
   */
   private class FontAction implements ActionListener
   {
      public void actionPerformed(ActionEvent event)
      {
         String fontFace = (String) face.getSelectedItem();
         int fontStyle = (bold.isSelected() ? Font.BOLD : 0)
            + (italic.isSelected() ? Font.ITALIC : 0);
         int fontSize = Integer.parseInt((String) size.getSelectedItem());
         Font font = new Font(fontFace, fontStyle, fontSize);
         sample.setFont(font);
         sample.repaint();
      }
   }
}
```

API **javax.swing.SpringLayout 1.4**

- `SpringLayout.Constraints getConstraints(Component c)`
  gets the constraints of the given component.

  Parameters: `c` One of the components or the container managed by this layout manager

- `void putConstraint(String endSide, Component end, Spring s, String startSide, Component start)`
- `void putConstraint(String endSide, Component end, int pad, String startSide, Component start)`
  set the given side of the `end` component to a spring that is obtained by adding the spring `s`, or a strut with size `pad`, to the spring that reaches from the left end of the container to the given side of the `start` container.

Parameters:	endSide, startSide	WEST, EAST, NORTH, or SOUTH
	end	The component to which a spring is added
	s	One of the summands of the added spring
	pad	The size of the strut summand
	start	The component to which the other summand spring reaches

javax.swing.SpringLayout.Constraints 1.4

- `Constraints(Component c)` **5.0**
  constructs a `Constraints` object whose positions, width, and springs match the given component.
- `Spring getX()`
- `Spring getY()`
  return the spring reaching from the start of the container to the west or north end of the constrained component.
- `Spring getWidth()`
- `Spring getHeight()`
  return the spring spanning the width or height of the constrained component.
- `Spring getConstraint(String side)`
- `void setConstraint(String edge, Spring s)`
  get or set a spring reaching from the start of the container to the given side of the constrained component.

Parameters:	side	One of the constants WEST, EAST, NORTH, or SOUTH of the SpringLayout class
	s	The spring to set

javax.swing.Spring 1.4

- `static Spring constant(int preferred)`
  constructs a strut with the given preferred size. The minimum and maximum sizes are set to the preferred size.
- `static Spring constant(int minimum, int preferred, int maximum)`
  constructs a spring with the given minimum, preferred, and maximum sizes.
- `static Spring sum(Spring s, Spring t)`
  returns the spring sum of `s` and `t`.
- `static Spring max(Spring s, Spring t)`
  returns the spring maximum of `s` and `t`.
- `static Spring minus(Spring s)`
  returns the opposite of the spring `s`.
- `static Spring scale(Spring s, float factor)` **5.0**
  scales the minimum, preferred, and maximum sizes of `s` by the given factor. If the factor is negative, the scaled opposite of `s` is returned.
- `static Spring width(Component c)` **5.0**
- `static Spring height(Component c)` **5.0**
  return a spring whose minimum, preferred, and maximum sizes equal the minimum, preferred, and maximum width or height of the given component.

- `int getMinimumValue()`
- `int getPreferredValue()`
- `int getMaximumValue()`

  return the minimum, preferred, and maximum value of this spring.
- `int getValue()`
- `void setValue(int newValue)`

  get and set the spring value. When setting the value of a compound spring, the values of the components are set as well.

Using No Layout Manager

There will be times when you don't want to bother with layout managers but just want to drop a component at a fixed location (sometimes called *absolute positioning*). This is not a great idea for platform-independent applications, but there is nothing wrong with using it for a quick prototype.

Here is what you do to place a component at a fixed location:

1. Set the layout manager to `null`.
2. Add the component you want to the container.
3. Then specify the position and size that you want.

```
setLayout(null);
JButton ok = new JButton("Ok");
add(ok);
ok.setBounds(10, 10, 30, 15);
```

java.awt.Component 1.0

- `void setBounds(int x, int y, int width, int height)`

  moves and resizes a component.

Parameters:	`x, y`	The new top-left corner of the component
	`width, height`	The new size of the component

Custom Layout Managers

In principle, you can design your own `LayoutManager` class that manages components in a special way. For example, you could arrange all components in a container to form a circle. This will almost always be a major effort and a real time sink, but as Figure 9–44 shows, the results can be quite dramatic.

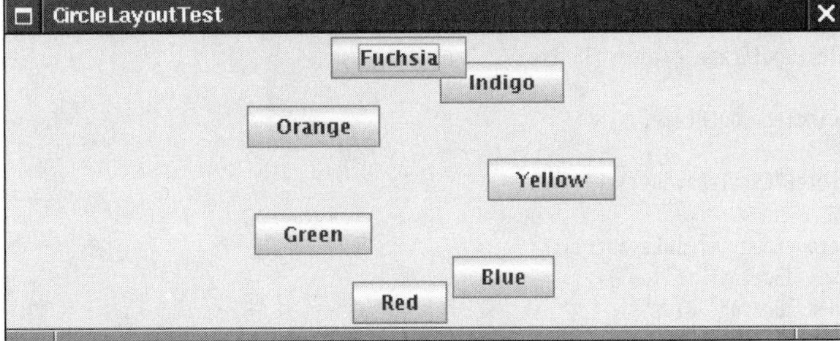

Figure 9–44: Circle layout

If you do feel you can't live without your own layout manager, here is what you do. Your own layout manager must implement the `LayoutManager` interface. You need to override the following five methods.

```
void addLayoutComponent(String s, Component c);
void removeLayoutComponent(Component c);
Dimension preferredLayoutSize(Container parent);
Dimension minimumLayoutSize(Container parent);
void layoutContainer(Container parent);
```

The first two functions are called when a component is added or removed. If you don't keep any additional information about the components, you can make them do nothing. The next two functions compute the space required for the minimum and the preferred layout of the components. These are usually the same quantity. The fifth function does the actual work and invokes `setBounds` on all components.

NOTE: The AWT has a second interface, called `LayoutManager2`, with 10 methods to implement rather than 5. The main point of the `LayoutManager2` interface is to allow the user to use the `add` method with constraints. For example, the `BorderLayout` and `GridBagLayout` implement the `LayoutManager2` interface.

Example 9–17 is a simple implementation of the `CircleLayout` manager, which, amazingly and uselessly enough, lays out the components along a circle inside the parent.

Example 9–17: CircleLayoutTest.java

```
import java.awt.*;
import java.awt.event.*;
import javax.swing.*;

public class CircleLayoutTest
{
   public static void main(String[] args)
   {
      CircleLayoutFrame frame = new CircleLayoutFrame();
      frame.setDefaultCloseOperation(JFrame.EXIT_ON_CLOSE);
      frame.pack();
      frame.setVisible(true);
   }
}

/**
   A frame that shows buttons arranged along a circle.
*/
class CircleLayoutFrame extends JFrame
{
   public CircleLayoutFrame()
   {
      setTitle("CircleLayoutTest");

      setLayout(new CircleLayout());
      add(new JButton("Yellow"));
      add(new JButton("Blue"));
      add(new JButton("Red"));
      add(new JButton("Green"));
      add(new JButton("Orange"));
      add(new JButton("Fuchsia"));
      add(new JButton("Indigo"));
```

```
   }
}

/**
   A layout manager that lays out components along a circle.
*/
class CircleLayout implements LayoutManager
{
   public void addLayoutComponent(String name, Component comp)
   {}

   public void removeLayoutComponent(Component comp)
   {}

   public void setSizes(Container parent)
   {
      if (sizesSet) return;
      int n = parent.getComponentCount();

      preferredWidth = 0;
      preferredHeight = 0;
      minWidth = 0;
      minHeight = 0;
      maxComponentWidth = 0;
      maxComponentHeight = 0;

      // compute the maximum component widths and heights
      // and set the preferred size to the sum of the component sizes.
      for (int i = 0; i < n; i++)
      {
         Component c = parent.getComponent(i);
         if (c.isVisible())
         {
            Dimension d = c.getPreferredSize();
            maxComponentWidth = Math.max(maxComponentWidth, d.width);
            maxComponentHeight = Math.max(maxComponentHeight, d.height);
            preferredWidth += d.width;
            preferredHeight += d.height;
         }
      }
      minWidth = preferredWidth / 2;
      minHeight = preferredHeight / 2;
      sizesSet = true;
   }

   public Dimension preferredLayoutSize(Container parent)
   {
      setSizes(parent);
      Insets insets = parent.getInsets();
      int width = preferredWidth + insets.left + insets.right;
      int height = preferredHeight + insets.top + insets.bottom;
      return new Dimension(width, height);
   }

   public Dimension minimumLayoutSize(Container parent)
   {
```

```
      setSizes(parent);
      Insets insets = parent.getInsets();
      int width = minWidth + insets.left + insets.right;
      int height = minHeight + insets.top + insets.bottom;
      return new Dimension(width, height);
   }

   public void layoutContainer(Container parent)
   {
      setSizes(parent);

      // compute center of the circle

      Insets insets = parent.getInsets();
      int containerWidth = parent.getSize().width - insets.left - insets.right;
      int containerHeight = parent.getSize().height - insets.top - insets.bottom;

      int xcenter = insets.left + containerWidth / 2;
      int ycenter = insets.top + containerHeight / 2;

      // compute radius of the circle

      int xradius = (containerWidth - maxComponentWidth) / 2;
      int yradius = (containerHeight - maxComponentHeight) / 2;
      int radius = Math.min(xradius, yradius);

      // lay out components along the circle

      int n = parent.getComponentCount();
      for (int i = 0; i < n; i++)
      {
         Component c = parent.getComponent(i);
         if (c.isVisible())
         {
            double angle = 2 * Math.PI * i / n;

            // center point of component
            int x = xcenter + (int)(Math.cos(angle) * radius);
            int y = ycenter + (int)(Math.sin(angle) * radius);

            // move component so that its center is (x, y)
            // and its size is its preferred size
            Dimension d = c.getPreferredSize();
            c.setBounds(x - d.width / 2, y - d.height / 2, d.width, d.height);
         }
      }
   }

   private int minWidth = 0;
   private int minHeight = 0;
   private int preferredWidth = 0;
   private int preferredHeight = 0;
   private boolean sizesSet = false;
   private int maxComponentWidth = 0;
   private int maxComponentHeight = 0;
}
```

java.awt.LayoutManager 1.0

- `void addLayoutComponent(String name, Component comp)`
  adds a component to the layout.

Parameters:	`name`	An identifier for the component placement
	`comp`	The component to be added

- `void removeLayoutComponent(Component comp)`
  removes a component from the layout.

Parameters:	`comp`	The component to be removed

- `Dimension preferredLayoutSize(Container parent)`
  returns the preferred size dimensions for the container under this layout.

Parameters:	`parent`	The container whose components are being laid out

- `Dimension minimumLayoutSize(Container parent)`
  returns the minimum size dimensions for the container under this layout.

Parameters:	`parent`	The container whose components are being laid out

- `void layoutContainer(Container parent)`
  lays out the components in a container.

Parameters:	`parent`	The container whose components are being laid out

Traversal Order

When you add many components into a window, you need to give some thought to the *traversal order.* When a window is first displayed, the first component in the traversal order has the keyboard focus. Each time the user presses the TAB key, the next component gains focus. (Recall that a component that has the keyboard focus can be manipulated with the keyboard. For example, a button can be "clicked" with the space bar when it has focus.) You may not personally care about using the TAB key to navigate through a set of controls, but plenty of users do. Among them are the mouse haters and those who cannot use a mouse, perhaps because of a handicap or because they are navigating the user interface by voice. For that reason, you need to know how Swing handles traversal order.

The traversal order is straightforward, first left to right and then top to bottom. For example, in the font dialog example, the components are traversed in the following order (see Figure 9–45):

1. Face combo box
2. Sample text area (press CTRL+TAB to move to the next field; the TAB character is considered text input)
3. Size combo box
4. Bold checkbox
5. Italic checkbox

NOTE: In the old AWT, the traversal order was determined by the order in which you inserted components into a container. In Swing, the insertion order does not matter—only the layout of the components is considered.

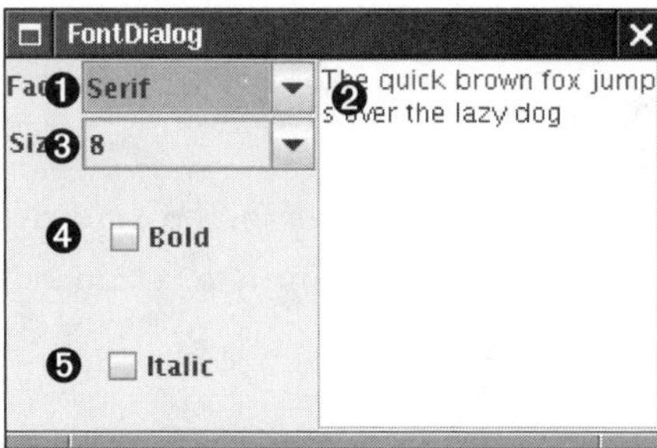

Figure 9–45: Geometric traversal order

The situation is more complex if your container contains other containers. When the focus is given to another container, it automatically ends up within the top-left component in that container and then it traverses all other components in that container. Finally, the focus is given to the component following the container.

You can use this to your advantage by grouping related elements in another container such as a panel.

NOTE: As of JDK 1.4, you call

```
component.setFocusable(false);
```

to remove a component from the focus traversal. In older versions of the JDK, you had to override the `isFocusTraversable` method, but that method is now deprecated.

In summary, there are two standard traversal policies in JDK 1.4:

- Pure AWT applications use the `DefaultFocusTraversalPolicy`. Components are included in the focus traversal if they are visible, displayable, enabled, and focusable, and if their native peers are focusable. The components are traversed in the order in which they were inserted in the container.
- Swing applications use the `LayoutFocusTraversalPolicy`. Components are included in the focus traversal if they are visible, displayable, enabled, and focusable. The components are traversed in geometric order: left to right, then top to bottom. However, a container introduces a new "cycle"—its components are traversed first before the successor of the container gains focus.

NOTE: The "cycle" notion is a bit confusing. After reaching the last element in a child container, the focus does not go back to its first element, but instead to the container's successor. The API supports true cycles, including keystrokes that move up and down in a cycle hierarchy. However, the standard traversal policy does not use hierarchical cycles. It flattens the cycle hierarchy into a linear (depth-first) traversal.

NOTE: In JDK 1.3, you could change the default traversal order by calling the `setNextFocusableComponent` method of the `JComponent` class. That method is now deprecated. To change the traversal order, try grouping related components into panels so that they form cycles. If that doesn't work, you have to either install a comparator that sorts the components differently or completely replace the traversal policy. Neither operation seems intended for the faint of heart—see the Sun API documentation for details.

Dialog Boxes

So far, all our user interface components have appeared inside a frame window that was created in the application. This is the most common situation if you write *applets* that run inside a web browser. But if you write applications, you usually want separate dialog boxes to pop up to give information to or get information from the user.

Just as with most windowing systems, AWT distinguishes between *modal* and *modeless* dialog boxes. A modal dialog box won't let users interact with the remaining windows of the application until he or she deals with it. You use a modal dialog box when you need information from the user before you can proceed with execution. For example, when the user wants to read a file, a modal file dialog box is the one to pop up. The user must specify a file name before the program can begin the read operation. Only when the user closes the (modal) dialog box can the application proceed.

A modeless dialog box lets the user enter information in both the dialog box and the remainder of the application. One example of a modeless dialog is a toolbar. The toolbar can stay in place as long as needed, and the user can interact with both the application window and the toolbar as needed.

We start this section with the simplest dialogs—modal dialogs with just a single message. Swing has a convenient `JOptionPane` class that lets you put up a simple dialog without writing any special dialog box code. Next, you see how to write more complex dialogs by implementing your own dialog windows. Finally, you see how to transfer data from your application into a dialog and back.

We conclude this section by looking at two standard dialogs: file dialogs and color dialogs. File dialogs are complex, and you definitely want to be familiar with the Swing `JFileChooser` for this purpose—it would be a real challenge to write your own. The `JColorChooser` dialog is useful when you want users to pick colors.

Option Dialogs

Swing has a set of ready-made simple dialogs that suffice when you need to ask the user for a single piece of information. The `JOptionPane` has four static methods to show these simple dialogs:

`showMessageDialog`	Show a message and wait for the user to click OK
`showConfirmDialog`	Show a message and get a confirmation (like OK/Cancel)
`showOptionDialog`	Show a message and get a user option from a set of options
`showInputDialog`	Show a message and get one line of user input

Figure 9–46 shows a typical dialog. As you can see, the dialog has the following components:

- An icon
- A message
- One or more option buttons

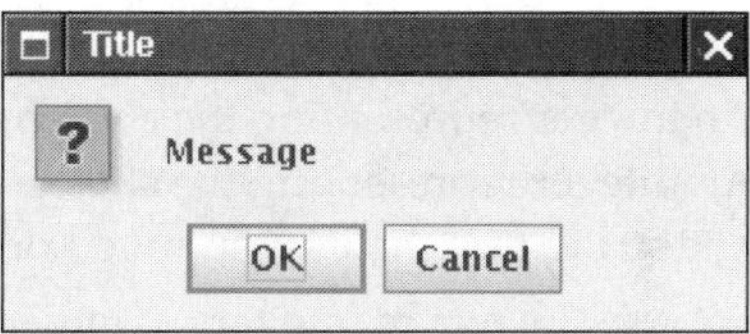

Figure 9–46: An option dialog

The input dialog has an additional component for user input. This can be a text field into which the user can type an arbitrary string, or a combo box from which the user can select one item.

The exact layout of these dialogs, and the choice of icons for standard message types, depend on the pluggable look and feel.

The icon on the left side depends on one of five *message types*:

```
ERROR_MESSAGE
INFORMATION_MESSAGE
WARNING_MESSAGE
QUESTION_MESSAGE
PLAIN_MESSAGE
```

The `PLAIN_MESSAGE` type has no icon. Each dialog type also has a method that lets you supply your own icon instead.

For each dialog type, you can specify a message. This message can be a string, an icon, a user interface component, or any other object. Here is how the message object is displayed:

`String`:	Draw the string
`Icon`:	Show the icon
`Component`:	Show the component
`Object[]`:	Show all objects in the array, stacked on top of each other
any other object:	Apply `toString` and show the resulting string

You can see these options by running the program in Example 9–18.

Of course, supplying a message string is by far the most common case. Supplying a `Component` gives you ultimate flexibility because you can make the `paintComponent` method draw anything you want.

The buttons on the bottom depend on the dialog type and the *option type*. When calling `showMessageDialog` and `showInputDialog`, you get only a standard set of buttons (OK and OK/Cancel, respectively). When calling `showConfirmDialog`, you can choose among four option types:

```
DEFAULT_OPTION
YES_NO_OPTION
YES_NO_CANCEL_OPTION
OK_CANCEL_OPTION
```

With the `showOptionDialog` you can specify an arbitrary set of options. You supply an array of objects for the options. Each array element is rendered as follows:

`String`:	Make a button with the string as label
`Icon`:	Make a button with the icon as label
`Component`:	Show the component
any other object:	Apply `toString` and make a button with the resulting string as label

The return values of these functions are as follows:

`showMessageDialog`	None
`showConfirmDialog`	An integer representing the chosen option
`showOptionDialog`	An integer representing the chosen option
`showInputDialog`	The string that the user supplied or selected

The `showConfirmDialog` and `showOptionDialog` return integers to indicate which button the user chose. For the option dialog, this is simply the index of the chosen option or the value `CLOSED_OPTION` if the user closed the dialog instead of choosing an option. For the confirmation dialog, the return value can be one of the following:

```
OK_OPTION
CANCEL_OPTION
YES_OPTION
NO_OPTION
CLOSED_OPTION
```

This all sounds like a bewildering set of choices, but in practice it is simple:

1. Choose the dialog type (message, confirmation, option, or input).
2. Choose the icon (error, information, warning, question, none, or custom).
3. Choose the message (string, icon, custom component, or a stack of them).
4. For a confirmation dialog, choose the option type (default, Yes/No, Yes/No/Cancel, or OK/Cancel).
5. For an option dialog, choose the options (strings, icons, or custom components) and the default option.
6. For an input dialog, choose between a text field and a combo box.
7. Locate the appropriate method to call in the `JOptionPane` API.

For example, suppose you want to show the dialog in Figure 9–46. The dialog shows a message and asks the user to confirm or cancel. Thus, it is a confirmation dialog. The icon is a warning icon. The message is a string. The option type is `OK_CANCEL_OPTION`. Here is the call you would make:

```
int selection = JOptionPane.showConfirmDialog(parent,
   "Message", "Title",
   JOptionPane.OK_CANCEL_OPTION,
   JOptionPane.WARNING_MESSAGE);
if (selection == JOptionPane.OK_OPTION) . . .
```

TIP: The message string can contain newline (`'\n'`) characters. Such a string is displayed in multiple lines.

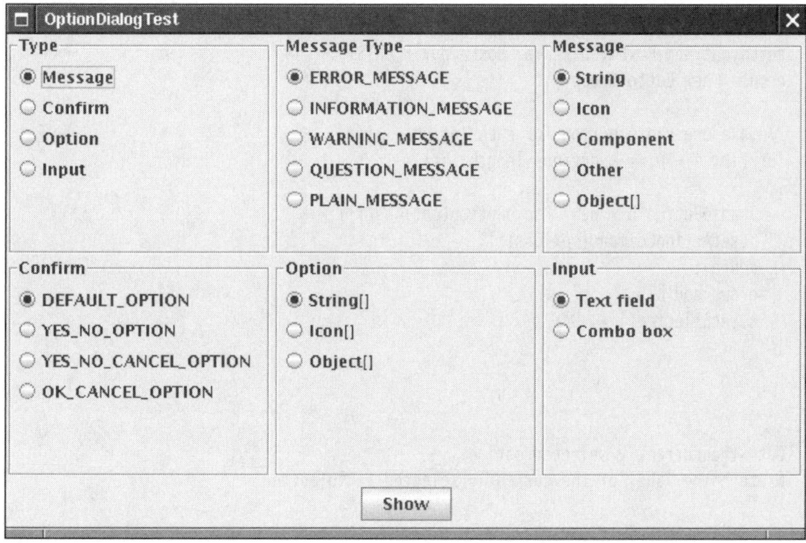

Figure 9–47: The `OptionDialogTest` program

The program in Example 9–18 lets you make the selections shown in Figure 9–47. It then shows you the resulting dialog.

Example 9–18: OptionDialogTest.java

```
import java.awt.*;
import java.awt.event.*;
import java.awt.geom.*;
import java.util.*;
import javax.swing.*;
import javax.swing.border.*;

public class OptionDialogTest
{
   public static void main(String[] args)
   {
      OptionDialogFrame frame = new OptionDialogFrame();
      frame.setDefaultCloseOperation(JFrame.EXIT_ON_CLOSE);
      frame.setVisible(true);
   }
}

/**
    A panel with radio buttons inside a titled border.
*/
class ButtonPanel extends JPanel
{
   /**
      Constructs a button panel.
      @param title the title shown in the border
      @param options an array of radio button labels
   */
   public ButtonPanel(String title, String[] options)
   {
      setBorder(BorderFactory.createTitledBorder(BorderFactory.createEtchedBorder(), title));
      setLayout(new BoxLayout(this, BoxLayout.Y_AXIS));
      group = new ButtonGroup();

      // make one radio button for each option
      for (int i = 0; i < options.length; i++)
      {
         JRadioButton b = new JRadioButton(options[i]);
         b.setActionCommand(options[i]);
         add(b);
         group.add(b);
         b.setSelected(i == 0);
      }
   }

   /**
      Gets the currently selected option.
      @return the label of the currently selected radio button.
   */
   public String getSelection()
   {
      return group.getSelection().getActionCommand();
   }
```

```

   private ButtonGroup group;
}

/**
   A frame that contains settings for selecting various option
   dialogs.
*/
class OptionDialogFrame extends JFrame
{
   public OptionDialogFrame()
   {
      setTitle("OptionDialogTest");
      setSize(DEFAULT_WIDTH, DEFAULT_HEIGHT);

      JPanel gridPanel = new JPanel();
      gridPanel.setLayout(new GridLayout(2, 3));

      typePanel = new ButtonPanel("Type",
         new String[]
         {
            "Message",
            "Confirm",
            "Option",
            "Input"
         });

      messageTypePanel = new ButtonPanel("Message Type",
         new String[]
         {
            "ERROR_MESSAGE",
            "INFORMATION_MESSAGE",
            "WARNING_MESSAGE",
            "QUESTION_MESSAGE",
            "PLAIN_MESSAGE"
         });

      messagePanel = new ButtonPanel("Message",
         new String[]
         {
            "String",
            "Icon",
            "Component",
            "Other",
            "Object[]"
         });

      optionTypePanel = new ButtonPanel("Confirm",
         new String[]
         {
            "DEFAULT_OPTION",
            "YES_NO_OPTION",
            "YES_NO_CANCEL_OPTION",
            "OK_CANCEL_OPTION"
         });

```

```
      optionsPanel = new ButtonPanel("Option",
         new String[]
         {
            "String[]",
            "Icon[]",
            "Object[]"
         });

      inputPanel = new ButtonPanel("Input",
         new String[]
         {
            "Text field",
            "Combo box"
         });

      gridPanel.add(typePanel);
      gridPanel.add(messageTypePanel);
      gridPanel.add(messagePanel);
      gridPanel.add(optionTypePanel);
      gridPanel.add(optionsPanel);
      gridPanel.add(inputPanel);

      // add a panel with a Show button

      JPanel showPanel = new JPanel();
      JButton showButton = new JButton("Show");
      showButton.addActionListener(new ShowAction());
      showPanel.add(showButton);

      add(gridPanel, BorderLayout.CENTER);
      add(showPanel, BorderLayout.SOUTH);
   }

   /**
      Gets the currently selected message.
      @return a string, icon, component, or object array,
      depending on the Message panel selection
   */
   public Object getMessage()
   {
      String s = messagePanel.getSelection();
      if (s.equals("String"))
         return messageString;
      else if (s.equals("Icon"))
         return messageIcon;
      else if (s.equals("Component"))
         return messageComponent;
      else if (s.equals("Object[]"))
         return new Object[]
         {
            messageString,
            messageIcon,
            messageComponent,
            messageObject
         };
      else if (s.equals("Other"))
```

```
         return messageObject;
      else return null;
   }

   /**
      Gets the currently selected options.
      @return an array of strings, icons, or objects, depending
      on the Option panel selection
   */
   public Object[] getOptions()
   {
      String s = optionsPanel.getSelection();
      if (s.equals("String[]"))
         return new String[] { "Yellow", "Blue", "Red" };
      else if (s.equals("Icon[]"))
         return new Icon[]
         {
            new ImageIcon("yellow-ball.gif"),
            new ImageIcon("blue-ball.gif"),
            new ImageIcon("red-ball.gif")
         };
      else if (s.equals("Object[]"))
         return new Object[]
         {
            messageString,
            messageIcon,
            messageComponent,
            messageObject
         };
      else
         return null;
   }

   /**
      Gets the selected message or option type
      @param panel the Message Type or Confirm panel
      @return the selected XXX_MESSAGE or XXX_OPTION constant
      from the JOptionPane class
   */
   public int getType(ButtonPanel panel)
   {
      String s = panel.getSelection();
      try
      {
         return JOptionPane.class.getField(s).getInt(null);
      }
      catch(Exception e)
      {
         return -1;
      }
   }

   /**
      The action listener for the Show button shows a
      Confirm, Input, Message, or Option dialog depending
      on the Type panel selection.
```

```
*/
private class ShowAction implements ActionListener
{
   public void actionPerformed(ActionEvent event)
   {
      if (typePanel.getSelection().equals("Confirm"))
         JOptionPane.showConfirmDialog(
            OptionDialogFrame.this,
            getMessage(),
            "Title",
            getType(optionTypePanel),
            getType(messageTypePanel));
      else if (typePanel.getSelection().equals("Input"))
      {
         if (inputPanel.getSelection().equals("Text field"))
            JOptionPane.showInputDialog(
               OptionDialogFrame.this,
               getMessage(),
               "Title",
               getType(messageTypePanel));
         else
            JOptionPane.showInputDialog(
               OptionDialogFrame.this,
               getMessage(),
               "Title",
               getType(messageTypePanel),
               null,
               new String[] { "Yellow", "Blue", "Red" },
               "Blue");
      }
      else if (typePanel.getSelection().equals("Message"))
         JOptionPane.showMessageDialog(
            OptionDialogFrame.this,
            getMessage(),
            "Title",
            getType(messageTypePanel));
      else if (typePanel.getSelection().equals("Option"))
         JOptionPane.showOptionDialog(
            OptionDialogFrame.this,
            getMessage(),
            "Title",
            getType(optionTypePanel),
            getType(messageTypePanel),
            null,
            getOptions(),
            getOptions()[0]);
   }
}

public static final int DEFAULT_WIDTH = 600;
public static final int DEFAULT_HEIGHT = 400;

private ButtonPanel typePanel;
private ButtonPanel messagePanel;
private ButtonPanel messageTypePanel;
private ButtonPanel optionTypePanel;
```

```
   private ButtonPanel optionsPanel;
   private ButtonPanel inputPanel;

   private String messageString = "Message";
   private Icon messageIcon = new ImageIcon("blue-ball.gif");
   private Object messageObject = new Date();
   private Component messageComponent = new SamplePanel();
}

/**
   A panel with a painted surface
*/

class SamplePanel extends JPanel
{
   public void paintComponent(Graphics g)
   {
      super.paintComponent(g);
      Graphics2D g2 = (Graphics2D) g;
      Rectangle2D rect = new Rectangle2D.Double(0, 0, getWidth() - 1, getHeight() - 1);
      g2.setPaint(Color.YELLOW);
      g2.fill(rect);
      g2.setPaint(Color.BLUE);
      g2.draw(rect);
   }

   public Dimension getMinimumSize()
   {
      return new Dimension(10, 10);
   }
}
```

API **javax.swing.JOptionPane 1.2**

- `static void showMessageDialog(Component parent, Object message, String title, int messageType, Icon icon)`
- `static void showMessageDialog(Component parent, Object message, String title, int messageType)`
- `static void showMessageDialog(Component parent, Object message)`
- `static void showInternalMessageDialog(Component parent, Object message, String title, int messageType, Icon icon)`
- `static void showInternalMessageDialog(Component parent, Object message, String title, int messageType)`
- `static void showInternalMessageDialog(Component parent, Object message)`

  show a message dialog or an internal message dialog. (An internal dialog is rendered entirely within its owner frame.)

Parameters:	`parent`	The parent component (can be `null`)
	`message`	The message to show on the dialog (can be a string, icon, component, or an array of them)
	`title`	The string in the title bar of the dialog
	`messageType`	One of `ERROR_MESSAGE`, `INFORMATION_MESSAGE`, `WARNING_MESSAGE`, `QUESTION_MESSAGE`, `PLAIN_MESSAGE`
	`icon`	An icon to show instead of one of the standard icons

- `static int showConfirmDialog(Component parent, Object message, String title, int optionType, int messageType, Icon icon)`
- `static int showConfirmDialog(Component parent, Object message, String title, int optionType, int messageType)`
- `static int showConfirmDialog(Component parent, Object message, String title, int optionType)`
- `static int showConfirmDialog(Component parent, Object message)`
- `static int showInternalConfirmDialog(Component parent, Object message, String title, int optionType, int messageType, Icon icon)`
- `static int showInternalConfirmDialog(Component parent, Object message, String title, int optionType, int messageType)`
- `static int showInternalConfirmDialog(Component parent, Object message, String title, int optionType)`
- `static int showInternalConfirmDialog(Component parent, Object message)`

  show a confirmation dialog or an internal confirmation dialog. (An internal dialog is rendered entirely within its owner frame.) Returns the option selected by the user (one of `OK_OPTION`, `CANCEL_OPTION`, `YES_OPTION`, `NO_OPTION`), or `CLOSED_OPTION` if the user closed the dialog.

Parameters:	`parent`	The parent component (can be `null`)
	`message`	The message to show on the dialog (can be a string, icon, component, or an array of them)
	`title`	The string in the title bar of the dialog
	`messageType`	One of `ERROR_MESSAGE`, `INFORMATION_MESSAGE`, `WARNING_MESSAGE`, `QUESTION_MESSAGE`, `PLAIN_MESSAGE`
	`optionType`	One of `DEFAULT_OPTION`, `YES_NO_OPTION`, `YES_NO_CANCEL_OPTION`, `OK_CANCEL_OPTION`
	`icon`	An icon to show instead of one of the standard icons

- `static int showOptionDialog(Component parent, Object message, String title, int optionType, int messageType, Icon icon, Object[] options, Object default)`
- `static int showInternalOptionDialog(Component parent, Object message, String title, int optionType, int messageType, Icon icon, Object[] options, Object default)`

  show an option dialog or an internal option dialog. (An internal dialog is rendered entirely within its owner frame.) Returns the index of the option selected by the user, or `CLOSED_OPTION` if the user canceled the dialog.

Parameters:	`parent`	The parent component (can be `null`)
	`message`	The message to show on the dialog (can be a string, icon, component, or an array of them)
	`title`	The string in the title bar of the dialog
	`messageType`	One of `ERROR_MESSAGE`, `INFORMATION_MESSAGE`, `WARNING_MESSAGE`, `QUESTION_MESSAGE`, `PLAIN_MESSAGE`
	`optionType`	One of `DEFAULT_OPTION`, `YES_NO_OPTION`, `YES_NO_CANCEL_OPTION`, `OK_CANCEL_OPTION`
	`icon`	An icon to show instead of one of the standard icons
	`options`	An array of options (can be strings, icons, or components)
	`default`	The default option to present to the user

- `static Object showInputDialog(Component parent, Object message, String title, int messageType, Icon icon, Object[] values, Object default)`
- `static String showInputDialog(Component parent, Object message, String title, int messageType)`
- `static String showInputDialog(Component parent, Object message)`
- `static String showInputDialog(Object message)`
- `static String showInputDialog(Component parent, Object message, Object default)` **1.4**
- `static String showInputDialog(Object message, Object default)` **1.4**
- `static Object showInternalInputDialog(Component parent, Object message, String title, int messageType, Icon icon, Object[] values, Object default)`
- `static String showInternalInputDialog(Component parent, Object message, String title, int messageType)`
- `static String showInternalInputDialog(Component parent, Object message)`

  show an input dialog or an internal input dialog. (An internal dialog is rendered entirely within its owner frame.) Returns the input string typed by the user, or `null` if the user canceled the dialog.

Parameters:	`parent`	The parent component (can be `null`)
	`message`	The message to show on the dialog (can be a string, icon, component, or an array of them)
	`title`	The string in the title bar of the dialog
	`messageType`	One of `ERROR_MESSAGE`, `INFORMATION_MESSAGE`, `WARNING_MESSAGE`, `QUESTION_MESSAGE`, `PLAIN_MESSAGE`
	`icon`	An icon to show instead of one of the standard icons
	`values`	An array of values to show in a combo box
	`default`	The default value to present to the user

Creating Dialogs

In the last section, you saw how to use the `JOptionPane` class to show a simple dialog. In this section, you see how to create such a dialog by hand.

Figure 9–48 shows a typical modal dialog box, a program information box that is displayed when the user clicks the About button.

To implement a dialog box, you derive a class from `JDialog`. This is essentially the same process as deriving the main window for an application from `JFrame`. More precisely:

1. In the constructor of your dialog box, call the constructor of the superclass `JDialog`. You will need to tell it the *owner frame* (the frame window over which the dialog pops up), the title of the dialog frame, and a Boolean flag to indicate if the dialog box is modal or modeless.

   You should supply the owner frame so that the dialog can be displayed on top of its owner. Windowing systems typically require that every pop-up window is owned by another frame. You can also supply a `null` owner, but that is a bit risky—the dialog might be hidden behind other windows. (Dialogs with a `null` owner are actually owned by a shared hidden frame.)
2. Add the user interface components of the dialog box.
3. Add the event handlers.
4. Set the size for the dialog box.

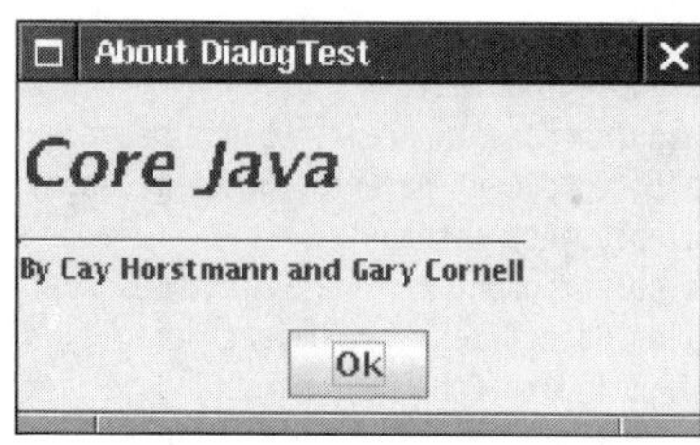

Figure 9–48: An About dialog box

Here's an example dialog box:

```
public AboutDialog extends JDialog
{
   public AboutDialog(JFrame owner)
   {
      super(owner, "About DialogTest", true);
      add(new JLabel(
         "<html><h1><i>Core Java</i></h1><hr>By Cay Horstmann and Gary Cornell</html>"),
         BorderLayout.CENTER);

      JPanel panel = new JPanel();
      JButton ok = new JButton("Ok");

      ok.addActionListener(new
         ActionListener()
         {
            public void actionPerformed(ActionEvent event)
            {
               setVisible(false);
            }
         });

      panel.add(ok);
      add(panel, BorderLayout.SOUTH);

      setSize(250, 150);
   }
}
```

As you can see, the constructor adds user interface elements: in this case, labels and a button. It adds a handler to the button and sets the size of the dialog.

To display the dialog box, you create a new dialog object and make it visible:

```
JDialog dialog = new AboutDialog(this);
dialog.setVisible(true);
```

Actually, in the sample code below, we create the dialog box only once, and we can reuse it whenever the user clicks the About button.

```
if (dialog == null) // first time
   dialog = new AboutDialog(this);
dialog.setVisible(true);
```

When the user clicks the Ok button, the dialog box should close. This is handled in the event handler of the Ok button:

```
ok.addActionListener(new
   ActionListener()
   {
```

```
      public void actionPerformed(ActionEvent event)
      {
         setVisible(false);
      }
   });
```

When the user closes the dialog by clicking on the Close box, then the dialog is also hidden. Just as with a `JFrame`, you can override this behavior with the `setDefaultCloseOperation` method.

Example 9–19 is the code for the About dialog box test program.

Example 9–19: DialogTest.java

```
import java.awt.*;
import java.awt.event.*;
import javax.swing.*;

public class DialogTest
{
   public static void main(String[] args)
   {
      DialogFrame frame = new DialogFrame();
      frame.setDefaultCloseOperation(JFrame.EXIT_ON_CLOSE);
      frame.setVisible(true);
   }
}

/**
   A frame with a menu whose File->About action shows a dialog.
*/
class DialogFrame extends JFrame
{
   public DialogFrame()
   {
      setTitle("DialogTest");
      setSize(DEFAULT_WIDTH, DEFAULT_HEIGHT);

      // construct a File menu

      JMenuBar menuBar = new JMenuBar();
      setJMenuBar(menuBar);
      JMenu fileMenu = new JMenu("File");
      menuBar.add(fileMenu);

      // add About and Exit menu items

      // The About item shows the About dialog

      JMenuItem aboutItem = new JMenuItem("About");
      aboutItem.addActionListener(new
         ActionListener()
         {
            public void actionPerformed(ActionEvent event)
            {
               if (dialog == null) // first time
                  dialog = new AboutDialog(DialogFrame.this);
               dialog.setVisible(true); // pop up dialog
```

```
            }
         });
      fileMenu.add(aboutItem);

      // The Exit item exits the program

      JMenuItem exitItem = new JMenuItem("Exit");
      exitItem.addActionListener(new
         ActionListener()
         {
            public void actionPerformed(ActionEvent event)
            {
               System.exit(0);
            }
         });
      fileMenu.add(exitItem);
   }

   public static final int DEFAULT_WIDTH = 300;
   public static final int DEFAULT_HEIGHT = 200;

   private AboutDialog dialog;
}

/**
   A sample modal dialog that displays a message and
   waits for the user to click the Ok button.
*/
class AboutDialog extends JDialog
{
   public AboutDialog(JFrame owner)
   {
      super(owner, "About DialogTest", true);

      // add HTML label to center

      add(new JLabel(
         "<html><h1><i>Core Java</i></h1><hr>By Cay Horstmann and Gary Cornell</html>"),
         BorderLayout.CENTER);

      // Ok button closes the dialog

      JButton ok = new JButton("Ok");
      ok.addActionListener(new
         ActionListener()
         {
            public void actionPerformed(ActionEvent event)
            {
               setVisible(false);
            }
         });

      // add Ok button to southern border

      JPanel panel = new JPanel();
```

```
        panel.add(ok);
        add(panel, BorderLayout.SOUTH);

        setSize(250, 150);
    }
}
```

API `javax.swing.JDialog` 1.2

- `public JDialog(Frame parent, String title, boolean modal)`
  constructs a dialog. The dialog is not visible until it is explicitly shown.

Parameters:	`parent`	The frame that is the owner of the dialog
	`title`	The title of the dialog
	`modal`	True for modal dialogs (a modal dialog blocks input to other windows)

Data Exchange

The most common reason to put up a dialog box is to get information from the user. You have already seen how easy it is to make a dialog box object: give it initial data and then call `setVisible(true)` to display the dialog box on the screen. Now let us see how to transfer data in and out of a dialog box.

Consider the dialog box in Figure 9–49 that could be used to obtain a user name and a password to connect to some on-line service.

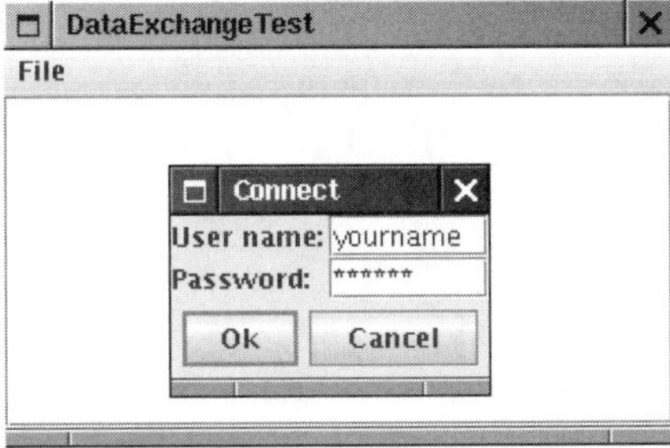

Figure 9–49: Password dialog box

Your dialog box should provide methods to set default data. For example, the `PasswordChooser` class of the example program has a method, `setUser`, to place default values into the next fields:

```
public void setUser(User u)
{
   username.setText(u.getName());
}
```

Once you set the defaults (if desired), you show the dialog by calling `setVisible(true)`. The dialog is now displayed.

The user then fills in the information and clicks the Ok or Cancel button. The event handlers for both buttons call `setVisible(false)`, which terminates the call to `setVisible(true)`. Alternatively, the user may close the dialog. If you did not install a window listener for the dialog, then the default window closing operation applies: the dialog becomes invisible, which also terminates the call to `setVisible(true)`.

The important issue is that the call to `setVisible(true)` blocks until the user has dismissed the dialog. This makes it easy to implement modal dialogs.

You want to know whether the user has accepted or canceled the dialog. Our sample code sets the `ok` flag to `false` before showing the dialog. Only the event handler for the Ok button sets the `ok` flag to `true`. In that case, you can retrieve the user input from the dialog.

NOTE: Transferring data out of a modeless dialog is not as simple. When a modeless dialog is displayed, the call to `setVisible(true)` does not block and the program continues running while the dialog is displayed. If the user selects items on a modeless dialog and then clicks Ok, the dialog needs to send an event to some listener in the program.

The example program contains another useful improvement. When you construct a `JDialog` object, you need to specify the owner frame. However, quite often you want to show the same dialog with different owner frames. It is better to pick the owner frame *when you are ready to show the dialog*, not when you construct the `PasswordChooser` object.

The trick is to have the `PasswordChooser` extend `JPanel` instead of `JDialog`. Build a `JDialog` object on the fly in the `showDialog` method:

```
public boolean showDialog(Frame owner, String title)
{
   ok = false;

   if (dialog == null || dialog.getOwner() != owner)
   {
      dialog = new JDialog(owner, true);
      dialog.add(this);
      dialog.pack();
   }

   dialog.setTitle(title);
   dialog.setVisible(true);
   return ok;
}
```

Note that it is safe to have `owner` equal to `null`.

You can do even better. Sometimes, the owner frame isn't readily available. It is easy enough to compute it from any `parent` component, like this:

```
Frame owner;
if (parent instanceof Frame)
   owner = (Frame) parent;
else
   owner = (Frame) SwingUtilities.getAncestorOfClass(Frame.class, parent);
```

We use this enhancement in our sample program. The `JOptionPane` class also uses this mechanism.

Many dialogs have a *default button*, which is automatically selected if the user presses a trigger key (ENTER in most "look and feel" implementations). The default button is specially marked, often with a thick outline.

You set the default button in the *root pane* of the dialog:

```
dialog.getRootPane().setDefaultButton(okButton);
```

If you follow our suggestion of laying out the dialog in a panel, then you must be careful to set the default button only after you wrapped the panel into a dialog. The panel itself has no root pane.

Example 9–20 is the complete code that illustrates the data flow into and out of a dialog box.

Example 9–20: DataExchangeTest.java

```
import java.awt.*;
import java.awt.event.*;
import javax.swing.*;

public class DataExchangeTest
{
   public static void main(String[] args)
   {
      DataExchangeFrame frame = new DataExchangeFrame();
      frame.setDefaultCloseOperation(JFrame.EXIT_ON_CLOSE);
      frame.setVisible(true);
   }
}

/**
   A frame with a menu whose File->Connect action shows a
   password dialog.
*/
class DataExchangeFrame extends JFrame
{
   public DataExchangeFrame()
   {
      setTitle("DataExchangeTest");
      setSize(DEFAULT_WIDTH, DEFAULT_HEIGHT);

      // construct a File menu

      JMenuBar mbar = new JMenuBar();
      setJMenuBar(mbar);
      JMenu fileMenu = new JMenu("File");
      mbar.add(fileMenu);

      // add Connect and Exit menu items

      JMenuItem connectItem = new JMenuItem("Connect");
      connectItem.addActionListener(new ConnectAction());
      fileMenu.add(connectItem);

      // The Exit item exits the program

      JMenuItem exitItem = new JMenuItem("Exit");
      exitItem.addActionListener(new
         ActionListener()
         {
            public void actionPerformed(ActionEvent event)
            {
               System.exit(0);
            }
         });
      fileMenu.add(exitItem);

      textArea = new JTextArea();
      add(new JScrollPane(textArea), BorderLayout.CENTER);
```

```
   }

   public static final int DEFAULT_WIDTH = 300;
   public static final int DEFAULT_HEIGHT = 200;

   private PasswordChooser dialog = null;
   private JTextArea textArea;

   /**
      The Connect action pops up the password dialog.
   */

   private class ConnectAction implements ActionListener
   {
      public void actionPerformed(ActionEvent event)
      {
         // if first time, construct dialog

         if (dialog == null)
            dialog = new PasswordChooser();

         // set default values
         dialog.setUser(new User("yourname", null));

         // pop up dialog
         if (dialog.showDialog(DataExchangeFrame.this, "Connect"))
         {
            // if accepted, retrieve user input
            User u = dialog.getUser();
            textArea.append(
               "user name = " + u.getName()
               + ", password = " + (new String(u.getPassword()))
               + "\n");
         }
      }
   }
}

/**
   A password chooser that is shown inside a dialog
*/
class PasswordChooser extends JPanel
{
   public PasswordChooser()
   {
      setLayout(new BorderLayout());

      // construct a panel with user name and password fields

      JPanel panel = new JPanel();
      panel.setLayout(new GridLayout(2, 2));
      panel.add(new JLabel("User name:"));
      panel.add(username = new JTextField(""));
      panel.add(new JLabel("Password:"));
      panel.add(password = new JPasswordField(""));
      add(panel, BorderLayout.CENTER);
```

```

      // create Ok and Cancel buttons that terminate the dialog

      okButton = new JButton("Ok");
      okButton.addActionListener(new
         ActionListener()
         {
            public void actionPerformed(ActionEvent event)
            {
               ok = true;
               dialog.setVisible(false);
            }
         });

      JButton cancelButton = new JButton("Cancel");
      cancelButton.addActionListener(new
         ActionListener()
         {
            public void actionPerformed(ActionEvent event)
            {
               dialog.setVisible(false);
            }
         });

      // add buttons to southern border

      JPanel buttonPanel = new JPanel();
      buttonPanel.add(okButton);
      buttonPanel.add(cancelButton);
      add(buttonPanel, BorderLayout.SOUTH);
   }

   /**
      Sets the dialog defaults.
      @param u the default user information
   */
   public void setUser(User u)
   {
      username.setText(u.getName());
   }

   /**
      Gets the dialog entries.
      @return a User object whose state represents
      the dialog entries
   */
   public User getUser()
   {
      return new User(username.getText(), password.getPassword());
   }

   /**
      Show the chooser panel in a dialog
      @param parent a component in the owner frame or null
      @param title the dialog window title
   */
```

```
   public boolean showDialog(Component parent, String title)
   {
      ok = false;

      // locate the owner frame

      Frame owner = null;
      if (parent instanceof Frame)
         owner = (Frame) parent;
      else
         owner = (Frame) SwingUtilities.getAncestorOfClass(Frame.class, parent);

      // if first time, or if owner has changed, make new dialog

      if (dialog == null || dialog.getOwner() != owner)
      {
         dialog = new JDialog(owner, true);
         dialog.add(this);
         dialog.getRootPane().setDefaultButton(okButton);
         dialog.pack();
      }

      // set title and show dialog

      dialog.setTitle(title);
      dialog.setVisible(true);
      return ok;
   }

   private JTextField username;
   private JPasswordField password;
   private JButton okButton;
   private boolean ok;
   private JDialog dialog;
}

/**
   A user has a name and password. For security reasons, the
   password is stored as a char[], not a String.
*/
class User
{
   public User(String aName, char[] aPassword)
   {
      name = aName;
      password = aPassword;
   }

   public String getName() { return name; }
   public char[] getPassword() { return password; }

   public void setName(String aName) { name = aName; }
   public void setPassword(char[] aPassword) { password = aPassword; }

   private String name;
   private char[] password;
}
```

javax.swing.SwingUtilities 1.2

- `Container getAncestorOfClass(Class c, Component comp)`
  returns the innermost parent container of the given component that belongs to the given class or one of its subclasses.

javax.swing.JComponent 1.2

- `JRootPane getRootPane()`
  gets the root pane enclosing this component, or `null` if this component does not have an ancestor with a root pane.

javax.swing.JRootPane 1.2

- `void setDefaultButton(JButton button)`
  sets the default button for this root pane. To deactivate the default button, call this method with a `null` parameter.

javax.swing.JButton 1.2

- `boolean isDefaultButton()`
  returns `true` if this button is the default button of its root pane.

File Dialogs

When you write an application, you often want to be able to open and save files. A good file dialog box that shows files and directories and lets the user navigate the file system is hard to write, and you definitely don't want to reinvent that wheel. Fortunately, Swing provides a `JFileChooser` class that allows you to display a file dialog box similar to the one that most native applications use. `JFileChooser` dialogs are always modal. Note that the `JFileChooser` class is not a subclass of `JDialog`. Instead of calling `setVisible(true)`, you call `showOpenDialog` to display a dialog for opening a file or you call `showSaveDialog` to display a dialog for saving a file. The button for accepting a file is then automatically labeled Open or Save. You can also supply your own button label with the `showDialog` method. Figure 9–50 shows an example of the file chooser dialog box.

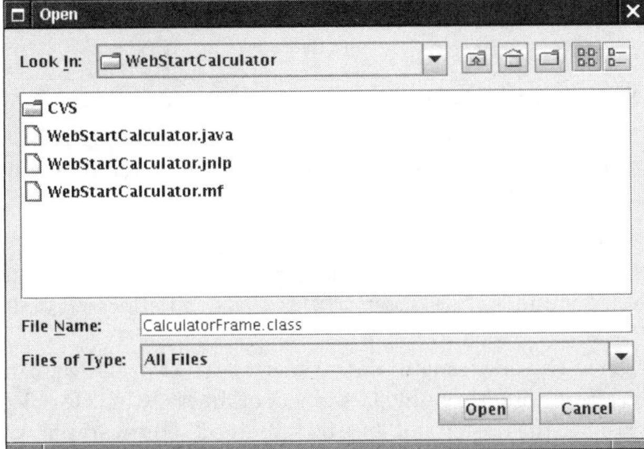

Figure 9–50: File chooser dialog box

Here are the steps needed to put up a file dialog box and recover what the user chooses from the box.

1. Make a `JFileChooser` object. Unlike the constructor for the `JDialog` class, you do not supply the parent component. This allows you to reuse a file chooser dialog with multiple frames.

   For example:

   ```
   JFileChooser chooser = new JFileChooser();
   ```

TIP: Reusing a file chooser object is a good idea because the `JFileChooser` constructor can be quite slow, especially on Windows if the user has many mapped network drives.

2. Set the directory by calling the `setCurrentDirectory` method.

   For example, to use the current working directory:

   ```
   chooser.setCurrentDirectory(new File("."));
   ```

   You need to supply a `File` object. `File` objects are explained in detail in Chapter 12. All you need to know for now is that the constructor `File(String filename)` turns a file or directory name into a `File` object.
3. If you have a default file name that you expect the user to choose, supply it with the `setSelectedFile` method:

   ```
   chooser.setSelectedFile(new File(filename));
   ```
4. To enable the user to select multiple files in the dialog, call the `setMultiSelectionEnabled` method. This is, of course, entirely optional and not all that common.

   ```
   chooser.setMultiSelectionEnabled(true);
   ```
5. If you want to restrict the display of files in the dialog to those of a particular type (for example, all files with extension `.gif`), then you need to set a *file filter*. We discuss file filters later in this section.
6. By default, a user can select only files with a file chooser. If you want the user to select directories, use the `setFileSelectionMode` method. Call it with `JFileChooser.FILES_ONLY` (the default), `JFileChooser.DIRECTORIES_ONLY`, or `JFileChooser.FILES_AND_DIRECTORIES`.
7. Show the dialog box by calling the `showOpenDialog` or `showSaveDialog` method. You must supply the parent component in these calls:

   ```
   int result = chooser.showOpenDialog(parent);
   ```

   or

   ```
   int result = chooser.showSaveDialog(parent);
   ```

   The only difference between these calls is the label of the "approve button," the button that the user clicks to finish the file selection. You can also call the `showDialog` method and pass an explicit text for the approve button:

   ```
   int result = chooser.showDialog(parent, "Select");
   ```

   These calls return only when the user has approved, canceled, or dismissed the file dialog. The return value is `JFileChooser.APPROVE_OPTION`, `JFileChooser.CANCEL_OPTION`, or `JFileChooser.ERROR_OPTION`
8. You get the selected file or files with the `getSelectedFile()` or `getSelectedFiles()` method. These methods return either a single `File` object or an array of `File` objects. If you just need the name of the file object, call its `getPath` method. For example,

   ```
   String filename = chooser.getSelectedFile().getPath();
   ```

For the most part, these steps are simple. The major difficulty with using a file dialog is to specify a subset of files from which the user should choose. For example, suppose the user should choose a GIF image file. Then, the file chooser should only display files with extension `.gif`. It should also give the user some kind of feedback that the displayed files are of a particular category, such as "GIF Images." But the situation can be more complex. If the user should choose a JPEG image file, then the extension can be either `.jpg` or `.jpeg`. Rather than coming up with a mechanism to codify these complexities, the designers of the file chooser supply a more elegant mechanism: to restrict the displayed files, you supply an object that extends the abstract class `javax.swing.filechooser.FileFilter`. The file chooser passes each file to the file filter and displays only the files that the file filter accepts.

At the time of this writing, only one such subclass is supplied: the default filter that accepts all files. However, it is easy to write ad hoc file filters. You simply implement the two abstract methods of the `FileFilter` superclass:

```
public boolean accept(File f);
public String getDescription();
```

NOTE: An unrelated `FileFilter` interface in the `java.io` package has a single method, `boolean accept(File f)`. It is used in the `listFiles` method of the `File` class to list files in a directory. We do not know why the designers of Swing didn't extend this interface—perhaps the Java class library has now become so complex that even the programmers at Sun are no longer aware of all the standard classes and interfaces.

You will need to resolve the name conflict between these two identically named types if you import both the `java.io` and the `javax.swing.filechooser` package. The simplest remedy is to import `javax.swing.filechooser.FileFilter`, not `javax.swing.filechooser.*`.

The first method tests whether a file should be accepted. The second method returns a description of the file type that can be displayed in the file chooser dialog. For example, to filter for GIF files, you might use

```
public class GifFilter extends FileFilter
{
   public boolean accept(File f)
   {
      return f.getName().toLowerCase().endsWith(".gif") || f.isDirectory();
   }
   public String getDescription()
   {
      return "GIF Image";
   }
}
```

Once you have a file filter object, you use the `setFileFilter` method of the `JFileChooser` class to install it into the file chooser object:

```
chooser.setFileFilter(new GifFilter());
```

In our sample program, we supply a class `ExtensionFileFilter`, to be used as follows:

```
ExtensionFileFilter filter = new ExtensionFileFilter();
filter.addExtension("jpg");
filter.addExtension("gif");
filter.setDescription("Image files");
```

The implementation of the `ExtensionFileFilter` is a straightforward generalization of the `GifFilter` class. You may want to use that class in your own programs.

NOTE: The JDK contains a similar class, ExampleFileFilter, in the demo/jfc/FileChooserDemo directory.

You can install multiple filters to the file chooser by calling

```
chooser.addChoosableFileFilter(new GifFilter());
chooser.addChoosableFileFilter(new JpegFilter());
. . .
```

The user selects a filter from the combo box at the bottom of the file dialog. By default, the "All files" filter is always present in the combo box. This is a good idea, just in case a user of your program needs to select a file with a nonstandard extension. However, if you want to suppress the "All files" filter, call

```
chooser.setAcceptAllFileFilterUsed(false)
```

CAUTION: If you reuse a single file chooser for loading and saving different file types, call

```
chooser.resetChoosableFilters()
```

to clear any old file filters before adding new ones.

Finally, you can customize the file chooser by providing special icons and file descriptions for each file that the file chooser displays. You do this by supplying an object of a class extending the FileView class in the javax.swing.filechooser package. This is definitely an advanced technique. Normally, you don't need to supply a file view—the pluggable look and feel supplies one for you. But if you want to show different icons for special file types, you can install your own file view. You need to extend the FileView class and implement five methods:

```
Icon getIcon(File f);
String getName(File f);
String getDescription(File f);
String getTypeDescription(File f);
Boolean isTraversable(File f);
```

Then you use the setFileView method to install your file view into the file chooser.

The file chooser calls your methods for each file or directory that it wants to display. If your method returns null for the icon, name, or description, the file chooser then consults the default file view of the look and feel. That is good, because it means you need to deal only with the file types for which you want to do something different.

The file chooser calls the isTraversable method to decide whether to open a directory when a user clicks on it. Note that this method returns a Boolean object, not a boolean value! This seems weird, but it is actually convenient—if you aren't interested in deviating from the default file view, just return null. The file chooser will then consult the default file view. In other words, the method returns a Boolean to let you choose among three options: true (Boolean.TRUE), false (Boolean.FALSE), and don't care (null).

The example program contains a simple file view class. That class shows a particular icon whenever a file matches a file filter. We use it to display a palette icon for all image files.

```
class FileIconView extends FileView
{
   public FileIconView(FileFilter aFilter, Icon anIcon)
   {
      filter = aFilter;
```

```
      icon = anIcon;
   }

   public Icon getIcon(File f)
   {
      if (!f.isDirectory() && filter.accept(f))
         return icon;
      else return null;
   }

   private FileFilter filter;
   private Icon icon;
}
```

CAUTION: In JDK version 1.2, you must define all five methods of your `FileView` subclass. Simply return `null` in the methods that you don't need. In JDK version 1.3, the `FileView` methods are no longer abstract.

You install this file view into your file chooser with the `setFileView` method:

```
chooser.setFileView(new FileIconView(filter,
   new ImageIcon("palette.gif")));
```

The file chooser will then show the palette icon next to all files that pass the `filter` and use the default file view to show all other files. Naturally, we use the same filter that we set in the file chooser.

TIP: You can find a more useful `ExampleFileView` class in the `demo/jfc/FileChooserDemo` directory of the JDK. That class lets you associate icons and descriptions with arbitrary extensions.

Finally, you can customize a file dialog by adding an *accessory* component. For example, Figure 9–51 shows a preview accessory next to the file list. This accessory displays a thumbnail view of the currently selected file.

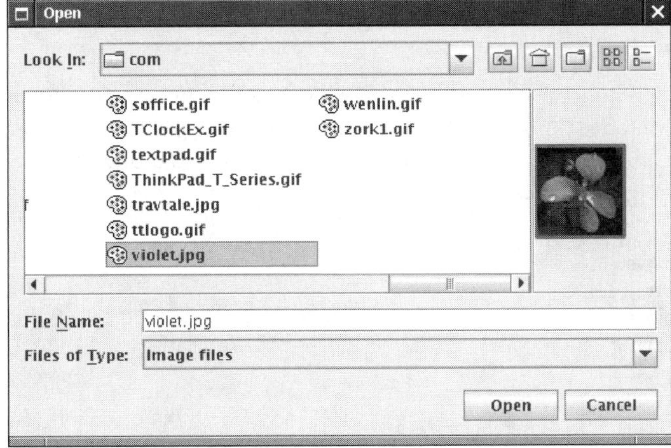

Figure 9–51: A file dialog with a preview accessory

An accessory can be any Swing component. In our case, we extend the `JLabel` class and set its icon to a scaled copy of the graphics image:

```
class ImagePreviewer extends JLabel
{
   public ImagePreviewer(JFileChooser chooser)
   {
      setPreferredSize(new Dimension(100, 100));
      setBorder(BorderFactory.createEtchedBorder());
   }

   public void loadImage(File f)
   {
      ImageIcon icon = new ImageIcon(f.getPath());
      if(icon.getIconWidth() > getWidth())
         icon = new ImageIcon(icon.getImage().getScaledInstance(
            getWidth(), -1, Image.SCALE_DEFAULT));
      setIcon(icon);
      repaint();
   }
}
```

There is just one challenge. We want to update the preview image whenever the user selects a different file. The file chooser uses the "JavaBeans" mechanism of notifying interested listeners whenever one of its properties changes. The selected file is a property that you can monitor by installing a `PropertyChangeListener`. We discuss this mechanism in greater detail in Volume 2. Here is the code that you need to trap the notifications:

```
chooser.addPropertyChangeListener(new
   PropertyChangeListener()
   {
      public void propertyChange(PropertyChangeEvent event)
      {
         if (event.getPropertyName() == JFileChooser.SELECTED_FILE_CHANGED_PROPERTY)
         {
            File newFile = (File) event.getNewValue()
             // update the accessory
             . . .
         }
      }
});
```

In our example program, we add this code to the `ImagePreviewer` constructor.

Example 9–21 contains a modification of the `ImageViewer` program from Chapter 2, in which the file chooser has been enhanced by a custom file view and a preview accessory.

Example 9–21: FileChooserTest.java

```
import java.awt.*;
import java.awt.event.*;
import java.awt.image.*;
import java.beans.*;
import java.util.*;
import java.io.*;
import javax.swing.*;
import javax.swing.filechooser.FileFilter;
import javax.swing.filechooser.FileView;

public class FileChooserTest
{
```

```
   public static void main(String[] args)
   {
      ImageViewerFrame frame = new ImageViewerFrame();
      frame.setDefaultCloseOperation(JFrame.EXIT_ON_CLOSE);
      frame.setVisible(true);
   }
}

/**
   A frame that has a menu for loading an image and a display
   area for the loaded image.
*/
class ImageViewerFrame extends JFrame
{
   public ImageViewerFrame()
   {
      setTitle("FileChooserTest");
      setSize(DEFAULT_WIDTH, DEFAULT_HEIGHT);

      // set up menu bar
      JMenuBar menuBar = new JMenuBar();
      setJMenuBar(menuBar);

      JMenu menu = new JMenu("File");
      menuBar.add(menu);

      JMenuItem openItem = new JMenuItem("Open");
      menu.add(openItem);
      openItem.addActionListener(new FileOpenListener());

      JMenuItem exitItem = new JMenuItem("Exit");
      menu.add(exitItem);
      exitItem.addActionListener(new
         ActionListener()
         {
            public void actionPerformed(ActionEvent event)
            {
               System.exit(0);
            }
         });

      // use a label to display the images
      label = new JLabel();
      add(label);

      // set up file chooser
      chooser = new JFileChooser();

      // accept all image files ending with .jpg, .jpeg, .gif
      final ExtensionFileFilter filter = new ExtensionFileFilter();
      filter.addExtension("jpg");
      filter.addExtension("jpeg");
      filter.addExtension("gif");
      filter.setDescription("Image files");
      chooser.setFileFilter(filter);

```

```
      chooser.setAccessory(new ImagePreviewer(chooser));

      chooser.setFileView(new FileIconView(filter, new ImageIcon("palette.gif")));
   }

   /**
      This is the listener for the File->Open menu item.
   */
   private class FileOpenListener implements ActionListener
   {
      public void actionPerformed(ActionEvent event)
      {
         chooser.setCurrentDirectory(new File("."));

         // show file chooser dialog
         int result = chooser.showOpenDialog(ImageViewerFrame.this);

         // if image file accepted, set it as icon of the label
         if(result == JFileChooser.APPROVE_OPTION)
         {
            String name = chooser.getSelectedFile().getPath();
            label.setIcon(new ImageIcon(name));
         }
      }
   }

   public static final int DEFAULT_WIDTH = 300;
   public static final int DEFAULT_HEIGHT = 400;

   private JLabel label;
   private JFileChooser chooser;
}

/**
   This file filter matches all files with a given set of
   extensions.
*/
class ExtensionFileFilter extends FileFilter
{
   /**
      Adds an extension that this file filter recognizes.
      @param extension a file extension (such as ".txt" or "txt")
   */
   public void addExtension(String extension)
   {
      if (!extension.startsWith("."))
         extension = "." + extension;
      extensions.add(extension.toLowerCase());
   }

   /**
      Sets a description for the file set that this file filter
      recognizes.
      @param aDescription a description for the file set
   */
   public void setDescription(String aDescription)
```

```
   {
      description = aDescription;
   }

   /**
      Returns a description for the file set that this file
      filter recognizes.
      @return a description for the file set
   */
   public String getDescription()
   {
      return description;
   }

   public boolean accept(File f)
   {
      if (f.isDirectory()) return true;
      String name = f.getName().toLowerCase();

      // check if the file name ends with any of the extensions
      for (String extension : extensions)
         if (name.endsWith(extension))
            return true;
      return false;
   }

   private String description = "";
   private ArrayList<String> extensions = new ArrayList<String>();
}

/**
   A file view that displays an icon for all files that match
   a file filter.
*/
class FileIconView extends FileView
{
   /**
       Constructs a FileIconView.
       @param aFilter a file filter--all files that this filter
       accepts will be shown with the icon.
       @param anIcon--the icon shown with all accepted files.
   */
   public FileIconView(FileFilter aFilter, Icon anIcon)
   {
      filter = aFilter;
      icon = anIcon;
   }

   public Icon getIcon(File f)
   {
      if (!f.isDirectory() && filter.accept(f))
         return icon;
      else return null;
   }

   private FileFilter filter;
```

```
   private Icon icon;
}

/**
   A file chooser accessory that previews images.
*/
class ImagePreviewer extends JLabel
{
   /**
      Constructs an ImagePreviewer.
      @param chooser the file chooser whose property changes
      trigger an image change in this previewer
   */
   public ImagePreviewer(JFileChooser chooser)
   {
      setPreferredSize(new Dimension(100, 100));
      setBorder(BorderFactory.createEtchedBorder());

      chooser.addPropertyChangeListener(new
         PropertyChangeListener()
         {
            public void propertyChange(PropertyChangeEvent
               event)
            {
               if (event.getPropertyName() ==
                  JFileChooser.SELECTED_FILE_CHANGED_PROPERTY)
               {
                  // the user has selected a new file
                  File f = (File) event.getNewValue();
                  if (f == null) { setIcon(null); return; }

                  // read the image into an icon
                  ImageIcon icon = new ImageIcon(f.getPath());

                  // if the icon is too large to fit, scale it
                  if(icon.getIconWidth() > getWidth())
                     icon = new ImageIcon(icon.getImage().getScaledInstance(
                        getWidth(), -1, Image.SCALE_DEFAULT));

                  setIcon(icon);
               }
            }
         });
   }
}
```

API `javax.swing.JFileChooser` 1.2

- `JFileChooser()`
  creates a file chooser dialog box that can be used for multiple frames.
- `void setCurrentDirectory(File dir)`
  sets the initial directory for the file dialog box.
- `void setSelectedFile(File file)`
- `void setSelectedFiles(File[] file)`
  set the default file choice for the file dialog box.

- `void setMultiSelectionEnabled(boolean b)`
  sets or clears multiple selection mode.
- `void setFileSelectionMode(int mode)`
  lets the user select files only (the default), directories only, or both files and directories. The `mode` parameter is one of `JFileChooser.FILES_ONLY`, `JFileChooser.DIRECTORIES_ONLY`, and `JFileChooser.FILES_AND_DIRECTORIES`.
- `int showOpenDialog(Component parent)`
- `int showSaveDialog(Component parent)`
- `int showDialog(Component parent, String approveButtonText)`
  show a dialog in which the approve button is labeled "Open", "Save", or with the `approveButtonText` string. Returns `APPROVE_OPTION`, `CANCEL_OPTION` (if the user selected the cancel button or dismissed the dialog), or `ERROR_OPTION` (if an error occurred).
- `File getSelectedFile()`
- `File[] getSelectedFiles()`
  get the file or files that the user selected (or return `null` if the user didn't select any file).
- `void setFileFilter(FileFilter filter)`
  sets the file mask for the file dialog box. All files for which `filter.accept` returns `true` will be displayed. Also adds the filter to the list of choosable filters.
- `void addChoosableFileFilter(FileFilter filter)`
  adds a file filter to the list of choosable filters.
- `void setAcceptAllFileFilterUsed(boolean b)`
  includes or suppresses an "All files" filter in the filter combo box.
- `void resetChoosableFileFilters()`
  clears the list of choosable filters. Only the "All files" filter remains unless it is explicitly suppressed.
- `void setFileView(FileView view)`
  sets a file view to provide information about the files that the file chooser displays.
- `void setAccessory(JComponent component)`
  sets an accessory component.

`javax.swing.filechooser.FileFilter` 1.2

- `boolean accept(File f)`
  returns `true` if the file chooser should display this file.
- `String getDescription()`
  returns a description of this file filter, for example, `"Image files (*.gif,*.jpeg)"`.

`javax.swing.filechooser.FileView` 1.2

- `String getName(File f)`
  returns the name of the file `f`, or `null`. Normally, this method simply returns `f.getName()`.
- `String getDescription(File f)`
  returns a humanly readable description of the file `f`, or `null`. For example, if `f` is an HTML document, this method might return its title.
- `String getTypeDescription(File f)`
  returns a humanly readable description of the type of the file `f`, or `null`. For example, if `f` is an HTML document, this method might return a string `"Hypertext document"`.

- `Icon getIcon(File f)`
  returns an icon for the file `f`, or `null`. For example, if `f` is a JPEG file, this method might return a thumbnail icon.
- `Boolean isTraversable(File f)`
  returns `Boolean.TRUE` if `f` is a directory that the user can open. This method might return `false` if a directory is conceptually a compound document. Like all `FileView` methods, this method can return `null` to signify that the file chooser should consult the default view instead.

Color Choosers

As you saw in the preceding section, a high-quality file chooser is an intricate user interface component that you definitely do not want to implement yourself. Many user interface toolkits provide other common dialogs: to choose a date/time, currency value, font, color, and so on. The benefit is twofold. Programmers can simply use a high-quality implementation rather than rolling their own. And users have a common experience for these selections.

At this point, Swing provides only one additional chooser, the `JColorChooser` (see Figures 9–52 through 9–54). You use it to let users pick a color value. Like the `JFileChooser` class, the color chooser is a component, not a dialog, but it contains convenience methods to create dialogs that contain a color chooser component.

Here is how you show a modal dialog with a color chooser:

```
Color selectedColor = JColorChooser.showDialog(parent,title, initialColor);
```

Alternatively, you can display a modeless color chooser dialog. You supply

- A parent component;
- The title of the dialog;
- A flag to select either a modal or a modeless dialog;
- A color chooser; and
- Listeners for the OK and Cancel buttons (or `null` if you don't want a listener).

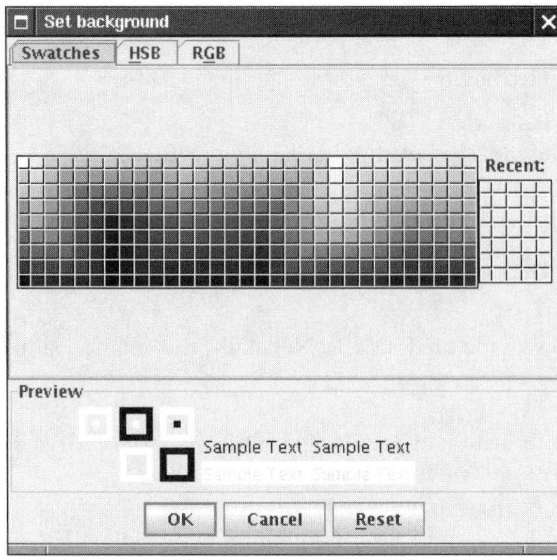

Figure 9–52: The "swatches" pane of a color chooser

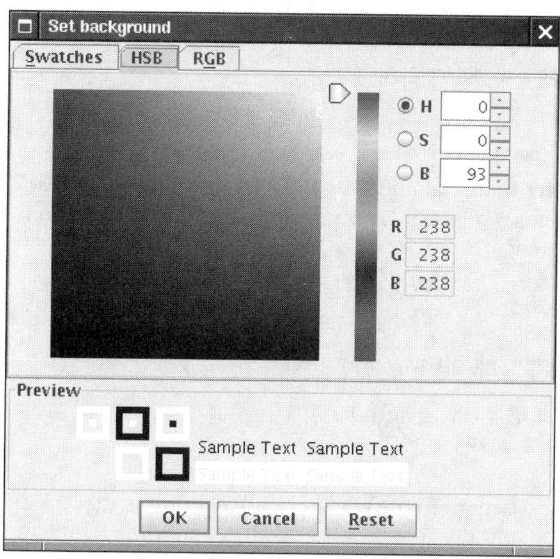

Figure 9–53: The HSB pane of a color chooser

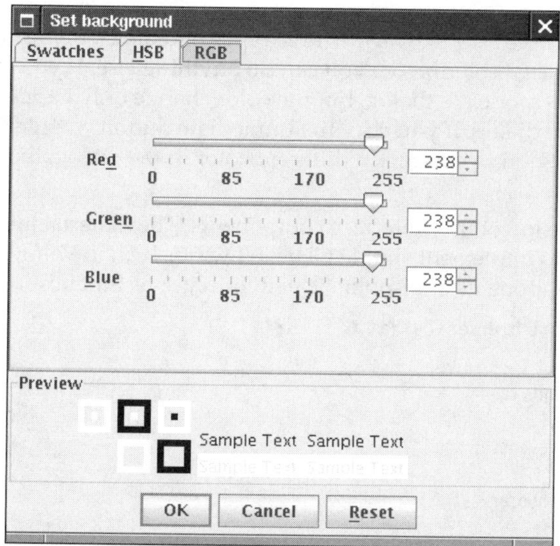

Figure 9–54: The RGB pane of a color chooser

Here is how you make a modeless dialog that sets the background color when the user clicks the OK button:

```
chooser = new JColorChooser();
dialog = JColorChooser.createDialog(
   parent,
   "Background Color",
   false /* not modal */,
   chooser,
   new ActionListener() // OK button listener
      {
```

```
          public void actionPerformed(ActionEvent event)
          {
             setBackground(chooser.getColor());
          }
       },
    null /* no Cancel button listener */);
```

You can do even better than that and give the user immediate feedback of the color selection. To monitor the color selections, you need to obtain the selection model of the chooser and add a change listener:

```
chooser.getSelectionModel().addChangeListener(new
   ChangeListener()
   {
      public void stateChanged(ChangeEvent event)
      {
         do something with chooser.getColor();
      }
   });
```

In this case, there is no benefit to the OK and Cancel buttons that the color chooser dialog provides. You can just add the color chooser component directly into a modeless dialog:

```
dialog = new JDialog(parent, false /* not modal */);
dialog.add(chooser);
dialog.pack();
```

The program in Example 9–22 shows the three types of dialogs. If you click on the Modal button, you must select a color before you can do anything else. If you click on the Modeless button, you get a modeless dialog, but the color change only happens when you click the OK button on the dialog. If you click the Immediate button, you get a modeless dialog without buttons. As soon as you pick a different color in the dialog, the background color of the panel is updated.

This ends our discussion of user interface components. The material in Chapters 7 through 9 showed you how to implement simple GUIs in Swing. Turn to Volume 2 for more advanced Swing components and sophisticated graphics techniques.

Example 9–22: ColorChooserTest.java

```
import java.awt.*;
import java.awt.event.*;
import javax.swing.*;
import javax.swing.event.*;

public class ColorChooserTest
{
   public static void main(String[] args)
   {
      ColorChooserFrame frame = new ColorChooserFrame();
      frame.setDefaultCloseOperation(JFrame.EXIT_ON_CLOSE);
      frame.setVisible(true);
   }
}

/**
   A frame with a color chooser panel
*/
class ColorChooserFrame extends JFrame
{
```

```
   public ColorChooserFrame()
   {
      setTitle("ColorChooserTest");
      setSize(DEFAULT_WIDTH, DEFAULT_HEIGHT);

      // add color chooser panel to frame

      ColorChooserPanel panel = new ColorChooserPanel();
      add(panel);
   }

   public static final int DEFAULT_WIDTH = 300;
   public static final int DEFAULT_HEIGHT = 200;
}

/**
   A panel with buttons to pop up three types of color choosers
*/
class ColorChooserPanel extends JPanel
{
   public ColorChooserPanel()
   {
      JButton modalButton = new JButton("Modal");
      modalButton.addActionListener(new ModalListener());
      add(modalButton);

      JButton modelessButton = new JButton("Modeless");
      modelessButton.addActionListener(new ModelessListener());
      add(modelessButton);

      JButton immediateButton = new JButton("Immediate");
      immediateButton.addActionListener(new ImmediateListener());
      add(immediateButton);
   }

   /**
      This listener pops up a modal color chooser
   */
   private class ModalListener implements ActionListener
   {
      public void actionPerformed(ActionEvent event)
      {
         Color defaultColor = getBackground();
         Color selected = JColorChooser.showDialog(
            ColorChooserPanel.this,
            "Set background",
            defaultColor);
         if (selected != null) setBackground(selected);
      }
   }

   /**
      This listener pops up a modeless color chooser.
      The panel color is changed when the user clicks the OK
      button.
   */
```

```
   private class ModelessListener implements ActionListener
   {
      public ModelessListener()
      {
         chooser = new JColorChooser();
         dialog = JColorChooser.createDialog(
            ColorChooserPanel.this,
            "Background Color",
            false /* not modal */,
            chooser,
            new ActionListener() // OK button listener
               {
                  public void actionPerformed(ActionEvent event)
                  {
                     setBackground(chooser.getColor());
                  }
               },
            null /* no Cancel button listener */);
      }

      public void actionPerformed(ActionEvent event)
      {
         chooser.setColor(getBackground());
         dialog.setVisible(true);
      }

      private JDialog dialog;
      private JColorChooser chooser;
   }

   /**
      This listener pops up a modeless color chooser.
      The panel color is changed immediately when the
      user picks a new color.
   */
   private class ImmediateListener implements ActionListener
   {
      public ImmediateListener()
      {
         chooser = new JColorChooser();
         chooser.getSelectionModel().addChangeListener(new
            ChangeListener()
            {
               public void stateChanged(ChangeEvent event)
               {
                  setBackground(chooser.getColor());
               }
            });

         dialog = new JDialog(
            (Frame) null,
            false /* not modal */);
         dialog.add(chooser);
         dialog.pack();
      }

```

```
      public void actionPerformed(ActionEvent event)
      {
         chooser.setColor(getBackground());
         dialog.setVisible(true);
      }

      private JDialog dialog;
      private JColorChooser chooser;
   }
}
```

API `javax.swing.JColorChooser` 1.2

- `JColorChooser()`
  constructs a color chooser with an initial color of white.
- `Color getColor()`
- `void setColor(Color c)`
  get and set the current color of this color chooser.
- `static Color showDialog(Component parent, String title, Color initialColor)`
  shows a modal dialog that contains a color chooser.

Parameters:	`parent`	The component over which to pop up the dialog
	`title`	The title for the dialog box frame
	`initialColor`	The initial color to show in the color chooser

- `static JDialog createDialog(Component parent, String title, boolean modal, JColorChooser chooser, ActionListener okListener, ActionListener cancelListener)`
  creates a dialog box that contains a color chooser.

Parameters:	`parent`	The component over which to pop up the dialog
	`title`	The title for the dialog box frame
	`modal`	`true` if this call should block until the dialog is closed
	`chooser`	The color chooser to add to the dialog
	`okListener`, `cancelListener`	The listeners of the OK and Cancel buttons

Chapter 10

Deploying Applets and Applications

- APPLET BASICS
- THE APPLET HTML TAGS AND ATTRIBUTES
- MULTIMEDIA
- THE APPLET CONTEXT
- JAR FILES
- APPLICATION PACKAGING
- JAVA WEB START
- STORAGE OF APPLICATION PREFERENCES

At this point, you should be comfortable with using most of the features of the Java programming language, and you had a pretty thorough introduction to basic graphics programming in Java. We hope that you agree with us that Java is a nice (albeit not perfect), general-purpose OOP language, and the Swing user interface libraries are flexible and useful. That's nice, but it isn't what created the original hype around Java. The unbelievable hype during the first few years of Java's life (as mentioned in Chapter 1) stemmed from *applets*. An applet is a special kind of Java program that a Java-enabled browser can download from the Internet and then run. The hopes were that users would be freed from the hassles of installing software and that they could access their software from any Java-enabled computer or device with an Internet connection.

For a number of reasons, applets never quite lived up to these expectations. Recently, Sun developed an alternative approach for Internet-based application delivery, called *Java Web Start*, that fixes some of the problems of applets.

This chapter shows you how to write and deploy applets and Java Web Start applications, how to package applets and applications for deployment, and how applications access and store configuration information.

Applet Basics

You use HTML (the hypertext markup language) to describe the layout of a web page. HTML is simply a vehicle to indicate elements of a hypertext page. For example, `<title>` indicates the title of the page, and any text that follows this tag becomes the title of the page. You indicate the end of the title with the `</title>` tag. (This is one of the general rules for tags: a slash followed by the name of the element indicates the end of the element.)

The basic idea of how to use applets in a web page is simple: the HTML page must tell the browser which applets to load and then where to put each applet on the web page. As you might expect, the tag needed to use an applet must tell the browser the following:

- Where to get the class files;
- How the applet is positioned on the web page (size, location, and so on).

The browser then retrieves the class files from the Internet (or from a directory on the user's machine) and automatically runs the applet, using an external Java runtime environment or its built-in Java virtual machine.

In addition to the applet itself, the web page can contain all the other HTML elements you have seen in use on web pages: multiple fonts, bulleted lists, graphics, links, and so on. Applets are just one part of the hypertext page. It is always worth keeping in mind that the Java programming language is *not* a tool for designing HTML pages; it is a tool for *bringing them to life*. This is not to say that the GUI design elements in a Java applet are not important, but that they must work with (and, in fact, are subservient to) the underlying HTML design of the web page.

NOTE: We do not cover general HTML tags; we assume that you know—or are working with someone who knows—the basics of HTML. Only a few special HTML tags are needed for Java applets. We do, of course, cover those later in this chapter. As for learning HTML, you can find dozens of HTML books at your local bookstore. One that covers what you need and that will not insult your intelligence is *HTML and XHTML: The Definitive Guide* by Chuck Musciano and Bill Kennedy from O'Reilly & Associates.

When applets were first developed, you had to use Sun's HotJava browser to view web pages that contained applets. Naturally, few users were willing to use a separate browser just to enjoy a new web feature. Java applets became really popular when Netscape included a Java virtual machine in its Navigator browser. Microsoft Internet Explorer soon followed suit. Unfortunately, two problems happened. Netscape didn't keep up with more modern versions of Java, and Microsoft vacillated between reluctantly supporting outdated Java versions and dropping Java support altogether.

To overcome this problem, Sun released a tool called the "Java Plug-in". Using the various extension mechanisms of Internet Explorer or Navigator, it seamlessly plugs in to both Netscape and Internet Explorer and allows both browsers to execute Java applets by using an external Java runtime environment that Sun supplies. By keeping the Plug-in up-to-date, you can always take advantage of the latest and greatest features of Java.

NOTE: To run the applets in this chapter in a browser, you need to install the current version of the Java Plug-in and make sure your browser is connected with the Plug-in. Go to `http://java.sun.com/getjava` for download and configuration information.

Admittedly, if you are designing web pages for a wide audience, it is probably unreasonable to ask the visitors to your web page to install the Java Plug-in, which is a fairly hefty (if one-time) download. Before turning to applets, you should check whether you can just use HTML forms, JavaScript, and animated GIF files to implement the client user interface. Then place the intelligence on the server, preferably with Java-based servlets and server pages.

On the other hand, if you roll out a very sophisticated Java program, you should ask yourself whether there is any benefit from using the web browser as a delivery vehicle. If not, then you can simply deliver Java applications that your users run on their local machines. You still have all the benefits of Java, such as platform independence, security management, and easy database and network access.

Of course, there are advantages to web deployment. For a user, it is often easier to locate an application on the Web than on the local file system. (This is particularly true for applications that aren't used every day.) For an administrator, it is easier to maintain and update an application on the web server than to push out bug fixes and improvements to lots of client desktops.

Thus, among the most successful Java programs are corporate *intranet* applications that interface with corporate information systems. For example, many companies have put expense reimbursement calculators, benefit tracking tools, schedule and vacation planners, purchase order requests, and so on, on their corporate intranet. These programs are relatively small, need to interface with databases, need more flexibility than web forms can provide, and need to be customized to the operations of a particular company. Applets and the Java Web Start mechanisms are excellent delivery technologies for these programs. Because the user population is constrained, it is less of a problem to manage the installation of the Java run time.

We start out with applets, both for the sake of tradition and because understanding applets gives you a head start with the Java Web Start technology.

A Simple Applet

For tradition's sake, let's write a `NotHelloWorld` program as an applet. Before we do that, we want to point out that, from a programming point of view, an applet isn't very strange. An applet is simply a Java class that extends the `java.applet.Applet` class. Note that although the `java.applet` package is not part of the `AWT` package, an applet is an AWT component, as the inheritance chain shown in Figure 10–1 illustrates. In this book, we will use Swing to implement applets. All of our applets will extend the `JApplet` class, the superclass for Swing applets. As you can see in Figure 10–1, `JApplet` is an immediate subclass of the ordinary `Applet` class.

NOTE: If your applet contains Swing components, you must extend the `JApplet` class. Swing components inside a plain `Applet` don't paint correctly.

Example 10–1 shows the code for an applet version of "Not Hello World".

Notice how similar this is to the corresponding program from Chapter 7. However, because the applet lives inside a web page, there is no need to specify a method for exiting the applet.

Example 10–1: NotHelloWorldApplet.java

```
/*
   The following HTML tags are required to display this applet in a browser:
   <applet code="NotHelloWorldApplet.class" width="300" height="100">
   </applet>
*/

import javax.swing.*;

public class NotHelloWorldApplet extends JApplet
{
   public void init()
   {
      JLabel label = new JLabel("Not a Hello, World applet", SwingConstants.CENTER);
      add(label);
   }
}
```

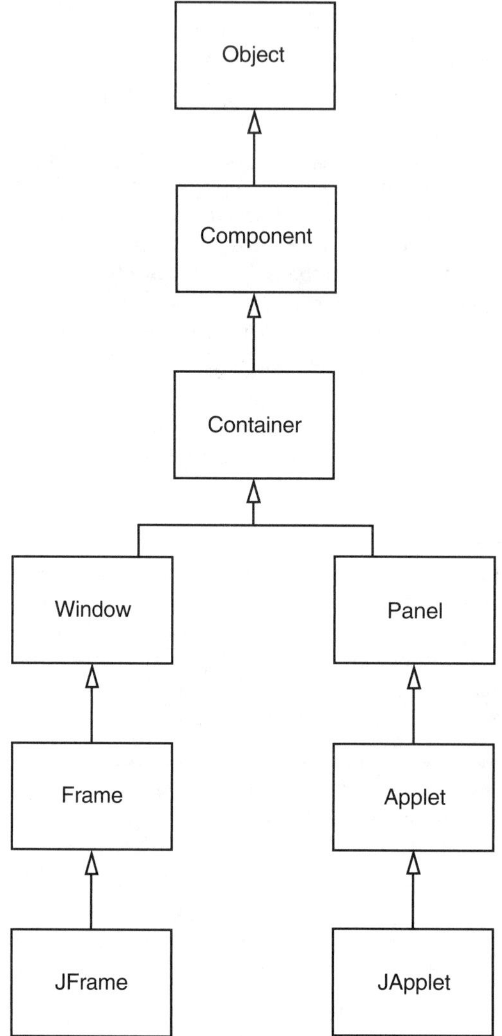

Figure 10–1: Applet inheritance hierarchy

Applet Viewing

To execute the applet, you carry out two steps:

1. Compile your Java source files into class files.
2. Create an HTML file that tells the browser which class file to load first and how to size the applet.

It is customary (but not necessary) to give the HTML file the same name as that of the applet class inside. So, following this tradition, we call the file `NotHelloWorldApplet.html`. Here are the contents of the file:

```
<applet code="NotHelloWorldApplet.class" width="300" height="300">
</applet>
```

Before you view the applet in a browser, it is a good idea to test it in the *applet viewer* program that is a part of the JDK. To use the applet viewer in our example, enter

```
appletviewer NotHelloWorldApplet.html
```

at the command line. The command-line argument for the applet viewer program is the name of the HTML file, not the class file. Figure 10–2 shows the applet viewer displaying this applet.

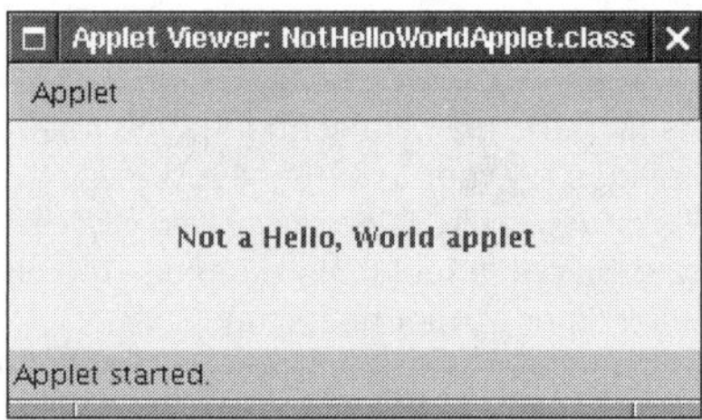

Figure 10–2: Viewing an applet in the applet viewer

TIP: You can also run applets from inside your editor or integrated environment. In Emacs, select JDE -> Run Applet from the menu. In Eclipse, you select Run -> Run as -> Java Applet from the menu.

TIP: Here is a weird trick to avoid the additional HTML file. Add an applet tag *as a comment inside the source file:*

```
/*
  <applet code="MyApplet.class" width="300" height="300">
  </applet>
*/
public class MyApplet extends JApplet
. . .
```

Then run the applet viewer *with the source file* as its command-line argument:

```
appletviewer NotHelloWorldApplet.java
```

We aren't recommending this as standard practice, but it can come in handy if you want to minimize the number of files that you need to worry about during testing.

The applet viewer is good for the first stage of testing, but at some point you need to run your applets in a browser to see them in the same way a user might use them. In particular, the applet viewer program shows you only the applet, not the surrounding HTML text. If an HTML file contains multiple `applet` tags, the applet viewer pops up multiple windows.

To properly view the applet, you need a Java 2-enabled browser. After installing and configuring the Java Plug-in, simply load the HTML file into the browser (see Figure 10–3). If the applet doesn't show up, your browser probably uses its built-in virtual machine, and you need to configure it to use the Java Plug-in instead.

TIP: If you make a change to your applet and recompile, you need to restart the browser so that it loads the new class files. Simply refreshing the HTML page will not load the new code. This is a hassle when you are debugging an applet. You can avoid the painful browser restart if you launch the Java console and issue the `x` command, which clears the classloader cache. Then you can reload the HTML page, and the new applet code is used. You can launch the Java console in Netscape and Mozilla from the menu. Under Windows, open the Java Plug-in console in the Windows control panel and request that the Java console be displayed.

NOTE: For older browsers (in particular, Netscape 4), you need to replace the `applet` tags with special `object` or `embed` tags in order to cause the browser to load the Plug-In. The page `http://java.sun.com/j2se/5.0/docs/guide/plugin/developer_guide/html_converter.html` describes this process and lets you download a tool that automates the web page conversion. With modern browsers, the conversion is no longer necessary.

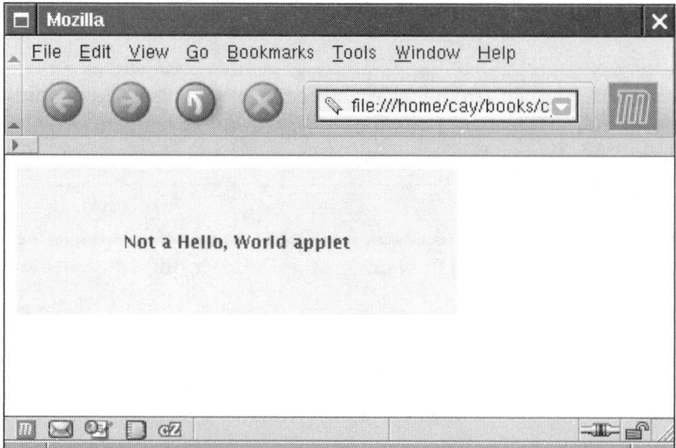

Figure 10–3: Viewing an applet in a browser

Application Conversion to Applets

It is easy to convert a graphical Java application (that is, an application that uses the AWT and that you can start with the `java` program launcher) into an applet that you can embed in a web page. Essentially, all of the user interface code can stay the same.

Here are the specific steps for converting an application to an applet.

1. Make an HTML page with the appropriate tag to load the applet code.
2. Supply a subclass of the `JApplet` class. Make this class `public`. Otherwise, the applet cannot be loaded.
3. Eliminate the `main` method in the application. Do not construct a frame window for the application. Your application will be displayed inside the browser.
4. Move any initialization code from the frame window constructor to the `init` method of the applet. You don't need to explicitly construct the applet object—the browser instantiates it for you and calls the `init` method.
5. Remove the call to `setSize`; for applets, sizing is done with the `width` and `height` parameters in the HTML file.

6. Remove the call to `setDefaultCloseOperation`. An applet cannot be closed; it terminates when the browser exits.
7. If the application calls `setTitle`, eliminate the call to the method. Applets cannot have title bars. (You can, of course, title the web page itself, using the HTML `title` tag.)
8. Don't call `setVisible(true)`. The applet is displayed automatically.

NOTE: On page 520, you will see how to implement a program that is both an applet and an application.

As an example of this transformation, we will change the calculator application from Chapter 9 into an applet. In Figure 10–4, you can see how it looks, sitting inside a web page.

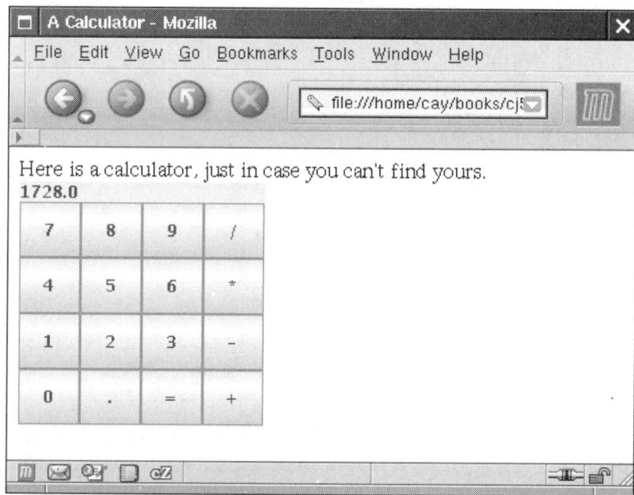

Figure 10–4: A calculator applet

Example 10–2 shows the HTML page. Note that there is some text in addition to the applet tags.

Example 10–2: Calculator.html

```
<html>
   <head><title>A Calculator</title></head>
   <body>
      <p>Here is a calculator, just in case you can't find yours.</p>
      <applet code="CalculatorApplet.class" width="180" height="180">
      </applet>
   </body>
</html>
```

Example 10–3 is the code for the applet. We introduced a subclass of `JApplet`, placed the initialization code into the `init` method, and removed the calls to `setTitle`, `setSize`, `setDefaultCloseOperation`, and `setVisible`. The `CalculatorPanel` class is taken from Chapter 9, and its code is omitted.

Example 10–3: CalculatorApplet.java

```
import java.awt.*;
import javax.swing.*;

public class CalculatorApplet extends JApplet
{
   public void init()
   {
      CalculatorPanel panel = new CalculatorPanel();
      add(panel);
   }
}
```

`java.applet.Applet` 1.0

- `void init()`
  is called when the applet is first loaded. Override this method and place all initialization code here.
- `void resize(int width, int height)`
  requests that the applet be resized. This would be a great method if it worked on web pages; unfortunately, it does not work in current browsers because it interferes with their page-layout mechanisms.

Life Cycle of an Applet

Four methods in the `Applet` class give you the framework on which you build any serious applet: `init`, `start`, `stop`, and `destroy`. What follows is a short description of these methods, occasions when these methods are called, and the code you should place into them.

- `init`

  This method is intended for whatever initialization is needed for your applet. It is called after the `param` tags inside the `applet` tag have been processed. Common actions in an applet include processing `param` values (see page 508) and adding user interface components.

  Applets can have a default constructor, but it is customary to perform all initialization in the `init` method instead of the default constructor.
- `start`

  This method is automatically called *after* the browser calls the `init` method. It is also called whenever the user returns to the page containing the applet after having gone off to other pages. This means that the `start` method can be called repeatedly, unlike the `init` method. For this reason, put the code that you want executed only once in the `init` method, rather than in the `start` method. The `start` method is where you usually restart a thread for your applet, for example, to resume an animation. If your applet does nothing that needs to be suspended when the user leaves the current web page, you do not need to implement this method (or the `stop` method).
- `stop`

  This method is automatically called when the user moves off the page on which the applet sits. It can, therefore, be called repeatedly in the same applet. Its purpose is to give you a chance to stop a time-consuming activity from slowing the system when the user is not paying attention to the applet. You would implement this method to stop an animation or audio playback.

- `destroy`
  This method is only called when the browser shuts down normally. Because applets are meant to live on an HTML page, you should not normally leave resources behind after a user leaves the page that contains the applet. But if you do, then you can close down the resources by overriding the `destroy` method.

API `java.applet.Applet` 1.0

- `void start()`
  override this method for code that needs to be executed *every time* the user visits the browser page containing this applet. A typical action is to reactivate a thread.
- `void stop()`
  override this method for code that needs to be executed *every time* the user leaves the browser page containing this applet. A typical action is to deactivate a thread.
- `void destroy()`
  override this method for code that needs to be executed when the user exits the browser.

Security Basics

Because applets are designed to be loaded from a remote site and then executed locally, security becomes vital. If a user enables Java in the browser, the browser will download all the applet code on the web page and execute it immediately. The user never gets a chance to confirm or to stop individual applets from running. For this reason, applets (unlike applications) are restricted in what they can do. The *applet security manager* throws a `SecurityException` whenever an applet attempts to violate one of the access rules.

What *can* applets do on all platforms? They can show images and play sounds, get keystrokes and mouse clicks from the user, and send user input back to the host from which they were loaded. That is enough functionality to show facts and figures or to get user input for placing an order. The restricted execution environment for applets is often called the "sandbox." Applets playing in the "sandbox" cannot alter the user's system or spy on it. In this chapter, we look only at applets that run inside the sandbox.

In particular, when running in the sandbox,

- Applets can *never* run any local executable program.
- Applets cannot communicate with any host other than the server from which they were downloaded; that server is called the *originating host*. This rule is often called "applets can only phone home." The rule protects applet users from applets that might try to spy on intranet resources.
- Applets cannot read from or write to the local computer's file system.
- Applets cannot find out any information about the local computer, except for the Java version used, the name and version of the operating system, and the characters used to separate files (for instance, / or \), paths (such as : or ;), and lines (such as `\n` or `\r\n`). In particular, applets cannot find out the user's name, e-mail address, and so on.
- All windows that an applet pops up carry a warning message.

All this is possible only because applets are executed by the Java virtual machine and not directly by the CPU on the user's computer. Because the virtual machine checks all critical instructions and program areas, a hostile (or poorly written) applet will almost certainly not be able to crash the computer, overwrite system memory, or change the privileges granted by the operating system.

These restrictions are too strong for some situations. For example, on a corporate intranet, you can certainly imagine an applet wanting to access local files. To allow for different levels of security under different situations, you can use *signed applets.* A signed applet carries with it a certificate that indicates the identity of the signer. Cryptographic techniques ensure that such a certificate cannot be forged. If you trust the signer, you can choose to give the applet additional rights. (We cover code signing in Volume 2.)

The point is that if you trust the signer of the applet, you can tell the browser to give the applet more privileges. You can, for example, give applets in your corporate intranet a higher level of trust than those from `www.cracker.com`. The configurable Java security model allows the continuum of privilege levels you need. You can give completely trusted applets the same privilege levels as local applications. Programs from vendors that are known to be somewhat flaky can be given access to some, but not all, privileges. Unknown applets can be restricted to the sandbox.

NOTE: Java Web Start applications (discussed later in this chapter) have a slightly more versatile sandbox. Some system resources can be accessed, provided the program user agrees.

To sum up, Java has three separate mechanisms for enforcing security:

1. Program code is interpreted by the Java virtual machine, not executed directly.
2. A security manager checks all sensitive operations in the Java runtime library.
3. Applets can be signed to identify their origin.

NOTE: In contrast, the security model of the ActiveX technology by Microsoft relies solely on the third option. If you want to run an ActiveX control at all, you must trust it completely. That model works fine when you deal with a small number of trusted suppliers, but it simply does not scale up to the World Wide Web. If you use Internet Explorer, you will see the ActiveX mechanism at work. You'll need to accept Sun's certificate to install the Java Plug-in on Internet Explorer. The certificate tells you that the code came from Sun. It doesn't tell you anything about the quality of the code. Once you accept the installation, the program runs without any further security checks.

Pop-Up Windows in Applets

An applet sits embedded in a web page, in a frame whose width is given by the `width` and `height` attributes in the applet tag. This can be quite limiting. Many programmers wonder whether they can have a pop-up window to make better use of the available space. It is indeed possible to create a pop-up frame. Here is a simple applet with a single button labeled Calculator. When you click on the button, a calculator pops up in a separate window.

The pop-up is easy to do. Simply use a `JFrame`, but don't call `setDefaultCloseOperation`.

```
frame = new CalculatorFrame();
frame.setTitle("Calculator");
frame.setSize(200, 200);
```

When the user clicks the button, toggle the frame so that it is shown if it isn't visible and hidden if it is. When you click on the calculator button, the dialog box pops up and floats over the web page. When you click on the button again, the calculator goes away.

```
JButton calcButton = new JButton("Calculator");
calcButton.addActionListener(new
   ActionListener()
   {
```

```
        public void actionPerformed(ActionEvent evt)
        {
           frame.setVisible(!frame.isVisible());
        }
     });
```

There is, however, an issue that you need to consider before you put this applet on your web page. To see how the calculator looks to a potential user, load the web page from a browser, not the applet viewer. The calculator will be surrounded by a border with a warning message (see Figure 10–5).

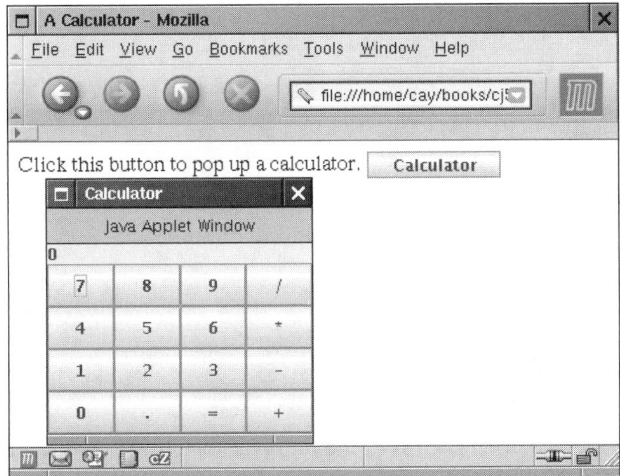

Figure 10–5: A window that pops up over a browser

In early browser versions, that message was very ominous: "Untrusted Java Applet Window". Every successive version of the JDK watered down the warning a bit—"Unauthenticated Java Applet Window", or "Warning: Java Applet Window". Now it is simply "Java Applet Window".

This message is a security feature of all web browsers. The browser wants to make sure that your applet does not launch a window that the user might mistake for a local application. The fear is that an unsuspecting user could visit a web page, which automatically launches the applets on it, and mistakenly type in a password or credit card number, which the applet could send back to its host.

To avoid any possibility of shenanigans like this, all pop-up windows launched by an applet bear a warning label. You can configure the Java Plug-in to omit the warning message for pop-up windows that are spawned by signed applets.

Example 10–4 shows the code for the `PopupCalculatorApplet` class.

Example 10–4: PopupCalculatorApplet.java

```
import java.awt.*;
import java.awt.event.*;
import javax.swing.*;

public class PopupCalculatorApplet extends JApplet
{
   public void init()
   {
```

```
      // create a frame with a calculator panel

      final JFrame frame = new JFrame();
      frame.setTitle("Calculator");
      frame.setSize(200, 200);
      frame.add(new CalculatorPanel());

      // add a button that pops up or hides the calculator

      JButton calcButton = new JButton("Calculator");
      add(calcButton);

      calcButton.addActionListener(new
         ActionListener()
         {
            public void actionPerformed(ActionEvent event)
            {
               frame.setVisible(!frame.isVisible());
            }
         });
   }
}
```

The Applet HTML Tags and Attributes

In its most basic form, an example for using the applet tag looks like this:

```
<applet code="NotHelloWorldApplet.class" width="300" height="100">
```

As you have seen, the code attribute gives the name of the class file and must include the .class extension; the width and height attributes size the window that will hold the applet. Both are measured in pixels. You also need a matching </applet> tag that marks the end of the HTML tagging needed for an applet. The text between the <applet> and </applet> tags is displayed only if the browser cannot show applets. The code, width, and height attributes are required. If any are missing, the browser cannot load your applet.

All this information would usually be embedded in an HTML page that, at the very least, might look like this:

```
<html>
   <head>
      <title>NotHelloWorldApplet</title>
   </head>
   <body>
      <p>The next line of text is displayed under the auspices of Java:</p>
      <applet code="NotHelloWorldApplet.class" width="100" height="100">
         If your browser could show Java, you would see an applet here.
      </applet>
   </body>
</html>
```

NOTE: According to the HTML specification, the HTML tags and attributes such as applet can be in upper or lower case. We use lower case because that is the recommendation of the newer XHTML specification. However, the name of the applet class is case sensitive! The letter case may be significant in other attributes, such as names of JAR files, if the web server file system is case sensitive.

Applet Attributes for Positioning

What follows are short discussions of the various attributes that you can (or must) use within the `applet` tag to position your applet. Readers familiar with HTML will recognize that many of these attributes are similar to those used with the `img` tag for image placement on a web page.

- `width, height`

  These attributes are required and give the width and height of the applet, measured in pixels. In the applet viewer, this is the initial size of the applet. You can resize any window that the applet viewer creates. In a browser, you *cannot* resize the applet. You will need to make a good guess about how much space your applet requires to show up well for all users.
- `align`

  This attribute specifies the alignment of the applet. There are two basic choices. The applet can be a block with text flowing around it, or the applet can be *inline,* floating inside a line of text as if it were an oversized text character. The first two values (`left` and `right`) make the text flow around the applet. The others make the applet flow with the text.

  The choices are described in Table 10–1.

Table 10–1: Applet Positioning Attributes

Attribute	What It Does
`left`	Places the applet at the left margin of the page. Text that follows on the page goes in the space to the right of the applet.
`right`	Places the applet at the right margin of the page. Text that follows on the page goes in the space to the left of the applet.
`top`	Places the top of the applet with the top of the current line.
`texttop`	Places the top of the applet with the top of the text in the current line.
`middle`	Places the middle of the applet with the baseline of the text in the current line.
`absmiddle`	Places the middle of the applet with the middle of the current line.
`baseline`	Places the bottom of the applet with the baseline of the text in the current line.
`bottom`	Places the bottom of the applet at the bottom of the text in the current line.
`absbottom`	Places the bottom of the applet with the bottom of the current line.
`vspace, hspace`	These optional attributes specify the number of pixels above and below the applet (`vspace`) and on each side of the applet (`hspace`).

Figure 10–6 shows all alignment options for an applet that floats with the surrounding text. The vertical bar at the beginning of each line is an image. Because the image is taller than the text, you can see the difference between alignment with the top or bottom of the line and the top or bottom of the text.

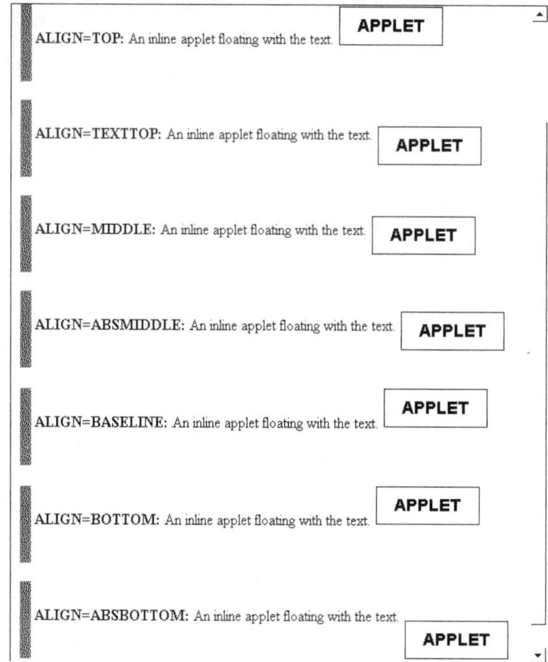

Figure 10–6: Applet alignment

Applet Attributes for Code

The following applet attributes tell the browser how to locate the applet code; here are short descriptions.

- `code`

  This attribute gives the name of the applet's class file. This name is taken relative to the codebase (see below) or relative to the current page if the codebase is not specified.

  The path name must match the package of the applet class. For example, if the applet class is in the package `com.mycompany`, then the attribute is `code="com/mycompany/MyApplet.class"`. The alternative `code="com.mycompany.MyApplet.class"` is also permitted. But you cannot use absolute path names here. Use the `codebase` attribute if your class file is located elsewhere.

  The `code` attribute specifies only the name of the class that contains the applet class. Of course, your applet may contain other class files. Once the browser's class loader loads the class containing the applet, it will realize that it needs more class files and will load them.

  Either the `code` or the `object` attribute (see below) is required.

- `codebase`

  This optional attribute is a URL for locating the class files. You can use an absolute URL, even to a different server. Most commonly, though, this is a relative URL that points to a subdirectory. For example, if the file layout looks like this:

```
aDirectory/
    ├── MyPage.html
    └── myApplets/
            └── CalculatorApplet.class
```

then you use the following tag in `MyPage.html`:

```
<applet code="CalculatorApplet.class" codebase="myApplets" width="100" height="150">
```

- `archive`

  This optional attribute lists the Java archive file or files containing classes and other resources for the applet. (See the section on JAR files later in this chapter for more on Java archive files.) These files are fetched from the web server before the applet is loaded. This technique speeds up the loading process significantly because only one HTTP request is necessary to load a JAR file that contains many smaller files. The JAR files are separated by commas. For example:

```
<applet code="CalculatorApplet.class"
   archive="CalculatorClasses.jar,corejava/CoreJavaClasses.jar"
   width="100" height="150">
```

- `object`

  This tag lets you specify the name of a file that contains the *serialized* applet object. (An object is *serialized* when you write all its instance fields to a file. We discuss serialization in Chapter 12.) To display the applet, the object is deserialized from the file to return it to its previous state. When you use this attribute, the `init` method is *not* called, but the applet's `start` method is called. Before serializing an applet object, you should call its `stop` method. This feature is useful for implementing a persistent browser that automatically reloads its applets and has them return to the same state that they were in when the browser was closed. This is a specialized feature, not normally encountered by web page designers.

  Either `code` or `object` must be present in every `applet` tag. For example,

```
<applet object="CalculatorApplet.ser" width="100" height="150">
```

- `name`

  Scripters will want to give the applet a `name` attribute that they can use to refer to the applet when scripting. Both Netscape and Internet Explorer let you call methods of an applet on a page through JavaScript. This is not a book on JavaScript, so we only give you a brief idea of the code that is required to call Java code from JavaScript.

NOTE: JavaScript is a scripting language that can be used inside web pages, invented by Netscape and originally called LiveScript. It has little to do with Java, except for some similarity in syntax. It was a marketing move to call it JavaScript. A subset (with the catchy name of ECMAScript) is standardized as ECMA-262. But, to nobody's surprise, Netscape and Microsoft support incompatible extensions of that standard in their browsers. For more information on JavaScript, we recommend the book *JavaScript: The Definitive Guide* by David Flanagan, published by O'Reilly & Associates.

To access an applet from JavaScript, you first have to give it a name.

```
<applet code="CalculatorApplet.class" width="100" height="150" name="calc">
</applet>
```

You can then refer to the object as `document.applets.`*appletname*. For example,

```
var calcApplet = document.applets.calc;
```

Through the magic of the integration between Java and JavaScript that both Netscape and Internet Explorer provide, you can call applet methods:

```
calcApplet.clear();
```

(Our calculator applet doesn't have a `clear` method; we just want to show you the syntax.)

The `name` attribute is also essential when you want two applets on the same page to communicate with each other directly. You specify a name for each current applet instance.

You pass this string to the `getApplet` method of the `AppletContext` class. We discuss this mechanism, called *inter-applet communication*, later in this chapter.

NOTE: In `http://www.javaworld.com/javatips/jw-javatip80.html`, Francis Lu uses JavaScript-to-Java communication to solve an age-old problem: to resize an applet so that it isn't bound by hardcoded `width` and `height` attributes. This is a good example of the integration between Java and JavaScript. It also shows how messy it is to write JavaScript that works on multiple browsers.

Applet Attributes for Java-Challenged Viewers

If a web page containing an `applet` tag is viewed by a browser that is not aware of Java applets, then the browser ignores the unknown `applet` and `param` tags. All text between the `<applet>` and `</applet>` tags is displayed by the browser. Conversely, Java-aware browsers do not display any text between the `<applet>` and `</applet>` tags. You can display messages inside these tags for those poor folks that use a prehistoric browser. For example,

```
<applet code="CalculatorApplet.class" width="100" height="150">
   If your browser could show Java, you would see a calculator here.
</applet>
```

Of course, nowadays most browsers know about Java, but Java may be deactivated, perhaps by the user or by a paranoid system administrator. You can then use the `alt` attribute to display a message to these unfortunate souls.

```
<applet code="CalculatorApplet.class" width="100" height="150"
   alt="If your browser could show Java, you would see a calculator here">
```

The `object` Tag

The `object` tag is part of the HTML 4.0 standard, and the W3 consortium suggests that people use it instead of the `applet` tag. There are 35 different attributes to the `object` tag, most of which (such as `onkeydown`) are relevant only to people writing Dynamic HTML. The various positioning attributes such as `align` and `height` work exactly as they did for the `applet` tag. The key attribute in the `object` tag for your Java applets is the `classid` attribute. This attribute specifies the location of the object. Of course, `object` tags can load different kinds of objects, such as Java applets or ActiveX components like the Java Plug-in itself. In the `codetype` attribute, you specify the nature of the object. For example, Java applets have a code type of `application/java`. Here is an `object` tag to load a Java applet:

```
<object
   codetype="application/java"
   classid="java:CalculatorApplet.class"
   width="100" height="150">
```

Note that the `classid` attribute can be followed by a `codebase` attribute that works exactly as it did with the `applet` tag.

Use of Parameters to Pass Information to Applets

Just as applications can use command-line information, applets can use parameters that are embedded in the HTML file. This is done by the HTML tag called `param` along with attributes that you define. For example, suppose you want to let the web page determine the style of the font to use in your applet. You could use the following HTML tags:

```
<applet code="FontParamApplet.class" width="200" height="200">
   <param name="font" value="Helvetica"/>
</applet>
```

You then pick up the value of the parameter, using the `getParameter` method of the `Applet` class, as in the following example:

```
public class FontParamApplet extends JApplet
{
   public void init()
   {
      String fontName = getParameter("font");
      . . .
   }
   . . .
}
```

NOTE: You can call the `getParameter` method only in the `init` method of the applet, not in the constructor. When the applet constructor is executed, the parameters are not yet prepared. Because the layout of most nontrivial applets is determined by parameters, we recommend that you don't supply constructors to applets. Simply place all initialization code into the `init` method.

Parameters are always returned as strings. You need to convert the string to a numeric type if that is what is called for. You do this in the standard way by using the appropriate method, such as `parseInt` of the `Integer` class.

For example, if we wanted to add a `size` parameter for the font, then the HTML code might look like this:

```
<applet code="FontParamApplet.class" width="200" height="200">
   <param name="font" value="Helvetica"/>
   <param name="size" value="24"/>
</applet>
```

The following source code shows how to read the integer parameter.

```
public class FontParamApplet extends JApplet
{
   public void init()
   {
      String fontName = getParameter("font");
      int fontSize = Integer.parseInt(getParameter("size"));
      . . .
   }
}
```

NOTE: The strings used when you define the parameters with the `param` tag and those used in the `getParameter` method must match exactly. In particular, both are case sensitive.

In addition to ensuring that the parameters match in your code, you should find out whether or not the `size` parameter was left out. You do this with a simple test for `null`. For example:

```
int fontsize;
String sizeString = getParameter("size");
if (sizeString == null) fontSize = 12;
else fontSize = Integer.parseInt(sizeString);
```

Here is a useful applet that uses parameters extensively. The applet draws a bar chart, shown in Figure 10–7.

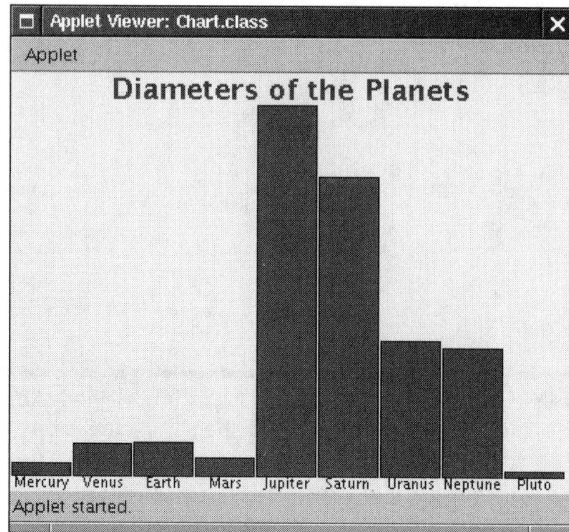

Figure 10–7: A chart applet

This applet takes the labels and the heights of the bars from the `param` values in the HTML file. Here is what the HTML file for Figure 10–7 looks like:

```
<applet code="Chart.class" width="400" height="300">
   <param name="title" value="Diameters of the Planets"/>
   <param name="values" value="9"/>
   <param name="name.1" value="Mercury"/>
   <param name="name.2" value="Venus"/>
   <param name="name.3" value="Earth"/>
   <param name="name.4" value="Mars"/>
   <param name="name.5" value="Jupiter"/>
   <param name="name.6" value="Saturn"/>
   <param name="name.7" value="Uranus"/>
   <param name="name.8" value="Neptune"/>
   <param name="name.9" value="Pluto"/>
   <param name="value.1" value="3100"/>
   <param name="value.2" value="7500"/>
   <param name="value.3" value="8000"/>
   <param name="value.4" value="4200"/>
   <param name="value.5" value="88000"/>
   <param name="value.6" value="71000"/>
   <param name="value.7" value="32000"/>
   <param name="value.8" value="30600"/>
   <param name="value.9" value="1430"/>
</applet>
```

You could have set up an array of strings and an array of numbers in the applet, but there are two advantages to using the parameter mechanism instead. You can have multiple copies of the same applet on your web page, showing different graphs: just put two `applet` tags with different sets of parameters on the page. And you can change the data that you want to chart. Admittedly, the diameters of the planets will stay the same for quite some time, but suppose your web page contains a chart of weekly sales data. It is easy to update the web page because it is plain text. Editing and recompiling a Java file weekly is more tedious.

In fact, there are commercial JavaBeans components (beans) that make much fancier graphs than the one in our chart applet. If you buy one, you can drop it into your web page and feed it parameters without ever needing to know how the applet renders the graphs.

Example 10–5 is the source code of our chart applet. Note that the `init` method reads the parameters, and the `paintComponent` method draws the chart.

Example 10–5: Chart.java

```
import java.awt.*;
import java.awt.font.*;
import java.awt.geom.*;
import javax.swing.*;

public class Chart extends JApplet
{
   public void init()
   {
      String v = getParameter("values");
      if (v == null) return;
      int n = Integer.parseInt(v);
      double[] values = new double[n];
      String[] names = new String[n];
      for (int i = 0; i < n; i++)
      {
         values[i] = Double.parseDouble(getParameter("value." + (i + 1)));
         names[i] = getParameter("name." + (i + 1));
      }

      add(new ChartPanel(values, names, getParameter("title")));
   }
}

/**
   A panel that draws a bar chart.
*/
class ChartPanel extends JPanel
{
   /**
       Constructs a ChartPanel.
       @param v the array of values for the chart
       @param n the array of names for the values
       @param t the title of the chart
   */
   public ChartPanel(double[] v, String[] n, String t)
   {
      values = v;
      names = n;
      title = t;
   }

   public void paintComponent(Graphics g)
   {
      super.paintComponent(g);
      Graphics2D g2 = (Graphics2D) g;

      // compute the minimum and maximum values
      if (values == null) return;
```

```
      double minValue = 0;
      double maxValue = 0;
      for (double v : values)
      {
         if (minValue > v) minValue = v;
         if (maxValue < v) maxValue = v;
      }
      if (maxValue == minValue) return;

      int panelWidth = getWidth();
      int panelHeight = getHeight();

      Font titleFont = new Font("SansSerif", Font.BOLD, 20);
      Font labelFont = new Font("SansSerif", Font.PLAIN, 10);

      // compute the extent of the title
      FontRenderContext context = g2.getFontRenderContext();
      Rectangle2D titleBounds = titleFont.getStringBounds(title, context);
      double titleWidth = titleBounds.getWidth();
      double top = titleBounds.getHeight();

      // draw the title
      double y = -titleBounds.getY(); // ascent
      double x = (panelWidth - titleWidth) / 2;
      g2.setFont(titleFont);
      g2.drawString(title, (float) x, (float) y);

      // compute the extent of the bar labels
      LineMetrics labelMetrics = labelFont.getLineMetrics("", context);
      double bottom = labelMetrics.getHeight();

      y = panelHeight - labelMetrics.getDescent();
      g2.setFont(labelFont);

      // get the scale factor and width for the bars
      double scale = (panelHeight - top - bottom) / (maxValue - minValue);
      int barWidth = panelWidth / values.length;

      // draw the bars
      for (int i = 0; i < values.length; i++)
      {
         // get the coordinates of the bar rectangle
         double x1 = i * barWidth + 1;
         double y1 = top;
         double height = values[i] * scale;
         if (values[i] >= 0)
            y1 += (maxValue - values[i]) * scale;
         else
         {
            y1 += maxValue * scale;
            height = -height;
         }

         // fill the bar and draw the bar outline
         Rectangle2D rect = new Rectangle2D.Double(x1, y1, barWidth - 2, height);
         g2.setPaint(Color.RED);
```

```
            g2.fill(rect);
            g2.setPaint(Color.BLACK);
            g2.draw(rect);

            // draw the centered label below the bar
            Rectangle2D labelBounds = labelFont.getStringBounds(names[i], context);

            double labelWidth = labelBounds.getWidth();
            x = x1 + (barWidth - labelWidth) / 2;
            g2.drawString(names[i], (float) x, (float) y);
         }
      }

   private double[] values;
   private String[] names;
   private String title;
}
```

API `java.applet.Applet` 1.0

- `public String getParameter(String name)`
  gets the value of a parameter defined with a `param` tag in the web page loading the applet. The string `name` is case sensitive.
- `public String getAppletInfo()`
  is a method that many applet authors override to return a string that contains information about the author, version, and copyright of the current applet. You need to create this information by overriding this method in your applet class.
- `public String[][] getParameterInfo()`
  is a method that you can override to return an array of `param` tag options that this applet supports. Each row contains three entries: the name, the type, and a description of the parameter. Here is an example:

```
"fps", "1-10", "frames per second"
"repeat", "boolean", "repeat image loop?"
"images", "url", "directory containing images"
```

Multimedia

Applets can handle both images and audio. As we write this, images must be in GIF, PNG, or JPEG form, audio files in AU, AIFF, WAV, or MIDI. Animated GIFs are supported, and the animation is displayed. Usually the files containing this information are specified as a URL, so we take up URLs first.

Encapsulating URLs

A URL is really nothing more than a description of a resource on the Internet. For example, `"http://java.sun.com/index.html"` tells the browser to use the hypertext transfer protocol on the file `index.html` located at `java.sun.com`. Java has the class `URL` that encapsulates URLs. The simplest way to make a URL is to give a string to the `URL` constructor:

```
URL u = new URL("http://java.sun.com/index.html");
```

This is called an *absolute* URL because we specify the entire resource name. Another useful URL constructor is a *relative* URL.

```
URL data = new URL(u, "data/planets.dat");
```

This specifies the file `planets.dat`, located in the `data` subdirectory of the URL `u`.

A common way of obtaining a URL is to ask an applet where it came from, in particular:

- What is the URL of the HTML page in which the applet is contained?
- What is the URL of the applet's codebase directory?

To find the former, use the `getDocumentBase` method; to find the latter, use `getCodeBase`.

NOTE: In prior versions of the JDK, there was considerable confusion about these methods—see bug #4456393 on the Java bug parade (`http://bugs.sun.com/bugdatabase/index.jsp`). The documentation has finally been clarified in JDK 5.0.

NOTE: You can access secure web pages (`https` URLs) from applets and through the Java Plug-in—see `http://java.sun.com/products/plugin/1.3/docs/https.html`. This uses the SSL capabilities of the underlying browser.

Obtaining Multimedia Files

You can retrieve images and audio files with the `getImage` and `getAudioClip` methods. For example:

```
Image cat = getImage(getCodeBase(), "images/cat.gif");
AudioClip meow = getAudioClip(getCodeBase(), "audio/meow.au");
```

Here, we use the `getCodeBase` method that returns the URL from which your applet code is loaded. The second argument of the method calls specifies where the image or audio clip is located, relative to the base document.

NOTE: The images and audio clips must be located on the same server that hosts the applet code. For security reasons, applets cannot access files on another server ("applets can only phone home").

You saw in Chapter 7 how to display an image. To play an audio clip, simply invoke its `play` method. You can also call the `play` method of the `Applet` class without first loading the audio clip.

```
play(getCodeBase(), "audio/meow.au");
```

For faster downloading, multimedia objects can be stored in JAR files (see the section below). The `getImage` and `getAudioClip/play` methods automatically search the JAR files of the applet. If the image or audio file is contained in the JAR file, it is loaded immediately. Otherwise, the browser requests it from the web server.

`java.net.URL` 1.0

- `URL(String name)`
  creates a URL object from a string describing an absolute URL.
- `URL(URL base, String name)`
  creates a relative URL object. If the string `name` describes an absolute URL, then the `base` URL is ignored. Otherwise, it is interpreted as a relative directory from the `base` URL.

API

`java.applet.Applet` 1.0

- `URL getDocumentBase()`
  gets the URL of the web page containing this applet.

- `URL getCodeBase()`
  gets the URL of the codebase directory from which this applet is loaded. That is either the absolute URL of the directory referenced by the `codebase` attribute or the directory of the HTML file if no `codebase` is specified.
- `void play(URL url)`
- `void play(URL url, String name)`
  The first form plays an audio file specified by the URL. The second form uses the string to provide a path relative to the URL in the first parameter. Nothing happens if the audio clip cannot be found.
- `AudioClip getAudioClip(URL url)`
- `AudioClip getAudioClip(URL url, String name)`
  The first form gets an audio clip from the given URL. The second form uses the string to provide a path relative to the URL in the first argument. The methods return `null` if the audio clip cannot be found.
- `Image getImage(URL url)`
- `Image getImage(URL url, String name)`
  return an image object that encapsulates the image specified by the URL. If the image does not exist, immediately returns `null`. Otherwise, a separate thread is launched to load the image.

The Applet Context

An applet runs inside a browser or the applet viewer. An applet can ask the browser to do things for it, for example, fetch an audio clip, show a short message in the status line, or display a different web page. The ambient browser can carry out these requests, or it can ignore them. For example, if an applet running inside the applet viewer asks the applet viewer program to display a web page, nothing happens.

To communicate with the browser, an applet calls the `getAppletContext` method. That method returns an object that implements an interface of type `AppletContext`. You can think of the concrete implementation of the `AppletContext` interface as a communication path between the applet and the ambient browser. In addition to `getAudioClip` and `getImage`, the `AppletContext` interface contains several useful methods, which we discuss in the next few sections.

Inter-Applet Communication

A web page can contain more than one applet. If a web page contains multiple applets from the same `codebase`, they can communicate with each other. Naturally, this is an advanced technique that you probably will not need very often.

If you give `name` attributes to each applet in the HTML file, you can use the `getApplet` method of the `AppletContext` interface to get a reference to the applet. For example, if your HTML file contains the tag

```
<applet code="Chart.class" width="100" height="100" name="Chart1">
```

then the call

```
Applet chart1 = getAppletContext().getApplet("Chart1");
```

gives you a reference to the applet. What can you do with the reference? Provided you give the `Chart` class a method to accept new data and redraw the chart, you can call this method by making the appropriate cast.

```
((Chart) chart1).setData(3, "Earth", 9000);
```

You can also list all applets on a web page, whether or not they have a `name` attribute. The `getApplets` method returns an *enumeration object.* (You learn more about enumeration objects in Volume 2.) Here is a loop that prints the class names of all applets on the current page.

```
Enumeration e = getAppletContext().getApplets();
while (e.hasMoreElements())
{
   Object a = e.nextElement();
   System.out.println(a.getClass().getName());
}
```

An applet cannot communicate with an applet on a different web page.

Display of Items in the Browser

You have access to two areas of the ambient browsers: the status line and the web page display area. Both use methods of the `AppletContext` class.

You can display a string in the status line at the bottom of the browser with the `showStatus` message, for example,

```
showStatus("Loading data . . . please wait");
```

TIP: In our experience, `showStatus` is of limited use. The browser is also using the status line, and, more often than not, it will overwrite your precious message with chatter like "`Applet running`." Use the status line for fluff messages like "`Loading data . . . please wait`," but not for something that the user cannot afford to miss.

You can tell the browser to show a different web page with the `showDocument` method. There are several ways to do this. The simplest is with a call to `showDocument` with one argument, the URL you want to show.

```
URL u = new URL("http://java.sun.com/index.html");
getAppletContext().showDocument(u);
```

The problem with this call is that it opens the new web page in the same window as your current page, thereby displacing your applet. To return to your applet, the user must click the Back button of the browser.

You can tell the browser to show the document in another window by giving a second parameter in the call to `showDocument` (see Table 10–2). If you supply the special string `"_blank"`, the browser opens a new window with the document, instead of displacing the current document. More important, if you take advantage of the frame feature in HTML, you can split a browser window into multiple frames, each of which has a name. You can put your applet into one frame and have it show documents in other frames. We show you an example of how to do this in the next section.

Table 10–2: The `showDocument` Method

Target Parameter	Location
`"_self"` or none	Show the document in the current frame.
`"_parent"`	Show the document in the parent frame.
`"_top"`	Show the document in the topmost frame.
`"_blank"`	Show in new, unnamed, top-level window.
Any other string	Show in the frame with that name. If no frame with that name exists, open a new window and give it that name.

NOTE: Sun's applet viewer does not show web pages. The `showDocument` method is ignored in the applet viewer.

java.applet.Applet 1.2

- `public AppletContext getAppletContext()`
  gives you a handle to the applet's browser environment. On most browsers, you can use this information to control the browser in which the applet is running.
- `void showStatus(String msg)`
  shows the string specified in the status line of the browser.

***java.applet.AppletContext* 1.2**

- `Enumeration getApplets()`
  returns an enumeration (see Volume 2) of all the applets in the same context, that is, the same web page.
- `Applet getApplet(String name)`
  returns the applet in the current context with the given name; returns `null` if none exists. Only the current web page is searched.
- `void showDocument(URL url)`
- `void showDocument(URL url, String target)`
  show a new web page in a frame in the browser. In the first form, the new page displaces the current page. The second form uses the `target` parameter to identify the target frame (see Table 10–2 on page 516).

A Bookmark Applet

This applet takes advantage of the frame feature in HTML. We divide the screen vertically into two frames. The left frame contains a Java applet that shows a list of bookmarks. When you select any of the bookmarks, the applet tells the browser to display the corresponding web page (see Figure 10–8).

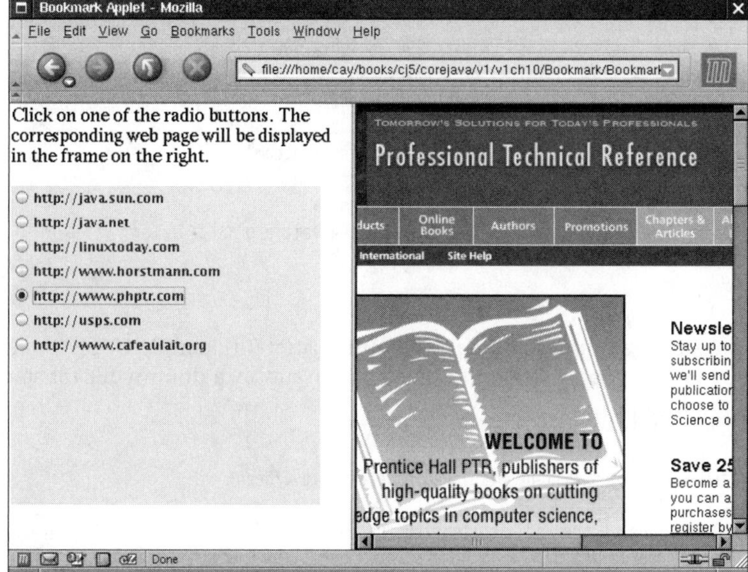

Figure 10–8: A bookmark applet

Example 10–6 shows the HTML file that defines the frames.

Example 10–6: Bookmark.html

```
<html>
   <head>
      <title>Bookmark Applet</title>
   </head>
   <frameset cols="320,*">
      <frame name="left" src="Left.html"
         marginheight="2" marginwidth="2"
         scrolling="no" noresize="noresize"/>
      <frame name="right" src="Right.html"
         marginheight="2" marginwidth="2"
         scrolling="yes" noresize="noresize"/>
   </frameset>
</html>
```

We do not go over the exact syntax elements. What is important is that each frame has two essential features: a name (given by the `name` attribute) and a URL (given by the `src` attribute). We could not think of any good names for the frames, so we simply named them `"left"` and `"right"`.

The left frame uses the `Left.html` file (Example 10–7) , which loads the applet into the left frame. It simply specifies the applet and the bookmarks. You can customize this file for your own web page by changing the bookmarks.

Example 10–7: Left.html

```
<html>
   <head><title>A Bookmark Applet</title></head>
   <body>
      <p>
         Click on one of the radio buttons.
         The corresponding web page
         will be displayed in the frame on the right.
      </p>
      <applet code="Bookmark.class" width="290" height="300">
         <param name="link.1" value="http://java.sun.com"/>
         <param name="link.2" value="http://java.net"/>
         <param name="link.3" value="http://linuxtoday.com"/>
         <param name="link.4" value="http://www.horstmann.com"/>
         <param name="link.5" value="http://www.phptr.com"/>
         <param name="link.6" value="http://usps.com"/>
         <param name="link.7" value="http://www.cafeaulait.org"/>
      </applet>
   </body>
</html>
```

The right frame loads a dummy file that we called `Right.html` (Example 10–8). (Some browsers do not approve when you leave a frame blank, so we supply a dummy file for starters.)

Example 10–8: Right.html

```
<html>
   <head><title>Web pages will be displayed here.</title></head>
   <body>
      <p>Click on one of the radio buttons to the left.
      The corresponding web page will be displayed here.</p>
   </body>
</html>
```

The code for the bookmark applet that is given in Example 10–9 is simple. It reads the values of the parameters `link.1`, `link.2`, and so on, and turns each of them into a radio

button. When you select one of the radio buttons, the showDocument method displays the corresponding page in the right frame.

Example 10–9: Bookmark.java

```
import java.awt.*;
import java.awt.event.*;
import java.applet.*;
import java.util.*;
import java.net.*;
import javax.swing.*;

public class Bookmark extends JApplet
{
   public void init()
   {
      Box box = Box.createVerticalBox();
      ButtonGroup group = new ButtonGroup();

      int i = 1;
      String urlString;

      // read all link.n parameters
      while ((urlString = getParameter("link." + i)) != null)
      {

         try
         {
            final URL url = new URL(urlString);

            // make a radio button for each link
            JRadioButton button = new JRadioButton(urlString);
            box.add(button);
            group.add(button);

            // selecting the radio button shows the URL in the "right" frame
            button.addActionListener(new
               ActionListener()
               {
                  public void actionPerformed(ActionEvent event)
                  {
                     AppletContext context = getAppletContext();
                     context.showDocument(url, "right");
                  }
               });
         }
         catch (MalformedURLException e)
         {
            e.printStackTrace();
         }

         i++;
      }

      add(box);
   }
}
```

It's an Applet. It's an Application. It's Both!

Quite a few years ago, a *Saturday Night Live* skit poking fun at a television commercial showed a couple arguing about a white, gelatinous substance. The husband said, "It's a dessert topping." The wife said, "It's a floor wax." And the announcer concluded triumphantly, "It's both!"

Well, in this section, we show you how to write a Java program that is *both* an applet and an application. That is, you can load the program with the applet viewer or a browser, or you can start it from the command line with the `java` program launcher. We are not sure how often this comes up—we found it interesting that this could be done at all and thought you would, too.

The screen shots in Figures 10–9 and 10–10 show the *same* program, launched from the command line as an application and viewed inside the applet viewer as an applet.

Let us see how this can be done. Every class file has exactly one public class. For the applet viewer to launch it, that class must derive from `Applet`. For Java to start the application, it must have a static `main` method. So far, we have

```
class MyAppletApplication extends JApplet
{
   public void init() { . . . }
   . . .
   public static void main(String[] args) { . . . }
}
```

Figure 10–9: The calculator as an application

Figure 10–10: The calculator as an applet

What can we put into `main`? Normally, we make an object of the class and invoke `setVisible(true)` on it. But this case is not so simple. You cannot call `setVisible` on a naked applet. The applet must be placed inside a frame.

To provide a frame, we create the class `AppletFrame`, like this:

```
public class AppletFrame extends JFrame
{
   public AppletFrame(Applet anApplet)
   {
      applet = anApplet;
      add(applet);
      . . .
   }
   . . .
}
```

The constructor of the frame puts the applet (which is a `Component`) inside the content pane of the frame.

In the `main` method of the applet/application, we construct and show an `AppletFrame`.

```
class MyAppletApplication extends JApplet
{
   public void init() { . . . }
   . . .
   public static void main(String args[])
   {
      AppletFrame frame = new AppletFrame(new MyAppletApplication());
      frame.setTitle("MyAppletApplication");
      frame.setSize(DEFAULT_WIDTH, DEFAULT_HEIGHT);
      frame.setDefaultCloseOperation(JFrame.EXIT_ON_CLOSE);
      frame.setVisible(true);
   }
}
```

When the applet starts, its `init` and `start` methods must be called. We achieve this by overriding the `setVisible` method of the `AppletFrame` class:

```
public void setVisible(boolean b)
{
   if (b)
   {
      applet.init();
      super.setVisible(true);
      applet.start();
   }
   else
   {
      applet.stop();
      super.setVisible(false);
      applet.destroy();
   }
}
```

There is one catch. If the program is started with the Java launcher and not the applet viewer, and it calls `getAppletContext`, it gets a `null` pointer because it has not been launched inside a browser. This causes a runtime crash whenever we have code like

```
getAppletContext().showStatus(message);
```

While we do not want to write a full-fledged browser, we do need to supply the bare minimum to make calls like this work. The call displays no message, but at least it will not crash the program. It turns out that all we need to do is implement two interfaces: `AppletStub` and `AppletContext`.

You have already seen applet contexts in action. They are responsible for fetching images and audio files and for displaying web pages. They can, however, politely refuse, and this is what our applet context will do. The major purpose of the `AppletStub` interface is to locate the applet context. Every applet has an applet stub (set with the `setStub` method of the `Applet` class).

In our case, `AppletFrame` implements both `AppletStub` and `AppletContext`. We supply the bare minimum functionality that is necessary to implement these two interfaces.

```
public class AppletFrame extends JFrame
   implements AppletStub, AppletContext
{
   . . .
   // AppletStub methods
   public boolean isActive() { return true; }
   public URL getDocumentBase() { return null; }
   public URL getCodeBase() { return null; }
   public String getParameter(String name) { return ""; }
   public AppletContext getAppletContext() { return this; }
   public void appletResize(int width, int height) {}

   // AppletContext methods
   public AudioClip getAudioClip(URL url) { return null; }
   public Image getImage(URL url) { return null; }
   public Applet getApplet(String name) { return null; }
   public Enumeration getApplets() { return null; }
   public void showDocument(URL url) {}
   public void showDocument(URL url, String target) {}
   public void showStatus(String status) {}
   public void setStream(String key, InputStream stream) {}
   public InputStream getStream(String key) { return null; }
   public Iterator getStreamKeys() { return null; }
}
```

NOTE: When you compile this file with the JDK 1.3 compiler, you will get a warning that the class `java.awt.Window` also has a method called `isActive` that has package visibility. Because our class is not in the same package as the `Window` class, it cannot override the `Window.isActive` method. That is fine with us—we want to supply a new `isActive` method for the `AppletStub` interface. And, interestingly enough, it is entirely legal to add a new method with the same signature to the subclass. Whenever the object is accessed through a `Window` reference inside the `java.awt` package, the package-visible `Window.isActive` method is called. But whenever the call is made through an `AppletFrame` or `AppletStub` reference, the `AppletFrame.isActive` method is called.

Next, the constructor of the frame class calls `setStub` on the applet to make itself its stub.

```
public AppletFrame(Applet anApplet)
{
   applet = anApplet
   Container contentPane = getContentPane();
   contentPane.add(applet);
   applet.setStub(this);
}
```

One final twist is possible. Suppose we want to use the calculator as an applet and application simultaneously. Rather than moving the methods of the CalculatorApplet class into the CalculatorAppletApplication class, we will just use inheritance. Here is the code for the class that does this.

```
public class CalculatorAppletApplication extends CalculatorApplet
{
   public static void main(String args[])
   {
      AppletFrame frame = new AppletFrame(new CalculatorApplet());
      . . .
   }
}
```

You can do this with any applet, not just with the calculator applet. All you do is derive a class MyAppletApplication from your applet class and pass a new MyApplet() object to the AppletFrame in the main method. The result is a class that is both an applet and an application.

Just for fun, we use the previously mentioned trick of adding the applet tag as a comment to the source file. Then you can invoke the applet viewer with the source file without requiring an additional HTML file.

Examples 10–10 and 10–11 list the code. You need to copy the CalculatorApplet.java file into the same directory to compile the program. Try running both the applet and the application:

```
appletviewer CalculatorAppletApplication.java
java CalculatorAppletApplication
```

Example 10–10: AppletFrame.java

```
import java.awt.*;
import java.awt.event.*;
import java.applet.*;
import java.io.*;
import java.net.*;
import java.util.*;
import javax.swing.*;

public class AppletFrame extends JFrame
   implements AppletStub, AppletContext
{
   public AppletFrame(Applet anApplet)
   {
      applet = anApplet;
      add(applet);
      applet.setStub(this);
   }

   public void setVisible(boolean b)
   {
      if (b)
      {
         applet.init();
         super.setVisible(true);
         applet.start();
      }
      else
      {
```

```
            applet.stop();
            super.setVisible(false);
            applet.destroy();
         }
      }

   // AppletStub methods
   public boolean isActive() { return true; }
   public URL getDocumentBase() { return null; }
   public URL getCodeBase() { return null; }
   public String getParameter(String name) { return ""; }
   public AppletContext getAppletContext() { return this; }
   public void appletResize(int width, int height) {}

   // AppletContext methods
   public AudioClip getAudioClip(URL url) { return null; }
   public Image getImage(URL url) { return null; }
   public Applet getApplet(String name) { return null; }
   public Enumeration getApplets() { return null; }
   public void showDocument(URL url) {}
   public void showDocument(URL url, String target) {}
   public void showStatus(String status) {}
   public void setStream(String key, InputStream stream) {}
   public InputStream getStream(String key) { return null; }
   public Iterator getStreamKeys() { return null; }

   private Applet applet;
}
```

Example 10–11: CalculatorAppletApplication.java

```
/*
  The applet viewer reads the tags below if you call it with
      appletviewer CalculatorAppletApplication.java (!)
  No separate HTML file is required.
  <applet code="CalculatorAppletApplication.class" width="200" height="200">
  </applet>
*/

import javax.swing.*;

public class CalculatorAppletApplication
   extends CalculatorApplet
// It's an applet. It's an application. It's BOTH!
{
   public static void main(String[] args)
   {
      AppletFrame frame = new AppletFrame(new CalculatorApplet());
      frame.setTitle("CalculatorAppletApplication");
      frame.setSize(DEFAULT_WIDTH, DEFAULT_HEIGHT);
      frame.setDefaultCloseOperation(JFrame.EXIT_ON_CLOSE);
      frame.setVisible(true);
   }

   public static final int DEFAULT_WIDTH = 200;
   public static final int DEFAULT_HEIGHT = 200;
}
```

JAR Files

The calculator applet from this chapter uses four classes: `CalculatorApplet`, `CalculatorPanel`, and two inner classes. You know that the applet tag references the class file that contains the applet class:

```
<applet code="CalculatorApplet.class" width="100" height="150">
```

When the browser reads this line, it makes a connection to the web server and fetches the file `CalculatorApplet.class`. The *class loader* of the browser's virtual machine loads the `CalculatorApplet` class from that file. During the loading process, the class loader must *resolve* the other classes used in this class. After doing so, it then knows it needs more classes to run the applet. The browser, therefore, makes additional connections to the web server, one for each class file. Loading such an applet over a slow network connection can take many minutes.

NOTE: It is important to remember that the reason for this long loading time is not the size of the class files—they are quite small. Rather it is because of the considerable overhead involved in establishing a connection to the web server.

Java supports an improved method for loading class files, allowing you to package all the needed class files into a single file. This file can then be downloaded with a *single* HTTP request to the server. Files that archive Java class files are called Java Archive (JAR) files. JAR files can contain both class files and other file types such as image and sound files. JAR files are compressed, using the familiar ZIP compression format, which further reduces the download time.

You use the `jar` tool to make JAR files. (In the default installation, it's in the `jdk/bin` directory.) The most common command to make a new JAR file uses the following syntax:

`jar cvf` *JARFileName File1 File2* . . .

For example,

```
jar cvf CalculatorClasses.jar *.class icon.gif
```

In general, the `jar` command has the format

`jar` *options File1 File2* . . .

Table 10–3 lists all the options for the `jar` program. They are similar to the options of the UNIX `tar` command.

Table 10–3: jar Program Options

Option	Description
`c`	Creates a new or empty archive and adds files to it. If any of the specified file names are directories, then the `jar` program processes them recursively.
`t`	Displays the table of contents.
`u`	Updates an existing JAR file.
`x`	Extracts files. If you supply one or more file names, only those files are extracted. Otherwise, all files are extracted.
`f`	Specifies the JAR file name as the second command-line argument. If this parameter is missing, then `jar` will write the result to standard output (when creating a JAR file) or read it from standard input (when extracting or tabulating a JAR file).
`v`	Generates verbose output.

Table 10–3: jar Program Options (continued)

Option	Description
m	Adds a *manifest* to the JAR file. A manifest is a description of the archive contents and origin. Every archive has a default manifest, but you can supply your own if you want to authenticate the contents of the archive.
0	Stores without ZIP compression.
M	Does not create a manifest file for the entries.
i	Creates an index file (see below for more information).
C	Temporarily changes the directory. For example, `jar cvf JARFileName.jar -C classes *.class` changes to the `classes` subdirectory to add class files.

Once you have a JAR file, you need to reference it in the `applet` tag, as in the following example.

```
<applet code="CalculatorApplet.class" archive="CalculatorClasses.jar" width="100" height="150">
```

Note that the `code` attribute must still be present. The `code` attribute tells the browser the name of the applet. The `archive` is merely a source where the applet class and other files may be located. Whenever a class, image, or sound file is needed, the browser searches the JAR files in the `archive` list first. Only if the file is not contained in the archive will it be fetched from the web server.

TIP: If you have a large applet, chances are that not all users require all of its functionality. To reduce the download time, you can break up the applet code into multiple JAR files and add an *index* to the main JAR file. The class loader then knows which JAR files contain a particular package or resource. See `http://java.sun.com/j2se/5.0/docs/guide/jar/jar.html#JAR%20Index` for details about the indexing procedure.

TIP: JDK 5.0 supports a new compression scheme, called "pack200", that is specifically tuned to compress class files more efficiently than the generic ZIP compression algorithm. Sun claims a compression rate of close to 90% with multi-megabyte JAR files that contain only class files. In order to deploy these files, you need to configure the web server so that it serves standard files for traditional clients and compressed files for new clients that indicate in the HTTP request that they are able to decompress them. See `http://java.sun.com/j2se/5.0/docs/guide/deployment/deployment-guide/pack200.html` for detailed instructions.

NOTE: The Java Plug-in will cache applet code. See `http://java.sun.com/j2se/5.0/docs/guide/plugin/developer_guide/applet_caching.html` for details on tweaking the cache.

Application Packaging

We now leave the world of applets and turn to the packaging of Java applications. When you ship an application, you don't want to deploy a mess of class files. Just as with applets, you should package the class files and other resources required by your program in a JAR file. Once the program is packaged, it can be loaded with a simple command or, if the operating system is configured appropriately, by double-clicking on the JAR file.

The Manifest

You can package application programs, program components (sometimes called "beans"—see Chapter 8 of Volume 2), and code libraries into JAR files. For example, the runtime library of the JDK is contained in a very large file `rt.jar`.

A JAR file is simply a ZIP file that contains classes, other files that a program may need (such as icon images), and a *manifest* file that describes special features of the archive.

The manifest file is called `MANIFEST.MF` and is located in a special `META-INF` subdirectory of the JAR file. The minimum legal manifest is quite boring: just

```
Manifest-Version: 1.0
```

Complex manifests can have many more entries. The manifest entries are grouped into sections. The first section in the manifest is called the *main section*. It applies to the whole JAR file. Subsequent entries can specify properties of named entities such as individual files, packages, or URLs. Those entries must begin with a `Name` entry. Sections are separated by blank lines. For example,

```
Manifest-Version: 1.0
lines describing this archive

Name: Woozle.class
lines describing this file

Name: com/mycompany/mypkg/
lines describing this package
```

To edit the manifest, place the lines that you want to add to the manifest into a text file. Then run

```
jar cfm JARFileName ManifestFileName . . .
```

For example, to make a new JAR file with a manifest, run:

```
jar cfm MyArchive.jar manifest.mf com/mycompany/mypkg/*.class
```

To add items to the manifest of an existing JAR file, place the additions into a text file and use a command such as

```
jar ufm MyArchive.jar manifest-additions.mf
```

See `http://java.sun.com/j2se/5.0/docs/guide/jar/jar.html` for more information on the JAR and manifest file formats.

Self-Running JAR Files

To package an application, place all files that your application needs into a JAR file and then add a manifest entry that specifies the *main class* of your program—the class that you would normally specify when invoking the `java` program launcher.

Make a file, say, `mainclass.mf`, containing a line such as

```
Main-Class: com/mycompany/mypkg/MainAppClass
```

CAUTION: The last line in the manifest must end with a newline character. Otherwise, the manifest will not be read correctly. It is a common error to produce a text file containing just the `Main-Class` line without a line terminator.

Do not add a `.class` extension to the main class name. Then run the `jar` command:

```
jar cvfm MyProgram.jar mainclass.mf files to add
```

Users can now simply start the program as

```
java -jar MyProgram.jar
```

Depending on the operating system configuration, you may be able to launch the application by double-clicking on the JAR file icon.

- On Windows, the Java runtime installer creates a file association for the ".jar" extension that launches the file with the `javaw -jar` command. (Unlike the `java` command, the `javaw` command doesn't open a shell window.)
- On Solaris, the operating system recognizes the "magic number" of a JAR file and starts it with the `java -jar` command.
- On Mac OS X, the operating system recognizes the ".jar" file extension and executes the Java program when you double-click on a JAR file. Furthermore, the application package utility `MRJAppBuilder` lets you turn a JAR file into a first-class, double-clickable Mac application with custom class paths, icons, and so on. For more information, see `http://developer.apple.com/qa/java/java29.html`.

Resources

Classes that are used in both applets and applications often use associated data files, such as

- Image and sound files;
- Text files with message strings and button labels;
- Files with binary data, for example, to describe the layout of a map.

In Java, such an associated file is called a *resource.*

NOTE: In Windows, the term "resource" has a more specialized meaning. Windows resources also consist of images, button labels, and so on, but they are attached to the executable file and accessed by a standard programming interface. In contrast, Java resources are stored as separate files, not as part of class files. And it is up to each class to access and interpret the resource data.

For example, consider a class, `AboutPanel`, that displays a message such as the one in Figure 10–11.

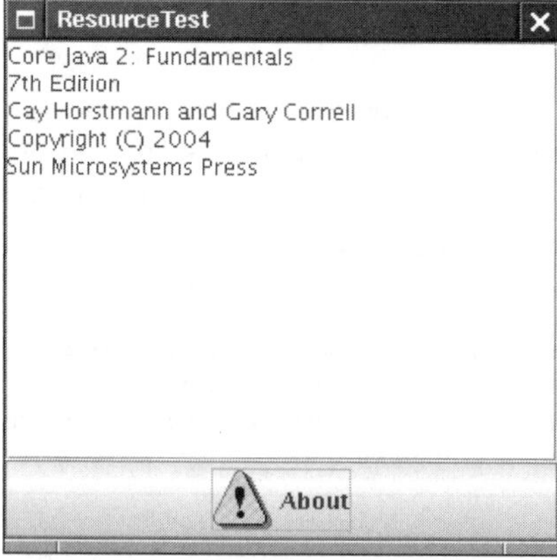

Figure 10–11: Displaying a resource from a JAR file

Of course, the book title and copyright year in the panel will change for the next edition of the book. To make it easy to track this change, we want to put the text inside a file and not hardcode it as a string.

But where should you put a file such as `about.txt`? Of course, it would be convenient if you simply placed it with the rest of the program files, for example, in a JAR file.

The class loader knows how to search for class files until it has located them somewhere on the class path, or in an archive, or on a web server. The resource mechanism gives you the same convenience for files that aren't class files. Here are the necessary steps:

1. Get the `Class` object of the class that has a resource, for example, `AboutPanel.class`.
2. Call `getResource(filename)` to get the resource location as a URL.
3. If the resource is an image or audio file, read it directly with the `getImage` or `getAudioClip` method.
4. Otherwise, use the `openStream` method on the URL to read in the data in the file. (See Chapter 12 for more on streams.)

The point is that the class loader remembers how to locate the class and it can then search for the associated resource in the same location.

For example, to make an icon with the image file `about.gif`, do the following:

```
URL url = AboutPanel.class.getResource("about.gif");
ImageIcon icon = new ImageIcon(url);
```

That means "locate the `about.gif` file at the same place where you find `AboutPanel.class`."

To read in the file `about.txt`, you can use similar commands:

```
URL url = AboutPanel.class.getResource("about.txt");
InputStream stream = url.openStream();
```

Because this combination is so common, there is a convenient shortcut method: `getResourceAsStream` returns an `InputStream`, not a `URL`.

```
InputStream stream = AboutPanel.class.getResourceAsStream("about.txt");
```

To read from this stream, you need to know how to process input (see Chapter 12 for details). In the sample program, we read the stream a line at a time with the following instructions:

```
InputStream stream = AboutPanel.class.getResourceAsStream("about.txt");
Scanner in = Scanner.create(stream);
while (in.hasNext())
   textArea.append(in.nextLine() + "\n");
```

The Core Java example files include a JAR file named `ResourceTest.jar` that contains all the class files for this example and the resource files `about.gif` and `about.txt`. This demonstrates that the program locates the resource file in the same location as the class file, namely, inside the JAR file. Example 10–12 shows the source code.

TIP: As you saw earlier in this chapter, applets can locate image and audio files with the `getImage` and `getAudioClip` methods—these methods automatically search JAR files. But to load other files from a JAR file, applets still need the `getResourceAsStream` method.

Instead of placing a resource file inside the same directory as the class file, you can place it in a subdirectory. You can use a hierarchical resource name such as

```
data/text/about.txt
```

This is a relative resource name, and it is interpreted relative to the package of the class that is loading the resource. Note that you must always use the / separator, regardless of the directory separator on the system that actually stores the resource files. For example, on the Windows file system, the resource loader automatically translates / to \ separators.

A resource name starting with a / is called an absolute resource name. It is located in the same way that a class inside a package would be located. For example, a resource

```
/corejava/title.txt
```

is located in the corejava directory (which may be a subdirectory of the class path, inside a JAR file, or, for applets, on a web server).

Automating the loading of files is all that the resource loading feature does. There are no standard methods for interpreting the contents of a resource file. Each program must have its own way of interpreting the contents of its resource files.

Another common application of resources is the internationalization of programs. Language-dependent strings, such as messages and user interface labels, are stored in resource files, with one file for each language. The *internationalization API*, which is discussed in Chapter 10 of Volume 2, supports a standard method for organizing and accessing these localization files.

Example 10–12: ResourceTest.java

```
import java.awt.*;
import java.awt.event.*;
import java.io.*;
import java.net.*;
import java.util.*;
import javax.swing.*;

public class ResourceTest
{
   public static void main(String[] args)
   {
      ResourceTestFrame frame = new ResourceTestFrame();
      frame.setDefaultCloseOperation(JFrame.EXIT_ON_CLOSE);
      frame.setVisible(true);
   }
}

/**
   A frame with a panel that has components demonstrating
   resource access from a JAR file.
*/
class ResourceTestFrame extends JFrame
{
   public ResourceTestFrame()
   {
      setTitle("ResourceTest");
      setSize(DEFAULT_WIDTH, DEFAULT_HEIGHT);
      add(new AboutPanel());
   }

   public static final int DEFAULT_WIDTH = 300;
   public static final int DEFAULT_HEIGHT = 300;
}

```

```
/**
   A panel with a text area and an "About" button. Pressing
   the button fills the text area with text from a resource.
*/
class AboutPanel extends JPanel
{
   public AboutPanel()
   {
      setLayout(new BorderLayout());

      // add text area
      textArea = new JTextArea();
      add(new JScrollPane(textArea), BorderLayout.CENTER);

      // add About button
      URL aboutURL = AboutPanel.class.getResource("about.gif");
      JButton aboutButton = new JButton("About", new ImageIcon(aboutURL));
      aboutButton.addActionListener(new AboutAction());
      add(aboutButton, BorderLayout.SOUTH);
   }

   private JTextArea textArea;

   private class AboutAction implements ActionListener
   {
      public void actionPerformed(ActionEvent event)
      {
         InputStream stream = AboutPanel.class.getResourceAsStream("about.txt");
         Scanner in = new Scanner(stream);
         while (in.hasNext())
            textArea.append(in.nextLine() + "\n");
      }
   }
}
```

API **java.lang.Class 1.0**

- URL getResource(String name) **1.1**
- InputStream getResourceAsStream(String name) **1.1**

  find the resource in the same place as the class and then return a URL or input stream you can use for loading the resource. Return `null` if the resource isn't found, and so do not throw an exception for an I/O error.

  Parameters: `name` The resource name

Sealing

We mentioned in Chapter 4 that you can *seal* a Java language package to ensure that no further classes can add themselves to it. You would want to seal a package if you use package-visible classes, methods, and fields in your code. Without sealing, other classes can place themselves into the same package and thereby gain access to its package-visible features.

For example, if you seal the package `com.mycompany.util`, then no class outside the sealed archive can be defined with the statement

```
package com.mycompany.util;
```

To achieve this, you put all classes of the package into a JAR file. By default, packages in a JAR file are not sealed. You can change that global default by placing the line

```
Sealed: true
```

into the main section of the manifest. For each individual package, you can specify whether you want the package sealed or not, by adding another section to the JAR file manifest, like this:

```
Name: com/mycompany/util/
Sealed: true

Name: com/mycompany/misc/
Sealed: false
```

To seal a package, make a text file with the manifest instructions. Then run the `jar` command in the usual way:

```
jar cvfm MyArchive.jar manifest.mf files to add
```

Java Web Start

Java Web Start is a newer technology that aims to improve on the user experience of Java programs that are delivered over the Internet. Here are the principal differences between Java Web Start applications and applets.

- Java Web Start delivers regular Java applications that are started by a call to the `main` method of a class. There is no need to inherit from `Applet`.
- A Java Web Start application does not live inside a browser. It is displayed outside the browser.
- A Java Web Start application can be launched through the browser, but the underlying mechanism is quite different from the launch of an applet. Browsers are tightly integrated with a Java runtime environment that executes applets. The Java Web Start integration is much looser. The browser simply launches an external application whenever it loads a Java Web Start application descriptor. That is the same mechanism that is used to launch other helper applications such as Adobe Acrobat or RealAudio. Even hostile browser vendors won't be able to interfere with this mechanism.
- Once a Java Web Start application has been downloaded, it can be started outside the browser.
- Java Web Start has a slightly relaxed "sandbox" that allows unsigned applications some access to local resources.

To prepare an application for delivery by Java Web Start, you package it in one or more JAR files. Then you prepare a descriptor file in Java Network Launch Protocol (JNLP) format. Place these files on a web server. Next, make sure that your web server reports a MIME type of `application/x-java-jnlp-file` for files with extension `.jnlp`. (Browsers use the MIME type to determine which helper application to launch.) Consult your web server documentation for details.

TIP: To experiment with Java Web Start, install Tomcat from `jakarta.apache.org/tomcat`. Tomcat is a container for servlets and JSP pages, but it also serves web pages. The current version is preconfigured to handle JNLP files.

Let's try out Java Web Start to deliver the calculator application from Chapter 9. Follow these steps.

1. Compile `Calculator.java`.

2. Prepare a manifest file `Calculator.mf` with the line

```
Main-Class: Calculator
```

3. Produce a JAR file with the command

```
jar cvfm Calculator.jar Calculator.mf *.class
```

4. Prepare the launch file `Calculator.jnlp` with the following contents:

```
<?xml version="1.0" encoding="utf-8"?>
<jnlp spec="1.0+"codebase="http://localhost:8080/calculator/" href="Calculator.jnlp">
  <information>
    <title>Calculator Demo Application</title>
    <vendor>Cay S. Horstmann</vendor>
    <description>A Calculator</description>
    <offline-allowed/>
  </information>
  <resources>
    <j2se version="5.0+"/>
    <jar href="Calculator.jar"/>
  </resources>
  <application-desc/>
</jnlp>
```

   The launch file format is fairly self-explanatory. For a full specification, see `http://java.sun.com/products/javawebstart/docs/developersguide.html`.

5. If you use Tomcat, make a directory *tomcat*`/webapps/calculator`, where *tomcat* is the base directory of your Tomcat installation. Make a subdirectory *tomcat*`/webapps/calculator/WEB-INF`, and place the following minimal `web.xml` file inside the `WEB-INF` subdirectory:

```
<?xml version="1.0" encoding="utf-8"?>
<!DOCTYPE web-app PUBLIC "-//Sun Microsystems, Inc.//DTD Web Application 2.3//EN"
   "http://java.sun.com/dtd/web-app_2_3.dtd">
<web-app>
</web-app>
```

6. Place the JAR file and the launch file on your web server so that the URL matches the `codebase` entry in the JNLP file. If you use Tomcat, put them into the *tomcat*`/webapps/calculator` directory.
7. Make sure that your browser has been configured for Java Web Start, by checking that the `application/x-java-jnlp-file` MIME type is associated with the `javaws` application. If you installed the JDK, the configuration should be automatic.
8. Start Tomcat.
9. Point your browser to the JNLP file. For example, if you use Tomcat, go to `http://localhost:8080/calculator/Calculator.jnlp`.
10. You should see the launch window for Java Web Start (see Figure 10–12). Soon afterward, the calculator should come up, with a border marking it as a Java Web Start application (see Figure 10–13).

Calculator Demo Application
Cay S. Horstmann

Figure 10–12: Launching Java Web Start

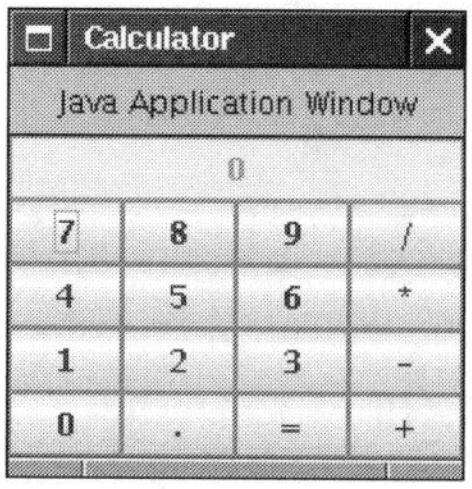

Figure 10–13: The calculator delivered by Java Web Start

11. When you access the JNLP file again, the application is retrieved from the cache. You can review the cache content by using the Java Plug-in control panel (see Figure 10–14). As of JDK 5.0, that control panel is used both for applets and Java Web Start applications. In Windows, look for the Java Plug-in control panel inside the Windows control panel. Under Linux, run *jdk*`/jre/bin/ControlPanel`.

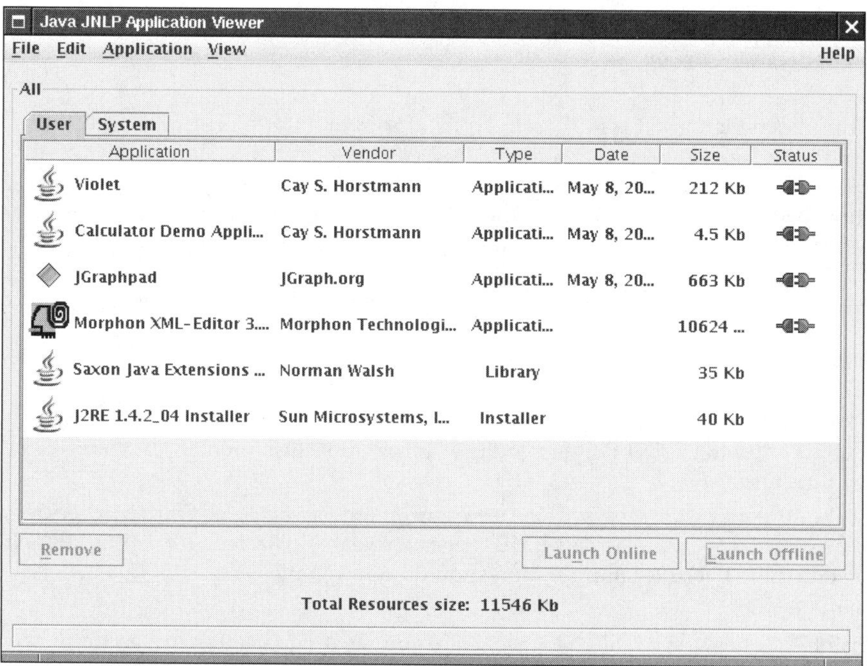

Figure 10–14: The application cache

The JNLP API

For a Java Web Start application to be granted full access to the local machine, the application must be digitally signed. (See Chapter 9 of Volume 2 for more information on digital signatures.) Just as with applets, an unsigned Java Web Start application that is downloaded from the Internet is inherently risky and runs in a sandbox, with minimal access to the local computer. However, with minimal security privileges, the JNLP API provides application developers some tools for accessing local resources.

For example, there are services to load and save files, but they are quite restrictive. The application can't look at the file system and it can't specify file names. Instead, a file dialog

is popped up, and the program user selects the file. Before the file dialog is popped up, the program user is alerted and must agree to proceed (see Figure 10–15). Furthermore, the API doesn't actually give the program access to a `File` object. In particular, the application has no way of finding out the file location. Thus, programmers are given the tools to implement standard "file open" and "file save" actions, but as much system information as possible is hidden from untrusted applications.

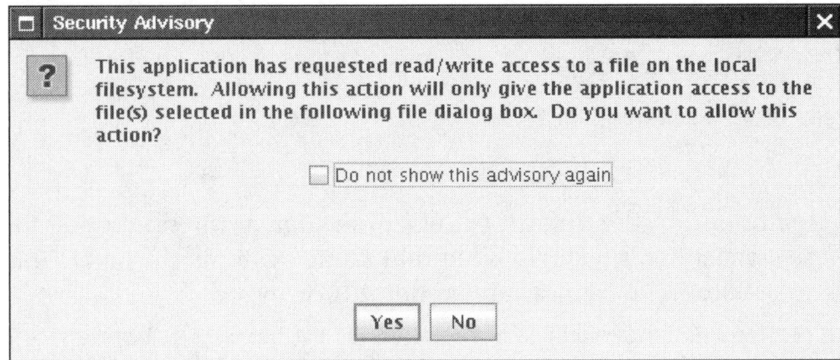

Figure 10–15: A Java Web Start security advisory

The API provides the following services:

- Loading and saving files
- Accessing the clipboard
- Downloading a file
- Printing
- Storing and retrieving persistent configuration information
- Displaying a document in the default browser
- Ensuring that only a single instance of an application executes (added in JDK 5.0)

To access a service, you use the `ServiceManager`, like this:

```
FileSaveService service = (FileSaveService) ServiceManager.lookup("javax.jnlp.FileSaveService");
```

This call throws an `UnavailableServiceException` if the service is not available.

NOTE: You must include the file `javaws.jar` in the class path if you want to compile programs that use the JNLP API. That file is included in the `jre/lib` subdirectory of the JDK.

We now discuss the most useful JNLP services. To save a file, you provide suggestions for the initial path name and file extensions for the file dialog, the data to be saved, and a suggested file name. For example,

```
service.saveFileDialog(".", new String[] { "txt" }, data, "calc.txt");
```

The data must be delivered in an `InputStream`. That can be somewhat tricky to arrange. The program in Example 10–13 uses the following strategy:

1. Create a `ByteArrayOutputStream` to hold the bytes to be saved.
2. Create a `PrintStream` that sends its data to the `ByteArrayOutputStream`.
3. Print the information to be saved to the `PrintStream`.
4. Create a `ByteArrayInputStream` to read the saved bytes.
5. Pass that stream to the `saveFileDialog` method.

You will learn more about streams in Chapter 12. For now, you can just gloss over the details in the sample program.

To read data from a file, you use the FileOpenService instead. Its openFileDialog receives suggestions for the initial path name and file extensions for the file dialog and returns a FileContents object. You can then call the getInputStream method to read the file data. If the user didn't choose a file, then the openFileDialog method returns null.

```
FileOpenService service = (FileOpenService) ServiceManager.lookup("javax.jnlp.FileOpenService");
FileContents contents =  service.openFileDialog(".", new String[] { "txt" });
if (contents != null)
{
   InputStream in = contents.getInputStream();
   . . .
}
```

To display a document on the default browser (similar to the showDocument method of an applet), use the BasicService interface. Note that some systems (in particular, many UNIX and Linux systems) may not have a default browser.

```
BasicService service = (BasicService) ServiceManager.lookup("javax.jnlp.BasicService");
if (service.isWebBrowserSupported())
   service.showDocument(url);
else . . .
```

A rudimentary PersistenceService lets an application store small amounts of configuration information and retrieve it when the application runs again. This service is necessary because an untrusted application cannot specify a location for a configuration file.

The mechanism is similar to HTTP cookies. The persistent store uses URLs as keys. The URLs don't have to point to a real web resource. The service simply uses them as a convenient hierarchical naming scheme. For any given URL key, an application can store arbitrary binary data. (The store may restrict the size of the data block.)

So that applications are isolated from each other, a particular application can only use URL keys that start with its codebase (as specified in the JNLP file). For example, if an application is downloaded from http://myserver.com/apps, then it can only use keys of the form http://myserver.com/apps/subkey1/subkey2/... Attempts to access other keys will fail.

An application can call the getCodeBase method of the BasicService to find its codebase.

You create a new key with the create method of the PersistenceService.

```
URL url = new URL(codeBase, "mykey");
service.create(url, maxSize);
```

To access the information associated with a particular key, call the get method. That method returns a FileContents object through which you can read and write the key data. For example,

```
FileContents contents = service.get(url);
InputStream in = contents.getInputStream();
OutputStream out = contents.getOutputStream(true); // true = overwrite
```

Unfortunately, there is no convenient way to find out whether a key already exists or whether you need to create it. You can hope that the key exists and call get. If the call throws a FileNotFoundException, then you need to create the key.

NOTE: Starting with JDK 5.0, both Java Web Start applications and applets can print, using the normal printing API. A security dialog pops up, asking the user for permission to access the printer. For more information on the printing API, turn to the Advanced AWT chapter in Volume 2.

The program in Example 10–13 is a simple enhancement of the calculator application. This calculator has a virtual paper tape that keeps track of all calculations. You can save and load the calculation history. To demonstrate the persistent store, the application lets you set the frame title. If you run the application again, it retrieves your title choice from the persistent store (see Figure 10–16).

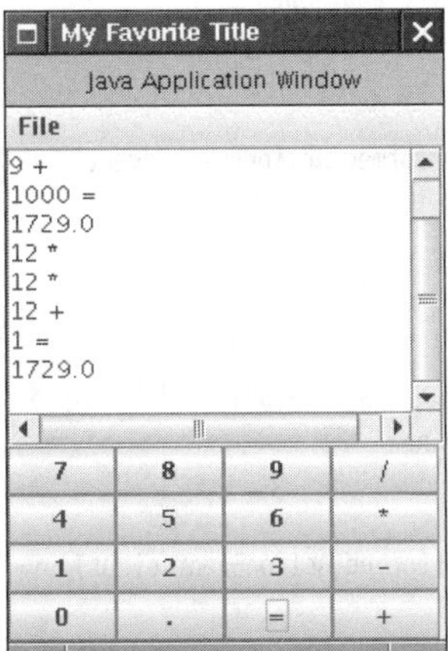

Figure 10–16: The WebStartCalculator application

Example 10–13: WebStartCalculator.java

```
import java.awt.*;
import java.awt.event.*;
import java.io.*;
import java.net.*;
import javax.swing.*;
import javax.swing.text.*;
import javax.jnlp.*;

/**
   A calculator with a calculation history that can be
   deployed as a Java Web Start application.
*/
public class WebStartCalculator
{
   public static void main(String[] args)
   {
      CalculatorFrame frame = new CalculatorFrame();
      frame.setDefaultCloseOperation(JFrame.EXIT_ON_CLOSE);
      frame.setVisible(true);
   }
}

/**
   A frame with a calculator panel and a menu to load and
   save the calculator history.
*/
class CalculatorFrame extends JFrame
{
   public CalculatorFrame()
   {
```

```
      setTitle();
      panel = new CalculatorPanel();
      add(panel);

      JMenu fileMenu = new JMenu("File");

      JMenuItem openItem = fileMenu.add("Open");
      openItem.addActionListener(new
         ActionListener()
         {
            public void actionPerformed(ActionEvent event)
            {
               open();
            }
         });

      JMenuItem saveItem = fileMenu.add("Save");
      saveItem.addActionListener(new
         ActionListener()
         {
            public void actionPerformed(ActionEvent event)
            {
               save();
            }
         });
      JMenuBar menuBar = new JMenuBar();
      menuBar.add(fileMenu);
      setJMenuBar(menuBar);

      pack();
   }

   /**
      Gets the title from the persistent store or
      asks the user for the title if there is no prior entry.
   */
   public void setTitle()
   {
      try
      {
         String title = null;

         BasicService basic = (BasicService) ServiceManager.lookup("javax.jnlp.BasicService");
         URL codeBase = basic.getCodeBase();

         PersistenceService service
            = (PersistenceService) ServiceManager.lookup("javax.jnlp.PersistenceService");
         URL key = new URL(codeBase, "title");

         try
         {
            FileContents contents = service.get(key);
            InputStream in = contents.getInputStream();
            BufferedReader reader = new BufferedReader(new InputStreamReader(in));
            title = reader.readLine();
         }
```

```
         catch (FileNotFoundException e)
         {
            title = JOptionPane.showInputDialog("Please supply a frame title:");
            if (title == null) return;

            service.create(key, 100);
            FileContents contents = service.get(key);
            OutputStream out = contents.getOutputStream(true);
            PrintStream printOut = new PrintStream(out);
            printOut.print(title);
         }
         setTitle(title);
      }
      catch (UnavailableServiceException e)
      {
         JOptionPane.showMessageDialog(this, e);
      }
      catch (MalformedURLException e)
      {
         JOptionPane.showMessageDialog(this, e);
      }
      catch (IOException e)
      {
         JOptionPane.showMessageDialog(this, e);
      }
   }

   /**
      Opens a history file and updates the display.
   */
   public void open()
   {
      try
      {
         FileOpenService service
            = (FileOpenService) ServiceManager.lookup("javax.jnlp.FileOpenService");
         FileContents contents = service.openFileDialog(".", new String[] { "txt" });

         JOptionPane.showMessageDialog(this, contents.getName());
         if (contents != null)
         {
            InputStream in = contents.getInputStream();
            BufferedReader reader = new BufferedReader(new InputStreamReader(in));
            String line;
            while ((line = reader.readLine()) != null)
            {
               panel.append(line);
               panel.append("\n");
            }
         }
      }
      catch (UnavailableServiceException e)
      {
         JOptionPane.showMessageDialog(this, e);
      }
      catch (IOException e)
```

```
         {
            JOptionPane.showMessageDialog(this, e);
         }
      }

      /**
         Saves the calculator history to a file.
      */
      public void save()
      {
         try
         {
            ByteArrayOutputStream out = new ByteArrayOutputStream();
            PrintStream printOut = new PrintStream(out);
            printOut.print(panel.getText());
            InputStream data = new ByteArrayInputStream(out.toByteArray());
            FileSaveService service
               = (FileSaveService) ServiceManager.lookup("javax.jnlp.FileSaveService");
            service.saveFileDialog(".", new String[] { "txt" }, data, "calc.txt");
         }
         catch (UnavailableServiceException e)
         {
            JOptionPane.showMessageDialog(this, e);
         }
         catch (IOException e)
         {
            JOptionPane.showMessageDialog(this, e);
         }
      }

      private CalculatorPanel panel;
   }


   /**
      A panel with calculator buttons and a result display.
   */
   class CalculatorPanel extends JPanel
   {
      /**
         Lays out the panel.
      */
      public CalculatorPanel()
      {
         setLayout(new BorderLayout());

         result = 0;
         lastCommand = "=";
         start = true;

         // add the display

         display = new JTextArea(10, 20);

         add(new JScrollPane(display), BorderLayout.NORTH);

```

```
      ActionListener insert = new InsertAction();
      ActionListener command = new CommandAction();

      // add the buttons in a 4 x 4 grid

      panel = new JPanel();
      panel.setLayout(new GridLayout(4, 4));

      addButton("7", insert);
      addButton("8", insert);
      addButton("9", insert);
      addButton("/", command);

      addButton("4", insert);
      addButton("5", insert);
      addButton("6", insert);
      addButton("*", command);

      addButton("1", insert);
      addButton("2", insert);
      addButton("3", insert);
      addButton("-", command);

      addButton("0", insert);
      addButton(".", insert);
      addButton("=", command);
      addButton("+", command);

      add(panel, BorderLayout.CENTER);
   }

   /**
      Gets the history text.
      @return the calculator history
   */
   public String getText()
   {
      return display.getText();
   }

   /**
      Appends a string to the history text.
      @param s the string to append
   */
   public void append(String s)
   {
      display.append(s);
   }

   /**
      Adds a button to the center panel.
      @param label the button label
      @param listener the button listener
   */
   private void addButton(String label, ActionListener listener)
   {
```

```
      JButton button = new JButton(label);
      button.addActionListener(listener);
      panel.add(button);
   }

   /**
      This action inserts the button action string to the
      end of the display text.
   */
   private class InsertAction implements ActionListener
   {
      public void actionPerformed(ActionEvent event)
      {
         String input = event.getActionCommand();
         start = false;
         display.append(input);
      }
   }

   /**
      This action executes the command that the button
      action string denotes.
   */
   private class CommandAction implements ActionListener
   {
      public void actionPerformed(ActionEvent event)
      {
         String command = event.getActionCommand();

         if (start)
         {
            if (command.equals("-"))
            {
               display.append(command);
               start = false;
            }
            else
               lastCommand = command;
         }
         else
         {
            try
            {
               int lines = display.getLineCount();
               int lineStart = display.getLineStartOffset(lines - 1);
               int lineEnd = display.getLineEndOffset(lines - 1);
               String value = display.getText(lineStart, lineEnd - lineStart);
               display.append(" ");
               display.append(command);
               calculate(Double.parseDouble(value));
               if (command.equals("="))
                  display.append("\n" + result);
               lastCommand = command;
               display.append("\n");
               start = true;
            }
```

```
            catch (BadLocationException e)
            {
               e.printStackTrace();
            }
         }
      }
   }

   /**
      Carries out the pending calculation.
      @param x the value to be accumulated with the prior result.
   */
   public void calculate(double x)
   {
      if (lastCommand.equals("+")) result += x;
      else if (lastCommand.equals("-")) result -= x;
      else if (lastCommand.equals("*")) result *= x;
      else if (lastCommand.equals("/")) result /= x;
      else if (lastCommand.equals("=")) result = x;
   }

   private JTextArea display;
   private JPanel panel;
   private double result;
   private String lastCommand;
   private boolean start;
}
```

API javax.jnlp.ServiceManager

- `static String[] getServiceNames()`
  returns the names of all available services.
- `static Object lookup(String name)`
  returns a service with a given name.

API javax.jnlp.BasicService

- `URL getCodeBase()`
  returns the codebase of this application.
- `boolean isWebBrowserSupported()`
  returns `true` if the Web Start environment can launch a web browser.
- `boolean showDocument(URL url)`
  attempts to show the given URL in a browser. Returns `true` if the request succeeded.

API javax.jnlp.FileContents

- `InputStream getInputStream()`
  returns an input stream to read the contents of the file.
- `OutputStream getOutputStream(boolean overwrite)`
  returns an output stream to write to the file. If `overwrite` is `true`, then the existing contents of the file are overwritten.
- `String getName()`
  returns the file name (but not the full directory path).

- `boolean canRead()`
- `boolean canWrite()`

  return `true` if the underlying file is readable or writable.

 **`javax.jnlp.FileOpenService`**

- `FileContents openFileDialog(String pathHint, String[] extensions)`
- `FileContents[] openMultiFileDialog(String pathHint, String[] extensions)`

  display a user warning and a file chooser. Return content descriptors of the file or files that the user selected, or `null` if the user didn't choose a file.

 **`javax.jnlp.FileSaveService`**

- `FileContents saveFileDialog(String pathHint, String[] extensions, InputStream data, String nameHint)`
- `FileContents saveAsFileDialog(String pathHint, String[] extensions, FileContents data)`

  display a user warning and a file chooser. Write the data and return content descriptors of the file or files that the user selected, or `null` if the user didn't choose a file.

 **`javax.jnlp.PersistenceService`**

- `long create(URL key, long maxsize)`

  creates a persistent store entry for the given key. Returns the maximum size granted by the persistent store.
- `void delete(URL key)`

  deletes the entry for the given key.
- `String[] getNames(URL url)`

  returns the relative key names of all keys that start with the given URL.
- `FileContents get(URL key)`

  gets a content descriptor through which you can modify the data associated with the given key. If no entry exists for the key, a `FileNotFoundException` is thrown.

Storage of Application Preferences

Most programs can be configured by their users. The programs must then save the user preferences and restore them when the application starts again. You already saw how a Java Web Start application can use a persistent store for that purpose. However, JDK 1.4 introduced a different and more powerful mechanism for local applications. We describe that mechanism, but first we cover the much simpler approach for storing configuration information that Java applications have traditionally taken.

Property Maps

A *property map* is a data structure that stores key/value pairs. Property maps are often used for storing configuration information. Property maps have three particular characteristics:

- The keys and values are strings.
- The set can easily be saved to a file and loaded from a file.
- There is a secondary table for default values.

The Java platform class that implements a property map is called `Properties`.

Property maps are useful in specifying configuration options for programs. For example,

```
Properties settings = new Properties();
settings.put("font", "Courier");
```

```
settings.put("size", "10");
settings.put("message", "Hello, World");
```

Use the store method to save this list of properties to a file. Here, we just save the property map in the file Myprog.properties. The second argument is a comment that is included in the file.

```
FileOutputStream out = new FileOutputStream("Myprog.properties");
settings.store(out, "Myprog Properties");
```

The sample set gives the following output.

```
#Myprog Properties
#Tue Jun 15 07:22:52  2004
font=Courier
size=10
message=Hello, World
```

To load the properties from a file, use

```
FileInputStream in = new FileInputStream("Myprog.properties");
settings.load(in);
```

We'll put this technique to work so that your users can customize the NotHelloWorld program to their hearts' content. We'll allow them to specify the following in the configuration file CustomWorld.properties:

- Window size
- Font
- Point size
- Text color
- Message string

If the user doesn't specify some of the settings, we will provide defaults.

The Properties class has two mechanisms for providing defaults. First, whenever you look up the value of a string, you can specify a default that should be used automatically when the key is not present.

```
String font = settings.getProperty("font", "Courier");
```

If there is a "font" property in the property table, then font is set to that string. Otherwise, font is set to "Courier".

If you find it too tedious to specify the default in every call to getProperty, then you can pack all the defaults into a secondary property map and supply that map in the constructor of your lookup table.

```
Properties defaultSettings = new Properties();
defaultSettings.put("font", "Courier");
defaultSettings.put("size", "10");
defaultSettings.put("color.red", "0");
. . .
Properties settings = new Properties(defaultSettings);
FileInputStream in = new FileInputStream("CustomWorld.properties");
settings.load(in);
. . .
```

Yes, you can even specify defaults to defaults if you give another property map parameter to the defaultSettings constructor, but it is not something one would normally do.

Example 10–14 is the customizable "Hello, Custom World" program. Just edit the .properties file to change the program's appearance to the way *you* want (see Figure 10–17).

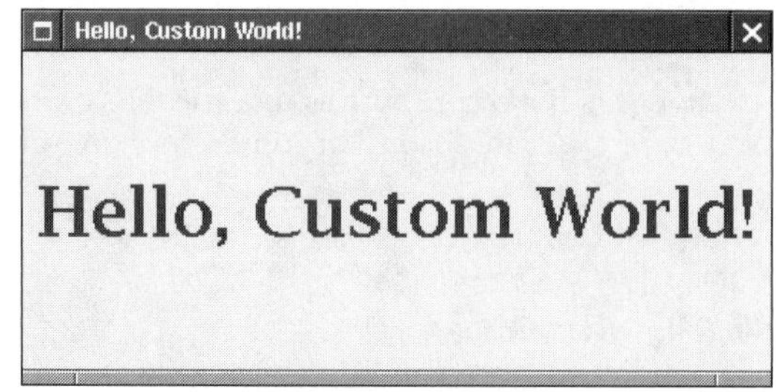

Figure 10–17: The customized Hello, World program

NOTE: Properties are simple tables without a hierarchical structure. It is common to introduce a fake hierarchy with key names such as `window.main.color`, `window.main.title`, and so on. But the `Properties` class has no methods that help organize such a hierarchy. If you store complex configuration information, you should use the `Preferences` class instead—see the next section.

NOTE: The `Properties` class *extends* the `Hashtable` class. That means that all `Hashtable` methods are available to `Properties` objects. Some methods are useful. For example, `size` returns the number of possible properties (well, it isn't *that* nice—it doesn't count the defaults). Similarly, `keys` returns an enumeration of all keys, except for the defaults. There is also a second method, called `propertyNames`, that returns all keys. The `put` method is downright dangerous. It doesn't check that you put strings into the table.

Does the *is-a* rule for using inheritance apply here? Is every property map a hash table? Not really. That these are true is really just an implementation detail. Maybe it is better to think of a property map as having a hash table. But then the hash table should be a private instance variable. Actually, in this case, a property map uses two hash tables: one for the defaults and one for the nondefault values.

We think a better design would be the following:

```
class Properties
{
   public String getProperty(String) { . . . }
   public void put(String, String) { . . . }
   . . .
   private Hashtable nonDefaults;
   private Hashtable defaults;
}
```

We don't want to tell you to avoid the `Properties` class in the Java library. Provided you are careful to put nothing but strings in it, it works just fine. But think twice before using "quick and dirty" inheritance in your own programs.

Example 10–14: CustomWorld.java

```
import java.awt.*;
import java.awt.event.*;
import java.util.*;
import java.io.*;
import javax.swing.*;

/**
   This program demonstrates how to customize a "Hello, World"
   program with a properties file.
```

```
*/
public class CustomWorld
{
   public static void main(String[] args)
   {
      CustomWorldFrame frame = new CustomWorldFrame();
      frame.setDefaultCloseOperation(JFrame.EXIT_ON_CLOSE);
      frame.setVisible(true);
   }
}

/**
   This frame displays a message. The frame size, message text,
   font, and color are set in a properties file.
*/
class CustomWorldFrame extends JFrame
{
   public CustomWorldFrame()
   {
      Properties defaultSettings = new Properties();
      defaultSettings.put("font", "Monospaced");
      defaultSettings.put("width", "300");
      defaultSettings.put("height", "200");
      defaultSettings.put("message", "Hello, World");
      defaultSettings.put("color.red", "0 50 50");
      defaultSettings.put("color.green", "50");
      defaultSettings.put("color.blue", "50");
      defaultSettings.put("ptsize", "12");

      Properties settings = new Properties(defaultSettings);
      try
      {
         FileInputStream in = new FileInputStream("CustomWorld.properties");
         settings.load(in);
      }
      catch (IOException e)
      {
         e.printStackTrace();
      }

      int red = Integer.parseInt(settings.getProperty("color.red"));
      int green = Integer.parseInt(settings.getProperty("color.green"));
      int blue = Integer.parseInt(settings.getProperty("color.blue"));

      Color foreground = new Color(red, green, blue);

      String name = settings.getProperty("font");
      int ptsize = Integer.parseInt(settings.getProperty("ptsize"));
      Font f = new Font(name, Font.BOLD, ptsize);

      int hsize = Integer.parseInt(settings.getProperty("width"));
      int vsize = Integer.parseInt(settings.getProperty("height"));
      setSize(hsize, vsize);
      setTitle(settings.getProperty("message"));

      JLabel label = new JLabel(settings.getProperty("message"), SwingConstants.CENTER);
```

```
        label.setFont(f);
        label.setForeground(foreground);
        add(label);
    }
}
```

java.util.Properties 1.0

- `Properties()`
  creates an empty property list.
- `Properties(Properties defaults)`
  creates an empty property list with a set of defaults.

Parameters:	`defaults`	The defaults to use for lookups

- `String getProperty(String key)`
  gets a property association. Returns the string associated with the key, or the string associated with the key in the default table if it wasn't present in the table, or `null` if the key wasn't present in the default table either.

Parameters:	`key`	The key whose associated string to get

- `String getProperty(String key, String defaultValue)`
  gets a property with a default value if the key is not found. Returns the string associated with the key, or the default string if it wasn't present in the table.

Parameters:	`key`	The key whose associated string to get
	`defaultValue`	The string to return if the key is not present

- `void load(InputStream in) throws IOException`
  loads a property map from an input stream.

Parameters:	`in`	The input stream

- `void store(OutputStream out, String header)` 1.2
  saves a property map to an output stream.

Parameters:	`out`	The output stream
	`header`	The header in the first line of the stored file

System Information

Here's another example of the ubiquity of the `Properties` set. Information about your system is stored in a `Properties` object that is returned by the static `getProperties` method of the `System` class:

```
Properties sysprops = System.getProperties();
```

To access a single property, call

```
String value = System.getProperty(key);
```

Applications that run without a security manager have complete access to this information, but applets and other untrusted programs can access only the following keys:

```
java.version
java.vendor
java.vendor.url
java.class.version
os.name
os.version
os.arch
```

```
file.separator
path.separator
line.separator
java.specification.version
java.vm.specification.version
java.vm.specification.vendor
java.vm.specification.name
java.vm.version
java.vm.vendor
java.vm.name
```

If an applet attempts to read another key (or all properties), then a security exception is thrown.

NOTE: You can find the names of the freely accessible system properties in the file `security/java.policy` in the directory of the Java run time.

The program in Example 10–15 prints out the key/value pairs in the `Properties` object that stores the system properties.

Here is an example of what you would see when you run the program. You can see all the values stored in this `Properties` object. (What you would get will, of course, reflect your machine's settings.)

```
#System Properties
#Sat May 08 08:27:34 PDT 2004
java.runtime.name=Java(TM) 2 Runtime Environment, Standard Edition
sun.boot.library.path=/usr/local/jdk5.0/jre/lib/i386
java.vm.version=5.0
java.vm.vendor=Sun Microsystems Inc.
java.vendor.url=http\://java.sun.com/
path.separator=\:
java.vm.name=Java HotSpot(TM) Client VM
file.encoding.pkg=sun.io
user.country=US
sun.os.patch.level=unknown
java.vm.specification.name=Java Virtual Machine Specification
user.dir=/home/cay/books/cj5/corejava/v1/v1ch10/SystemInfo
java.runtime.version=5.0
java.awt.graphicsenv=sun.awt.X11GraphicsEnvironment
java.endorsed.dirs=/usr/local/jdk5.0/jre/lib/endorsed
os.arch=i386
java.io.tmpdir=/tmp
line.separator=\n
java.vm.specification.vendor=Sun Microsystems Inc.
os.name=Linux
java.library.path=/usr/local/jdk5.0/jre/lib/i386/client\:/usr/local/jdk5.0/jre/lib/i386\:/usr/
local/jdk5.0/jre/../lib/i386
java.specification.name=Java Platform API Specification
java.class.version=48.0
sun.management.compiler=HotSpot Client Compiler
java.util.prefs.PreferencesFactory=java.util.prefs.FileSystemPreferencesFactory
os.version=2.4.20-8
user.home=/home/cay
user.timezone=America/Los_Angeles
java.awt.printerjob=sun.print.PSPrinterJob
```

```
file.encoding=UTF-8
java.specification.version=5.0
java.class.path=.
user.name=cay
java.vm.specification.version=1.0
java.home=/usr/local/jdk5.0/jre
sun.arch.data.model=32
user.language=en
java.specification.vendor=Sun Microsystems Inc.
java.vm.info=mixed mode
java.version=5.0
java.ext.dirs=/usr/local/jdk5.0/jre/lib/ext
sun.boot.class.path=/usr/local/jdk5.0/jre/lib/rt.jar\:/usr/local/jdk5.0/jre/lib/i18n.jar\:/usr/
local/jdk5.0/jre/lib/sunrsasign.jar\:/usr/local/jdk5.0/jre/lib/jsse.jar\:/usr/local/jdk5.0/jre/lib/
jce.jar\:/usr/local/jdk5.0/jre/lib/charsets.jar\:/usr/local/jdk5.0/jre/classes
java.vendor=Sun Microsystems Inc.
file.separator=/
java.vendor.url.bug=http\://java.sun.com/cgi-bin/bugreport.cgi
sun.io.unicode.encoding=UnicodeLittle
sun.cpu.endian=little
sun.cpu.isalist=
```

Example 10–15: SystemInfo.java

```
import java.applet.*;
import java.io.*;
import java.util.*;

/**
   This program prints out all system properties.
*/
public class SystemInfo
{
   public static void main(String args[])
   {
      try
      {
         Properties sysprops = System.getProperties();
         sysprops.store(System.out, "System Properties");
      }
      catch (IOException e)
      {
         e.printStackTrace();
      }
   }
}
```

API `java.lang.System` 1.0

- `Properties getProperties()`
  retrieves all system properties. The application must have permission to retrieve all properties or a security exception is thrown.
- `String getProperty(String key)`
  retrieves the system property with the given key name. The application must have permission to retrieve the property or a security exception is thrown.

The Preferences API

As you have seen, the `Properties` class makes it simple to load and save configuration information. However, using property files has a number of disadvantages.

- The configuration files cannot always be stored in the same location as the program because that location may not be writable. For example, it may be a read-only directory or a JAR file.
- Multiple users may want to configure the same application in different ways.
- Configuration files cannot always be stored in the user's home directory. Some operating systems (such as Windows 9x) have no concept of a home directory.
- There is no standard convention for naming configuration files, increasing the likelihood of name clashes as users install multiple Java applications.

Some operating systems have a central repository for configuration information. The best-known example is the registry in Microsoft Windows. The `Preferences` class of JDK 1.4 provides such a central repository in a platform-independent manner. In Windows, the `Preferences` class uses the registry for storage; on Linux, the information is stored in the local file system instead. Of course, the repository implementation is transparent to the programmer using the `Preferences` class.

The `Preferences` repository has a tree structure, with node path names such as `/com/mycompany/myapp`. As with package names, name clashes are avoided as long as programmers start the paths with reversed domain names. In fact, the designers of the API suggest that the configuration node paths match the package names in your program.

Each node in the repository has a separate table of key/value pairs that you can use to store numbers, strings, or byte arrays. No provision is made for storing serializable objects. The API designers felt that the serialization format is too fragile for long-term storage. Of course, if you disagree, you can save serialized objects in byte arrays.

For additional flexibility, there are multiple parallel trees. Each program user has one tree, and an additional tree, called the system tree, is available for settings that are common to all users. The `Preferences` class uses the operating system notion of the "current user" for accessing the appropriate user tree.

To access a node in the tree, start with the user or system root:

```
Preferences root = Preferences.userRoot();
```

or

```
Preferences root = Preferences.systemRoot();
```

Then access the node. You can simply provide a node path name:

```
Preferences node = root.node("/com/mycompany/myapp");
```

A convenient shortcut gets a node whose path name equals the package name of a class. Simply take an object of that class and call

```
Preferences node = Preferences.userNodeForPackage(obj.getClass());
```

or

```
Preferences node = Preferences.systemNodeForPackage(obj.getClass());
```

Typically, `obj` will be the `this` reference.

Once you have a node, you can access the key/value table with methods

```
String get(String key, String defval)
int getInt(String key, int defval)
long getLong(String key, long defval)
float getFloat(String key, float defval)
```

```
double getDouble(String key, double defval)
boolean getBoolean(String key, boolean defval)
byte[] getByteArray(String key, byte[] defval)
```

Note that you must specify a default value when reading the information, in case the repository data is not available. Defaults are required for several reasons. The data might be missing because the user never specified a preference. Certain resource-constrained platforms might not have a repository, and mobile devices might be temporarily disconnected from the repository.

Conversely, you can write data to the repository with `put` methods such as

```
put(String key, String value)
putInt(String key, int value)
```

and so on.

You can enumerate all keys stored in a node with the method

```
String[] keys
```

But there is currently no way to find out the type of the value of a particular key.

Central repositories such as the Windows registry traditionally suffer from two problems.

- They turn into a "dumping ground," filled with obsolete information.
- Configuration data gets entangled into the repository, making it difficult to move preferences to a new platform.

The `Preferences` class has a solution for the second problem. You can export the preferences of a subtree (or, less commonly, a single node) by calling the methods

```
void exportSubtree(OutputStream out)
void exportNode(OutputStream out)
```

The data are saved in XML format. You can import them into another repository by calling

```
void importPreferences(InputStream in)
```

Here is a sample file:

```
<?xml version="1.0" encoding="UTF-8"?>
<!DOCTYPE preferences SYSTEM "http://java.sun.com/dtd/preferences.dtd">
<preferences EXTERNAL_XML_VERSION="1.0">
  <root type="user">
    <map/>
    <node name="com">
      <map/>
      <node name="horstmann">
        <map/>
        <node name="corejava">
          <map>
            <entry key="left" value="11"/>
            <entry key="top" value="9"/>
            <entry key="width" value="453"/>
            <entry key="height" value="365"/>
          </map>
        </node>
      </node>
    </node>
  </root>
</preferences>
```

If your program uses preferences, you should give your users the opportunity of exporting and importing them, so they can easily migrate their settings from one computer to

another. The program in Example 10–16 demonstrates this technique. The program simply saves the position and size of the main window. Try resizing the window, then exit and restart the application. The window will be just like you left it when you exited.

Example 10–16: PreferencesTest.java

```
import java.awt.*;
import java.awt.event.*;
import java.io.*;
import java.util.logging.*;
import java.util.prefs.*;
import javax.swing.*;
import javax.swing.event.*;

/**
   A program to test preference settings. The program
   remembers the frame position and size.
*/
public class PreferencesTest
{
   public static void main(String[] args)
   {
      PreferencesFrame frame = new PreferencesFrame();
      frame.setDefaultCloseOperation(JFrame.EXIT_ON_CLOSE);
      frame.setVisible(true);
   }
}

/**
   A frame that restores position and size from user
   preferences and updates the preferences upon exit.
*/
class PreferencesFrame extends JFrame
{
   public PreferencesFrame()
   {
      setTitle("PreferencesTest");

      // get position, size from preferences

      Preferences root = Preferences.userRoot();
      final Preferences node = root.node("/com/horstmann/corejava");
      int left = node.getInt("left", 0);
      int top = node.getInt("top", 0);
      int width = node.getInt("width", DEFAULT_WIDTH);
      int height = node.getInt("height", DEFAULT_HEIGHT);
      setBounds(left, top, width, height);

      // set up file chooser that shows XML files

      final JFileChooser chooser = new JFileChooser();
      chooser.setCurrentDirectory(new File("."));

      // accept all files ending with .xml
      chooser.setFileFilter(new
         javax.swing.filechooser.FileFilter()
         {
```

```
            public boolean accept(File f)
            {
               return f.getName().toLowerCase().endsWith(".xml") || f.isDirectory();
            }
            public String getDescription()
            {
               return "XML files";
            }
         });


      // set up menus
      JMenuBar menuBar = new JMenuBar();
      setJMenuBar(menuBar);
      JMenu menu = new JMenu("File");
      menuBar.add(menu);

      JMenuItem exportItem = new JMenuItem("Export preferences");
      menu.add(exportItem);
      exportItem.addActionListener(new
         ActionListener()
         {
            public void actionPerformed(ActionEvent event)
            {
               if(chooser.showSaveDialog(PreferencesFrame.this) == JFileChooser.APPROVE_OPTION)
               {
                  try
                  {
                     OutputStream out = new FileOutputStream(chooser.getSelectedFile());
                     node.exportSubtree(out);
                     out.close();
                  }
                  catch (Exception e)
                  {
                     e.printStackTrace();
                  }
               }
            }
         });

      JMenuItem importItem = new JMenuItem("Import preferences");
      menu.add(importItem);
      importItem.addActionListener(new
         ActionListener()
         {
            public void actionPerformed(ActionEvent event)
            {
               if(chooser.showOpenDialog(PreferencesFrame.this) == JFileChooser.APPROVE_OPTION)
               {
                  try
                  {
                     InputStream in = new FileInputStream(chooser.getSelectedFile());
                     node.importPreferences(in);
                     in.close();
                  }
                  catch (Exception e)
```

```
                  {
                     e.printStackTrace();
                  }
               }
            }
         });

      JMenuItem exitItem = new JMenuItem("Exit");
      menu.add(exitItem);
      exitItem.addActionListener(new
         ActionListener()
         {
            public void actionPerformed(ActionEvent event)
            {
               node.putInt("left", getX());
               node.putInt("top", getY());
               node.putInt("width", getWidth());
               node.putInt("height", getHeight());
               System.exit(0);
            }
         });
   }
   public static final int DEFAULT_WIDTH = 300;
   public static final int DEFAULT_HEIGHT = 200;
}
```

java.util.prefs.Preferences 1.4

- `Preferences userRoot()`
  returns the root preferences node of the user of the calling program.
- `Preferences systemRoot()`
  returns the systemwide root preferences node.
- `Preferences node(String path)`
  returns a node that can be reached from the current node by the given path. If `path` is absolute (that is, starts with a /), then the node is located starting from the root of the tree containing this preference node. If there isn't a node with the given path, it is created.
- `Preferences userNodeForPackage(Class cl)`
- `Preferences systemNodeForPackage(Class cl)`
  return a node in the current user's tree or the system tree whose absolute node path corresponds to the package name of the class `cl`.
- `String[] keys()`
  returns all keys belonging to this node.
- `String get(String key, String defval)`
- `int getInt(String key, int defval)`
- `long getLong(String key, long defval)`
- `float getFloat(String key, float defval)`
- `double getDouble(String key, double defval)`
- `boolean getBoolean(String key, boolean defval)`
- `byte[] getByteArray(String key, byte[] defval)`
  return the value associated with the given key, or the supplied default value if no value is associated with the key, or the associated value is not of the correct type, or the preferences store is unavailable.

- `void put(String key, String value)`
- `void putInt(String key, int value)`
- `void putLong(String key, long value)`
- `void putFloat(String key, float value)`
- `void putDouble(String key, double value)`
- `void putBoolean(String key, boolean value)`
- `void putByteArray(String key, byte[] value)`
  store a key/value pair with this node.
- `void exportSubtree(OutputStream out)`
  writes the preferences of this node and its children to the specified stream.
- `void exportNode(OutputStream out)`
  writes the preferences of this node (but not its children) to the specified stream.
- `void importPreferences(InputStream in)`
  imports the preferences contained in the specified stream.

This concludes our discussion of Java software deployment. In the next chapter, you learn how to use exceptions to tell your programs what to do when problems arise at run time. We also give you tips and techniques for testing and debugging so that not too many things will go wrong when your programs run.

Chapter 11

Exceptions and Debugging

- Dealing with Errors
- Catching Exceptions
- Tips for Using Exceptions
- Logging
- Using Assertions
- Debugging Techniques
- Using a Debugger

In a perfect world, users would never enter data in the wrong form, files they choose to open would always exist, and code would never have bugs. So far, we have mostly presented code as though we lived in this kind of perfect world. It is now time to turn to the mechanisms the Java programming language has for dealing with the real world of bad data and buggy code.

Encountering errors is unpleasant. If a user loses all the work he or she did during a program session because of a programming mistake or some external circumstance, that user may forever turn away from your program. At the very least, you must

- Notify the user of an error;
- Save all work;
- Allow users to gracefully exit the program.

For exceptional situations, such as bad input data with the potential to bomb the program, Java uses a form of error trapping called, naturally enough, *exception handling*. Exception handling in Java is similar to that in C++ or Delphi. The first part of this chapter covers Java's exceptions.

The second part of this chapter concerns finding bugs in your code before they cause exceptions at run time. Unfortunately, if you use just the JDK, then bug detection is the same as it was back in the Dark Ages. We give you some tips and a few tools to ease the pain. Then, we explain how to use the command-line debugger as a tool of last resort.

For the serious Java developer, products such as Eclipse, NetBeans, and JBuilder have quite useful debuggers. We introduce you to the Eclipse debugger.

Dealing with Errors

Suppose an error occurs while a Java program is running. The error might be caused by a file containing wrong information, a flaky network connection, or (we hate to mention it) use of an invalid array index or an attempt to use an object reference that hasn't yet been assigned to an object. Users expect that programs will act sensibly when errors happen. If an operation cannot be completed because of an error, the program ought to either

- Return to a safe state and enable the user to execute other commands; or
- Allow the user to save all work and terminate the program gracefully.

This may not be easy to do, because the code that detects (or even causes) the error condition is usually far removed from the code that can roll back the data to a safe state or the code that can save the user's work and exit cheerfully. The mission of exception handling is to transfer control from where the error occurred to an error handler that can deal with the situation. To handle exceptional situations in your program, you must take into account the errors and problems that may occur. What sorts of problems do you need to consider?

User input errors. In addition to the inevitable typos, some users like to blaze their own trail instead of following directions. Suppose, for example, that a user asks to connect to a URL that is syntactically wrong. Your code should check the syntax, but suppose it does not. Then the network package will complain.

Device errors. Hardware does not always do what you want it to. The printer may be turned off. A web page may be temporarily unavailable. Devices will often fail in the middle of a task. For example, a printer may run out of paper in the middle of a printout.

Physical limitations. Disks can fill up; you can run out of available memory.

Code errors. A method may not perform correctly. For example, it could deliver wrong answers or use other methods incorrectly. Computing an invalid array index, trying to find a nonexistent entry in a hash table, and trying to pop an empty stack are all examples of a code error.

The traditional reaction to an error in a method is to return a special error code that the calling method analyzes. For example, methods that read information back from files often return a –1 end-of-file value marker rather than a standard character. This can be an efficient method for dealing with many exceptional conditions. Another common return value to denote an error condition is the `null` reference. In Chapter 10, you saw an example of this with the `getParameter` method of the `Applet` class that returns `null` if the queried parameter is not present.

Unfortunately, it is not always possible to return an error code. There may be no obvious way of distinguishing valid and invalid data. A method returning an integer cannot simply return –1 to denote the error—the value –1 might be a perfectly valid result.

Instead, as we mentioned back in Chapter 5, Java allows every method an alternative exit path if it is unable to complete its task in the normal way. In this situation, the method does not return a value. Instead, it *throws* an object that encapsulates the error information. Note that the method exits immediately; it does not return its normal (or any) value. Moreover, execution does not resume at the code that called the method; instead, the exception-handling mechanism begins its search for an *exception handler* that can deal with this particular error condition.

Exceptions have their own syntax and are part of a special inheritance hierarchy. We take up the syntax first and then give a few hints on how to use this language feature effectively.

The Classification of Exceptions

In the Java programming language, an exception object is always an instance of a class derived from `Throwable`. As you will soon see, you can create your own exception classes if the ones built into Java do not suit your needs.

Figure 11–1 is a simplified diagram of the exception hierarchy in Java.

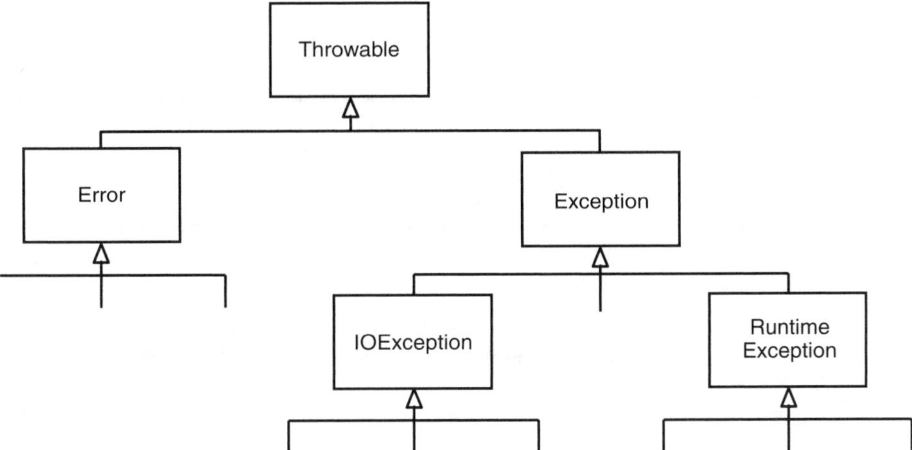

Figure 11–1: Exception hierarchy in Java

Notice that all exceptions descend from `Throwable`, but the hierarchy immediately splits into two branches: `Error` and `Exception`.

The `Error` hierarchy describes internal errors and resource exhaustion inside the Java runtime system. You should not throw an object of this type. There is little you can do if such an internal error occurs, beyond notifying the user and trying to terminate the program gracefully. These situations are quite rare.

When doing Java programming, you focus on the `Exception` hierarchy. The `Exception` hierarchy also splits into two branches: exceptions that derive from `RuntimeException` and those that do not. The general rule is this: A `RuntimeException` happens because you made a programming error. Any other exception occurs because a bad thing, such as an I/O error, happened to your otherwise good program.

Exceptions that inherit from `RuntimeException` include such problems as

- A bad cast;
- An out-of-bounds array access;
- A null pointer access.

Exceptions that do not inherit from `RuntimeException` include

- Trying to read past the end of a file;
- Trying to open a malformed URL;
- Trying to find a `Class` object for a string that does not denote an existing class.

The rule "If it is a RuntimeException, it was your fault" works pretty well. You could have avoided that ArrayIndexOutOfBoundsException by testing the array index against the array bounds. The NullPointerException would not have happened had you checked whether the variable was null before using it.

How about a malformed URL? Isn't it also possible to find out whether it is "malformed" before using it? Well, different browsers can handle different kinds of URLs. For example, Netscape can deal with a mailto: URL, whereas the applet viewer cannot. Thus, the notion of "malformed" depends on the environment, not just on your code.

The Java Language Specification calls any exception that derives from the class Error or the class RuntimeException an *unchecked* exception. All other exceptions are called *checked* exceptions. This is useful terminology that we also adopt. The compiler checks that you provide exception handlers for all checked exceptions.

NOTE: The name RuntimeException is somewhat confusing. Of course, all of the errors we are discussing occur at run time.

C++ NOTE: If you are familiar with the (much more limited) exception hierarchy of the standard C++ library, you will be really confused at this point. C++ has two fundamental exception classes, runtime_error and logic_error. The logic_error class is the equivalent of Java's RuntimeException and also denotes logical errors in the program. The runtime_error class is the base class for exceptions caused by unpredictable problems. It is equivalent to exceptions in Java that are not of type RuntimeException.

Declaring Checked Exceptions

A Java method can throw an exception if it encounters a situation it cannot handle. The idea is simple: a method will not only tell the Java compiler what values it can return, *it is also going to tell the compiler what can go wrong*. For example, code that attempts to read from a file knows that the file might not exist or that it might be empty. The code that tries to process the information in a file therefore will need to notify the compiler that it can throw some sort of IOException.

The place in which you advertise that your method can throw an exception is the header of the method; the header changes to reflect the checked exceptions the method can throw. For example, here is the declaration of one of the constructors of the FileInputStream class from the standard library. (See Chapter 12 for more on streams.)

```
public FileInputStream(String name) throws FileNotFoundException
```

The declaration says that this constructor produces a FileInputStream object from a String parameter but that it *also* can go wrong in a special way—by throwing a FileNotFoundException. If this sad state should come to pass, the constructor call will not initialize a new FileInputStream object but instead will throw an object of the FileNotFoundException class. If it does, then the runtime system will begin to search for an exception handler that knows how to deal with FileNotFoundException objects.

When you write your own methods, you don't have to advertise every possible throwable object that your method might actually throw. To understand when (and what) you have to advertise in the throws clause of the methods you write, keep in mind that an exception is thrown in any of the following four situations:

1. You call a method that throws a checked exception, for example, the `FileInputStream` constructor.
2. You detect an error and throw a checked exception with the `throw` statement (we cover the `throw` statement in the next section).
3. You make a programming error, such as `a[-1] = 0` that gives rise to an unchecked exception such as an `ArrayIndexOutOfBoundsException`.
4. An internal error occurs in the virtual machine or runtime library.

If either of the first two scenarios occurs, you must tell the programmers who will use your method about the possibility of an exception. Why? Any method that throws an exception is a potential death trap. If no handler catches the exception, the current thread of execution terminates.

As with Java methods that are part of the supplied classes, you declare that your method may throw an exception with an *exception specification* in the method header.

```
class MyAnimation
{
   . . .

   public Image loadImage(String s) throws IOException
   {
      . . .
   }
}
```

If a method might throw more than one checked exception type, you must list all exception classes in the header. Separate them by a comma as in the following example:

```
class MyAnimation
{
   . . .
   public Image loadImage(String s) throws EOFException, MalformedURLException
   {
      . . .
   }
}
```

However, you do not need to advertise internal Java errors, that is, exceptions inheriting from `Error`. Any code could potentially throw those exceptions, and they are entirely beyond your control.

Similarly, you should not advertise unchecked exceptions inheriting from `RuntimeException`.

```
class MyAnimation
{
   . . .
   void drawImage(int i) throws ArrayIndexOutOfBoundsException // bad style
   {
      . . .
   }
}
```

These runtime errors are completely under your control. If you are so concerned about array index errors, you should spend the time needed to fix them instead of advertising the possibility that they can happen.

In summary, a method must declare all the *checked* exceptions that it might throw. Unchecked exceptions are either beyond your control (`Error`) or result from conditions that you should not have allowed in the first place (`RuntimeException`). If your method fails to faithfully declare all checked exceptions, the compiler will issue an error message.

Of course, as you have already seen in quite a few examples, instead of declaring the exception, you can also catch it. Then the exception won't be thrown out of the method, and no `throws` specification is necessary. You see later in this chapter how to decide whether to catch an exception or to enable someone else to catch it.

CAUTION: If you override a method from a superclass, the checked exceptions that the subclass method declares cannot be more general than those of the superclass method. (It is Ok to throw more specific exceptions, or not to throw any exceptions in the subclass method.) In particular, if the superclass method throws no checked exception at all, neither can the subclass. For example, if you override `JComponent.paintComponent`, your `paintComponent` method must not throw any checked exceptions, because the superclass method doesn't throw any.

When a method in a class declares that it throws an exception that is an instance of a particular class, then it may throw an exception of that class or of any of its subclasses. For example, the `FileInputStream` constructor could have declared that it throws an `IOException`. In that case, you would not have known what kind of `IOException`. It could be a plain `IOException` or an object of one of the various subclasses, such as `FileNotFoundException`.

C++ NOTE: The `throws` specifier is the same as the `throw` specifier in C++, with one important difference. In C++, `throw` specifiers are enforced at run time, not at compile time. That is, the C++ compiler pays no attention to exception specifications. But if an exception is thrown in a function that is not part of the `throw` list, then the `unexpected` function is called, and, by default, the program terminates.

Also, in C++, a function may throw any exception if no `throw` specification is given. In Java, a method without a `throws` specifier may not throw any checked exception at all.

How to Throw an Exception

Let us suppose something terrible has happened in your code. You have a method, `readData`, that is reading in a file whose header promised

```
Content-length: 1024
```

But, you get an end of file after 733 characters. You decide this situation is so abnormal that you want to throw an exception.

You need to decide what exception type to throw. Some kind of `IOException` would be a good choice. Perusing the Java API documentation, you find an `EOFException` with the description "Signals that an EOF has been reached unexpectedly during input." Perfect. Here is how you throw it:

```
throw new EOFException();
```

or, if you prefer,

```
EOFException e = new EOFException();
throw e;
```

Here is how it all fits together:

```
String readData(Scanner in) throws EOFException
{
```

```
      . . .
      while (. . .)
      {
         if (!in.hasNext()) // EOF encountered
         {
            if (n < len)
               throw new EOFException();
         }
         . . .
      }
      return s;
   }
```

The EOFException has a second constructor that takes a string argument. You can put this to good use by describing the exceptional condition more carefully.

```
String gripe = "Content-length: " + len + ", Received: " + n;
throw new EOFException(gripe);
```

As you can see, throwing an exception is easy if one of the existing exception classes works for you. In this case:

1. Find an appropriate exception class.
2. Make an object of that class.
3. Throw it.

Once a method throws an exception, the method does not return to its caller. This means that you do not have to worry about cooking up a default return value or an error code.

C++ NOTE: Throwing an exception is the same in C++ and in Java, with one small exception. In Java, you can throw only objects of subclasses of Throwable. In C++, you can throw values of any type.

Creating Exception Classes

Your code may run into a problem that is not adequately described by any of the standard exception classes. In this case, it is easy enough to create your own exception class. Just derive it from Exception or from a child class of Exception such as IOException. It is customary to give both a default constructor and a constructor that contains a detailed message. (The toString method of the Throwable superclass prints that detailed message, which is handy for debugging.)

```
class FileFormatException extends IOException
{
   public FileFormatException() {}
   public FileFormatException(String gripe)
   {
      super(gripe);
   }
}
```

Now you are ready to throw your very own exception type.

```
String readData(BufferedReader in) throws FileFormatException
{
   . . .
```

```
    while (. . .)
    {
        if (ch == -1) // EOF encountered
        {
            if (n < len)
                throw new FileFormatException();
        }
        . . .
    }
    return s;
}
```

java.lang.Throwable 1.0

- `Throwable()`
  constructs a new `Throwable` object with no detailed message.
- `Throwable(String message)`
  constructs a new `Throwable` object with the specified detailed message. By convention, all derived exception classes support both a default constructor and a constructor with a detailed message.
- `String getMessage()`
  gets the detailed message of the `Throwable` object.

Catching Exceptions

You now know how to throw an exception. It is pretty easy. You throw it and you forget it. Of course, some code has to catch the exception. Catching exceptions requires more planning.

If an exception occurs that is not caught anywhere, the program will terminate and print a message to the console, giving the type of the exception and a stack trace. Graphics programs (both applets and applications) catch exceptions, print stack trace messages, and then go back to the user interface processing loop. (When you are debugging a graphically based program, it is a good idea to keep the console available on the screen and not minimized.)

To catch an exception, you set up a `try`/`catch` block. The simplest form of the `try` block is as follows:

```
try
{
    code
    more code
    more code
}
catch (ExceptionType e)
{
    handler for this type
}
```

If any of the code inside the `try` block throws an exception of the class specified in the `catch` clause, then

1. The program skips the remainder of the code in the `try` block;
2. The program executes the handler code inside the `catch` clause.

If none of the code inside the `try` block throws an exception, then the program skips the `catch` clause.

If any of the code in a method throws an exception of a type other than the one named in the `catch` clause, this method exits immediately. (Hopefully, one of its callers has already coded a `catch` clause for that type.)

To show this at work, we show some fairly typical code for reading in text:

```
public void read(String filename)
{
   try
   {
      InputStream in = new FileInputStream(filename);
      int b;
      while ((b = in.read()) !=-1)
      {
         process input
      }
   }
   catch (IOException exception)
   {
      exception.printStackTrace();
   }
}
```

Notice that most of the code in the `try` clause is straightforward: it reads and processes lines until we encounter the end of the file. As you can see by looking at the Java API, there is the possibility that the `read` method will throw an `IOException`. In that case, we skip out of the entire `while` loop, enter the `catch` clause and generate a stack trace. For a toy program, that seems like a reasonable way to deal with this exception. What other choice do you have?

Often, the best choice is to do nothing at all and simply pass the exception on to the caller. If an error occurs in the `read` method, let the caller of the `read` method worry about it! If we take that approach, then we have to advertise the fact that the method may throw an `IOException`.

```
public void read(String filename) throws IOException
{
   InputStream in = new FileInputStream(filename);
   int b;
   while ((b = in.read()) !=-1)
   {
      process input
   }
}
```

Remember, the compiler strictly enforces the `throws` specifiers. If you call a method that throws a checked exception, you must either handle it or pass it on.

Which of the two is better? As a general rule, you should catch those exceptions that you know how to handle and propagate those that you do not know how to handle. When you propagate an exception, you must add a `throws` specifier to alert the caller that an exception may be thrown.

Look at the Java API documentation to see what methods throw which exceptions. Then decide whether you should handle them or add them to the `throws` list. There is nothing embarrassing about the latter choice. It is better to direct an exception to a competent handler than to squelch it.

Please keep in mind that there is one exception to this rule, as we mentioned earlier. If you are writing a method that overrides a superclass method that throws no exceptions (such as paintComponent in JComponent), then you *must* catch each checked exception in the method's code. You are not allowed to add more throws specifiers to a subclass method than are present in the superclass method.

C++ NOTE: Catching exceptions is almost the same in Java and in C++. Strictly speaking, the analog of

```
catch (Exception e) // Java
```

is

```
catch (Exception& e) // C++
```

There is no analog to the C++ catch (...). This is not needed in Java because all exceptions derive from a common superclass.

Catching Multiple Exceptions

You can catch multiple exception types in a try block and handle each type differently. You use a separate catch clause for each type as in the following example:

```
try
{
   code that might throw exceptions
}
catch (MalformedURLException e1)
{
   emergency action for malformed URLs
}
catch (UnknownHostException e2)
{
   emergency action for unknown hosts
}
catch (IOException e3)
{
   emergency action for all other I/O problems
}
```

The exception object (e1, e2, e3) may contain information about the nature of the exception. To find out more about the object, try

```
e3.getMessage()
```

to get the detailed error message (if there is one), or

```
e3.getClass().getName()
```

to get the actual type of the exception object.

Rethrowing and Chaining Exceptions

You can throw an exception in a catch clause. Typically, you do this because you want to change the exception type. If you build a subsystem that other programmers use, it makes a lot of sense to use an exception type that indicates a failure of the subsystem. An example of such an exception type is the ServletException. The code that executes a servlet may not want to know in minute detail what went wrong, but it definitely wants to know that the servlet was at fault.

Here is how you can catch an exception and rethrow it.

```
try
{
   access the database
}
```

```
catch (SQLException e)
{
   throw new ServletException("database error: " + e.getMessage());
}
```

Here, the `ServletException` is constructed with the message text of the exception. As of JDK 1.4, you can do better than that and set the original exception as the "cause" of the new exception:

```
try
{
   access the database
}
catch (SQLException e)
{
   Throwable se = new ServletException("database error");
   se.setCause(e);
   throw se;
}
```

When the exception is caught, the original exception can be retrieved:

```
Throwable e = se.getCause();
```

This wrapping technique is highly recommended. It allows you to throw high-level exceptions in subsystems without losing the details of the original failure.

TIP: The wrapping technique is also useful if a checked exception occurs in a method that is not allowed to throw a checked exception. You can catch the checked exception and wrap it into a runtime exception.

NOTE: A number of exception classes, such as `ClassNotFoundException`, `InvocationTargetException`, and `RuntimeException`, have had their own chaining schemes. As of JDK 1.4, these have been brought into conformance with the "cause" mechanism. You can still retrieve the chained exception in the historical way or just call `getCause`. Unfortunately, the chained exception most commonly used by application programmers, `SQLException`, has not been retrofitted.

The `finally` Clause

When your code throws an exception, it stops processing the remaining code in your method and exits the method. This is a problem if the method has acquired some local resource that only it knows about and if that resource must be cleaned up. One solution is to catch and rethrow all exceptions. But this solution is tedious because you need to clean up the resource allocation in two places, in the normal code and in the exception code.

Java has a better solution, the `finally` clause. Here we show you how to properly dispose of a `Graphics` object. If you do any database programming in Java, you will need to use the same techniques to close connections to the database. As you will see in Chapter 4 of Volume 2, it is very important to close all database connections properly, even when exceptions occur.

The code in the `finally` clause executes whether or not an exception was caught. In the following example, the program will dispose of the graphics context *under all circumstances.*

```
Graphics g = image.getGraphics();
try
{
   // 1
   code that might throw exceptions
```

```
   // 2
}
catch (IOException e)
{
   // 3
   show error dialog
   // 4
}
finally
{
   // 5
   g.dispose();
}
// 6
```

Let us look at the three possible situations in which the program will execute the `finally` clause.

1. The code throws no exceptions. In this event, the program first executes all the code in the `try` block. Then, it executes the code in the `finally` clause. Afterwards, execution continues with the first statement after the `try` block. In other words, execution passes through points 1, 2, 5, and 6.
2. The code throws an exception that is caught in a `catch` clause, in our case, an `IOException`. For this, the program executes all code in the `try` block, up to the point at which the exception was thrown. The remaining code in the `try` block is skipped. The program then executes the code in the matching `catch` clause, then the code in the `finally` clause.

   If the `catch` clause does not throw an exception, then the program executes the first line after the `try` block. In this scenario, execution passes through points 1, 3, 4, 5, and 6.
   If the `catch` clause throws an exception, then the exception is thrown back to the caller of this method, and execution passes through points 1, 3, and 5 only.
3. The code throws an exception that is not caught in any `catch` clause. For this, the program executes all code in the `try` block until the exception is thrown. The remaining code in the `try` block is skipped. Then, the code in the `finally` clause is executed, and the exception is thrown back to the caller of this method. Execution passes through points 1 and 5 only.

You can use the `finally` clause without a `catch` clause. For example, consider the following `try` statement:

```
Graphics g = image.getGraphics();
try
{
   code that might throw exceptions
}
finally
{
   g.dispose();
}
```

The `g.dispose()` command in the `finally` clause is executed whether or not an exception is encountered in the `try` block. Of course, if an exception is encountered, it is rethrown and must be caught in another `catch` clause.

In fact, as explained in the following tip, we think it is a very good idea to use the `finally` clause in this way.

TIP: We strongly suggest that you *decouple* try/catch and try/finally blocks. This makes your code far less confusing. For example,

```
InputStream in = ...;
try
{
   try
   {
      code that might throw exceptions
   }
   finally
   {
      in.close();
   }
}
catch (IOException e)
{
   show error dialog
}
```

The inner try block has a single responsibility: to make sure that the input stream is closed. The outer try block has a single responsibility: to ensure that errors are reported. Not only is this solution clearer, it is also more functional: errors in the finally clause are reported.

CAUTION: A finally clause can yield unexpected results when it contains return statements. Suppose you exit the middle of a try block with a return statement. Before the method returns, the contents of the finally block are executed. If the finally block also contains a return statement, then it masks the original return value. Consider this contrived example:

```
public static int f(int n)
{
   try
   {
      int r = n * n;
      return r;
   }
   finally
   {
      if (n == 2) return 0;
   }
}
```

If you call f(2), then the try block computes r = 4 and executes the return statement. However, the finally clause is executed before the method actually returns. The finally clause causes the method to return 0, ignoring the original return value of 4.

Sometimes the finally clause gives you grief, namely if the cleanup method can also throw an exception. A typical case is closing a stream. (See Chapter 12 for more information on streams.) Suppose you want to make sure that you close a stream when an exception hits in the stream processing code.

```
InputStream in = ...;
try
{
   code that might throw exceptions
```

```
}
catch (IOException e)
{
   show error dialog
}
finally
{
   in.close();
}
```

Now suppose that the code in the try block throws some exception *other than an* IOException that is of interest to the caller of the code. The finally block executes, and the close method is called. That method can itself throw an IOException! When it does, then the original exception is lost and the IOException is thrown instead. That is very much against the spirit of exception handling.

It is always a good idea—unfortunately not one that the designers of the InputStream class chose to follow—to throw no exceptions in cleanup operations such as dispose, close, and so on, that you expect users to call in finally blocks.

C++ NOTE: There is one fundamental difference between C++ and Java with regard to exception handling. Java has no destructors; thus, there is no stack unwinding as in C++. This means that the Java programmer must manually place code to reclaim resources in finally blocks. Of course, because Java does garbage collection, there are far fewer resources that require manual deallocation.

Analyzing Stack Trace Elements

A *stack trace* is a listing of all pending method calls at a particular point in the execution of a program. You have almost certainly seen stack trace listings—they are displayed whenever a Java program terminates with an uncaught exception.

NOTE: The stack trace only traces back to the statement that throws the exception, not necessarily to the root cause of the error.

Before JDK 1.4, you could access the text description of a stack trace by calling the printStackTrace method of the Throwable class. Now you can call the getStackTrace method to get an array of StackTraceElement objects that you can analyze in your program. For example,

```
Throwable t = new Throwable();
StackTraceElement[] frames = t.getStackTrace();
for (StackTraceElement frame : frames)
   analyze frame
```

The StackTraceElement class has methods to obtain the file name and line number, as well as the class and method name, of the executing line of code. The toString method yields a formatted string containing all of this information.

JDK 5.0 adds the static Thread.getAllStackTraces method that yields the stack traces of all threads. Here is how you use that method:

```
Map<Thread, StackTraceElement[]> map = Thread.getAllStackTraces();
for (Thread t : map.keySet())
{
   StackTraceElement[] frames = map.get(t);
   analyze frames
}
```

See Volume 2 for more information on threads and the `Map` interface.

Example 11–1 prints the stack trace of a recursive factorial function. For example, if you compute `factorial(3)`, the printout is

```
factorial(3):
StackTraceTest.factorial(StackTraceTest.java:8)
StackTraceTest.main(StackTraceTest.java:23)
factorial(2):
StackTraceTest.factorial(StackTraceTest.java:8)
StackTraceTest.factorial(StackTraceTest.java:14)
StackTraceTest.main(StackTraceTest.java:23)
factorial(1):
StackTraceTest.factorial(StackTraceTest.java:8)
StackTraceTest.factorial(StackTraceTest.java:14)
StackTraceTest.factorial(StackTraceTest.java:14)
StackTraceTest.main(StackTraceTest.java:23)
return 1
return 2
return 6
```

Example 11–1: StackTraceTest.java

```
import java.util.*;

/**
   A program that displays a trace feature of a recursive
   method call.
*/
public class StackTraceTest
{
   /**
      Computes the factorial of a number
      @param n a nonnegative integer
      @return n! = 1 * 2 * . . . * n
   */
   public static int factorial(int n)
   {
      System.out.println("factorial(" + n + "):");
      Throwable t = new Throwable();
      StackTraceElement[] frames = t.getStackTrace();
      for (StackTraceElement f : frames)
         System.out.println(f);
      int r;
      if (n <= 1) r = 1;
      else r = n * factorial(n - 1);
      System.out.println("return " + r);
      return r;
   }

   public static void main(String[] args)
   {
      Scanner in = new Scanner(System.in);
      System.out.print("Enter n: ");
      int n = in.nextInt();
      factorial(n);
   }
}
```

`java.lang.Throwable` 1.0

- `Throwable(Throwable cause)` 1.4
- `Throwable(String message, Throwable cause)` 1.4
  construct a `Throwable` with a given cause.
- `Throwable initCause(Throwable cause)` 1.4
  sets the cause for this object or throws an exception if this object already has a cause. Returns `this`.
- `Throwable getCause()` 1.4
  gets the exception object that was set as the cause for this object, or `null` if no cause was set.
- `StackTraceElement[] getStackTrace()` 1.4
  gets the trace of the call stack at the time this object was constructed.

`java.lang.Exception` 1.0

- `Exception(Throwable cause)` 1.4
- `Exception(String message, Throwable cause)`
  construct an `Exception` with a given cause.

`java.lang.RuntimeException` 1.0

- `RuntimeException(Throwable cause)` 1.4
- `RuntimeException(String message, Throwable cause)` 1.4
  construct a `RuntimeException` with a given cause.

`java.lang.StackTraceElement` 1.4

- `String getFileName()`
  gets the name of the source file containing the execution point of this element, or `null` if the information is not available.
- `int getLineNumber()`
  gets the line number of the source file containing the execution point of this element, or –1 if the information is not available.
- `String getClassName()`
  gets the fully qualified name of the class containing the execution point of this element.
- `String getMethodName()`
  gets the name of the method containing the execution point of this element. The name of a constructor is `<init>`. The name of a static initializer is `<clinit>`. You can't distinguish between overloaded methods with the same name.
- `boolean isNativeMethod()`
  returns `true` if the execution point of this element is inside a native method.
- `String toString()`
  returns a formatted string containing the class and method name and the file name and line number, if available.

Taking a Final Look at Java Error and Exception Handling

Example 11–2 deliberately generates a number of different errors and catches various exceptions (see Figure 11–2).

ExceptTest
Integer divide by zero
Floating point divide by zero
Array bounds
Bad cast
Null pointer
sqrt(-1)
Overflow
No such file
Throw unknown
java.io.FileNotFoundException: woozle.txt (No such file or directory)

Figure 11–2: A program that generates exceptions

Try it out. Click on the buttons and see what exceptions are thrown.

As you know, a programmer error such as a bad array index throws a `RuntimeException`. An attempt to open a nonexistent file triggers an `IOException`. Perhaps surprisingly, floating-point computations such as dividing by 0.0 or taking the square root of −1 do not generate exceptions. Instead, they yield the special "infinity" and "not a number" values that we discussed in Chapter 3. However, integer division by 0 throws an `ArithmeticException`.

We trap the exceptions that the `actionPerformed` methods throw in the `fireActionPerformed` method of the radio buttons and display them in the text field. However, the `actionPerformed` method is declared to throw no checked exceptions. Thus, the handler for the "No such file" button must catch the `IOException`.

If you click on the "Throw unknown" button, an `UnknownError` object is thrown. This is not a subclass of `Exception`, so our program does not catch it. Instead, the user interface code prints an error message and a stack trace to the console.

Example 11–2: ExceptTest.java

```
import java.awt.*;
import java.awt.event.*;
import javax.swing.*;
import java.io.*;

public class ExceptTest
{
   public static void main(String[] args)
   {
      ExceptTestFrame frame = new ExceptTestFrame();
      frame.setDefaultCloseOperation(JFrame.EXIT_ON_CLOSE);
      frame.setVisible(true);
   }
}

/**
   A frame with a panel for testing various exceptions
*/
class ExceptTestFrame extends JFrame
{
   public ExceptTestFrame()
   {
      setTitle("ExceptTest");
      ExceptTestPanel panel = new ExceptTestPanel();
```

```
      add(panel);
      pack();
   }
}

/**
   A panel with radio buttons for running code snippets
   and studying their exception behavior
*/
class ExceptTestPanel extends Box
{
   public ExceptTestPanel()
   {
      super(BoxLayout.Y_AXIS);
      group = new ButtonGroup();

      // add radio buttons for code snippets

      addRadioButton("Integer divide by zero", new
         ActionListener()
         {
            public void actionPerformed(ActionEvent event)
            {
               a[1] = 1 / (a.length - a.length);
            }
         });

      addRadioButton("Floating point divide by zero", new
         ActionListener()
         {
            public void actionPerformed(ActionEvent event)
            {
               a[1] = a[2] / (a[3] - a[3]);
            }
         });

      addRadioButton("Array bounds", new
         ActionListener()
         {
            public void actionPerformed(ActionEvent event)
            {
               a[1] = a[10];
            }
         });

      addRadioButton("Bad cast", new
         ActionListener()
         {
            public void actionPerformed(ActionEvent event)
            {
               a = (double[])event.getSource();
            }
         });

      addRadioButton("Null pointer", new
         ActionListener()
         {
```

```
            public void actionPerformed(ActionEvent event)
            {
               event = null;
               System.out.println(event.getSource());
            }
         });

      addRadioButton("sqrt(-1)", new
         ActionListener()
         {
            public void actionPerformed(ActionEvent event)
            {
               a[1] = Math.sqrt(-1);
            }
         });

      addRadioButton("Overflow", new
         ActionListener()
         {
            public void actionPerformed(ActionEvent event)
            {
               a[1] = 1000 * 1000 * 1000 * 1000;
               int n = (int) a[1];
            }
         });

      addRadioButton("No such file", new
         ActionListener()
         {
            public void actionPerformed(ActionEvent event)
            {
               try
               {
                  InputStream in = new FileInputStream("woozle.txt");
               }
               catch (IOException e)
               {
                  textField.setText(e.toString());
               }
            }
         });

      addRadioButton("Throw unknown", new
         ActionListener()
         {
            public void actionPerformed(ActionEvent event)
            {
               throw new UnknownError();
            }
         });

      // add the text field for exception display
      textField = new JTextField(30);
      add(textField);
   }

   /**
```

```
      Adds a radio button with a given listener to the
      panel. Traps any exceptions in the actionPerformed
      method of the listener.
      @param s the label of the radio button
      @param listener the action listener for the radio button
   */
   private void addRadioButton(String s, ActionListener listener)
   {
      JRadioButton button = new JRadioButton(s, false)
         {
            // the button calls this method to fire an
            // action event. We override it to trap exceptions
            protected void fireActionPerformed(ActionEvent event)
            {
               try
               {
                  textField.setText("No exception");
                  super.fireActionPerformed(event);
               }
               catch (Exception e)
               {
                  textField.setText(e.toString());
               }
            }
         };

      button.addActionListener(listener);
      add(button);
      group.add(button);
   }

   private ButtonGroup group;
   private JTextField textField;
   private double[] a = new double[10];
}
```

Tips for Using Exceptions

There is a certain amount of controversy about the proper use of exceptions. Some programmers believe that all checked exceptions are a nuisance, others can't seem to throw enough of them. We think that exceptions (even checked exceptions) have their place, and offer you these tips for their proper use.

1. *Exception handling is not supposed to replace a simple test.*

   As an example of this, we wrote some code that uses the built-in `Stack` class. The code in Example 11–3 tries 1,000,000 times to pop an empty stack. It first does this by finding out whether the stack is empty.

   ```
   if (!s.empty()) s.pop();
   ```

   Next, we tell it to pop the stack no matter what. Then, we catch the `EmptyStackException` that tells us that we should not have done that.

   ```
   try()
   {
      s.pop();
   }
   catch (EmptyStackException e)
   {
   }
   ```

On our test machine, we got the timing data in Table 11–1.

Table 11–1: Timing Data

Test	Throw/Catch
154 milliseconds	10739 milliseconds

As you can see, it took far longer to catch an exception than it did to perform a simple test. The moral is: Use exceptions for exceptional circumstances only.

2. *Do not micromanage exceptions.*

Many programmers wrap every statement in a separate `try` block.

```
OutputStream out;
Stack s;

for (i = 0; i < 100; i++)
{
   try
   {
      n = s.pop();
   }
   catch (EmptyStackException s)
   {
      // stack was empty
   }
   try
   {
      out.writeInt(n);
   }
   catch (IOException e)
   {
      // problem writing to file
   }
}
```

This approach blows up your code dramatically. Think about the task that you want the code to accomplish. Here we want to pop 100 numbers off a stack and save them to a file. (Never mind why—it is just a toy example.) There is nothing we can do if a problem rears its ugly head. If the stack is empty, it will not become occupied. If the file contains an error, the error will not magically go away. It therefore makes sense to wrap the *entire task* in a `try` block. If any one operation fails, you can then abandon the task.

```
try
{
   for (i = 0; i < 100; i++)
   {
      n = s.pop();
      out.writeInt(n);
   }
}
catch (IOException e)
{
   // problem writing to file
}
catch (EmptyStackException s)
{
   // stack was empty
}
```

This code looks much cleaner. It fulfills one of the promises of exception handling, to *separate* normal processing from error handling.

3. *Make good use of the exception hierarchy.*

   Don't just throw a `RuntimeException`. Find an appropriate subclass or create your own.

   Don't just catch `Throwable`. It makes your code hard to read and maintain.

   Respect the difference between checked and unchecked exceptions. Checked exceptions are inherently burdensome—don't throw them for logic errors. (For example, the reflection library gets this wrong. Callers often need to catch exceptions that they know can never happen.)

   Do not hesitate to turn an exception into another exception that is more appropriate. For example, when you parse an integer in a file, catch the `NumberFormatException` and turn it into a subclass of `IOException` or `MySubsystemException`.

4. *Do not squelch exceptions.*

   In Java, there is the tremendous temptation to shut up exceptions. You write a method that calls a method that might throw an exception once a century. The compiler whines because you have not declared the exception in the `throws` list of your method. You do not want to put it in the `throws` list because then the compiler will whine about all the methods that call your method. So you just shut it up:

```
public Image loadImage(String s)
{
   try
   {
      code that threatens to throw checked exceptions
   }
   catch (Exception e)
   {} // so there
}
```

   Now your code will compile without a hitch. It will run fine, except when an exception occurs. Then, the exception will be silently ignored. If you believe that exceptions are at all important, you should make some effort to handle them right.

5. *When you detect an error, "tough love" works better than indulgence.*

   Some programmers worry about throwing exceptions when they detect errors. Maybe it would be better to return a dummy value rather than throw an exception when a method is called with invalid parameters. For example, should `Stack.pop` return `null` rather than throw an exception when a stack is empty? We think it is better to throw a `EmptyStackException` at the point of failure than to have a `NullPointerException` occur at later time.

6. *Propagating exceptions is not a sign of shame.*

   Many programmers feel compelled to catch all exceptions that are thrown. If they call a method that throws an exception, such as the `FileInputStream` constructor or the `readLine` method, they instinctively catch the exception that may be generated. Often, it is actually better to *propagate* the exception instead of catching it:

```
public void readStuff(String filename) throws IOException // not a sign of shame!
{
   InputStream in = new FileInputStream(filename);
   . . .
}
```

   Higher-level methods are often better equipped to inform the user of errors or to abandon unsuccessful commands.

NOTE: Rules 5 and 6 can be summarized as "throw early, catch late."

Example 11–3: ExceptionalTest.java

```
import java.util.*;

public class ExceptionalTest
{
   public static void main(String[] args)
   {
      int i = 0;
      int ntry = 1000000;
      Stack s = new Stack();
      long s1;
      long s2;

      // test a stack for emptiness ntry times
      System.out.println("Testing for empty stack");
      s1 = new Date().getTime();
      for (i = 0; i <= ntry; i++)
         if (!s.empty()) s.pop();
      s2 = new Date().getTime();
      System.out.println((s2 - s1) + " milliseconds");

      // pop an empty stack ntry times and catch the
      // resulting exception
      System.out.println("Catching EmptyStackException");
      s1 = new Date().getTime();
      for (i = 0; i <= ntry; i++)
      {
         try
         {
            s.pop();
         }
         catch(EmptyStackException e)
         {
         }
      }
      s2 = new Date().getTime();
      System.out.println((s2 - s1) + " milliseconds");
   }
}
```

Logging

Every Java programmer is familiar with the process of inserting calls to `System.out.println` into troublesome code to gain insight into program behavior. Of course, once you have figured out the cause of trouble, you remove the print statements, only to put them back in when the next problem surfaces. The logging API of JDK 1.4 is designed to overcome this problem. Here are the principal advantages of the API.

- It is easy to suppress all log records or just those below a certain level, and just as easy to turn them back on.

- Suppressed logs are very cheap, so that there is only a minimal penalty for leaving the logging code in your application.
- Log records can be directed to different handlers, for display in the console, for storage in a file, and so on.
- Both loggers and handlers can filter records. Filters discard boring log entries, using any criteria supplied by the filter implementor.
- Log records can be formatted in different ways, for example, in plain text or XML.
- Applications can use multiple loggers, with hierarchical names such as `com.mycompany.myapp`, similar to package names.
- By default, the logging configuration is controlled by a configuration file. Applications can replace this mechanism if desired.

Basic Logging

Let's get started with the simplest possible case. The logging system manages a default logger `Logger.global` that you can use instead of `System.out`. Use the `info` method to log an information message:

```
Logger.global.info("File->Open menu item selected");
```

By default, the record is printed like this:

```
May 10, 2004 10:12:15 PM LoggingImageViewer fileOpen
INFO: File->Open menu item selected
```

(Note that the time and the names of the calling class and method are automatically included.) But if you call

```
Logger.global.setLevel(Level.OFF);
```

at an appropriate place (such as the beginning of `main`), then all logging is suppressed.

Advanced Logging

Now that you have seen "logging for dummies," let's go on to industrial-strength logging. In a professional application, you wouldn't want to log all records to a single global logger. Instead, you can define your own loggers.

When you request a logger with a given name for the first time, it is created.

```
Logger myLogger = Logger.getLogger("com.mycompany.myapp");
```

Subsequent calls to the same name yield the same logger object.

Similar to package names, logger names are hierarchical. In fact, they are *more* hierarchical than packages. There is no semantic relationship between a package and its parent, but logger parents and children share certain properties. For example, if you set the log level on the logger `"com.mycompany"`, then the child loggers inherit that level.

There are seven logging levels:

- `SEVERE`
- `WARNING`
- `INFO`
- `CONFIG`
- `FINE`
- `FINER`
- `FINEST`

By default, the top three levels are actually logged. You can set a different level, for example,

```
logger.setLevel(Level.FINE);
```

Now all levels of `FINE` and higher are logged.

You can also use `Level.ALL` to turn on logging for all levels or `Level.OFF` to turn all logging off.

There are logging methods for all levels, such as

```
logger.warning(message);
logger.fine(message);
```

and so on. Alternatively, you can use the `log` method and supply the level, such as

```
logger.log(Level.FINE, message);
```

TIP: The default logging configuration logs all records with level of `INFO` or higher. Therefore, you should use the levels `CONFIG`, `FINE`, `FINER`, and `FINEST` for debugging messages that are useful for diagnostics but meaningless to the program user.

CAUTION: If you set the logging level to a value finer than `INFO`, then you also need to change the log handler configuration. The default log handler suppresses messages below `INFO`. See the next section for details.

The default log record shows the name of the class and method that contain the logging call, as inferred from the call stack. However, if the virtual machine optimizes execution, accurate call information may not be available. You can use the `logp` method to give the precise location of the calling class and method. The method signature is

```
void logp(Level l, String className, String methodName, String message)
```

There are convenience methods for tracing execution flow:

```
void entering(String className, String methodName)
void entering(String className, String methodName, Object param)
void entering(String className, String methodName, Object[] params)
void exiting(String className, String methodName)
void exiting(String className, String methodName, Object result)
```

For example,

```
int read(String file, String pattern)
{
   logger.entering("com.mycompany.mylib.Reader", "read",
      new Object[] { file, pattern });
   . . .
   logger.exiting("com.mycompany.mylib.Reader", "read", count);
   return count;
}
```

These calls generate log records of level `FINER` that start with the strings `ENTRY` and `RETURN`.

NOTE: At some point in the future, the logging methods will be rewritten to support variable parameter lists ("varargs"). Then you will be able to make calls such as `logger.entering("com.mycompany.mylib.Reader", "read", file, pattern)`.

A common use for logging is to log unexpected exceptions. Two convenience methods include a description of the exception in the log record.

```
void throwing(String className, String methodName, Throwable t)
void log(Level l, String message, Throwable t)
```

Typical uses are

```
if (. . .)
{
   IOException exception = new IOException(". . .");
   logger.throwing("com.mycompany.mylib.Reader", "read", exception);
   throw exception;
}
```

and

```
try
{
   . . .
}
catch (IOException e)
{
   Logger.getLogger("com.mycompany.myapp").log(Level.WARNING, "Reading image", e);
}
```

The `throwing` call logs a record with level `FINER` and a message that starts with `THROW`.

Changing the Log Manager Configuration

You can change various properties of the logging system by editing a configuration file. The default configuration file is located at

```
jre/lib/logging.properties
```

To use another file, set the `java.util.logging.config.file` property to the file location by starting your application with

```
java -Djava.util.logging.config.file=configFile MainClass
```

CAUTION: Calling `System.setProperty("java.util.logging.config.file", file)` in `main` has no effect because the log manager is initialized during VM startup, before `main` executes.

To change the default logging level, edit the configuration file and modify the line

```
.level=INFO
```

You can specify the logging levels for your own loggers by adding lines such as

```
com.mycompany.myapp.level=FINE
```

That is, append the `.level` suffix to the logger name.

As you see later in this section, the loggers don't actually send the messages to the console—that is the job of the handlers. Handlers also have levels. To see `FINE` messages on the console, you also need to set

```
java.util.logging.ConsoleHandler.level=FINE
```

CAUTION: The settings in the log manager configuration are *not* system properties. Starting a program with `-Dcom.mycompany.myapp.level=FINE` does not have any influence on the logger.

NOTE: The logging properties file is processed by the `java.util.logging.LogManager` class. It is possible to specify a different log manager by setting the `java.util.logging.manager` system property to the name of a subclass. Alternatively, you can keep the standard log manager and still bypass the initialization from the logging properties file. Set the `java.util.logging.config.class` system property to the name of a class that sets log manager properties in some other way. See the API documentation for the `LogManager` class for more information.

Localization

You may want to localize logging messages so that they are readable for international users. Internationalization of applications is the topic of Chapter 10 of Volume 2. Briefly, here are the points to keep in mind when localizing logging messages.

Localized applications contain locale-specific information in *resource bundles.* A resource bundle consists of a set of mappings for various locales (such as United States or Germany). For example, a resource bundle may map the string "readingFile" into strings "Reading file" in English or "Achtung! Datei wird eingelesen" in German.

A program may contain multiple resource bundles, perhaps one for menus and another for log messages. Each resource bundle has a name (such as "com.mycompany.logmessages"). To add mappings to a resource bundle, you supply a file for each locale. English message mappings are in a file com/mycompany/logmessages_en.properties, and German message mappings are in a file com/mycompany/logmessages_de.properties. (The en, de codes are the language codes.) You place the files together with the class files of your application, so that the ResourceBundle class will automatically locate them. These files are plain text files, consisting of entries such as

```
readingFile=Achtung! Datei wird eingelesen
renamingFile=Datei wird umbenannt
...
```

When requesting a logger, you can specify a resource bundle:

```
Logger logger = Logger.getLogger(loggerName, "com.mycompany.logmessages");
```

Then you specify the resource bundle key, not the actual message string, for the log message.

```
logger.info("readingFile");
```

You often need to include arguments into localized messages. Then the message should contain placeholders {0}, {1}, and so on. For example, to include the file name with a log message, include the placeholder like this:

```
Reading file {0}.
Achtung! Datei {0} wird eingelesen.
```

You then pass values into the placeholders by calling one of the following methods:

```
logger.log(Level.INFO, "readingFile", fileName);
logger.log(Level.INFO, "renamingFile", new Object[] { oldName, newName });
```

Handlers

By default, loggers send records to a ConsoleHandler that prints them to the System.err stream. Specifically, the logger sends the record to the parent handler, and the ultimate ancestor (with name "") has a ConsoleHandler.

Like loggers, handlers have a logging level. For a record to be logged, its logging level must be above the threshold of *both* the logger and the handler. The log manager configuration file sets the logging level of the default console handler as

```
java.util.logging.ConsoleHandler.level=INFO
```

To log records with level FINE, change both the default logger level and the handler level in the configuration. Alternatively, you can bypass the configuration file altogether and install your own handler.

```
Logger logger = Logger.getLogger("com.mycompany.myapp");
logger.setLevel(Level.FINE);
logger.setUseParentHandlers(false);
Handler handler = new ConsoleHandler();
```

```
handler.setLevel(Level.FINE);
logger.addHandler(handler);
```

By default, a logger sends records both to its own handlers and the handlers of the parent. Our logger is a child of the primordial logger (with name "") that sends all records with level INFO or higher to the console. But we don't want to see those records twice. For that reason, we set the useParentHandlers property to false.

To send log records elsewhere, add another handler. The logging API provides two useful handlers for this purpose, a FileHandler and a SocketHandler. The SocketHandler sends records to a specified host and port. Of greater interest is the FileHandler that collects records in a file.

You can simply send records to a default file handler, like this:

```
FileHandler handler = new FileHandler();
logger.addHandler(handler);
```

The records are sent to a file javan.log in the user's home directory, where *n* is a number to make the file unique. If a user's system has no concept of the user's home directory (for example, in Windows 95/98/Me), then the file is stored in a default location such as C:\Windows. By default, the records are formatted in XML. A typical log record has the form

```
<record>
  <date>2002-02-04T07:45:15</date>
  <millis>1012837515710</millis>
  <sequence>1</sequence>
  <logger>com.mycompany.myapp</logger>
  <level>INFO</level>
  <class>com.mycompany.mylib.Reader</class>
  <method>read</method>
  <thread>10</thread>
  <message>Reading file corejava.gif</message>
</record>
```

You can modify the default behavior of the file handler by setting various parameters in the log manager configuration (see Table 11–2), or by using another constructor (see the API notes at the end of this section).

You probably don't want to use the default log file name. Therefore, you should use another pattern, such as %h/myapp.log. (See Table 11–3 for an explanation of the pattern variables.)

If multiple applications (or multiple copies of the same application) use the same log file, then you should turn the "append" flag on. Alternatively, use %u in the file name pattern so that each application creates a unique copy of the log.

It is also a good idea to turn file rotation on. Log files are kept in a rotation sequence, such as myapp.log.0, myapp.log.1, myapp.log.2, and so on. Whenever a file exceeds the size limit, the oldest log is deleted, the other files are renamed, and a new file with generation number 0 is created.

Table 11–2: File Handler Configuration Parameters

Configuration Property	Description	Default
java.util.logging.FileHandler.level	The handler level.	Level.ALL
java.util.logging.FileHandler.append	Controls whether the handler should append to an existing file, or open a new file for each program run.	false

Table 11–2: File Handler Configuration Parameters (continued)

Configuration Property	Description	Default
`java.util.logging.FileHandler.limit`	The approximate maximum number of bytes to write in a file before opening another. (0 = no limit).	0 (no limit) in the `FileHandler` class, 50000 in the default log manager configuration
`java.util.logging.FileHandler.pattern`	The pattern for the log file name. See Table 11–3 for pattern variables.	`%h/java%u.log`
`java.util.logging.FileHandler.count`	The number of logs in a rotation sequence.	1 (no rotation)
`java.util.logging.FileHandler.filter`	The filter class to use.	No filtering
`java.util.logging.FileHandler.encoding`	The character encoding to use.	The platform encoding
`java.util.logging.FileHandler.formatter`	The record formatter.	`java.util.logging.XMLFormatter`

TIP: Many programmers use logging as an aid for the technical support staff. If a program misbehaves in the field, then the user can send back the log files for inspection. In that case, you should turn the "append" flag on, use rotating logs, or both.

Table 11–3: Log File Pattern Variables

Variable	Description
`%h`	The value of the `user.home` system property.
`%t`	The system temporary directory.
`%u`	A unique number to resolve conflicts.
`%g`	The generation number for rotated logs. (A `.%g` suffix is used if rotation is specified and the pattern doesn't contain `%g`.)
`%%`	The `%` character.

You can also define your own handlers by extending the `Handler` or the `StreamHandler` class. We define such a handler in the example program at the end of this section. That handler displays the records in a window (see Figure 11–3).

The handler extends the `StreamHandler` class and installs a stream whose `write` methods display the stream output in a text area.

```
class WindowHandler extends StreamHandler
{
   public WindowHandler()
   {
      . . .
      final JTextArea output = new JTextArea();
      setOutputStream(new
         OutputStream()
         {
```

```
            public void write(int b) {} // not called
            public void write(byte[] b, int off, int len)
            {
               output.append(new String(b, off, len));
            }
         });
   }
   . . .
}
```

```
May 10, 2004 10:59:55 AM ImageViewerFrame <init>
FINER: ENTRY
May 10, 2004 10:59:55 AM ImageViewerFrame <init>
FINER: RETURN
May 10, 2004 10:59:55 AM LoggingImageViewer main
FINE: Showing frame
May 10, 2004 11:00:04 AM ImageViewerFrame.FileOpenListener actio
FINER: ENTRY java.awt.event.ActionEvent[ACTION_PERFORMED,cmd=C
May 10, 2004 11:00:08 AM ImageViewerFrame$FileOpenListener acti
FINE: File open dialog canceled.
May 10, 2004 11:00:09 AM ImageViewerFrame.FileOpenListener actio
FINER: RETURN
```

Figure 11–3: A log handler that displays records in a window

There is just one problem with this approach—the handler buffers the records and only writes them to the stream when the buffer is full. Therefore, we override the `publish` method to flush the buffer after each record:

```
class WindowHandler extends StreamHandler
{
   . . .
   public void publish(LogRecord record)
   {
      super.publish(record);
      flush();
   }
}
```

If you want to write more exotic stream handlers, extend the `Handler` class and define the `publish`, `flush`, and `close` methods.

Filters

By default, records are filtered according to their logging levels. Each logger and handler can have an optional filter to perform added filtering. You define a filter by implementing the `Filter` interface and defining the method

```
boolean isLoggable(LogRecord record)
```

Analyze the log record, using any criteria that you desire, and return `true` for those records that should be included in the log. For example, a particular filter may only be interested in the messages generated by the `entering` and `exiting` methods. The filter should then call `record.getMessage()` and check whether it starts with ENTRY or RETURN.

To install a filter into a logger or handler, simply call the `setFilter` method. Note that you can have at most one filter at a time.

Formatters

The ConsoleHandler and FileHandler classes emit the log records in text and XML formats. However, you can define your own formats as well. You need to extend the Formatter class and override the method

```
String format(LogRecord record)
```

Format the information in the record in any way you like and return the resulting string. In your format method, you may want to call the method

```
String formatMessage(LogRecord record)
```

That method formats the message part of the record, substituting parameters and applying localization.

Many file formats (such as XML) require a head and tail part that surrounds the formatted records. In that case, override the methods

```
String getHead(Handler h)
String getTail(Handler h)
```

Finally, call the setFormatter method to install the formatter into the handler.

With so many options for logging, it is easy to lose track of the fundamentals. The "Logging Cookbook" sidebar summarizes the most common operations.

Logging Cookbook

1. For a simple application, choose a single logger. It is a good idea to give the logger the same name as your main application package, such as com.mycompany.myprog. You can always get the logger by calling

   ```
   Logger logger = Logger.getLogger("com.mycompany.myprog");
   ```

   For convenience, you may want to add static fields

   ```
   private static final Logger logger = Logger.getLogger("com.mycompany.myprog");
   ```

   to classes with a lot of logging activity.

2. The default logging configuration logs all messages of level INFO or higher to the console. Users can override the default configuration, but as you have seen, the process is a bit involved. Therefore, it is a good idea to install a more reasonable default in your application.

   The following code ensures that all messages are logged to an application-specific file. Place the code into the main method of your application.

   ```
   if (System.getProperty("java.util.logging.config.class") == null
         && System.getProperty("java.util.logging.config.file") == null)
   {
      try
      {
         Logger.getLogger("").setLevel(Level.ALL);
         final int LOG_ROTATION_COUNT = 10;
         Handler handler = new FileHandler("%h/myapp.log", 0,  LOG_ROTATION_COUNT);
         Logger.getLogger("").addHandler(handler);
      }
      catch (IOException e)
      {
         logger.log(Level.SEVERE, "Can't create log file handler", e);
      }
   }
   ```

Logging Cookbook

3. Now you are ready to log to your heart's content. Keep in mind that all messages with level `INFO`, `WARNING`, and `SEVERE` show up on the console. Therefore, reserve these levels for messages that are meaningful to the users of your program. The level `FINE` is a good choice for logging messages that are intended for programmers.

   Whenever you are tempted to call `System.out.println`, emit a log message instead:

   ```
   logger.fine("File open dialog canceled");
   ```

   It is also a good idea to log unexpected exceptions, for example,

   ```
   try
   {
      . . .
   }
   catch (SomeException e)
   {
      logger.log(Level.FINE, "explanation", e);
   }
   ```

Example 11–4 presents the code for the image viewer that logs events to a log window.

Example 11–4: LoggingImageViewer.java

```
import java.awt.*;
import java.awt.event.*;
import java.awt.image.*;
import java.io.*;
import java.util.logging.*;
import javax.swing.*;

/**
   A modification of the image viewer program that logs
   various events.
*/
public class LoggingImageViewer
{
   public static void main(String[] args)
   {

      if (System.getProperty("java.util.logging.config.class") == null
         && System.getProperty("java.util.logging.config.file") == null)
      {
         try
         {
            Logger.getLogger("").setLevel(Level.ALL);
            final int LOG_ROTATION_COUNT = 10;
            Handler handler = new FileHandler("%h/LoggingImageViewer.log", 0, LOG_ROTATION_COUNT);
            Logger.getLogger("").addHandler(handler);
         }
         catch (IOException e)
         {
            Logger.getLogger("com.horstmann.corejava").log(Level.SEVERE,
               "Can't create log file handler", e);
         }
      }
```

```

      Handler windowHandler = new WindowHandler();
      windowHandler.setLevel(Level.ALL);
      Logger.getLogger("com.horstmann.corejava").addHandler(windowHandler);

      JFrame frame = new ImageViewerFrame();
      frame.setTitle("LoggingImageViewer");
      frame.setSize(300, 400);
      frame.setDefaultCloseOperation(JFrame.EXIT_ON_CLOSE);

      Logger.getLogger("com.horstmann.corejava").fine("Showing frame");
      frame.setVisible(true);
   }
}

/**
   The frame that shows the image.
*/
class ImageViewerFrame extends JFrame
{
   public ImageViewerFrame()
   {
      logger.entering("ImageViewerFrame", "<init>");
      // set up menu bar
      JMenuBar menuBar = new JMenuBar();
      setJMenuBar(menuBar);

      JMenu menu = new JMenu("File");
      menuBar.add(menu);

      JMenuItem openItem = new JMenuItem("Open");
      menu.add(openItem);
      openItem.addActionListener(new FileOpenListener());

      JMenuItem exitItem = new JMenuItem("Exit");
      menu.add(exitItem);
      exitItem.addActionListener(new
         ActionListener()
         {
            public void actionPerformed(ActionEvent event)
            {
               logger.fine("Exiting.");
               System.exit(0);
            }
         });

      // use a label to display the images
      label = new JLabel();
      add(label);
      logger.exiting("ImageViewerFrame", "<init>");
   }

   private class FileOpenListener implements ActionListener
   {
      public void actionPerformed(ActionEvent event)
```

```
      {
         logger.entering("ImageViewerFrame.FileOpenListener", "actionPerformed", event);

         // set up file chooser
         JFileChooser chooser = new JFileChooser();
         chooser.setCurrentDirectory(new File("."));

         // accept all files ending with .gif
         chooser.setFileFilter(new
            javax.swing.filechooser.FileFilter()
            {
               public boolean accept(File f)
               {
                  return f.getName().toLowerCase().endsWith(".gif") || f.isDirectory();
               }
               public String getDescription()
               {
                  return "GIF Images";
               }
            });

         // show file chooser dialog
         int r = chooser.showOpenDialog(ImageViewerFrame.this);

         // if image file accepted, set it as icon of the label
         if (r == JFileChooser.APPROVE_OPTION)
         {
            String name = chooser.getSelectedFile().getPath();
            logger.log(Level.FINE, "Reading file {0}", name);
            label.setIcon(new ImageIcon(name));
         }
         else
            logger.fine("File open dialog canceled.");
         logger.exiting("ImageViewerFrame.FileOpenListener", "actionPerformed");
      }
   }

   private JLabel label;
   private static Logger logger = Logger.getLogger("com.horstmann.corejava");
}

/**
   A handler for displaying log records in a window.
*/
class WindowHandler extends StreamHandler
{
   public WindowHandler()
   {
      frame = new JFrame();
      final JTextArea output = new JTextArea();
      output.setEditable(false);
      frame.setSize(200, 200);
      frame.add(new JScrollPane(output));
      frame.setFocusableWindowState(false);
      frame.setVisible(true);
      setOutputStream(new
```

```
         OutputStream()
         {
            public void write(int b) {} // not called
            public void write(byte[] b, int off, int len)
            {
               output.append(new String(b, off, len));
            }
         });
   }

   public void publish(LogRecord record)
   {
      if (!frame.isVisible()) return;
      super.publish(record);
      flush();
   }

   private JFrame frame;
}
```

API java.util.logging.Logger 1.4

- `Logger getLogger(String loggerName)`
- `Logger getLogger(String loggerName, String bundleName)`

  get the logger with the given name. If the logger doesn't exist, it is created.

  Parameters:

`loggerName`	The hierarchical logger name, such as `com.mycompany.myapp`
`bundleName`	The name of the resource bundle for looking up localized messages

- `void severe(String message)`
- `void warning(String message)`
- `void info(String message)`
- `void config(String message)`
- `void fine(String message)`
- `void finer(String message)`
- `void finest(String message)`

  log a record with the level indicated by the method name and the given message.

- `void entering(String className, String methodName)`
- `void entering(String className, String methodName, Object param)`
- `void entering(String className, String methodName, Object[] param)`
- `void exiting(String className, String methodName)`
- `void exiting(String className, String methodName, Object result)`

  log a record that describes entering or exiting a method with the given parameter(s) or return value.

- `void throwing(String className, String methodName, Throwable t)`

  logs a record that describes throwing of the given exception object.

- `void log(Level level, String message)`
- `void log(Level level, String message, Object obj)`
- `void log(Level level, String message, Object[] objs)`
- `void log(Level level, String message, Throwable t)`

  log a record with the given level and message, optionally including objects or a throwable. To include objects, the message must contain formatting placeholders `{0}`, `{1}`, and so on.

- `void logp(Level level, String className, String methodName, String message)`
- `void logp(Level level, String className, String methodName, String message, Object obj)`
- `void logp(Level level, String className, String methodName, String message, Object[] objs)`
- `void logp(Level level, String className, String methodName, String message, Throwable t)`

  log a record with the given level, precise caller information, and message, optionally including objects or a throwable.

- `void logrb(Level level, String className, String methodName, String bundleName, String message)`
- `void logrb(Level level, String className, String methodName, String bundleName, String message, Object obj)`
- `void logrb(Level level, String className, String methodName, String bundleName, String message, Object[] objs)`
- `void logrb(Level level, String className, String methodName, String bundleName, String message, Throwable t)`

  log a record with the given level, precise caller information, resource bundle name, and message, optionally including objects or a throwable.

- `Level getLevel()`
- `void setLevel(Level l)`

  get and set the level of this logger.

- `Logger getParent()`
- `void setParent(Logger l)`

  get and set the parent logger of this logger.

- `Handler[] getHandlers()`

  gets all handlers of this logger.

- `void addHandler(Handler h)`
- `void removeHandler(Handler h)`

  add or remove a handler for this logger.

- `boolean getUseParentHandlers()`
- `void setUseParentHandlers(boolean b)`

  get and set the "use parent handler" property. If this property is `true`, the logger forwards all logged records to the handlers of its parent.

- `Filter getFilter()`
- `void setFilter(Filter f)`

  get and set the filter of this logger.

API **java.util.logging.Handler** 1.4

- `abstract void publish(LogRecord record)`

  sends the record to the intended destination.

- `abstract void flush()`

  flushes any buffered data.

- `abstract void close()`

  flushes any buffered data and releases all associated resources.

- `Filter getFilter()`
- `void setFilter(Filter f)`

  get and set the filter of this handler.

- `Formatter getFormatter()`
- `void setFormatter(Formatter f)`

  get and set the formatter of this handler.

- `Level getLevel()`
- `void setLevel(Level l)`

  get and set the level of this handler.

java.util.logging.ConsoleHandler 1.4

- `ConsoleHandler()`
  constructs a new console handler.

java.util.logging.FileHandler 1.4

- `FileHandler(String pattern)`
- `FileHandler(String pattern, boolean append)`
- `FileHandler(String pattern, int limit, int count)`
- `FileHandler(String pattern, int limit, int count, boolean append)`
  construct a file handler.

  Parameters:

`pattern`	The pattern for constructing the log file name. See Table 11–3 on page 585 for pattern variables.
`limit`	The approximate maximum number of bytes before a new log file is opened.
`count`	The number of files in a rotation sequence.
`append`	`true` if a newly constructed file handler object should append to an existing log file.

java.util.logging.LogRecord 1.4

- `Level getLevel()`
  gets the logging level of this record.
- `String getLoggerName()`
  gets the name of the logger that is logging this record.
- `ResourceBundle getResourceBundle()`
- `String getResourceBundleName()`
  get the resource bundle, or its name, to be used for localizing the message, or `null` if none is provided.
- `String getMessage()`
  gets the "raw" message before localization or formatting.
- `Object[] getParameters()`
  gets the parameter objects, or `null` if none is provided.
- `Throwable getThrown()`
  gets the thrown object, or `null` if none is provided.
- `String getSourceClassName()`
- `String getSourceMethodName()`
  get the location of the code that logged this record. This information may be supplied by the logging code or automatically inferred from the runtime stack. It might be inaccurate, if the logging code supplied the wrong value or if the running code was optimized and the exact location cannot be inferred.
- `long getMillis()`
  gets the creation time, in milliseconds, since 1970.
- `long getSequenceNumber()`
  gets the unique sequence number of this record.
- `int getThreadID()`
  gets the unique ID for the thread in which this record was created. These IDs are assigned by the `LogRecord` class and have no relationship to other thread IDs.

java.util.logging.Filter 1.4

- `boolean isLoggable(LogRecord record)`
  returns `true` if the given log record should be logged.

java.util.logging.Formatter 1.4

- `abstract String format(LogRecord record)`
  returns the string that results from formatting the given log record.
- `String getHead(Handler h)`
- `String getTail(Handler h)`
  return the strings that should appear at the head and tail of the document containing the log records. The `Formatter` superclass defines these methods to return the empty string; override them if necessary.
- `String formatMessage(LogRecord record)`
  returns the localized and formatted message part of the log record.

Using Assertions

Assertions are a commonly used idiom for defensive programming. Suppose you are convinced that a particular property is fulfilled, and you rely on that property in your code. For example, you may be computing

```
double y = Math.sqrt(x);
```

You are certain that `x` is not negative. Perhaps it is the result of another computation that can't have a negative result, or it is a parameter of a method that requires its callers to supply only positive inputs. Still, you want to double-check rather than having confusing "not a number" floating-point values creep into your computation. You could, of course, throw an exception:

```
if (x < 0) throw new IllegalArgumentException("x < 0");
```

But this code stays in the program, even after testing is complete. If you have lots of checks of this kind, the program runs quite a bit slower than it should.

The assertion mechanism allows you to put in checks during testing and to have them automatically removed in the production code.

As of JDK 1.4, the Java language has a keyword `assert`. There are two forms:

```
assert condition;
```

and

```
assert condition : expression;
```

Both statements evaluate the condition and throw an `AssertionError` if it is `false`. In the second statement, the expression is passed to the constructor of the `AssertionError` object and turned into a message string.

NOTE: The sole purpose of the *expression* part is to produce a message string. The `AssertionError` object does not store the actual expression value, so you can't query it later. As the JDK documentation states with paternalistic charm, doing so "would encourage programmers to attempt to recover from assertion failure, which defeats the purpose of the facility."

To assert that `x` is nonnegative, you can simply use the statement

```
assert x >= 0;
```

Or you can pass the actual value of `x` into the `AssertionError` object, so that it gets displayed later.

```
assert x >= 0 : x;
```

C++ NOTE: The `assert` macro of the C language turns the assertion condition into a string that is printed if the assertion fails. For example, if `assert(x >= 0)` fails, it prints that `"x >= 0"` is the failing condition. In Java, the condition is not automatically part of the error report. If you want to see it, you have to pass it as a string into the `AssertionError` object: `assert x >= 0 : "x >= 0"`.

If you use JDK 1.4, you must tell the compiler that you are using the `assert` keyword. Use the `-source 1.4` option, like this:

```
javac -source 1.4 MyClass.java
```

Starting with JDK 5.0, support for assertions is enabled by default.

Assertion Enabling and Disabling

By default, assertions are disabled. You enable them by running the program with the `-enableassertions` or `-ea` option:

```
java -enableassertions MyApp
```

Note that you do not have to recompile your program to enable or disable assertions. Enabling or disabling assertions is a function of the *class loader*. When assertions are disabled, the class loader strips out the assertion code so that it won't slow execution.

You can even turn on assertions in specific classes or in entire packages. For example,

```
java -ea:MyClass -ea:com.mycompany.mylib... MyApp
```

This command turns on assertions for the class `MyClass` and all classes in the `com.mycompany.mylib` package *and its subpackages*. The option `-ea...` turns on assertions in all classes of the default package.

You can also disable assertions in certain classes and packages with the `-disableassertions` or `-da` option:

```
java -ea:... -da:MyClass MyApp
```

Some classes are not loaded by a class loader but directly by the virtual machine. You can use these switches to selectively enable or disable assertions in those classes. However, the `-ea` and `-da` switches that enable or disable all assertions do not apply to the "system classes" without class loaders. Use the `-enablesystemassertions/-esa` switch to enable assertions in system classes.

It is also possible to programmatically control the assertion status of class loaders. See the API notes at the end of this section.

Usage Hints for Assertions

The Java language gives you three mechanisms to deal with system failures:

- Throwing an exception
- Logging
- Using assertions

When should you choose assertions? Keep these points in mind:

- Assertion failures are intended to be fatal, unrecoverable errors.

- Assertion checks are turned on only during development and testing. (This is sometimes jokingly described as "wearing a life jacket when you are close to shore, and throwing it overboard once you are in the middle of the ocean.")

Therefore, you would not use assertions for signaling recoverable conditions to another part of the program or for communicating problems to the program user. Assertions should only be used to locate internal program errors during testing.

Let's look at a common scenario—the checking of method parameters. Should you use assertions to check for illegal index values or `null` references? To answer that question, you have to look at the documentation of the method. For example, consider the `Arrays.sort` method from the standard library.

```
/**
   Sorts the specified range of the specified array into
   ascending numerical order.  The range to be sorted extends
   from fromIndex, inclusive, to toIndex, exclusive.
   @param a the array to be sorted.
   @param fromIndex the index of the first element (inclusive) to be sorted.
   @param toIndex the index of the last element (exclusive) to be sorted.
   @throws IllegalArgumentException if fromIndex > toIndex
   @throws ArrayIndexOutOfBoundsException if fromIndex < 0 or toIndex > a.length
*/
static void sort(int[] a, int fromIndex, int toIndex)
```

The documentation states that the method throws an exception if the index values are incorrect. That behavior is part of the contract that the method makes with its callers. If you implement the method, you have to respect that contract and throw the indicated exceptions. It would not be appropriate to use assertions instead.

Should you assert that `a` is not `null`? That is not appropriate either. The method documentation is silent on the behavior of the method when `a` is `null`. The callers have the right to assume that the method will return successfully in that case and not throw an assertion error.

However, suppose the method contract had been slightly different:

```
@param a the array to be sorted. (Must not be null)
```

Now the callers of the method have been put on notice that it is illegal to call the method with a `null` array. Then the method may start with the assertion

```
assert a != null;
```

Computer scientists call this kind of contract a *precondition*. The original method had no preconditions on its parameters—it promised a well-defined behavior in all cases. The revised method has a single precondition: that `a` is not `null`. If the caller fails to fulfill the precondition, then all bets are off and the method can do anything it wants. In fact, with the assertion in place, the method has a rather unpredictable behavior when it is called illegally. It sometimes throws an assertion error, and sometimes a null pointer exception, depending on how its class loader is configured.

NOTE: In JDK 5.0, the `Arrays.sort` method throws a `NullPointerException` if you call it with a `null` array. That is a bug, either in the specification or the implementation.

Many programmers use comments to document their underlying assumptions. The JDK documentation contains a good example:

```
if (i % 3 == 0)
   . . .
```

```
else if (i % 3 == 1)
   . . .
else // (i % 3 == 2)
   . . .
```

In this case, it makes a lot of sense to use an assertion instead.

```
if (i % 3 == 0)
   . . .
else if (i % 3 == 1)
   . . .
else
{
   assert i % 3 == 2;
   . . .
}
```

Of course, it would make even more sense to think through the issue a bit more thoroughly. What are the possible values of `i % 3`? If `i` is positive, the remainders must be 0, 1, or 2. If `i` is negative, then the remainders can be −1 or −2. Thus, the real assumption is that `i` is not negative. A better assertion would be

```
assert i >= 0;
```

before the `if` statement.

At any rate, this example shows a good use of assertions as a self-check for the programmer. As you can see, assertions are a tactical tool for testing and debugging, whereas logging is a strategic tool for the entire life cycle of a program.

java.lang.ClassLoader 1.0

- `void setDefaultAssertionStatus(boolean b)` 1.4
  enables or disables assertions for all classes loaded by this class loader that don't have an explicit class or package assertion status.
- `void setClassAssertionStatus(String className, boolean b)` 1.4
  enables or disables assertions for the given class and its inner classes.
- `void setPackageAssertionStatus(String packageName, boolean b)` 1.4
  enables or disables assertions for all classes in the given package and its subpackages.
- `void clearAssertionStatus()` 1.4
  removes all explicit class and package assertion status settings and disables assertions for all classes loaded by this class loader.

Debugging Techniques

Suppose you wrote your program and made it bulletproof by catching and properly handling all exceptions. Then you run it, and it does not work right. Now what? (If you never have this problem, you can skip the remainder of this chapter.)

Of course, it is best if you have a convenient and powerful debugger. Debuggers are available as a part of professional development environments such as Eclipse, NetBeans, or JBuilder. However, if you use a new version of Java that is not yet supported by development environments or if you work on an unusual platform, you will need to do a great deal of debugging by the time-honored method of inserting logging statements into your code.

Useful Tricks for Debugging

Here are some tips for efficient debugging if you have to do it all yourself.

1. You can print or log the value of any variable with code like this:

```
System.out.println("x=" + x);
```

   or

```
Logger.global.info("x=" + x);
```

   If x is a number, it is converted to its string equivalent. If x is an object, then Java calls its toString method. To get the state of the implicit parameter object, print the state of the this object.

```
Logger.global.info("this=" + this);
```

   Most of the classes in the Java library are very conscientious about overriding the toString method to give you useful information about the class. This is a real boon for debugging. You should make the same effort in your classes.

2. One seemingly little-known but very useful trick is that you can put a separate main method in each class. Inside it, you can put a unit test stub that lets you test the class in isolation.

```
public class MyClass
{
   methods and fields
   . . .
   public static void main(String[] args)
   {
      test code
   }
}
```

   Make a few objects, call all methods, and check that each of them does the right thing. You can leave all these main methods in place and launch the Java virtual machine separately on each of the files to run the tests. When you run an applet, none of these main methods are ever called. When you run an application, the Java virtual machine calls only the main method of the startup class.

3. If you liked the preceding tip, you should check out JUnit from http://junit.org. JUnit is a very popular unit testing framework that makes it easy to organize suites of test cases. Run the tests whenever you make changes to a class, and add another test case whenever you find a bug.

4. A *logging proxy* is an object of a subclass that intercepts method calls, logs them, and then calls the superclass. For example, if you have trouble with the setBackground method of a panel, you can create a proxy object as an instance of an anonymous subclass:

```
JPanel panel = new
   JPanel()
   {
      public void setBackground(Color c)
      {
         Logger.global.info("setBackground: c=" + c);
         super.setBackground(c);
      }
   };
```

   Whenever the setBackground method is called, a log message is generated. To find out who called the method, generate a stack trace—see the next tip.

5. You can get a stack trace from any exception object with the `printStackTrace` method in the `Throwable` class. The following code catches any exception, prints the exception object and the stack trace, and rethrows the exception so it can find its intended handler.

```
try
{
   . . .
}
catch (Throwable t)
{
   t.printStackTrace();
   throw t;
}
```

   You don't even need to catch an exception to generate a stack trace. Simply insert the statement

```
Thread.dumpStack();
```

   anywhere into your code to get a stack trace.

6. Normally, the stack trace is displayed on `System.err`. You can send it to a file with the `void printStackTrace(PrintWriter s)` method. Or, if you want to log or display the stack trace, here is how you can capture it into a string:

```
StringWriter out = new StringWriter();
new Throwable().printStackTrace(new PrintWriter(out));
String trace = out.toString();
```

   (See Chapter 12 for the `PrintWriter` and `StringWriter` classes.)

7. It is often handy to trap program errors in a file. However, errors are sent to `System.err`, not `System.out`. Therefore, you cannot simply trap them by running

```
java MyProgram > errors.txt
```

   In UNIX and Windows NT/2000/XP, this is not a problem. For example, if you use `bash` as your shell, simply capture the error stream as

```
java MyProgram 2> errors.txt
```

   To capture both `System.err` and `System.out` in the same file, use

```
java MyProgram 2>&1 errors.txt
```

   Some operating systems (such as Windows 95/98/Me) do not have such a convenient method. Here is a remedy. Use the following Java program:

```
import java.io.*;
public class Errout
{
   public static void main(String[] args) throws IOException
   {
      Process p = Runtime.getRuntime().exec(args);
      BufferedReader err = new BufferedReader(new InputStreamReader(p.getErrorStream()));
      String line;
      while ((line = err.readLine()) != null)
         System.out.println(line);
   }
}
```

   Then run your program as

```
java Errout java MyProgram > errors.txt
```

C++ NOTE: A more efficient way of getting the same result in Windows is to compile this C program into a file, `errout.exe`:

```
#include <io.h>
#include <stdio.h>
#include <process.h>
int main(int argc, char* argv[])
{
   dup2(1, 2); /* make stderr go to stdout */
   execvp(argv[1], argv + 1);
   return 0;
}
```

Then you can run

```
errout java MyProgram > errors.txt
```

8. To watch class loading, launch the Java virtual machine with the `-verbose` flag. You get a printout such as:

```
[Opened /usr/local/jdk5.0/jre/lib/rt.jar]
[Opened /usr/local/jdk5.0/jre/lib/jsse.jar]
[Opened /usr/local/jdk5.0/jre/lib/jce.jar]
[Opened /usr/local/jdk5.0/jre/lib/charsets.jar]
[Loaded java.lang.Object from shared objects file]
[Loaded java.io.Serializable from shared objects file]
[Loaded java.lang.Comparable from shared objects file]
[Loaded java.lang.CharSequence from shared objects file]
[Loaded java.lang.String from shared objects file]
[Loaded java.lang.reflect.GenericDeclaration from shared objects file]
[Loaded java.lang.reflect.Type from shared objects file]
[Loaded java.lang.reflect.AnnotatedElement from shared objects file]
[Loaded java.lang.Class from shared objects file]
[Loaded java.lang.Cloneable from shared objects file]
...
```

This can occasionally be helpful to diagnose class path problems.

9. If you ever looked at a Swing window and wondered how its designer managed to get all the components to line up so nicely, you can spy on the contents. Press CTRL+SHIFT+F1, and you get a printout of all components in the hierarchy:

```
FontDialog[frame0,0,0,300x200,layout=java.awt.BorderLayout,...
  javax.swing.JRootPane[,4,23,292x173,layout=javax.swing.JRootPane$RootLayout,...
   javax.swing.JPanel[null.glassPane,0,0,292x173,hidden,layout=java.awt.FlowLayout,...
   javax.swing.JLayeredPane[null.layeredPane,0,0,292x173,...
     javax.swing.JPanel[null.contentPane,0,0,292x173,layout=java.awt.GridBagLayout,...
       javax.swing.JList[,0,0,73x152,alignmentX=null,alignmentY=null,...
         javax.swing.CellRendererPane[,0,0,0x0,hidden]
          javax.swing.DefaultListCellRenderer$UIResource[,-73,-19,0x0,...
       javax.swing.JCheckBox[,157,13,50x25,layout=javax.swing.OverlayLayout,...
       javax.swing.JCheckBox[,156,65,52x25,layout=javax.swing.OverlayLayout,...
       javax.swing.JLabel[,114,119,30x17,alignmentX=0.0,alignmentY=null,...
       javax.swing.JTextField[,186,117,105x21,alignmentX=null,alignmentY=null,...
       javax.swing.JTextField[,0,152,291x21,alignmentX=null,alignmentY=null,...
```

10. If you design your own custom Swing component and it doesn't seem to be displayed correctly, you'll really love the *Swing graphics debugger.* And even if you don't write your own component classes, it is instructive and fun to see exactly how the contents of a

component are drawn. To turn on debugging for a Swing component, use the `setDebugGraphicsOptions` method of the `JComponent` class. The following options are available:

`DebugGraphics.FLASH_OPTION`	Flashes each line, rectangle, and text in red before drawing it
`DebugGraphics.LOG_OPTION`	Prints a message for each drawing operation
`DebugGraphics.BUFFERED_OPTION`	Displays the operations that are performed on the off-screen buffer
`DebugGraphics.NONE_OPTION`	Turns graphics debugging off

We have found that for the flash option to work, you must disable "double buffering," the strategy used by Swing to reduce flicker when updating a window. The magic incantation for turning on the flash option is:

```
RepaintManager.currentManager(getRootPane()).setDoubleBufferingEnabled(false);
((JComponent) getContentPane()).setDebugGraphicsOptions(DebugGraphics.FLASH_OPTION);
```

Simply place these lines at the end of your frame constructor. When the program runs, you will see the content pane filled in slow motion. Or, for more localized debugging, just call `setDebugGraphicsOptions` for a single component. Control freaks can set the duration, count, and color of the flashes—see the on-line documentation of the `DebugGraphics` class for details.

11. JDK 5.0 adds the `-Xlint` option to the compiler for spotting common code problems. For example, if you compile with the command

```
javac -Xlint:fallthrough
```

then the compiler reports missing `break` statements in `switch` statements. (The term "lint" originally described a tool for locating potential problems in C programs, and is now generically applied to tools that flag constructs that are questionable but not illegal.) The following options are available:

`-Xlint` or `-Xlint:all`	Carries out all checks
`-Xlint:deprecation`	Same as `-deprecation`, checks for deprecated methods
`-Xlint:fallthrough`	Checks for missing `break` statements in `switch` statements
`-Xlint:finally`	Warns about `finally` clauses that cannot complete normally
`-Xlint:none`	Carries out none of the checks
`-Xlint:path`	Checks that all directories on the class path and source path exist
`-Xlint:serial`	Warns about serializable classes without `serialVersionUID` (see Chapter 12)
`-Xlint:unchecked`	Warns of unsafe conversions between generic and raw types (see Chapter 13)

12. JDK 5.0 adds support for *monitoring and management* of Java applications, allowing the installation of agents in the virtual machine that track memory consumption, thread usage, class loading, and so on. This feature is particularly important for large and long-running Java programs such as application servers. As a demonstration of these capabilities, the JDK ships with a graphical tool called `jconsole` that displays statistics about the performance of a virtual machine (see Figure 11–4). To enable monitoring,

start the virtual machine with the `-Dcom.sun.management.jmxremote` option. Then find out the ID of the operating system process that runs the virtual machine. In UNIX/Linux, run the `ps` utility; in Windows, use the task manager. Then launch the `jconsole` program:

```
java -Dcom.sun.management.jmxremote MyProgram.java
jconsole processID
```

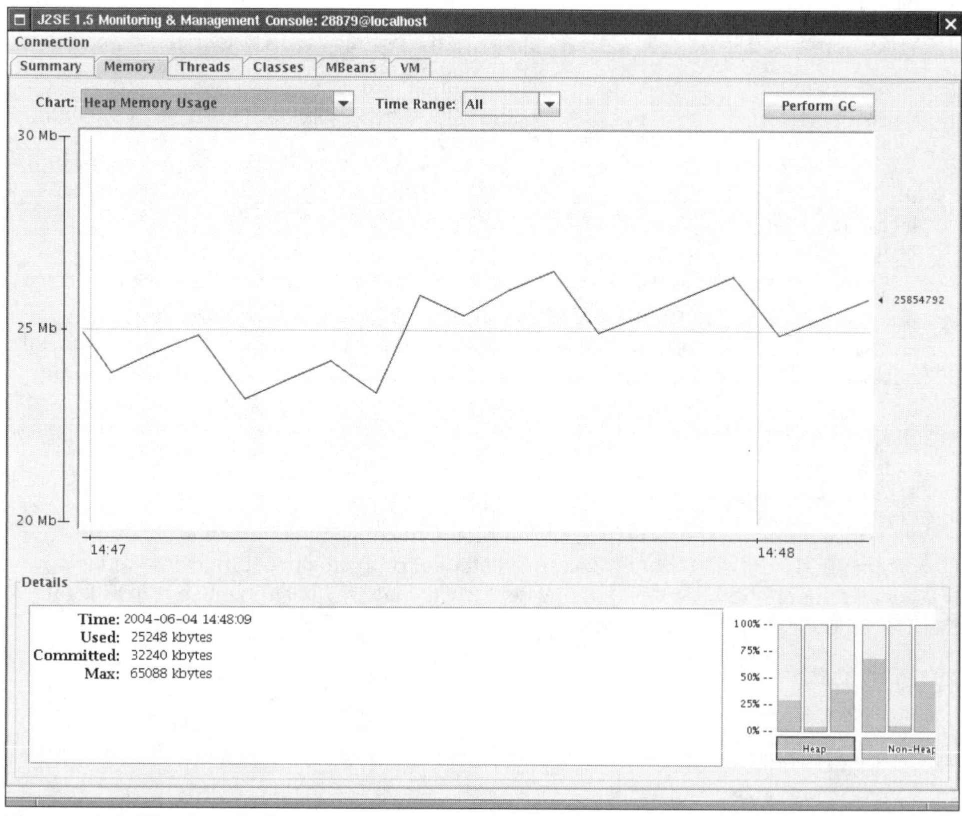

Figure 11–4: The `jconsole` Program

13. If you launch the Java virtual machine with the `-Xprof` flag, it runs a rudimentary *profiler* that keeps track of the methods in your code that were executed most often. The profiling information is sent to `System.out`. The output also tells you which methods were compiled by the just-in-time compiler.

CAUTION: The `-X` options of the compiler are not officially supported and may not be present in all versions of the JDK. Run `java -X` to get a listing of all nonstandard options.

Using a Console Window

If you run an applet inside a browser, you may not be able to see any messages that are sent to `System.out`. Most browsers will have some sort of Java Console window. (Check the help system for your browser.) For example, Netscape Navigator has one, as does Internet Explorer 4 and above. If you use the Java Plug-in, check the Show Java Console box in the configuration panel (see Chapter 10).

Moreover, the Java Console window has a set of scrollbars, so you can retrieve messages that have scrolled off the window. Windows users will find this a definite advantage over the DOS shell window in which the `System.out` output normally appears.

We give you a similar window class so you can enjoy the same benefit of seeing your debugging messages in a window when debugging a program. Figure 11–5 shows our `ConsoleWindow` class in action.

The class is easy to use. Simply call:

```
ConsoleWindow.init()
```

Then print to `System.out` or `System.err` in the normal way.

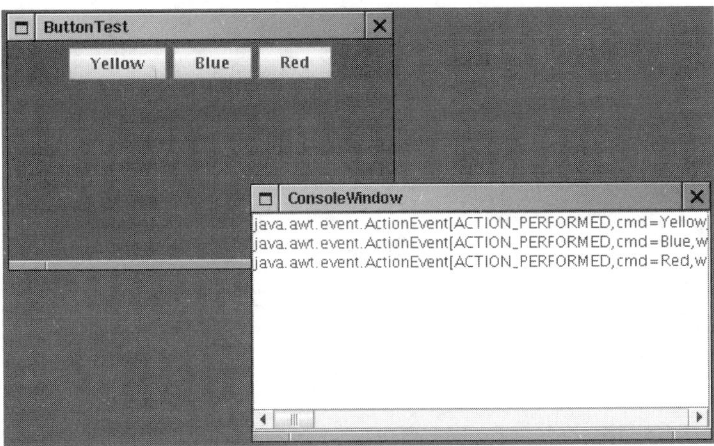

Figure 11–5: The console window

Example 11–5 lists the code for the `ConsoleWindow` class. As you can see, the class is quite simple. Messages are displayed in a `JTextArea` inside a `JScrollPane`. We call the `System.setOut` and `System.setErr` methods to set the output and error streams to a special stream that adds all messages to the text area.

Example 11–5: ConsoleWindow.java

```
import java.awt.*;
import java.awt.event.*;
import javax.swing.*;
import java.io.*;

/**
   A window that displays the bytes sent to System.out
   and System.err
*/
public class ConsoleWindow
{
   public static void init()
   {
      JFrame frame = new JFrame();
      frame.setTitle("ConsoleWindow");
      final JTextArea output = new JTextArea();
      output.setEditable(false);
      frame.add(new JScrollPane(output));
```

```
      frame.setSize(DEFAULT_WIDTH, DEFAULT_HEIGHT);
      frame.setLocation(DEFAULT_LEFT, DEFAULT_TOP);
      frame.setFocusableWindowState(false);
      frame.setVisible(true);

      // define a PrintStream that sends its bytes to the
      // output text area
      PrintStream consoleStream = new PrintStream(new
         OutputStream()
         {
            public void write(int b) {} // never called
            public void write(byte[] b, int off, int len)
            {
               output.append(new String(b, off, len));
            }
         });

      // set both System.out and System.err to that stream
      System.setOut(consoleStream);
      System.setErr(consoleStream);
   }

   public static final int DEFAULT_WIDTH = 300;
   public static final int DEFAULT_HEIGHT = 200;
   public static final int DEFAULT_LEFT = 200;
   public static final int DEFAULT_TOP = 200;
}
```

Tracing AWT Events

When you write a fancy user interface in Java, you need to know what events AWT sends to what components. Unfortunately, the AWT documentation is somewhat sketchy in this regard. For example, suppose you want to show hints in the status line when the user moves the mouse over different parts of the screen. The AWT generates mouse and focus events that you may be able to trap.

We give you a useful EventTrace class to spy on these events. It prints out all event handling methods and their parameters. See Figure 11–6 for a display of the traced events.

To spy on messages, add the component whose events you want to trace to an event tracer:

```
EventTracer tracer = new EventTracer();
tracer.add(frame);
```

That prints a textual description of all events, like this:

```
public abstract void java.awt.event.MouseListener.mouseExited(java.awt.event.MouseEvent):
java.awt.event.MouseEvent[MOUSE_EXITED,(408,14),button=0,clickCount=0] on javax.swing.JButton[,0,345,400x25,...]
public abstract void java.awt.event.FocusListener.focusLost(java.awt.event.FocusEvent):
java.awt.event.FocusEvent[FOCUS_LOST,temporary,opposite=null] on javax.swing.JButton[,0,345,400x25,...]
```

You may want to capture this output in a file or a console window, as explained in the preceding sections.

Example 11–6 is the EventTracer class. The idea behind the class is easy even if the implementation is a bit mysterious.

1. When you add a component to the event tracer in the add method, the JavaBeans introspection class analyzes the component for methods of the form void addXxxListener(XxxEvent). (See Chapter 8 of Volume 2 for more information on JavaBeans.) For each matching method, an EventSetDescriptor is generated. We pass each descriptor to the addListener method.

2. If the component is a container, we enumerate its components and recursively call `add` for each of them.
3. The `addListener` method is called with two parameters: the component on whose events we want to spy and the event set descriptor. The `getListenerType` method of the `EventSetDescriptor` class returns a `Class` object that describes the event listener interface such as `ActionListener` or `ChangeListener`. We create a proxy object for that interface. The proxy handler simply prints the name and event parameter of the invoked event method. The `getAddListenerMethod` method of the `EventSetDescriptor` class returns a `Method` object that we use to add the proxy object as the event listener to the component.

   This program is a good example of the power of the reflection mechanism. We don't have to hardwire the fact that the `JButton` class has a method `addActionListener` whereas a `JSlider` has a method `addChangeListener`. The reflection mechanism discovers these facts for us.

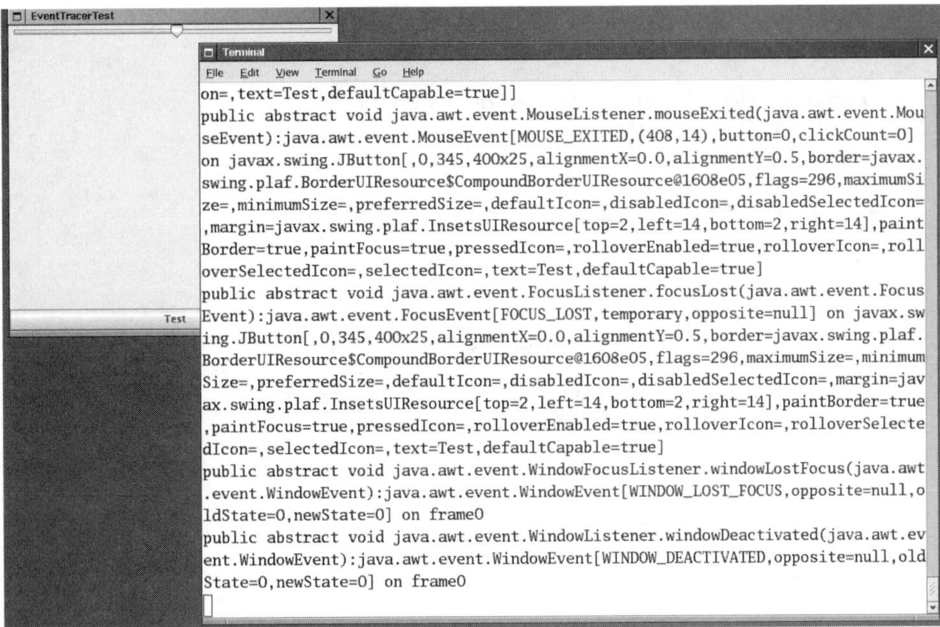

Figure 11–6: The `EventTracer` class at work

NOTE: The proxy mechanism makes this program dramatically easier. In prior editions of this book, we needed to define a listener that simultaneously implements the `MouseListener`, `ComponentListener`, `FocusListener`, `KeyListener`, `ContainerListener`, `WindowListener`, `TextListener`, `AdjustmentListener`, `ActionListener`, and `ItemListener` interfaces and a couple of dozen methods that print the event parameter. The proxy mechanism is explained at the end of Chapter 6.

Example 11–7 tests the event tracer. The program displays a frame with a button and a slider and traces the events that these components generate.

Example 11–6: EventTracer.java

```
import java.awt.*;
import java.awt.event.*;
import java.beans.*;
```

```
import java.lang.reflect.*;

public class EventTracer
{
   public EventTracer()
   {
      // the handler for all event proxies
      handler = new
         InvocationHandler()
         {
            public Object invoke(Object proxy, Method method, Object[] args)
            {
               System.out.println(method + ":" + args[0]);
               return null;
            }
         };
   }

   /**
      Adds event tracers for all events to which this component
      and its children can listen
      @param c a component
   */
   public void add(Component c)
   {
      try
      {
         // get all events to which this component can listen
         BeanInfo info = Introspector.getBeanInfo(c.getClass());

         EventSetDescriptor[] eventSets = info.getEventSetDescriptors();
         for (EventSetDescriptor eventSet : eventSets)
            addListener(c, eventSet);
      }
      catch (IntrospectionException e) {}
      // ok not to add listeners if exception is thrown

      if (c instanceof Container)
      {
         // get all children and call add recursively
         for (Component comp : ((Container) c).getComponents())
            add(comp);
      }
   }

   /**
      Add a listener to the given event set
      @param c a component
      @param eventSet a descriptor of a listener interface
   */
   public void addListener(Component c, EventSetDescriptor eventSet)
   {
      // make proxy object for this listener type and route all calls to the handler
      Object proxy = Proxy.newProxyInstance(null,
         new Class[] { eventSet.getListenerType() }, handler);

```

```
      // add the proxy as a listener to the component
      Method addListenerMethod = eventSet.getAddListenerMethod();
      try
      {
         addListenerMethod.invoke(c, proxy);
      }
      catch(InvocationTargetException e) {}
      catch(IllegalAccessException e) {}
      // ok not to add listener if exception is thrown
   }

   private InvocationHandler handler;
}
```

Example 11–7: EventTracerTest.java

```
import java.awt.*;
import java.awt.event.*;
import javax.swing.*;

public class EventTracerTest
{
   public static void main(String[] args)
   {
      JFrame frame = new EventTracerFrame();
      frame.setDefaultCloseOperation(JFrame.EXIT_ON_CLOSE);
      frame.setVisible(true);
   }
}

class EventTracerFrame extends JFrame
{
   public EventTracerFrame()
   {
      setTitle("EventTracerTest");
      setSize(DEFAULT_WIDTH, DEFAULT_HEIGHT);

      // add a slider and a button
      add(new JSlider(), BorderLayout.NORTH);
      add(new JButton("Test"), BorderLayout.SOUTH);

      // trap all events of components inside the frame
      EventTracer tracer = new EventTracer();
      tracer.add(this);
   }

   public static final int DEFAULT_WIDTH = 400;
   public static final int DEFAULT_HEIGHT = 400;
}
```

Letting the AWT Robot Do the Work

Version 1.3 of the Java 2 Platform adds a `Robot` class that you can use to send keystrokes and mouse clicks to any AWT program. This class is intended for automatic testing of user interfaces.

To get a robot, you need to first get a `GraphicsDevice` object. You get the default screen device through the sequence of calls:

```
GraphicsEnvironment environment = GraphicsEnvironment.getLocalGraphicsEnvironment();
GraphicsDevice screen = environment.getDefaultScreenDevice();
```

Then you construct a robot as:

```
Robot robot = new Robot(screen);
```

To send a keystroke, tell the robot to simulate a key press and a key release:

```
robot.keyPress(KeyEvent.VK_TAB);
robot.keyRelease(KeyEvent.VK_TAB);
```

For a mouse click, you first need to move the mouse and then press and release a button:

```
robot.mouseMove(x, y); // x and y are absolute screen pixel coordinates.
robot.mousePress(InputEvent.BUTTON1_MASK);
robot.mouseRelease(InputEvent.BUTTON1_MASK);
```

The idea is that you simulate key and mouse input and afterwards take a screen snapshot to see whether the application did what it was supposed to. You capture the screen with the `createScreenCapture` method:

```
Rectangle rect = new Rectangle(x, y, width, height);
BufferedImage image = robot.createScreenCapture(rect);
```

The rectangle coordinates also refer to absolute screen pixels.

Finally, you usually want to add a small delay between robot instructions so that the application can catch up. Use the `delay` method and give it the number of milliseconds to delay. For example:

```
robot.delay(1000); // delay by 1000 milliseconds
```

The program in Example 11–8 shows how you can use the robot. A robot tests the button test program that you saw in Chapter 8. First, pressing the space bar activates the leftmost button. Then the robot waits for two seconds so that you can see what it has done. After the delay, the robot simulates the tab key and another space bar press to click on the next button. Finally, we simulate a mouse click on the third button. (You may need to adjust the `x` and `y` coordinates of the program to actually press the button.) The program ends by taking a screen capture and displaying it in another frame (see Figure 11–7).

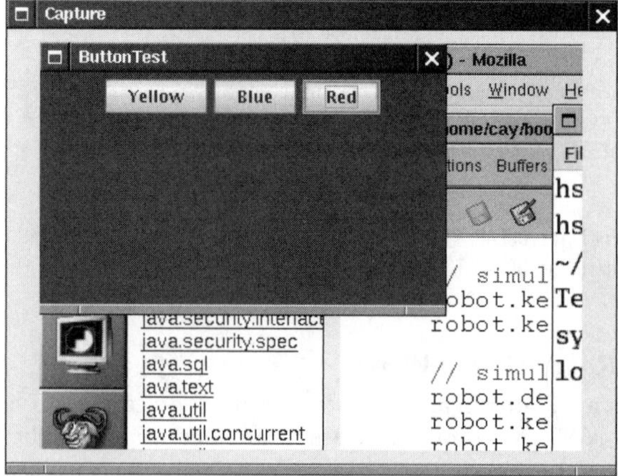

Figure 11–7: Capturing the screen with the AWT robot

As you can see from this example, the Robot class is not by itself suitable for convenient user interface testing. Instead, it is a basic building block that can be a foundational part of a testing tool. A professional testing tool can capture, store, and replay user interaction scenarios and find out the screen locations of the components so that mouse clicks aren't guesswork. At the time of this writing, the robot is brand new and we are not aware of any sophisticated testing tools for Java user interfaces. We expect these tools to materialize in the future.

Example 11–8: RobotTest.java

```
import java.awt.*;
import java.awt.event.*;
import java.awt.image.*;
import javax.swing.*;

public class RobotTest
{
   public static void main(String[] args)
   {
      // make frame with a button panel

      ButtonFrame frame = new ButtonFrame();
      frame.setDefaultCloseOperation(JFrame.EXIT_ON_CLOSE);
      frame.setVisible(true);

      // attach a robot to the screen device

      GraphicsEnvironment environment = GraphicsEnvironment.getLocalGraphicsEnvironment();
      GraphicsDevice screen = environment.getDefaultScreenDevice();

      try
      {
         Robot robot = new Robot(screen);
         run(robot);
      }
      catch (AWTException e)
      {
         e.printStackTrace();
      }
   }

   /**
      Runs a sample test procedure
      @param robot the robot attached to the screen device
   */
   public static void run(Robot robot)
   {
      // simulate a space bar press
      robot.keyPress(' ');
      robot.keyRelease(' ');

      // simulate a tab key followed by a space
      robot.delay(2000);
      robot.keyPress(KeyEvent.VK_TAB);
      robot.keyRelease(KeyEvent.VK_TAB);
      robot.keyPress(' ');
      robot.keyRelease(' ');

```

```
      // simulate a mouse click over the rightmost button
      robot.delay(2000);
      robot.mouseMove(200, 50);
      robot.mousePress(InputEvent.BUTTON1_MASK);
      robot.mouseRelease(InputEvent.BUTTON1_MASK);

      // capture the screen and show the resulting image
      robot.delay(2000);
      BufferedImage image = robot.createScreenCapture(new Rectangle(0, 0, 400, 300));

      ImageFrame frame = new ImageFrame(image);
      frame.setVisible(true);
   }
}

/**
   A frame to display a captured image
*/
class ImageFrame extends JFrame
{
   /**
      @param image the image to display
   */
   public ImageFrame(Image image)
   {
      setTitle("Capture");
      setSize(DEFAULT_WIDTH, DEFAULT_HEIGHT);

      JLabel label = new JLabel(new ImageIcon(image));
      add(label);
   }

   public static final int DEFAULT_WIDTH = 450;
   public static final int DEFAULT_HEIGHT = 350;
}
```

API **java.awt.GraphicsEnvironment 1.2**

- `static GraphicsEnvironment getLocalGraphicsEnvironment()`
  returns the local graphics environment.
- `GraphicsDevice getDefaultScreenDevice()`
  returns the default screen device. Note that computers with multiple monitors have one graphics device per screen—use the `getScreenDevices` method to obtain an array of all screen devices.

API **java.awt.Robot 1.3**

- `Robot(GraphicsDevice device)`
  constructs a robot that can interact with the given device.
- `void keyPress(int key)`
- `void keyRelease(int key)`
  simulate a key press or release.

  Parameters: `key` The key code. See the `KeyStroke` class for more information on key codes

- `void mouseMove(int x, int y)`
  simulates a mouse move.

  Parameters: `x, y` The mouse position in absolute pixel coordinates

- `void mousePress(int eventMask)`
- `void mouseRelease(int eventMask)`
  simulate a mouse button press or release.

  Parameters: `eventMask` The event mask describing the mouse buttons. See the `InputEvent` class for more information on event masks

- `void delay(int milliseconds)`
  delays the robot for the given number of milliseconds.
- `BufferedImage createScreenCapture(Rectangle rect)`
  captures a portion of the screen.

  Parameters: `rect` The rectangle to be captured, in absolute pixel coordinates

Using a Debugger

Debugging with print statements is not one of life's more joyful experiences. You constantly find yourself adding and removing the statements, then recompiling the program. Using a debugger is better. A debugger runs your program in full motion until it reaches a breakpoint, and then you can look at everything that interests you.

The JDB Debugger

The JDK includes JDB, an extremely rudimentary command-line debugger. Its user interface is so minimal that you will not want to use it except as a last resort. It really is more a proof of concept than a usable tool. We nevertheless briefly introduce it because there are situations in which it is better than no debugger at all. Of course, many Java programming environments have far more convenient debuggers. The main principles of all debuggers are the same, and you may want to use the example in this section to learn to use the debugger in your environment instead of JDB.

Examples 11–9 through 11–11 show a deliberately corrupted version of the `ButtonTest` program from Chapter 8. (We broke up the program and placed each class into a separate file because some debuggers have trouble dealing with multiple classes in the same file.)

When you click on any of the buttons, nothing happens. Look at the source code—button clicks are supposed to set the background color to the color specified by the button name.

Example 11–9: BuggyButtonTest.java

```
import javax.swing.*;

public class BuggyButtonTest
{
  public static void main(String[] args)
  {
    BuggyButtonFrame frame = new BuggyButtonFrame();
    frame.setDefaultCloseOperation(JFrame.EXIT_ON_CLOSE);
    frame.setVisible(true);
  }
}
```

Example 11–10: BuggyButtonFrame.java

```
import java.awt.*;
import javax.swing.*;

public class BuggyButtonFrame extends JFrame
{
   public BuggyButtonFrame()
   {
      setTitle("BuggyButtonTest");
      setSize(DEFAULT_WIDTH, DEFAULT_HEIGHT);

      // add panel to frame

      BuggyButtonPanel panel = new BuggyButtonPanel();
      add(panel);
   }

   public static final int DEFAULT_WIDTH = 300;
   public static final int DEFAULT_HEIGHT = 200;
}
```

Example 11–11: BuggyButtonPanel.java

```
import java.awt.*;
import java.awt.event.*;
import javax.swing.*;

class BuggyButtonPanel extends JPanel
{
   public BuggyButtonPanel()
   {
      ActionListener listener = new ButtonListener();

      JButton yellowButton = new JButton("Yellow");
      add(yellowButton);
      yellowButton.addActionListener(listener);

      JButton blueButton = new JButton("Blue");
      add(blueButton);
      blueButton.addActionListener(listener);

      JButton redButton = new JButton("Red");
      add(redButton);
      redButton.addActionListener(listener);
   }

   private class ButtonListener implements ActionListener
   {
      public void actionPerformed(ActionEvent event)
      {
         String arg = event.getActionCommand();
         if (arg.equals("yellow"))
            setBackground(Color.yellow);
         else if (arg.equals("blue"))
            setBackground(Color.blue);
         else if (arg.equals("red"))
```

```
            setBackground(Color.red);
        }
    }
}
```

In a program this short, you may be able to find the bug just by reading the source code. Let us pretend that scanning the source code for errors is not practical. Here is how you can run the debugger to locate the error.

To use JDB, you must first compile your program with the `-g` option, for example:

```
javac -g BuggyButtonTest.java BuggyButtonFrame.java BuggyButtonPanel.java
```

When you compile with this option, the compiler adds the names of local variables and other debugging information into the class files. Then you launch the debugger:

```
jdb BuggyButtonTest
```

Once you launch the debugger, you will see a display that looks something like this:

```
Initializing jdb...
>
```

The > prompt indicates the debugger is waiting for a command. Table 11–4 shows all the debugger commands. Items enclosed in [...] are optional, and the suffix (s) means that you can supply one or more arguments separated by spaces.

Table 11–4: Debugging Commands

`threads` [*threadgroup*]	Lists threads
`thread` *thread_id*	Sets default thread
`suspend` [*thread_id(s)*]	Suspends threads (default: `all`)
`resume` [*thread_id(s)*]	Resumes threads (default: `all`)
`where` [*thread_id*] or `all`	Dumps a thread's stack
`wherei` [*thread_id*] or `all`	Dumps a thread's stack and program counter info
`threadgroups`	Lists thread groups
`threadgroup` *name*	Sets current thread group
`print` *name(s)*	Prints object or field
`dump` *name(s)*	Prints all object information
`locals`	Prints all current local variables
`classes`	Lists currently known classes
`methods` *class*	Lists a class's methods
`stop in` *class.method*	Sets a breakpoint in a method
`stop at` *class:line*	Sets a breakpoint at a line
`up` [*n*]	Moves up a thread's stack
`down` [*n*]	Moves down a thread's stack
`clear` *class:line*	Clears a breakpoint
`step`	Executes the current line, stepping inside calls
`stepi`	Executes the current instruction
`step up`	Executes until the end of the current method
`next`	Executes the current line, stepping over calls
`cont`	Continues execution from breakpoint
`catch` *class*	Breaks for the specified exception
`ignore` *class*	Ignores the specified exception
`list` [*line*]	Prints source code

Table 11–4: Debugging Commands (continued)

`use` [*path*]	Displays or changes the source path
`memory`	Reports memory usage
`gc`	Frees unused objects
`load` *class*	Loads Java class to be debugged
`run` [*class* [*args*]]	Starts execution of a loaded Java class
`!!`	Repeats last command
`help` (or `?`)	Lists commands
`exit` (or `quit`)	Exits debugger

We cover only the most useful JDB commands in this section. The basic idea, though, is simple: you set one or more breakpoints, then run the program. When the program reaches one of the breakpoints you set, it stops. You can inspect the values of the local variables to see if they are what they are supposed to be.

To set a breakpoint, use

```
stop in class.method
```

or the command

```
stop at class:line
```

For example, let us set a breakpoint in the `actionPerformed` method of `BuggyButtonTest`. To do this, enter

```
stop in BuggyButtonPanel$ButtonListener.actionPerformed
```

Now we want to run the program up to the breakpoint, so enter

```
run
```

The program will run, but the breakpoint won't be hit until Java starts processing code in the `actionPerformed` method. For this, click on the Yellow button. The debugger breaks at the *start* of the `actionPerformed` method. You'll see:

```
Breakpoint hit: thread="AWT-EventQueue-0", BuggyButtonPanel$ButtonListener.actionPerformed(),
line=28, bci=0
  28         String arg = event.getActionCommand();
```

The `list` command lets you find out where you are. The debugger will show you the current line and a few lines above and below. You also see the line numbers. For example:

```
24      private class ButtonListener implements ActionListener
25      {
26         public void actionPerformed(ActionEvent event)
27         {
28=>           String arg = event.getActionCommand();
29            if (arg.equals("yellow"))
30               setBackground(Color.yellow);
31            else if (arg.equals("blue"))
32               setBackground(Color.blue);
33            else if (arg.equals("red"))
```

Type `locals` to see all local variables. For example,

```
Method arguments:
  event = instance of java.awt.event.ActionEvent(id=698)
Local variables:
```

For more detail, use

```
dump variable
```

For example,

```
dump event
```

displays all instance fields of the evt variable.

```
event = instance of java.awt.event.ActionEvent(id=698) {
   SHIFT_MASK: 1
   CTRL_MASK: 2
   META_MASK: 4
   ALT_MASK: 8
   ACTION_FIRST: 1001
   ACTION_LAST: 1001
   ACTION_PERFORMED: 1001
   actionCommand: "Yellow"
   modifiers: 0
   serialVersionUID: -7671078796273832149
   . . .
```

There are two basic commands to single-step through a program. The step command steps into every method call. The next command goes to the next line without stepping inside any further method calls. Type next twice and then type list to see where you are.

The program stops in line 31.

```
27          {
28             String arg = event.getActionCommand();
29             if (arg.equals("yellow"))
30                setBackground(Color.yellow);
31=>           else if (arg.equals("blue"))
32                setBackground(Color.blue);
33             else if (arg.equals("red"))
34                setBackground(Color.red);
35          }
```

That is not what should have happened. The program was supposed to call setColor(Color.yellow) and then exit the method.

Dump the arg variable.

```
arg = "Yellow"
```

Now you can see what happened. The value of arg was "Yellow", with an uppercase Y, but the comparison tested

```
if (arg.equals("yellow"))
```

with a lowercase y. Mystery solved.

To quit the debugger, type:

```
quit
```

As you can see from this example, the jdb debugger can be used to find an error, but the command-line interface is very inconvenient. Remember to use list and locals whenever you are confused about where you are. But if you have any choice at all, use a better debugger for serious debugging work.

The Eclipse Debugger

Eclipse has a modern and convenient debugger that has many of the amenities that you would expect. In particular, you can set breakpoints, inspect variables, and single-step through a program.

To set a breakpoint, move the cursor to the desired line and select Run -> Toggle Line Breakpoint from the menu. The breakpoint line is highlighted (see Figure 11–8).

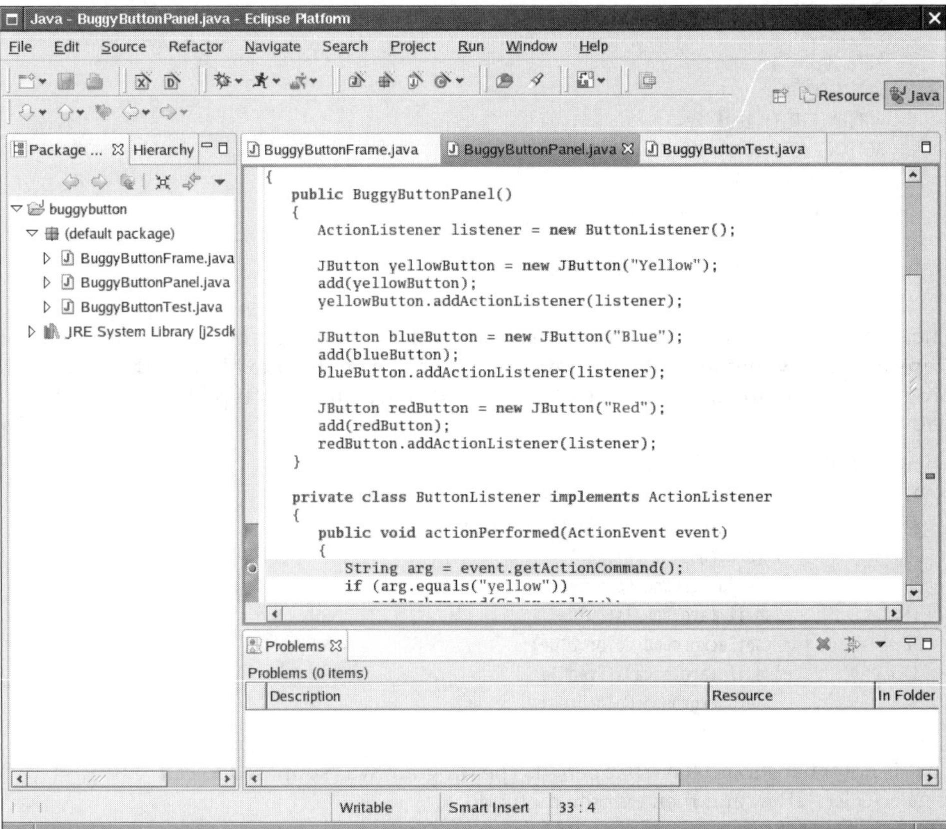

Figure 11–8: Breakpoints in the Eclipse debugger

To start debugging, select Run -> Debug As -> Java Application from the menu. The program starts running. Set a breakpoint in the first line of the `actionPerformed` method.

When the debugger stops at a breakpoint, you can see the call stack and the local variables (see Figure 11–9).

To single-step through the application, use the Run -> Step into (F5) or Run -> Step over (F6) commands. In our example, press the F6 key twice to see how the program skips over the `setBackground(Color.yellow)` command. Then watch the value of `arg` to see the reason (see Figure 11–10).

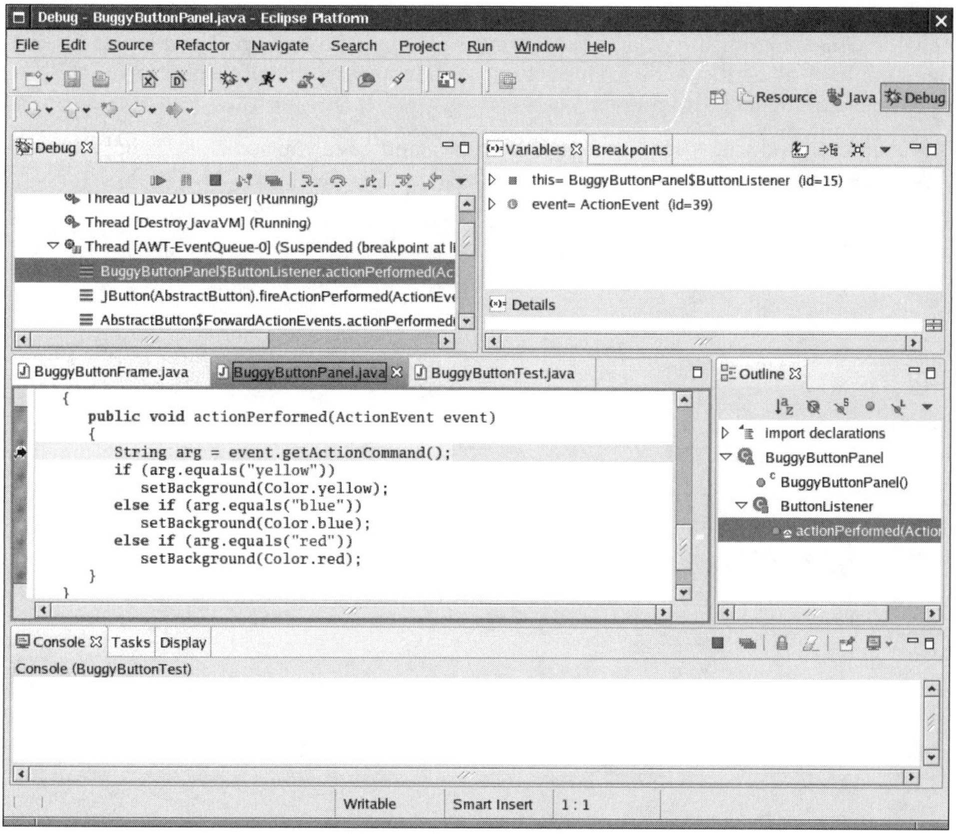

Figure 11–9: Stopping at a breakpoint

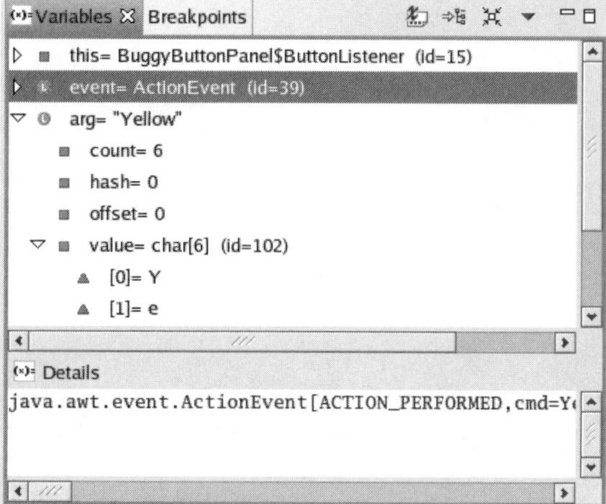

Figure 11–10: Inspecting variables

As you can see, the Eclipse debugger is much easier to use than JDB because you have visual feedback to indicate where you are in the program. Setting breakpoints and inspecting variables is also much easier. This is typical of debuggers that are a part of an integrated development environment.

This chapter introduced you to exception handling and gave you some useful hints for testing and debugging. The next chapter covers streams.

Chapter 12

Streams and Files

- STREAMS
- THE COMPLETE STREAM ZOO
- ZIP FILE STREAMS
- USE OF STREAMS
- OBJECT STREAMS
- FILE MANAGEMENT
- NEW I/O
- REGULAR EXPRESSIONS

In this chapter, we cover the methods for handling files and directories as well as the methods for actually writing and reading data. This chapter also shows you the object serialization mechanism that lets you store objects as easily as you can store text or numeric data. Next, we turn to several improvements that were made in the "new I/O" package `java.nio`, introduced in JDK 1.4 We finish the chapter with a discussion of regular expressions, even though they are not actually related to streams and files. We couldn't find a better place to handle that topic, and apparently neither could the Java team—the regular expression API specification was attached to the specification request for the "new I/O" features of JDK 1.4.

Streams

Input/output techniques are not particularly exciting, but without the ability to read and write data, your programs are severely limited. This chapter is about how to get input from any source of data that can send out a sequence of bytes and how to send output to any destination that can receive a sequence of bytes. These sources and destinations of byte sequences can be—and often are—files, but they can also be network connections and even blocks of memory. There is a nice payback to keeping this generality in mind: for example, information stored in files and information retrieved from a network connection are handled in *essentially the same way.* (See Volume 2 for more information about programming with networks.) Of course, while data are always *ultimately* stored as a sequence of bytes, it is often more convenient to think of data as having some higher-level structure such as being a sequence of characters or objects. For that reason, we dispense with low-level input/output quickly and focus on higher-level facilities for the majority of the chapter.

In the Java programming language, an object from which we can read a sequence of bytes is called an *input stream.* An object to which we can write a sequence of bytes is called an *output stream.* These are specified in the abstract classes `InputStream` and `OutputStream`. Because byte-oriented streams are inconvenient for processing information stored in Unicode (recall that Unicode uses two bytes per code unit), there is a separate hierarchy of classes for processing Unicode characters that inherit from the abstract `Reader` and `Writer` classes. These classes have read and write operations that are based on two-byte Unicode code units rather than on single-byte characters.

You saw abstract classes in Chapter 5. Recall that the point of an abstract class is to provide a mechanism for factoring out the common behavior of classes to a higher level. This leads to cleaner code and makes the inheritance tree easier to understand. The same game is at work with input and output in the Java programming language.

As you will soon see, Java derives from these four abstract classes a zoo of concrete classes. You can visit almost any conceivable input/output creature in this zoo.

Reading and Writing Bytes

The `InputStream` class has an abstract method:

```
abstract int read()
```

This method reads one byte and returns the byte that was read, or –1 if it encounters the end of the input source. The designer of a concrete input stream class overrides this method to provide useful functionality. For example, in the `FileInputStream` class, this method reads one byte from a file. `System.in` is a predefined object of a subclass of `InputStream` that allows you to read information from the keyboard.

The `InputStream` class also has nonabstract methods to read an array of bytes or to skip a number of bytes. These methods call the abstract `read` method, so subclasses need to override only one method.

Similarly, the `OutputStream` class defines the abstract method

```
abstract void write(int b)
```

which writes one byte to an output location.

Both the `read` and `write` methods can *block* a thread until the byte is actually read or written. This means that if the stream cannot immediately be read from or written to (usually because of a busy network connection), Java suspends the thread containing this call. This gives other threads the chance to do useful work while the method is waiting for the stream to again become available. (We discuss threads in depth in Volume 2.)

The `available` method lets you check the number of bytes that are currently available for reading. This means a fragment like the following is unlikely to ever block:

```
int bytesAvailable = in.available();
if (bytesAvailable > 0)
{
   byte[] data = new byte[bytesAvailable];
   in.read(data);
}
```

When you have finished reading or writing to a stream, close it by calling the `close` method. This call frees up operating system resources that are in limited supply. If an application opens too many streams without closing them, system resources may become depleted. Closing an output stream also *flushes* the buffer used for the output stream: any characters

that were temporarily placed in a buffer so that they could be delivered as a larger packet are sent off. In particular, if you do not close a file, the last packet of bytes may never be delivered. You can also manually flush the output with the `flush` method.

Even if a stream class provides concrete methods to work with the raw `read` and `write` functions, Java programmers rarely use them because programs rarely need to read and write streams of bytes. The data that you are interested in probably contain numbers, strings, and objects.

Java gives you many stream classes derived from the basic `InputStream` and `OutputStream` classes that let you work with data in the forms that you usually use rather than at the low byte-level.

java.io.InputStream 1.0

- `abstract int read()`
  reads a byte of data and returns the byte read. The `read` method returns a –1 at the end of the stream.
- `int read(byte[] b)`
  reads into an array of bytes and returns the actual number of bytes read, or –1 at the end of the stream. The `read` method reads at most `b.length` bytes.
- `int read(byte[] b, int off, int len)`
  reads into an array of bytes. The `read` method returns the actual number of bytes read, or –1 at the end of the stream.

Parameters:	`b`	The array into which the data is read
	`off`	The offset into `b` where the first bytes should be placed
	`len`	The maximum number of bytes to read

- `long skip(long n)`
  skips `n` bytes in the input stream. Returns the actual number of bytes skipped (which may be less than `n` if the end of the stream was encountered).
- `int available()`
  returns the number of bytes available without blocking. (Recall that blocking means that the current thread loses its turn.)
- `void close()`
  closes the input stream.
- `void mark(int readlimit)`
  puts a marker at the current position in the input stream. (Not all streams support this feature.) If more than `readlimit` bytes have been read from the input stream, then the stream is allowed to forget the marker.
- `void reset()`
  returns to the last marker. Subsequent calls to `read` reread the bytes. If there is no current marker, then the stream is not reset.
- `boolean markSupported()`
  returns `true` if the stream supports marking.

java.io.OutputStream 1.0

- `abstract void write(int n)`
  writes a byte of data.
- `void write(byte[] b)`
  writes all bytes in the array `b`.

- `void write(byte[] b, int off, int len)`
  writes a range of bytes in the array `b`.

Parameters:	`b`	The array from which to write the data
	`off`	The offset into `b` to the first byte that will be written
	`len`	The number of bytes to write

- `void close()`
  flushes and closes the output stream.
- `void flush()`
  flushes the output stream, that is, sends any buffered data to its destination.

The Complete Stream Zoo

Unlike C, which gets by just fine with a single type `FILE*`, Java has a whole zoo of more than 60 (!) different stream types (see Figures 12–1 and 12–2). Library designers claim that there is a good reason to give users a wide choice of stream types: it is supposed to reduce programming errors. For example, in C, some people think it is a common mistake to send output to a file that was open only for reading. (Well, it is not actually that common.) Naturally, if you do this, the output is ignored at run time. In Java and C++, the compiler catches that kind of mistake because an `InputStream` (Java) or `istream` (C++) has no methods for output.

(We would argue that in C++, and even more so in Java, the main tool that the stream interface designers have against programming errors is intimidation. The sheer complexity of the stream libraries keeps programmers on their toes.)

C++ NOTE: ANSI C++ gives you more stream types than you want, such as `istream`, `ostream`, `iostream`, `ifstream`, `ofstream`, `fstream`, `wistream`, `wifstream`, `istrstream`, and so on (18 classes in all). But Java really goes overboard with streams and gives you separate classes for selecting buffering, lookahead, random access, text formatting, and binary data.

Let us divide the animals in the stream class zoo by how they are used. Four abstract classes are at the base of the zoo: `InputStream`, `OutputStream`, `Reader`, and `Writer`. You do not make objects of these types, but other methods can return them. For example, as you saw in Chapter 10, the `URL` class has the method `openStream` that returns an `InputStream`. You then use this `InputStream` object to read from the URL. As we said, the `InputStream` and `OutputStream` classes let you read and write only individual bytes and arrays of bytes; they have no methods to read and write strings and numbers. You need more capable child classes for this. For example, `DataInputStream` and `DataOutputStream` let you read and write all the basic Java types.

For Unicode text, on the other hand, as we said, you use classes that descend from `Reader` and `Writer`. The basic methods of the `Reader` and `Writer` classes are similar to the ones for `InputStream` and `OutputStream`.

```
abstract int read()
abstract void write(int b)
```

They work just as the comparable methods do in the `InputStream` and `OutputStream` classes except, of course, the `read` method returns either a Unicode code unit (as an integer between 0 and 65535) or –1 when you have reached the end of the file.

Finally, there are streams that do useful stuff, for example, the `ZipInputStream` and `ZipOutputStream` that let you read and write files in the familiar ZIP compression format.

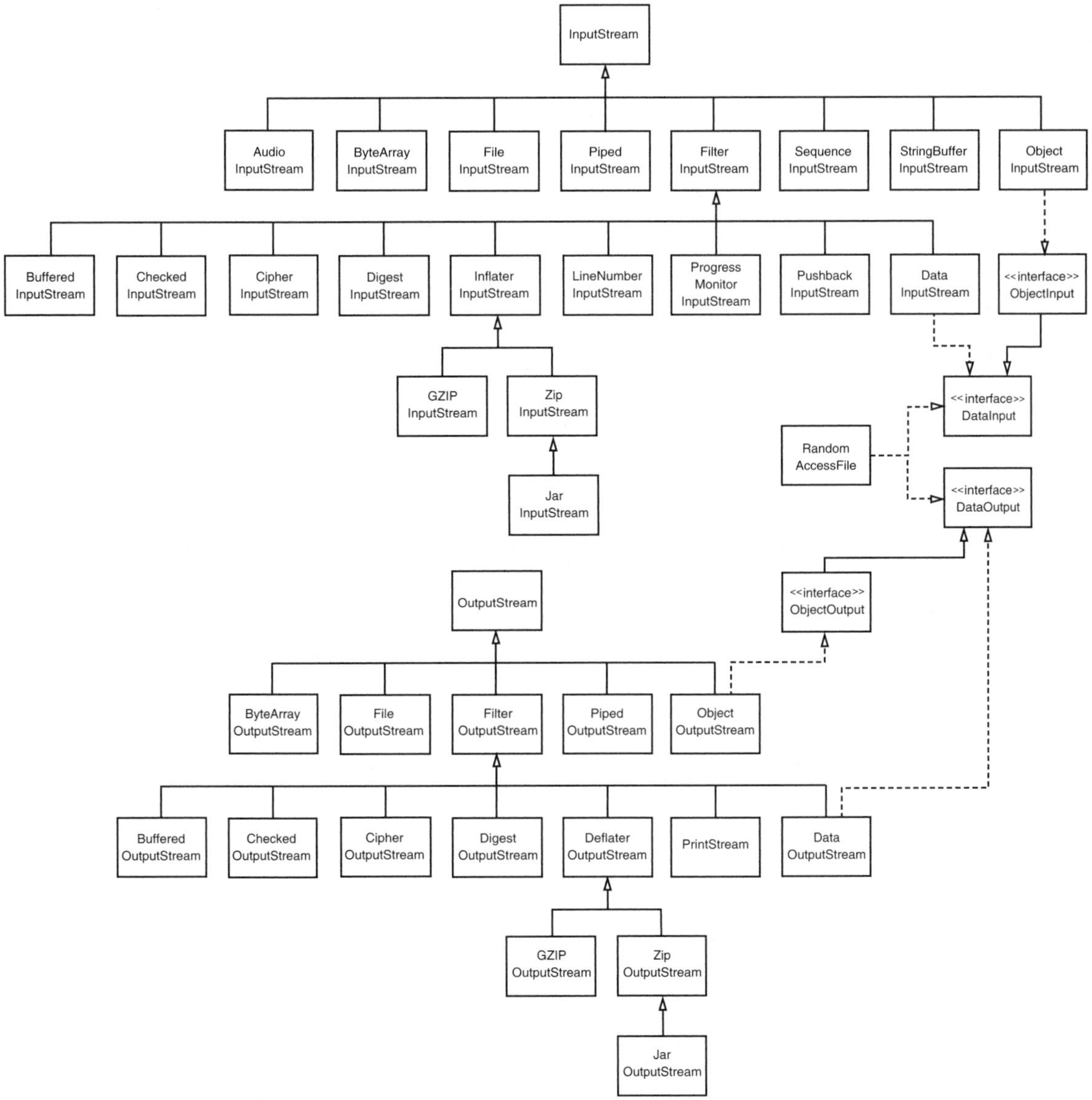

Figure 12–1: Input and output stream hierarchy

Moreover, JDK 5.0 introduces four new interfaces: `Closeable`, `Flushable`, `Readable`, and `Appendable` (see Figure 12–3). The first two interfaces are very simple, with methods

```
void close() throws IOException
```

and

```
void flush()
```

respectively. The classes `InputStream`, `OutputStream`, `Reader`, and `Writer` all implement the `Closeable` interface. `OutputStream` and `Writer` implement the `Flushable` interface.

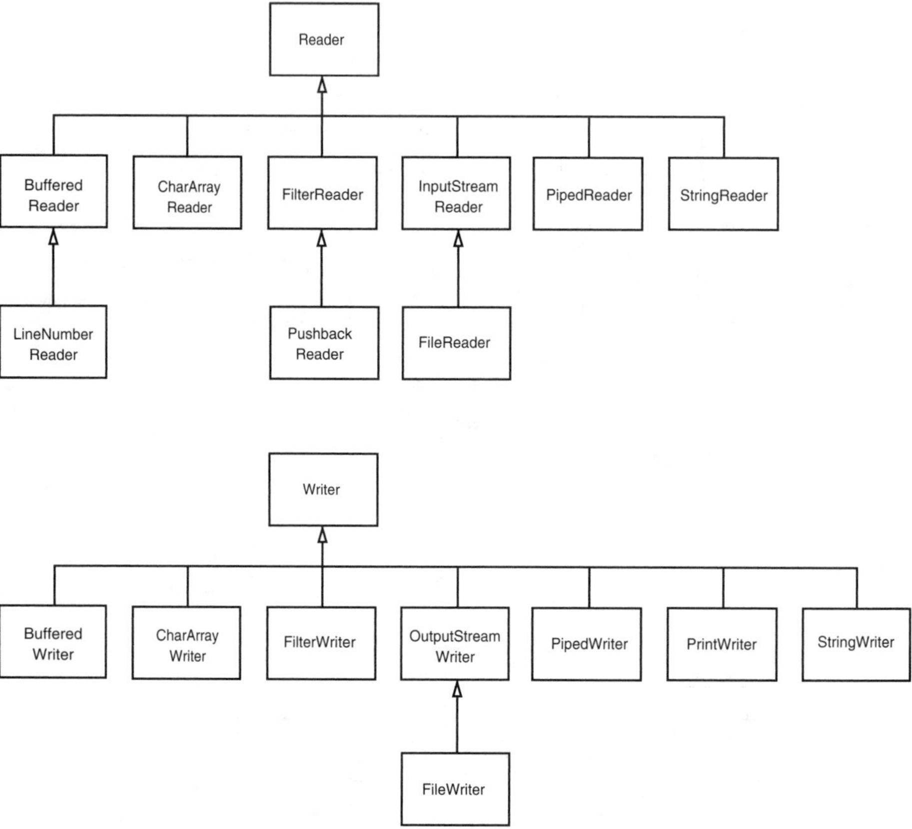

Figure 12–2: Reader and writer hierarchy

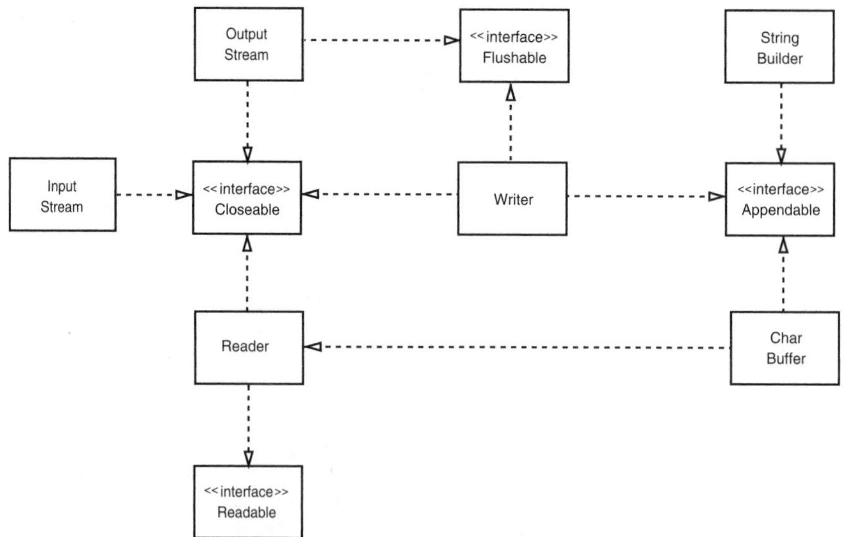

Figure 12–3: The `Closeable`, `Flushable`, `Readable`, and `Appendable` interfaces

The Readable interface has a single method

```
int read(CharBuffer cb)
```

The CharBuffer class has methods for sequential and random read/write access. It represents an in-memory buffer or a memory-mapped file (see page 694).

The Appendable interface has two methods, for appending single characters and character sequences:

```
Appendable append(char c)
Appendable append(CharSequence s)
```

The CharSequence type is yet another interface, describing minimal properties of a sequence of char values. It is implemented by String, CharBuffer, and StringBuilder/StringBuffer (see page 656).

Of the stream zoo classes, only Writer implements Appendable.

java.io.Closeable 5.0

- `void close()`
  closes this Closeable. This method may throw an IOException.

java.io.Flushable 5.0

- `void flush()`
  flushes this Flushable.

java.lang.Readable 5.0

- `int read(CharBuffer cb)`
  attempts to read as many char values into cb as it can hold. Returns the number of values read, or -1 if no further values are available from this Readable.

java.lang.Appendable 5.0

- `Appendable append(char c)`
  appends the code unit c to this Appendable; returns this.
- `Appendable append(CharSequence cs)`
  appends all code units in cs to this Appendable; returns this.

java.lang.CharSequence 1.4

- `char charAt(int index)`
  returns the code unit at the given index.
- `int length()`
  returns the number of code units in this sequence.
- `CharSequence subSequence(int startIndex, int endIndex)`
  returns a CharSequence consisting of the code units stored at index startIndex to endIndex - 1.
- `String toString()`
  returns a string consisting of the code units of this sequence.

Layering Stream Filters

FileInputStream and FileOutputStream give you input and output streams attached to a disk file. You give the file name or full path name of the file in the constructor. For example,

```
FileInputStream fin = new FileInputStream("employee.dat");
```

looks in the current directory for a file named "employee.dat".

CAUTION: Because the backslash character is the escape character in Java strings, be sure to use \\ for Windows-style path names ("C:\\Windows\\win.ini"). In Windows, you can also use a single forward slash ("C:/Windows/win.ini") because most Windows file handling system calls will interpret forward slashes as file separators. However, this is not recommended—the behavior of the Windows system functions is subject to change, and on other operating systems, the file separator may yet be different. Instead, for portable programs, you should use the correct file separator character. It is stored in the constant string `File.separator`.

You can also use a `File` object (see page 684 for more on file objects):

```
File f = new File("employee.dat");
FileInputStream fin = new FileInputStream(f);
```

Like the abstract `InputStream` and `OutputStream` classes, these classes support only reading and writing on the byte level. That is, we can only read bytes and byte arrays from the object `fin`.

```
byte b = (byte) fin.read();
```

TIP: Because all the classes in `java.io` interpret relative path names as starting with the user's current working directory, you may want to know this directory. You can get at this information by a call to `System.getProperty("user.dir")`.

As you will see in the next section, if we just had a `DataInputStream`, then we could read numeric types:

```
DataInputStream din = . . .;
double s = din.readDouble();
```

But just as the `FileInputStream` has no methods to read numeric types, the `DataInputStream` has no method to get data from a file.

Java uses a clever mechanism to separate two kinds of responsibilities. Some streams (such as the `FileInputStream` and the input stream returned by the `openStream` method of the URL class) can retrieve bytes from files and other more exotic locations. Other streams (such as the `DataInputStream` and the `PrintWriter`) can assemble bytes into more useful data types. The Java programmer has to combine the two into what are often called *filtered streams* by feeding an existing stream to the constructor of another stream. For example, to be able to read numbers from a file, first create a `FileInputStream` and then pass it to the constructor of a `DataInputStream`.

```
FileInputStream fin = new FileInputStream("employee.dat");
DataInputStream din = new DataInputStream(fin);
double s = din.readDouble();
```

It is important to keep in mind that the data input stream that we created with the above code does not correspond to a new disk file. The newly created stream *still* accesses the data from the file attached to the file input stream, but the point is that it now has a more capable interface.

If you look at Figure 12–1 again, you can see the classes `FilterInputStream` and `FilterOutputStream`. You combine their subclasses into a new filtered stream to construct the streams you want. For example, by default, streams are not buffered. That is, every call to `read` contacts the operating system to ask it to dole out yet another byte. If you want buffering *and* the data input methods for a file named `employee.dat` in the current directory, you need to use the following rather monstrous sequence of constructors:

```
DataInputStream din = new DataInputStream(
   new BufferedInputStream(
      new FileInputStream("employee.dat")));
```

Notice that we put the DataInputStream *last* in the chain of constructors because we want to use the DataInputStream methods, and we want *them* to use the buffered read method. Regardless of the ugliness of the above code, it is necessary: you must be prepared to continue layering stream constructors until you have access to the functionality you want.

Sometimes you'll need to keep track of the intermediate streams when chaining them together. For example, when reading input, you often need to peek at the next byte to see if it is the value that you expect. Java provides the PushbackInputStream for this purpose.

```
PushbackInputStream pbin = new PushbackInputStream(
   new BufferedInputStream(
      new FileInputStream("employee.dat")));
```

Now you can speculatively read the next byte

```
int b = pbin.read();
```

and throw it back if it isn't what you wanted.

```
if (b != '<') pbin.unread(b);
```

But reading and unreading are the *only* methods that apply to the pushback input stream. If you want to look ahead and also read numbers, then you need both a pushback input stream and a data input stream reference.

```
DataInputStream din = new DataInputStream(
   pbin = new PushbackInputStream(
      new BufferedInputStream(
         new FileInputStream("employee.dat"))));
```

Of course, in the stream libraries of other programming languages, niceties such as buffering and lookahead are automatically taken care of, so it is a bit of a hassle in Java that one has to resort to layering stream filters in these cases. But the ability to mix and match filter classes to construct truly useful sequences of streams does give you an immense amount of flexibility. For example, you can read numbers from a compressed ZIP file by using the following sequence of streams (see Figure 12–4).

```
ZipInputStream zin = new ZipInputStream(new FileInputStream("employee.zip"));
DataInputStream din = new DataInputStream(zin);
```

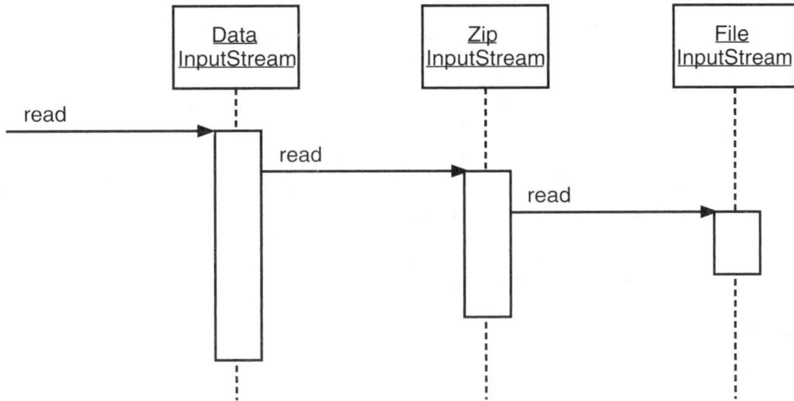

Figure 12–4: A sequence of filtered streams

(See the section on ZIP file streams starting on page 643 for more on Java's ability to handle ZIP files.)

All in all, apart from the rather monstrous constructors that are needed to layer streams, the ability to mix and match streams is a very useful feature of Java!

java.io.FileInputStream 1.0

- `FileInputStream(String name)`
  creates a new file input stream, using the file whose path name is specified by the `name` string.
- `FileInputStream(File f)`
  creates a new file input stream, using the information encapsulated in the `File` object. (The `File` class is described at the end of this chapter.)

java.io.FileOutputStream 1.0

- `FileOutputStream(String name)`
  creates a new file output stream specified by the `name` string. Path names that are not absolute are resolved relative to the current working directory. *Caution:* This method automatically deletes any existing file with the same name.
- `FileOutputStream(String name, boolean append)`
  creates a new file output stream specified by the `name` string. Path names that are not absolute are resolved relative to the current working directory. If the `append` parameter is `true`, then data are added at the end of the file. An existing file with the same name will not be deleted.
- `FileOutputStream(File f)`
  creates a new file output stream using the information encapsulated in the `File` object. (The `File` class is described at the end of this chapter.) *Caution:* This method automatically deletes any existing file with the same name as the name of `f`.

java.io.BufferedInputStream 1.0

- `BufferedInputStream(InputStream in)`
  creates a new buffered stream with a default buffer size. A buffered input stream reads characters from a stream without causing a device access every time. When the buffer is empty, a new block of data is read into the buffer.
- `BufferedInputStream(InputStream in, int n)`
  creates a new buffered stream with a user-defined buffer size.

java.io.BufferedOutputStream 1.0

- `BufferedOutputStream(OutputStream out)`
  creates a new buffered stream with a default buffer size. A buffered output stream collects characters to be written without causing a device access every time. When the buffer fills up or when the stream is flushed, the data are written.
- `BufferedOutputStream(OutputStream out, int n)`
  creates a new buffered stream with a user-defined buffer size.

java.io.PushbackInputStream 1.0

- `PushbackInputStream(InputStream in)`
  constructs a stream with one-byte lookahead.

- `PushbackInputStream(InputStream in, int size)`
  constructs a stream with a pushback buffer of specified size.
- `void unread(int b)`
  pushes back a byte, which is retrieved again by the next call to read. You can push back only one byte at a time.

  Parameters: `b` The byte to be read again

Data Streams

You often need to write the result of a computation or read one back. The data streams support methods for reading back all the basic Java types. To write a number, character, Boolean value, or string, use one of the following methods of the `DataOutput` interface:

```
writeChars
writeByte
writeInt
writeShort
writeLong
writeFloat
writeDouble
writeChar
writeBoolean
writeUTF
```

For example, `writeInt` always writes an integer as a 4-byte binary quantity regardless of the number of digits, and `writeDouble` always writes a `double` as an 8-byte binary quantity. The resulting output is not humanly readable, but the space needed will be the same for each value of a given type and reading it back in will be faster. (See the section on the `PrintWriter` class later in this chapter for how to output numbers as human-readable text.)

NOTE: There are two different methods of storing integers and floating-point numbers in memory, depending on the platform you are using. Suppose, for example, you are working with a 4-byte `int`, say the decimal number 1234, or 4D2 in hexadecimal (1234 = 4 x 256 + 13 x 16 + 2). This can be stored in such a way that the first of the 4 bytes in memory holds the most significant byte (MSB) of the value: `00 00 04 D2`. This is the so-called big-endian method. Or we can start with the least significant byte (LSB) first: `D2 04 00 00`. This is called, naturally enough, the little-endian method. For example, the SPARC uses big-endian; the Pentium, little-endian. This can lead to problems. When a C or C++ file is saved, the data are saved exactly as the processor stores them. That makes it challenging to move even the simplest data files from one platform to another. In Java, all values are written in the big-endian fashion, regardless of the processor. That makes Java data files platform independent.

The `writeUTF` method writes string data by using a modified version of 8-bit Unicode Transformation Format. Instead of simply using the standard UTF-8 encoding (which is shown in Table 12–1), character strings are first represented in UTF-16 (see Table 12–2) and then the result is encoded using the UTF-8 rules. The modified encoding is different for characters with code higher than `0xFFFF`. It is used for backwards compatibility with virtual machines that were built when Unicode had not yet grown beyond 16 bits.

Because nobody else uses this modification of UTF-8, you should only use the `writeUTF` method to write strings that are intended for a Java virtual machine; for example, if you write a program that generates bytecodes. Use the `writeChars` method for other purposes.

Table 12–1: UTF-8 Encoding

Character Range	Encoding
0...7F	$0a_6a_5a_4a_3a_2a_1a_0$
80...7FF	$110a_{10}a_9a_8a_7a_6$ $10a_5a_4a_3a_2a_1a_0$
800...FFFF	$1110a_{15}a_{14}a_{13}a_{12}$ $10a_{11}a_{10}a_9a_8a_7a_6$ $10a_5a_4a_3a_2a_1a_0$
10000...10FFFF	$11110a_{20}a_{19}a_{18}$ $10a_{17}a_{16}a_{15}a_{14}a_{13}a_{12}$ $10a_{11}a_{10}a_9a_8a_7a_6$ $10a_5a_4a_3a_2a_1a_0$

Table 12–2: UTF-16 Encoding

Character Range	Encoding
0...FFFF	$a_{15}a_{14}a_{13}a_{12}a_{11}a_{10}a_9a_8$ $a_7a_6a_5a_4a_3a_2a_1a_0$
10000...10FFFF	$110110b_{19}b_{18}$ $b_{17}a_{16}a_{15}a_{14}a_{13}a_{12}a_{11}a_{10}$ $110111a_9a_8$ $a_7a_6a_5a_4a_3a_2a_1a_0$ where $b_{19}b_{18}b_{17}b_{16} = a_{20}a_{19}a_{18}a_{17}a_{16}$ -1

NOTE: See RFC 2279 (`http://ietf.org/rfc/rfc2279.txt`) and RFC 2781 (`http://ietf.org/rfc/rfc2781.txt`) for definitions of UTF-8 and UTF-16.

To read the data back in, use the following methods:

`readInt`	`readDouble`
`readShort`	`readChar`
`readLong`	`readBoolean`
`readFloat`	`readUTF`

NOTE: The binary data format is compact and platform independent. Except for the UTF strings, it is also suited to random access. The major drawback is that binary files are not readable by humans.

java.io.DataInput 1.0

- `boolean readBoolean()`
  reads in a Boolean value.
- `byte readByte()`
  reads an 8-bit byte.
- `char readChar()`
  reads a 16-bit Unicode character.
- `double readDouble()`
  reads a 64-bit double.
- `float readFloat()`
  reads a 32-bit float.
- `void readFully(byte[] b)`
  reads bytes into the array `b`, blocking until all bytes are read.

  Parameters: `b` The buffer into which the data is read

- `void readFully(byte[] b, int off, int len)`
  reads bytes into the array `b`, blocking until all bytes are read.

Parameters:	`b`	The buffer into which the data is read
	`off`	The start offset of the data
	`len`	The maximum number of bytes to read

- `int readInt()`
  reads a 32-bit integer.
- `String readLine()`
  reads in a line that has been terminated by a `\n`, `\r`, `\r\n`, or `EOF`. Returns a string containing all bytes in the line converted to Unicode characters.
- `long readLong()`
  reads a 64-bit long integer.
- `short readShort()`
  reads a 16-bit short integer.
- `String readUTF()`
  reads a string of characters in "modified UTF-8" format.
- `int skipBytes(int n)`
  skips `n` bytes, blocking until all bytes are skipped.

Parameters:	`n`	The number of bytes to be skipped

`java.io.DataOutput` 1.0

- `void writeBoolean(boolean b)`
  writes a Boolean value.
- `void writeByte(int b)`
  writes an 8-bit byte.
- `void writeChar(int c)`
  writes a 16-bit Unicode character.
- `void writeChars(String s)`
  writes all characters in the string.
- `void writeDouble(double d)`
  writes a 64-bit double.
- `void writeFloat(float f)`
  writes a 32-bit float.
- `void writeInt(int i)`
  writes a 32-bit integer.
- `void writeLong(long l)`
  writes a 64-bit long integer.
- `void writeShort(int s)`
  writes a 16-bit short integer.
- `void writeUTF(String s)`
  writes a string of characters in "modified UTF-8" format.

Random-Access File Streams

The `RandomAccessFile` stream class lets you find or write data anywhere in a file. It implements both the `DataInput` and `DataOutput` interfaces. Disk files are random access, but streams of data from a network are not. You open a random-access file either for reading only or for both reading and writing. You specify the option by using the string "r" (for read access) or "rw" (for read/write access) as the second argument in the constructor.

```
RandomAccessFile in = new RandomAccessFile("employee.dat", "r");
RandomAccessFile inOut = new RandomAccessFile("employee.dat", "rw");
```

When you open an existing file as a RandomAccessFile, it does not get deleted.

A random-access file also has a *file pointer* setting that comes with it. The file pointer always indicates the position of the next record that will be read or written. The seek method sets the file pointer to an arbitrary byte position within the file. The argument to seek is a long integer between zero and the length of the file in bytes.

The getFilePointer method returns the current position of the file pointer.

To read from a random-access file, you use the same methods—such as readInt and readChar—as for DataInputStream objects. That is no accident. These methods are actually defined in the DataInput interface that both DataInputStream and RandomAccessFile implement.

Similarly, to write a random-access file, you use the same writeInt and writeChar methods as in the DataOutputStream class. These methods are defined in the DataOutput interface that is common to both classes.

The advantage of having the RandomAccessFile class implement both DataInput and DataOutput is that this lets you use or write methods whose argument types are the DataInput and DataOutput *interfaces.*

```
class Employee
{  . . .
   read(DataInput in) { . . . }
   write(DataOutput out) { . . . }
}
```

Note that the read method can handle either a DataInputStream or a RandomAccessFile object because both of these classes implement the DataInput interface. The same is true for the write method.

API **java.io.RandomAccessFile 1.0**

- RandomAccessFile(String file, String mode)
- RandomAccessFile(File file, String mode)

Parameters:	file	The file to be opened
	mode	"r" for read-only mode, "rw" for read/write mode, "rws" for read/write mode with synchronous disk writes of data and metadata for every update, and "rwd" for read/write mode with synchronous disk writes of data only.

- long getFilePointer()
  returns the current location of the file pointer.
- void seek(long pos)
  sets the file pointer to pos bytes from the beginning of the file.
- long length()
  returns the length of the file in bytes.

Text Streams

In the last section, we discussed *binary* input and output. While binary I/O is fast and efficient, it is not easily readable by humans. In this section, we will focus on *text* I/O. For example, if the integer 1234 is saved in binary, it is written as the sequence of bytes `00 00 04 D2` (in hexadecimal notation). In text format, it is saved as the string `"1234"`.

Unfortunately, doing this in Java requires a bit of work, because, as you know, Java uses Unicode characters. That is, the character encoding for the string `"1234"` really is `00 31 00 32 00 33 00 34` (in hex). However, at the present time most environments in which your Java programs will run use their own character encoding. This may be a single-byte, double-byte, or variable-byte scheme. For example, if you use Windows, the string would be written in ASCII, as `31 32 33 34`, without the extra zero bytes. If the Unicode encoding were written into a text file, then it would be quite unlikely that the resulting file would be humanly readable with the tools of the host environment. To overcome this problem, Java has a set of stream filters that bridges the gap between Unicode-encoded strings and the character encoding used by the local operating system. All of these classes descend from the abstract `Reader` and `Writer` classes, and the names are reminiscent of the ones used for binary data. For example, the `InputStreamReader` class turns an input stream that contains bytes in a particular character encoding into a reader that emits Unicode characters. Similarly, the `OutputStreamWriter` class turns a stream of Unicode characters into a stream of bytes in a particular character encoding.

For example, here is how you make an input reader that reads keystrokes from the console and automatically converts them to Unicode.

```
InputStreamReader in = new InputStreamReader(System.in);
```

This input stream reader assumes the normal character encoding used by the host system. For example, under Windows, it uses the ISO 8859-1 encoding (also known as ISO Latin-1 or, among Windows programmers, as "ANSI code"). You can choose a different encoding by specifying it in the constructor for the `InputStreamReader`. This takes the form

```
InputStreamReader(InputStream, String)
```

where the string describes the encoding scheme that you want to use. For example,

```
InputStreamReader in = new InputStreamReader(
   new FileInputStream("kremlin.dat"), "ISO8859_5");
```

The next section has more information on character sets.

Because it is so common to want to attach a reader or writer to a file, a pair of convenience classes, `FileReader` and `FileWriter`, is provided for this purpose. For example, the writer definition

```
FileWriter out = new FileWriter("output.txt");
```

is equivalent to

```
FileWriter out = new FileWriter(new FileOutputStream("output.txt"));
```

Character Sets

In the past, international character sets have been handled rather unsystematically throughout the Java library. The `java.nio` package—introduced in JDK 1.4—unifies character set conversion with the introduction of the `Charset` class. (Note that the `s` is lower case.)

A character set maps between sequences of two-byte Unicode code units and byte sequences used in a local character encoding. One of the most popular character encodings is ISO-8859-1, a single-byte encoding of the first 256 Unicode characters. Gaining in importance is

ISO-8859-15, which replaces some of the less useful characters of ISO-8859-1 with accented letters used in French and Finnish, and, more important, replaces the "international currency" character ¤ with the Euro symbol (€) in code point `0xA4`. Other examples for character encodings are the variable-byte encodings commonly used for Japanese and Chinese.

The `Charset` class uses the character set names standardized in the IANA Character Set Registry (`http://www.iana.org/assignments/character-sets`). These names differ slightly from those used in previous versions. For example, the "official" name of ISO-8859-1 is now `"ISO-8859-1"` and no longer `"ISO8859_1"`, which was the preferred name up to JDK 1.3. For compatibility with other naming conventions, each character set can have a number of aliases. For example, ISO-8859-1 has aliases

```
ISO8859-1
ISO_8859_1
ISO8859_1
ISO_8859-1
ISO_8859-1:1987
8859_1
latin1
l1
csISOLatin1
iso-ir-100
cp819
IBM819
IBM-819
819
```

Character set names are case insensitive.

You obtain a `Charset` by calling the static `forName` method with either the official name or one of its aliases:

```
Charset cset = Charset.forName("ISO-8859-1");
```

The `aliases` method returns a `Set` object of the aliases. A `Set` is a collection that we discuss in Volume 2; here is the code to iterate through the set elements:

```
Set<String> aliases = cset.aliases();
for (String alias : aliases)
   System.out.println(alias);
```

NOTE: An excellent reference for the "ISO 8859 alphabet soup" is `http://czyborra.com/charsets/iso8859.html`.

International versions of Java support many more encodings. There is even a mechanism for adding additional character set providers—see the JDK documentation for details. To find out which character sets are available in a particular implementation, call the static `availableCharsets` method. It returns a `SortedMap`, another collection class. Use this code to find out the names of all available character sets:

```
Set<String, Charset> charsets = Charset.availableCharsets();
for (String name : charsets.keySet())
   System.out.println(name);
```

Table 12–3 lists the character encodings that every Java implementation is required to have. Table 12–4 lists the encoding schemes that the JDK installs by default. The character sets in Tables 12–5 and 12–6 are installed only on operating systems that use non-European languages. The encoding schemes in Table 12–6 are supplied for compatibility with previous versions of the JDK.

Local encoding schemes cannot represent all Unicode characters. If a character cannot be represented, it is transformed to a ?.

Table 12–3: Required Character Encodings

Charset Standard Name	Legacy Name	Description
US-ASCII	ASCII	American Standard Code for Information Exchange
ISO-8859-1	ISO8859_1	ISO 8859-1, Latin alphabet No. 1
UTF-8	UTF8	Eight-bit Unicode Transformation Format
UTF-16	UTF-16	Sixteen-bit Unicode Transformation Format, byte order specified by an optional initial byte-order mark
UTF-16BE	UnicodeBigUnmarked	Sixteen-bit Unicode Transformation Format, big-endian byte order
UTF-16LE	UnicodeLittleUnmarked	Sixteen-bit Unicode Transformation Format, little-endian byte order

Table 12–4: Basic Character Encodings

Charset Standard Name	Legacy Name	Description
ISO8859-2	ISO8859_2	ISO 8859-2, Latin alphabet No. 2
ISO8859-4	ISO8859_4	ISO 8859-4, Latin alphabet No. 4
ISO8859-5	ISO8859_5	ISO 8859-5, Latin/Cyrillic alphabet
ISO8859-7	ISO8859_7	ISO 8859-7, Latin/Greek alphabet
ISO8859-9	ISO8859_9	ISO 8859-9, Latin alphabet No. 5
ISO8859-13	ISO8859_13	ISO 8859-13, Latin alphabet No. 7
ISO8859-15	ISO8859_15	ISO 8859-15, Latin alphabet No. 9
windows-1250	Cp1250	Windows Eastern European
windows-1251	Cp1251	Windows Cyrillic
windows-1252	Cp1252	Windows Latin-1
windows-1253	Cp1253	Windows Greek
windows-1254	Cp1254	Windows Turkish
windows-1257	Cp1257	Windows Baltic

Table 12–5: Extended Character Encodings

Charset Standard Name	Legacy Name	Description
Big5	Big5	Big5, Traditional Chinese
Big5-HKSCS	Big5_HKSCS	Big5 with Hong Kong extensions, Traditional Chinese
EUC-JP	EUC_JP	JIS X 0201, 0208, 0212, EUC encoding, Japanese
EUC-KR	EUC_KR	KS C 5601, EUC encoding, Korean

Table 12–5: Extended Character Encodings (continued)

Charset Standard Name	Legacy Name	Description
GB18030	GB18030	Simplified Chinese, PRC Standard
GBK	GBK	GBK, Simplified Chinese
ISCII91	ISCII91	ISCII91 encoding of Indic scripts
ISO-2022-JP	ISO2022JP	JIS X 0201, 0208 in ISO 2022 form, Japanese
ISO-2022-KR	ISO2022KR	ISO 2022 KR, Korean
ISO8859-3	ISO8859_3	ISO 8859-3, Latin alphabet No. 3
ISO8859-6	ISO8859_6	ISO 8859-6, Latin/Arabic alphabet
ISO8859-8	ISO8859_8	ISO 8859-8, Latin/Hebrew alphabet
Shift_JIS	SJIS	Shift-JIS, Japanese
TIS-620	TIS620	TIS620, Thai
windows-1255	Cp1255	Windows Hebrew
windows-1256	Cp1256	Windows Arabic
windows-1258	Cp1258	Windows Vietnamese
windows-31j	MS932	Windows Japanese
x-EUC-CN	EUC_CN	GB2312, EUC encoding, Simplified Chinese
x-EUC-JP-LINUX	EUC_JP_LINUX	JIS X 0201, 0208, EUC encoding, Japanese
x-EUC-TW	EUC_TW	CNS11643 (Plane 1-3), EUC encoding, Traditional Chinese
x-MS950-HKSCS	MS950_HKSCS	Windows Traditional Chinese with Hong Kong extensions
x-mswin-936	MS936	Windows Simplified Chinese
x-windows-949	MS949	Windows Korean
x-windows-950	MS950	Windows Traditional Chinese

Table 12–6: Legacy Character Encodings

Legacy Name	Description
Cp037	USA, Canada (Bilingual, French), Netherlands, Portugal, Brazil, Australia
Cp273	IBM Austria, Germany
Cp277	IBM Denmark, Norway
Cp278	IBM Finland, Sweden
Cp280	IBM Italy
Cp284	IBM Catalan/Spain, Spanish Latin America
Cp285	IBM United Kingdom, Ireland
Cp297	IBM France
Cp420	IBM Arabic
Cp424	IBM Hebrew
Cp437	MS-DOS United States, Australia, New Zealand, South Africa
Cp500	EBCDIC 500V1
Cp737	PC Greek

Table 12–6: Legacy Character Encodings (continued)

Legacy Name	Description
Cp775	PC Baltic
Cp838	IBM Thailand extended SBCS
Cp850	MS-DOS Latin-1
Cp852	MS-DOS Latin-2
Cp855	IBM Cyrillic
Cp856	IBM Hebrew
Cp857	IBM Turkish
Cp858	Variant of Cp850 with Euro character
Cp860	MS-DOS Portuguese
Cp861	MS-DOS Icelandic
Cp862	PC Hebrew
Cp863	MS-DOS Canadian French
Cp864	PC Arabic
Cp865	MS-DOS Nordic
Cp866	MS-DOS Russian
Cp868	MS-DOS Pakistan
Cp869	IBM Modern Greek
Cp870	IBM Multilingual Latin-2
Cp871	IBM Iceland
Cp874	IBM Thai
Cp875	IBM Greek
Cp918	IBM Pakistan (Urdu)
Cp921	IBM Latvia, Lithuania (AIX, DOS)
Cp922	IBM Estonia (AIX, DOS)
Cp930	Japanese Katakana-Kanji mixed with 4370 UDC, superset of 5026
Cp933	Korean Mixed with 1880 UDC, superset of 5029
Cp935	Simplified Chinese Host mixed with 1880 UDC, superset of 5031
Cp937	Traditional Chinese Host mixed with 6204 UDC, superset of 5033
Cp939	Japanese Latin Kanji mixed with 4370 UDC, superset of 5035
Cp942	IBM OS/2 Japanese, superset of Cp932
Cp942C	Variant of Cp942
Cp943	IBM OS/2 Japanese, superset of Cp932 and Shift-JIS
Cp943C	Variant of Cp943
Cp948	OS/2 Chinese (Taiwan) superset of 938
Cp949	PC Korean
Cp949C	Variant of Cp949
Cp950	PC Chinese (Hong Kong, Taiwan)
Cp964	AIX Chinese (Taiwan)

Table 12–6: Legacy Character Encodings (continued)

Legacy Name	Description
Cp970	AIX Korean
Cp1006	IBM AIX Pakistan (Urdu)
Cp1025	IBM Multilingual Cyrillic: Bulgaria, Bosnia, Herzegovina, Macedonia (FYR)
Cp1026	IBM Latin-5, Turkey
Cp1046	IBM Arabic - Windows
Cp1097	IBM Iran (Farsi)/Persian
Cp1098	IBM Iran (Farsi)/Persian (PC)
Cp1112	IBM Latvia, Lithuania
Cp1122	IBM Estonia
Cp1123	IBM Ukraine
Cp1124	IBM AIX Ukraine
Cp1140	Variant of Cp037 with Euro character
Cp1141	Variant of Cp273 with Euro character
Cp1142	Variant of Cp277 with Euro character
Cp1143	Variant of Cp278 with Euro character
Cp1144	Variant of Cp280 with Euro character
Cp1145	Variant of Cp284 with Euro character
Cp1146	Variant of Cp285 with Euro character
Cp1147	Variant of Cp297 with Euro character
Cp1148	Variant of Cp500 with Euro character
Cp1149	Variant of Cp871 with Euro character
Cp1381	IBM OS/2, DOS People's Republic of China (PRC)
Cp1383	IBM AIX People's Republic of China (PRC)
Cp33722	IBM-eucJP - Japanese (superset of 5050)
ISO2022CN	ISO 2022 CN, Chinese (conversion to Unicode only)
ISO2022CN_CNS	CNS 11643 in ISO 2022 CN form, Traditional Chinese (conversion from Unicode only)
ISO2022CN_GB	GB 2312 in ISO 2022 CN form, Simplified Chinese (conversion from Unicode only)
JIS0201	JIS X 0201, Japanese
JIS0208	JIS X 0208, Japanese
JIS0212	JIS X 0212, Japanese
JISAutoDetect	Detects and converts from Shift-JIS, EUC-JP, ISO 2022 JP (conversion to Unicode only)
Johab	Johab, Korean
MS874	Windows Thai
MacArabic	Macintosh Arabic
MacCentralEurope	Macintosh Latin-2
MacCroatian	Macintosh Croatian
MacCyrillic	Macintosh Cyrillic

Table 12–6: Legacy Character Encodings (continued)

Legacy Name	Description
MacDingbat	Macintosh Dingbat
MacGreek	Macintosh Greek
MacHebrew	Macintosh Hebrew
MacIceland	Macintosh Iceland
MacRoman	Macintosh Roman
MacRomania	Macintosh Romania
MacSymbol	Macintosh Symbol
MacThai	Macintosh Thai
MacTurkish	Macintosh Turkish
MacUkraine	Macintosh Ukraine

Once you have a character set, you can use it to convert between Unicode strings and encoded byte sequences. Here is how you encode a Unicode string.

```
String str = . . .;
ByteBuffer buffer = cset.encode(str);
byte[] bytes = buffer.array();
```

Conversely, to decode a byte sequence, you need a byte buffer. Use the static `wrap` method of the `ByteBuffer` array to turn a byte array into a byte buffer. The result of the `decode` method is a `CharBuffer`. Call its `toString` method to get a string.

```
byte[] bytes = . . .;
ByteBuffer bbuf = ByteBuffer.wrap(bytes, offset, length);
CharBuffer cbuf = cset.decode(bbuf);
String str = cbuf.toString();
```

API **java.nio.charset.Charset 1.4**

- `static SortedMap availableCharsets()`
  gets all available character sets for this virtual machine. Returns a map whose keys are character set names and whose values are character sets.
- `static Charset forName(String name)`
  gets a character set for the given name.
- `Set aliases()`
  returns the set of alias names for this character set.
- `ByteBuffer encode(String str)`
  encodes the given string into a sequence of bytes.
- `CharBuffer decode(ByteBuffer buffer)`
  decodes the given character sequence. Unrecognized inputs are converted to the Unicode "replacement character" (`'\uFFFD'`).

API **java.nio.ByteBuffer 1.4**

- `byte[] array()`
  returns the array of bytes that this buffer manages.
- `static ByteBuffer wrap(byte[] bytes)`
- `static ByteBuffer wrap(byte[] bytes, int offset, int length)`
  return a byte buffer that manages the given array of bytes or the given range.

 **java.nio.CharBuffer**

- `char[] array()`
  returns the array of code units that this buffer manages.
- `char charAt(int index)`
  returns the code unit at the given index.
- `String toString()`
  returns a string consisting of the code units that this buffer manages

How to Write Text Output

For text output, you want to use a `PrintWriter`. A print writer can print strings and numbers in text format. Just as a `DataOutputStream` has useful output methods but no destination, a `PrintWriter` must be combined with a destination writer.

```
PrintWriter out = new PrintWriter(new FileWriter("employee.txt"));
```

You can also combine a print writer with a destination (output) stream.

```
PrintWriter out = new PrintWriter(new FileOutputStream("employee.txt"));
```

The `PrintWriter(OutputStream)` constructor automatically adds an `OutputStreamWriter` to convert Unicode characters to bytes in the stream.

To write to a print writer, you use the same `print` and `println` methods that you used with `System.out`. You can use these methods to print numbers (`int`, `short`, `long`, `float`, `double`), characters, Boolean values, strings, and objects.

 NOTE: Java veterans may wonder whatever happened to the `PrintStream` class and to `System.out`. In Java 1.0, the `PrintStream` class simply truncated all Unicode characters to ASCII characters by dropping the top byte. Conversely, the `readLine` method of the `DataInputStream` turned ASCII to Unicode by setting the top byte to 0. Clearly, that was not a clean or portable approach, and it was fixed with the introduction of readers and writers in Java 1.1. For compatibility with existing code, `System.in`, `System.out`, and `System.err` are still streams, not readers and writers. But now the `PrintStream` class internally converts Unicode characters to the default host encoding in the same way as the `PrintWriter` does. Objects of type `PrintStream` act exactly like print writers when you use the `print` and `println` methods, but unlike print writers, they allow you to send raw bytes to them with the `write(int)` and `write(byte[])` methods.

For example, consider this code:

```
String name = "Harry Hacker";
double salary = 75000;
out.print(name);
out.print(' ');
out.println(salary);
```

This writes the characters

```
Harry Hacker 75000
```

to the stream `out`. The characters are then converted to bytes and end up in the file `employee.txt`.

The `println` method automatically adds the correct end-of-line character for the target system ("`\r\n`" on Windows, "`\n`" on UNIX, "`\r`" on Macs) to the line. This is the string obtained by the call `System.getProperty("line.separator")`.

If the writer is set to *autoflush mode*, then all characters in the buffer are sent to their destination whenever `println` is called. (Print writers are always buffered.) By default, autoflushing is *not* enabled. You can enable or disable autoflushing by using the `PrintWriter(Writer, boolean)` constructor and passing the appropriate Boolean as the second argument.

```
PrintWriter out = new PrintWriter(new FileWriter("employee.txt"), true); // autoflush
```

The `print` methods don't throw exceptions. You can call the `checkError` method to see if something went wrong with the stream.

NOTE: You cannot write raw bytes to a `PrintWriter`. Print writers are designed for text output only.

`java.io.PrintWriter` 1.1

- `PrintWriter(Writer out)`
  creates a new `PrintWriter`, without automatic line flushing.

Parameters:	`out`	A character-output writer

- `PrintWriter(Writer out, boolean autoFlush)`
  creates a new `PrintWriter`.

Parameters:	`out`	A character-output writer
	`autoFlush`	If `true`, the `println` methods will flush the output buffer

- `PrintWriter(OutputStream out)`
  creates a new `PrintWriter`, without automatic line flushing, from an existing `OutputStream` by automatically creating the necessary intermediate `OutputStreamWriter`.

Parameters:	`out`	An output stream

- `PrintWriter(OutputStream out, boolean autoFlush)`
  creates a new `PrintWriter` from an existing `OutputStream` but allows you to determine whether the writer autoflushes or not.

Parameters:	`out`	An output stream
	`autoFlush`	If `true`, the `println` methods will flush the output buffer

- `void print(Object obj)`
  prints an object by printing the string resulting from `toString`.

Parameters:	`obj`	The object to be printed

- `void print(String s)`
  prints a Unicode string.
- `void println(String s)`
  prints a string followed by a line terminator. Flushes the stream if the stream is in autoflush mode.
- `void print(char[] s)`
  prints an array of Unicode characters.
- `void print(char c)`
  prints a Unicode character.
- `void print(int i)`
  prints an integer in text format.

- `void print(long l)`
  prints a long integer in text format.
- `void print(float f)`
  prints a floating-point number in text format.
- `void print(double d)`
  prints a double-precision floating-point number in text format.
- `void print(boolean b)`
  prints a Boolean value in text format.
- `boolean checkError()`
  returns `true` if a formatting or output error occurred. Once the stream has encountered an error, it is tainted and all calls to `checkError` return `true`.

How to Read Text Input

As you know:

- To write data in binary format, you use a `DataOutputStream`.
- To write in text format, you use a `PrintWriter`.

Therefore, you might expect that there is an analog to the `DataInputStream` that lets you read data in text format. The closest analog is the `Scanner` class that we have used extensively. However, before JDK 5.0, the only game in town for processing text input was the `BufferedReader` method—it has a method, `readLine`, that lets you read a line of text. You need to combine a buffered reader with an input source.

```
BufferedReader in = new BufferedReader(new FileReader("employee.txt"));
```

The `readLine` method returns `null` when no more input is available. A typical input loop, therefore, looks like this:

```
String line;
while ((line = in.readLine()) != null)
{
   do something with line
}
```

The `FileReader` class already converts bytes to Unicode characters. For other input sources, you need to use the `InputStreamReader`—unlike the `PrintWriter`, the `InputStreamReader` has no automatic convenience method to bridge the gap between bytes and Unicode characters.

```
BufferedReader in2 = new BufferedReader(new InputStreamReader(System.in));
BufferedReader in3 = new BufferedReader(new InputStreamReader(url.openStream()));
```

To read numbers from text input, you need to read a string first and then convert it.

```
String s = in.readLine();
double x = Double.parseDouble(s);
```

That works if there is a single number on each line. Otherwise, you must work harder and break up the input string, for example, by using the `StringTokenizer` utility class. We see an example of this later in this chapter.

TIP: Java has `StringReader` and `StringWriter` classes that allow you to treat a string as if it were a data stream. This can be quite convenient if you want to use the same code to parse both strings and data from a stream.

ZIP File Streams

ZIP files are archives that store one or more files in (usually) compressed format. Java 1.1 can handle both GZIP and ZIP format. (See RFC 1950, RFC 1951, and RFC 1952, for example, at `http://www.faqs.org/rfcs`.) In this section we concentrate on the more familiar (but somewhat more complicated) ZIP format and leave the GZIP classes to you if you need them. (They work in much the same way.)

NOTE: The classes for handling ZIP files are in `java.util.zip` and not in `java.io`, so remember to add the necessary `import` statement. Although not part of `java.io`, the `GZIP` and `ZIP` classes subclass `java.io.FilterInputStream` and `java.io.FilterOutputStream`. The `java.util.zip` packages also contain classes for computing cyclic redundancy check (CRC) checksums. (CRC is a method to generate a hashlike code that the receiver of a file can use to check the integrity of the data.)

Each ZIP file has a header with information such as the name of the file and the compression method that was used. In Java, you use a `ZipInputStream` to read a ZIP file by layering the `ZipInputStream` constructor onto a `FileInputStream`. You then need to look at the individual entries in the archive. The `getNextEntry` method returns an object of type `ZipEntry` that describes the entry. The `read` method of the `ZipInputStream` is modified to return –1 at the end of the current entry (instead of just at the end of the ZIP file). You must then call `closeEntry` to read the next entry. Here is a typical code sequence to read through a ZIP file:

```
ZipInputStream zin = new ZipInputStream(new FileInputStream(zipname));
ZipEntry entry;
while ((entry = zin.getNextEntry()) != null)
{
   analyze entry;
   read the contents of zin;
   zin.closeEntry();
}
zin.close();
```

To read the contents of a ZIP entry, you will probably not want to use the raw `read` method; usually, you will use the methods of a more competent stream filter. For example, to read a text file inside a ZIP file, you can use the following loop:

```
BufferedReader in = new BufferedReader(new InputStreamReader(zin));
String s;
while ((s = in.readLine()) != null)
   do something with s;
```

The program in Example 12–1 lets you open a ZIP file. It then displays the files stored in the ZIP archive in the combo box at the bottom of the screen. If you double-click on one of the files, the contents of the file are displayed in the text area, as shown in Figure 12–5.

Example 12–1: ZipTest.java

```
import java.awt.*;
import java.awt.event.*;
import java.io.*;
import java.util.*;
import java.util.zip.*;
import javax.swing.*;
import javax.swing.filechooser.FileFilter;

public class ZipTest
{
   public static void main(String[] args)
```

```
   {
      ZipTestFrame frame = new ZipTestFrame();
      frame.setDefaultCloseOperation(JFrame.EXIT_ON_CLOSE);
      frame.setVisible(true);
   }
}

/**
   A frame with a text area to show the contents of a file inside
   a zip archive, a combo box to select different files in the
   archive, and a menu to load a new archive.
*/
class ZipTestFrame extends JFrame
{
   public ZipTestFrame()
   {
      setTitle("ZipTest");
      setSize(DEFAULT_WIDTH, DEFAULT_HEIGHT);

      // add the menu and the Open and Exit menu items
      JMenuBar menuBar = new JMenuBar();
      JMenu menu = new JMenu("File");

      JMenuItem openItem = new JMenuItem("Open");
      menu.add(openItem);
      openItem.addActionListener(new OpenAction());

      JMenuItem exitItem = new JMenuItem("Exit");
      menu.add(exitItem);
      exitItem.addActionListener(new
         ActionListener()
         {
            public void actionPerformed(ActionEvent event)
            {
               System.exit(0);
            }
         });

      menuBar.add(menu);
      setJMenuBar(menuBar);

      // add the text area and combo box
      fileText = new JTextArea();
      fileCombo = new JComboBox();
      fileCombo.addActionListener(new
         ActionListener()
         {
            public void actionPerformed(ActionEvent event)
            {
               loadZipFile((String) fileCombo.getSelectedItem());
            }
         });

      add(fileCombo, BorderLayout.SOUTH);
      add(new JScrollPane(fileText), BorderLayout.CENTER);
   }

```

```
   /**
      This is the listener for the File->Open menu item.
   */
   private class OpenAction implements ActionListener
   {
      public void actionPerformed(ActionEvent event)
      {
         // prompt the user for a zip file
         JFileChooser chooser = new JFileChooser();
         chooser.setCurrentDirectory(new File("."));
         ExtensionFileFilter filter = new ExtensionFileFilter();
         filter.addExtension(".zip");
         filter.addExtension(".jar");
         filter.setDescription("ZIP archives");
         chooser.setFileFilter(filter);
         int r = chooser.showOpenDialog(ZipTestFrame.this);
         if (r == JFileChooser.APPROVE_OPTION)
         {
            zipname = chooser.getSelectedFile().getPath();
            scanZipFile();
         }
      }
   }

   /**
      Scans the contents of the zip archive and populates
      the combo box.
   */
   public void scanZipFile()
   {
      fileCombo.removeAllItems();
      try
      {
         ZipInputStream zin = new ZipInputStream(new FileInputStream(zipname));
         ZipEntry entry;
         while ((entry = zin.getNextEntry()) != null)
         {
            fileCombo.addItem(entry.getName());
            zin.closeEntry();
         }
         zin.close();
      }
      catch (IOException e)
      {
         e.printStackTrace();
      }
   }

   /**
      Loads a file from the zip archive into the text area
      @param name the name of the file in the archive
   */
   public void loadZipFile(String name)
   {
      try
      {
         ZipInputStream zin = new ZipInputStream(new FileInputStream(zipname));
```

```
         ZipEntry entry;
         fileText.setText("");

         // find entry with matching name in archive
         while ((entry = zin.getNextEntry()) != null)
         {
            if (entry.getName().equals(name))
            {
               // read entry into text area
               BufferedReader in = new BufferedReader(new InputStreamReader(zin));
               String line;
               while ((line = in.readLine()) != null)
               {
                  fileText.append(line);
                  fileText.append("\n");
               }
            }
            zin.closeEntry();
         }
         zin.close();
      }
      catch (IOException e)
      {
         e.printStackTrace();
      }
   }

   public static final int DEFAULT_WIDTH = 400;
   public static final int DEFAULT_HEIGHT = 300;

   private JComboBox fileCombo;
   private JTextArea fileText;
   private String zipname;
}

/**
   This file filter matches all files with a given set of
   extensions. From FileChooserTest in chapter 9
*/
class ExtensionFileFilter extends FileFilter
{
   /**
      Adds an extension that this file filter recognizes.
      @param extension a file extension (such as ".txt" or "txt")
   */
   public void addExtension(String extension)
   {
      if (!extension.startsWith("."))
         extension = "." + extension;
      extensions.add(extension.toLowerCase());
   }

   /**
      Sets a description for the file set that this file filter
      recognizes.
      @param aDescription a description for the file set
   */
```

```
   public void setDescription(String aDescription)
   {
      description = aDescription;
   }

   /**
      Returns a description for the file set that this file
      filter recognizes.
      @return a description for the file set
   */
   public String getDescription()
   {
      return description;
   }

   public boolean accept(File f)
   {
      if (f.isDirectory()) return true;
      String name = f.getName().toLowerCase();

      // check if the file name ends with any of the extensions
      for (String e : extensions)
         if (name.endsWith(e))
            return true;
      return false;
   }

   private String description = "";
   private ArrayList<String> extensions = new ArrayList<String>();
}
```

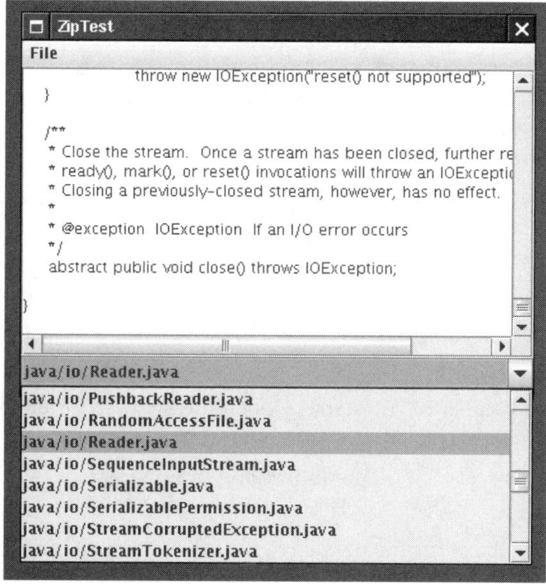

Figure 12–5: The ZipTest program

NOTE: The ZIP input stream throws a `ZipException` when there is an error in reading a ZIP file. Normally this error occurs when the ZIP file has been corrupted.

To write a ZIP file, you open a `ZipOutputStream` by layering it onto a `FileOutputStream`. For each entry that you want to place into the ZIP file, you create a `ZipEntry` object. You pass the file name to the `ZipEntry` constructor; it sets the other parameters such as file date and decompression method automatically. You can override these settings if you like. Then, you call the `putNextEntry` method of the `ZipOutputStream` to begin writing a new file. Send the file data to the ZIP stream. When you are done, call `closeEntry`. Repeat for all the files you want to store. Here is a code skeleton:

```
FileOutputStream fout = new FileOutputStream("test.zip");
ZipOutputStream zout = new ZipOutputStream(fout);
for all files
{
   ZipEntry ze = new ZipEntry(filename);
   zout.putNextEntry(ze);
   send data to zout;
   zout.closeEntry();
}
zout.close();
```

NOTE: JAR files (which were discussed in Chapter 10) are simply ZIP files with another entry, the so-called manifest. You use the `JarInputStream` and `JarOutputStream` classes to read and write the manifest entry.

ZIP streams are a good example of the power of the stream abstraction. Both the source and the destination of the ZIP data are completely flexible. You layer the most convenient reader stream onto the ZIP file stream to read the data that are stored in compressed form, and that reader doesn't even realize that the data are being decompressed as they are being requested. And the source of the bytes in ZIP formats need not be a file—the ZIP data can come from a network connection. In fact, the JAR files that we discussed in Chapter 10 are ZIP-formatted files. Whenever the class loader of an applet reads a JAR file, it reads and decompresses data from the network.

NOTE: The article at `http://www.javaworld.com/javaworld/jw-10-2000/jw-1027-toolbox.html` shows you how to modify a ZIP archive.

`java.util.zip.ZipInputStream` 1.1

- `ZipInputStream(InputStream in)`
  This constructor creates a `ZipInputStream` that allows you to inflate data from the given `InputStream`.

  Parameters: `in` The underlying input stream

- `ZipEntry getNextEntry()`
  returns a `ZipEntry` object for the next entry, or `null` if there are no more entries.

- `void closeEntry()`
  closes the current open entry in the ZIP file. You can then read the next entry by using `getNextEntry()`.

API **java.util.zip.ZipOutputStream 1.1**

- `ZipOutputStream(OutputStream out)`
  this constructor creates a `ZipOutputStream` that you use to write compressed data to the specified `OutputStream`.

  Parameters: `out` The underlying output stream

- `void putNextEntry(ZipEntry ze)`
  writes the information in the given `ZipEntry` to the stream and positions the stream for the data. The data can then be written to the stream by `write()`.

  Parameters: `ze` The new entry

- `void closeEntry()`
  closes the currently open entry in the ZIP file. Use the `putNextEntry` method to start the next entry.
- `void setLevel(int level)`
  sets the default compression level of subsequent `DEFLATED` entries. The default value is `Deflater.DEFAULT_COMPRESSION`. Throws an `IllegalArgumentException` if the level is not valid.

  Parameters: `level` A compression level, from 0 (`NO_COMPRESSION`) to 9 (`BEST_COMPRESSION`)

- `void setMethod(int method)`
  sets the default compression method for this `ZipOutputStream` for any entries that do not specify a method.

  Parameters: `method` The compression method, either `DEFLATED` or `STORED`

java.util.zip.ZipEntry 1.1

- `ZipEntry(String name)`

  Parameters: `name` The name of the entry

- `long getCrc()`
  returns the CRC32 checksum value for this `ZipEntry`.
- `String getName()`
  returns the name of this entry.
- `long getSize()`
  returns the uncompressed size of this entry, or –1 if the uncompressed size is not known.
- `boolean isDirectory()`
  returns a Boolean that indicates whether this entry is a directory.
- `void setMethod(int method)`

  Parameters: `method` The compression method for the entry; must be either `DEFLATED` or `STORED`

- `void setSize(long size)`
  sets the size of this entry. Only required if the compression method is `STORED`.

  Parameters: `size` The uncompressed size of this entry

- `void setCrc(long crc)`
  sets the CRC32 checksum of this entry. Use the `CRC32` class to compute this checksum. Only required if the compression method is `STORED`.

  Parameters: `crc` The checksum of this entry

`java.util.zip.ZipFile` 1.1

- `ZipFile(String name)`
  this constructor creates a `ZipFile` for reading from the given string.

  Parameters: `name` A string that contains the path name of the file

- `ZipFile(File file)`
  this constructor creates a `ZipFile` for reading from the given `File` object.

  Parameters: `file` The file to read; the `File` class is described at the end of this chapter

- `Enumeration entries()`
  returns an `Enumeration` object that enumerates the `ZipEntry` objects that describe the entries of the `ZipFile`.

- `ZipEntry getEntry(String name)`
  returns the entry corresponding to the given name, or `null` if there is no such entry.

  Parameters: `name` The entry name

- `InputStream getInputStream(ZipEntry ze)`
  returns an `InputStream` for the given entry.

  Parameters: `ze` A `ZipEntry` in the ZIP file

- `String getName()`
  returns the path of this ZIP file.

Use of Streams

In the next four sections, we show you how to put some of the creatures in the stream zoo to good use. For these examples, we assume you are working with the `Employee` class and some of its subclasses, such as `Manager`. (See Chapters 4 and 5 for more on these example classes.) We consider four separate scenarios for saving an array of employee records to a file and then reading them back into memory:

1. Saving data of the same type (`Employee`) in text format
2. Saving data of the same type in binary format
3. Saving and restoring polymorphic data (a mixture of `Employee` and `Manager` objects)
4. Saving and restoring data containing embedded references (managers with pointers to other employees)

Writing Delimited Output

In this section, you learn how to store an array of `Employee` records in the time-honored *delimited* format. This means that each record is stored in a separate line. Instance fields are separated from each other by delimiters. We use a vertical bar (`|`) as our delimiter. (A colon (:) is another popular choice. Part of the fun is that everyone uses a different delimiter.) Naturally, we punt on the issue of what might happen if a `|` actually occurred in one of the strings we save.

NOTE: Especially on UNIX systems, an amazing number of files are stored in exactly this format. We have seen entire employee databases with thousands of records in this format, queried with nothing more than the UNIX `awk`, `sort`, and `join` utilities. (In the PC world, where desktop database programs are available at low cost, this kind of ad hoc storage is much less common.)

Here is a sample set of records:

```
Harry Hacker|35500|1989|10|1
Carl Cracker|75000|1987|12|15
Tony Tester|38000|1990|3|15
```

Writing records is simple. Because we write to a text file, we use the `PrintWriter` class. We simply write all fields, followed by either a `|` or, for the last field, a `\n`. Finally, in keeping with the idea that we want the *class* to be responsible for responding to messages, we add a method, `writeData`, to our `Employee` class.

```
public void writeData(PrintWriter out) throws IOException
{
   GregorianCalendar calendar = new GregorianCalendar();
   calendar.setTime(hireDay);
   out.println(name + "|"
      + salary + "|"
      + calendar.get(Calendar.YEAR) + "|"
      + (calendar.get(Calendar.MONTH) + 1) + "|"
      + calendar.get(Calendar.DAY_OF_MONTH));
}
```

To read records, we read in a line at a time and separate the fields. This is the topic of the next section, in which we use a utility class supplied with Java to make our job easier.

String Tokenizers and Delimited Text

When reading a line of input, we get a single long string. We want to split it into individual strings. This means finding the `|` delimiters and then separating out the individual pieces, that is, the sequence of characters up to the next delimiter. (These are usually called `tokens`.) The `StringTokenizer` class in `java.util` is designed for exactly this purpose. It gives you an easy way to break up a large string that contains delimited text. The idea is that a string tokenizer object attaches to a string. When you construct the tokenizer object, you specify which characters are the delimiters. For example, we need to use

```
StringTokenizer tokenizer = new StringTokenizer(line, "|");
```

You can specify multiple delimiters in the string, for example:

```
StringTokenizer tokenizer = new StringTokenizer(line, "|,;");
```

This means that any of the characters in the string can serve as delimiters.

If you don't specify a delimiter set, the default is `" \t\n\r"`, that is, all whitespace characters (space, tab, newline, and carriage return)

Once you have constructed a string tokenizer, you can use its methods to quickly extract the tokens from the string. The `nextToken` method returns the next unread token. The `hasMoreTokens` method returns `true` if more tokens are available. The following loop processes all tokens:

```
while (tokenizer.hasMoreTokens())
{
   String token = tokenizer.nextToken();
   process token
}
```

NOTE: An alternative to the `StringTokenizer` is the `split` method of the `String` class. The call `line.split("[|,;]")` returns a `String[]` array consisting of all tokens, using the delimiters inside the brackets. You can use any regular expression to describe delimiters—we will discuss regular expression on page 698.

java.util.StringTokenizer 1.0

- `StringTokenizer(String str, String delim)`
  constructs a string tokenizer with the given delimiter set.

Parameters:	`str`	The input string from which tokens are read
	`delim`	A string containing delimiter characters (every character in this string is a delimiter)

- `StringTokenizer(String str)`
  constructs a string tokenizer with the default delimiter set `" \t\n\r"`.
- `boolean hasMoreTokens()`
  returns `true` if more tokens exist.
- `String nextToken()`
  returns the next token; throws a `NoSuchElementException` if there are no more tokens.
- `String nextToken(String delim)`
  returns the next token after switching to the new delimiter set. The new delimiter set is subsequently used.
- `int countTokens()`
  returns the number of tokens still in the string.

Reading Delimited Input

Reading in an `Employee` record is simple. We simply read in a line of input with the `readLine` method of the `BufferedReader` class. Here is the code needed to read one record into a string.

```
BufferedReader in = new BufferedReader(new FileReader("employee.dat"));
. . .
String line = in.readLine();
```

Next, we need to extract the individual tokens. When we do this, we end up with *strings*, so we need to convert them to numbers.

Just as with the `writeData` method, we add a `readData` method of the `Employee` class. When you call

```
e.readData(in);
```

this method overwrites the previous contents of `e`. Note that the method may throw an `IOException` if the `readLine` method throws that exception. This method can do nothing if an `IOException` occurs, so we just let it propagate up the call chain.

Here is the code for this method:

```
public void readData(BufferedReader in) throws IOException
{
   String s = in.readLine();
   StringTokenizer t = new StringTokenizer(s, "|");
   name = t.nextToken();
   salary = Double.parseDouble(t.nextToken());
   int y = Integer.parseInt(t.nextToken());
```

```
      int m = Integer.parseInt(t.nextToken());
      int d = Integer.parseInt(t.nextToken());
      GregorianCalendar calendar = new GregorianCalendar(y, m - 1, d);
         // GregorianCalendar uses 0 = January
      hireDay = calendar.getTime();
   }
```

Finally, in the code for a program that tests these methods, the static method

```
void writeData(Employee[] e, PrintWriter out)
```

first writes the length of the array, then writes each record. The static method

```
Employee[] readData(BufferedReader in)
```

first reads in the length of the array, then reads in each record, as illustrated in Example 12–2.

Example 12–2: DataFileTest.java

```
import java.io.*;
import java.util.*;

public class DataFileTest
{
   public static void main(String[] args)
   {
      Employee[] staff = new Employee[3];

      staff[0] = new Employee("Carl Cracker", 75000, 1987, 12, 15);
      staff[1] = new Employee("Harry Hacker", 50000, 1989, 10, 1);
      staff[2] = new Employee("Tony Tester", 40000, 1990, 3, 15);

      try
      {
         // save all employee records to the file employee.dat
         PrintWriter out = new PrintWriter(new FileWriter("employee.dat"));
         writeData(staff, out);
         out.close();

         // retrieve all records into a new array
         BufferedReader in = new BufferedReader(new FileReader("employee.dat"));
         Employee[] newStaff = readData(in);
         in.close();

         // print the newly read employee records
         for (Employee e : newStaff)
            System.out.println(e);
      }
      catch(IOException exception)
      {
         exception.printStackTrace();
      }
   }

   /**
      Writes all employees in an array to a print writer
      @param employees an array of employees
      @param out a print writer
   */
```

```
   static void writeData(Employee[] employees, PrintWriter out)
      throws IOException
   {
      // write number of employees
      out.println(employees.length);

      for (Employee e : employees)
         e.writeData(out);
   }

   /**
      Reads an array of employees from a buffered reader
      @param in the buffered reader
      @return the array of employees
   */
   static Employee[] readData(BufferedReader in)
      throws IOException
   {
      // retrieve the array size
      int n = Integer.parseInt(in.readLine());

      Employee[] employees = new Employee[n];
      for (int i = 0; i < n; i++)
      {
         employees[i] = new Employee();
         employees[i].readData(in);
      }
      return employees;
   }
}

class Employee
{
   public Employee() {}

   public Employee(String n, double s, int year, int month, int day)
   {
      name = n;
      salary = s;
      GregorianCalendar calendar = new GregorianCalendar(year, month - 1, day);
      hireDay = calendar.getTime();
   }

   public String getName()
   {
      return name;
   }

   public double getSalary()
   {
      return salary;
   }

   public Date getHireDay()
   {
```

```
      return hireDay;
   }

   public void raiseSalary(double byPercent)
   {
      double raise = salary * byPercent / 100;
      salary += raise;
   }

   public String toString()
   {
      return getClass().getName()
         + "[name=" + name
         + ",salary=" + salary
         + ",hireDay=" + hireDay
         + "]";
   }

   /**
      Writes employee data to a print writer
      @param out the print writer
   */
   public void writeData(PrintWriter out) throws IOException
   {
      GregorianCalendar calendar = new GregorianCalendar();
      calendar.setTime(hireDay);
      out.println(name + "|"
         + salary + "|"
         + calendar.get(Calendar.YEAR) + "|"
         + (calendar.get(Calendar.MONTH) + 1) + "|"
         + calendar.get(Calendar.DAY_OF_MONTH));
   }

   /**
      Reads employee data from a buffered reader
      @param in the buffered reader
   */
   public void readData(BufferedReader in) throws IOException
   {
      String s = in.readLine();
      StringTokenizer t = new StringTokenizer(s, "|");
      name = t.nextToken();
      salary = Double.parseDouble(t.nextToken());
      int y = Integer.parseInt(t.nextToken());
      int m = Integer.parseInt(t.nextToken());
      int d = Integer.parseInt(t.nextToken());
      GregorianCalendar calendar = new GregorianCalendar(y, m - 1, d);
      hireDay = calendar.getTime();
   }

   private String name;
   private double salary;
   private Date hireDay;
}
```

The `StringBuilder` Class

When you process input, you often need to construct strings from individual characters or Unicode code units. It would be inefficient to use string concatenation for this purpose. Every time you append characters to a string, the string object needs to find new memory to hold the larger string: this is time consuming. Appending even more characters means the string needs to be relocated again and again. Using the `StringBuilder` class avoids this problem.

In contrast, a `StringBuilder` works much like an `ArrayList`. It manages a `char[]` array that can grow and shrink on demand. You can append, insert, or remove code units until the string builder holds the desired string. Then you use the `toString` method to convert the contents to an actual `String` object.

NOTE: The `StringBuilder` class was introduced in JDK 5.0. Its predecessor, `StringBuffer`, is slightly less efficient, but it allows multiple threads to add or remove characters. If all string editing happens in a single thread, you should use `StringBuilder` instead. The APIs of both classes are identical.

The following API notes contain the most important methods for the `StringBuilder` and `StringBuffer` classes.

`java.lang.StringBuilder` 5.0

`java.lang.StringBuffer` 1.0

- `StringBuilder/StringBuffer()`
  constructs an empty string builder or string buffer.
- `StringBuilder/StringBuffer(int length)`
  constructs an empty string builder or string buffer with the initial capacity `length`.
- `StringBuilder/StringBuffer(String str)`
  constructs a string builder or string buffer with the initial contents `str`.
- `int length()`
  returns the number of code units of the builder or buffer.
- `StringBuilder/StringBuffer append(String str)`
  appends a string and returns `this`.
- `StringBuilder/StringBuffer append(char c)`
  appends a code unit and returns `this`.
- `StringBuilder/StringBuffer appendCodePoint(int cp)` 5.0
  appends a code point, converting it into one or two code units, and returns `this`.
- `void setCharAt(int i, char c)`
  sets the `i`th code unit to `c`.
- `StringBuilder/StringBuffer insert(int offset, String str)`
  inserts a string at position `offset` and returns `this`.
- `StringBuilder/StringBuffer insert(int offset, char c)`
  inserts a code unit at position `offset` and returns `this`.
- `StringBuilder/StringBuffer delete(int startIndex, int endIndex)`
  deletes the code units with offsets `startIndex` to `endIndex - 1` and returns `this`.
- `String toString()`
  returns a string with the same data as the builder or buffer contents.

Working with Random-Access Streams

If you have a large number of employee records of variable length, the storage technique used in the preceding section suffers from one limitation: it is not possible to read a record in the middle of the file without first reading all records that come before it. In this section, we make all records the same length. This lets us implement a random-access method for reading back the information by using the `RandomAccessFile` class that you saw earlier—we can use this to get at any record in the same amount of time.

We will store the numbers in the instance fields in our classes in a binary format. We do that with the `writeInt` and `writeDouble` methods of the `DataOutput` interface. (As we mentioned earlier, this is the common interface of the `DataOutputStream` and the `RandomAccessFile` classes.)

However, because the size of each record must remain constant, we need to make all the strings the same size when we save them. The variable-size UTF format does not do this, and the rest of the Java library provides no convenient means of accomplishing this. We need to write a bit of code to implement two helper methods to make the strings the same size. We will call the methods `writeFixedString` and `readFixedString`. These methods read and write Unicode strings that always have the same length.

The `writeFixedString` method takes the parameter `size`. Then, it writes the specified number of code units, starting at the beginning of the string. (If there are too few code units, the method pads the string, using zero values.) Here is the code for the `writeFixedString` method:

```
static void writeFixedString(String s, int size, DataOutput out)
   throws IOException
{
   int i;
   for (i = 0; i < size; i++)
   {
      char ch = 0;
      if (i < s.length()) ch = s.charAt(i);
      out.writeChar(ch);
   }
}
```

The `readFixedString` method reads characters from the input stream until it has consumed `size` code units or until it encounters a character with a zero value. Then, it should skip past the remaining zero values in the input field. For added efficiency, this method uses the `StringBuilder` class to read in a string.

```
static String readFixedString(int size, DataInput in)
   throws IOException
{
   StringBuilder b = new StringBuilder(size);
   int i = 0;
   boolean more = true;
   while (more && i < size)
   {
      char ch = in.readChar();
      i++;
      if (ch == 0) more = false;
      else b.append(ch);
   }
   in.skipBytes(2 * (size - i));
   return b.toString();
}
```

NOTE: We placed the `writeFixedString` and `readFixedString` methods inside the `DataIO` helper class.

To write a fixed-size record, we simply write all fields in binary.

```
public void writeData(DataOutput out) throws IOException
{
   DataIO.writeFixedString(name, NAME_SIZE, out);
   out.writeDouble(salary);

   GregorianCalendar calendar = new GregorianCalendar();
   calendar.setTime(hireDay);
   out.writeInt(calendar.get(Calendar.YEAR));
   out.writeInt(calendar.get(Calendar.MONTH) + 1);
   out.writeInt(calendar.get(Calendar.DAY_OF_MONTH));
}
```

Reading the data back is just as simple.

```
public void readData(DataInput in) throws IOException
{
   name = DataIO.readFixedString(NAME_SIZE, in);
   salary = in.readDouble();
   int y = in.readInt();
   int m = in.readInt();
   int d = in.readInt();
   GregorianCalendar calendar = new GregorianCalendar(y, m - 1, d);
   hireDay = calendar.getTime();
}
```

In our example, each employee record is 100 bytes long because we specified that the name field would always be written using 40 characters. This gives us a breakdown as indicated in the following:

40 characters = 80 bytes for the name

1 `double` = 8 bytes

3 `int` = 12 bytes

As an example, suppose you want to position the file pointer to the third record. You can use the following version of the `seek` method:

```
long n = 3;
int RECORD_SIZE = 100;
in.seek((n - 1) * RECORD_SIZE);
```

Then you can read a record:

```
Employee e = new Employee();
e.readData(in);
```

If you want to modify the record and then save it back into the same location, remember to set the file pointer back to the beginning of the record:

```
in.seek((n - 1) * RECORD_SIZE);
e.writeData(out);
```

To determine the total number of bytes in a file, use the `length` method. The total number of records is the length divided by the size of each record.

```
long int nbytes = in.length(); // length in bytes
int nrecords = (int) (nbytes / RECORD_SIZE);
```

The test program shown in Example 12–3 writes three records into a data file and then reads them from the file in reverse order. To do this efficiently requires random access—we need to get at the third record first.

Example 12–3: RandomFileTest.java

```
import java.io.*;
import java.util.*;

public class RandomFileTest
{
   public static void main(String[] args)
   {
      Employee[] staff = new Employee[3];

      staff[0] = new Employee("Carl Cracker", 75000, 1987, 12, 15);
      staff[1] = new Employee("Harry Hacker", 50000, 1989, 10, 1);
      staff[2] = new Employee("Tony Tester", 40000, 1990, 3, 15);

      try
      {
         // save all employee records to the file employee.dat
         DataOutputStream out = new DataOutputStream(new FileOutputStream("employee.dat"));
         for (Employee e : staff)
            e.writeData(out);
         out.close();

         // retrieve all records into a new array
         RandomAccessFile in = new RandomAccessFile("employee.dat", "r");
         // compute the array size
         int n = (int)(in.length() / Employee.RECORD_SIZE);
         Employee[] newStaff = new Employee[n];

         // read employees in reverse order
         for (int i = n - 1; i >= 0; i--)
         {
            newStaff[i] = new Employee();
            in.seek(i * Employee.RECORD_SIZE);
            newStaff[i].readData(in);
         }
         in.close();

         // print the newly read employee records
         for (Employee e : newStaff)
            System.out.println(e);
      }
      catch(IOException e)
      {
         e.printStackTrace();
      }
   }
}

class Employee
{
   public Employee() {}

```

```
   public Employee(String n, double s, int year, int month, int day)
   {
      name = n;
      salary = s;
      GregorianCalendar calendar = new GregorianCalendar(year, month - 1, day);
      hireDay = calendar.getTime();
   }

   public String getName()
   {
      return name;
   }

   public double getSalary()
   {
      return salary;
   }

   public Date getHireDay()
   {
      return hireDay;
   }

   /**
      Writes employee data to a data output
      @param out the data output
   */
   public void raiseSalary(double byPercent)
   {
      double raise = salary * byPercent / 100;
      salary += raise;
   }

   public String toString()
   {
      return getClass().getName()
         + "[name=" + name
         + ",salary=" + salary
         + ",hireDay=" + hireDay
         + "]";
   }

   /**
      Writes employee data to a data output
      @param out the data output
   */
   public void writeData(DataOutput out) throws IOException
   {
      DataIO.writeFixedString(name, NAME_SIZE, out);
      out.writeDouble(salary);

      GregorianCalendar calendar = new GregorianCalendar();
      calendar.setTime(hireDay);
      out.writeInt(calendar.get(Calendar.YEAR));
      out.writeInt(calendar.get(Calendar.MONTH) + 1);
      out.writeInt(calendar.get(Calendar.DAY_OF_MONTH));
```

```
   }

   /**
      Reads employee data from a data input
      @param in the data input
   */
   public void readData(DataInput in) throws IOException
   {
      name = DataIO.readFixedString(NAME_SIZE, in);
      salary = in.readDouble();
      int y = in.readInt();
      int m = in.readInt();
      int d = in.readInt();
      GregorianCalendar calendar = new GregorianCalendar(y, m - 1, d);
      hireDay = calendar.getTime();
   }

   public static final int NAME_SIZE = 40;
   public static final int RECORD_SIZE = 2 * NAME_SIZE + 8 + 4 + 4 + 4;

   private String name;
   private double salary;
   private Date hireDay;
}

class DataIO
{
   public static String readFixedString(int size, DataInput in)
      throws IOException
   {
      StringBuilder b = new StringBuilder(size);
      int i = 0;
      boolean more = true;
      while (more && i < size)
      {
         char ch = in.readChar();
         i++;
         if (ch == 0) more = false;
         else b.append(ch);
      }
      in.skipBytes(2 * (size - i));
      return b.toString();
   }

   public static void writeFixedString(String s, int size, DataOutput out)
      throws IOException
   {
      int i;
      for (i = 0; i < size; i++)
      {
         char ch = 0;
         if (i < s.length()) ch = s.charAt(i);
         out.writeChar(ch);
      }
   }
}
```

Object Streams

Using a fixed-length record format is a good choice if you need to store data of the same type. However, objects that you create in an object-oriented program are rarely all of the same type. For example, you may have an array called `staff` that is nominally an array of `Employee` records but contains objects that are actually instances of a subclass such as `Manager`.

If we want to save files that contain this kind of information, we must first save the type of each object and then the data that define the current state of the object. When we read this information back from a file, we must

- Read the object type;
- Create a blank object of that type;
- Fill it with the data that we stored in the file.

It is entirely possible (if very tedious) to do this by hand, and in the first edition of this book we did exactly this. However, Sun Microsystems developed a powerful mechanism that allows this to be done with much less effort. As you will soon see, this mechanism, called *object serialization*, almost completely automates what was previously a very tedious process. (You see later in this chapter where the term "serialization" comes from.)

Storing Objects of Variable Type

To save object data, you first need to open an `ObjectOutputStream` object:

```
ObjectOutputStream out = new ObjectOutputStream(new FileOutputStream("employee.dat"));
```

Now, to save an object, you simply use the `writeObject` method of the `ObjectOutputStream` class as in the following fragment:

```
Employee harry = new Employee("Harry Hacker", 50000, 1989, 10, 1);
Manager boss = new Manager("Carl Cracker", 80000, 1987, 12, 15);
out.writeObject(harry);
out.writeObject(boss);
```

To read the objects back in, first get an `ObjectInputStream` object:

```
ObjectInputStream in = new ObjectInputStream(new FileInputStream("employee.dat"));
```

Then, retrieve the objects in the same order in which they were written, using the `readObject` method.

```
Employee e1 = (Employee) in.readObject();
Employee e2 = (Employee) in.readObject();
```

When reading back objects, you must carefully keep track of the number of objects that were saved, their order, and their types. Each call to `readObject` reads in another object of the type `Object`. You therefore will need to cast it to its correct type.

If you don't need the exact type or you don't remember it, then you can cast it to any superclass or even leave it as type `Object`. For example, `e2` is an `Employee` object variable even though it actually refers to a `Manager` object. If you need to dynamically query the type of the object, you can use the `getClass` method that we described in Chapter 5.

You can write and read only *objects* with the `writeObject`/`readObject` methods. For primitive type values, you use methods such as `writeInt`/`readInt` or `writeDouble`/`readDouble`. (The object stream classes implement the `DataInput`/`DataOutput` interfaces.) Of course, numbers inside objects (such as the `salary` field of an `Employee` object) are saved and restored automatically. Recall that, in Java, strings and arrays are objects and can, therefore, be processed with the `writeObject`/`readObject` methods.

There is, however, one change you need to make to any class that you want to save and restore in an object stream. The class must implement the `Serializable` interface:

```
class Employee implements Serializable { . . . }
```

The `Serializable` interface has no methods, so you don't need to change your classes in any way. In this regard, it is similar to the `Cloneable` interface that we also discussed in Chapter 6. However, to make a class cloneable, you still had to override the `clone` method of the `Object` class. To make a class serializable, you do not need to do *anything* else.

Example 12–4 is a test program that writes an array containing two employees and one manager to disk and then restores it. Writing an array is done with a single operation:

```
Employee[] staff = new Employee[3];
. . .
out.writeObject(staff);
```

Similarly, reading in the result is done with a single operation. However, we must apply a cast to the return value of the `readObject` method:

```
Employee[] newStaff = (Employee[]) in.readObject();
```

Once the information is restored, we print each employee because you can easily distinguish employee and manager objects by their different `toString` results. This should convince you that we did restore the correct types.

Example 12–4: ObjectFileTest.java

```
import java.io.*;
import java.util.*;

class ObjectFileTest
{
   public static void main(String[] args)
   {
      Manager boss = new Manager("Carl Cracker", 80000, 1987, 12, 15);
      boss.setBonus(5000);

      Employee[] staff = new Employee[3];

      staff[0] = boss;
      staff[1] = new Employee("Harry Hacker", 50000, 1989, 10, 1);
      staff[2] = new Employee("Tony Tester", 40000, 1990, 3, 15);

      try
      {
         // save all employee records to the file employee.dat
         ObjectOutputStream out = new ObjectOutputStream(new FileOutputStream("employee.dat"));
         out.writeObject(staff);
         out.close();

         // retrieve all records into a new array
         ObjectInputStream in =  new ObjectInputStream(new FileInputStream("employee.dat"));
         Employee[] newStaff = (Employee[]) in.readObject();
         in.close();

         // print the newly read employee records
         for (Employee e : newStaff)
            System.out.println(e);
      }
      catch (Exception e)
```

```
      {
         e.printStackTrace();
      }
   }
}

class Employee implements Serializable
{
   public Employee() {}

   public Employee(String n, double s, int year, int month, int day)
   {
      name = n;
      salary = s;
      GregorianCalendar calendar = new GregorianCalendar(year, month - 1, day);
      hireDay = calendar.getTime();
   }

   public String getName()
   {
      return name;
   }

   public double getSalary()
   {
      return salary;
   }

   public Date getHireDay()
   {
      return hireDay;
   }

   public void raiseSalary(double byPercent)
   {
      double raise = salary * byPercent / 100;
      salary += raise;
   }

   public String toString()
   {
      return getClass().getName()
         + "[name=" + name
         + ",salary=" + salary
         + ",hireDay=" + hireDay
         + "]";
   }

   private String name;
   private double salary;
   private Date hireDay;
}

class Manager extends Employee
{
```

```
   /**
      @param n the employee's name
      @param s the salary
      @param year the hire year
      @param month the hire month
      @param day the hire day
   */
   public Manager(String n, double s, int year, int month, int day)
   {
      super(n, s, year, month, day);
      bonus = 0;
   }

   public double getSalary()
   {
      double baseSalary = super.getSalary();
      return baseSalary + bonus;
   }

   public void setBonus(double b)
   {
      bonus = b;
   }

   public String toString()
   {
      return super.toString()
        + "[bonus=" + bonus
        + "]";
   }

   private double bonus;
}
```

API **java.io.ObjectOutputStream 1.1**

- `ObjectOutputStream(OutputStream out)`
  creates an `ObjectOutputStream` so that you can write objects to the specified `OutputStream`.
- `void writeObject(Object obj)`
  writes the specified object to the `ObjectOutputStream`. This method saves the class of the object, the signature of the class, and the values of any nonstatic, nontransient field of the class and its superclasses.

java.io.ObjectInputStream 1.1

- `ObjectInputStream(InputStream is)`
  creates an `ObjectInputStream` to read back object information from the specified `InputStream`.
- `Object readObject()`
  reads an object from the `ObjectInputStream`. In particular, this method reads back the class of the object, the signature of the class, and the values of the nontransient and nonstatic fields of the class and all its superclasses. It does deserializing to allow multiple object references to be recovered.

Understanding the Object Serialization File Format

Object serialization saves object data in a particular file format. Of course, you can use the `writeObject/readObject` methods without having to know the exact sequence of bytes that represents objects in a file. Nonetheless, we found studying the data format to be extremely helpful for gaining insight into the object streaming process. We did this by looking at hex dumps of various saved object files. However, the details are somewhat technical, so feel free to skip this section if you are not interested in the implementation.

Every file begins with the two-byte "magic number"

```
AC ED
```

followed by the version number of the object serialization format, which is currently

```
00 05
```

(We use hexadecimal numbers throughout this section to denote bytes.) Then, it contains a sequence of objects, in the order that they were saved.

String objects are saved as

74	two-byte length	characters

For example, the string "Harry" is saved as

```
74 00 05 Harry
```

The Unicode characters of the string are saved in "modified UTF-8" format.

When an object is saved, the class of that object must be saved as well. The class description contains

1. The name of the class;
2. The *serial version unique ID,* which is a fingerprint of the data field types and method signatures;
3. A set of flags describing the serialization method; and
4. A description of the data fields.

Java gets the fingerprint by

1. Ordering descriptions of the class, superclass, interfaces, field types, and method signatures in a canonical way;
2. Then applying the so-called Secure Hash Algorithm (SHA) to that data.

SHA is a fast algorithm that gives a "fingerprint" to a larger block of information. This fingerprint is always a 20-byte data packet, regardless of the size of the original data. It is created by a clever sequence of bit operations on the data that makes it essentially 100 percent certain that the fingerprint will change if the information is altered in any way. SHA is a U.S. standard, recommended by the National Institute for Science and Technology (NIST). (For more details on SHA, see, for example, *Cryptography and Network Security: Principles and Practice,* by William Stallings [Prentice Hall, 2002].) However, Java uses only the first 8 bytes of the SHA code as a class fingerprint. It is still very likely that the class fingerprint will change if the data fields or methods change in any way.

Java can then check the class fingerprint to protect us from the following scenario: An object is saved to a disk file. Later, the designer of the class makes a change, for example, by removing a data field. Then, the old disk file is read in again. Now the data layout on the disk no longer matches the data layout in memory. If the data were read back in its old form, it could corrupt memory. Java takes great care to make such memory corruption close to impossible. Hence, it checks, using the fingerprint, that the class definition has not changed when it restores an object. It does this by comparing the fingerprint on disk with the fingerprint of the current class.

NOTE: Technically, as long as the data layout of a class has not changed, it ought to be safe to read objects back in. But Java is conservative and checks that the methods have not changed either. (After all, the methods describe the meaning of the stored data.) Of course, in practice, classes do evolve, and it may be necessary for a program to read in older versions of objects. We discuss this later in the section entitled "Versioning" on page 679.

Here is how a class identifier is stored:

`72`
2-byte length of class name
class name
8-byte fingerprint
1-byte flag
2-byte count of data field descriptors
data field descriptors
`78` (end marker)
superclass type (`70` if none)

The flag byte is composed of three bit masks, defined in `java.io.ObjectStreamConstants`:

```
static final byte SC_WRITE_METHOD = 1;
   // class has writeObject method that writes additional data
static final byte SC_SERIALIZABLE = 2;
   // class implements Serializable interface
static final byte SC_EXTERNALIZABLE = 4;
   // class implements Externalizable interface
```

We discuss the `Externalizable` interface later in this chapter. Externalizable classes supply custom read and write methods that take over the output of their instance fields. The classes that we write implement the `Serializable` interface and will have a flag value of `02`. The `java.util.Date` class defines its own `readObject`/`writeObject` methods and has a flag of `03`.

Each data field descriptor has the format:

1-byte type code
2-byte length of field name
field name
class name (if field is an object)

The type code is one of the following:

`B`	`byte`
`C`	`char`
`D`	`double`
`F`	`float`
`I`	`int`
`J`	`long`
`L`	object
`S`	`short`
`Z`	`boolean`
`[`	array

When the type code is `L`, the field name is followed by the field type. Class and field name strings do not start with the string code `74`, but field types do. Field types use a slightly

different encoding of their names, namely, the format used by native methods. (See Volume 2 for native methods.)

For example, the salary field of the `Employee` class is encoded as:

```
D 00 06 salary
```

Here is the complete class descriptor of the `Employee` class:

`72 00 08 Employee`	
`E6 D2 86 7D AE AC 18 1B 02`	Fingerprint and flags
`00 03`	Number of instance fields
`D 00 06 salary`	Instance field type and name
`L 00 07 hireDay`	Instance field type and name
`74 00 10 Ljava/util/Date;`	Instance field class name—`Date`
`L 00 04 name`	Instance field type and name
`74 00 12 Ljava/lang/String;`	Instance field class name—`String`
`78`	End marker
`70`	No superclass

These descriptors are fairly long. If the *same* class descriptor is needed again in the file, then an abbreviated form is used:

`71`	4-byte serial number

The serial number refers to the previous explicit class descriptor. We discuss the numbering scheme later.

An object is stored as

`73`	class descriptor	object data

For example, here is how an `Employee` object is stored:

`40 E8 6A 00 00 00 00 00`	`salary` field value—`double`
`73`	`hireDay` field value—new object
`71 00 7E 00 08`	Existing class `java.util.Date`
`77 08 00 00 00 91 1B 4E B1 80 78`	External storage—details later
`74 00 0C Harry Hacker`	`name` field value—`String`

As you can see, the data file contains enough information to restore the `Employee` object.

Arrays are saved in the following format:

`75`	class descriptor	4-byte number of entries	entries

The array class name in the class descriptor is in the same format as that used by native methods (which is slightly different from the class name used by class names in other class descriptors). In this format, class names start with an `L` and end with a semicolon.

For example, an array of three `Employee` objects starts out like this:

`75`	Array
`72 00 0B [LEmployee;`	New class, string length, class name `Employee[]`
`FC BF 36 11 C5 91 11 C7 02`	Fingerprint and flags
`00 00`	Number of instance fields

78	End marker
70	No superclass
00 00 00 03	Number of array entries

Note that the fingerprint for an array of `Employee` objects is different from a fingerprint of the `Employee` class itself.

Of course, studying these codes can be about as exciting as reading the average phone book. But it is still instructive to know that the object stream contains a detailed description of all the objects that it contains, with sufficient detail to allow reconstruction of both objects and arrays of objects.

Solving the Problem of Saving Object References

We now know how to save objects that contain numbers, strings, or other simple objects. However, there is one important situation that we still need to consider. What happens when one object is shared by several objects as part of its state?

To illustrate the problem, let us make a slight modification to the `Manager` class. Let's assume that each manager has a secretary, implemented as an instance variable `secretary` of type `Employee`. (It would make sense to derive a class `Secretary` from `Employee` for this purpose, but we don't do that here.)

```
class Manager extends Employee
{
   . . .
   private Employee secretary;
}
```

Having done this, you must keep in mind that the `Manager` object now contains a *reference* to the `Employee` object that describes the secretary, *not* a separate copy of the object.

In particular, two managers can share the same secretary, as is the case in Figure 12–6 and the following code:

```
harry = new Employee("Harry Hacker", . . .);
Manager carl = new Manager("Carl Cracker", . . .);
carl.setSecretary(harry);
Manager tony = new Manager("Tony Tester", . . .);
tony.setSecretary(harry);
```

Now, suppose we write the employee data to disk. What we *don't* want is for the `Manager` to save its information according to the following logic:

- Save employee data;
- Save secretary data.

Then, the data for `harry` would be saved *three times*. When reloaded, the objects would have the configuration shown in Figure 12–7.

This is not what we want. Suppose the secretary gets a raise. We would not want to hunt for all other copies of that object and apply the raise as well. We want to save and restore only *one copy* of the secretary. To do this, we must copy and restore the original references to the objects. In other words, we want the object layout on disk to be exactly like the object layout in memory. This is called *persistence* in object-oriented circles.

Of course, we cannot save and restore the memory addresses for the secretary objects. When an object is reloaded, it will likely occupy a completely different memory address than it originally did.

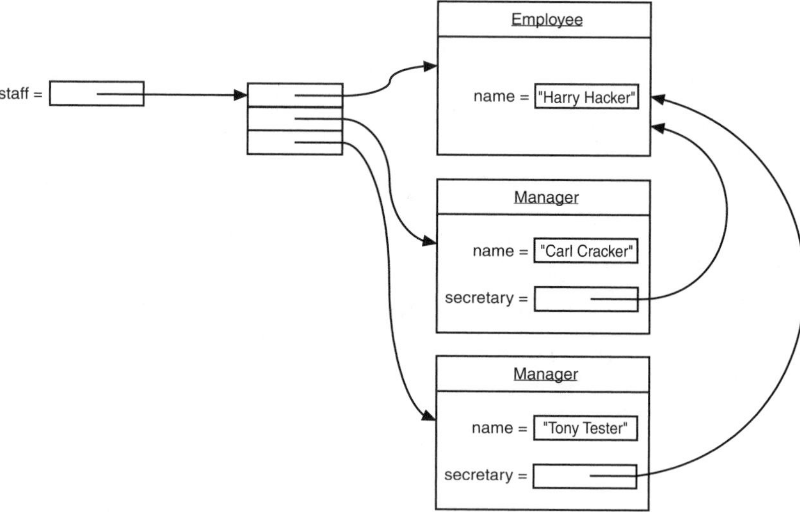

Figure 12–6: Two managers can share a mutual employee

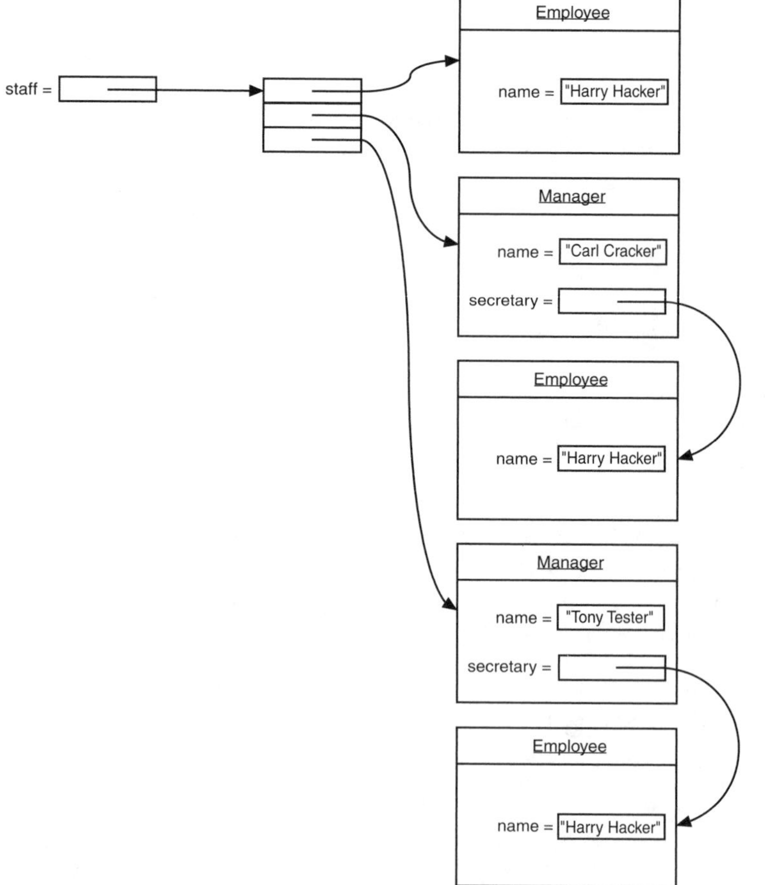

Figure 12–7: Here, Harry is saved three times

Instead, Java uses a *serialization* approach. Hence, the name *object serialization* for this mechanism. Here is the algorithm:

- All objects that are saved to disk are given a serial number (1, 2, 3, and so on, as shown in Figure 12–8).
- When saving an object to disk, find out if the same object has already been stored.
- If it has been stored previously, just write "same as previously saved object with serial number *x*." If not, store all its data.

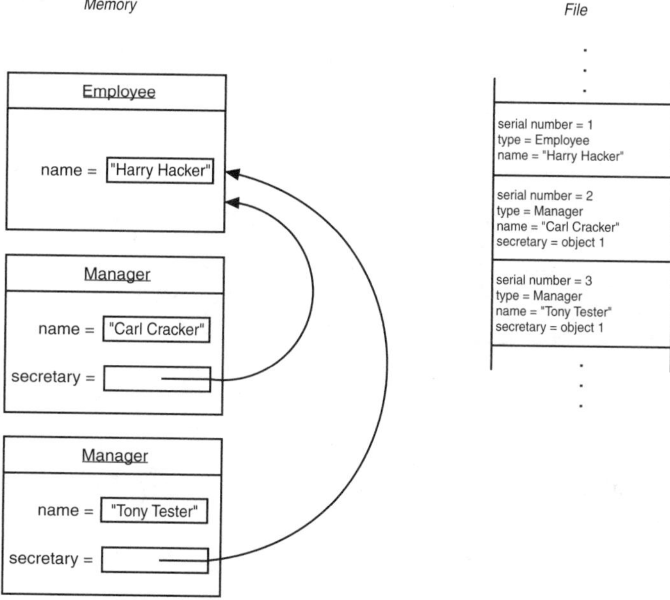

Figure 12–8: An example of object serialization

When reading back the objects, simply reverse the procedure. For each object that you load, note its sequence number and remember where you put it in memory. When you encounter the tag "same as previously saved object with serial number *x*," you look up where you put the object with serial number *x* and set the object reference to that memory address.

Note that the objects need not be saved in any particular order. Figure 12–9 shows what happens when a manager occurs first in the staff array.

All of this sounds confusing, and it is. Fortunately, when object streams are used, the process is also *completely automatic*. Object streams assign the serial numbers and keep track of duplicate objects. The exact numbering scheme is slightly different from that used in the figures—see the next section.

NOTE: In this chapter, we use serialization to save a collection of objects to a disk file and retrieve it exactly as we stored it. Another very important application is the transmittal of a collection of objects across a network connection to another computer. Just as raw memory addresses are meaningless in a file, they are also meaningless when communicating with a different processor. Because serialization replaces memory addresses with serial numbers, it permits the transport of object collections from one machine to another. We study that use of serialization when discussing remote method invocation in Volume 2.

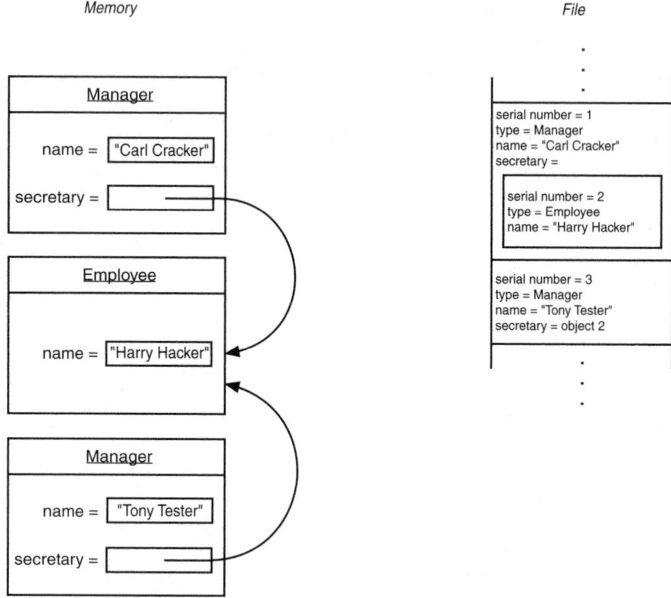

Figure 12–9: Objects saved in random order

Example 12–5 is a program that saves and reloads a network of `Employee` and `Manager` objects (some of which share the same employee as a secretary). Note that the secretary object is unique after reloading—when `newStaff[1]` gets a raise, that is reflected in the `secretary` fields of the managers.

Example 12–5: ObjectRefTest.java

```
import java.io.*;
import java.util.*;

class ObjectRefTest
{
   public static void main(String[] args)
   {
      Employee harry = new Employee("Harry Hacker", 50000, 1989, 10, 1);
      Manager boss = new Manager("Carl Cracker", 80000, 1987, 12, 15);
      boss.setSecretary(harry);

      Employee[] staff = new Employee[3];

      staff[0] = boss;
      staff[1] = harry;
      staff[2] = new Employee("Tony Tester", 40000, 1990, 3, 15);

      try
      {
         // save all employee records to the file employee.dat
         ObjectOutputStream out = new ObjectOutputStream(new FileOutputStream("employee.dat"));
         out.writeObject(staff);
         out.close();
```

```
         // retrieve all records into a new array
         ObjectInputStream in =  new ObjectInputStream(new FileInputStream("employee.dat"));
         Employee[] newStaff = (Employee[]) in.readObject();
         in.close();

         // raise secretary's salary
         newStaff[1].raiseSalary(10);

         // print the newly read employee records
         for (Employee e : newStaff)
            System.out.println(e);
      }
      catch (Exception e)
      {
         e.printStackTrace();
      }
   }
}

class Employee implements Serializable
{
   public Employee() {}

   public Employee(String n, double s, int year, int month, int day)
   {
      name = n;
      salary = s;
      GregorianCalendar calendar = new GregorianCalendar(year, month - 1, day);
      hireDay = calendar.getTime();
   }

   public String getName()
   {
      return name;
   }

   public double getSalary()
   {
      return salary;
   }

   public Date getHireDay()
   {
      return hireDay;
   }

   public void raiseSalary(double byPercent)
   {
      double raise = salary * byPercent / 100;
      salary += raise;
   }

   public String toString()
```

```
   {
      return getClass().getName()
         + "[name=" + name
         + ",salary=" + salary
         + ",hireDay=" + hireDay
         + "]";
   }

   private String name;
   private double salary;
   private Date hireDay;
}

class Manager extends Employee
{
   /**
      Constructs a Manager without a secretary
      @param n the employee's name
      @param s the salary
      @param year the hire year
      @param month the hire month
      @param day the hire day
   */
   public Manager(String n, double s, int year, int month, int day)
   {
      super(n, s, year, month, day);
      secretary = null;
   }

   /**
      Assigns a secretary to the manager.
      @param s the secretary
   */
   public void setSecretary(Employee s)
   {
      secretary = s;
   }

   public String toString()
   {
      return super.toString()
        + "[secretary=" + secretary
        + "]";
   }

   private Employee secretary;
}
```

Understanding the Output Format for Object References

This section continues the discussion of the output format of object streams. If you skipped the previous discussion, you should skip this section as well.

All objects (including arrays and strings) and all class descriptors are given serial numbers as they are saved in the output file. This process is referred to as *serialization* because every saved object is assigned a serial number. (The count starts at `00 7E 00 00`.)

We already saw that a full class descriptor for any given class occurs only once. Subsequent descriptors refer to it. For example, in our previous example, a repeated reference to the Date class was coded as

```
71 00 7E 00 08
```

The same mechanism is used for objects. If a reference to a previously saved object is written, it is saved in exactly the same way, that is, 71 followed by the serial number. It is always clear from the context whether the particular serial reference denotes a class descriptor or an object.

Finally, a null reference is stored as

```
70
```

Here is the commented output of the ObjectRefTest program of the preceding section. If you like, run the program, look at a hex dump of its data file employee.dat, and compare it with the commented listing. The important lines toward the end of the output show the reference to a previously saved object.

AC ED 00 05	File header
75	Array staff (serial #1)
72 00 0B [LEmployee;	New class, string length, class name Employee[] (serial #0)
FC BF 36 11 C5 91 11 C7 02	Fingerprint and flags
00 00	Number of instance fields
78	End marker
70	No superclass
00 00 00 03	Number of array entries
73	staff[0]—new object (serial #7)
72 00 07 Manager	New class, string length, class name (serial #2)
36 06 AE 13 63 8F 59 B7 02	Fingerprint and flags
00 01	Number of data fields
L 00 09 secretary	Instance field type and name
74 00 0A LEmployee;	Instance field class name—String (serial #3)
78	End marker
72 00 08 Employee	Superclass—new class, string length, class name (serial #4)
E6 D2 86 7D AE AC 18 1B 02	Fingerprint and flags
00 03	Number of instance fields
D 00 06 salary	Instance field type and name
L 00 07 hireDay	Instance field type and name
74 00 10 Ljava/util/Date;	Instance field class name—String (serial #5)
L 00 04 name	Instance field type and name
74 00 12 Ljava/lang/String;	Instance field class name—String (serial #6)
78	End marker
70	No superclass
40 F3 88 00 00 00 00 00	salary field value—double

`73`	`hireDay` field value—new object (serial #9)
`72 00 0E java.util.Date`	New class, string length, class name (serial #8)
`68 6A 81 01 4B 59 74 19 03`	Fingerprint and flags
`00 00`	No instance variables
`78`	End marker
`70`	No superclass
`77 08`	External storage, number of bytes
`00 00 00 83 E9 39 E0 00`	Date
`78`	End marker
`74 00 0C Carl Cracker`	`name` field value—`String` (serial #10)
`73`	`secretary` field value—new object (serial #11)
`71 00 7E 00 04`	existing class (use serial #4)
`40 E8 6A 00 00 00 00 00`	`salary` field value—`double`
`73`	`hireDay` field value—new object (serial #12)
`71 00 7E 00 08`	Existing class (use serial #8)
`77 08`	External storage, number of bytes
`00 00 00 91 1B 4E B1 80`	Date
`78`	End marker
`74 00 0C Harry Hacker`	`name` field value—`String` (serial #13)
`71 00 7E 00 0B`	`staff[1]`—existing object (use serial #11)
`73`	`staff[2]`—new object (serial #14)
`71 00 7E 00 04`	Existing class (use serial #4)
`40 E3 88 00 00 00 00 00`	`salary` field value—`double`
`73`	`hireDay` field value—new object (serial #15)
`71 00 7E 00 08`	Existing class (use serial #8)
`77 08`	External storage, number of bytes
`00 00 00 94 6D 3E EC 00 00`	Date
`78`	End marker
`74 00 0B Tony Tester`	`name` field value—`String` (serial # 16)

It is usually not important to know the exact file format (unless you are trying to create an evil effect by modifying the data). What you should remember is this:

- The object stream output contains the types and data fields of all objects.
- Each object is assigned a serial number.
- Repeated occurrences of the same object are stored as references to that serial number.

Modifying the Default Serialization Mechanism

Certain data fields should never be serialized, for example, integer values that store file handles or handles of windows that are only meaningful to native methods. Such information is guaranteed to be useless when you reload an object at a later time or transport it to a different

machine. In fact, improper values for such fields can actually cause native methods to crash. Java has an easy mechanism to prevent such fields from ever being serialized. Mark them with the keyword `transient`. You also need to tag fields as `transient` if they belong to nonserializable classes. Transient fields are always skipped when objects are serialized.

The serialization mechanism provides a way for individual classes to add validation or any other desired action to the default read and write behavior. A serializable class can define methods with the signature

```
private void readObject(ObjectInputStream in)
   throws IOException, ClassNotFoundException;
private void writeObject(ObjectOutputStream out)
   throws IOException;
```

Then, the data fields are no longer automatically serialized, and these methods are called instead.

Here is a typical example. A number of classes in the `java.awt.geom` package, such as `Point2D.Double`, are not serializable. Now suppose you want to serialize a class `LabeledPoint` that stores a `String` and a `Point2D.Double`. First, you need to mark the `Point2D.Double` field as `transient` to avoid a `NotSerializableException`.

```
public class LabeledPoint implements Serializable
{
   . . .
   private String label;
   private transient Point2D.Double point;
}
```

In the `writeObject` method, we first write the object descriptor and the `String` field, state, by calling the `defaultWriteObject` method. This is a special method of the `ObjectOutputStream` class that can only be called from within a `writeObject` method of a serializable class. Then we write the point coordinates, using the standard `DataOutput` calls.

```
private void writeObject(ObjectOutputStream out)
   throws IOException
{
   out.defaultWriteObject();
   out.writeDouble(point.getX());
   out.writeDouble(point.getY());
}
```

In the `readObject` method, we reverse the process:

```
private void readObject(ObjectInputStream in)
   throws IOException
{
   in.defaultReadObject();
   double x = in.readDouble();
   double y = in.readDouble();
   point = new Point2D.Double(x, y);
}
```

Another example is the `java.util.Date` class that supplies its own `readObject` and `writeObject` methods. These methods write the date as a number of milliseconds from the epoch (January 1, 1970, midnight UTC). The `Date` class has a complex internal representation that stores both a `Calendar` object and a millisecond count, to optimize lookups. The state of the `Calendar` is redundant and does not have to be saved.

The `readObject` and `writeObject` methods only need to save and load their data fields. They should not concern themselves with superclass data or any other class information.

Rather than letting the serialization mechanism save and restore object data, a class can define its own mechanism. To do this, a class must implement the Externalizable interface. This in turn requires it to define two methods:

```
public void readExternal(ObjectInputStream in)
  throws IOException, ClassNotFoundException;
public void writeExternal(ObjectOutputStream out)
  throws IOException;
```

Unlike the readObject and writeObject methods that were described in the preceding section, these methods are fully responsible for saving and restoring the entire object, *including the superclass data*. The serialization mechanism merely records the class of the object in the stream. When reading an externalizable object, the object stream creates an object with the default constructor and then calls the readExternal method. Here is how you can implement these methods for the Employee class:

```
public void readExternal(ObjectInput s)
   throws IOException
{
   name = s.readUTF();
   salary = s.readDouble();
   hireDay = new Date(s.readLong());
}

public void writeExternal(ObjectOutput s)
   throws IOException
{
  s.writeUTF(name);
  s.writeDouble(salary);
  s.writeLong(hireDay.getTime());
}
```

TIP: Serialization is somewhat slow because the virtual machine must discover the structure of each object. If you are concerned about performance and if you read and write a large number of objects of a particular class, you should investigate the use of the Externalizable interface. The tech tip http://developer.java.sun.com/developer/TechTips/txtarchive/Apr00_Stu.txt demonstrates that in the case of an employee class, using external reading and writing was about 35%–40% faster than the default serialization.

CAUTION: Unlike the readObject and writeObject methods, which are private and can only be called by the serialization mechanism, the readExternal and writeExternal methods are public. In particular, readExternal potentially permits modification of the state of an existing object.

NOTE: For even more exotic variations of serialization, see http://www.absolutejava.com/serialization.

Serializing Singletons and Typesafe Enumerations

You have to pay particular attention when serializing and deserializing objects that are assumed to be unique. This commonly happens when you are implementing singletons and typesafe enumerations.

If you use the enum construct of JDK 5.0, then you need not worry about serialization—it just works. However, suppose you maintain legacy code that contains an enumerated type such as

```
public class Orientation
{
   public static final Orientation HORIZONTAL = new Orientation(1);
   public static final Orientation VERTICAL  = new Orientation(2);
   private Orientation(int v) { value = v; }
   private int value;
}
```

This idiom was common before enumerations were added to the Java language. Note that the constructor is private. Thus, no objects can be created beyond Orientation.HORIZONTAL and Orientation.VERTICAL. In particular, you can use the == operator to test for object equality:

```
if (orientation == Orientation.HORIZONTAL) . . .
```

There is an important twist that you need to remember when a typesafe enumeration implements the Serializable interface. The default serialization mechanism is not appropriate. Suppose we write a value of type Orientation and read it in again:

```
Orientation original = Orientation.HORIZONTAL;
ObjectOutputStream out = . . .;
out.write(value);
out.close();
ObjectInputStream in = . . .;
Orientation saved = (Orientation) in.read();
```

Now the test

```
if (saved == Orientation.HORIZONTAL) . . .
```

will fail. In fact, the saved value is a completely new object of the Orientation type and not equal to any of the predefined constants. Even though the constructor is private, the serialization mechanism can create new objects!

To solve this problem, you need to define another special serialization method, called readResolve. If the readResolve method is defined, it is called after the object is deserialized. It must return an object that then becomes the return value of the readObject method. In our case, the readResolve method will inspect the value field and return the appropriate enumerated constant:

```
protected Object readResolve() throws ObjectStreamException
{
   if (value == 1) return Orientation.HORIZONTAL;
   if (value == 2) return Orientation.VERTICAL;
   return null; // this shouldn't happen
}
```

Remember to add a readResolve method to all typesafe enumerations in your legacy code and to all classes that follow the singleton design pattern.

Versioning

In the previous sections, we showed you how to save relatively small collections of objects by means of an object stream. But those were just demonstration programs. With object streams, it helps to think big. Suppose you write a program that lets the user produce a document. This document contains paragraphs of text, tables, graphs, and so on. You can stream out the entire document object with a single call to writeObject:

```
out.writeObject(doc);
```

The paragraph, table, and graph objects are automatically streamed out as well. One user of your program can then give the output file to another user who also has a copy of your program, and that program loads the entire document with a single call to `readObject`:

```
doc = (Document) in.readObject();
```

This is very useful, but your program will inevitably change, and you will release a version 1.1. Can version 1.1 read the old files? Can the users who still use 1.0 read the files that the new version is now producing? Clearly, it would be desirable if object files could cope with the evolution of classes.

At first glance it seems that this would not be possible. When a class definition changes in any way, then its SHA fingerprint also changes, and you know that object streams will refuse to read in objects with different fingerprints. However, a class can indicate that it is *compatible* with an earlier version of itself. To do this, you must first obtain the fingerprint of the *earlier* version of the class. You use the stand-alone `serialver` program that is part of the JDK to obtain this number. For example, running

```
serialver Employee
```

prints

```
Employee: static final long serialVersionUID = -1814239825517340645L;
```

If you start the `serialver` program with the `-show` option, then the program brings up a graphical dialog box (see Figure 12–10).

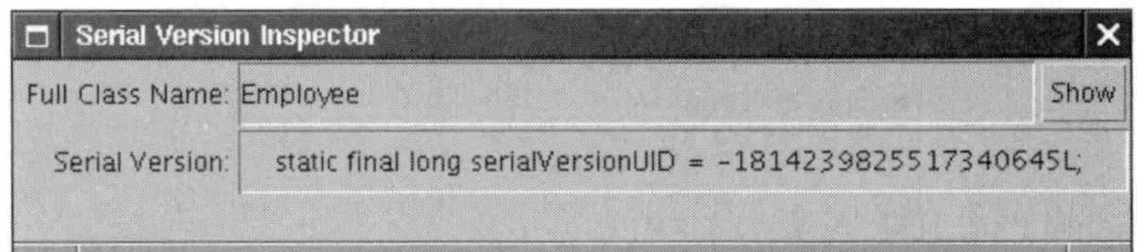

Figure 12–10: The graphical version of the `serialver` program

All *later* versions of the class must define the `serialVersionUID` constant to the same fingerprint as the original.

```
class Employee implements Serializable // version 1.1
{
   . . .
   public static final long serialVersionUID = -1814239825517340645L;
}
```

When a class has a static data member named `serialVersionUID`, it will not compute the fingerprint manually but instead will use that value.

Once that static data member has been placed inside a class, the serialization system is now willing to read in different versions of objects of that class.

If only the methods of the class change, then there is no problem with reading the new object data. However, if data fields change, then you may have problems. For example, the old file object may have more or fewer data fields than the one in the program, or the types of the data fields may be different. In that case, the object stream makes an effort to convert the stream object to the current version of the class.

The object stream compares the data fields of the current version of the class with the data fields of the version in the stream. Of course, the object stream considers only the nontransient and nonstatic data fields. If two fields have matching names but different types, then the object stream makes no effort to convert one type to the other—the objects are incompatible. If the object in the stream has data fields that are not present in the current version,

then the object stream ignores the additional data. If the current version has data fields that are not present in the streamed object, the added fields are set to their default (`null` for objects, zero for numbers, and `false` for Boolean values).

Here is an example. Suppose we have saved a number of employee records on disk, using the original version (1.0) of the class. Now we change the `Employee` class to version 2.0 by adding a data field called `department`. Figure 12–11 shows what happens when a 1.0 object is read into a program that uses 2.0 objects. The department field is set to `null`. Figure 12–12 shows the opposite scenario: a program using 1.0 objects reads a 2.0 object. The additional `department` field is ignored.

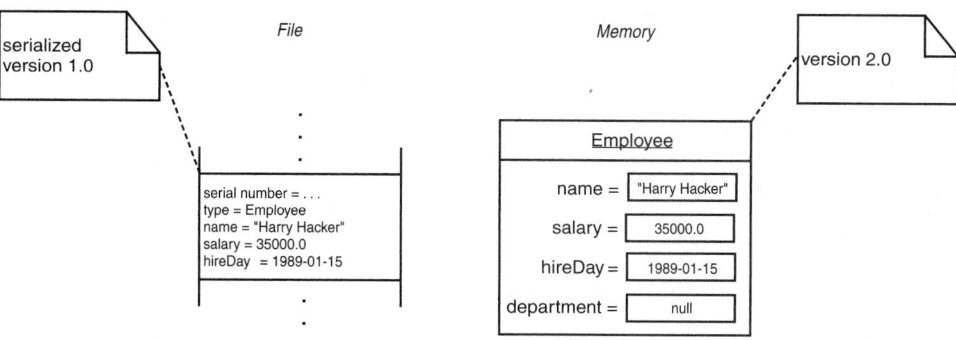

Figure 12–11: Reading an object with fewer data fields

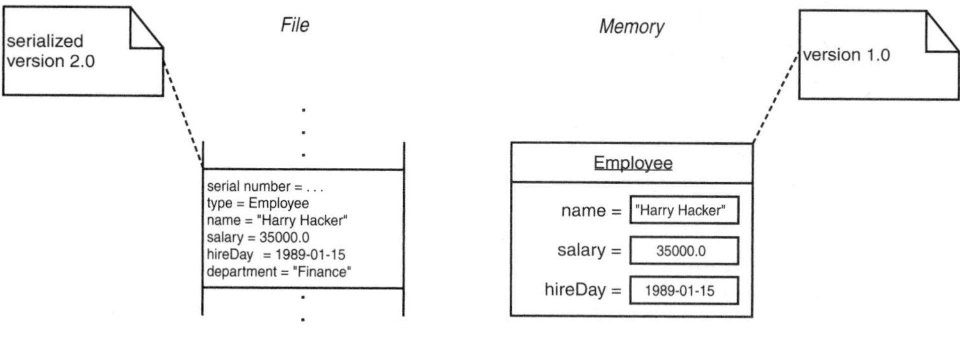

Figure 12–12: Reading an object with more data fields

Is this process safe? It depends. Dropping a data field seems harmless—the recipient still has all the data that it knew how to manipulate. Setting a data field to `null` may not be so safe. Many classes work hard to initialize all data fields in all constructors to non-`null` values, so that the methods don't have to be prepared to handle `null` data. It is up to the class designer to implement additional code in the `readObject` method to fix version incompatibilities or to make sure the methods are robust enough to handle `null` data.

Using Serialization for Cloning

There is an amusing (and, occasionally, very useful) use for the serialization mechanism: it gives you an easy way to clone an object provided the class is serializable. (Recall from Chapter 6 that you need to do a bit of work to allow an object to be cloned.)

To clone a serializable object, simply serialize it to an output stream and then read it back in. The result is a new object that is a deep copy of the existing object. You don't have to write the object to a file—you can use a `ByteArrayOutputStream` to save the data into a byte array.

As Example 12–6 shows, to get `clone` for free, simply extend the `SerialCloneable` class, and you are done.

You should be aware that this method, although clever, will usually be much slower than a clone method that explicitly constructs a new object and copies or clones the data fields (as you saw in Chapter 6).

Example 12–6: SerialCloneTest.java

```
import java.io.*;
import java.util.*;

public class SerialCloneTest
{
   public static void main(String[] args)
   {
      Employee harry = new Employee("Harry Hacker", 35000, 1989, 10, 1);
      // clone harry
      Employee harry2 = (Employee) harry.clone();

      // mutate harry
      harry.raiseSalary(10);

      // now harry and the clone are different
      System.out.println(harry);
      System.out.println(harry2);
   }
}

/**
   A class whose clone method uses serialization.
*/
class SerialCloneable implements Cloneable, Serializable
{
   public Object clone()
   {
      try
      {
         // save the object to a byte array
         ByteArrayOutputStream bout = new ByteArrayOutputStream();
         ObjectOutputStream out = new ObjectOutputStream(bout);
         out.writeObject(this);
         out.close();

         // read a clone of the object from the byte array
         ByteArrayInputStream bin = new ByteArrayInputStream(bout.toByteArray());
         ObjectInputStream in = new ObjectInputStream(bin);
         Object ret = in.readObject();
         in.close();

         return ret;
      }
```

```
      catch (Exception e)
      {
         return null;
      }
   }
}

/**
   The familiar Employee class, redefined to extend the
   SerialCloneable class.
*/
class Employee extends SerialCloneable
{
   public Employee(String n, double s, int year, int month, int day)
   {
      name = n;
      salary = s;
      GregorianCalendar calendar = new GregorianCalendar(year, month - 1, day);
      hireDay = calendar.getTime();
   }

   public String getName()
   {
      return name;
   }

   public double getSalary()
   {
      return salary;
   }

   public Date getHireDay()
   {
      return hireDay;
   }

   public void raiseSalary(double byPercent)
   {
      double raise = salary * byPercent / 100;
      salary += raise;
   }

   public String toString()
   {
      return getClass().getName()
         + "[name=" + name
         + ",salary=" + salary
         + ",hireDay=" + hireDay
         + "]";
   }

   private String name;
   private double salary;
   private Date hireDay;
}
```

File Management

You have learned how to read and write data from a file. However, there is more to file management than reading and writing. The File class encapsulates the functionality that you will need in order to work with the file system on the user's machine. For example, you use the File class to find out when a file was last modified or to remove or rename the file. In other words, the stream classes are concerned with the contents of the file, whereas the File class is concerned with the storage of the file on a disk.

NOTE: As is so often the case in Java, the File class takes the least common denominator approach. For example, under Windows, you can find out (or set) the read-only flag for a file, but while you can find out if it is a hidden file, you can't hide it without using a native method (see Volume 2).

The simplest constructor for a File object takes a (full) file name. If you don't supply a path name, then Java uses the current directory. For example,

```
File f = new File("test.txt");
```

gives you a file object with this name in the current directory. (The "current directory" is the current directory of the process that executes the virtual machine. If you launched the virtual machine from the command line, it is the directory from which you started the java executable.)

A call to this constructor *does not create a file with this name if it doesn't exist*. Actually, creating a file from a File object is done with one of the stream class constructors or the createNewFile method in the File class. The createNewFile method only creates a file if no file with that name exists, and it returns a boolean to tell you whether it was successful.

On the other hand, once you have a File object, the exists method in the File class tells you whether a file exists with that name. For example, the following trial program would almost certainly print "false" on anyone's machine, and yet it can print out a path name to this nonexistent file.

```
import java.io.*;

public class Test
{
   public static void main(String args[])
   {
      File f = new File("afilethatprobablydoesntexist");
      System.out.println(f.getAbsolutePath());
      System.out.println(f.exists());
   }
}
```

There are two other constructors for File objects:

```
File(String path, String name)
```

which creates a File object with the given name in the directory specified by the path parameter. (If the path parameter is null, this constructor creates a File object, using the current directory.)

Finally, you can use an existing File object in the constructor:

```
File(File dir, String name)
```

where the File object represents a directory and, as before, if dir is null, the constructor creates a File object in the current directory.

Somewhat confusingly, a `File` object can represent either a file or a directory (perhaps because the operating system that the Java designers were most familiar with happens to implement directories as files). You use the `isDirectory` and `isFile` methods to tell whether the file object represents a file or a directory. This is surprising—in an object-oriented system, you might have expected a separate `Directory` class, perhaps extending the `File` class.

To make an object representing a directory, you simply supply the directory name in the `File` constructor:

```
File tempDir = new File(File.separator + "temp");
```

If this directory does not yet exist, you can create it with the `mkdir` method:

```
tempDir.mkdir();
```

If a file object represents a directory, use `list()` to get an array of the file names in that directory. The program in Example 12–7 uses all these methods to print out the directory substructure of whatever path is entered on the command line. (It would be easy enough to change this program into a utility class that returns a vector of the subdirectories for further processing.)

TIP: Always use `File` objects, not strings, when manipulating file or directory names. For example, the `equals` method of the `File` class knows that some file systems are not case significant and that a trailing / in a directory name doesn't matter.

Example 12–7: FindDirectories.java

```
import java.io.*;

public class FindDirectories
{
   public static void main(String[] args)
   {
      // if no arguments provided, start at the parent directory
      if (args.length == 0) args = new String[] { ".." };

      try
      {
         File pathName = new File(args[0]);
         String[] fileNames = pathName.list();

         // enumerate all files in the directory
         for (int i = 0; i < fileNames.length; i++)
         {
            File f = new File(pathName.getPath(), fileNames[i]);

            // if the file is again a directory, call the main method recursively
            if (f.isDirectory())
            {
               System.out.println(f.getCanonicalPath());
               main(new String [] { f.getPath() });
            }
         }
      }
      catch(IOException e)
      {
         e.printStackTrace();
```

```
        }
    }
}
```

Rather than listing all files in a directory, you can use a `FileNameFilter` object as a parameter to the `list` method to narrow down the list. These objects are simply instances of a class that satisfies the `FilenameFilter` interface.

All a class needs to do to implement the `FilenameFilter` interface is define a method called `accept`. Here is an example of a simple `FilenameFilter` class that allows only files with a specified extension:

```
public class ExtensionFilter implements FilenameFilter
{
   public ExtensionFilter(String ext)
   {
      extension = "." + ext;
   }

   public boolean accept(File dir, String name)
   {
      return name.endsWith(extension);
   }

   private String extension;
}
```

When writing portable programs, it is a challenge to specify file names with subdirectories. As we mentioned earlier, it turns out that you can use a forward slash (the UNIX separator) as the directory separator in Windows as well, but other operating systems might not permit this, so we don't recommend using a forward slash.

CAUTION: If you do use forward slashes as directory separators in Windows when constructing a `File` object, the `getAbsolutePath` method returns a file name that contains forward slashes, which will look strange to Windows users. Instead, use the `getCanonicalPath` method—it replaces the forward slashes with backslashes.

It is much better to use the information about the current directory separator that the `File` class stores in a static instance field called `separator`. (In a Windows environment, this is a backslash (\); in a UNIX environment, it is a forward slash (/). For example:

```
File foo = new File("Documents" + File.separator + "data.txt")
```

Of course, if you use the second alternate version of the `File` constructor

```
File foo = new File("Documents", "data.txt")
```

then the constructor will supply the correct separator.

The API notes that follow give you what we think are the most important remaining methods of the `File` class; their use should be straightforward.

java.io.File 1.0

- `boolean canRead()`
  indicates whether the file can be read by the current application.
- `boolean canWrite()`
  indicates whether the file is writable or read-only.

- `static boolean createTempFile(String prefix, String suffix)` **1.2**
- `static boolean createTempFile(String prefix, String suffix, File directory)` **1.2**
  create a temporary file in the system's default temp directory or the given directory, using the given prefix and suffix to generate the temporary name.

Parameters:	`prefix`	A prefix string that is at least three characters long
	`suffix`	An optional suffix. If `null`, `.tmp` is used
	`directory`	The directory in which the file is created. If it is `null`, the file is created in the current working directory

- `boolean delete()`
  tries to delete the file. Returns `true` if the file was deleted, `false` otherwise.
- `void deleteOnExit()`
  requests that the file be deleted when the virtual machine shuts down.
- `boolean exists()`
  `true` if the file or directory exists; `false` otherwise.
- `String getAbsolutePath()`
  returns a string that contains the absolute path name. Tip: Use `getCanonicalPath` instead.
- `File getCanonicalFile()` **1.2**
  returns a `File` object that contains the canonical path name for the file. In particular, redundant "." directories are removed, the correct directory separator is used, and the capitalization preferred by the underlying file system is obtained.
- `String getCanonicalPath()` **1.1**
  returns a string that contains the canonical path name. In particular, redundant "." directories are removed, the correct directory separator is used, and the capitalization preferred by the underlying file system is obtained.
- `String getName()`
  returns a string that contains the file name of the `File` object (does not include path information).
- `String getParent()`
  returns a string that contains the name of the parent of this `File` object. If this `File` object is a file, then the parent is the directory containing it. If it is a directory, then the parent is the parent directory or `null` if there is no parent directory.
- `File getParentFile()` **1.2**
  returns a `File` object for the parent of this `File` directory. See `getParent` for a definition of "parent."
- `String getPath()`
  returns a string that contains the path name of the file.
- `boolean isDirectory()`
  returns `true` if the `File` represents a directory; `false` otherwise.
- `boolean isFile()`
  returns `true` if the `File` object represents a file as opposed to a directory or a device.
- `boolean isHidden()` **1.2**
  returns `true` if the `File` object represents a hidden file or directory.
- `long lastModified()`
  returns the time the file was last modified (counted in milliseconds since Midnight January 1, 1970 GMT), or 0 if the file does not exist. Use the `Date(long)` constructor to convert this value to a date.

- `long length()`
  returns the length of the file in bytes, or 0 if the file does not exist.
- `String[] list()`
  returns an array of strings that contain the names of the files and directories contained by this `File` object, or `null` if this `File` was not representing a directory.
- `String[] list(FilenameFilter filter)`
  returns an array of the names of the files and directories contained by this `File` that satisfy the filter, or `null` if none exist.

Parameters:	`filter`	The `FilenameFilter` object to use

- `File[] listFiles()` **1.2**
  returns an array of `File` objects corresponding to the files and directories contained by this `File` object, or `null` if this `File` was not representing a directory.
- `File[] listFiles(FilenameFilter filter)` **1.2**
  returns an array of `File` objects for the files and directories contained by this `File` that satisfy the filter, or `null` if none exist.

Parameters:	`filter`	The `FilenameFilter` object to use

- `static File[] listRoots()` **1.2**
  returns an array of `File` objects corresponding to all the available file roots. (For example, on a Windows system, you get the `File` objects representing the installed drives (both local drives and mapped network drives). On a UNIX system, you simply get "/".)
- `boolean createNewFile()` **1.2**
  automatically makes a new file whose name is given by the `File` object if no file with that name exists. That is, the checking for the file name and the creation are not interrupted by other file system activity. Returns `true` if the method created the file.
- `boolean mkdir()`
  makes a subdirectory whose name is given by the `File` object. Returns `true` if the directory was successfully created; `false` otherwise.
- `boolean mkdirs()`
  unlike `mkdir`, creates the parent directories if necessary. Returns `false` if any of the necessary directories could not be created.
- `boolean renameTo(File dest)`
  returns `true` if the name was changed; `false` otherwise.

Parameters:	`dest`	A `File` object that specifies the new name

- `boolean setLastModified(long time)` **1.2**
  sets the last modified time of the file. Returns `true` if successful, `false` otherwise.

Parameters:	`time`	A long integer representing the number of milliseconds since Midnight January 1, 1970, GMT. Use the `getTime` method of the `Date` class to calculate this value

- `boolean setReadOnly()` **1.2**
  sets the file to be read-only. Returns `true` if successful, `false` otherwise.
- `URL toURL()` **1.2**
  converts the `File` object to a file `URL`.

java.io.FilenameFilter 1.0

- `boolean accept(File dir, String name)`
  should be defined to return `true` if the file matches the filter criterion.

  Parameters: `dir` — A `File` object representing the directory that contains the file
  `name` — The name of the file

New I/O

JDK 1.4 contains a number of features for improved input/output processing, collectively called the "new I/O," in the `java.nio` package. (Of course, the "new" moniker is somewhat regrettable because, a few years down the road, the package won't be new any longer.)

The package includes support for the following features:

- Memory-mapped files
- File locking
- Character set encoders and decoders
- Nonblocking I/O

We already introduced character sets on page 633. In this section, we discuss only the first two features. Nonblocking I/O requires the use of threads, which are covered in Volume 2.

Memory-Mapped Files

Most operating systems can take advantage of the virtual memory implementation to "map" a file, or a region of a file, into memory. Then the file can be accessed as if it were an in-memory array, which is much faster than the traditional file operations.

At the end of this section, you can find a program that computes the CRC32 checksum of a file, using traditional file input and a memory-mapped file. On one machine, we got the timing data shown in Table 12–7 when computing the checksum of the 37-Mbyte file `rt.jar` in the `jre/lib` directory of the JDK.

Table 12–7: Timing Data for File Operations

Method	Time
Plain Input Stream	110 seconds
Buffered Input Stream	9.9 seconds
Random Access File	162 seconds
Memory Mapped file	7.2 seconds

As you can see, on this particular machine, memory mapping is a bit faster than using buffered sequential input and dramatically faster than using a `RandomAccessFile`.

Of course, the exact values will differ greatly from one machine to another, but it is obvious that the performance gain can be substantial if you need to use random access. For sequential reading of files of moderate size, on the other hand, there is no reason to use memory mapping.

The `java.nio` package makes memory mapping quite simple. Here is what you do.

First, get a *channel* from the file. A channel is an abstraction for disk files that lets you access operating system features such as memory mapping, file locking, and fast data transfers between files. You get a channel by calling the `getChannel` method that has been added to the `FileInputStream`, `FileOutputStream`, and `RandomAccessFile` class.

```
FileInputStream in = new FileInputStream(. . .);
FileChannel channel = in.getChannel();
```

Then you get a `MappedByteBuffer` from the channel by calling the `map` method of the `FileChannel` class. You specify the area of the file that you want to map and a *mapping mode*. Three modes are supported:

- `FileChannel.MapMode.READ_ONLY`: The resulting buffer is read-only. Any attempt to write to the buffer results in a `ReadOnlyBufferException`.
- `FileChannel.MapMode.READ_WRITE`: The resulting buffer is writable, and the changes will be written back to the file at some time. Note that other programs that have mapped the same file may not see those changes immediately. The exact behavior of simultaneous file mapping by multiple programs is operating-system dependent.
- `FileChannel.MapMode.PRIVATE`: The resulting buffer is writable, but any changes are private to this buffer and are *not* propagated to the file.

Once you have the buffer, you can read and write data, using the methods of the `ByteBuffer` class and the `Buffer` superclass.

Buffers support both sequential and random data access. A buffer has a *position* that is advanced by `get` and `put` operations. For example, you can sequentially traverse all bytes in the buffer as

```
while (buffer.hasRemaining())
{
   byte b = buffer.get();
   . . .
}
```

Alternatively, you can use random access:

```
for (int i = 0; i < buffer.limit(); i++)
{
   byte b = buffer.get(i);
   . . .
}
```

You can also read and write arrays of bytes with the methods

```
get(byte[] bytes)
get(byte[], int offset, int length)
```

Finally, there are methods

```
getInt
getLong
getShort
getChar
getFloat
getDouble
```

to read primitive type values that are stored as *binary* values in the file. As we already mentioned, Java uses big-endian ordering for binary data. However, if you need to process a file containing binary numbers in little-endian order, simply call

```
buffer.order(ByteOrder.LITTLE_ENDIAN);
```

To find out the current byte order of a buffer, call

```
ByteOrder b = buffer.order()
```

CAUTION: This pair of methods does not use the `set/get` naming convention.

To write numbers to a buffer, use one of the methods

```
putInt
putLong
putShort
putChar
putFloat
putDouble
```

Example 12–8 computes the 32-bit cyclic redundancy checksum (CRC32) of a file. That quantity is a checksum that is often used to determine whether a file has been corrupted. Corruption of a file makes it very likely that the checksum has changed. The `java.util.zip` package contains a class `CRC32` that computes the checksum of a sequence of bytes, using the following loop:

```
CRC32 crc = new CRC32();
while (more bytes)
   crc.update(next byte)
long checksum = crc.getValue();
```

NOTE: For a nice explanation of the CRC algorithm, see `http://www.relisoft.com/Science/CrcMath.html`.

The details of the CRC computation are not important. We just use it as an example of a useful file operation.

Run the program as

```
java NIOTest filename
```

Example 12–8: NIOTest.java

```
import java.io.*;
import java.nio.*;
import java.nio.channels.*;
import java.util.zip.*;

/**
   This program computes the CRC checksum of a file.
   Usage: java NIOTest filename
*/
public class NIOTest
{
   public static long checksumInputStream(String filename)
      throws IOException
   {
      InputStream in = new FileInputStream(filename);
      CRC32 crc = new CRC32();

      int c;
      while((c = in.read()) != -1)
         crc.update(c);
      return crc.getValue();
   }
```

```
   public static long checksumBufferedInputStream(String filename)
      throws IOException
   {
      InputStream in = new BufferedInputStream(new FileInputStream(filename));
      CRC32 crc = new CRC32();

      int c;
      while((c = in.read()) != -1)
         crc.update(c);
      return crc.getValue();
   }

   public static long checksumRandomAccessFile(String filename)
      throws IOException
   {
      RandomAccessFile file = new RandomAccessFile(filename, "r");
      long length = file.length();
      CRC32 crc = new CRC32();

      for (long p = 0; p < length; p++)
      {
         file.seek(p);
         int c = file.readByte();
         crc.update(c);
      }
      return crc.getValue();
   }

   public static long checksumMappedFile(String filename)
      throws IOException
   {
      FileInputStream in = new FileInputStream(filename);
      FileChannel channel = in.getChannel();

      CRC32 crc = new CRC32();
      int length = (int) channel.size();
      MappedByteBuffer buffer = channel.map(FileChannel.MapMode.READ_ONLY, 0, length);

      for (int p = 0; p < length; p++)
      {
         int c = buffer.get(p);
         crc.update(c);
      }
      return crc.getValue();
   }

   public static void main(String[] args)
      throws IOException
   {
      System.out.println("Input Stream:");
      long start = System.currentTimeMillis();
      long crcValue = checksumInputStream(args[0]);
      long end = System.currentTimeMillis();
      System.out.println(Long.toHexString(crcValue));
      System.out.println((end - start) + " milliseconds");
```

```
        System.out.println("Buffered Input Stream:");
        start = System.currentTimeMillis();
        crcValue = checksumBufferedInputStream(args[0]);
        end = System.currentTimeMillis();
        System.out.println(Long.toHexString(crcValue));
        System.out.println((end - start) + " milliseconds");

        System.out.println("Random Access File:");
        start = System.currentTimeMillis();
        crcValue = checksumRandomAccessFile(args[0]);
        end = System.currentTimeMillis();
        System.out.println(Long.toHexString(crcValue));
        System.out.println((end - start) + " milliseconds");

        System.out.println("Mapped File:");
        start = System.currentTimeMillis();
        crcValue = checksumMappedFile(args[0]);
        end = System.currentTimeMillis();
        System.out.println(Long.toHexString(crcValue));
        System.out.println((end - start) + " milliseconds");
    }
}
```

java.io.FileInputStream 1.0

- `FileChannel getChannel()` 1.4
  returns a channel for accessing this stream.

java.io.FileOutputStream 1.0

- `FileChannel getChannel()` 1.4
  returns a channel for accessing this stream.

java.io.RandomAccessFile 1.0

- `FileChannel getChannel()` 1.4
  returns a channel for accessing this file.

java.nio.channels.FileChannel 1.4

- `MappedByteBuffer map(FileChannel.MapMode mode, long position, long size)`
  maps a region of the file to memory.

Parameters:	`mode`	One of the constants `READ_ONLY`, `READ_WRITE`, or `PRIVATE` in the `FileChannel.MapMode` class
	`position`	The start of the mapped region
	`size`	The size of the mapped region

java.nio.Buffer 1.4

- `boolean hasRemaining()`
  returns `true` if the current buffer position has not yet reached the buffer's limit position.
- `int limit()`
  returns the limit position of the buffer, that is, the first position at which no more values are available.

java.nio.ByteBuffer 1.4

- `byte get()`
  gets a byte from the current position and advances the current position to the next byte.
- `byte get(int index)`
  gets a byte from the specified index.
- `ByteBuffer put(byte b)`
  puts a byte to the current position and advances the current position to the next byte. Returns a reference to this buffer.
- `ByteBuffer put(int index, byte b)`
  puts a byte at the specified index. Returns a reference to this buffer.
- `ByteBuffer get(byte[] destination)`
- `ByteBuffer get(byte[] destination, int offset, int length)`
  fill a byte array, or a region of a byte array, with bytes from the buffer, and advance the current position by the number of bytes read. If not enough bytes remain in the buffer, then no bytes are read, and a `BufferUnderflowException` is thrown. Return a reference to this buffer.

Parameters:	`destination`	The byte array to be filled
	`offset`	The offset of the region to be filled
	`length`	The length of the region to be filled

- `ByteBuffer put(byte[] source)`
- `ByteBuffer put(byte[] source, int offset, int length)`
  put all bytes from a byte array, or the bytes from a region of a byte array, into the buffer, and advance the current position by the number of bytes read. If not enough bytes remain in the buffer, then no bytes are written, and a `BufferOverflowException` is thrown. Returns a reference to this buffer.

Parameters:	`source`	The byte array to be written
	`offset`	The offset of the region to be written
	`length`	The length of the region to be written

- *Xxx* `get`*Xxx*`()`
- *Xxx* `get`*Xxx*`(int index)`
- `ByteBuffer put`*Xxx*`(`*xxx* `value)`
- `ByteBuffer put`*Xxx*`(int index,` *xxx* `value)`
  are used for relative and absolute reading and writing of binary numbers. *Xxx* is one of `Int`, `Long`, `Short`, `Char`, `Float`, or `Double`.
- `ByteBuffer order(ByteOrder order)`
- `ByteOrder order()`
  set or get the byte order. The value for `order` is one of the constants `BIG_ENDIAN` or `LITTLE_ENDIAN` of the `ByteOrder` class.

The Buffer Data Structure

When you use memory mapping, you make a single buffer that spans the entire file, or the area of the file in which you are interested. You can also use buffers to read and write more modest chunks of information.

In this section, we briefly describe the basic operations on `Buffer` objects. A buffer is an array of values of the same type. The `Buffer` class is an abstract class with concrete subclasses `Byte-`

Buffer, CharBuffer, DoubleBuffer, FloatBuffer, IntBuffer, LongBuffer, and ShortBuffer. In practice, you will most commonly use ByteBuffer and CharBuffer. As shown in Figure 12–13, a buffer has

- a *capacity* that never changes
- a *position* at which the next value is read or written
- a *limit* beyond which reading and writing is meaningless
- optionally, a *mark* for repeating a read or write operation

These values fulfill the condition

$0 \leq mark \leq position \leq limit \leq capacity$

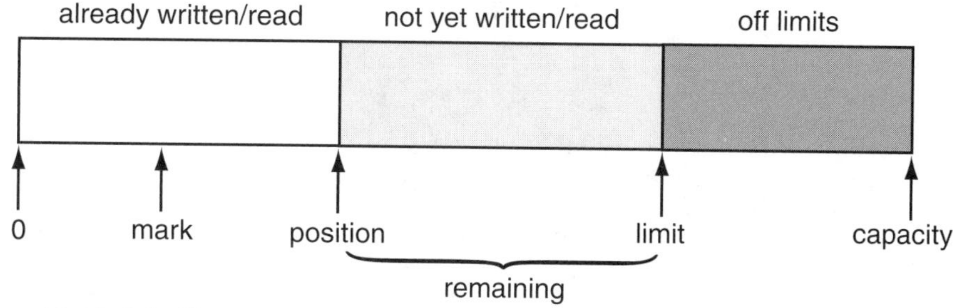

Figure 12–13: A buffer

The principal purpose for a buffer is a "write, then read" cycle. At the outset, the buffer's position is 0 and the limit is the capacity. Keep calling put to add values to the buffer. When you run out of data or you reach the capacity, it is time to switch to reading.

Call flip to set the limit to the current position and the position to 0. Now keep calling get while the remaining method (which returns *limit - position*) is positive. When you have read all values in the buffer, call clear to prepare the buffer for the next writing cycle. The clear method resets the position to 0 and the limit to the capacity.

If you want to re-read the buffer, use rewind or mark/reset—see the API notes for details.

java.nio.Buffer 1.4

- Buffer clear()
  prepares this buffer for writing by setting the position to zero and the limit to the capacity; returns this.
- Buffer flip()
  prepares this buffer for reading by setting the limit to the position and the position to zero; returns this.
- Buffer rewind()
  prepares this buffer for re-reading the same values by setting the position to zero and leaving the limit unchanged; returns this.
- Buffer mark()
  sets the mark of this buffer to the position; returns this.
- Buffer reset()
  sets the position of this buffer to the mark, thus allowing the marked portion to be read or written again; returns this.
- int remaining()
  returns the remaining number of readable or writable values, that is, the difference between limit and position.

- `int position()`
  returns the position of this buffer.
- `int capacity()`
  returns the capacity of this buffer.

java.nio.CharBuffer 1.4

- `char get()`
- `CharBuffer get(char[] destination)`
- `CharBuffer get(char[] destination, int offset, int length)`
  gets one `char` value, or a range of `char` values, starting at the buffer's position and moving the position past the characters that were read. The last two methods return `this`.
- `CharBuffer put(char c)`
- `CharBuffer put(char[] source)`
- `CharBuffer put(char[] source, int offset, int length)`
- `CharBuffer put(String source)`
- `CharBuffer put(CharBuffer source)`
  puts one `char` value, or a range of `char` values, starting at the buffer's position and advancing the position past the characters that were written. When reading from a `CharBuffer`, all remaining characters are read. All methods return `this`.
- `CharBuffer read(CharBuffer destination)`
  gets `char` values from this buffer and puts them into the destination until the destination's limit is reached. Returns `this`.

File Locking

Consider a situation in which multiple simultaneously executing programs need to modify the same file. Clearly, the programs need to communicate in some way, or the file can easily become damaged.

File locks control access to a file or a range of bytes within a file. However, file locking varies greatly among operating systems, which explains why file locking capabilities were absent from prior versions of the JDK.

Frankly, file locking is not all that common in application programs. Many applications use a database for data storage, and the database has mechanisms for resolving concurrent access problems. If you store information in flat files and are worried about concurrent access, you may well find it simpler to start using a database rather than designing complex file locking schemes.

Still, there are situations in which file locking is essential. Suppose your application saves a configuration file with user preferences. If a user invokes two instances of the application, it could happen that both of them want to write the configuration file at the same time. In that situation, the first instance should lock the file. When the second instance finds the file locked, it can decide to wait until the file is unlocked or simply skip the writing process.

To lock a file, call either the `lock` or `tryLock` method of the `FileChannel` class:

```
FileLock lock = channel.lock();
```

or

```
FileLock lock = channel.tryLock();
```

The first call blocks until the lock becomes available. The second call returns immediately, either with the lock or `null` if the lock is not available. The file remains locked until the channel is closed or the `release` method is invoked on the lock.

You can also lock a portion of the file with the call

```
FileLock lock(long start, long size, boolean exclusive)
```

or

```
FileLock tryLock(long start, long size, boolean exclusive)
```

The `exclusive` flag is `true` to lock the file for both reading and writing. It is `false` for a *shared* lock, which allows multiple processes to read from the file, while preventing any process from acquiring an exclusive lock. Not all operating systems support shared locks. You may get an exclusive lock even if you just asked for a shared one. Call the `isShared` method of the `FileLock` class to find out which kind you have.

NOTE: If you lock the tail portion of a file and the file subsequently grows beyond the locked portion, the additional area is not locked. To lock all bytes, use a size of `Long.MAX_VALUE`.

Keep in mind that file locking is system dependent. Here are some points to watch for:

- On some systems, file locking is merely *advisory*. If an application fails to get a lock, it may still write to a file that another application has currently locked.
- On some systems, you cannot simultaneously lock a file and map it into memory.
- File locks are held by the entire Java virtual machine. If two programs are launched by the same virtual machine (such as an applet or application launcher), then they can't each acquire a lock on the same file. The `lock` and `tryLock` methods will throw an `OverlappingFileLockException` if the virtual machine already holds another overlapping lock on the same file.
- On some systems, closing a channel releases all locks on the underlying file held by the Java virtual machine. You should therefore avoid multiple channels on the same locked file.
- Locking files on a networked file system is highly system dependent and should probably be avoided.

API `java.nio.channels.FileChannel` 1.4

- `FileLock lock()`
  acquires an exclusive lock on the entire file. This method blocks until the lock is acquired.
- `FileLock tryLock()`
  acquires an exclusive lock on the entire file, or returns `null` if the lock cannot be acquired.
- `FileLock lock(long position, long size, boolean shared)`
- `FileLock tryLock(long position, long size, boolean shared)`
  acquire a lock on a region of the file. The first method blocks until the lock is acquired, and the second method returns `null` if the lock cannot be acquired.

Parameters:	`position`	The start of the region to be locked
	`size`	The size of the region to be locked
	`shared`	`true` for a shared lock, `false` for an exclusive lock

`java.nio.channels.FileLock` 1.4

- `void release()`
  releases this lock.

Regular Expressions

Regular expressions are used to specify string patterns. You can use regular expressions whenever you need to locate strings that match a particular pattern. For example, one of our sample programs locates all hyperlinks in an HTML file by looking for strings of the pattern `<a href="...">`.

Of course, for specifying a pattern, the ... notation is not precise enough. You need to specify precisely what sequence of characters is a legal match. You need to use a special syntax whenever you describe a pattern.

Here is a simple example. The regular expression

```
[Jj]ava.+
```

matches any string of the following form:

- The first letter is a `J` or `j`.
- The next three letters are `ava`.
- The remainder of the string consists of one or more arbitrary characters.

For example, the string `"javanese"` matches the particular regular expression, but the string `"Core Java"` does not.

As you can see, you need to know a bit of syntax to understand the meaning of a regular expression. Fortunately, for most purposes, a small number of straightforward constructs are sufficient.

- A *character class* is a set of character alternatives, enclosed in brackets, such as `[Jj]`, `[0-9]`, `[A-Za-z]`, or `[^0-9]`. Here the `-` denotes a range (all characters whose Unicode value falls between the two bounds), and `^` denotes the complement (all characters except the ones specified).
- There are many predefined character classes such as `\d` (digits) or `\p{Sc}` (Unicode currency symbol). See Tables 12–8 and 12–9.
- Most characters match themselves, such as the `ava` characters in the example above.
- The `.` symbol matches any character (except possibly line terminators, depending on flag settings).
- Use `\` as an escape character, for example `\.` matches a period and `\\` matches a backslash.
- `^` and `$` match the beginning and end of a line respectively.
- If *X* and *Y* are regular expressions, then *XY* means "any match for *X* followed by a match for *Y*". X | Y means "any match for *X* or *Y*".
- You can apply *quantifiers* X+ (1 or more), X* (0 or more), and X? (0 or 1) to an expression X.
- By default, a quantifier matches the largest possible repetition that makes the overall match succeed. You can modify that behavior with suffixes ? (reluctant or stingy match—match the smallest repetition count) and + (possessive or greedy match—match the largest count even if that makes the overall match fail).

  For example, the string `cab` matches `[a-z]*ab` but not `[a-z]*+ab`. In the first case, the expression `[a-z]*` only matches the character `c`, so that the characters `ab` match the remainder of the pattern. But the greedy version `[a-z]*+` matches the characters `cab`, leaving the remainder of the pattern unmatched.
- You can use *groups* to define subexpressions. Enclose the groups in `( )`, for example `([+-]?)([0-9]+)`. You can then ask the pattern matcher to return the match of each group or to refer back to a group with `\n`, where `n` is the group number (starting with `\1`).

For example, here is a somewhat complex but potentially useful regular expression—it describes decimal or hexadecimal integers:

```
[+-]?[0-9]+|0[Xx][0-9A-Fa-f]+
```

Unfortunately, the expression syntax is not completely standardized between the various programs and libraries that use regular expressions. While there is consensus on the basic constructs, there are many maddening differences in the details. The Java regular expression classes use a syntax that is similar to, but not quite the same as, the one used in the Perl language. Table 12–8 shows all constructs of the Java syntax. For more information on the regular expression syntax, consult the API documentation for the `Pattern` class or the book *Mastering Regular Expressions* by Jeffrey E. F. Friedl (O'Reilly and Associates, 1997).

The simplest use for a regular expression is to test whether a particular string matches it. Here is how you program that test in Java. First construct a `Pattern` object from the string denoting the regular expression. Then get a `Matcher` object from the pattern, and call its `matches` method:

```
Pattern pattern = Pattern.compile(patternString);
Matcher matcher = pattern.matcher(input);
if (matcher.matches()) . . .
```

Table 12–8: Regular Expression Syntax

Syntax	Explanation
Characters	
c	The character *c*
`\u`*nnnn*, `\x`*nn*, `\0`*n*, `\0`*nn*, `\0`*nnn*	The code unit with the given hex or octal value
`\t`, `\n`, `\r`, `\f`, `\a`, `\e`	The control characters tab, newline, return, form feed, alert, and escape
`\c`*c*	The control character corresponding to the character *c*
Character Classes	
`[`C_1C_2. . .`]`	Any of the characters represented by C_1, C_2, . . . The C_i are characters, character ranges (c_1-c_2), or character classes
`[^. . .]`	Complement of character class
`[. . .&&. . .]`	Intersection of two character classes
Predefined Character Classes	
`.`	Any character except line terminators (or any character if the `DOTALL` flag is set)
`\d`	A digit `[0-9]`
`\D`	A nondigit `[^0-9]`
`\s`	A whitespace character `[ \t\n\r\f\x0B]`
`\S`	A non-whitespace character
`\w`	A word character `[a-zA-Z0-9_]`
`\W`	A nonword character
`\p{`*name*`}`	A named character class—see Table 12–9
`\P{`*name*`}`	The complement of a named character class
Boundary Matchers	
`^ $`	Beginning, end of input (or beginning, end of line in multiline mode)
`\b`	A word boundary
`\B`	A nonword boundary

Table 12–8: Regular Expression Syntax (continued)

Syntax	Explanation
\A	Beginning of input
\z	End of input
\Z	End of input except final line terminator
\G	End of previous match
Quantifiers	
X?	Optional X
X*	X, 0 or more times
X+	X, 1 or more times
X{*n*} *X*{*n*,} *X*{*n*,*m*}	X *n* times, at least *n* times, between *n* and *m* times
Quantifier Suffixes	
?	Turn default (greedy) match into reluctant match
+	Turn default (greedy) match into possessive match
Set Operations	
XY	Any string from *X*, followed by any string from *Y*
X|Y	Any string from *X* or *Y*
Grouping	
(X)	Capture the string matching *X* as a group
n	The match of the *n*th group
Escapes	
c	The character *c* (must not be an alphabetic character)
\Q...\E	Quote . . . verbatim
(?...)	Special construct—see API notes of `Pattern` class

Table 12–9: Predefined Character Class Names

`Lower`	ASCII lower case `[a-z]`
`Upper`	ASCII upper case `[A-Z]`
`Alpha`	ASCII alphabetic `[A-Za-z]`
`Digit`	ASCII digits `[0-9]`
`Alnum`	ASCII alphabetic or digit `[A-Za-z0-9]`
`XDigit`	Hex digits `[0-9A-Fa-f]`
`Print` or `Graph`	Printable ASCII character `[\x21-\x7E]`
`Punct`	ASCII non-alpha or digit `[\p{Print}&&\P{Alnum}]`
`ASCII`	All ASCII `[\x00-\x7F]`
`Cntrl`	ASCII Control character `[\x00-\x1F]`
`Blank`	Space or tab `[ \t]`
`Space`	Whitespace `[ \t\n\r\f\0x0B]`

Table 12–9: Predefined Character Class Names (continued)

javaLowerCase	Lower case, as determined by Character.isLowerCase()
javaUpperCase	Upper case, as determined by Character.isUpperCase()
javaWhitespace	Whitespace, as determined by Character.isWhitespace()
javaMirrored	Mirrored, as determined by Character.isMirrored()
In*Block*	*Block* is the name of a Unicode character block, with spaces removed, such as BasicLatin or Mongolian. See http://www.unicode.org for a list of block names.
Category or In*Category*	*Category* is the name of a Unicode character category such as L (letter) or Sc (currency symbol). See http://www.unicode.org for a list of category names.

The input of the matcher is an object of any class that implements the CharSequence interface, such as a String, StringBuilder, or CharBuffer.

When compiling the pattern, you can set one or more flags, for example,

```
Pattern pattern = Pattern.compile(patternString,
   Pattern.CASE_INSENSITIVE + Pattern.UNICODE_CASE);
```

The following six flags are supported:

- CASE_INSENSITIVE: Match characters independently of the letter case. By default, this flag takes only US ASCII characters into account.
- UNICODE_CASE: When used in combination with CASE_INSENSITIVE, use Unicode letter case for matching.
- MULTILINE: ^ and $ match the beginning and end of a line, not the entire input.
- UNIX_LINES: Only '\n' is recognized as a line terminator when matching ^ and $ in multiline mode.
- DOTALL: When using this flag, the . symbol matches all characters, including line terminators.
- CANON_EQ: Takes canonical equivalence of Unicode characters into account. For example, u followed by ¨ (diaeresis) matches ü.

If the regular expression contains groups, then the Matcher object can reveal the group boundaries. The methods

```
int start(int groupIndex)
int end(int groupIndex)
```

yield the starting index and the past-the-end index of a particular group.

You can simply extract the matched string by calling

```
String group(int groupIndex)
```

Group 0 is the entire input; the group index for the first actual group is 1. Call the groupCount method to get the total group count.

Nested groups are ordered by the opening parentheses. For example, given the pattern

```
((1?[0-9]):([0-5][0-9]))[ap]m
```

and the input

```
11:59am
```

the matcher reports the following groups

Group Index	Start	End	String
0	0	7	11;59am
1	0	5	11:59
2	0	2	11
3	3	5	59

Example 12–9 prompts for a pattern, then for strings to match. It prints out whether or not the input matches the pattern. If the input matches and the pattern contains groups, then the program prints the group boundaries as parentheses, such as

```
((11):(59))am
```

Example 12–9: RegexTest.java

```
import java.util.*;
import java.util.regex.*;

/**
   This program tests regular expression matching.
   Enter a pattern and strings to match, or hit Cancel
   to exit. If the pattern contains groups, the group
   boundaries are displayed in the match.
*/
public class RegExTest
{
   public static void main(String[] args)
   {
      Scanner in = new Scanner(System.in);
      System.out.println("Enter pattern: ");
      String patternString = in.nextLine();

      Pattern pattern = null;
      try
      {
         pattern = Pattern.compile(patternString);
      }
      catch (PatternSyntaxException e)
      {
         System.out.println("Pattern syntax error");
         System.exit(1);
      }

      while (true)
      {
         System.out.println("Enter string to match: ");
         String input = in.nextLine();
         if (input == null || input.equals("")) return;
         Matcher matcher = pattern.matcher(input);
         if (matcher.matches())
         {
            System.out.println("Match");
            int g = matcher.groupCount();
            if (g > 0)
            {
               for (int i = 0; i < input.length(); i++)
               {
```

```
                  for (int j = 1; j <= g; j++)
                     if (i == matcher.start(j))
                        System.out.print('(');
                  System.out.print(input.charAt(i));
                  for (int j = 1; j <= g; j++)
                     if (i + 1 == matcher.end(j))
                        System.out.print(')');
               }
               System.out.println();
            }
         }
         else
            System.out.println("No match");
      }
   }
}
```

Usually, you don't want to match the entire input against a regular expression, but you want to find one or more matching substrings in the input. Use the `find` method of the `Matcher` class to find the next match. If it returns `true`, use the `start` and `end` methods to find the extent of the match.

```
while (matcher.find())
{
   int start = matcher.start();
   int end = matcher.end();
   String match = input.substring(start, end);
   . . .
}
```

Example 12–10 puts this mechanism to work. It locates all hypertext references in a web page and prints them. To run the program, supply a URL on the command line, such as

```
java HrefMatch http://www.horstmann.com
```

Example 12–10: HrefMatch.java

```
import java.io.*;
import java.net.*;
import java.util.regex.*;

/**
   This program displays all URLs in a web page by
   matching a regular expression that describes the
   <a href=...> HTML tag. Start the program as
   java HrefMatch URL
*/
public class HrefMatch
{
   public static void main(String[] args)
   {
      try
      {
         // get URL string from command line or use default
         String urlString;
         if (args.length > 0) urlString = args[0];
         else urlString = "http://java.sun.com";

         // open reader for URL
```

```
         InputStreamReader in = new InputStreamReader(new URL(urlString).openStream());

         // read contents into string buffer
         StringBuilder input = new StringBuilder();
         int ch;
         while ((ch = in.read()) != -1) input.append((char) ch);

         // search for all occurrences of pattern
         String patternString = "<a\\s+href\\s*=\\s*(\"[^\"]*\"|[^\\s>])\\s*>";
         Pattern pattern = Pattern.compile(patternString, Pattern.CASE_INSENSITIVE);
         Matcher matcher = pattern.matcher(input);

         while (matcher.find())
         {
            int start = matcher.start();
            int end = matcher.end();
            String match = input.substring(start, end);
            System.out.println(match);
         }
      }
      catch (IOException e)
      {
         e.printStackTrace();
      }
      catch (PatternSyntaxException e)
      {
         e.printStackTrace();
      }
   }
}
```

The `replaceAll` method of the `Matcher` class replaces all occurrences of a regular expression with a replacement string. For example, the following instructions replace all sequences of digits with a # character.

```
Pattern pattern = Pattern.compile("[0-9]+");
Matcher matcher = pattern.matcher(input);
String output = matcher.replaceAll("#");
```

The replacement string can contain references to groups in the pattern: `$n` is replaced with the *n*th group. Use `\$` to include a `$` character in the replacement text.

The `replaceFirst` method replaces only the first occurrence of the pattern.

Finally, the `Pattern` class has a `split` method that works like a string tokenizer on steroids. It splits an input into an array of strings, using the regular expression matches as boundaries. For example, the following instructions split the input into tokens, where the delimiters are punctuation marks surrounded by optional whitespace.

```
Pattern pattern = Pattern.compile("\\s*\\p{Punct}\\s*");
String[] tokens = pattern.split(input);
```

java.util.regex.Pattern 1.4

- `static Pattern compile(String expression)`
- `static Pattern compile(String expression, int flags)`

  compile the regular expression string into a pattern object for fast processing of matches.

Parameters: `expression` The regular expression

`flags` One or more of the flags `CASE_INSENSITIVE`, `UNICODE_CASE`, `MULTILINE`, `UNIX_LINES`, `DOTALL`, and `CANON_EQ`

- `Matcher matcher(CharSequence input)`
  returns a `matcher` object that you can use to locate the matches of the pattern in the input.
- `String[] split(CharSequence input)`
- `String[] split(CharSequence input, int limit)`
  split the input string into tokens, where the pattern specifies the form of the delimiters. Return an array of tokens. The delimiters are not part of the tokens.

  Parameters: `input` The string to be split into tokens

  `limit` The maximum number of strings to produce. If `limit - 1` matching delimiters have been found, then the last entry of the returned array contains the remaining unsplit input. If `limit` is ≤ 0, then the entire input is split. If `limit` is 0, then trailing empty strings are not placed in the returned array

java.util.regex.Matcher 1.4

- `boolean matches()`
  returns `true` if the input matches the pattern.
- `boolean lookingAt()`
  returns `true` if the beginning of the input matches the pattern.
- `boolean find()`
- `boolean find(int start)`
  attempt to find the next match and return `true` if another match is found.

  Parameters: `start` The index at which to start searching
- `int start()`
- `int end()`
  return the start and past-the-end position of the current match.
- `String group()`
  returns the current match.
- `int groupCount()`
  returns the number of groups in the input pattern.
- `int start(int groupIndex)`
- `int end(int groupIndex)`
  return the start and past-the-end position of a given group in the current match.

  Parameters: `groupIndex` The group index (starting with 1), or 0 to indicate the entire match
- `String group(int groupIndex)`
  returns the string matching a given group.

  Parameters: `groupIndex` The group index (starting with 1), or 0 to indicate the entire match

- `String replaceAll(String replacement)`
- `String replaceFirst(String replacement)`
  return a string obtained from the matcher input by replacing all matches, or the first match, with the replacement string.

Parameters:	`replacement`	The replacement string. It can contain references to a pattern group as `$`*n*. Use \\$ to include a `$` symbol

- `Matcher reset()`
- `Matcher reset(CharSequence input)`
  reset the matcher state. The second method makes the matcher work on a different input. Both methods return `this`.

Chapter 13

Generic Programming

- WHY GENERIC PROGRAMMING?
- DEFINITION OF A SIMPLE GENERIC CLASS
- GENERIC METHODS
- BOUNDS FOR TYPE VARIABLES
- GENERIC CODE AND THE VIRTUAL MACHINE
- RESTRICTIONS AND LIMITATIONS
- INHERITANCE RULES FOR GENERIC TYPES
- WILDCARD TYPES
- REFLECTION AND GENERICS

Generics constitute the most significant change in the Java programming language since the 1.0 release. The addition of generics to JDK 5.0 is the result of one of the first Java Specification Requests, JSR 14, that was formulated in 1999. The expert group spent about five years on specifications and test implementations.

Generics are desirable because they let you write code that is safer and easier to read than code that is littered with `Object` variables and casts. Generics are particularly useful for collection classes, such as the ubiquitous `ArrayList`.

Generics are—at least on the surface—similar to templates in C++. In C++, as in Java, templates were first added to the language to support strongly typed collections. However, over the years, other uses were discovered. After reading this chapter, perhaps you will find novel uses for Java generics in your programs.

Why Generic Programming?

Generic programming means to write code that can be reused for objects of many different types. For example, you don't want to program separate classes to collect `String` and `File` objects. And you don't have to—the single class `ArrayList` collects objects of any class. This is one example of generic programming.

Before JDK 5.0, generic programming in Java was always achieved with *inheritance*. The `ArrayList` class simply maintained an array of `Object` references:

```
public class ArrayList // before JDK 5.0
{
   public Object get(int i) { . . . }
   public void add(Object o) { . . . }
   . . .
   private Object[] elementData;
}
```

This approach has two problems. A cast is necessary whenever you retrieve a value:

```
ArrayList files = new ArrayList();
. . .
String filename = (String) names.get(0);
```

Moreover, there is no error checking. You can add values of any class:

```
files.add(new File(". . ."));
```

This call compiles and runs without error. Elsewhere, casting the result of `get` to a `String` will cause an error.

JDK 5.0 offers a better solution: *type parameters*. The `ArrayList` class now has a type parameter that indicates the element type:

```
ArrayList<String> files = new ArrayList<String>();
```

This makes your code easier to read. You can tell right away that this particular array list contains `String` objects.

The compiler can make good use of this information too. No cast is required for calling `get`: the compiler knows that the return type is `String`, not `Object`:

```
String filename = files.get(0);
```

The compiler also knows that the `add` method of an `ArrayList<String>` has a parameter of type `String`. That is a lot safer than having an `Object` parameter. Now the compiler can check that you don't insert objects of the wrong type. For example, the statement

```
files.add(new File(". . .")); // can only add String objects to an ArrayList<String>
```

will not compile. A compiler error is much better than a class cast exception at run time.

This is the appeal of type parameters: they make your programs easier to read and safer.

Who Wants to Be a Generic Programmer?

It is easy to use a generic class such as `ArrayList`. Most Java programmers will simply use types such as `ArrayList<String>` as if they had been built into the language, just like `String[]` arrays. (Of course, array lists are better than arrays because they can expand automatically.)

However, it is not so easy to implement a generic class. The programmers who use your code will want to plug in all sorts of classes for your type parameters. They expect everything to work without onerous restrictions and confusing error messages. Your job as a generic programmer, therefore, is to anticipate all the potential future uses of your class.

How hard can this get? Here is a typical issue that the designers of the standard class library had to grapple with. The `ArrayList` class has a method `addAll` to add all elements of another collection. A programmer may want to add all elements from an `ArrayList<Manager>` to an `ArrayList<Employee>`. But, of course, doing it the other way around should not be legal. How do you allow one call and disallow the other? The Java language designers invented an ingenious new concept, the *wildcard type*, to solve this problem. Wildcard types are rather abstract, but they allow a library builder to make methods as flexible as possible.

Generic programming falls into three skill levels. At a basic level, you just use generic classes—typically, collections such as `ArrayList`—without thinking how and why they work.

Most application programmers will want to stay at that level until something goes wrong. You may encounter a confusing error message when mixing different generic classes, or when interfacing with legacy code that knows nothing about type parameters. At that point, you need to learn enough about Java generics to solve problems systematically rather than through random tinkering. Finally, of course, you may want to implement your own generic classes and methods.

Application programmers probably won't write lots of generic code. The folks at Sun have already done the heavy lifting and supplied type parameters for all the collection classes. As a rule of thumb, only code that traditionally involved lots of casts from very general types (such as `Object` or the `Comparable` interface) will benefit from using type parameters.

In this chapter, we tell you everything you need to know to implement your own generic code. However, we expect most readers to use this knowledge primarily for help with troubleshooting, and to satisfy their curiosity about the inner workings of the parameterized collection classes.

Definition of a Simple Generic Class

A *generic class* is a class with one or more type variables. In this chapter, we use a simple `Pair` class as an example. This class allows us to focus on generics without being distracted by data storage details. Here is the code for the generic `Pair` class:

```
public class Pair<T>
{
   public Pair() { first = null; second = null; }
   public Pair(T first, T second) { this.first = first;  this.second = second; }

   public T getFirst() { return first; }
   public T getSecond() { return second; }

   public void setFirst(T newValue) { first = newValue; }
   public void setSecond(T newValue) { second = newValue; }

   private T first;
   private T second;
}
```

The `Pair` class introduces a type variable `T`, enclosed in angle brackets < >, after the class name. A generic class can have more than one type variable. For example, we could have defined the `Pair` class with separate types for the first and second field:

```
public class Pair<T, U> { . . . }
```

The type variables are used throughout the class definition to specify method return types and the types of fields and local variables. For example,

```
private T first; // uses type variable
```

NOTE: It is common practice to use uppercase letters for type variables, and to keep them short. The Java library uses the variable `E` for the element type of a collection, `K` and `V` for key and value types of a table, and `T` (and the neighboring letters `U` and `S`, if necessary) for "any type at all".

You *instantiate* the generic type by substituting types for the type variables, such as

```
Pair<String>
```

You can think of the result as an ordinary class with constructors

```
Pair<String>()
Pair<String>(String, String)
```

and methods

```
String getFirst()
String getSecond()
void setFirst(String)
void setSecond(String)
```

In other words, the generic class acts as a factory for ordinary classes.

The program in Example 13–1 puts the `Pair` class to work. The static `minmax` method traverses an array and simultaneously computes the minimum and maximum value. It uses a `Pair` object to return both results. Recall that the `compareTo` method compares two strings, returning 0 if the strings are identical, a negative integer if the first string comes before the second in dictionary order, and a positive integer otherwise.

C++ NOTE: Superficially, generic classes in Java are similar to template classes in C++. The only obvious difference is that Java has no special `template` keyword. However, as you will see throughout this chapter, there are substantial differences between these two mechanisms.

Example 13–1 PairTest1.java

```
public class PairTest1
{
   public static void main(String[] args)
   {
      String[] words = { "Mary", "had", "a", "little", "lamb" };
      Pair<String> mm = ArrayAlg.minmax(words);
      System.out.println("min = " + mm.getFirst());
      System.out.println("max = " + mm.getSecond());
   }
}

class ArrayAlg
{
   /**
      Gets the minimum and maximum of an array of strings.
      @param a an array of strings
      @return a pair with the min and max value, or null if a is
      null or empty
   */
   public static Pair<String> minmax(String[] a)
   {
      if (a == null || a.length == 0) return null;
      String min = a[0];
      String max = a[0];
      for (int i = 1; i < a.length; i++)
      {
         if (min.compareTo(a[i]) > 0) min = a[i];
         if (max.compareTo(a[i]) < 0) max = a[i];
      }
      return new Pair<String>(min, max);
   }
}
```

Generic Methods

In the preceding section, you have seen how to define a generic class. You can also define a single method with type parameters.

```
class ArrayAlg
{
   public static <T> T getMiddle(T[] a)
   {
      return a[a.length / 2]);
   }
}
```

This method is defined inside an ordinary class, not inside a generic class. However, it is a generic method, as you can see from the angle brackets and the type variable. Note that the type variables are inserted after the modifiers (`public static`, in our case) and before the return type.

You can define generic methods both inside ordinary classes and inside generic classes.

When you call a generic method, you can place the actual types, enclosed in angle brackets, before the method name:

```
String[] names = { "John", "Q.", "Public" };
String middle = ArrayAlg.<String>getMiddle(names);
```

In this case (and indeed in most cases), you can omit the `<String>` type parameter from the method call. The compiler has enough information to infer the method that you want. It matches the type of `names` (that is, `String[]`) against the generic type `T[]` and deduces that `T` must be `String`. That is, you can simply call

```
String middle = ArrayAlg.getMiddle(names);
```

C++ NOTE: In C++, you place the type parameters after the method name. That can lead to nasty parsing ambiguities. For example, `g(f<a,b>(c))` can mean "call `g` with the result of `f<a,b>(c)`", or "call `g` with the two Boolean values `f<a` and `b>(c)`".

Bounds for Type Variables

Sometimes, a class or a method needs to place restrictions on type variables. Here is a typical example. We want to compute the smallest element of an array:

```
class ArrayAlg
{
   public static <T> T min(T[] a) // almost correct
   {
      if (a == null || a.length == 0) return null;
      T smallest = a[0];
      for (int i = 1; i < a.length; i++)
         if (smallest.compareTo(a[i]) > 0) smallest = a[i];
      return smallest;
   }
}
```

But there is a problem. Look inside the code of the `min` method. The variable `smallest` has type `T`, which means that it could be an object of an arbitrary class. How do we know that the class to which `T` belongs has a `compareTo` method?

The solution is to restrict `T` to a class that implements the `Comparable` interface—a standard interface with a single method, `compareTo`. You achieve this by giving a *bound* for the type variable `T`:

```
public static <T extends Comparable> T min(T[] a) . . .
```

Actually, the `Comparable` interface is itself a generic type. For now, we will ignore that complexity.

Now, the generic `min` method can only be called with arrays of classes that implement the `Comparable` interface, such as `String`, `Date`, and so on. Calling `min` with a `Rectangle` array is a compile-time error because the `Rectangle` class does not implement `Comparable`.

C++ NOTE: In C++, you cannot restrict the types of template parameters. If a programmer instantiates a template with an inappropriate type, an (often obscure) error message is reported inside the template code.

You may wonder why you use the `extends` keyword rather than the `implements` keyword in this situation—after all, `Comparable` is an interface. The notation

<T extends *BoundingType*>

expresses that `T` should be a *subtype* of the bounding type. Both `T` and the bounding type can be either a class or an interface. The `extends` keyword was chosen because it is a reasonable approximation of the subtype concept, and the Java designers did not want to add a new keyword (such as `sub`) to the language.

A type variable or wildcard can have multiple bounds, for example,

```
T extends Comparable & Serializable
```

The bounding types are separated by ampersands (`&`) because commas are used to separate type variables.

As with Java inheritance, you can have as many interface supertypes as you like, but at most one of the bounds can be a class. If you have a class as a bound, it must be the first one in the bounds list.

In the next sample program (Example 13–2), we rewrite the `minmax` method to be generic. The method computes the minimum and maximum of a generic array, returning a `Pair<T>`.

Example 13–2: PairTest2.java

```
import java.util.*;

public class PairTest2
{
   public static void main(String[] args)
   {
      GregorianCalendar[] birthdays =
         {
            new GregorianCalendar(1906, Calendar.DECEMBER, 9), // G. Hopper
            new GregorianCalendar(1815, Calendar.DECEMBER, 10), // A. Lovelace
            new GregorianCalendar(1903, Calendar.DECEMBER, 3), // J. von Neumann
            new GregorianCalendar(1910, Calendar.JUNE, 22), // K. Zuse
         };
      Pair<GregorianCalendar> mm = ArrayAlg.minmax(birthdays);
      System.out.println("min = " + mm.getFirst().getTime());
      System.out.println("max = " + mm.getSecond().getTime());
   }
}

class ArrayAlg
{
   /**
      Gets the minimum and maximum of an array of objects of type T.
```

```
      @param a an array of objects of type T
      @return a pair with the min and max value, or null if a is
      null or empty
   */
   public static <T extends Comparable> Pair<T> minmax(T[] a)
   {
      if (a == null || a.length == 0) return null;
      T min = a[0];
      T max = a[0];
      for (int i = 1; i < a.length; i++)
      {
         if (min.compareTo(a[i]) > 0) min = a[i];
         if (max.compareTo(a[i]) < 0) max = a[i];
      }
      return new Pair<T>(min, max);
   }
}
```

Generic Code and the Virtual Machine

The virtual machine does not have objects of generic types—all objects belong to ordinary classes. An earlier version of the generics implementation was even able compile a program that uses generics into class files that executed on 1.0 virtual machines! This backward compatibility was only abandoned fairly late in the development for Java generics. If you use the Sun compiler to compile code that uses Java generics, the resulting class files will *not* execute on pre-5.0 virtual machines.

NOTE: If you want to have the benefits of the JDK 5.0 language features while retaining byte-code compatibility with older virtual machines, check out `http://sourceforge.net/projects/retroweaver`. The Retroweaver program rewrites class files so that they are compatible with older virtual machines.

Whenever you define a generic type, a corresponding *raw* type is automatically provided. The name of the raw type is simply the name of the generic type, with the type parameters removed. The type variables are *erased* and replaced by their bounding types (or `Object` for variables without bounds.)

For example, the raw type for `Pair<T>` looks like this:

```
public class Pair
{
   public Pair(Object first, Object second)
   {
      this.first = first;
      this.second = second;
   }

   public Object getFirst() { return first; }
   public Object getSecond() { return second; }

   public void setFirst(Object newValue) { first = newValue; }
   public void setSecond(Object newValue) { second = newValue; }

   private Object first;
   private Object second;
}
```

Because T is an unbounded type variable, it is simply replaced by Object.

The result is an ordinary class, just as you might have implemented it before generics were added to the Java programming language.

Your programs may contain different kinds of Pair, such as Pair<String> or Pair<GregorianCalendar>, but erasure turns them all into raw Pair types.

C++ NOTE: In this regard, Java generics are very different from C++ templates. C++ produces different types for each template instantiation, a phenomenon called "template code bloat." Java does not suffer from this problem.

The raw type replaces type variables with the first bound, or Object if no bounds are given. For example, the type variable in the class Pair<T> has no explicit bounds, hence the raw type replaces T with Object. Suppose we declare a slightly different type

```
public class Interval<T extends Comparable & Serializable> implements Serializable
{
   public Interval(T first, T second)
   {
      if (first.compareTo(second) <= 0) { lower = first; upper = second; }
      else { lower = second; upper = first; }
   }
   . . .
   private T lower;
   private T upper;
}
```

The raw type Interval looks like this:

```
public class Interval implements Serializable
{
   public Interval(Comparable first, Comparable second) { . . . }
   . . .
   private Comparable lower;
   private Comparable upper;
}
```

NOTE: You may wonder what happens if you switch the bounds: class Interval<Serializable & Comparable>. In that case, the raw type replaces T with Serializable, and the compiler inserts casts to Comparable when necessary. For efficiency, you should therefore put tagging interfaces (that is, interfaces without methods) at the end of the bounds list.

Translating Generic Expressions

When you program a call to a generic method, the compiler inserts casts when the return type has been erased. For example, consider the sequence of statements

```
Pair<Employee> buddies = . . .;
Employee buddy = buddies.getFirst();
```

The erasure of getFirst has return type Object. The compiler automatically inserts the cast to Employee. That is, the compiler translates the method call into two virtual machine instructions:

- a call to the raw method Pair.getFirst
- a cast of the returned Object to the Employee type

Casts are also inserted when you access a generic field. Suppose the `first` and `second` fields of the `Pair` class were public. (Not a good programming style, perhaps, but it is legal Java.) Then the expression

```
Employee buddy = buddies.first;
```

also has a cast inserted in the resulting byte codes.

Translating Generic Methods

Type erasure also happens for generic methods. Programmers usually think of a generic method such as

```
public static <T extends Comparable> T min(T[] a)
```

as a whole family of methods, but after erasure, only a single method is left:

```
public static Comparable min(Comparable[] a)
```

Note that the type parameter `T` has been erased, leaving only its bounding type `Comparable`.

Erasure of method brings up a couple of complexities. Consider this example:

```
class DateInterval extends Pair<Date>
{
   public void setSecond(Date second)
   {
      if (second.compareTo(getFirst()) >= 0)
         super.setSecond(second);
   }
   . . .
}
```

A date interval is a pair of `Date` objects, and we'll want to override the methods to ensure that the second value is never smaller than the first. This class is erased to

```
class DateInterval extends Pair // after erasure
{
   public void setSecond(Date second) { . . . }
   . . .
}
```

Perhaps surprisingly, there is another `setSecond` method, inherited from `Pair`, namely,

```
public void setSecond(Object second)
```

This is clearly a different method because it has a parameter of a different type—`Object` instead of `Date`. But it *shouldn't* be different. Consider this sequence of statements:

```
DateInterval interval = new DateInterval(. . .);
Pair<Date> pair = interval; // OK--assignment to superclass
pair.setSecond(aDate);
```

Our expectation is that the call to `setSecond` is polymorphic and that the appropriate method is called. Because `pair` refers to a `DateInterval` object, that should be `DateInterval.setSecond`. The problem is that the type erasure interferes with polymorphism. To fix this problem, the compiler generates a *bridge method* in the `DateInterval` class:

```
public void setSecond(Object second) { setSecond((Date) second); }
```

To see why this works, let us carefully follow the execution of the statement

```
pair.setSecond(aDate)
```

The variable `pair` has declared type `Pair<Date>`, and that type only has a single method called `setSecond`, namely `setSecond(Object)`. The virtual machine calls that method on the object to which `pair` refers. That object is of type `DateInterval`. Therefore, the method

DateInterval.setSecond(Object) is called. That method is the synthesized bridge method. It calls DateInterval.setSecond(Date), which is what we want.

Bridge methods can get even stranger. Suppose the DateInterval method also overrides the getSecond method:

```
class DateInterval extends Pair<Date>
{
   public Date getSecond() { return (Date) super.getSecond().clone(); }
   . . .
}
```

In the erased type, there are two getSecond methods:

```
Date getSecond() // defined in DateInterval
Object getSecond() // defined in Pair
```

You could not write Java code like that—it would be illegal to have two methods with the same parameter types—here, no parameters. However, in the virtual machine, the parameter types *and the return type* specify a method. Therefore, the compiler can produce bytecodes for two methods that differ only in their return type, and the virtual machine will handle this situation correctly.

NOTE: Bridge methods are not limited to generic types. We already noted in Chapter 5 that, starting with JDK 5.0, it is legal for a method to specify a more restrictive return type when overriding another method. For example,

```
public class Employee implements Cloneable
{
   public Employee clone() throws CloneNotSupportedException { ... }
}
```

The Object.clone and Employee.clone methods are said to have *covariant return types.*

Actually, the Employee class has *two* clone methods:

```
Employee clone() // defined above
Object clone() // synthesized bridge method, overrides Object.clone
```

The synthesized bridge method calls the newly defined method.

In summary, you need to remember these facts about translation of Java generics:

- There are no generics in the virtual machines, only ordinary classes and methods.
- All type parameters are replaced by their bounds.
- Bridge methods are synthesized to preserve polymorphism.
- Casts are inserted as necessary to preserve type safety.

Calling Legacy Code

Lots of Java code was written before JDK 5.0. If generic classes could not interoperate with that code, they would probably not be widely used. Fortunately, it is straightforward to use generic classes together with their raw equivalents in legacy APIs.

Let us look at a concrete example. To set the labels of a JSlider, you use the method

```
void setLabelTable(Dictionary table)
```

In Chapter 9, we used the following code to populate the label table:

```
Dictionary<Integer, Component> labelTable = new Hashtable<Integer, Component>();
labelTable.put(0, new JLabel(new ImageIcon("nine.gif")));
```

```
labelTable.put(20, new JLabel(new ImageIcon("ten.gif")));
. . .
slider.setLabelTable(labelTable); // WARNING
```

NOTE: The Hashtable class is a concrete subclass of the abstract Dictionary class. Both Dictionary and Hashtable have been declared as "obsolete" ever since they were superseded by the Map interface and the HashMap class of JDK 1.2. Apparently though, they are still alive and kicking. After all, the JSlider class was only added in JDK 1.3. Didn't its programmers know about the Map class by then? Does this make you hopeful that they are going to adopt generics in the near future? Well, that's the way it goes with legacy code.

In JDK 5.0, the Dictionary and Hashtable classes were turned into a generic class. Therefore, we are able to form Dictionary<Integer, Component> instead of using a raw Dictionary. However, when you pass the Dictionary<Integer, Component> object to setLabelTable, the compiler issues a warning.

```
Dictionary<Integer, Components> labelTable = . . .;
slider.setLabelTable(labelTable); // WARNING
```

After all, the compiler has no assurance about what the setLabelTable might do to the Dictionary object. That method might replace all the keys with strings. That breaks the guarantee that the keys have type Integer, and future operations may cause bad cast exceptions.

There isn't much you can do with this warning, except ponder it and ask what the JSlider is likely going to do with this Dictionary object. In our case, it is pretty clear that the JSlider only reads the information, so we can ignore the warning.

Now consider the opposite case, in which you get an object of a raw type from a legacy class. You can assign it to a parameterized type variable, but of course you will get a warning. For example,

```
Dictionary<Integer, Components> labelTable = slider.getLabelTable(); // WARNING
```

That's ok—review the warning and make sure that the label table really contains Integer and Component objects. Of course, there never is an absolute guarantee. A malicious coder might have installed a different Dictionary in the slider. But again, the situation is no worse than it was before JDK 5.0. In the worst case, your program will throw an exception.

It is unfortunate that you can't turn off the warnings after you reviewed them. It seems impractical to review every warning every time you recompile a source file. The Java language designers are planning to add a more flexible warning mechanism to a future version of the JDK.

Restrictions and Limitations

In the following sections, we discuss a number of restrictions that you need to consider when working with Java generics. Most of these restrictions are a consequence of type erasure.

Primitive Types

You cannot substitute a primitive type for a type parameter. Thus, there is no Pair<double>, only Pair<Double>. The reason is, of course, type erasure. After erasure, the Pair class has fields of type Object, and you can't use them to store double values.

This is an annoyance, to be sure, but it is consistent with the separate status of primitive types in the Java language. It is not a fatal flaw—there are only eight primitive types, and you can always handle them with separate classes and methods when wrapper types are not an acceptable substitute.

Runtime Type Inquiry

Objects in the virtual machine always have a specific nongeneric type. Therefore, all type inquiries yield only the raw type. For example,

```
if (a instanceof Pair<String>) // same as a instanceof Pair
```

really only tests whether a is a Pair of any type. The same is true for the test

```
if (a instanceof Pair<T>) // T is ignored
```

or the cast

```
Pair<String> p = (Pair<String>) a; // WARNING--can only test that a is a Pair
```

To remind you of the risk, you will get a compiler warning whenever you use instanceof or cast expressions that involve generic types.

In the same spirit, the getClass method always returns the raw type. For example,

```
Pair<String> stringPair = . . .;
Pair<Employee> employeePair = . . .;
if (stringPair.getClass() == employeePair.getClass()) // they are equal
```

The comparison yields true because both calls to getClass return Pair.class.

Exceptions

You can neither throw nor catch objects of a generic class. In fact, it is not even legal for a generic class to extend Throwable. For example, the following definition will not compile:

```
public class Problem<T> extends Exception { /* . . . */ } // ERROR--can't extend Throwable
```

You cannot use a type variable in a catch clause. For example, the following method will not compile:

```
public static <T extends Throwable> void doWork(Class<T> t)
{
   try
   {
      do work
   }
   catch (T e) // ERROR--can't catch type variable
   {
      Logger.global.info(...)
   }
}
```

However, it is ok to use type variables in exception specifications. The following method is legal:

```
public static <T extends Throwable> void doWork(T t) throws T // OK
{
   try
   {
      do work
   }
   catch (Throwable realCause)
   {
      t.initCause(realCause);
      throw t;
   }
}
```

Arrays

You cannot declare arrays of parameterized types, such as

```
Pair<String>[] table = new Pair<String>(10); // ERROR
```

What's wrong with that? After erasure, the type of table is Pair[]. You can convert it to Object[]:

```
Object[] objarray = table;
```

We discussed in Chapter 5 that an array remembers its component type and throws an ArrayStoreException if you try to store an element of the wrong type:

```
objarray[0] = "Hello"; // ERROR--component type is Pair
```

But erasure renders this mechanism ineffective for generic types. The assignment

```
objarray[0] = new Pair<Employee>();
```

would pass the array store check but still result in a type error. For this reason, arrays of parameterized types are outlawed.

TIP: If you need to collect parameterized type objects, simply use an ArrayList: ArrayList<Pair<String>> is safe and effective.

Instantiation of Generic Types

You cannot instantiate generic types. For example, the following Pair<T> constructor is illegal:

```
public Pair() { first = new T(); second = new T(); } // ERROR
```

Type erasure would change T to Object, and surely you don't want to call new Object().

Similarly, you cannot make a generic array:

```
public <T> T[] minMax(T[] a) { T[] mm = new T[2]; . . . } // ERROR
```

Type erasure would cause this method to always construct an array Object[2].

However, you can construct generic objects and arrays through reflection, by calling the Class.newInstance and Array.newInstance methods.

Static Contexts

You cannot reference type variables in static fields or methods. For example, the following clever idea won't work:

```
public class Singleton<T>
{
   public static T getSingleInstance() // ERROR
   {
      if (singleInstance == null) construct new instance of T
      return singleInstance;
   }
   private static T singleInstance; // ERROR
}
```

If this could be done, then a program could declare a Singleton<Random> to share a random number generator and a Singleton<JFileChooser> to share a file chooser dialog. But it can't work. After type erasure there is only one Singleton class, and only one singleInstance field. For that reason, static fields and methods with type variables are simply outlawed.

Clashes after Erasure

It is illegal to create conditions that cause clashes when generic types are erased. Here is an example. Suppose we add an equals method to the Pair class, like this:

```
public class Pair<T>
{
   public boolean equals(T value) { return first.equals(value) && second.equals(value); }
   . . .
}
```

Consider a Pair<String>. Conceptually, it has two equals methods:

```
boolean equals(String) // defined in Pair<T>
boolean equals(Object) // inherited from Object
```

But the intuition leads us astray. The erasure of the method

```
boolean equals(T)
```

is

```
boolean equals(Object)
```

which clashes with the Object.equals method.

The remedy is, of course, to rename the offending method.

The generics specification cites another rule: "To support translation by erasure, we impose the restriction that a class or type variable may not at the same time be a subtype of two interface types which are different parameterizations of the same interface." For example, the following is illegal:

```
class Calendar implements Comparable<Calendar> { . . . }
class GregorianCalendar extends Calendar implements Comparable<GregorianCalendar> { . . . } // ERROR
```

GregorianCalendar would then implement both Comparable<Calendar> and Comparable<GregorianCalendar>, which are different parameterizations of the same interface.

It is not clear what this restriction has to do with type erasure. The nongeneric version

```
class Employee implements Comparable { . . . }
class Manager extends Employee implements Comparable { . . . }
```

is legal.

Inheritance Rules for Generic Types

When you work with generic classes, you need to learn a few rules about inheritance and subtypes. Let's start with a situation that many programmers find unintuitive. Consider a class and a subclass, such as Employee and Manager. Is Pair<Manager> a subclass of Pair<Employee>? Perhaps surprisingly, the answer is "no." For example, the following code will not compile

```
Manager[] topHonchos = . . .;
Pair<Employee> = ArrayAlg.minmax(topHonchos); // ERROR
```

The minmax method returns a Pair<Manager>, not a Pair<Employee>, and it is illegal to assign one to the other.

In general, there is *no* relationship between Pair<S> and Pair<T>, no matter how S and T are related (see Figure 13–1).

This seems like a cruel restriction, but it is necessary for type safety. Suppose we were allowed to convert a Pair<Manager> to a Pair<Employee>. Consider this code.

```
Pair<Manager> managerBuddies = new Pair<Manager>(ceo, cfo);
Pair<Employee> employeeBuddies = managerBuddies; // illegal, but suppose it wasn't
employeeBuddies.setFirst(lowlyEmployee);
```

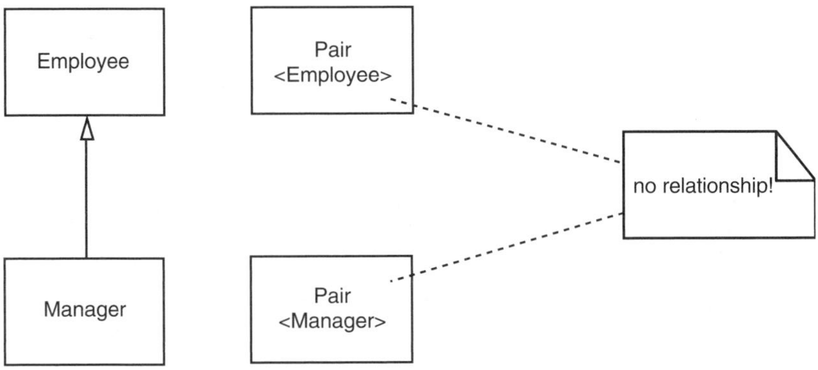

Figure 13–1: No inheritance relationship between pair classes

Clearly, the last statement is legal. But `employeeBuddies` and `managerBuddies` refer to the *same object*. We now managed to pair up the CFO with a lowly employee, which should not be possible for a `Pair<Manager>`.

In contrast, you can always convert a parameterized type to a raw type. For example, `Pair<Employee>` is a subtype of the raw type `Pair`. This conversion is necessary for interfacing with legacy code.

Can you convert to the raw type and then cause a type error? Unfortunately, you can. Consider this example:

```
Pair<Manager> managerBuddies = new Pair<Manager>(ceo, cfo);
Pair rawBuddies = managerBuddies; // OK
rawBuddies.setFirst(new File(". . .")); // only a compile-time warning
```

This sounds scary. However, keep in mind that you are no worse off than you were with older versions of Java. The security of the virtual machine is not at stake. When the foreign object is retrieved with `getFirst` and assigned to a `Manager` variable, a `ClassCastException` is thrown, just as in the good old days. You merely lose the added safety that generic programming normally provides.

Finally, generic classes can extend or implement other generic classes. In this regard, they are no different from ordinary classes. For example, the class `ArrayList<T>` implements the interface `List<T>`. That means, an `ArrayList<Manager>` can be converted to a `List<Manager>`. However, as you just saw, an `ArrayList<Manager>` is *not* an `ArrayList<Employee>` or `List<Employee>`. Figure 13–2 shows these relationships.

Wildcard Types

It was known for some time among researchers of type systems that a rigid system of generic types is quite unpleasant to use. The Java designers invented an ingenious (but nevertheless safe) "escape hatch": the *wildcard type*. For example, the wildcard type

```
Pair<? extends Employee>
```

denotes any generic `Pair` type whose type parameter is a subclass of `Employee`, such as `Pair<Manager>`, but not `Pair<String>`.

Let's say you want to write a method that prints out pairs of employees, like this:

```
public static void printBuddies(Pair<Employee> p)
{
   Employee first = p.getFirst();
   Employee second = p.getSecond();
   System.out.println(first.getName() + " and " + second.getName() + " are buddies.";
}
```

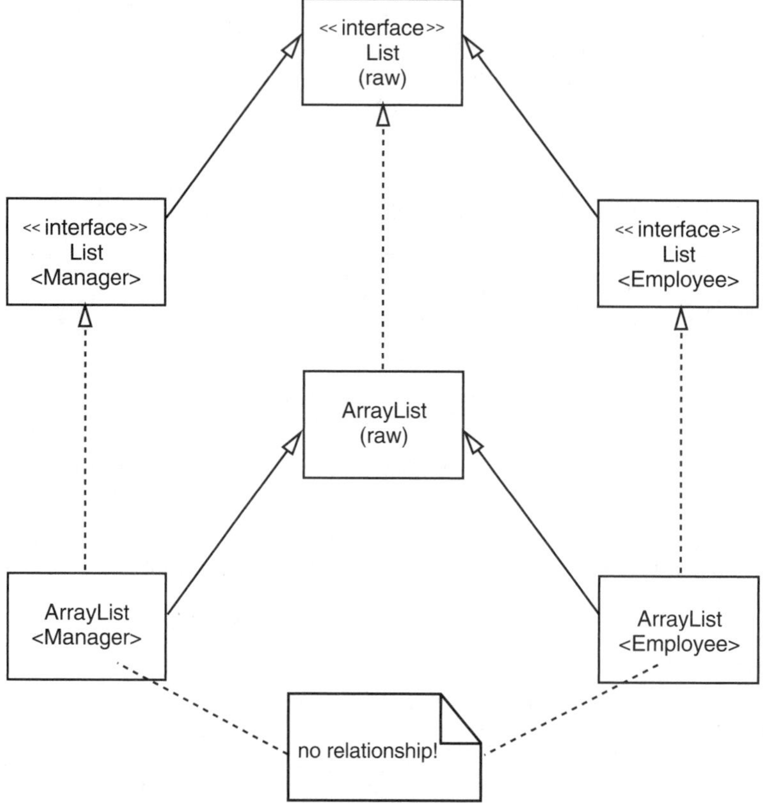

Figure 13–2: Subtype relationships among generic list types

As you saw in the preceding section, you cannot pass a `Pair<Manager>` to that method, which is rather limiting. But the solution is simple: use a wildcard type:

```
public static void printBuddies(Pair<? extends Employee> p)
```

The type `Pair<Manager>` is a subtype of `Pair<? extends Employee>` (see Figure 13–3).

Can we use wildcards to corrupt a `Pair<Manager>` through a `Pair<? extends Employee>` reference?

```
Pair<Manager> managerBuddies = new Pair<Manager>(ceo, cfo);
Pair<? extends Employee> wildcardBuddies = managerBuddies; // OK
wildcardBuddies.setFirst(lowlyEmployee); // compile-time error
```

No corruption is possible. The call to `setFirst` is a type error. To see why, let us have a closer look at the type `Pair<? extends Employee>`. Its methods look like this:

```
? extends Employee getFirst()
void setFirst(? extends Employee)
```

This makes it impossible to call the `setFirst` method. The compiler only knows that it needs some subtype of `Employee`, but it doesn't know which type. It refuses to pass any specific type—after all, ? might not match it.

We don't have this problem with `getFirst`: It is perfectly legal to assign the return value of `getFirst` to an `Employee` reference.

This is the key idea behind bounded wildcards. We now have a way of distinguishing between the safe accessor methods and the unsafe mutator methods.

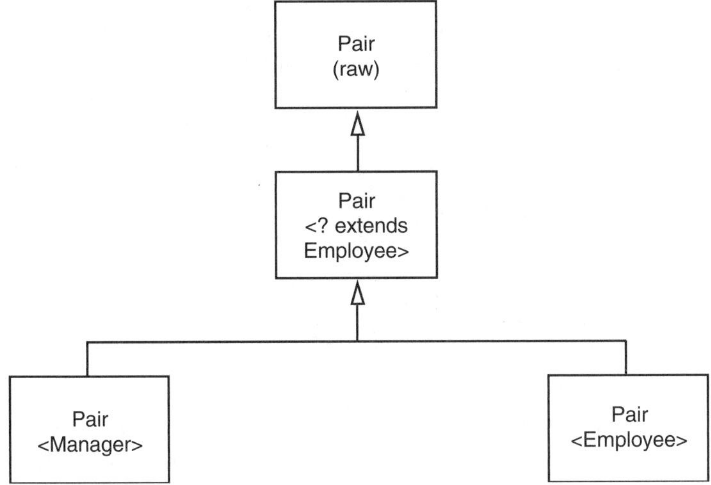

Figure 13–3: Subtype relationships with wildcards

Supertype Bounds for Wildcards

Wildcard bounds are similar to type variable bounds, but they have an added capability—you can specify a *supertype bound,* like this:

```
? super Manager
```

This wildcard is restricted to all supertypes of `Manager`. (It was a stroke of good luck that the existing `super` keyword describes the relationship so accurately.)

Why would you want to do this? A wildcard with a supertype bound gives you the opposite behavior of the wildcards described on page 721. You can supply parameters to methods, but you can't use the return values. For example, `Pair<? super Manager>` has methods

```
void set(? super Manager)
? super Manager get()
```

The compiler doesn't know the exact type of the `set` method but can call it with any `Manager` object (or a subtype such as `Executive`), but not with an `Employee`. However, if you call `get`, there is no guarantee about the type of the returned object. You can only assign it to an `Object`.

Here is a typical example. We have an array of managers and want to put the manager with the lowest and highest bonus into a `Pair` object. What kind of `Pair`? A `Pair<Employee>` should be fair game or, for that matter, a `Pair<Object>` (see Figure 13–4). The following method will accept any appropriate `Pair`:

```
public static void minMaxBonus(Manager[] a, Pair<? super Manager> result)
{
   if (a == null || a.length == 0) return;
   Manager min = a[0];
   Manager max = a[0];
   for (int i = 1; i < a.length; i++)
   {
      if (min.getBonus() > a[i].getBonus()) min = a[i];
      if (max.getBonus() < a[i].getBonus()) max = a[i];
   }
   result.setFirst(min);
   result.setSecond(max);
}
```

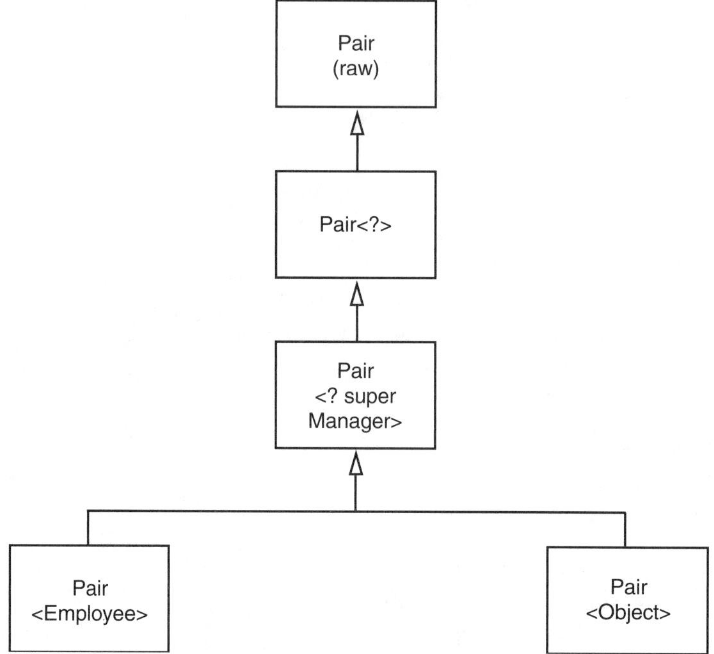

Figure 13–4: A wildcard with a supertype bound

Intuitively speaking, wildcards with supertype bounds let you write to a generic object, wildcards with subtype bounds let you read from a generic objects.

Here is another use for supertype bounds. The `Comparable` interface is itself a generic type. It is declared as follows:

```
public interface Comparable<T>
{
    public int compareTo(T other);
}
```

Here, the type variable indicates the type of the `other` parameter. For example, the `String` class implements `Comparable<String>`, and its `compareTo` method is declared as

```
public int compareTo(String other)
```

This is nice—the explicit parameter has the correct type. Before JDK 5.0, `other` was an `Object`, and a cast was necessary in the implementation of the method.

Because `Comparable` is a generic type, perhaps we should have done a better job with the `min` method of the `ArrayAlg` class? We could have declared it as

```
public static <T extends Comparable<T>> T min(T[] a) . . .
```

This looks more thorough than just using `T extends Comparable`, and it would work fine for many classes. For example, if you compute the minimum of a `String` array, then `T` is the type `String`, and `String` is a subtype of `Comparable<String>`. But we run into a problem when processing an array of `GregorianCalendar` objects. As it happens, `GregorianCalendar` is a subclass of `Calendar`, and `Calendar` implements `Comparable<Calendar>`. Thus, `GregorianCalendar` implements `Comparable<Calendar>` but not `Comparable<GregorianCalendar>`.

In a situation such as this one, supertypes come to the rescue:

```
public static <T extends Comparable<? super T>> T min(T[] a) . . .
```

Now the compareTo method has the form

```
int compareTo(? super T)
```

Maybe it is declared to take an object of type T, or—for example, when T is GregorianCalendar—a supertype of T. At any rate, it is safe to pass an object of type T to the compareTo method.

To the uninitiated, a declaration such as <T **extends Comparable<? super** T>> is bound to look intimidating. This is unfortunate, because the intent of this declaration is to help application programmers by removing unnecessary restrictions on the call parameters. Application programmers with no interest in generics will probably learn quickly to gloss over these declarations and just take for granted that library programmers will do the right thing. If you are a library programmer, you'll need to get used to wildcards, or your users will curse you and throw random casts at their code until it compiles.

Unbounded Wildcards

You can even use wildcards with no bounds at all, for example, Pair<?>. At first glance, this looks identical to the raw Pair type. Actually, the types are very different. The type Pair<?> has methods such as

```
? getFirst()
void setFirst(?)
```

The return value of getFirst can only be assigned to an Object. The setFirst method can never be called, *not even with an* Object. That's the essential difference between Pair<?> and Pair: you can call the setObject method of the raw Pair class with *any* Object.

Why would you ever want such a wimpy type? It is useful for very simple operations. For example, the following method tests whether a pair contains a given object. It never needs the actual type.

```
public static boolean hasNulls(Pair<?> p)
{
   return p.getFirst() == null || p.getSecond() == null;
}
```

You could have avoided the wildcard type by turning contains into a generic method:

```
public static <T> boolean hasNulls(Pair<T> p)
```

However, the version with the wildcard type seems easier to read.

Wildcard Capture

Let us write a method that swaps the elements of a pair:

```
public static void swap(Pair<?> p)
```

A wildcard is not a type variable, so we can't write code that uses ? as a type. In other words, the following would be illegal:

```
? t = p.getFirst(); // ERROR
p.setFirst(p.getSecond());
p.setSecond(t);
```

That's a problem because we need to temporarily hold the first element when we do the swapping. Fortunately, there is an interesting solution to this problem. We can write a helper method, swapHelper, like this:

```
public static <T> void swapHelper(Pair<T> p)
{
   T t = p.getFirst();
   p.setFirst(p.getSecond());
   p.setSecond(t);
}
```

Note that swapHelper is a generic method, whereas swap is not—it has a fixed parameter of type Pair<?>.

Now we can call swapHelper from swap:

```
public static void swap(Pair<?> p) { swapHelper(p); }
```

In this case, the parameter T of the swapHelper method *captures the wildcard*. It isn't known what type the wildcard denotes, but it is a definite type, and the definition of <T>swapHelper makes perfect sense when T denotes that type.

Of course, in this case, we were not compelled to use a wildcard—there is nothing wrong with using a type parameter, as in the swapHelper method. However, consider this example in which a wildcard type occurs naturally in the middle of a computation:

```
public static void maxMinBonus(Manager[] a, Pair<? super Manager> result)
{
   minMaxBonus(a, result);
   PairAlg.swapHelper(result); // OK--swapHelper captures wildcard type
}
```

Here, the wildcard capture mechanism cannot be avoided.

Wildcard capture is only legal in very limited circumstances. The compiler must be able to guarantee that the wildcard represents a single, definite type. For example, the T in ArrayList<Pair<T>> can never capture the wildcard in ArrayList<Pair<?>>. The array list might hold two Pair<?>, each of which has a different type for ?.

The test program in Example 13–3 gathers up the various methods that we discussed in the preceding sections, so that you can see them in context.

Example 13–3: PairTest3.java

```
import java.util.*;

public class PairTest3
{
   public static void main(String[] args)
   {
      Manager ceo = new Manager("Gus Greedy", 800000, 2003, 12, 15);
      Manager cfo = new Manager("Sid Sneaky", 600000, 2003, 12, 15);
      Pair<Manager> buddies = new Pair<Manager>(ceo, cfo);
      printBuddies(buddies);

      ceo.setBonus(1000000);
      cfo.setBonus(500000);
      Manager[] managers = { ceo, cfo };

      Pair<Employee> result = new Pair<Employee>();
      minMaxBonus(managers, result);
      System.out.println("first: " + result.getFirst().getName()
         + ", second: " + result.getSecond().getName());
      maxMinBonus(managers, result);
      System.out.println("first: " + result.getFirst().getName()
         + ", second: " + result.getSecond().getName());
   }

   public static void printBuddies(Pair<? extends Employee> p)
   {
      Employee first = p.getFirst();
```

```
      Employee second = p.getSecond();
      System.out.println(first.getName() + " and " + second.getName() + " are buddies.");
   }

   public static void minMaxBonus(Manager[] a, Pair<? super Manager> result)
   {
      if (a == null || a.length == 0) return;
      Manager min = a[0];
      Manager max = a[0];
      for (int i = 1; i < a.length; i++)
      {
         if (min.getBonus() > a[i].getBonus()) min = a[i];
         if (max.getBonus() < a[i].getBonus()) max = a[i];
      }
      result.setFirst(min);
      result.setSecond(max);
   }

   public static void maxMinBonus(Manager[] a, Pair<? super Manager> result)
   {
      minMaxBonus(a, result);
      PairAlg.swapHelper(result); // OK--swapHelper captures wildcard type
   }
}

class PairAlg
{
   public static boolean hasNulls(Pair<?> p)
   {
      return p.getFirst() == null || p.getSecond() == null;
   }

   public static void swap(Pair<?> p) { swapHelper(p); }

   public static <T> void swapHelper(Pair<T> p)
   {
      T t = p.getFirst();
      p.setFirst(p.getSecond());
      p.setSecond(t);
   }
}

class Employee
{
   public Employee(String n, double s, int year, int month, int day)
   {
      name = n;
      salary = s;
      GregorianCalendar calendar = new GregorianCalendar(year, month - 1, day);
      hireDay = calendar.getTime();
   }

   public String getName()
   {
      return name;
   }
```

```

   public double getSalary()
   {
      return salary;
   }

   public Date getHireDay()
   {
      return hireDay;
   }

   public void raiseSalary(double byPercent)
   {
      double raise = salary * byPercent / 100;
      salary += raise;
   }

   private String name;
   private double salary;
   private Date hireDay;
}

class Manager extends Employee
{
   /**
      @param n the employee's name
      @param s the salary
      @param year the hire year
      @param month the hire month
      @param day the hire day
   */
   public Manager(String n, double s, int year, int month, int day)
   {
      super(n, s, year, month, day);
      bonus = 0;
   }

   public double getSalary()
   {
      double baseSalary = super.getSalary();
      return baseSalary + bonus;
   }

   public void setBonus(double b)
   {
      bonus = b;
   }

   public double getBonus()
   {
      return bonus;
   }

   private double bonus;
}
```

Reflection and Generics

The `Class` class is now generic. For example, `String.class` is actually an object (in fact, the sole object) of the class `Class<String>`.

The type parameter is useful because it allows the methods of `Class<T>` to be more specific about their return types. The following methods of `Class<T>` take advantage of the type parameter:

```
T newInstance()
T cast(Object obj)
T[] getEnumConstants()
Class<? super T> getSuperclass()
Constructor<T> getConstructor(Class... parameterTypes)
Constructor<T> getDeclaredConstructor(Class... parameterTypes)
```

The `newInstance` method returns an instance of the class, obtained from the default constructor. Its return type can now be declared to be `T`, the same type as the class that is being described by `Class<T>`. That saves a cast.

The `cast` method returns the given object, now declared as type `T` if its type is indeed a subtype of `T`. Otherwise, it throws a `BadCastException`.

The `getEnumConstants` method returns `null` if this class is not an `enum` class or an array of the enumeration values, which are known to be of type `T`.

Finally, the `getConstructor` and `getDeclaredConstructor` methods return a `Constructor<T>` object. The `Constructor` class has also been made generic so that its `newInstance` method has the correct return type.

API `java.lang.Class<T>` 1.0

- `T newInstance()` **5.0**
  returns a new instance constructed with the default constructor.
- `T cast(Object obj)` **5.0**
  returns `obj` if it is `null` or can be converted to the type `T`, or throws a `BadCastException` otherwise.
- `T[] getEnumConstants()` **5.0**
  returns an array of all values if `T` is an enumerated type, `null` otherwise.
- `Class<? super T> getSuperclass()` **5.0**
  returns the superclass of this class, or `null` if `T` is not a class or the class `Object`.
- `Constructor<T> getConstructor(Class... parameterTypes)` **5.0**
- `Constructor<T> getDeclaredConstructor(Class... parameterTypes)` **5.0**
  get the public constructor, or the constructor with the given parameter types.

`java.lang.reflect.Constructor<T>` 1.1

- `T newInstance(Object... parameters)` **5.0**
  returns a new instance constructed with the given parameters.

Using Class<T> Parameters for Type Matching

It is sometimes useful to match the type variable of a `Class<T>` parameter in a generic method. Here is the canonical example:

```
public static <T> Pair<T> makePair(Class<T> c) throws InstantiationException, IllegalAccessException
{
   return new Pair<T>(c.newInstance(), c.newInstance());
}
```

If you call

```
makePair(Employee.class)
```

then `Employee.class` is an object of type `Class<Employee>`. The type parameter `T` of the `makePair` method matches `Employee`, and the compiler can infer that the method returns a `Pair<Employee>`.

Generic Type Information in the Virtual Machine

One of the notable features of Java generics is the erasure of generic types in the virtual machine. Perhaps surprisingly, the erased classes still retain some faint memory of their generic origin. For example, the raw `Pair` class knows that it originated from the generic class `Pair<T>`, even though an object of type `Pair` can't tell whether it was constructed as a `Pair<String>` or `Pair<Employee>`.

Similarly, consider a method

```
public static Comparable min(Comparable[] a)
```

that is the erasure of a generic method

```
public static <T extends Comparable<? super T>> T min(T[] a)
```

You can use the reflection API enhancements of JDK 5.0 to determine that

- the generic method has a type parameter called `T`;
- the type parameter has a subtype bound that is itself a generic type;
- the bounding type has a wildcard parameter;
- the wildcard parameter has a supertype bound; and
- the generic method has a generic array parameter.

In other words, you get to reconstruct everything about generic classes and methods that their implementors declared. However, you won't know how the type parameters were resolved for specific objects or method calls.

NOTE: The type information that is contained in class files to enable reflection of generics is incompatible with older virtual machines.

In order to express generic type declarations, JDK 5.0 provides a new interface `Type` in the `java.lang.reflect` package. The interface has the following subtypes:

- the `Class` class, describing concrete types
- the `TypeVariable` interface, describing type variables (such as `T extends Comparable<? super T>`)
- the `WildcardType` interface, describing wildcards (such as `? super T`)
- the `ParameterizedType` interface, describing generic class or interface types (such as `Comparable<? super T>`)
- the `GenericArrayType` interface, describing generic arrays (such as `T[]`)

Figure 13–5 shows the inheritance hierarchy. Note that the last four subtypes are interfaces—the virtual machine instantiates suitable classes that implement these interfaces.

Example 13–4 uses the generic reflection API to print out what it discovers about a given class. If you run it with the `Pair` class, you get this report:

```
class Pair<T extends java.lang.Object> extends java.lang.Object
public T extends java.lang.Object getSecond()
public void setFirst(T extends java.lang.Object)
public void setSecond(T extends java.lang.Object)
public T extends java.lang.Object getFirst()
```

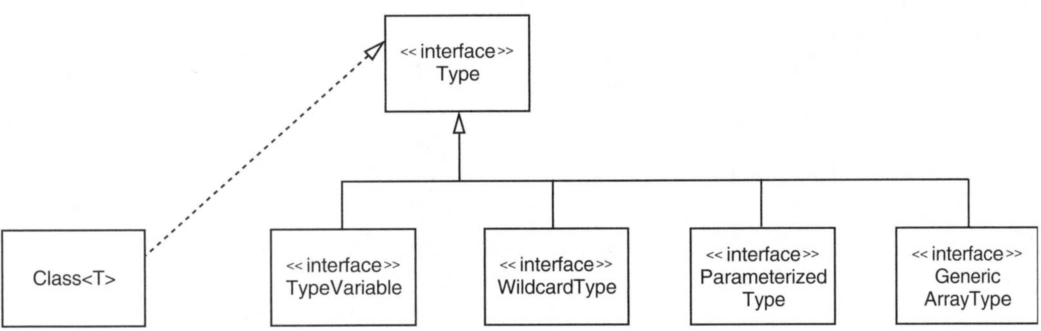

Figure 13–5: The `Type` class and its descendants

If you run it with `ArrayAlg` in the `PairTest2` directory, the report displays the following method:

```
public static <T extends java.lang.Comparable> Pair<T extends java.lang.Comparable> minmax(T extends
java.lang.Comparable[])
```

The API notes at the end of this section describe the methods used in the example program.

Example 13–4: GenericReflectionTest.java

```
import java.lang.reflect.*;
import java.util.*;

public class GenericReflectionTest
{
   public static void main(String[] args)
   {
      // read class name from command-line args or user input
      String name;
      if (args.length > 0)
         name = args[0];
      else
      {
         Scanner in = new Scanner(System.in);
         System.out.println("Enter class name (e.g. java.util.Date): ");
         name = in.next();
      }

      try
      {
         // print generic info for class and public methods
         Class cl = Class.forName(name);
         printClass(cl);
         for (Method m : cl.getDeclaredMethods())
            printMethod(m);
      }
      catch (ClassNotFoundException e)
      {
         e.printStackTrace();
      }
   }

   public static void printClass(Class cl)
```

```
   {
      System.out.print(cl);
      printTypes(cl.getTypeParameters(), "<", ", ", ">");
      Type sc = cl.getGenericSuperclass();
      if (sc != null)
      {
         System.out.print(" extends ");
         printType(sc);
      }
      printTypes(cl.getGenericInterfaces(), " implements ", ", ", "");
      System.out.println();
   }

   public static void printMethod(Method m)
   {
      String name = m.getName();
      System.out.print(Modifier.toString(m.getModifiers()));
      System.out.print(" ");
      printTypes(m.getTypeParameters(), "<", ", ", "> ");

      printType(m.getGenericReturnType());
      System.out.print(" ");
      System.out.print(name);
      System.out.print("(");
      printTypes(m.getGenericParameterTypes(), "", ", ", "");
      System.out.println(")");
   }

   public static void printTypes(Type[] types, String pre, String sep, String suf)
   {
      if (types.length > 0) System.out.print(pre);
      for (int i = 0; i < types.length; i++)
      {
         if (i > 0) System.out.print(sep);
         printType(types[i]);
      }
      if (types.length > 0) System.out.print(suf);
   }

   public static void printType(Type type)
   {
      if (type instanceof Class)
      {
         Class t = (Class) type;
         System.out.print(t.getName());
      }
      else if (type instanceof TypeVariable)
      {
         TypeVariable t = (TypeVariable) type;
         System.out.print(t.getName());
         printTypes(t.getBounds(), " extends ", " & ", "");
      }
      else if (type instanceof WildcardType)
      {
         WildcardType t = (WildcardType) type;
         System.out.print("?");
```

```
         printTypes(t.getLowerBounds(), " extends ", " & ", "");
         printTypes(t.getUpperBounds(), " super ", " & ", "");
      }
      else if (type instanceof ParameterizedType)
      {
         ParameterizedType t = (ParameterizedType) type;
         Type owner = t.getOwnerType();
         if (owner != null) { printType(owner); System.out.print("."); }
         printType(t.getRawType());
         printTypes(t.getActualTypeArguments(), "<", ", ", ">");
      }
      else if (type instanceof GenericArrayType)
      {
         GenericArrayType t = (GenericArrayType) type;
         System.out.print("");
         printType(t.getGenericComponentType());
         System.out.print("[]");
      }

   }
}
```

java.lang.Class<T> 1.0

- `TypeVariable[] getTypeParameters()` 5.0
  gets the generic type variables if this type was declared as a generic type, or an array of length 0 otherwise.
- `Type getGenericSuperclass()` 5.0
  gets the generic type of the superclass that was declared for this type, or `null` if this type is `Object` or not a class type.
- `Type[] getGenericInterfaces()` 5.0
  gets the generic types of the interfaces that were declared for this type, in declaration order, or an array of length 0 if this type doesn't implement interfaces.

java.lang.reflect.Method 1.1

- `TypeVariable[] getTypeParameters()` 5.0
  gets the generic type variables if this method was declared as a generic method, or an array of length 0 otherwise.
- `Type getGenericReturnType()` 5.0
  gets the generic return type with which this method was declared.
- `Type[] getGenericParameterTypes()` 5.0
  gets the generic parameter types with which this method was declared. If the method has no parameters, an array of length 0 is returned.

java.lang.reflect.TypeVariable 5.0

- `String getName()`
  gets the name of this type variable.
- `Type[] getBounds()`
  gets the subclass bounds of this type variable, or an array of length 0 if the variable is unbounded.

java.lang.reflect.WildcardType> 5.0

- `Type[] getLowerBounds()`
  gets the subclass (`extends`) bounds of this type variable, or an array of length 0 has no subclass bounds
- `Type[] getUpperBounds()`
  gets the superclass (`super`) bounds of this type variable, or an array of length 0 has no superclass bounds.

java.lang.reflect.ParameterizedType 5.0

- `Type getRawType()`
  gets the raw type of this parameterized type.
- `Type[] getActualTypeArguments()`
  gets the type parameters with which this parameterized type was declared.
- `Type getOwnerType()`
  gets the outer class type if this is an inner type, or `null` if this is a top-level type.

java.lang.reflect.GenericArrayType 5.0

- `Type getGenericComponentType()`
  gets the generic component type with which this array type was declared.

You have now reached the end of the first volume of Core Java. This volume covered the fundamentals of the Java programming language and the parts of the standard library that you need for most programming projects. We hope that you enjoyed your tour through the Java fundamentals and that you found useful information along the way. For advanced topics, such as networking, multithreading, security, and internationalization, please turn to the second volume.

Appendix A

Java Keywords

Keyword	Meaning	See Chapter
`abstract`	an abstract class or method	5
`assert`	used to locate internal program errors	11
`boolean`	the Boolean type	3
`break`	breaks out of a `switch` or loop	3
`byte`	the 8-bit integer type	3
`case`	a case of a `switch`	3
`catch`	the clause of a `try` block catching an exception	11
`char`	the Unicode character type	3
`class`	defines a class type	4
`const`	not used	
`continue`	continues at the end of a loop	3
`default`	the default clause of a `switch`	3
`do`	the top of a `do/while` loop	3
`double`	the double-precision floating-number type	3
`else`	the `else` clause of an `if` statement	3
`extends`	defines the parent class of a class	4
`final`	a constant, or a class or method that cannot be overridden	5
`finally`	the part of a `try` block that is always executed	11
`float`	the single-precision floating-point type	3
`for`	a loop type	3
`goto`	not used	
`if`	a conditional statement	3
`implements`	defines the interface(s) that a class implements	6
`import`	imports a package	4
`instanceof`	tests if an object is an instance of a class	5

Keyword	Meaning	See Chapter
`int`	the 32-bit integer type	3
`interface`	an abstract type with methods that a class can implement	6
`long`	the 64-bit long integer type	3
`native`	a method implemented by the host system	Volume 2
`new`	allocates a new object or array	3
`null`	a null reference	3
`package`	a package of classes	4
`private`	a feature that is accessible only by methods of this class	4
`protected`	a feature that is accessible only by methods of this class, its children, and other classes in the same package	5
`public`	a feature that is accessible by methods of all classes	4
`return`	returns from a method	3
`short`	the 16-bit integer type	3
`static`	a feature that is unique to its class, not to objects of its class	3
`strictfp`	Use strict rules for floating-point computations	2
`super`	the superclass object or constructor	5
`switch`	a selection statement	3
`synchronized`	a method or code block that is atomic to a thread	Volume 2
`this`	the implicit argument of a method, or a constructor of this class	4
`throw`	throws an exception	11
`throws`	the exceptions that a method can throw	11
`transient`	marks data that should not be persistent	12
`try`	a block of code that traps exceptions	11
`void`	denotes a method that returns no value	3
`volatile`	ensures that a field is coherently accessed by multiple threads	Volume 2
`while`	a loop	3

Appendix B

Retrofitting JDK 5.0 Code

This book uses JDK 5.0 features in many of its programs. This appendix summarizes the changes that you need to make to the sample programs so that they compile and run with JDK 1.4.

Enhanced for Loop

The enhanced `for` loop (or "for each" loop) must be turned into a traditional loop.

5.0	1.4

`for (type variable : array)`
`{`
`   body`
`}`
	`for (int i = 0; i < array.length; i++)`
	`{`
	`   type variable = array[i];`
	`   body`
	`}`

`for (type variable : arrayList)`
`{`
`   body`
`}`
	`for (int i = 0; i < arrayList.size(); i++)`
	`{`
	`   type variable = (type) arrayList.get(i);`
	`   body`
	`}`

Generic Array Lists

You need to remove the type parameters and add casts to any `get` operations.

5.0	1.4
`ArrayList<Type> arrayList = new ArrayList<Type>()`	`ArrayList arrayList = new ArrayList();`
`arrayList.get(i)`	`(Type) arrayList.get(i)`

Autoboxing

Before JDK 5.0, the conversion between primitive types and their wrapper classes was not automatic. To convert from a primitive type to a wrapper object, add a constructor call.

5.0	1.4
`Integer wrapper = n;`	`Integer wrapper = new Integer(n);`

To convert a wrapper to a primitive type value, add calls to methods `intValue`, `doubleValue`, and so on.

5.0	1.4
`int n = wrapper;`	`int n = wrapper.intValue();`

Variable Parameter Lists

You need to bundle up the parameters into an array.

5.0	1.4
method(*other params*, p_1, p_2, p_3)	*method*(*other params*, new *Type*[] { p_1, p_2, p_3 })

Covariant Return Types

Prior to JDK 5.0, the return type could not change when overriding a method. It is now legal to use a subtype in the overriding method. A typical example is the `clone` method.

5.0	1.4

`public Employee clone() { ... }`
`...`
`Employee cloned = e.clone();`
	`public Object clone() { ... }`
	`...`
	`Employee cloned = (Employee) e.clone();`

Static Import

Static import is not supported prior to JDK 5.0. Add the class name to the static feature.

5.0	1.4

`import static java.lang.Math;`
`import static java.lang.System;`
`...`
`out.println(sqrt(PI));`
	`System.out.println(Math.sqrt(Math.PI));`

Console Input

Prior to JDK 5.0, there was no `Scanner` class. Use `JOptionPane.showInputDialog` instead.

5.0	1.4

`Scanner in = new Scanner(System.in);`
`System.out.print(prompt);`
`int n = in.nextInt();`
`double x = in.nextDouble();`
`String s = in.nextLine();`
	`String input = JOptionPane.showInputDialog(prompt);`
	`int n = Integer.parseInt(input);`
	`double x = Double.parseDouble(input);`
	`s = input;`

Formatted Output

Prior to JDK 5.0, there was no `printf` method. Use `NumberFormat.getNumberInstance` instead.

5.0	1.4

`System.out.printf("%8.2f", x);`	`NumberFormat formatter`
	`   = NumberFormat.getNumberInstance();`
	`formatter.setMinimumFractionDigits(2);`
	`formatter.setMaximumFractionDigits(2);`
	`String formatted = formatter.format(x);`
	`for (int i = formatted.length(); i < 8; i++)`
	`   System.out.print(" ");`
	`System.out.print(formatted);`

Content Pane Delegation

Prior to JDK 5.0, the `JFrame`, `JDialog`, and `JApplet` classes did not delegate `add` and `setLayout` calls to the content pane. Note that this issue is only reported at run time.

5.0	1.4
`add(component)`	`getContentPane().add(component)`
`setLayout(manager)`	`getContentPane().setLayout(manager)`

Unicode Code Points

JDK 5.0 supports Unicode 4.0, in which the "supplementary" characters are encoded with two consecutive `char` values.

5.0	1.4
`int cp = string.codePointAt(i)`	`char cp = string.charAt(i)`
`if (Character.isSupplementaryCharacter(cp))` `   . . .`	omit—there are no supplementary characters prior to JDK 5.0

Building Strings

JDK 5.0 introduces a `StringBuilder` class whose methods are not synchronized, making it slightly more efficient than `StringBuffer`.

5.0	1.4
`StringBuilder`	`StringBuffer`

Index

Symbols

Numerics

A

743

745

D

E

G

H

I

751

J

K

L

755

P

757

S

759

761

X

Y

Z